A History of Fort Worth in Black & White

A History of Fort Worth in Black & White

165 Years of African-American Life

by Richard F. Selcer

Denton, Texas

Printed in the United States of America.

10 9 8 7 6 5 4 3 2 1

Permissions:
University of North Texas Press
1155 Union Circle #311336
Denton, TX 76203-5017

The paper used in this book meets the minimum requirements of the American National Standard for Permanence of Paper for Printed Library Materials, z39.48.1984. Binding materials have been chosen for durability.

Library of Congress Cataloging-in-Publication Data

Selcer, Richard F., author.

A history of Fort Worth in black & white : 165 years of African-American life / by Richard Selcer. -- Edition: first.

pages cm

Includes bibliographical references and index.

ISBN 978-1-57441-616-9 (cloth : alk. paper)

978-1-57441-630-5 (ebook)

1. African Americans--Texas--Fort Worth. 2. Fort Worth (Tex.)--Social conditions--19th century. 3. Fort Worth (Tex.)--Social conditions--20th century. 4. Fort Worth (Tex.)--Social conditions--21st century. I. Title. II. Title: History of Fort Worth in black and white.

F394.F7.S454 2015

305.896'07307645315--dc23

2015032742

Front cover: "The Caddy" by Vivian Sloan Yarborough, 1933 oil on canvas. Courtesy of Edmund P. Cranz. Cover photographs courtesy of *Fort Worth Star-Telegram* Photograph Collection, Special Collections, University of Texas at Arlington Library, Arlington, TX.; Scott and Linda Jo Barker's Collections; and the I.M. Terrell 1960 "Panther" Annual.

Back cover: "Moon over Mount Gilead."
Photograph courtesy of Brian Luenser of Fort Worth.

The electronic edition of this book was made possible
by the support of the Vick Family Foundation.

Dedication

To Jan Jones, friend, fellow author, and Sister in Christ.

"Until the lions have their own historians, the history of the hunt will always glorify the hunter."

—African proverb, quoted by Chinua Achebe (1930-2013), Nobel-winning Nigerian novelist

"We have a heritage worth preserving. We have a past worth researching. We have ancestors worthy of being remembered."

—Lenora Rolla, age 95 (1999)

"For the most part, this country's history, as recited in our schools and colleges, has been its 'white' history."

—Bob Ray Sanders, *Fort Worth Star-Telegram* columnist and I.M. Terrell alumnus

Table of Contents

List of Photos

ACKNOWLEDGMENTS

Every historian is indebted to legions of friends, colleagues, librarians, and archivists for what in the end is published under his or her name only. The support group provides the raw material; the historian alone is responsible for how it's put together and any mistakes that occur in the writing. Every Fort Worth book I've written—seven and counting—has benefitted from the input of that mostly anonymous cohort. I often wonder if anyone actually reads acknowledgments, but I would be remiss if I did not thank in black and white the good folks who went above and beyond professional courtesy in their contributions to this volume.

Thanks to Hollace Weiner, Fort Worth's Jewish historian, author, and archivist at Beth-El Congregation for serving as an unofficial reader and offering invaluable critique of the manuscript. Hollace's Jewish heritage makes her especially sensitive to the travails of other minorities in American history, a fact that is reflected in her writing. She also contributed information from her personal files and from the Beth-El archives that I would never have found on my own.

Thanks to Max Hill, librarian-turned-researcher retired from the Fort Worth Public Library. Over the years Max has spent hundreds of hours reading back issues of the *Fort Worth Press* on microfilm, taking copious notes. He graciously dug through his files pulling out all the black-Fort Worth history stories he could find and passing them along to me without any *quid pro quo*. For all the hours you put in (unknowingly) researching for me and for sharing the fruits of your labor, thanks, Max!

Thanks to Bob Smith for spending countless hours as my mapmaker, creating the graphics that have helped bring several of my books to life.

Ruth Karbach is a research dynamo in Fort Worth women's history and an extremely generous colleague when it comes to sharing her research. She put me on several new trails that I would not have thought of otherwise. Thanks, Ruth.

As usual, staff members of the Fort Worth Public Library were invaluable researchers who fortunately for me are on the payroll of the City of Fort Worth. Otherwise, I couldn't have afforded them. Standing at the forefront of the helpers on this book are archivist Betty Shankle and Senior Librarian Jabari Jones. Of great help in the later stages of my research was Senior Librarian Rene Gomez, whose research on the Trinity river-bottom settlements and forgotten buildings of Fort Worth was enlightening. He graciously shared the fruits of his photographic expeditions into some of the darker corners of the city.

Members of the Tarrant County Historical Commission, specifically Susan Kline, provided encouragement to this project. Susan's research into the old Riverside Colored School provided much useful information on the whole system of segregated education in Fort Worth.

You can't write anything about Fort Worth's African American history without consulting Reby Cary, who has not only written nine or ten books about local black history, but also lived it first-person. Brenda Sanders-Wise and Sarah Walker each wear at least two hats, one of which is keeping the Tarrant County Black Historical and Genealogical Society open.

Thanks to Jan Jones for being a sounding board for my occasionally far-out ideas and interpretations and for helping fill in some of the holes in my knowledge about what was going on in the black community in the old days. She was generous in sharing the fruits of her research on the life of William M. McDonald.

Eternal thanks as well to Gayle Hanson, Fort Worth's only black historian working full-time on black history. Gayle has long been my sounding board and conscience in all things related to black history. She tries to keep me from stumbling over my ignorance and embarrassing myself. Any missteps in the present volume are all on me.

Profuse thanks to Professor Marvin Dulaney of the History Department at the University of Texas, Arlington. He was that rare peer reviewer who actually did a close reading of the manuscript, 600+ endnotes and all, and made numerous suggestions for improvement. My ego eventually recovered, and the final product is much the better for his knowledgeable involvement. Any mistakes still remaining are my own.

Thanks to Scott Barker, Dalton Hoffman, Jan Jones, Hollace Weiner, Greg Dow, Taurean Washington, Kevin Foster, Bill Wynn, and Byron Hill for generously sharing photo treasures from their personal collections to illustrate this book. Ditto for Brian Luenser, who calls himself an "amateur," but who possesses the heart of a professional photographer. His images of familiar buildings under night skies make us see them in new and different ways. Thanks to Kevin also for being my IT person whenever there was scanning and Photoshopping to be done. Without the contributions of all these folks, this would have been a much poorer volume visually speaking. Kevin Foster is also my Johnny-on-the-spot I.T. man who can scan and Photoshop images with the best of 'em.

And finally, thanks to Ron Chrisman and Karen DeVinney at UNT Press for green-lighting this project to begin with. If Ron, the Director, and Karen, the editor-in-chief, hadn't gotten on board, there would be no book.

To Ron, Karen, Marvin, Gayle, Susan, Kevin, Max, and Hollace and all others who helped move this project along, you have proved decisively that "it takes a village" —not only to raise a child but also to write a book!

A History of Fort Worth in Black & White

Introduction

There have always been two Fort Worths living side-by-side, one white and one black. The black community for too long existed in the shadow of the white community, more ignored than oppressed. Those of us who grew up on the white side of the racial divide were barely aware of the black community unless we had a black maid or yard man. Not until the 1960s, by which time I was finishing high school and going off to college, did that start to change. Thanks to the Civil Rights movement, the black community finally emerged from the shadows. White Fort Worth has been trying to adjust ever since. That adjustment is still painful sometimes.

The book's title went through several permutations, from "Shadow People" to "Fifty Shades of Black," but the former was too clichéd and the latter was a little too cute. The idea of "Shadow People" arose because African Americans have always lived in the shadows of this city, barely registering in the historical record, but that title had already been staked out by other authors. As for "Fifty Shades of Black," everyone who has ever taken an art course knows that there are no shades of black because it is an absolute, not a color. But when you look at something black, common sense tells you there are different degrees of blackness from almost gray to pitch-black. Fort Worth's black community has never been monochromatic or monolithic. There have always been numerous and diverse elements within that community. This volume is about those differences; it is not a simple story of victims and oppressors.

What terminology to use in speaking of the black community had to be addressed early on. During more than 150 years of black-white interaction, attitudes have changed and so has language. We no longer refer to African Americans as "coloreds," which was the polite term used by white people of my parents' generation. "African American" is more politically correct but too much of a mouthful in a world where K.I.S.S. ("Keep it short and simple") is the operating rule. It may come as a shock to learn that the thoroughly modern-sounding term "Afro-Americans" was being used in the mainstream press as early as 1897 in Fort Worth; it just took sixty or seventy years to catch on.[1]

The descriptive term "Negro" carries so much baggage it can only be used today in a historical context, and even then it can provoke a visceral reaction in readers. So how to describe that minority segment of our community that has at different times been referred to by all four names? In this work I alternate between "black" and "African American," using the other two names only when unavoidable, *i.e.*, when quoting someone or when it is part of the name of an organization. As for the occasional use of the "N" word, it has no place in our language today because it is so hateful, but it cannot be wiped from history. The emotion and anger it carries cannot be conveyed by substituting a nicer word. Apologies in advance to anyone who is offended by its use in quotations in this book.[2]

The name "Fort Worth" as it frequently appears in this volume is often used as shorthand for the white majority. Since they had the numbers and all the power this seems a reasonable way to characterize public opinion without running the descriptor "white" into the ground. "Caucasian," which is used by some writers, calls too much attention to itself for this author's taste.

Since Fort Worth has had a black community almost from the beginning, why has no one to date attempted to tell their story in its entirety? We have a number of "saddle-and-sirloin" histories of the city that celebrate our Western heritage, plus a few more narrowly focused volumes on certain demographics such as women, law enforcement, the military, even the Hispanic community, but not African Americans. Why? The answer to that question is complicated—and awkward.

Beloved Texas historian Walter Prescott Webb used to tell this story about a crusty Weatherford rancher and his faithful old black servant, Sam. The rancher gave Sam a copy of a new book on Weatherford's history and kept after him to read it because, "You're in it." Sam dodged and ducked until finally he explained his complete lack of interest in the book this way: "When a Negro get old, he jes' sit around and talk to hisself. When a white man get old, he write a book."[3] Take away the Uncle Remus dialect, and the essence of the story is still true today.

W.E. B. DuBois said it more elegantly in responding to historian Hutchins Hapgood's request that he contribute to a planned history of African Americans. DuBois turned him down flat, explaining, "The Negroes do not wish to be written about by white men, even when they know they will be treated sympathetically." White novelist Carl Van Vechten commented on the same issue in the mid-1920s when he noted the "tendency on the part of the Negro to be sensitive concerning all that is written about him, particularly by a white man." That has not changed in a hundred years.[4]

The first "black history" of Fort Worth was written in 1907 by J. A. Hamilton, for which he raised the money by selling advertising in the booklet. It was a glorified business directory and "Who's Who" of black Fort Worth. He peddled copies for a buyer-friendly $2.50. Its target audience (the black community), limited print run, and cheap quality quickly made it a collector's item. Not even the public library owned a copy. Hamilton's research consisted of chats with prominent members of the black community. As he himself ruefully admitted, "There are only a few printed reminiscences of [our] history extant. Lots of it is lost entirely." Even at this early date, the city's black history was dependent upon oral recollections. For all practical purposes, Fort Worth history remained the private preserve of white writers.[5]

And that is the problem. White writers naturally tend to write for white audiences. This is not because of some vast conspiracy but because we all write from our own experience and perspective, and local historians have grown up with an image of Fort Worth as "The City Where the West Begins." As for race, racial attitudes are like genetic tags imbedded in our cultural DNA. Fort Worth history is no different from any other; it reflects its authors' biases. In 1927, a TCU graduate student writing the very first thesis at that white bastion of higher education to tackle any aspect of the black community wrote, "Fort Worth's inter-racial problems deserve serious consideration." She went on to say we should "neither disparage the shortcomings of the Negro nor demerit the sentiments and attitudes of the Southern white." Those well-intentioned words sound quaintly racist today. In 1927 they were quite liberal.[6]

The standard histories of our city to date have virtually ignored the roughly 10 percent of the population that was black. Oliver Knight's *Outpost on the Trinity* (1953), the standard history of our city, does not mention African Americans by any name in the index. To find out anything about that segment of the community, the reader has to go through the book page by page to discover that William "Gooseneck Bill" McDonald was black. McDonald, a wealthy entrepreneur and landowner of national standing in his day, is mentioned on just one page. TCU Press' 1990 reissue of *Fort Worth: Outpost on the Trinity*, claiming to "bring the book up to the present," includes both "Negroes" and "Blacks" in the new index, but it is old wine in new skins. McDonald remains the only African American mentioned by name. Julia Kathryn Garrett's *Fort Worth, A Frontier Triumph* (1973) is the definitive history of the city's early pioneers, a genuine classic. Yet when she tells of the Allen family settling in the area in 1854 she describes the scene this way: "The songs of slaves vibrated through the timber during [that] fall and winter." Presumably, these were happy slaves singing familiar plantation songs.[7]

Things haven't changed much over the past half-century. The only history of "the Fort Worth medical community" does not mention a single black doctor or the "Negro sanitariums" (black doctors' clinics) of the Jim Crow era. And the outstanding history of "Fort Worth's military legacy" published in 2011 devotes an entire chapter to World War I's Camp Bowie without mentioning the 3,000 black soldiers who trained there in 1918 and 1919. Neither omission is because the authors had a racist agenda; nothing could be further from the truth. It is because the "usual suspects" in the Fort Worth historical community are white, and we were all either self-taught or studied under white professors in white colleges. On top of that, all of our favorite primary sources—Julia Katherine Garrett, Mack Williams, Buckley B. Paddock, Mary Daggett Lake—were as white as Mrs. Baird's bread.[8]

All of this raises another troubling issue: Most of my African-American students in forty years of teaching have showed as much interest in history as in watching dressage on television. In taking up this topic I faced the question why there are there no academic histories of black Fort Worth, no biographies (to date) of black leaders? Fort Worth has produced articulate and knowledgeable spokespersons in the black community but to date not a single published work that meets the rigorous standards of Academe.

Of course, why should African Americans care anything about the city's history? Although Fort Worth has always prided itself on "its freedom and its hospitality," those qualities extended mainly to whites.[9] The black community has always suffered discrimination and mistreatment. The story is rooted in oppression, but it is not a simple story of victims and oppressors; it is far more complicated than that. Fort Worth's black community has always had both good people and bad people, ennobling acts and despicable acts, just like the white community. This volume aims to tell the story of that community, warts and all. It has been necessary to scrape down through layers of myth and deal with the dearth of nineteenth-century sources. Unfortunately, the slim records of the Tarrant County Black Historical & Genealogical Society are comprised mostly of the papers of Society founder Lenora Rolla, with most of those dating from the 1940s and forward when she was working in Fort Worth. Neither Ms. Rolla nor those who have carried on her work are trained historians; they are collectors and archivists. Writing history is not their passion or even their day job; it is an avocation. Their perspective is also colored, if you will, by their personal connection to many of the people they are writing about. We turn to professionals when we want our cars fixed, our lawsuits defended, and our medical problems treated, but we regard history as a hobby that anybody can grasp.

The writing of black history has always been shaped by the oral record. During the years of slavery blacks were rarely taught to read and write; their lives were not documented in the same way that white Americans' lives were—through birth, death, and marriage records, census reports, and personal papers—but only as property. There is a saying among historians, "what counts is what is counted," meaning you can't write about something if there are no historical records. What we know about early Fort Worth blacks either comes from collective memory—a very unreliable source—or what whites wrote about them, also unreliable. We must weigh carefully all the hand-me-down stories in the black community as well as mainstream newspaper reports, which focused on criminals and celebrities. Thus we have Tommie Lee (criminal—see Chap. 4) and "Gooseneck Bill" McDonald (celebrity—see sidebar), and almost no record of ordinary folks.

Additionally, the historian of black history finds his job complicated by the fact that African Americans typically have not been preservers of their own history. The black community has a poor collective memory, whether it's the history of their schools, churches, or what have you. Bishop College, the oldest black college in north Texas for years, did not even include on its list of "Notable Alumni" Lacey K. Williams, a 1905 graduate who went on to an unbroken string of successes, first as the pastor of the largest black church in Texas (Mount Gilead Baptist), then pastoring the largest black church in the world (Chicago's Olivet Baptist), and ultimately serving as president of the National Baptist Convention,

U.S.A. The "Minister's Institute" program at Bishop College was even named for him! Yet years later, he is completely forgotten.[10]

The modern historian has access to an almost bottomless source of Fort Worth history in the form of old newspapers preserved on microfilm. But those that have survived and made it onto microfilm were all white-owned publications. Fort Worth also had a succession of short-lived black newspapers, known today only through the odd surviving copy or by being mentioned in the major newspapers like the *Democrat* or *Morning Register.* What this means for the historian is that the daily lives of black residents went unnoticed in print.

A large part of the blame rests squarely on the shoulders of the Fourth Estate. Fort Worth's major newspapers never covered the routine stories in the black community—"passages" (marriages, births, deaths), social gatherings, and business openings. For much of the twentieth century *The Press* and *Star-Telegram* battled it out to be Fort Worth's number one newspaper. *The Press* tended to cover the black community better than its rival, perhaps because *The Press* wanted to be the hometown newspaper while the *Star-Telegram* aimed at a wider audience. For example, *The Press* did a better job with its annual coverage of Juneteenth (the celebration of emancipation in Texas) than the *Star-Telegram.* And on the rare occasions when angry racial feelings bubbled to the surface, *The Press* was more likely to report it than the *Star-Telegram.* (The best coverage of racial troubles in Fort Worth was to be found in the Dallas newspapers.)

More than one editorial policy was at work when it came to deciding what to cover. The *Star-Telegram,* with a much larger staff and bigger budget, for most of its history has given short shrift to neighborhood news in favor of national and international news. *The Press* was only marginally better. Since old newspapers are a prime source of information about daily life, we can glean frustratingly little about black daily life when the newspapers were not paying attention. *Star-Telegram* practice seems to have been to avoid such sensitive issues as substandard housing ("shotgun shacks"), civil rights protests, racial politics and fair employment—in other words, anything that might cast the home town in a bad light. For years, about the only black stories the major dailies were interested in were crime-driven, and the more sensational, the better.[11]

Dallas' Fourth Estate had a far better track record covering the black community than Fort Worth's leading dailies. For years the *Dallas Morning News* had regular columnist Lynn W. Landrum covering the "black beat." Landrum was white, but that did not prevent him from being an advocate of the black community, and he wrote passionately about black issues. His advocacy did not sit well with all the paper's readers. In 1940, one reader complained in a letter to the editor about one unnamed "well-known columnist [that] has done more to antagonize the Negroes than any other person." That could only have been Landrum. By contrast, neither of Fort Worth's two modern dailies—the *Star-Telegram* (1909–the present) or *The Press* (1922–1975)—had that problem, at least in part because neither newspaper had a beat writer covering the black community. *The Press* daringly gave a by-line to a black writer in 1934, but the *Star-Telegram* resolutely remained white Fort Worth's newspaper until the late 1960s. Even after it added an African American to the staff, his contributions were buried deep inside the newspaper.[12]

The black community was not completely without a black press; it's just that no black-owned newspaper enjoyed as big a circulation or as long a run as *The Press* and *Star-Telegram.* A better question is why didn't the black community try to preserve those newspaper runs? The obvious reason was a lack of means to create archives, no surprise when the majority of a community has trouble putting food on the table and a roof over their heads. Add to this a lack of archival training and ignorance of basic historical methodology, and the scope of the problem begins to come into focus.

There is one more reason blacks are nearly invisible in the historical record: They were not recognized by most early photographers as members of a community worthy of being photographed. The only two professionally produced photo albums of old Fort Worth contain scores of pictures of public buildings, streets, homes, even livestock, but not a single photo of a black person or building where blacks gathered. David Swartz and Charles Swartz were (with their brother John) Fort Worth's preeminent photographers around the turn of the century. David published his book in 1889, Charles in 1901. Both books represent countless hours invested by their creators to create a visual image of their hometown. Either volume might be titled "Portrait of a City"; they are that thorough. What were the brothers thinking when they chose to ignore a significant segment of the city? Nothing, and that's the point. Neither David nor Charles Swartz was a racist; on the contrary, both men took numerous studio shots of black customers who paid for a sitting; this much is apparent from surviving pictures held in various collections today. Yet even as they went about the city snapping pictures of every conceivable location, neither man felt obliged to point their camera at anything connected to the black community. From looking at their books, a modern viewer might conclude that Fort Worth was an all-white city in 1889 and 1901. No, David and Charles Swartz were not part of some sinister conspiracy to scrub the black community from the public consciousness; they just never thought of them as part of the city.

In 165 years of Fort Worth history, the history of the black community has never been properly told. In 1976 on the occasion of the U.S. Bicentennial a small group of the black intellectual leaders privately published a cursory retrospective of the city's black history that they called a "souvenir book." *Fort Worth, the Black Prospective* [sic] was by admission of the authors, not a "historical masterpiece." Its purpose was to "pause and take a glance back into Black Fort Worth in this Bicentennial year." It received limited distribution and disappeared as soon as the Bicentennial was over. For whatever reason, no one picked up the ball and pushed forward with a thoroughgoing history of black Fort Worth.[13]

Today, the history of the black community still derives mostly from living memory and oral tradition with a smattering of primary documents. The letters, diaries, memoirs, newspaper clippings, photographs, and other primary sources that we typically use to write scholarly history scarcely exist because a barely literate black population for too long had virtually no sense of its own identity, much less its own history. To date, research in the public records by recognized historians is either non-existent or insubstantial. It is telling that the best study of slavery in Texas, Randolph Campbell's *An Empire for Slavery*, examined the records of forty-seven counties but not Tarrant County, which was certainly a slave county from 1850 to 1865. Sadly, there is not much more documentation of Fort Worth's black history *after* emancipation.[14]

None of which is to say it's impossible to reconstruct a usable history of Fort Worth's black community from available records. The Tarrant County Black Historical & Genealogical Society is a start at doing so. In the early 1980s an interviewer asked Lenora Rolla if she thought a black historical society was really necessary since there already existed the Tarrant County Historical Society, Tarrant County Genealogical Society, and Fort Worth Library archives. Her response was both telling and wildly optimistic: "Perhaps by 1990 or the year 2000 there be no need for the 'Black' in Tarrant County Black Historical & Genealogical Society. . . . This black-white situation erases family-hood, and we can't deny it, and we can't change it." Thirty years later there is still a need for a *black* historical and genealogical society.[15]

One big reason I wanted to write a history of the black community is because a lot of oral tradition in that community paints their history in stark terms of us vs. them and larger-than-life heroes and villains. For instance, during Black History Month in 2013, a *Star-Telegram* article about pioneering black physician Dr. Marion Brooks, quoted one community leader describing Brooks this way: "He had the status and intelligence to stand up to a white-dominated society. Not everyone had those kinds of guts. Those kinds of guts would land you in jail, or shot or worse." In 2015, members of the black community recalling Martin Luther King, Jr.'s visit to Fort Worth in 1959 told the *Star-Telegram* that people were afraid to go hear him speak because they were afraid if their white bosses found out, they would be fired. Another called white TCU professors who invited King into their home "courageous" because of what their neighbors probably thought. At least that's the way those telling it now remember it, and who's to disagree?[16]

The full story is much more complex than that. Some of the leading figures in the great struggle for equality were far less than saints, Jeff Daggett for instance (sidebar, end of Chap. 4) or Hiram McGar (sidebar, end of Chap. 3). Not even the subjects of the later mythology took themselves so seriously. Dr. Brooks responding to a newspaper reporter's question about his place in the civil rights struggle described his role as "little bitty." But everyone needs heroes to believe in, so sometimes we burnish the historical record to create them. This is not just a problem with black history.[17]

We have to be careful not to retroactively apply modern sensibilities to the past. This is especially true when writing minority history. It is useful to keep in mind that the concept of "racism" as it is understood today had barely begun to emerge in the nineteenth century; it was a foreign concept outside of a few New England drawing rooms and religious circles. The historian can relate examples of racism in the old days without offering easy judgments based on modern, politically correct standards.

Despite the seriousness of racial prejudice and oppression, there are some lighter moments in the story of black Fort Worth. There has always been a tradition of black humor where "black" has nothing to do with race; it means when things are so bad you have to laugh to keep from crying. The dialect-flavored quote or the occasional example of situational humor are funny in the same "can-you-believe-it" way that black-face minstrelsy is to modern-day sensibilities. Even angry black director Spike Lee has mined humor in the old black-face performance tradition. Humor can be a sharp-edged weapon in social commentary. "Black humor" is about finding humor in the misfortunes life throws our way. In the pre-P.C. era, newspaper reporters regularly wrote racially insensitive remarks because their white readership found them hilarious, and the black community's feelings did not have to be considered. Today those remarks are dredged up because they give us the flavor of the times, sometimes even more than the dry facts of the news stories themselves.[18]

A History of Fort Worth in Black & White is really an examination of two communities who have lived simultaneously together and at arm's length for 165 years. The relationship has never been equal; often it's been quite rocky. The "Black & White" part of the title is shorthand for the two races, not about judging them.

Photo 1. Victims of the June 1915 flood

When disaster strikes, communities come together. It doesn't matter what color you are or how many legs you have! Five victims of the June 1915 flood find comfort together around a coffee urn. Courtesy of *Fort Worth Star-Telegram* Photograph Collection, Special Collections, University of Texas at Arlington Library, Arlington, TX.

Notes

1. *Fort Worth Register*, January 8, 1897. *Cf.* The *Baltimore Afro-American*, a weekly, began publishing in 1892.
2. The equally historical term "Negress" is not heard at all today. For examples of its common use formerly, see *Fort Worth Telegram*, December 24, 1908; and *Fort Worth Star-Telegram*, June 19, 1915.
3. As related by Paul Crume in his "Big D" column, *Dallas Morning News*, March 23, 1955.
4. DuBois is quoted without identifying when in Leslie E. Fishbein, *Rebels in Bohemia: The Radicals of the Masses, 1911–1967* (Chapel Hill: University of North Carolina Press, 1982), 164. Van Vechten, author of *Nigger Heaven* (1926) and similar novels, is quoted in David Levering Lewis, *When Harlem Was in Vogue* (New York: Alfred A. Knopf, 1981), 184, hereafter Lewis, *Harlem.*
5. James A. Hamilton, *History and Directory of Fort Worth, Giving an Account of Its Early Settlers, Founders and Growth* (Fort Worth: privately printed, 1907), 34 for quote, hereafter Hamilton, *History and Directory.*
6. Dorothy Lasseter Doggett, "Survey of Fort Worth's Negro Schools," Master's Thesis for Dept. of Education, June 1927, Special Collections, Mary Couts Burnett Library, Texas Christian University. Hereafter, Doggett, "Survey."
7. Julia Kathryn Garrett, *Fort Worth, A Frontier Triumph* (repr., Fort Worth: Texas Christian University Press, 1995), 98, hereafter cited as Garrett.
8. Ann Arnold, *A History of the Fort Worth Medical Community* (Arlington, TX: Landa Press, 2002); J'Nell L. Pate, *Arsenal of Defense: Fort Worth's Military Legacy* (Denton: Texas State Historical Association, 2011), 40–57, hereafter Pate, *Arsenal.* For example of "negro sanitariums" (clinics), see *Dallas Morning News*, April 4, 1912. For the contributions of specific primary sources mentioned, see bibliography.
9. The quote comes from Howard W. Peak who claimed to be the first (white) male child born in Fort Worth (1856–1939), and in a second career, was the self-appointed historian of the city. *Fort Worth Star-Telegram*, August 20, 1922.
10. Bishop College was founded in east Texas in 1881 and transplanted to Dallas in 1961. For information on Lacey, see Reby Cary, "Black Leadership in Fort Worth," in *Fort Worth, The Black Prospective* [*sic*], no

author (Fort Worth: Black Citizens Concerned with the Bicentennial, 1976), 2, cited hereafter as *Fort Worth, The Black Prospective (sic)*. See also *Fort Worth Star-Telegram*, August 3, 1913; and October 12, 1921. *Dallas Morning News*, April 8, 1963; and April 29, 1970. For "Notable Alumni" list, see Bishop College entry in Wikipedia, http://en.wikipedia.org/wiki/Bishop_College.

11. For recent change in *Star-Telegram* editorial policy toward more neighborhood coverage, see "New section to add more coverage of local news," *Fort Worth Star-Telegram*, July 17, 2013.
12. For Landrum, see *Dallas Morning News*, November 3, 1940. The first black writer to appear in the pages of *The Press* was Dr. T.S. Boone who wrote a story for Juneteenth in 1934. *Fort Worth Press*, June 19, 1934, p. 14. The lead-in to the story detailed his credentials including his five college degrees. The topic of his article: "the contributions of the negro to American civilization." Cecil Johnson, the first black writer on the *Star-Telegram* staff, joined the newspaper in 1970.
13. *Fort Worth, The Black Prospective* [*sic*]. The authors made a conscious decision to publish their work on June 19, 1976 ("Juneteenth").
14. Lenora Rolla founded the Tarrant County Black Historical and Genealogical Society in 1974 and started its collections with her personal papers. Since 1996 her papers have been held by the Fort Worth Library, Central Branch, Local History, Genealogy and Archives Unit. Hereafter cited as Lenora Rolla Papers. Almost none of the documents date from before the 1930s. For the best study of slavery in Texas, see Randolph B. Campbell, *An Empire for Slavery: The Peculiar Institution in Texas, 1821–1865* (Baton Rouge: Louisiana State University Press, 1989), 270–71, hereafter Campbell, *Empire.*
15. Quoted in Phyllis Wonjou Allen, "These Women Lived!", Katie Sherrod, ed., *Grace and Gumption: Stories of Fort Worth Women* (Fort Worth, TX: TCU Press, 2007), 195, hereafter Allen (Sherrod), *Grace and Gumption.*
16. Mitch Mitchell, "Trailblazing African-American Doctor Honored in Fort Worth Museum Display," *Fort Worth Star-Telegram*, February 10, 2013. Bud Kennedy, "Memories Fading of MLK's Fort Worth Visit," ibid., January 17, 2015.
17. Quoted in *Fort Worth Star-Telegram*, February 10, 2013. Dr. Brooks died in 2003, and the occasion for this article was a memorial exhibit to his life and legacy set up in the Lenora Rolla Heritage Center Museum for Black History Month, 2013, part of the Tarrant County Black Historical & Genealogical Society, 1020 E. Humbolt.

18. See Spike Lee, *Bamboozled* (2000), ranked by reviewers Will Leitch and Tim Grierson as #7 among Lee's 22 films, ca. 2012. They call it both "tone-deaf" and incisive "satire." www.vulture.com. "Spike Lee Films Rated from Best to Worst."

Chapter 1

The Antebellum and Civil War Years

From the beginning, Fort Worth, Texas, has been a community where Southern values and attitudes intersected with Western values and attitudes; both are part of our genetic code today, but they had to come from somewhere. Fort Worth began life in the mid-nineteenth century as a frontier settlement built by migrants from the Deep South who combined the racial prejudices of that region with the greater tolerance and openness of the Wild West. This combination could not help but have an effect on blacks and whites alike.

Slavery arrived on the twin forks of the Trinity almost with the first white men. The earliest settler in the area was Tennessee-born Edward S. Terrell who arrived in 1843. He was a contract supplier for the U.S. Army who made a killing in 1856 by selling his entire herd to the Fort Richardson garrison. He then invested some of the proceeds in slaves to sell to the incoming homesteaders who like himself were mostly Southerners.[1]

While Fort Worth was still a military outpost (1849–1853), there were also slave-owners among the officers. Major Ripley Arnold, the post's founder, owned a body servant, and so did his First Lieutenant, Washington P. Street. In that day and age, white men who grew up in the South, regardless of where they had been born, considered slavery part of the normal order of things. Men owned slaves, not necessarily a field full, but more than likely a personal or body servant if they could afford one. Lieutenant Washington Street grew up in the upper Midwest of Illinois, Wisconsin, and Iowa—abolitionist country. But when military service took him to Texas he was accompanied by London Triplett, a black man who had worked for the family in some unspecified capacity for years. Family lore has it that Triplett was a free man, and having a last name suggests that, but it is also hard to imagine a black man in antebellum Texas being able to come and go as he pleased. It is equally hard to imagine a young Army lieutenant paying servant's wages out of his meager salary. Army life on the frontier was different from the world that gentlemen officers came from. Far beyond the pale of civilization, they might keep a black slave or live with an Indian squaw when they would never have done either back home.[2]

Colonel Middleton Tate Johnson, one of the five men who helped Major Arnold select the site, later dubbed "the Father of Tarrant County," had at least thirty-nine slaves in 1850 on his plantation in nearby Navarro County. When he settled in Tarrant County that same year at a spot about fifteen miles east of Fort Worth, he brought his slaves with him. One of those slaves many years later told an interviewer that Johnson had "about" eighty-six slaves on his place in Tarrant County, which suggests that as his wealth and status rose he bought additional slaves.[3]

Most of those early settlers came from the Deep South; they came west to farm a piece of land and realize the American Dream, a dream built on slavery. They were slave-owners who saw the rich, black soil as their ticket, in the process unwittingly extending the cotton empire onto the Great Plains. Fort Worth's location on the edge of the eastern prairie where it merged with the Cross Timbers offered the kind of hot, dry climate that was favorable for cotton cultivation although not as favorable as the deep delta lands of the Mississippi River valley. Statistically, Tarrant County did not even register when it came to calculating national cotton production; tables and charts showing the distribution of the twelve million acres under cultivation in 1859 do not even include Tarrant County. Since cotton was the single largest employer of slaves and Tarrant County was such an insignificant player in the cotton empire, it seems clear that slaves did not compose a large part of the local population.[4]

There is no historical consensus about the number of slaves living in the county between 1850 and 1865, and even less agreement when it comes to Fort Worth. At best we have a snapshot of the population for certain years. Tax rolls show a steady increase in the number of slaves county-wide before the Civil War: from 32 in 1850 to 280 in 1855 to either 699 or 730 in 1860. The earliest number conflicts with some records that show 65 slaves *total* in Tarrant County including the little community calling itself "Fort Town." One of those who make the error of conflating the county and the town is B. B. Paddock, earliest chronicler of the city's history, who uses the number sixty-five as the number "in Fort Worth in 1850 out of a total population of 664." The fact is, it is virtually impossible to distinguish the number of slaves owned by residents of the town from those belonging to slave-owners in the rest of the county. Logically, we would expect the overwhelming majority of slaves to be engaged in agricultural work as opposed to the "house servants" and "body servants" that tended to be found in town. More confusion was created by later recollections. In 1893, which was still within living memory of the first generation of Fort Worthers, the *Dallas Morning News* states there were 115 slaves in Fort Worth in 1850 out of a total population of 500. Julia Kathryn Garrett, the respected modern-day historian of early Fort Worth, says there were 756 slaves in the county in 1861 but provides no source for that figure. At this late date we cannot make an accurate accounting of slave numbers in Tarrant County or Fort Worth because the primary sources are so unreliable. All we can say with confidence is that Fort

Worth as a small frontier community contributed little to the total slave population of Texas in the antebellum period.[5]

What we can do is put a face on the slave-owners if not the slaves themselves. Their ranks included the most distinguished citizens of the county: Ephraim Daggett, Lawrence Steele, Middleton Tate Johnson, Charles Turner, Dr. G.M. Standifer, Nathaniel Terry, and brothers Otis and Paul Isbell. All were planters who came to Fort Worth from elsewhere across the South, bringing their slaves with them to start over in the new land. Even Dr. Standifer only practiced medicine out of necessity while improving his spread. Among the others were occasional Indian fighters and slave traders, two well-known avocations on the Texas frontier.[6]

The man called the "Father of Fort Worth," Captain Ephraim M. Daggett, was a big-time slave-owner. He and his family arrived in 1852 with what was described by contemporaries as "a large contingent" of slaves, meaning not just house servants but field hands as well. Lawrence Steele and his wife Elizabeth arrived that same year in two wagons with thirty-six slaves. Why Steele needed that many slaves is a mystery because he was in the merchandising business, unless they were an investment and he planned to sell them. Slave-trading was looked down on by Southern elites although not slave-owning. People were less squeamish on the frontier about such things. Supporting the slave-trading theory, the following year Steele was down to ten slaves, all registered in his wife's name although he paid the taxes on them. His business partner, Julian Feild [*sic*], was paying taxes on fourteen slaves before the Civil War.[7]

The biggest slave-owner in Tarrant County on the eve of the Civil War was either Middleton Tate Johnson or Charles Turner. The two men had served together in the Mexican War and together guided Major Ripley Arnold to the bluffs of the Trinity in 1849. Turner owned 640 acres north of the river where Greenwood Cemetery is today and was active buying slaves on the local market. By 1861 he owned 150. Johnson owned a sprawling spread east of Fort Worth in present-day Arlington which served as a way station on the road to Dallas. He, too, owned more than

100 slaves. Turner saw no contradiction between being a Union man and owning slaves during the secession crisis of 1861. Both men cast their lot with the Confederacy after Texas seceded from the Union.[8]

Another large slave-owner, also with a spread just north of town, was Nathaniel Terry, known locally as "Colonel Terry." He first came to Texas in 1854 from Alabama with his family and thirty-six slaves hoping to recreate the plantation life he had known back home. Within a few years, he had acquired more than eighty slaves. The area where both Turner and Terry settled was what later came to be known as "White Settlement." The origins of the name are still debated today, whether it refers to whites as opposed to Indians or whites as opposed to blacks.[9]

All of these men are counted today among the founding fathers of Fort Worth, so the fact that they were not just slave-owners but big-time slave-owners is significant. It shows that slavery was considered respectable and was rooted in the community right from the beginning. It was the economic bedrock of the local economy. Approval even crossed whatever lines were drawn between secessionists and unionists in 1860–61.

What kind of masters were these men? They may have been pillars of the community in their day, but we judge our pillars differently today. Captain J. C. Terrell, who knew most of them, says in his *Reminiscences of the Early Days of Fort Worth* that Johnson and Daggett were "grand men... morally" while admitting that neither was "exemplary or saintly." He calls them authentic "heroes" because "we loved them for the manifold good they did... [and because] both were good Masons." Colonel Johnson may have put his guns away, but he never accepted the freedmen on equal terms. At the end of the war he opposed "granting the Negroes any political rights whatever" although he was not averse to treating them with "justice and kindness."[10]

We know more about Charles Turner as a slave-owner than either of the other two. Reportedly he allowed his slaves an extended Christmas holiday every year that continued as long as a huge Yule log burned. He also went down to the "negro quarters" with Christmas gifts for all. It is suggested that such acts of kindness were far more than the average slave-owner did. When the Civil War came, Turner refused to convert his considerable gold stash into Confederate notes. Instead he buried it under a giant live oak "with the aid of a trusted slave," Uncle Jake. Since the location of the gold was never revealed to Union authorities even after the war, we can presume that it was a very strong relationship between Turner and Uncle Jake. Turner died in 1873. Reportedly, the "faithful" *former* slave was buried at Turner's side when he died. We do not have similar details on Nathaniel Terry, only that he was likewise a kindly master. However, we do have independent testimony that says lumped together as a group Texas slave-owners were less harsh than many of their brethren in the Deep South. Testimony to this effect comes from visitors to the state. There were no slave auctions, no underground railroad to serve as an escape valve for runaways, and the sketchy historical record does not contain any mention of any Simon Legree types. On a relative scale, therefore, slavery in Tarrant County (Fort Worth) was fairly benign, which should not be confused with being a good thing.[11]

Compared to the big slave-owners, men like Ripley Arnold and Washington Street with their "body servants" were small cogs in the system. Their slaves were faithful retainers treated more like companions than chattel. Master and slave worked and ate together and sometimes slept under the same roof. Such owners were not economically dependent on slavery for their livelihood; having a "man servant" was a perk of being a gentleman in the Old South. It was the big plantation owners employing scores if not hundreds of slaves that drove the system. But most slave-owners, whether they owned one body servant or 100 field-hands, would have believed that they were doing the right thing for all concerned.

In the decade before the Civil War, black-white relations in the tiny community seem to have been not just peaceful but congenial. The local slave population was far from restive, and Fort Worth was safely removed from the strongholds of Northern abolitionism. Some prominent locals could even advocate for blacks without arousing the hostility of their white neighbors. The fact that such kindly souls were not willing to go all the way by arguing for emancipation does not mean they were hypocrites or completely heartless. One of the most solicitous was Florence Peak, the wife of Dr. Carroll Peak, who made herself a "friend to the helpless" among blacks and whites. Word got around in the slave community that a black man facing a whipping might even appeal to Mrs. Peak to intercede in his behalf. Her countless acts of kindness produced one unforeseen consequence; it was said that "numbers of [black] girl babies" were named "Florence" in her honor.[12]

Acts of charity like Florence Peak performed, while admirable, did not change the law. Slaves were still property in the eyes of the law and could be treated as such, meaning they could be bought and sold at their owner's whim without any concern for what they might want. They had no legal protection; even the sanctity of the family unit that was a cornerstone of both English Common Law and Napoleonic law did not apply. Families could be broken up and sold off or gifted just like livestock. Slaves could also be seized by the sheriff in bankruptcy proceedings. When Colonel Terry suffered a financial setback, eighty of his slaves were sold at auction on the Tarrant County courthouse steps in a single sale. Neither the law nor the Colonel was entirely heartless; he got to keep his faithful "body servant," Uncle Daniel.[13]

Uncle Daniel was one of the fortunate ones, but even he had no expectation of ever enjoying due process. The only protection he had came from his master, and that protection could be taken away arbitrarily for even the smallest misstep. It would have been big news if an accused black man did receive due process in any proceeding. The first known hanging in Tarrant County was of an unnamed black man, and reportedly it went by the book. According to a brief news items in 1859, the "Negro man of Col. Harton of Navarro County" was accused of robbing and murdering "Mr. English" of Fort Worth. He was tried—before an all-white court, of course—and convicted on the basis of some of the stolen money found in his wife's possession. The newspaper summarized the trial this way: The accused was "examined, found guilty, and hung by the citizens."[14]

The hanging of Colonel Harton's man was noteworthy because it cannot be categorized as a lynching like the hanging of three black men in Dallas a year later in the super-heated atmosphere before the Civil War. The coming of the war shattered the established order between the two races, ultimately replacing it with something scarcely better, legalized segregation. The abolition of slavery was a noble goal, but lifelong docility and loyal service could not be swept away with the stroke of a presidential pen. Two and a half centuries of American slavery had created a comfortable if unequal relationship between slaves and masters. In the run-up to the Civil War the status quo was undermined by talk of war and rumors of abolitionist plots to incite a slave uprising. The closer the election of 1860 came with the possibility of an "abolitionist" President (Abraham Lincoln, *sic*), the more slave-owners became hypersensitive to anything resembling rebellion or even insubordination. Suspicions focused not on slaves alone but on white provocateurs (Northern abolitionists).[15]

A series of events that summer dubbed the "Texas Troubles" in newspapers across the nation raised white fears of a vast plot to torch towns and murder citizens in their beds. It started with a wave of fires on July 8 that hit several north Texas towns, including Dallas (but not Fort Worth). In the public mind the fires were linked together and constituted the beginning of a slave revolt. The *Dallas Herald* stoked the worst white fears, which involved not just arson and murder but deep-seated fear of black men raping white women. Dallas citizens formed a vigilance committee to hunt down the conspirators, and Fort Worth was not far behind. In August, Col. Nathaniel Terry wrote to a friend in east Texas, "We are in an intense excitement, growing out of these organized burnings that have been going on." Another Fort Worth citizen, unnamed, declared that "universal sentiment" thereabouts was that it was better to hang ninety-nine (suspicious) men than "let one guilty man pass, for the guilty one endangers the peace of society." The lucky ones were hanged; there were reports that some men were burned alive.[16]

As many as fifty men were lynched across the region that summer without regard for due process of law, including three black Dallas residents accused of arson. One was "the notorious negro named Uncle Cato." Fort Worth's "vigilance committee" hanged two white men for being guilty of nothing worse than being abolitionists. The body of one, William H. Crawford, was discovered by passers-by on July 17 swinging from a pecan tree. He had been accused of being "an agent of the underground railroad" and urging slaves to kill their masters. Reportedly, he had distributed six-shooters to fifty slaves to accomplish that fiendish end. The other victim, Anthony Bewley, was a Methodist minister from Missouri with well-known abolitionist leanings. In September he fled town but was pursued by the vigilance committee all the way to Missouri and brought back in chains. On the night of September 13, they hanged him from the same tree used to dispatch William Crawford. Months later Bewley's wife, safely relocated to New York, named two pillars of the Fort Worth community, Ephraim Daggett and Charles Turner, as leaders of the mob that abducted and lynched her husband.[17]

The newspapers did not report any more hangings of abolitionists in Fort Worth after September 13 or any hangings of blacks in Tarrant County during the Texas Troubles, but that does not mean Fort Worth was more law-abiding than some other communities with more murders on their record. In the same letter cited above, Colonel Terry confided that seven white men had been lynched and added, "I expect before it is over not less than fifty Negroes will be hung." Terry was one of the more moderate and compassionate of the local slave-owners.[18]

Whites were more afraid of white instigators coming down from the North than they were of their slaves. Conventional wisdom said that slaves would never rise up on their own, only if they were "enticed by some white man," which really meant some Yankee. As every Southerner knew, Yankees were even lower on the evolutionary scale than blacks.

"We should never forget that treachery, falsehood and deception are the peculiar characteristics of Yankees," thundered the *Galveston News.* Blacks, on the other hand, if left to their own devices, were docile and simple-minded creatures, or at least that is what conventional wisdom said. Ultimately, this sort of thinking would make it impossible for whites to accept blacks as equals under any circumstances.[19]

The Texas Troubles finally wound down in October, less than a month before the national elections to determine who would lead the nation for the next four years. One historian calls the Texas Troubles "the worst Southern slave panic" since the infamous Nat Turner slave rebellion in Virginia in 1830. How hard the hysteria hit Fort Worth is hard to gauge because the town's only newspaper at the time, *The Whig,* is lost to history, and personal accounts from that period are likewise virtually non-existent. We are forced to depend upon reports of the situation in north Texas carried in other newspapers. Those suggest that, Nathaniel Terry's dire warnings aside, Tarrant County masters deterred any rebellious tendencies among their slaves with the whip rather than lynchings. Whether there was ever any real threat of a slave uprising in Tarrant County seems extremely unlikely based on the available evidence.[20]

Before it was over, the Texas Troubles probably claimed as many whites as blacks, but its impact on the two races was quite different. White abolitionists, and those suspected of abolitionist sympathies, were free to leave the state, but slaves did not have that option; they could not simply pack up and depart. They had to ride things out and hope for the best. A whipping was preferable to a lynching, and life under slavery was preferable to death. The latter part of 1860 found blacks walking on egg shells. With rumors swirling that slaves possessed arms and poison (strychnine), the local vigilance committee became the self-appointed guardian of law and order. If the truth be known, the white community had little to fear. A lifetime of bowing and scraping had made most slaves incapable of resistance, much less open revolt. Northern abolitionists encouraging them to rise up or run away did not inspire action, only fear of punishment. It was their minds that were chained, not their bodies.[21]

It is hard to say how many slaves were in Fort Worth or even Tarrant County when Texas seceded. Two sources survive today that give us a snapshot of how many slaves were in Tarrant County in 1860–61. The federal census shows 699 slaves in the entire county. (Slaves were enumerated by county not by city.) Tarrant County tax records for 1861, just before the war started, show 756 slaves. Tarrant County's slave population must be measured against the total slave population of the state, which in 1860 was 182,566.[22]

The county's slave population might be expected to have decreased during the Civil War as blacks sought freedom by fleeing to the safety of Union lines or Indian Territory (Oklahoma). It is true that as increasing numbers of white men went off to fight, flight became less risky. But just the opposite occurred; the local slave population grew. In 1865 the number of Tarrant County slaves was more than twice what it had been in 1860 (1,722 vs. 699). Some sources credit this increase to the area's importance as a cattle market, attracting lots of cattle traders and their slaves, but since the cattle trade through Fort Worth did not take off until 1867, it seems more likely that the spike in the slave population occurred because slave-owners from elsewhere in the Confederacy either fled to north Texas with their property or sent their slaves here for safe-keeping. It is estimated that 150,000 slaves were "refugeed" into the state from across the South by the end of 1864.[23]

The anecdotal evidence strongly suggests as much. Jamie Wilson, a slave brought down from Arkansas by his master in a group of nearly a hundred slaves, was unceremoniously cut loose. The master tried to sell the lot to the locals but kept getting the same answer: "We have more niggers than we know what to do with." Finally, he abandoned them and returned to Arkansas, leaving them to fend for themselves. Many years later, Wilson still remembered his introduction to freedom, working for handouts and begging for a roof over his head. A teen-aged Charles Ellis

Mitchell (white), who spent time in Dallas and Fort Worth, knew of two widows, Mrs. Routh and Mrs. Worthington, who arrived in Dallas with a large number of slaves in tow. Overwhelmed by having to provide for so many, they offered to give away the lot to anyone who would take them in, which included clothing and shoeing them. Mitchell's mother took in three girls who knew how to weave and spin and put them to work producing uniforms for the Confederate army. As he recalled many years later, this proved a happy arrangement for all parties to the transaction.[24]

Some slave-owners fared better when it came to dumping their slaves on the bearish local market. A Mr. Lewis who was slave-poor when he arrived in town during the war saw the writing on the wall. He decided to put down roots and traded his slaves for 264 prime acres southeast of town. Whatever the value of the land, he came out much better than the unnamed buyer who probably lost his entire investment when emancipation came.[25]

Some local owners, recognizing the same writing on the wall by 1864, simply called their slaves together and told them they were free. That spring, Charles Turner told his 150 slaves they were free to go. Around the same time, Paul Isbell gathered his 200 slaves, men, women, and children under the huge pecan tree on his property, climbed atop a table so all could hear him, and said,

> The war is [almost over]. You are free to come or to go. The roads and fields are open to travel where you will.[26]

The reaction by Turner's and Isbell's slaves was the same, and duplicated on other plantations all over the South—stunned silence. A lifetime of servitude made them afraid to cheer or dance in joy. Some packed up and took off as soon as possible. Many stayed on because they had nowhere else to go. Their lives had been circumscribed by the boundaries of the plantation and slave quarters. Paul Isbell's overseer, "Uncle Ott," spoke for many when he asked plaintively, where were they to go, and what were they to do. It was a question that Isbell could not answer. It has been estimated that about half of Tarrant County's slaves left the area after being emancipated. There is no way to confirm or deny this figure.[27]

Slavery's legacy in Fort Worth is a delicate subject. We want to get past stereotypes however. Slaves who were part of the town's population would have been mostly personal servants, not field hands, keeping the numbers very small. (Fort Worth did not become an actual "city" until 1873.) They would have been better treated than the average field hand although at the end of the day, they were still slaves. Trying to get a handle on how Fort Worth masters treated their slaves is tricky because it entails a lot of extrapolation from limited sources. Texas newspapers of the day spoke of "trusty negroes" traveling with their masters, even into Mexico and back, suggesting that such slaves were well-treated. All of the available anecdotal evidence, from both black and white sources, agrees that Tarrant County masters fall into the vague category of "kindly masters," the kind that would extend a helping hand to their former slaves after emancipation, providing shelter, employment, and protection from the KKK. Former slaves interviewed for the "Texas Slave Narratives" in the 1930s spoke well of their old masters. For instance, Betty Bormer, one of M.T. Johnson's slaves along with her parents and nine siblings, recalled "Marster Johnson was good to us cullud folks and he feeds us good." She went on to say that Johnson provided entertainment for his slaves, and his children taught any slave who expressed an interest how to read and write. After the war, he even set them up on their own and continued to help them when they were in trouble. When he died they mourned him because he "twas our pappy. . . . he was a blessed man." All this came from a woman who had no reason to gloss over the truth with a WPA interviewer seventy years after the events.[28]

Photo 2. Betty Bormer

An elderly Betty Bormer, former slave, interviewed for the WPA's "Slave Narratives," *ca.* 1937. Her fading memory is part of the slim record we have of slave times locally. Courtesy of Library of Congress.

The good and the bad of slavery locally are equally difficult to deal with dispassionately: the notion of kindly masters treating their slaves as members of the family is as hard to swallow as the notion that every master was a whip-wielding "Simon Legree." There is much evidence that Fort Worth masters were decent human beings as far as it went. Most would have agreed with Georgian Thomas R. Cobb's description of his state's slaves as "the most happy and contented of workers," well cared for and never abused or over-worked. Cobb would have found a like-minded soul in Ida Loving Turner, a member of Fort Worth's pioneer generation married to Charles Turner, and one of the few to leave a memoir behind. Mrs. Turner was kindly disposed towards the Turner slaves and totally clueless about how the other half lived and felt about things. Hers was a sheltered world of dutiful, humble servants who all apparently loved their master, her husband. And as far as she was concerned, the feeling was reciprocated. Looking back many years later, this was how she remembered the relationship:

> Speaking of Negroes, I want to say that they were gentle and peaceable people. I never heard of murders committed or harm done to their own race or to white people. Many of the old Negroes were friends and protectors of their White Folks, left in their care after the men joined the army. They were always courteous and helpful to children. My mother [Mary Loving] had deep sympathy, as most of the whites did, for the Negro people.[29]

It may be true that Fort Worth masters as a rule did not abuse their slaves, but that was not the only evil consequence of slavery. A lifetime of servitude destroys the human spirit, stunting ambition, character development, and independent thought, and those effects could not be erased in a generation or even several generations.

There was something else, too. The same closeness that could produce loving paternal relationships also produced slavery's dirty little secret, namely that some masters had intimate relations with their female slaves. For instance, M. T. Johnson, fondly remembered as the "Father of Tarrant

County," had ten unexplained mulattos among his scores of slaves in 1850, ranging in age from forty down to one year old. This does not necessarily mean Johnson was the father, but it raises the question of what white man was the father of those children. It is not difficult to understand how illicit relations occurred between masters and slaves. Some may have actually been caring relationships. E. B. Daggett, son of E. M. Daggett the "Father of Fort Worth," produced a son, Jeff Daggett, with one of his father's slaves. He grew up to become a prominent fixture in Fort Worth society for many years, until being gunned down in a courthouse elevator in 1917. Hiram McGar, a highly successful Fort Worth entrepreneur who helped bring the Negro League baseball to town (see McGar sidebar), was also mulatto. Legendary white cattleman John Chisum had two daughters by his slave mistress, Jensie, whose descendants still live in Fort Worth today. The most famous African-American evangelist around the turn of the century, J. L. "Sin Killer" Griffin, was a mulatto born into slavery during the Civil War. And recently, an African American, Isaiah Edwards, Jr. has come forward claiming to be the great-grandson of Major Ripley Arnold. While the supporting evidence is problematic, the fact that his claim is taken seriously by so many suggests not just how far we have come as a society, but how pervasive those master-slave relationships were.[30]

Mixed-race offspring of a black and white parent at least had the best of all possible role models, Frederick Douglass, a mulatto whose remarkable career did not seem to suffer from the circumstances of his heritage. And mixed racial heritage was not limited to the offspring of white masters and black slave women. Native Americans and African Americans also got together, producing children who struggled to fit into mutually hostile societies. In the 1890s, when the U.S. Government was trying to decide whether to pay annuities to mixed race offspring of Native Americans or only pure-blood Indians, one local wag said, "All the Negroes in Fort Worth are hunting up their pedigrees." The issue of racial heritage, while it arose during slavery, lingered long after the slaves were freed.[31]

Lincoln's Emancipation Proclamation, coming in the third year of the war, did not change anything in north Texas. Most Southern slaves learned they were free when Union troops marched into Rebel territory and spread the word that they were legally free. But slaves in north Texas received no such word, so they continued in their labors just as they always had until June 1865. That is when Union General Gordon Granger arrived at Galveston to establish federal authority over Texas. He landed without resistance on the nineteenth with eighteen hundred men to administer the entire state of Texas. One of his first actions was to declare that all laws enacted in the state since 1861 were null and void and all slaves were freed. It was that simple. Slavery was over in Texas.

There is no telling when the word got to north Texas, but the grapevine would have seen to it that the word got to everyone in the state, black as well as white. One thing is certain, Tarrant County slaves were not freed by force of arms. Unlike what happened in so many communities in the Deep South, no federal troops showed up to enforce emancipation. There was no Jubilee of freedom. Blacks in Tarrant County would not have dared have a joyous celebration. Their reaction would have been just to walk off the job—or more likely, not, because the slave's life was all they had ever known. There are no reports of a mass exodus of freedmen from the area.

Welcoming General Granger was the provisional government of Union General A. J. Hamilton, appointed by President Andrew Johnson in May. In 1866 a state convention limited to Unionists and pardoned Confederates drafted a new constitution. Ex-Confederate James W. Throckmorton was elected governor under the new regime, and other ex-Confederates filled the legislature. This signaled to freedmen that for them things were not going to change any time soon. They would continue to work for their former masters as slaves in everything but name. The new boss looked a lot like the old boss.

The legacy of slavery would hang over the black community forever after in the nation's history. African Americans coped with that legacy in different ways. Some never got over the anger and resentment. Others coped with selective memories that included feelings of nostalgia. The further from slavery they got, the more nostalgia colored memories. In 1903, an editorial in the *Fort Worth Telegram* (by a white writer) recalled,

> a time when the Southern people would trust the negro with his home, his family, and his gold. The negro of slavery days was such a character. . . . But times have changed. The negro as a general proposition is altogether different in the twentieth century. While there are some of his race who are worthy of good words, there are many who have brought the black people into disrepute because of the idle, shiftless characters which they have.[32]

And the myth-making was not all on the white side. That same year, in fact that same month, one hundred elderly former slaves calling themselves the "Congress of Ex-slaves" marched peacefully through Dallas. They were not protesting. They carried no signs and displayed no "emblems or regalia" except an American flag. An unspecified number of Tarrant County blacks participated in the march and in the three-day reunion that accompanied it. The only message other than patriotism may have been in the timing. The event coincided with the annual state fair in Dallas, which blacks could attend only one day during its run.[33]

"Colored People's Day" at the state fair was considered by the fair's white organizers to be a symbol of racial reconciliation—"a day devoted to the colored race of Texas." It went along with the myth that slavery in Texas had not been all that bad, at least compared to states in the Deep South, and that afterwards the black man had become "partners" with the white man in the state's economy. According to white thinking, they had provided the brains and blacks the "willing and able" labor in a mutually agreeable arrangement. In 1936, an unnamed editorial writer in the *Dallas Morning News* said,

> The Negro has had a part in the development of Texas that has created an acknowledged debt. . . . Texas never had a large slave

> population. The negro participation in growth has been largely as a free race.[34]

Of course, this was all part of the mythology that whites created to erase the guilt of slavery. "It wasn't really *that* bad. . . was it?"

Notes

1. Popularly known as "Captain Terrell." See Edward S. Terrell vertical file, Tarrant County Archives; and B.B. Paddock, ed., *A Twentieth Century History and Biographical Record of North and West Texas* (Chicago: Lewis Publishing Co., 1906), 86.
2. For Arnold, see Clay Perkins, *The Fort in Fort Worth* (Keller, TX: Cross-Timbers Heritage Publishing Co., 2001), 44. For London Triplett, see Introduction to "Letters from First Lieutenant Washington P. Street to His Sister, Miss Sarah Eleanor Street," *Footprints* 45, no. 3 (August 2002): 97.
3. Johnson's slave numbers are all over the place. For instance, see Garrett, 60–61, 109, and 129. *Cf.* Betty Bormer, former slave, interviewed for "Texas Slave Narratives" in the 1930s, "Federal Writers' Project," "Slave Narratives, A Folk History of Slavery in the United States from Interviews with Former Slaves," 1938, on-line at feepages.genealogy.rootsweb.ancestry.com, hereafter cited by interviewee's name, "Slave Narratives." *Cf.* U.S. Census Slave Schedules for Navarro/Ellis County, 1850. "U.S. Federal Census, Slave Schedule" for Navarro District, Ellis County, Seventh Census of the United States, 1850, Washington, D.C.: National Archives and Records Administration, 1850 (database on-line at Ancestry.com). Note: Tarrant was part of Navarro County until it was split off at the end of 1849. For county tax rolls, see Campbell, *Empire,* Appendix 2, p. 266.
4. Stuart Bruchey, ed., *Cotton and the Growth of the American Economy, 1790–1860* (New York: Harcourt, Brace & World, 1967).
5. The slave counts are all over the map for those years. U.S. Census records show 65 slaves in Tarrant County (*cf.* Fort Worth) in 1850, a number that was fewer than in three of the four surrounding counties. (Only Denton County had fewer than Tarrant with ten.) However, the issue is complicated by the fact that Tarrant County was part of Navarro County for much of 1850. Still, the number 65 is used by most historical sources. See, for example, B.B. Paddock, ed., *Fort Worth and the Texas Northwest,* vol. 2 (Chicago: Lewis Pub. Co., 1922), 834, hereafter Paddock, *Fort Worth and the Texas Northwest*; and Frank W. Johnson, *A History of Texas and Texans,* vol. 2 (Chicago: American Historical Society, 1914), 816. The most reliable number for 1860 comes from the Tax Assessment of Tarrant

County which lists 699 slaves. See Paul N. Geisel, *Historical Vignette of the Black Population of Fort Worth, Texas* (College Park, MD: Dr. Charles M. Christian and the Dept. of Geography, University of MD., 1991), 4, hereafter Geisel, *Historical Vignette*. For 1861 numbers, see Garrett, 215 and 217. The 1850 "U.S. Federal Census Slave Schedule," ibid., gives the total number of slaves in Texas as 54,634, so Fort Worth was barely a blip on the demographic map. The 1860 federal census records for Tarrant County no longer exist to confirm or repudiate figures for 1860–61. For numbers from that year, see *Dallas Morning News*, July 22, 1893. *Cf.* Campbell, *Empire*, Appendix 2, p. 266.

6. Garrett, *Frontier Triumph*, 99, Geisel, *Historical Vignette*, 1.
7. For Daggett, see Garrett, 129. For Steele, see Garrett, *Fort Worth*, 129. For Steele and Feild [*sic*], see Eudora Hodges, "Lawrence Steel [*sic*]—Early Settler," *Footprints* 34, no. 4 (November 1991): 197–98, 200, fnts. 5 and 12.
8. For Johnson, see Garrett, *Frontier Triumph*, 58-64. For Turner, see Garrett, ibid., 215 and 217; and vertical files in Tarrant County Archives. Slave-owners with 100 or more slaves constituted just 10 percent of the slave-owning population, putting both men in exclusive company.
9. For Nathaniel Terry, see "Something of Col. Terry," *Dallas Morning News*, Feb. 7, 1904.
10. J.C. Terrell, *Reminiscences of the Early Days of Fort Worth* (Fort Worth: Texas Printing Co., 1906; reprinted TCU Press, 1999), 15; Garrett, *Frontier Triumph*, 61, 247–48.
11. Terry's stories are part of local and family lore. See vertical files in Tarrant County archives. The story of "faithful Uncle Jake" comes from hand-written MS in the Turner family file in Ruby Schmidt's papers, Tarrant County Archives, hereafter, Turner files, Schmidt. (Schmidt was the long-time president of the Tarrant County Historical Society.) For travelers, see Marilyn McAdams Sibley, *Travelers in Texas, 1761–1860* (Austin: University of Texas Press, 1967), 133–34. The most famous traveler through Texas before the Civil War was Frederick Law Olmsted, although he did not get to Fort Worth. See Frederick Law Olmsted, *A Journey Through Texas* (1857, reprinted New York: Time-Life Education, 1982); and ibid., *Journeys and Explorations in the Cotton Kingdom* (1861, reprinted Charleston, SC: Nabu Press, 2010). Simon Legree was the villainous slave-owner in Harriet Beecher Stowe's classic novel, *Uncle Tom's Cabin* (1852). He has his overseer whip poor Uncle Tom to death. For generations of Americans ever since the novel appeared, Legree has been the personification of heartless cruelty.

12. Mary Daggett Lake, "Tarrant's First Hundred Families," unidentified newspaper clipping in Peak Family Papers, Tarrant County Archives.
13. Or it may have been that Uncle Daniel was also an excellent jockey who rode the Colonel's prize horse to successful finishes in match races. "Something of Colonel Terry," the recollections of Captain J. C. Terrell in *Dallas Morning News*, February 7, 1904.
14. [Austin] *Texas State Gazette*, August 6, 1859.
15. Since usable public records for Fort Worth from this era no longer exist, we must reconstruct a history of this period through received lore, newspaper reports of other towns, and a handful of surviving private letters, some written many years later. For a good overview of the era, see Garrett, 175–182.
16. Terry's letter is reported in the *New York Evening Post*, August 24, 1860, reprinted from the *New Orleans Crescent*, August 20, 1860. It is also reported in the *Marshall* [Texas] *Republican*, August 18, 1860. Letter by anonymous Texas writer printed in *New York Daily Tribune*, August 22, 1860; cited in Donald E. Reynolds, *Editors Make War*, 2nd ed. (Carbondale: Southern Illinois University Press, 2006), 103-04, hereafter Reynolds, *Editors.*
17. For three Dallas hangings, see recollections of eighty-two-year-old J.M. Murrell, *Dallas Morning News*, July 14, 1929. For William H. Crawford, see *Dallas Herald*, May 1 and May 15 ("Letter to the Editor"), 1861; Richard B. McCaslin, *Tainted Breeze* (Baton Rouge: Louisiana State University Press, 1994), 26. For Reverend Anthony Bewley, see Robert L. Rooke, "Proclaiming the Injustice of Slavery Led to a Texas Preacher's Violent Death," *Fort Worth Star-Telegram*, February 5, 2010; Campbell, *Empire*, 227–28; and David Pickering and Judy Falls, *Brush Men and Vigilantes* (College Station: Texas A&M University Press, 2000), 44. For overview of events, see Donald E. Reynolds, *Texas Terror: The Slave Insurrection Panic of 1860 and the Secession of the Lower South* (Baton Rouge: Louisiana State University Press, 2007).
18. Besides the previously cited sources, Terry's letter is quoted in Reynolds, *Editors*, 106.
19. The "enticement" quote is from a "Wanted" notice for a runaway slave, issued in 1863 by Georgia slave-owner Louis Manigault, and cited in Stephanie McCurry, "No More Driver's Lash for Me," *America's Civil War* 25, no. 5 (November 2012): 21. For "Yankees," see *Galveston Weekly News*, February 15, 1865.

20. The editor of *The Whig*, A.B. Norton, was also a Unionist who had to tread lightly in his reporting. Ultimately, he was forced to leave town anyway. Reynolds, *Editors*, 107, 113, 133.
21. For Texas hysteria, see David Keehn, "Strong Arm of Secession," *North & South Magazine* 10, no. 6 (June, 2008): 42 ff. Newspapers reporting the hysteria included the *New York Times*, *New York Herald*, New Haven [Connecticut] *Columbian Register*, *Baltimore Sun*, Yazoo [Mississippi] *Democrat*, *Galveston* [Texas] *News*, Corpus Christi [Texas] *Ranchero*, and Marshall [Texas} *Harrison Flag*.
22. Appraised value of Tarrant County slaves in 1861 was $337,662. For tax records, see Bill Fairley, "Tarrant County Chronicles," *Fort Worth Star-Telegram*, June 19, 2002. The 1860 census figures are reported in "The Progress of Abolition," *Civil War Times* 48, no. 6 (December 2009): 36–37; and Geisel, *Historical Vignette*, 2.
23. For "cattle market" hypothesis, see Geisel, *Historical Vignette*, 2. For numbers, see Bruce Levine, *The Fall of the House of Dixie* (New York: Random House, 2013), 239.
24. Jamie Wilson's recollections are among the ex-slave interviews conducted by newspaperman Zeke Chandler in the 1930s. For Wilson's recollections, see Mack Williams, ed., "Memories of Tarrant County Slaves," "In Old Fort Worth" (collected columns), *The News-Tribune In Old Fort Worth* 13, no. 1 (July 2–4, 1976): 15, hereafter Williams, "Memories of Tarrant County Slaves." For Mitchell's recollections, see Charles Ellis Mitchell, "When Every Man Carried a Six-shooter," *In Old Fort Worth*, ed. Mack Williams (Fort Worth: privately printed, 1986), 46, hereafter Williams, *In Old Fort Worth*, 1986. This story was related by Mitchell more than half a century later. According to his recollections the women had 4,000 slaves between them, which is far more than the total number of slaves ever reported on the upper Trinity by any other source. The story is questionable on several counts: First, he would have been barely fifteen years old when this took place and not likely to have conducted a count. Second, the idea of two women virtually alone driving so many slaves through wartime Texas is incredible. The conclusion here is to discount the numbers while giving credence to the rest of the story.
25. Recollections of B. Frank Lewis, "The First Time I Saw Fort Worth," in Mack Williams, ed., "In Old Fort Worth," collection of columns from the *News-Tribune* 13, no. 1 (July 2, 3, 4, 1976): 4.
26. Bill Fairley, "Tarrant County Chronicles," *Fort Worth Star-Telegram*, June 19, 2002.

27. Ibid.
28. For "trusty negroes," see Levine, *Fall of the House of Dixie*, 239. Bormer, "Slave Narratives."
29. For Cobb quote, see Harold Holzer, "Secession Fever Revisited," *Civil War Times* 24, no. 2 (May 2011): 21. Ida Loving was born in Mississippi in 1856 and came to Fort Worth from Louisiana in the 1870s. Her recollections of slavery are from growing up in Mississippi and Louisiana, but her attitudes are consistent with upper-class white Southerners of her time. Ida Turner memoir., Box 1, Folder 4, Fort Worth Library, Central Branch, Local History, Genealogy, & Archives Unit.
30. For Johnson, see 1850 U.S. Federal Census, Slave Schedules, ibid. E.B. Daggett produced at least one child by the slave woman Matilda. For his story, see Richard Selcer, "Black Sheep Jeff Daggett," in *Fort Worth Characters* (Denton: University of North Texas Press, 2009), 131–148. For Chisum, see Delbert Willis, "A Great Cattle King," *Fort Worth Press*, October 6, 1966; and interview with Byron Hill of Fort Worth, a descendant of Chisum and Jensie, March 12, 2015. For Griffin, see Thomas H. Smith, "A Poor Pilgrim of Sorrow," *Legacies: A Journal for Dallas and North Central Texas* 17, no. 2 (Fall 2005): 7, Hereafter Thomas, "A Poor Pilgrim," and *Legacies Journal.*; and *Dallas Morning News*, May 28, 1933. Isaiah Edwards' evidence has yet to be thoroughly investigated by a professional historian or genealogist, but he was an invited guest to the dedication of Major Ripley Arnold's statue in 2014. Until his claim can be thoroughly vetted it must be treated carefully. For a brief overview of his case, see Bob Ray Sanders, "A Long-awaited Monument Will Be Dedicated to City's Founder," *Fort Worth Star-Telegram*, April 27, 2014.
31. For Douglass, see William S. McFeely, *Frederick Douglass* (New York: W.W. Norton, 1991); and Maria Diedrich, *Love across Color Lines: Ottilie Assing and Frederick Douglass* (New York: Hill and Wang, 1999). *Dallas Morning News*, September 26, 1891.
32. *Fort Worth Telegram*, October 6, 1903.
33. *Fort Worth Telegram*, October 8, 1903.
34. For "Colored People's Day," see Texas State Fair program, 1899, in Frances Allen Collection, Series II, Box 3 ("Family Papers"), Tarrant County Archives. *Dallas Morning News*, February 25, 1936.

Chapter 2

Reconstruction and the City's Beginnings (1865–1879)

At the end of the Civil War, Fort Worth was as low as it would ever be. If the residents had been polled, most would probably have agreed with Khleber Van Zandt, an ex-Confederate who arrived in August 1865, that Fort Worth was a "sad and gloomy" place. Nonetheless, Van Zandt saw something that made him decide to stay. He hired three young freedmen to help bring his family and belongings from Marshall. That simple financial arrangement alone was a sign of how things had changed. Before emancipation he would have expected to pay their master to hire their services. Times had changed in ways both large and small.[1]

In 1865 what was left of Fort Worth's white population numbered only about 250. By 1870 that number had risen to about 500 thanks to the seasonal cattle drives that came through headed north to Kansas railheads. The black population of Tarrant County in 1870 numbered 672. All those freedmen had to be doing some kind of work if they stayed on after being granted their freedom. Most still worked in virtual servitude for their former masters. Emancipation was unenforceable beyond the power of the U.S. Army. Significantly, there is no record of Fort Worth blacks celebrating the news of emancipation, probably because they didn't dare. When ex-Confederates like R.E. Beckham, B.B. Paddock, and Abe Harris came home to post-emancipation Fort Worth they found race relations virtually unchanged from pre-war.[2]

Most white Texans saw Reconstruction not as a fresh start but as a foreign occupation, the "foreigners" being Yankee carpetbaggers and bluecoats. Ex-Confederate and former Texas Governor Francis R. Lubbock wrote in his memoirs that Texas was "writhing under the heel of military despotism. . . [with a] premium on ignorance and barbarism." The latter were code words for elevation of the freedmen. When Lubbock got home from the war in December 1865 he found the state's principal cities "crowded with lazy negroes [begging] for rations, clothing, and everything else they could secure." He lamented the loss of his home, which had been destroyed, and adding insult to injury, "all our negroes are gone."[3]

When prominent white men like John Peter Smith and B. B. Paddock returned home to Fort Worth after the war they found what they believed to be a restive black population. Some Dallas men, including June Peak, the brother of Fort Worth's Dr. Carroll Peak, organized a Ku Klux Klan chapter to nip resistance to white rule in the bud. "Notices of warning" appeared on both sides of the Trinity directed at blacks and their sympathizers. The show of force apparently worked because no troubles occurred.[4]

Local efforts were supported by the Texas legislature. Soon after the war, those gentlemen passed a series of restrictive laws known as the "black codes" that created a system of virtual slavery to fill the void left by the abolition of the real thing. The codes applied a variety of civil and criminal statutes differently to blacks versus whites, restricting freedom of movement, property rights, and labor contracts, to name just a few areas. Specifically, the line dividing whites from blacks was drawn at having one-eighth African blood, which meant if even one grandparent had been black, the person was considered "black" under the law. These laws, which applied to blacks in Fort Worth the same as elsewhere in Texas, were officially enforced until 1867, and unofficially after that. For instance, with no legal definition of what constituted "negro-ness," white Texans depended on the "eyeball test"—if you looked black, you were black. On the other hand, for many years this allowed persons of mixed race to "pass" as white with no questions asked.[5]

Reconstruction barely touched Fort Worth. No federal troops were posted here or in Dallas. The city would not see numbers of U.S. troops until 1917 (World War I). There was a garrison of U.S. Colored Troops at Shreveport, Louisiana, 220 miles to the east, but they had no reason to visit Fort Worth. A young Bud Daggett, a member of one of the First Families of Fort Worth, encountered them when he helped drive a herd of cattle to Shreveport in 1865, and was glad to get home to Fort Worth afterwards because not only did Fort Worth not have to live under the heel of the U.S. army, but carpetbaggers did not descend on the area after the war. The big landowners from before the war, such as Nathaniel Terry, Paul Isbell, Ephraim Daggett, and Charles Turner, were still calling all the shots. Neither the Freedmen's Bureau nor the Union League, the champions of black freedom and equality, had outposts in north Texas for the first three years of Reconstruction. In 1868 Fort Worth and Dallas were placed in Sub-district No. 40 of the Freedmen's Bureau as part of an administrative re-organization. There is no record that the Bureau's agents ever came to town. The only federal presence in town was the U.S. Post Office. As long as Fort Worth did not draw attention to itself with mob violence or Klan activities, life could go on pretty much as it always had. True, slavery had been abolished, but freedmen still needed jobs and a roof over their heads and the whites controlled every aspect of social and economic life.[6]

A New Relationship

The end of Reconstruction could not come fast enough for men like Francis Lubbock and Nathaniel Terry. It meant not just the end of military occupation in their state, but the "restoration of white supremacy," and there were tens of thousands of whites just like them all over Texas. Eventually, even die-hard Rebels had to accept the reality of emancipation and the Fifteenth Amendment (ratified December 18, 1865). Fortunately for the small black population that still called Fort Worth home, there were a few enlightened citizens to set a good example, starting with former Confederate Major K. M. Van Zandt. The Tennessee-born Van Zandt had been raised in Texas with a slave as a "playmate." His childhood playmate accompanied him to war in 1861 and was still with him when he settled down in Fort Worth after the war. Van Zandt used freedmen as sharecroppers on his 600-acre spread west of town (located where the current cultural district is) and even patronized the only black entrepreneur in town, a blacksmith. Many years later, long after he had reinvented himself as a banker and businessman, Van Zandt continued to rely on the faithful "old negro" and another black man to work the farm.[7]

If blacks and whites were going to live together still, they were going to have to forge a new relationship. The two races could not simply go their own way; there was too much history between them. Whites needed black labor to keep an agricultural economy going. Blacks needed the structure and services of white-run society, at least until they could build their own social and political institutions. Naturally, in the beginning the new relationship looked a lot like the old one with blacks doing all the heavy labor and whites calling the shots. Many blacks hired themselves out to white families to do everything from cooking to plowing and harvesting. The long tradition of blacks in the cotton fields was an especially hard one to break.[8]

The new order would require some wrenching adjustments, starting with replacing the old state constitution that codified slavery. For blacks, the path from chattel to full-fledged citizens would be long and hard. For whites, the steady erosion of their historic power and position would also be difficult. One lingering effect of slavery that did not change much was names. During slavery, blacks did not have family names;

they were called by their first names or by "Uncle" or "Mammy" or some other demeaning name. After emancipation, needing a surname now to function in society, most freedmen simply took the last name of their former master. Thus, Fort Worth blacks show up in city directories and census records years later with familiar-sounding last names like Johnson, Tucker, Standifer, Daggett, and Turner.[9]

Emancipation's biggest economic impact on whites was on the big landowners who had relied on slave labor to work their land. Wealthy by pre-emancipation standards, they lost the equivalent of $1,200–$1,500 for every field hand who took his freedom and ran. Multiplied by twenty to fifty field hands, this was a financial blow from which many never recovered. By contrast, household slaves and "personal servants" tended to stay with their white families. Their masters had usually treated them well, even taking a paternalistic interest in their welfare. So close were those relationships that they were stunned if faithful servant chose freedom over the status quo. During the war Francis Lubbock had taken his man Eli to Richmond with him "at great expense" when joining Jefferson Davis' cabinet. When Eli disappeared near the end of the war after it became obvious that the South was going to lose, Lubbock presumed he had been killed because "He would have returned to me or to Texas for he was devoted to me." Instead, Lubbock never heard from Eli again. Lubbock expressed pity for the "poor boy."[10]

Some former masters were shocked at the perceived lack of loyalty displayed by their former slaves. Diehard Virginia secessionist Edmund Ruffin wrote in his diary in late 1864, "I had before believed in the general prevalence of much attachment & affection of negro slaves for the families of their masters," but what he was seeing instead was "signal ingratitude & treachery" toward even the "most considerate & kind of masters."[11]

The record of a few notable former Tarrant County masters is heart-warming insofar as it goes. They behaved with commendable charity toward their freed slaves, perhaps because making nice could save them the cost of hiring workers on the open market. Any freedman who could be convinced to stick around and work in return for a roof over their head and a percentage of the crop saved the landowner money out of pocket that most could not afford. We don't know their motives, however; we only know the results. Middleton Tate Johnson took care of Betty Bormer and her family; Paul Isbell looked after "Old Uncle Ott"; William B. Tucker extended a hand to Hagar (who even took his former master's last name); Edward Terrell took care of "Old Nath"; Nathaniel Terry did the same for "Uncle Dan'l," and Charles Turner for "Uncle Jake" until the day Turner died in 1873. Lore even has it that Turner and Uncle Jake were buried side-by-side at Turner's request. Then there was Baldwin Samuels, a familiar sight around town driving a "shiny black buggy" with his former slave as a "constant companion perched on the back." These old masters represent a Who's Who of Fort Worth's First Families. Their faithful servants may have been "freed" in the legal sense, but not even the strongest bonds of love and devotion could guarantee financial security and the sort of independence that comes with such security. Out of necessity many were forced to continue working for the old master. What they got for their continued loyalty and service was a roof over their head, food, and protection from roving bands of night riders. However, the fact that in more than a few cases this generosity continued years after the former slave had become too old or too infirm to do a full day's work also suggests that it was not entirely calculating. [12]

It was the fortunate freedman after the Civil War who was able to place himself or herself under the protection of a powerful white patron. Captain E.M. Daggett, for instance, took care of Matilda, the mammy who had largely raised his son "Bud"; she remained on the Daggett plantation as a household servant for many years after being emancipated. Daggett was famously solicitous toward all of his former slaves. If we can believe surviving accounts, they "worshipped him" and "were ever ready to go to him. . . at his bidding." Such an arrangement benefitted both sides; the black person had a protector in a cruel, unforgiving world, and the Captain never lacked for willing hands to work his fields.[13]

The benefactor relationship endured long after the curtain was rung down on Reconstruction. In 1890, after an elderly Hagar Tucker had fallen on hard times, his old master William B. Tucker allowed him to live in the servants' quarters behind his mansion on Tucker Hill. And sometime after 1889, when black cattleman Daniel Webster Wallace was down on his luck, he came to Fort Worth to see Winfield Scott, the cattle baron/real estate tycoon. Wallace had once worked for Scott, and now when he reached out to Scott, the old boss gave him a letter of credit for $10,000 which helped Wallace get back on his feet. Kindnesses such as these were admirable, even heart-warming, although they were not the same as genuine equality.[14]

Beloved personal servants were just one part of the equation. Far more numerous were the field hands under slavery who were totally unprepared for freedom when it came. For them life as freedmen proved to be little different from slavery. In Tarrant County they formed an insignificant percentage of the total population. The 1871 *Texas Almanac* reported that the county had 64,000 acres planted in corn, wheat, and cotton, and nine-tenths of the farm work was done by white men, which would have included both landowners and hired laborers. African Americans, the *Almanac* went on, "never own lands but generally lease," meaning they were sharecroppers and tenant farmers. Big landowners like Khleber Van Zandt became irritated when one of their tenant farmers "saw fit to move back to town." This was one of the reasons they were reluctant to let their workers go into town. The possibility of getting drunk and not coming back, or getting into trouble with the law, or even being grabbed by another white landowner needing workers were also concerns. For all these reasons, tenant farmers would only have been seen around town when they came in for supplies, although on the occasions that did happen the rare black face would certainly have stood out among the town's 1,500 white residents. And since there was no black business district at this time they would have had to buy their supplies from the same merchants as white residents, which would not have been an issue as long as they bought what they needed and left, not tarrying in the saloons or public places.[15]

"Good Darkies" vs. "Unruly Negroes"

In white thinking of the time there were two kinds of blacks: "good darkies," the term applied to those who were respectful and did what they were told, and "unruly negroes," the name applied to those who were considered trouble-makers or simply did not know their place. It was this sort of thinking that spawned rumors in 1879 of widespread attacks on white women in the area. There is no evidence that any such attacks took place, and even the *Fort Worth Democrat* (owned and published by Confederate veteran Buckley B. Paddock) called them "alleged attacks," but that did not put an end to the wild rumors. Those fears of murder and rapine faded with time, to be replaced by the warm glow of nostalgia. Late in life lifetime Fort Worth resident Howard W. Peak recalled the "old-time darkeys [*sic*]" he had known in his youth with fondness, including Old Dan Hall, Dan Daggett, and John Pratt. Another of the "good negroes" was "Uncle Tom" Washington, whose passing was lamented by the *Fort Worth Telegram* in 1907. Peak called such men "mighty faithful negroes," putting his finger on the one quality that endeared them to whites of Peak's generation. Washington's flattering obituary in the *Telegram* was all the more remarkable because that newspaper seldom had anything good to say about blacks, but Uncle Tom had also been a deacon in the Colored Baptist Church on the North Side. He rang the bell for Sunday services for many years. The newspaper did not know his real first name; "Uncle Tom" was an affectionate sobriquet for "one of the most religious among the colored people." "Uncle Tom" was shorthand for any loyal, well-mannered black man of a certain age, and had been since antebellum times when Harriet Beecher Stowe created the fictional "Uncle Tom."[16]

For decades after the Civil War, "faithful (old) negro" was the highest compliment whites could apply to a black man. It was more than just a cliché; it became shorthand in newspaper reports for any black who accepted his assigned place in society. By the same token, it was the second-most demeaning label that could be put on a black man. The term does not drop out of usage until well into the twentieth century.[17]

The emancipated generation found the way smoother if they continued to behave in the old ways while raising their children to take their rightful place in society. Parents invested all their hopes and dreams in the next generation. One of those was Alexander Terrell, father of beloved Fort Worth educator Isaiah M. Terrell. The elder Terrell lived most of his life in Grimes County, east Texas, where local whites considered him a good "colored citizen" of the county. When he died in 1901 they took the almost unheard-of action of publishing a testimonial in the *Houston Post* that said his "walk through life" had been "upright. . . though his color be black," and that he bore himself "at all times as a man should. . . by realizing his own position in life and not attempting to depart from it." They praised him as a man who "made it his duty. . . to preserve a friendly feeling in his heart for the white people of this community." The unspoken message between the lines was that if all blacks were like "Old Uncle Alex" the races would get along fine. Later black activists would criticize men like Alexander Terrell for holding back the progress of the black man in the South by being content just to get along.[18]

On the other end of the spectrum were troublesome "uppity" blacks who would not accept their approved position in the natural order, instead agitating for equality. Their kind was hated and feared by whites because they threatened the very pillars Southern society was built on: white superiority and black subservience. The old order was threatened by the Freedmen's Bureau and its successor, the Union League, both of which were universally hated by whites. To keep African Americans in line and smooth the transition from slavery to emancipation, the white ruling class attempted to keep blacks in the fields with "labor contracts" and tenant farming. With no skills, no education, and no money, most freedmen found themselves with no options but to go back to work on the land of their former masters while their women continued to work as domestics, also without pay.

Whites who even noticed freedmen on the street during the Reconstruction era thought nothing of engaging in a little "harmless fun" at black expense. Charles Ellis Mitchell, who came to Fort Worth as a boy in 1856, witnessed white men firing their pistols into the ground at the feet of blacks just to see them "dance." As Mitchell recalled the scene years later, it was nothing special; the boys did this to all "newcomers" in town.[19]

Socially, the difference between slavery and freedom was not very large. In the legal system, things changed scarcely at all. Written into the state constitution of 1876 were prohibitions against blacks sitting on juries, testifying in court, or bringing suit against white persons. Emancipation had changed nothing. The legal system was still as firmly in the hands of whites as it had always been.[20]

THE KLAN AND THREATS OF VIOLENCE

Always lingering in the background of their new life was the threat of violence. Lynching was a fact of life for freedmen in Texas as elsewhere in the South. Lynching in its various forms was not just about punishing one unfortunate; it sent a message to the entire black community. Stories of horrific murders and whippings were told and re-told in both the black and white communities even when they were completely spurious. In 1869 the *Denton Monitor* told the story of a white school teacher of black schoolchildren in Tarrant County who had been hanged for daring to "procure a license to marry one of his pupils." It never happened, but the newspaper underscored the evils of miscegenation for both races by reporting that it was a "colored mob" who hanged the white teacher! Not only is there no independent verification of the story in any historical record, but the whole episode is preposterous on the face of it. Still, the message was loud and clear; the last line of the newspaper story emphasized it mockingly: "It seems the negroes apprehended that if miscegenation was not checked the whites would soon get all the best-looking wenches."[21]

Serious enforcement of the social order was not left up to "colored mobs," however. It was the job of the Ku Klux Klan, the extra-legal organization that functioned as a virtual auxiliary to legitimate law enforcement. In 1868 a group of unnamed Tarrant County men organized a local chapter of the group founded in Tennessee two years earlier. The local Klavern was strongest in the rural, eastern part of the county. It is impossible to say today whether it kept a low profile or was just weak because we have scant references to its activities. What survives is contained in a few private letters and "Slave Narrative" interviews, the latter recorded many years later. While there are reports of whippings and night ridings in the county, Fort Worth seems to have enjoyed remarkably peaceful race relations. The threat of mob action never seems to have been carried out judging by surviving records.[22]

With the end of Reconstruction in Texas, the Klan "waned and disappeared" after 1871 according to Julia Kathryn Garrett, the pre-eminent historian of early Fort Worth. The entire Reconstruction period, roughly 1865–1877, is very vague in Fort Worth history. But two things are clear: Former masters, specifically E. M. Daggett, K. M. Van Zandt, and William B. Tucker, were remarkably tolerant and kindly to their former slaves. After the Holocaust, Europe's Jews had the concept of "the Righteous Gentile," meaning non-Jews who saved individual Jews or small groups from genocide. During Reconstruction it seems there were "righteous whites" who tried to ease the transition of blacks from slavery to freedom, which is not to say they were saintly, just that they tried to do the right thing. Second, the stories of terrified African American men spending every night in the woods to avoid the sweeps of Klan night-riders through the countryside strains credulity. Such stories were related decades later to WPA interviewers for the "Slave Narratives." Setting aside the passage of decades, the stories seem too contrived, too melodramatic to be genuine. Still, they cannot be dismissed out of hand.

They may be true or they may be the product of failing memories and over-active imaginations. They are a window to attitudes in the 1930s as much as the 1870s.[23]

"GIVE US THIS DAY OUR DAILY BREAD"

This well-known line from the Lord's Prayer reminds us that freedom is about more than exercising the rights of citizenship. Freedmen had to earn a living in this brave, new world. The compassion of some former masters obscures the fact that all were not reduced to peonage or begging for handouts. Historian Augusta Gooch lists more than a dozen jobs "colored people" could go into between 1870 and 1880, that include but are not limited to wood-cutter, dray operator, boot-black, tinsmith, white-washer, rag-picker, expressman, domestic, porter, hod carrier, and farrier. Most of these jobs no longer exist today, but they represent a good cross-section of unskilled jobs available in a frontier town in the nineteenth century. They were the bottom of the economic scale, but at least they paid wages and allowed a worker one of the essential freedoms—freedom of contract—that had been denied slaves.[24]

Two freedmen, Hagar Tucker and John Pratt, showed their people the path to the future. The city council hired Tucker as a "special policeman" in 1873 based (grudgingly) on the ancient, unwritten right of a community to "police their own." In Reconstruction Texas only whites could be official policemen; blacks were reduced to being "special officers." A black special officer was the eyes and ears of the white city council in the black community, with the understanding that he had no authority over whites. Tucker performed a difficult job successfully, but was let go nonetheless within a year with Reconstruction in full retreat and the economy in the doldrums. John Pratt became the first "Negro businessman of Fort Worth" when he opened a blacksmith shop near the public square. He was not well-received until Major Van Zandt, the Confederate war hero, began taking his horse to Pratt's shop.[25]

The ugly, racist side of the Reconstruction era can be seen in the 1874 hanging of Sol Bragg, a black man convicted of killing Matthew Green, a white man. Reportedly, the accused got a "fair trial" before being hanged by Sheriff Tom James. Bragg was the first man legally hanged in Tarrant County, but with no lawyer for the defendant and a white judge (Hardin Hart) and jury, it is questionable how fair his trial was. On May 8, a crowd estimated at 4,000, including women and children, gathered in "the hollow west of town" to watch justice administered. Sol Bragg was incorporated into local lore as a cautionary tale that demonstrates the insidious nature of racism: as white Fort Worthers remembered it years later, his crime was "assaulting a white woman."[26]

The case of John Pratt illustrates an important aspect of the post-emancipation social contract between blacks and whites. Independent entrepreneurs like Pratt were regarded with contempt unless they had a white patron. Van Zandt along with a handful of other more enlightened or more compassionate men, like William Tucker and the Reverend Lacey K. Williams, opened a few doors to their black neighbors who were trying to better themselves. In the process, Tucker and Williams and others like them whose names have not come down to us also helped keep racial incidents to a minimum.

Something else kept racial incidents to a minimum, and that was living apart. The white community had its own reasons for imposing segregation, but the fact remains that it helped keep racial tensions down. On the other side of the segregation line, blacks who had been slaves found life easier if they lived as far from town as possible. In the early 1870s the largest concentration of freedmen was to be found in bucolic Mosier Valley, fourteen miles east of Fort Worth between Euless and Arlington. There a few families settled on a tract of empty land covering about 900 acres (1.4 square miles) with a stream running through it and a stand of timber. The original settlers were former farm laborers who wanted to keep doing the only kind of work they knew but not as sharecroppers. Over the years that followed they were joined by others looking for a safe place and a life among their own people. They became a real community after they built a church (1874) and a schoolhouse (1883). The population of Mosier Valley eventually peaked at about 300 in the 1930s.[27]

While Mosier Valley offered security and friendly faces, what it would not offer for the next century were municipal services: no sewers or water lines, no fire and police protection, no public park, streetlights, or sidewalks, even after being annexed by Fort Worth in 1963. Mosier Valley would live in a time warp for almost 100 years. In 1983 it received a historical marker from the Texas Historical Commission as "the oldest black settlement in the state of Texas," and in 2014 it was designated "an under-served area of the city."[28]

Mosier Valley is a microcosm of the experience of African Americans in many areas of the South after emancipation. On the one hand, they were marginalized and treated like second-class citizens. On the other hand, as one resident said many years later about growing up in Mosier Valley and attending the school there, "The community was small, and the relationship we had with each other . . . . was more like a family." This was an experience they would have missed living in a more integrated community.[29]

SCHOOLS

Schooling for children of freedmen was one of the great challenges of the new order. Reconstruction policy set in Washington decreed that all children go to school together regardless of race. It was unenforceable. As a result, black children either went to private schools or did not go to school at all. Private schooling meant being taught by white teachers, many of them Northerners who came south after the war to take on a noble mission. White Southerners labeled them "carpetbaggers," i.e., invaders who had come into their communities to carry off everything that wasn't nailed down.

The first schools for blacks in Fort Worth were set up by Charles C. Cummings, who arrived from Mississippi in 1873 as a Confederate veteran. After being elected county judge in 1876 he approached James A. Cavile, a leader of the black community, and asked him to head up a "colored board of trustees" tasked with organizing the first colored schools in the county. Cavile and his fellow trustees rolled up their sleeves and soon had schools in Fort Worth, Village Creek, Mosier Valley, Johnson's Station (Arlington), Mansfield, Live Oak Grove, and White Settlement. Under Judge Cummings' patronage, they operated this "colored school system" for the next "six or eight years." The schools were funded by a combination of white donations and fees paid by black parents. In later years, Cavile was dubbed "the Father of Negro Schools and education" in Fort Worth before being ultimately overshadowed in the historical record by Isaiah M. Terrell and James E. Guinn.[30]

Meanwhile, teaching black children the "3Rs" was proceeding on another, parallel track in churches and private homes. Private "negro schools" were run by Belle Murray Burchill and Henry H. Butler. They charged three dollars per month tuition, a not-inconsequential sum in those days for whites or blacks. Burchill was white; Butler was African-American.[31]

Burchill had come to Fort Worth from Illinois with her husband George in 1874. By that date the "carpetbagger" designation had lost some of its sting. Not content to be a stay-at-home wife or society maven, Burchill opened a school for black children in her home on Houston St. The classes were both a source of extra income and an act of benevolence. In 1878 she moved her school to the Allen Chapel building, an outpost of the African Methodist Episcopal (A.M.E.) church close to where the Eastern cattle trail passed through town. Enrollment reportedly soared to 130.[32]

Another colored school was started by the Methodist Episcopal Church. They hired Henry H. Butler—one of those rarest of frontier types, a black educator—to teach classes. Little is known about Butler's early life, only that he arrived in town about 1876 as a Union army veteran with a fierce commitment to educating his people. Because he had a degree in English from Washburn College in Kansas he was invited by the church to operate a school in their building. Butler later told an interviewer he was driven by "a determination I possessed, partly because of my own volition and partly because of what my father had told me. . . to educate myself if I had the opportunity." He spent the next twenty-two years giving the same opportunity to others of his race. When he started he had thirty-five paying pupils and split the tuition with the congregation.[33]

Thanks to the vision of people like James A. Cavile, Belle Burchill, and Henry H. Butler, black Fort Worth children got the chance to develop their minds, something they had been denied under slavery. In Cavile and Butler they also had something else, black role models, demonstrating that a black man could aspire to something more than a life of back-breaking labor.

Even with willing teachers and classrooms, the obstacles to learning were still daunting. The modest tuition was beyond the means of 99 percent of black families, and money was not the only issue. Teachers had the children for at most six months out of the year. During growing season their pupils had to work in the fields to help support their families. Still, inadequate schooling was better than no schooling at all, so parents did their best to come up with the tuition and juggle the chores during the school year. Because of the sacrifices parents had to make to send their children to school, teachers were among the most respected members of the community.

CHURCHES

There was not a lot of organized religion to nourish the African-American spirit during this era. They had no church buildings, no preachers, no congregations in the beginning. Most had been exposed to Christianity during slavery and continued on that path after they were freed. Congregations were the first social groups they formed, and the church quickly became the center of the black community. It was the one place where they could gather in peace, comforted by the scriptural teaching that all men are equal before God. Not until the very end of the era did the first church buildings go up. They were havens from the world, community centers, and providers of social services besides being houses of worship.

In early Fort Worth, denominational options for African Americans were limited to either the Baptist or Methodist creed. Both denominations had split over the issue of slavery before the Civil War, the Methodists in 1844 and the Baptists in 1845. The Methodist Episcopal Church South included both masters and slaves although not on an equal basis. Slaves were only allowed to participate in worship services by either sitting quietly in the back of the room or listening at an open window. Nobody, black or white, met in their own building for many years. They either met at the Masonic Hall, over the livery stable, or in some other public building. The first church buildings were erected after the Civil War, by which time the racial lines were firmly drawn. Not even emancipation made blacks welcome in white congregations. Some black Methodists pulled out of the Methodist Episcopal Church South and formed the Colored Methodist Episcopal Church. Mostly, the freedmen were unfazed by ecclesiastical purity and worshipped as they always had. Those who identified with one denomination or the other formed unauthorized congregations and worshipped together wherever they could. It was not easy. In 1866 the Methodist Conference of Texas divided black and white faithful into two "divisions" and ordered them to meet separately. And if the black faithful of any denomination wanted a house of worship they would have to build it themselves.[34]

The black Methodist faithful were the first to organize a Fort Worth church, under the direction of a white circuit preacher who came to town in 1870 and started a flock with just five members. Methodists had an advantage over most other denominations because they had a well-established system of circuit-riding preachers that brought the Word to even the most remote and desolate outposts. The first meeting place of black Methodists was a "shanty" with a "cobblestone" floor. That little flock became the genesis of the later Allen Chapel African Methodist Episcopal (A.M.E.) Church at First and Elm which still exists today. Meanwhile, another group of black Methodists, organized under the banner of the Christian Methodist Episcopal (C.M.E.) Church was meeting at what is today Sixth and Crump. They were close to where the McCoy Trail (aka, the Chisholm Trail) passed through Fort Worth. Church lore says that black cowboys driving cattle up the trail worshipped with the congregation, but this cannot be verified from the historical record.[35]

The black faithful of the Baptists and Disciples of Christ denominations did not formally organize in Fort Worth until years later. If there were black Presbyterians, Episcopalians, and Catholics, they were too few to be considered congregations.

Politics

In the 1870s black residents of Fort Worth could participate in the political process but only at the pleasure of the white majority. Come election time, black voters were recruited by white candidates to tip the balance in their favor in the event of a tight election. Otherwise, the black vote was insignificant. Since there were never any black candidates for public office, if the black community wanted to have any influence whatsoever on the election they had to cut a deal with whichever candidate promised them the most. It was old-fashioned democracy with a racial twist. One barely remembered deal was cut in the 1875 election for county judge. One of the candidates, Charles C. Cummings, cut a deal with James A. Cavile, a prominent black landowner and spokesman for the black community. Cummings asked Cavile to "represent" him in the "colored community," meaning get out the vote for him. The other part of the deal was that Cummings would see that the white community, his community, got behind the establishment of the area's first "colored schools." This constitutes the first black-white political deal in Fort Worth history. Cummings went on to win (the first of two terms, 1876–1880) and kept his promise.[36]

This deal is particularly instructive because Cummings and Cavile did not have any relationship at the time the candidate invited the black man over to his house to offer him the deal. Even a proud Confederate veteran could not be too proud when it came to running for public office. The black vote, as insignificant as it was, could not be ignored. Other prominent white men like Khleber Van Zandt might have long-standing personal relationships with former slaves, but Cummings and Cavile were simply cutting a political deal, and that based on nothing more than a hand-shake. Cavile had not even been Cummings' slave; he had belonged to Nathaniel Terry until 1865.

The black vote was not always solicited by whites running for public office. In the 1879 marshal's race, one candidate took out an ad in the *Fort Worth Democrat* announcing that he did not want the vote of "any Negro" or Union army veteran, two groups of voters considered *persona non grata* by unreconstructed whites. This was fourteen years after Appomattox. The passions of the war lasted long after the firing stopped.[37]

When Reconstruction officially ended in Texas (1873), the incremental progress being made by blacks during the previous nine years ground to a halt. Post-Reconstruction, both parties angled to control the African-American vote, the Republicans by turning their backs on any black who voted Democrat, and the Democrats by discouraging blacks from voting at all. Identified with emancipation and carpetbaggers, the Republican Party grew weaker by the year while the Democrats won state and local offices with machine-like regularity. When, after the mid-1880s, control of the Republican Party passed into the hands of Norris Wright Cuney, an African American, the party was practically doomed as an effective opposition party.

The 1876 Texas constitution could not completely disfranchise blacks because of the Fifteenth Amendment to the U.S. Constitution, but there were other, extra-legal ways of keeping blacks away from the polls, such as literacy tests and poll taxes. In 1888 there were still enough Republicans locally to hold a county convention in the run-up to the presidential election, but when the convention tried to allow black members to vote for delegates to the state convention, thirty white members walked out in protest.[38]

The Reconstruction era remained vivid in the collective memory of the black community even decades later. Those once known as "freedmen" became celebrities to those whose only knowledge of slavery was what they heard from old-timers. The recollections of those old-timers became the stuff of oral history *and* of legend. Among former Tarrant County slaves who lived well into the twentieth century were Lucinda Clayton, Sam Kilgore, and A.J. Anderson. Far enough removed from the bad old days for nostalgia to take over, they were feted by whites and blacks alike when Juneteenth rolled around every year. In the 1930s, retired newspaper reporter Zeke Handler interviewed as many as he could round up, and Mrs. Charles Scheuber of the Fort Worth Public Library made his notes part of the library's holdings. Those notes then became part of the "Slave Narratives" in the "Federal Writers' Project." They give us the only glimpse we have today of the other side of the great racial divide before 1865.[39]

HAGAR TUCKER—KEEPING THE PEACE[40]

He was born into slavery in Kentucky in 1842 and given a proper Old Testament name, "Hagar," by his parents. The surname "Tucker" came from the fact that his master was William B. Tucker, and when emancipation came, freedmen just naturally took their master's family name to gout in the white man's world. He grew up without an education and never learned to write his own name. As an adult he signed documents with an "X."

Hagar came to Texas with William B. Tucker's family in the 1850s and was emancipated along with the rest of the slaves in 1865. For the rest of his life, he maintained an extraordinarily good relationship with his former master, which may explain why he stayed on in Fort Worth as a free man despite the lack of opportunities for people of color. His wife Amy had also been a Tucker slave. Their marriage is not recorded, but the union lasted thirty-two years and produced at least eight children.

Within two years of emancipation Hagar Tucker owned property and was registered to vote in Tarrant County. When Fort Worth incorporated in 1873, Reconstruction was still going on and the city had both a black and a white community living uneasily together. To maintain order in the black community and help keep peace between the races, city fathers wanted a black officer on the tiny police force. Tucker was a natural choice. Not only was he respected in the black community, but his former master was on the city council and vouched for "Hague." The council appointed him a "special policeman" which meant he was not a member of the regular force. He was paid less and restricted to policing his own people.

Officer Hague performed his duties capably and with due deference to whites. It is not known how long he was a special policeman, but when Fort Worth experienced its first case of racial conflict in the fall of 1874, it was Irish cop Columbus Fitzgerald who brought in the black ringleaders of the trouble.

After leaving law enforcement, Tucker found employment as a saloon "porter" (janitor) then went into the grocery business, selling locally grown fruits and vegetables out of his house. On the tax records he was listed as a "free man of color," a term carried over from slavery days. He and Amy taught all their children to read and write. One eventually became a teacher. Tucker was also the earliest known member of the Prince Hall (black) Masons in Fort Worth. His membership must have pleased William B. Tucker who was a charter member of Masonic Grand Lodge No. 148.

By 1890, forty-eight-year-old Hague Tucker was in bad health and old beyond his years. A daughter worked for William B. Tucker on the Tucker Hill estate. She was allowed to move her mother and father into the servants' quarters behind the big house. Hague and Amy did light work for Mr. Tucker as domestics. Life had come full circle.

On October 2, 1892, Hagar Tucker died and was buried in the Trinity [African-American] section of Oakwood Cemetery. An engraved stone obelisk, probably paid for by William Tucker, was placed over the grave. At the time of his death, Hagar Tucker owned personal property worth $500. He left it to "my beloved wife Amy Tucker." Hagar Tucker was Fort Worth's first black resident of note. There would not be another black officer with the Fort Worth Police Department until 1953.

Isaiah Milligan Terrell—Pioneering educator[41]

Isaiah M. Terrell is the father of black education in Fort Worth. He was one of the first two black teachers hired when the city created a public school system in 1882. Like his role model, Booker T. Washington, he was born into slavery, in Grimes County, Texas, sometime in the 1850s. (Since birth records for slaves do not exist, his exact birth date is unknown.) He learned to read and write and do simple sums at a time when book-learning was not just unavailable for blacks; it was unlawful. After emancipation he attended Straight University in New Orleans where he earned both bachelor's and master's degrees by 1880. At Straight he also met his future wife, a Fort Worth girl named Marcelite Landry. Until 1882 Terrell taught at a private school in Grimes County, but then he was offered a teaching job in Fort Worth. He took it and married Marcelite the next year. She, too, was a classroom teacher, and they would teach together for the rest of their careers. They also collaborated in producing two sons, Alexander Bismarck Terrell and Wendell Terrell.

Terrell had many fine qualities, including a powerful mind and a relentless ambition, but a sweet disposition was not among them. School Superintendent Alexander Hogg brought Terrell to Fort Worth in 1882 and remained his mentor for the next thirty-three years. This sometimes meant protecting Terrell from himself. If Terrell didn't exactly pick fights, he did not back down from them either. He acquired more than his share of powerful enemies over the years. In 1889 the school board fired him for the first but not last time in his life. He took a job as superintendent of Waxahachie's black elementary school, but returned to Fort Worth a year later and added the title "superintendent" of black schools to his credentials. Six years later he was out on the street again, but landed a teaching job in Dallas. In 1901 it was back to Fort Worth for him and Marcelite, again as superintendent of black schools. By now, even the white newspapers were calling him "Professor," a remarkable compliment in the Jim Crow era. That same year, the city's most conservative newspaper admitted that the credit for the "excellent" state of the city's two "colored schools" belonged to "I.M. Terrell and his wife."

So why did a man whose talent for education was recognized by even the most bigoted observers change jobs so often? Terrell was never much good at the bowing and scraping required of black men in the Jim Crow era. He wore his principles on his sleeve and provided his bosses with plenty of reasons to give him the gate. Fortunately, Alexander Hogg was always there to bring him back after the latest tempest had subsided. That changed after the 1908–09 school year when Hogg retired. One of his last acts was pushing through Terrell's appointment as principal of the South Side Colored School, the city's first black secondary school. Marcelite was part of the package, teaching voice.

In 1915 the latest blow-up with the school board forced him out for good. Isaiah Terrell had burned his last bridge in Fort Worth. Looking back, the *Fort Worth Star-Telegram* described his thirty-three-year tenure in the Fort Worth school system as "stormy." Undeterred, Prairie View Normal School hired him as president. Having made the jump to higher education, he moved on to Houston Baptist College, the last stop for him and Marcelite. She died in 1924, and seven years later he joined her on September 28, 1931. They are buried beside each other in Houston. The headstone misspells his name "Isiah [*sic*] M. Terrell."

In 1921, six years after he left town for good, the Fort Worth school board renamed the old South Side Colored School at Twelfth and Steadman "I.M. Terrell High School" in his honor. That name followed it in its move to Eighteenth and Chambers in 1937. Over the next three decades it was enlarged and upgraded to meet the growing demands on the area's only black high school. It offered a unique educational experience to both students and teachers, including such extra-curricular activities as a debate society and an interior decorating club.

The school board closed the high school in 1973 in response to court-ordered school desegregation. In the years that followed, an active alumni association continued to raise the Terrell banner high, honoring both the man and the school that was named for him. It was their efforts that got the building designated a Texas historic landmark in 1986, and in 1998 Terrell received a six-million-dollar facelift and was reborn as an elementary school and neighborhood civic center. In 2004, East Eighteenth on Chambers Hill was renamed I.M. Terrell Circle. In 2014 the school experienced its second renaissance when the Fort Worth school board designated it the future home of the new Visual and Performing Arts School *and* the Science, Technology, Engineering, and Math (STEM) Academy—open to all Fort Worth students. In a building bearing the name of legendary educator Isaiah M. Terrell, black students can achieve their dreams just the same as white students.

NOTES

1. Whether they stayed on in Fort Worth or returned to Marshall is not known. K.M. Van Zandt, *Force without Fanfare: The Autobiography of K.M. Van Zandt,* ed. Sandra L. Myers (Fort Worth: Texas Christian University Press, 1968), 113, 116.
2. Teresa Palomo Acosta, "Juneteenth," *The New Handbook of Texas,* Ron Tyler *et al.*, eds. (Austin: Texas State Historical Association, 1996), hereafter *New Handbook of Texas.* Statistics come from "Federal Writers' Project, Research Data: Fort Worth and Tarrant County, Texas," Series I, Fort Worth Library Unit, 1941, Fort Worth Library, Central Branch, Local History, Archives and Genealogy Unit., pp. 251, 638, and 4,045; hereafter "Federal Writers' Project."
3. Francis Richard Lubbock, *Six Decades in Texas* (Austin: Pemberton Press, 1968), 592, 604–05, hereafter Lubbock, *Six Decades.*
4. Recollections of Worth Peak (June Peak's brother), undated, Peak Papers, Tarrant County Archives. The Peak family was prominent in both Dallas and Fort Worth from the earliest days.
5. Carl H. Moneyhon, "Black Codes," *New Handbook of Texas.*
6. Garrett, *Frontier Triumph,* 185; A. Ray Stephens, *Texas: A Historical Atlas* (Norman: University of Oklahoma Press, 2010), 177–78. For Daggett, see William H. Leahy, "Pioneer Citizen [Col. H.M. "Bud" Daggett] Is Reminiscent over Days of Old," unidentified newspaper clipping in Daggett files, Tarrant County Archives.
7. Lubbock, *Six Decades,* 60–5; *Fort Worth Telegram,* March 17, 1907.
8. Bill Fairley, "Tarrant Chronicles," *Fort Worth Star-Telegram,* February 17, 1999.
9. For constitutional changes, see Lubbock, *Six Decades,* 604. For adopted surnames, see Geisel, *Historical Vignette,* p. 1. Another likely but unprovable surname connection was Trezevant. Former Confederate Colonel J. T. Trezevant (white) arrived in Dallas in 1876 and made a name for himself as a business entrepreneur in the following decades. Meanwhile, William and Naomi Trezevant (black) arrived in Fort Worth in 1877 from no-one-knew-where, and their son William, Jr. was born that same year. Like Hagar Tucker and Jeff Daggett, Travezant, Jr. grew up well-spoken, educated, and burning with ambition. For Trezevant, Jr., see Max Hill,

"William Trezevant, Jr.," *Fort Worth Genealogical Society's Footprints* 47, no. 3 (August 2004): 107, hereafter cited as Hill, "Trezevant".

10. Lubbock, *Six Decades*, 554–55.
11. Edmund Ruffin, *The Diary of Edmund Ruffin*, vol. 3, William Kaufman Scarborough, ed. (Baton Rouge: Louisiana State University, 1972-1989), 692.
12. Garrett, 275–76, 279. For price of slaves, "mighty faithful negroes," and "Old Nath," see reminiscences of Howard W. Peak in a series of articles in *Fort Worth Star-Telegram*, October 1, 1922. For "Hagar," see Selcer, "Hagar Tucker: Fort Worth's First Black Policeman," in *Fort Worth Characters*, 59–66. For Terry and "Old Dan'l," see J.C. Terrell's reminiscences in *Fort Worth Telegram* (predecessor of *Star-Telegram*), February 7, 1904. Either Nathaniel Terry was particularly kind to his slaves or memories played tricks on white pioneers years later because Terry was also reportedly the master of "Uncle Billy Mays," who had nothing bad to say about his former master. See *Fort Worth Weekly Gazette*, February 6, 1890. For Turner and "Uncle Jake," see Turner files, Schmidt. For Samuels, see biographical file in Tarrant County Historical Commission's archives. The freedman is not identified by name.
13. For white protection, see reminiscences of Sam Kilgore, Williams, "Memories of Tarrant County Slaves," p. 15. For Daggett's relationship with his former slaves, see biographical sketch in *Fort Worth City Directory*, 1877, on microfiche, Fort Worth Public Library, Central Branch, Local History, Genealogy, & Archives Unit, hereafter *Fort Worth City Directory* and date.
14. For Hagar Tucker, see Richard Selcer, "Hagar Tucker: Fort Worth's First Black Policeman," *Fort Worth Characters*, 64-65, hereafter Selcer, "Tucker." For Wallace, see Joyce Gibson Roach, "Daniel Webster Wallace," in *Black Cowboys of Texas*, ed. Sara R. Massey (College Station: Texas A&M University Press, 2000), 187.
15. *The Texas Almanac for 1871, and Emigrant's Guide to Texas* (Austin, 1871), 151. For Van Zandt, see *Fort Worth Telegram*, March 17, 1907.
16. For "unruly negroes," see *Dallas Morning News*, July 21, 1892. For "alleged attacks," see *Fort Worth Daily Democrat*, November 30, 1879. For Peak, see recollections in *Fort Worth Star-Telegram*, September 24, 1922. For "Uncle Tom" Washington, see obituary in *Fort Worth Telegram*, October 2, 1907. (He was buried in the "colored" section of Oakwood Cemetery.)

17. For random examples of how the term was used, see *Dallas Morning News*, October 3, 1894; and *Fort Worth Mail-Telegram*, September 23, 1902.
18. Reprinted from the *Houston Post* in the *Fort Worth Morning Register*, August 14, 1901.
19. Charles Ellis Mitchell, "When Every Man Carried a Six-shooter," *In Old Fort Worth*, ed. Mack Williams (Fort Worth: privately printed, 1986), 46.
20. H.N. P. Gammel, comp. *The Laws of Texas, 1822–1897*, vol. 1 (Austin: The Gammel Book Co., 1898), 1265–66.
21. *Fiske's Bulletin* (Galveston, TX.), July 31, 1869. This sensational story, picked up by the Galveston newspaper, was not even carried by the Dallas newspaper, adding further doubt to its credibility.
22. For whipping, see recollections of William Hamilton, Williams, ed. "Memories of Tarrant County Slaves," 15.
23. The term "righteous whites" is borrowed from Jewish history. The Jews used the term "righteous gentiles" to describe non-Jews in Europe who tried to protect Jews from the Nazis during the Holocaust. For "scant evidence" and "waned and disappear," see Garrett, 276. See also James Farber, *Fort Worth in the Civil War* (Belton, TX: Peter Hansbrough Bell Press, 1960), 55. For "kindly" Tucker and Daggett, see Selcer, *Fort Worth Characters*, 59–64, and 133. For sleeping in the woods, see Bill Fairley, "Ex-slave Recounts Horrors of Klan," one of a series in "Tales from Where the West Begins," *Fort Worth Star-Telegram*, February 12, 1997. Hiding in the woods every night is a theme that appears frequently in freedmen's interviews with historians many years later. This is not to say such stories were made up out of whole cloth, rather that they may have been learned as part of the lore of the black community, not experienced personally.
24. This list is not identical to Gooch's but includes some additional jobs that show up in other sources, e.g., city directories. And Gooch lists "hostler" although there is no evidence that Fort Worth blacks were running hotels in this period. Porters were all-purpose handymen and janitors. The identification of the job with African Americans can be seen in the screen name of one Hollywood's most popular African-American actors during the Golden Age, "Stepin Fetchit." Augusta Gooch, *Life of Lenora Rolla* (Seattle, WA: CreateSpace, 2013), 116, hereafter Gooch, *Life of Rolla*.
25. For "unwritten right," see Jon Pareles, "Ernest Withers Brings Memphis Back Home," *International Herald Tribune*, March 22, 2002. For Hagar

Tucker, see Selcer, "Tucker," 60–61; and Jeanette Keith, *Fever Season* (New York: Bloomsbury Press, 2012), 83 and 201, hereafter Keith, *Fever Season.* For Pratt, see James Farber, *Fort Worth in the Civil War* (Belton, TX: Peter Hansbrough Bell Press, 1960), 54; and Garrett, 279. (Curiously, Pratt's story is not told in Van Zandt's autobiography, *Force without Fanfare*, ed. Sandra Myres [Fort Worth: Texas Christian University Press, 1968]; it comes from oral tradition.) For another view of black police in the South, see W. Marvin Dulaney, *Black Police in America* (Bloomington: Indiana University Press, 1996).

26. Bragg was the first man legally hanged in Fort Worth. *Dallas Weekly Herald*, May 9, 1874; and recollections of J.B. Roberts in Roberts, "Memories of an Early Police Reporter," *Fort Worth News-Tribune*, July 2–4, 1976, p. 28, hereafter cited as Roberts, "Memories". For lore, see interview with J.L. Terry, 1938, in *"Federal Writers' Project,"* Vol. 2, pp. 535-36. Terry's faulty memory confuses Sol Bragg with Isham Capps, another black man, executed in Fort Worth in 1880.
27. Mosier Valley was named for a plantation in the area settled by a Tennessee slave-owner. "Mosier Valley Study," City of Fort Worth Planning Department, August 21, 1985, Fort Worth Library, Central Branch, Local History, Genealogy, and Archives Unit, hereafter "Mosier Valley Study." Bob Ray Sanders, "It's Time to Keep Promises to Mosier Valley," *Fort Worth Star-Telegram*, January 26, 2014, hereafter Sanders, "Time to Keep Promises." "Mosier Valley. . . Finally Gets Park," ibid., February 12, 2014.
28. Mosier Valley's designation as "oldest black settlement" is arguable since post-Civil War freedmen's communities do not have official founding dates; therefore, it is impossible to say that one, say Mosier Valley, began earlier than another, say Waco's Willow Grove. Both date from the 1870s. There were also *slave* communities in east Texas that predated the Civil War. For claim to be oldest in the state, see "Mosier Valley Study," p. 1 and attachment A. *Cf.* "oldest black community in Tarrant County," Sanders, "Time to Keep Promises." For "under-served," see ibid., February 12, 2014.
29. Quote comes from Rose Renee Tucker who grew up in Mosier Valley and attended school there in the 1960s. Her recollections in particular were about attending the Mosier Valley school. *Fort Worth Star-Telegram*, February 12, 2014.
30. Hamilton, *History and Directory*, 50.
31. For tuition, see *Fort Worth Star-Telegram*, January 4, 1914.

32. A good Republican, Belle Burchill was appointed postmistress of Fort Worth in 1881 by President James Garfield, giving up school-teaching for her new duties. Her story is told by Howard Peak in the *Fort Worth Star-Telegram*, September 24, 1922; by Bill Fairley, "Terrell Was Early Black School Leader," ibid., February 20, 2002; and biographical sketch, ibid., March 4, 2013. Allen Chapel was named for Richard Allen, an African-American minister of Philadelphia who became the first bishop of the African Methodist Episcopal Church. The present Allen Chapel dating from 1914 is located at 116 Elm.
33. It is unclear whether it was the African Methodist Episcopal or Colored Methodist Episcopal group. Since Belle Burchill taught at Allen Chapel, which was part of the A.M.E. Church, Henry Butler probably taught at Morning Chapel, part of the Colored Methodist Episcopal Church. Liz Stevens, "Who Was Mr. Butler?" *Fort Worth Star-Telegram*, August 17, 1997. For Terrell, see Fairley, "Terrell," ibid., February 20, 2002.
34. For a history of "Fort Worth Methodism," see *Fort Worth Star-Telegram*, November 11, 1920; and "Church Plans... 125th Anniversary," ibid., May 15, 1993.
35. It has been said that that Methodist circuit rider was Tom Moody, but to date no record can be found supporting that claim, and the name "Moody" is iconic in the history of the Methodist Church, U.S.A. Ruby Schmidt, ed., *Fort Worth and Tarrant County: A Historical Guide* (Fort Worth: Texas Christian University Press, 1984), 83. "Tarrant's African-Americans Find Spiritual Sanctuary within Historic Treasure of Architecture," *Fort Worth Star-Telegram*, February 17, 1991; and "Church Plans... 125th Anniversary," ibid., May 15, 1993.
36. Hamilton, *History and Directory*, 50.
37. The two top candidates for the marshal's office that year, Sam Farmer and Timothy Isaiah Courtright, had both been Union men during the Civil War, but neither made any public pronouncements one way or the other about the black vote. *Fort Worth Democrat*, March 29, 1879.
38. *Austin Daily Statesman*, September 14, 1888.
39. Williams, ed., "Memories of Tarrant County Slaves," 15. *Fort Worth Star-Telegram*, June 19, 1939. Silas Graham and Jamie Wilson, "Slave Narratives."
40. All historical sources for Hagar Tucker can be found in Richard Selcer, "Hagar Tucker: Fort Worth's First Black Policeman," *Fort Worth Characters* (Denton: University of North Texas Press, 2009), 59–66.

41. Sources: Gayle W. Hanson, "Isaiah Milligan Terrell," in *The Handbook of Texas Online.* www.tshaonline.org. *Fort Worth Morning Register,* August 14 and Sept. 1, 1901. Bill Fairley, "Terrell Was Early Black School Leader," *Fort Worth Star-Telegram,* February 20, 2002; Bob Ray Sanders, "A Family Linked by Generations of Learning," ibid., July 20, 2011; and Sanders, "New Arts, Science Academies Will Have the Perfect Location, ibid., February 8, 2015; Cecil Johnson, "This Nation has Only One I.M. Terrell," ibid., July 16, 2006. Program from the I.M. Terrell High School "All Student" Reunion of 1985, TCBH&GS, Series II (Individual Collections), Box 1, File 4. Most sources incorrectly give the name of Terrell's school as "North Side Colored School No. 11." This was probably a typo in an early source repeated over the years. The city directories and a basic knowledge of geography clearly show it to be the "South Side Colored School No. 11." For Terrell's final blow-up, see *Fort Worth Star-Telegram,* October 3, 1915.

Chapter 3

A Growing Sense of Identity (1880–1900)

The 1880s to the end of the century were mostly good times for the citizens of Fort Worth. The economy was booming thanks to the cattle and railroad industries, and the population was growing exponentially: more than 400 percent in the twenty years. Most of the newcomers were white, but the black population also grew modestly. In 1880, the city had a total population of 6,718 out of a county of 24,671 people. There are no numbers for the black population of the city, but the county as a whole had 2,160 or roughly 11.4 percent of the total population. Five years later, the white population of the city had increased to approximately 9,000 of whom 4 percent were black, which comes out to 360 black residents. The numbers are hard to correlate since we are dealing with two different sets of numbers (county and city), but the disparity between black population of the county versus that of the city suggests that the great majority of blacks in Tarrant County resided outside the city. That makes sense because most were engaged in agricultural work. The percentage of blacks in the city's population would continue to rise until by 1900 it reached 10 percent.[1]

During these years the city also endured epidemic outbreaks (dengue fever and smallpox), a bloody railroad strike (1886), and a national depression (1893–95). As if those were not enough, the city wrestled with rampant crime and vice. These problems affected the black community as much as the white, the chief difference being that their stories went largely untold.

The last two decades of the nineteenth century brought not just a population increase in the black community but a growing sense of identity. Neither slaves nor "freedmen" any longer, African Americans struggled to establish a new identity while keeping a low profile. It was a tall hill to climb.[2]

A COMMUNITY OF FREE MEN AND WOMEN

Emerging from Reconstruction, the black population of Fort Worth was scarcely a community in the sense of having a collective consciousness or sense of purpose. Fifteen years after the end of the Civil War they were still adjusting to freedom. Life was mostly about survival, which included, besides acquiring the basics of food and shelter, not antagonizing the white majority.

Black Fort Worthers left little record of their lives, either public or private. The best sources on the city's black residents in this era are city directories, newspaper accounts, and the U.S. Census. These sources reveal that most blacks were menials—"cattle drivers," teamsters, porters, servants, housekeepers, cooks, "washer women," and common laborers. The common denominator among all these jobs is that no particular skill set or training was involved, and their employers were white. A little higher on the employment ladder were "railroad workers," most of whom worked for the Texas & Pacific. For black women, the largest occupation seems to have been "washing & ironing," which could mean either working as a domestic in a white household or taking in laundry. Neither the census nor city directories include transients (e.g., cow punchers, itinerant gamblers) or persons openly engaged in the sex trade. We can, however, read between the lines and assume that single girls ("Miss So-and-so") living together at the same address on the south end of town were probably prostitutes. Combining the information gleaned from city directories, Sanborn fire insurance maps, and newspapers, it seems the majority of those who were not domestics or railroad workers were part of the underworld known as "the Acre."[3]

For a black man there were few paths to the good life. About the only jobs readily available were tenant farming and domestic service. A black man with a will to work and a strong back could always find a job, and if he saved his money, even a humble express man like William Trezevant could eventually buy a piece of land to call his own. Trezevant's son, William, Jr., continued the all-American success story, climbing still higher up the socio-economic ladder. He started out as a porter in one of the Acre's saloons, always an attractive job for an African-American man because it was indoors and had the potential for upward mobility. Every saloon from the top-end fancy ones to the low dives employed one or more black porters around the place. They did everything from emptying spittoons to delivering drink orders to the gaming tables. A black porter could start at one of the low-end joints and work his way up to a high-class establishment like Joe Wheat's Stag Saloon, which is exactly what Will Trezevant, Jr. did. He eventually opened his own "club," thereby announcing his arrival as a member of the small black middle class.[4]

Being a saloon porter, while a respectable line of work, did bring a man into daily contact with two notorious types: 1) "sporting men;" and 2) pimps. These were not exactly role models, but if a man were ambitious and not too squeamish about the company he kept, either of these lines of work was a sure path out of poverty and dependence. Although they later became black stereotypes in the literature of the West, both sport and pimp were semi-respectable callings in a community where the deck was historically stacked against African Americans. Joe Pervis, for instance, was a gentleman sport in Fort Worth's black community. One Dallas newspaper enumerated the attributes that made him a "big man": He "conducts a big coon gambling house, wears flashy store clothes and at least a dozen immense paste diamonds . . . and walked with a swagger." [5]

Or if a black man had ambitions to be something more than a sport or a pimp and possessed some entrepreneurial talent, he might open a full-service saloon like Will Trezevant, Jr. did. Tom Mason and Bill Love also got their starts as saloon men, and Hiram McGar parlayed a pool hall into a second career as the Father of Negro League Baseball in Fort Worth. Their stories are just as much a part of Fort Worth's black history as I. M. Terrell's or Henry H. Butler's.

Other than the vice trade, the surest path to the good life was to have a skill in the trades. It's harder to find examples of men who followed this path, however. Toward the end of the century, two hard-working black men, Gus Adams and Sam Kilgore, carved out places as an independent carpenter and a cement contractor, respectively. The work was not as glamorous as the sporting life, but offered another path to success and self-respect, and did not entail rubbing elbows with prostitutes and gamblers.[6]

A very few highly successful men like William McDonald managed to bypass the saloon and gambling routes by shrewdly investing in real estate, buying up property on the cheap when it came up for sale. They turned their fraternal and religious ties into a clientele base, which was about the only way a black man had to make business contacts in an overwhelmingly white community. He lacked the old school ties and army pals that whites had. What he had were fraternal and church connections. Unfortunately, there were too few male role models in the black community to offset all the bad examples—a few ministers and teachers, but mostly common laborers stuck in dead-end jobs. The city directories, which include a man's occupation with his name, carry the same notation beside name after name: "laborer," sometimes "porter" or "servant."

For black women wanting to work, the options were even more limited: maid, cook, and seamstress were about the only honest jobs available outside the home. Then there was the "oldest profession." Prostitution was the easiest and most lucrative line of work for a young black woman. No training required; she already had all the "job skills" needed. There were plenty of young white girls in the West working as prostitutes, too, but polite society's attitude toward them was different. Westerners called white prostitutes "soiled doves" and treated them with indulgence. Black prostitutes were usually labeled "vile wenches" or something similar and targeted by police. In 1874 the *Fort Worth Democrat* called them "a disgrace" to the city, and Officer Columbus Fitzgerald vowed to "lock them up every day until they learn to behave themselves." The same line of work, only different skin color. Market demand trumped moral outrage, however, because black bawds were a fixture of the lower end of Fort Worth. The *Dallas Morning News* even took the time to count them; there were "eleven or twelve" in the summer of 1886.[7]

One of them was Lula Jackson, described in the *Gazette* as "a soiled dove of ginger-cake hue." Lula got into the newspaper because she was accused of robbing a railroad man whom she had "artfully. . . lured to her abode." Police arrested Lula on his complaint, but released her the next day "for lack of evidence." Her case is interesting because both her skin color ("ginger-cake") and her ethnic heritage ("mulatto") were reported, neither of which ever happened with white prostitutes.[8]

The world's oldest profession created Fort Worth's first black female entrepreneur, Emeline Gooden, a madam who ran a highly successful bordello. "Madam Emeline," however, was no Madam C. J. Walker (1867–1919), the millionaire queen of black hair-care products who ran her national empire from St. Louis. Gooden was providing a different service out of one of the most popular establishments in the Acre and living quite well off the proceeds. The exact location of her bordello is unknown today, only that it was in the lower end of town known as Hell's Half-acre. Even where she came from before landing in Fort Worth in the 1870s is unknown. She employed black prostitutes —one newspaper called them "colored Cyprians"—and her customers included both black and white "Romeos." The only color Emeline recognized was green. She was also one tough customer who defended her turf against all comers, male or female, sometimes with knives or broken bottles, leading the *Fort Worth Gazette* to dub her "the she-terror of the Third Ward." Despite achieving the dream of financial security, her life was not happy. In 1887 a jealous rival stabbed her. She recovered, but a few months later tried to take her own life with an overdose of morphine. She survived that, too, and ran her bawdy house for another two years before one of the periodic "clean-up-the-Acre" campaigns shut her down in October 1889, and she left town. As the city's most notorious African-American madam, Emeline was the black Mary Porter of Fort Worth (another high-profile madam, white) but without Mary's happy ending.[9]

Vice was one of the gray areas in racial protocols. White men could patronize black prostitutes, but the reverse was never true: black customers and white prostitutes. This unwritten rule carried over well into the twentieth century. In 1917, police raided a black bordello on East Seventeenth. They arrested nineteen blacks, three "Mexicans," and one "American" for vagrancy. The diversity of the haul was nothing out of the ordinary for arresting officers.[10]

While white Fort Worth tolerated the unconventional Emeline Gooden because of the useful service she provided, they preferred their black men to be less like the assertive Thomas Mason or William McDonald and more like the lovable Uncle Billy Mays. Twenty-five years after emancipation, Uncle Billy was a familiar sight shuffling along the city's streets "with a stout cane as his support," going about his business. On a slow news day in the winter of 1890, a *Fort Worth Gazette* reporter tracked down Mays for an interview. He calculated that Uncle Billy was 105 years old and gave him the title of "oldest negro in Texas." More importantly, everyone in Fort Worth—white as well as black—loved "Uncle Billy" like a member of the family. He had come to Fort Worth before the Civil War as the property of Nathaniel Terry, remaining with him for fifty years first as a slave then as a servant before he got too old to work. Uncle

Billy could have left when he was freed, but Fort Worth was his home. A lifetime of servitude taught him how to keep a low profile and always be pleasant, and the city adopted him. Mays was the wise, snowy-headed old black man, the sort whites called "Uncle Tom," meaning no insult. The problem as they saw it was that there were not more Uncle Billy's.[11]

Whites were not above applauding success in the black community—within the bounds of existing social structures. The *Fort Worth Democrat* praised a Dr. Franklin Trabue who had come to Fort Worth as a slave many years before, but by 1882 was a practicing physician. The newspaper called him "a shining example of what hard work could do for his race."[12]

For working-class African Americans, the only advocacy group was the Noble Order of the Knights of Labor, the first broad-based national organization for working men. Under Terence V. Powderly's leadership, the union's open membership policy included not just men of all trades but also all races. The Knights reached their height in the mid-1880s with some 702,000 members nationwide. Fort Worth had a white lodge and a "colored lodge," the latter composed mostly of railroad workers. In December 1885 the colored lodge took over the "union hall" for their Christmas party. Within two years, however, the national Knights of Labor were no more. After that, efforts to organize black workers in Fort Worth were weak and ineffective. In 1900, members of local Protective Laborers Union No. 8104 petitioned the city council for "a share" of the contract work on city streets for their union. There is no record that the council responded.[13]

Photo 3. Middle-class African American man.

The distinguished-looking young gentleman in this David Swartz photograph is proof positive of a black middle class in Fort Worth before the turn of the century. Unfortunately, his identity is unknown. Note: Photographs of nineteenth–century, middle-class African Americans are exceedingly rare. Courtesy of historian Jan Jones.

By the mid-1880s the first stirrings of a black middle class in Fort Worth could be seen in the variety of fraternal and benevolent societies that established themselves here during the decade: the Masons, the United Brothers of Friendship, the Willing Workers, the Wide-Awake Society, and the Youth Society. All but one were part of larger national organizations with long histories. They also represented an early form of networking in the city's small, black community that was geographically at least cut off from the centers of African-American life in the nation. The earliest of the bunch was the United Brothers of Friendship (UBF) when Lodge No. 15 was chartered in 1877. The UBF was a benevolent society that began in Louisville, Kentucky, in 1861 and after the Civil War became a secret society that eventually attracted more than 60,000 members, men as well as women, worldwide. By 1890 the Fort Worth lodge had their own meeting hall at Eleventh and Calhoun. The second was the "Willing Workers," also known as the "Seven Stars of Consolidation," which arrived in Fort Worth with Lodge No. 19, chartered on September 11, 1881. Little of the organization's history is known today.

1885 saw a flurry of organizing, which reflected the city's growing black population. First came the Wide Awake Society, Lodge No. 1, whose members hoped would be the beginning of a new political movement in Texas. The original national organization was composed of young men's marching clubs that did yeoman's work for the Republican Party during its early years. By the 1880s what had begun as an all-white paramilitary organization was just a memory among Republican Party loyalists. A group of Fort Worth blacks resurrected the name in May 1885 to demonstrate that their political sympathies still lay with the Republican Party. Next came the Young Men of St. Paul, a church-affiliated group that formed Youth Lodge No. 1 in Fort Worth in August 1885. It is not clear whether they were an entirely local group or the first of a new movement in Texas.[14]

Most important of all was the Prince Hall Masons, the oldest African-American fraternal order in the United States. Their origins went back to

1808 when a group of free blacks in Boston, Massachusetts, organized the Prince Hall or African Grand Lodge of Masons, named for their founder. Their guiding principles were truth, charity, temperance, and fraternity. As the movement spread it split American Freemasonry into separate black and white lodges. Texas was one of the states where white Masonic lodges did not recognize black lodges as brothers. A veritable "Who's Who" of Fort Worth founding fathers organized (white) Lodge No. 148 in 1855.[15] Another thirty years would pass before the Prince Hall Masons establish a foothold in Fort Worth when in 1885 a fledgling group of fifty-four black Masons in Fort Worth organized the Rescue Lodge. In the early years, they held their weekly meetings in a "hall" at Fifteenth and Houston. In 1907 they built a three-story structure of white pressed brick at E. Ninth and Jones as their "temple." Appropriately, it was in the heart of the black business district. The location was no coincidence since the lodge was virtually a businessman's club on top of being a fraternal order. In the years to follow, the Rescue Lodge's most famous member would be William M. "Gooseneck Bill" McDonald who joined about 1898, rose to the post of corresponding secretary, and served as unofficial banker of the state organization for more than thirty years.[16]

Black Masonry in Fort Worth prospered. They were strong enough financially and numerically to host the fourteenth annual state convention in 1889, and by 1906 they boasted the largest membership of any lodge in Texas, a remarkable accomplishment considering the nineteen other lodges that had been founded before them. In 1924 the Fort Worth lodge built a magnificent Mosque on First Street, the largest African-American fraternal hall in the United States, covering two square blocks built in the form of a central rotunda and four wings. It could seat 3,000 people for public events and was often rented out for conventions, musical concerts, and church functions. It was not only the biggest structure, but also the pride and joy of the black community in Fort Worth.[17]

None of these organizations for all their titles and fraternal solidarity posed a threat to Jim Crow. The Rescue Lodge of Prince Hall Masons might have sixty or seventy members and a treasury of a couple of thousand dollars, but the white A.F.&A.M. Lodge No. 148 had three or four times that many members and a treasury at least ten times as large. In 1886 membership in all five Fort Worth fraternal groups may have totaled 224, ranging from a high of 65 members in the UBF to just eighteen members in the Young Men of St. Paul, and the total number was probably much smaller because many men belonged to more than one group. William McDonald, for instance, belonged to both the Masons and the Seven Stars of Consolidation while living in Fort Worth. The Prince Hall Masons and their like were shadows of familiar white organizations, and for the black community they filled the same needs: providing a safety net in a cruel world. One limitation on the growth of such organizations was finding a regular meeting place. There were not too many places in Fort Worth where fifty or sixty black men could freely assemble. They could rent the city hall auditorium for five dollars or meet in one of the larger churches. Black fraternal groups also built, or they may have just borrowed (the record is not clear) "meeting halls" at two locations in the "colored" section of town: Fifteenth and Houston and Eleventh and Calhoun. For all their high-falutin' names, none of the black fraternal organizations possessed any particular political or economic power; they were simply social networking groups. The creation of business and professional organizations had to wait a few more years.[18]

One of the surest signs of a black middle class was holding a formal wedding in one's home as opposed to borrowing a church or standing up in front of a Justice of the Peace. That is exactly was what Rev. E. Handsofr and Mrs. J.T.M. Lindsay did on November 8, 1899, when they tied the knot at the home of J.A. Blackburn on the city's Near South Side. The importance of the event wasn't just the nice ceremony or the impressive guest list, but the "feast" put out afterwards and the announcement carried the next day in the (white) *Fort Worth Morning Register.*[19]

THE "NEGRO DISTRICT"

The Thirteenth Amendment may have freed the slaves and the Fourteenth and Fifteenth amendments guaranteed their rights, but that did not make them equal in the eyes of the white majority; they were second-class citizens. It started with where they lived. Black neighborhoods lacked such basic amenities as water wells and garbage removal from the streets, and street lamps. Life was not much different than it had been in the slave quarters during antebellum times. Decent white folks stayed as far away as possible from the vile haunts of the city's "negro section" or "negro district," which could not even be called a neighborhood. The newspapers were very clear about that.

In the 1880s, the "negro section" consisted of pockets of black residents hemmed in by nature (the Trinity River), railroad tracks (the Texas & Pacific), and white attitudes. Most of that population was concentrated in a few "colonies" as one newspaper called them on Main and Rusk scattered from Fourth down to Ninth. A few more lived in the Trinity River bottoms and just beyond the city limits as tenant farmers or sharecroppers so not really a part of the city's population. As the black population grew in the years that followed, it tended to cluster on the eastern edge of town. That land was less desirable because the West Fork of the Trinity encircled the area creating extensive bottom lands, and also because the cattle drives for many years had come up Rusk St. (Commerce St. after 1911) on the way north, making living conditions nearby almost unbearable during cattle season. The east side of town below the public square was the working-class section.[20]

There were not separate black residential and business districts as in the white part of town, just streets where blacks lived and worked. The city had no need for zoning laws because everyone knew where the white and "colored" sections were. Starting on Main Street, one could walk east two blocks to Calhoun and find what Sanborn fire insurance maps labeled "Negro tenements," meaning hovels. The same was true on the next block to the east, Jones Street, which was as far as the city was platted. Tenement housing started at Bluff St. on the north end of town and stretched down to the Railroad Reservation, extending also onto the numbered side-streets between Seventh and Fourteenth. The largest concentration of black residences was in the southeast quadrant of the city, what on political maps was labeled the "Third Ward." None of the streets in this section were paved, nor did they have streetlights, gutters, or sidewalks. First labeled "Irish Town" after the T&P arrived (1876), this area was renamed "Little Africa" by the turn of the century, reflecting the new untouchable class.

As the city grew, the black section was pushed farther out to the east and south of town, jumping the railroad reservations that marked the southern and eastern edges of the city. The T&P Reservation blocked the south end of town after 1876. A second reservation was created on the east side after the Gulf, Colorado & Santa Fe and the Missouri, Kansas & Texas (the "KATY") arrived in 1881, followed by the Fort Worth & Denver City in 1882 and the Chicago, Rock Island, & Texas in 1893. The two reservations created a barrier to city growth eastward and southward just as surely as if a wall had been erected. From this time forward, black urban growth was literally on "the other side of the tracks" in both directions. What business decisions created, racial prejudice hardened into policy. Land along the railroad right of way was undesirable due to noise, smoke, and the ever-present danger of derailment. What was unfit for whites was perfect for second-class citizens. In 1909 when the school board announced it was relocating the (white) First Ward School to a new site farther from the Santa Fe tracks that ran nearby, the gentlemen gave two reasons: the old site was noisy and unsafe; and "a great deal of the nearby property is occupied by negroes." It was no coincidence that the two issues were linked.[21]

On the south end of town, blacks settled on Terrell Ave. (named for I.M. Terrell) and Rosedale, which were lines on a map more than proper residential thoroughfares. Blocks were not laid out; streets were not graded, grass was not cut. In 1890 Terrell marked the southern boundary of the city. As late as 1900, both Terrell and Rosedale were little more than rural tracks "out in the country, lacking all city services including police patrols"—and fire protection. A 1904 newspaper story called this section of town "the ragged end of nowhere."[22]

Beyond the east-side railroad tracks lay a slight rise known as Baptist Hill and then the Trinity River. The geographic landmark known as Baptist Hill became known as Chambers Hill after the man who developed it into a residential property. Unfortunately for the residents it was hemmed in on all sides by railroad tracks and therefore less than desirable real estate. Blacks were kept off Chambers Hill in the early years only to move in *en masse* in later years after the railroads had completed their encirclement. Its brief tenure as a racially mixed neighborhood has been held up as a badge of honor, although in truth that was actually only a transitory phase.[23]

Farther east beyond the Trinity was the western edge of the cross-timbers and prairie land extending all the way to Arlington. This area was still dotted with small farms at the end of the century. West of Calhoun the black section was hemmed in by Hell's Half-acre, described in an 1891 newspaper story as "a rendezvous for thieves and thugs of the worst character," and increasingly, black people. The Acre was so low on the social scale that traditional color lines had long been blurred. Rusk and Main were off-limits to black residences or businesses because those were the two main thoroughfares that connected the T&P train station to courthouse square.

There was another reason the concept of "neighborhoods" did not have a lot of relevance for African Americans: most black residents were either renters or squatters because they could not afford mortgages. Whites owned even the undesirable land on the east and south sides of town, but did not live there. Black residences were the type that could be vacated quickly on demand such as when a railroad reservation had to be created or land was needed for a warehouse. White landowners and the city generally left squatters alone until the city's population outgrew its existing boundaries and needed new land for development; then it was time for poor folks to move. The police did not even patrol these areas of town, and the volunteer fire brigade did not consider them part of their jurisdiction either. The population of black squatters was tolerated until they were "cleared from the land" like so much undergrowth in the name of progress. This made life in the black community very precarious and discouraged development of any sense of neighborhood in areas of black concentration.[24]

Even lower than the "Negro tenements" (as the Sanborn Fire Maps put it) on the quality-of-life scale were the settlements in the Trinity River bottoms. Later chroniclers would describe them as rat-holes, shantytowns, colonies, but white Fort Worthers of their day gave them more colorful names like "Battercake Flats" (below the bluff north and west of the courthouse near the confluence of the Clear Fork and West Fork), "Yellow Row" (almost due north of town on the West Fork), and "Stick Town" (east of Samuels Ave. between the Rock Island tracks and the West Fork). The poorest of the poor lived there along with criminals and vagrants of every race and ethnic group. Whites did not covet the land, and the police seldom intruded. The areas were not platted, so residents were squatters with no legal rights. On the other hand, they did not have to pay taxes or maintain the property. The bottom lands were vulnerable to flooding in the spring and were home to all kinds of creepy-crawly creatures. And since the city still dumped its raw sewage in the river below the town, the area was also a breeding ground for disease. The combination of all these things is why one Fort Worth newspaper called the river bottoms "no-man's land" and urged police to make a clean sweep of the area, driving the residents out. A grand jury charged with investigating them called them "a disgrace" to the city.[25]

As the city grew outward in the late nineteenth century, the white population jumped the eastern limits of the business district to settle on Chambers Hill and, beyond that, the Polytechnic area. The latter was four miles from the business district. The black population was squeezed between the center of the city and Polytechnic with Chambers Hill existing as a white island for years until the white residents all fled to other neighborhoods.

Filling the area in-between was the Alford and Veal Addition that included the "state streets" —Arizona, Louisiana, Missouri, and Kentucky avenues—running north to south. The state streets started at the T&P Reservation and stretched to the city limits on the south. The streets were platted in the 1880s and by the end of the century homes were filling in the map.[26]

After 1896 another black residential area sprang up out of nowhere. That was the year Amanda Davis bought property several miles southeast of town at the bargain rate of $45 an acre. She purchased several acres and built a home—a crude cabin without electricity or running water—but it was hers free and clear, which was more than the tenement-dwellers could say. In the beginning her nearest neighbors were miles away and the city did not know she existed. Fortunately, Village Creek ran through the area and provided a reliable source of water. Other blacks followed Davis, like the Cowans, the Stalcups, and the Brockmans, and together they created a rural, "family-oriented community" that they named Cowanville. They supported themselves by farming the vacant land, and in time shops and churches came to the area, saving them the trek into town. Life was not perfect—they lacked police protection and the city was in no hurry to extend municipal services their way—but it was good. After the Interurban rail line to Dallas came through in 1902, the area became a regular stop on the thirty-five-mile route. It was the sixth stop coming out of Fort Worth—after Virginia, Nona, Oakland, Sycamore Heights, and College Hill—so the new neighborhood was dubbed "Stop Six." After the Interurban shut down in 1934, the Stop Six name remained for the neighborhood that today is located between Miller and East Loop 820 (west to east) and Rosedale and Berry (north to south). For three generations of residents it was what one African-American writer called "a safe and nurturing environment" in which to live and raise children.[27]

Hell's Half-acre was the only area of the city proper where blacks could walk the streets freely and even open a little saloon, the only sure-fire business for a black entrepreneur. During the cattle-drive era of the 1870s and '80s, some of the drovers were black, and like their white counterparts they wanted someplace to wet their whistle and blow off steam. Black-owned saloons like the Red Star sprang up on the fringes of the Acre, catering to a black clientele and any white customer with eclectic taste. Such places differed from white joints only in the color of the clientele, not in the level of depravity. Most of those black hole-in-the-wall places came and went without leaving any imprint on history. Only the most notorious, such as the Red Star, the Bucket of Blood, and the Black Elephant, are even remembered today.[28]

Newspapers of the day paint a grim picture of African Americans in that section. The *Dallas Herald* in 1883 called Hell's Half-acre the "low quarter of the city," suggesting that the reason for that had something to do with the racial makeup of the district. Said the *Herald*, "The negroes have been creating considerable disturbance for three nights past by engaging in shooting affrays." Fort Worth Marshal William Rea ordered "a number" of them (blacks) to "leave the city at once." It was not necessary to warn them twice.[29]

The situation did not improve. Two years later the same newspaper found "monstrous negro dives" in the Acre "where more sin, iniquity and crime can be found than in any quarter, be it ever so low, in the city of New York." Being compared unfavorably to the sin capital of the nation was not a good sign. And it was not just Dallas newspapers that were critical. The *Fort Worth Gazette* in 1887 estimated that "more than one-half" of all the prostitutes in the Acre were black. The accuracy of the statement is less important than the perception that insisted on putting a black face on crime and immorality. In 1906 the *Fort Worth Record* declared, "For foul filth, nothing in the Acre can compare with the Black Elephant," a saloon that was no worse than a dozen other dives.[30]

With many disreputable houses in the Acre doubling as residences for the owners and their employees who lived upstairs or out back, it was nearly impossible to separate black residences from black businesses, which contributed to the unsavory reputation of the black community in general. Legitimate black entrepreneurs could not even open a business outside the vague boundaries of the Acre without risking prosecution or worse. The north or business end of town was strictly off-limits, and the city directories—put out annually starting in 1877—leave the impression that the only black businesses were "disorderly houses," which could describe either a saloon or a brothel. We know that black residents of Fort Worth patronized other businesses besides disorderly houses, but daily comings and goings did not get into the public record.[31]

For those blacks who felt unwelcome or even unsafe in Fort Worth, there was the siren call of the Oklahoma Immigration Society. Toward the end of the century this organization was working hard to attract blacks from across the South to fill in empty spaces of the Oklahoma Territory. The Territory had long been seen as a dumping ground for both Native Americans and African Americans. The Society sent agents into north Texas to invite black residents to relocate to the "new country" where they were actually wanted. There are no exact numbers, but reports were that "several thousand" made the move.[32]

Schools

After Belle Burchill quit the classroom and the Freedmen's Bureau schools shut down, the education of black children was left in the hands of the city's churches. In the 1880s both the Methodists and Baptists operated "colored schools," the Methodists out of the Morning Chapel Methodist Episcopal Church (Third and Crump), and the Baptists out of the Mount Gilead Missionary Baptist Church (Thirteenth and Jones). The teachers and principals at both schools were black. To be hired to teach — if indeed they were paid—did not require training at a "normal" (i.e., teaching) college; they only had to be members of the denomination, of good moral character, and have a little book-learning. The Baptists' school was taught by Isaiah M. Terrell, assisted by the preacher, Thomas V.B. Davis.[33]

In 1882, the schooling of Fort Worth children changed dramatically. The city created a free public-school system, forerunner of what would eventually become the Fort Worth Independent School District. The school year began the first week of October 1882, serving roughly 1,200 white pupils in rented buildings. The city's black children, numbering fewer than 300 by official count, were not enrolled until the next school year (1883–84). That year the city's schools had twenty-four white teachers and four black. The black teachers were Isaiah Milligan Terrell, Henry H. Butler, J. W. Johnson, and the Rev. Thomas V. B. Davis, all of whom had moved over from church schools to the new public schools. The facilities they had to teach in were, if anything, worse than before. Classes were held in a single, four-room school house (designated "building no. 6") on the southwest corner of E. Ninth and Terry. Before the opening of school in 1884, it was enlarged to six rooms, and an additional two teachers ("assistants") hired, one of whom was Isaiah Terrell's wife, Marcelite. All the pupils were boys. By contrast, the white schools were teaching the 3Rs to girls and boys both. By 1886, the six black teachers were teaching 294 children for a pupil-teacher ratio of 49:1. By contrast, the ratio in the white schools with their 1,362 pupils and 39 teachers was 35:1.[34]

The size of one black schoolhouse and the number of teachers remained constant for the next decade while during that same period the number of white pupils and classrooms grew rapidly. There was something else about the East Ninth St. School. Its location put it on the eastern edge of the Third Ward, uncomfortably close to the red-light district known as Hell's Half-acre. It is likely the pupils could hear the sound of occasional gunfire and full-time hell-raising from the "Acre" during their studies as newspaper reports shows those things going on just a few blocks away. In the following years there was also a large year-to-year turnover in the faculty. The only holdovers were Henry Butler and Isaiah Terrell, but regardless of who taught, they all shared the same goal, which in the words of Butler, was "to advance [our] race."[35]

In 1886 the lone "colored school" moved to East Ninth and Pecan. By then it was bursting at the seams with 450 pupils in grades one through eleven. The building's official designation was now "School No. 10" according to the simple numerical system of naming schools in the order in which they were built. The Fort Worth school district expanded in the late 1880s by adding two high schools, one for boys and the other for girls (whites only). Finally, in 1899 city fathers were forced to address the urgent need for a second schoolhouse for black children. The city council closed on a small piece of property only 100 x 200 feet in size that did not even allow room for a playground. It was in the segregated district, "opposite the colored church in the Seventh Ward" (1217 Arizona Ave.) and designated "South Side School No. 11" or more simply, "South Side Colored School." The building was already inadequate when it opened, a fact finessed by newspaper reports describing it as "modest." What that really meant was a wood-frame building containing just two rooms into which 72 of the oldest children were squeezed. (It was not a high school.) A single stove heated both rooms in the winter. The school board hired two new teachers, one of whom was "Principal" James Guinn. Even disinterested white observers recognized the miserly accommodations for what they were. The *Morning Register* said hopefully, "There is good promise of an enlargement and better facilities being given the [colored] pupils there." It would be years before that vague "promise" was fulfilled.[36]

According to existing records, what was still generally referred to as "the Ninth St. Colored School" graduated its first class of young men in 1893, but since it did not offer a high school curriculum, they could not really be called high school graduates. The four young men represented the best of the East Ninth St. School, and included A. F. Brashear who went on to become the first principal of the new South Side Colored School when it opened in 1899.[37]

Photo 4. Graduates of the Colored High School

These five distinguished-looking young men are reputed to be the first five graduates of Fort Worth's Colored High School in 1893. The only problem is Fort Worth did not have a Colored High School in 1893. This is not to say they were not products of the East Ninth St. Colored School. Courtesy of Billy W. Sills Center for Archives, Fort Worth Independent School District.

Because education was the ticket out of poverty and dependence, the black community prized its schools only slightly less than its churches. The Guinn family who came to Fort Worth from Missouri during Reconstruction, recognized that education was a "pearl of great price" and though the parents were themselves illiterate, they made sure their son James Elvis got an education. Growing up in Fort Worth, James Guinn was a product of the city's early, privately operated African-American schools. He matriculated out of the local school system after the eighth grade, but his parents found tutors to prepare him for college. He attended

Central College in Nashville, Tennessee, and after graduating returned to Texas to teach, first at Prairie View Normal and Industrial School, then in Fort Worth's public school system, which had opened up to blacks in the meantime.[38]

Kindergarten, which reached American shores in 1860 and spread westward from Boston, was part of many public school systems by the turn of the century. Fort Worth, no less progressive than larger cities, jumped on the bandwagon in 1896 when a group of progressive society matrons formed the Free Kindergarten Association (FKA) and opened two schools, one of them (at Eleventh and Calhoun) for black children. There is no record whether the teachers were white or black, but their sense of purpose would have been the same. Since kindergarten was not part of the public school system, and few black parents could afford tuition, the ladies of the FKA had to support the African-American kindergarten out of their own pockets. To raise funds, they held what history showed would be a sure-fire money-maker, a "negro minstrel jubilee," at the Worth Hotel. To fill out the evening's program they recruited local black talent to perform comedy sketches and song and dance numbers for the paying white audience. In the end, however, the dream of a black kindergarten as a precursor to segregated public schools proved unworkable, but for a couple of years, the experiment showed that Fort Worth's more progressive citizens were not insensitive to the educational needs of black children in their community.[39]

Without any sense of irony, community leaders at the turn of the century bragged, "The [city's] negro schools have been built up to a standing not excelled, if equaled, by those of any city of the state." There is no telling what colored schools were like elsewhere in the state, but both of Fort Worth's were shameful.[40]

Churches

Black churches, like black schools, were a source of pride for their community; they offered comfort in an unfair world and hope for a better world to come. The earliest black congregations (see Chap. 2) were "mission churches" planted by established churches. This remained true for many years. Baptists and Methodists established the first beachheads in Fort Worth's black community. A.R. Griggs of the New Hope Baptist Church of Dallas was known as "the pioneering preacher" for the number of mission churches he planted in Fort Worth and elsewhere.[41]

Mount Gilead Baptist Church, which has the distinction of being the first black church ever listed in the city directory, traces its roots back to September 1875 when twenty-six worshippers joined together to form a congregation. Their first meeting place (hardly a church building) was in the vicinity of Fifteenth and Crump, but they put up a building at Thirteenth and Jones in 1882. What distinguished Mount Gilead from other black churches was that it drew not just from the nearby neighborhood but from all over the city. It is considered the "mother church" of Fort Worth's black Baptists. Its pulpit ministers could legitimately claim to speak for the entire black community, and its rolls included many of the best black families and most distinguished leaders.[42]

By the 1880s Fort Worth had eighteen congregations in all, which included eight different denominations. Three were black, representing the African Methodist Episcopal, Methodist Episcopal, and Baptist churches. All offered spiritual nourishment to a community that was short on all the other comforts of life. The Mount Gilead Baptist congregation was a mission outreach of the (white) First Baptist Church of Fort Worth, but it was counted separately because it met in its own building. All three black churches were on the east side of town: the A.M.E. church at First and Elm, the Methodist church at Fifth and Crump, and the Missionary Baptist Church (aka, Mount Gilead) at Thirteenth and Jones. Because churches spring up wherever people settle, it is easy to tell from these locations where the city's black population was concentrated.[43]

In the next few years the number of black churches increased along with the city's black population. By 1890 Mount Pisgah Baptist Church had joined Mount Gilead as the representatives of the Baptist faith in the black community. Two years later Fort Worth black worshippers could choose from among five Methodist and Baptist congregations, all of them still situated on the east side of town in the area between First and Fifteenth north-to-south and Elm to Pecan west-to-east. No other mainstream denominations had a presence in Fort Worth's black community at this time, not even as mission outreach efforts. Presbyterians, Churches of Christ, and others would come later.[44]

Black congregations that were not mission outposts of the white establishment found themselves marginalized or completely excluded by the Southern Baptist Convention (SBC), the umbrella organization for white Baptists across the South. The sign over the door might say "Baptist," but there were Baptists and then there were "Baptists"; the two races did not commune together. Feeling unwelcome in the SBC, some black Baptist congregations broke away in 1895 to form the National Baptist Convention (NBC). The split divided local communities just as it did the national fellowship. The Mount Gilead and Mount Pisgah congregations stayed with the SBC while some other Fort Worth congregations went with the NBC. Fort Worth had always prided itself on being a city of many churches, and now some said it had twice as many as it needed because of the split between black and white Baptists, black and white Methodists, and other color-conscious denominations.

Black church-goers were not even safe within the walls of their sanctuaries. The Mount Gilead Church on the edge of Hell's Half-acre was plagued by crime and vice from the district. In 1881 they petitioned the city council to appoint two "special policemen" to guard the premises during worship. The council refused to take up the request, probably because the idea of putting armed black men on the street with police powers was too disturbing to consider.[45]

Not everyone liked their religion nicely packaged and delivered from a pulpit. There was also a strong tradition in American Protestantism of the outdoor camp meeting, and no one did it better than the Reverend J. L. "Sin Killer" Griffin. Griffin was an African-American revival preacher whose meetings were Holy-Roller style. Sin Killer was built like a bowling ball, possessed a set of leather lungs, and was a mesmerizing speaker whose theology was self-taught. He received his colorful name from a Dallas publisher impressed by his paint-peeling style of preaching. During most of a career lasting more than half a century, he did not have his own church but was content to preach wherever he could get a public space—in rented auditoriums, city halls, on the lawn in front of city hall or even the county jail, and at trolley parks. He eventually acquired a giant tent for his meetings. Pre-tent, Sin Killer made his first appearance in Fort Worth in 1883 but did not make much of a splash. One newspaper said that he received the usual "bad treatment among Christians of his color." If so, it did not discourage him. He was back six years later by which time he had polished his message and his methods, and after 1893 he became a regular visitor to the city. His popularity soared higher with every visit, crossing racial and gender lines. His meetings could last up to a week and attract crowds that numbered from a few hundred up to 5,000 a night![46]

Although Griffin billed himself an "Independent Baptist," regular pulpit ministers, both black and white, shunned him. He told an 1896 audience that "certain preachers" in Fort Worth were "not in sympathy" with his meetings. Two years earlier he had suggested conspiratorially that some of his own race might wish him harm: "Some of these big nigger preachers come to me and says, 'Brother Griffin, you better not preach tonight for sho' as you are alive you'll get hurt.'" But he assured his audience, "The Lord has been caring for me all these years, and I haven't been hurt yet." He threw his net wide, speaking all over the country but mostly in the Deep South. As a denominational outcast he was forced to support himself by passing the hat, which he was not shy about doing. Huge crowds came to hear and see him and were willing to pay for the show.[47]

Sin Killer spoke bluntly if colorfully to his own people. As he liked to say, he didn't know a lot about theology but he did about "niggerology." He used the "N" word frequently and unabashedly. By all accounts, his black followers ate it up, shouting "amen!" and hollering back at him when he made a good point. Sometimes he invited them to come down front and "testify," which many did. He traveled with a five- or six-person choir and led them himself in his favorite gospel hymns. (He also wrote some of the music they sang.) His sermons were equal parts scripture, self-help, and humorous stories. He used many of the same methods as two more famous, white revival-style preachers that he is often compared to: Sam Jones and J. Frank Norris. One thing they all had in common was self-promotion. Sin Killer could have written the book on self-promotion. He wrote letters to editors asking them to "say something about me in your paper," let them know his schedules and sermon titles in advance, and the first thing he did when he got to a new town was call up the leading newspaper to alert them that he was holding a meeting. The luckiest thing that happened to him was the *Dallas Morning News* got behind him and started sending stenographers to record his sermons, which it then printed in the next morning's edition. It was priceless advertising and it was free. The Fort Worth newspapers, on the other hand, were not as enamored with him and may have even decided he had gotten too big for his britches. In 1897 a *Morning Register* reporter interviewed him at the train station and made it a point to report that Sin Killer had greeted him "while holding on to a fried-chicken drumstick with one hand" and "cordially" extending the other.[48]

Sin Killer's home base for many years was Dallas although he spent more time on the road than he did at home. He tried to take his show to Chicago but found out his message did not play as well up North, so he came back to Texas. There were also reports in Cincinnati and New Orleans that he had debauched white girls. He made frequent visits to Fort Worth to address the faithful whom he called his "Gospel Army." It wasn't until 1903, however, that he finally achieved a certain amount of mainstream acceptance here; that was the year he preached a week-long revival at Mount Pisgah Baptist Church.[49]

Sin Killer Griffin was a force of nature. But the most interesting thing about him is that even deep in the heart of Jim Crow Texas, he pulled in audiences that were equal parts white and black. He made it a point to invite white audiences and bragged that "the white people come to hear me in Fort Worth the same as they do elsewhere." Naturally he saw to it that whites had reserved seats, and he even preached differently to the two different segments of his audience—what he called "lecturing" to the whites and "preaching" to the African Americans or "two-text sermons." The latter shouted and clapped and leaped up in ecstasy. Some even rushed the platform and had to be subdued. It is hard to say how many whites came for the scriptural message and how many came for the show, but he never lacked for white followers. The police department always posted officers at his meetings to keep an eye on things. A thousand or more black people in the throes of religious fervor could be a scary thing to the authorities. For that reason alone, the presence of white folks in the audience could have been reassuring.[50]

In later years Griffin tried to drop the moniker "Sin Killer," going by the more dignified "Reverend J. L. Griffin." His last known appearance in Fort Worth was 1911 although he continued to tour until at least 1937. His last meeting was held in a tent on the railroad reservation at the south end of town, not in one of the churches. The announced topic was "The Elevation of the Negro Race." There is no explanation for why he bypassed Fort Worth after 1911, although it could have something to do with the Dixie Theater race riot that occurred here that year, which may have signaled a less friendly climate for his brand of highly emotional preaching.[51]

THE BLACK PRESS, PART 1

Sin Killer Griffin's frequent appearances in Fort Worth never got much coverage in the city's mainstream newspapers, and it was not because whites took no interest in his revivals. On the contrary, the faithful of both races turned out *en masse*. Yet, almost everything we know about his visits comes from the *Dallas Morning News*. Fort Worth's white dailies virtually ignored him. His visits would have been natural subjects for the black press to cover, but there are no surviving issues of black-owned newspapers from those days. We know from the historical record that there were such newspapers; we just know next-to-nothing about them.

Fort Worth's first black-owned newspaper was the weekly *Fort Worth Enterprise*, which began publishing in 1886. Starved for advertising and unable to afford to subscribe to a wire service, it soon went under. Three years later the *Fort Worth Sunday Globe* was publishing in the city. Nothing is known about it today except that its editor-publisher was "colored," and he kept the doors open by reprinting news items from other newspapers. The *Globe* faced the same problems as the *Enterprise*, a small readership and too little advertising to pay the bills, and in the end it suffered the same fate. In 1894 Jay W. Taylor and James C. Scott began publishing *The Item* out of an office over 109 Main. This was the third attempt at a locally-owned-and-operated black newspaper. It came out once a week, on Saturdays. By the time the first *Fort Worth Colored City Directory* came out in 1909 *The Item* was the "oldest Negro newspaper in Texas." Not even that claim to fame was enough to keep the doors open, however, and it was not long after that before its owners too had to face reality.[52]

The reality was that Fort Worth was a lonely outpost for black members of the Fourth Estate. Sin-Killer Griffin excoriated his people during an 1896 revival in Fort Worth for not keeping up with the news. "You people hain't [*sic*] got sense enough to read a newspaper, and those of you as can, won't!" he thundered. No black-owned newspaper was able to make a go of it in the nineteenth century. The black Fourth Estate was so poorly represented in Fort Worth that in 1899 when the Texas Colored Press Association held its first convention, no Fort Worth publication was represented—and this despite the fact that the convention was held just thirty miles away in Dallas. Seventeen other black-owned newspapers from across the state did send representatives.[53]

At the turn of the century, one other black-owned-and-operated newspaper besides *The Item* called Fort Worth home, the *Baptist Star*, published with church backing by the Rev. E.W.D. Isaac. It had started out in Dallas before moving to Fort Worth in 1898 after an incident with the local "white caps" (Klansmen) convinced Isaac that Dallas was no longer a good fit for his brand of journalism. The *Baptist Star* had a statewide readership, and by 1915 it also had the Fort Worth field all to itself. That was the year the Colored Progressive Club called for "the immediate establishment" of a newspaper in the city "devoted to the interests of the negro race." Their cry went unanswered for more than a decade. [54]

One of many Jim Crow stereotypes believed by whites was the "natural tendency of Negroes to spread the news" in some mystical way. Supposedly, blacks possessed some sort of clandestine grapevine that whites weren't privy to. The myth was encouraged by the fact that many blacks were not able to read or write and therefore could not keep up with the news in the usual way, by reading the newspaper.[55] Widespread illiteracy was only part of the problem. Starting up a newspaper required deep pockets, a steady stream of advertising revenue, access to newsmakers, and a distribution network. None of those things was readily available to a would-be black publisher. Even if he had the start-up money he would have found himself cut off from news sources and advertising in the white community, denied access for reasons of race to the larger (white) half of the community.

Still, the city's black residents were not completely cut off from news of events in the national black community. After 1905 they could catch up with the news in copies of the *Chicago Defender*, the largest black-circulation newspaper in the country. It was carried to Fort Worth by

Pullman porters during their travels and passed from hand to hand in the city. The *Chicago Defender* was both a source of news and an inspiration to local black publishers, and it repudiated the myth that blacks got all their news via the grapevine.[56]

Politics and Public Life

After Reconstruction ended, black participation in politics declined almost to nothing as the Republican party deserted them and the Democratic party snubbed them. Rather than demand admission to the political system, many whites felt they should focus on raising themselves up by their bootstraps. In 1889 black Texas activists marched through Austin to protest their treatment. The convention, albeit peaceful, was not well-received. Sniffed one newspaper, "The fact that they did not meet as citizens, but as negroes, shows that they do not yet fairly understand their relations to the state." The newspaper went on to editorialize that whatever wrongs Texas blacks suffered from, they could "never be righted by conventions or by politics." Rather, black Texans had to "develop" their intelligence and individuality, which could only be done through "patience and forbearance." The newspaper further observed that the state's black citizens were was not really so bad off, considering the thousands of acres of land they owned, the taxes they paid, and the numbers of doctors, lawyers, teachers and even inventors they had. "Texas negroes," the writer concluded, ought to be proud of their accomplishments, not worrying about politics.[57]

Preaching patience and forbearance was all well and good for the white population, but it was not going to change things for the black population like political activism would. Unfortunately, in Fort Worth politics black influence even without racial prejudice was severely limited by the fact that the black population was so small and confined to a single ward. Fort Worth was divided up into three wards until 1885, which grew to nine wards by 1892, each represented by two aldermen on the city council. The Third Ward south of Ninth and east of Main was the only ward where blacks lived, and since the Third was also home to the Acre, it was not the most respectable section of the city. The kind of representatives it sent to city hall tended to be saloon keepers and variety-theater owners, so blacks lost twice in Fort Worth politics. As if that were not enough, without any knowledge of the issues or incentive to vote, most black citizens did not even attempt to exercise the franchise. As a result, there was not a single black representative on any elected body, city, county, or precinct; blacks were completely excluded.

Not surprisingly, the most visible members of the black community were a mixed bag. While men like the Trezevants, father and son, were all-American success stories, others were usually described as "notorious characters" in the newspaper, among them the aforementioned sport Joe Pervis and William "Crack-shot" Smith. Smith was no sporting gent like Pervis, but he was just as flamboyant. His tools of the trade were pistols rather than playing cards. He was a sharp-shooting dandy who put on demonstrations that would have made him a featured performer in a Wild West Show had he only been white.[58]

Besides hard-working anonymities like the Trezevants and notorious characters like Joe Pervis and William Smith, Fort Worth was also home to a handful of professional men who should have been role models. At the top of that list were educators Isaiah Milligan Terrell and Henry H. Butler, the Reverend Franklin Pearce Gipson, who led the small, black Methodist congregation, and Dr. William E. Davis, Fort Worth's first black physician. Somewhere between the rascals and the role models were saloon men like Bill Love and Thomas Mason. One newspaper in 1887 called Love Fort Worth's "leading colored politician," a man who regularly rubbed shoulders with the white power brokers who ran the city, while Mason, described euphemistically in the white press as a "Senagambian," leveraged his saloon business into a real estate portfolio and kept moving up until he became president of the city's first black-owned financial institution, the Fraternal Bank & Trust. The number of black men who were able to climb out of slavery and poverty, acquire property, and achieve middle-class status was miniscule but significant. Most of them would probably have agreed with Fort Worth educator Hazel Harvey Peace years later when she described her life as "just trying to do the best I can with what I got." Indeed, that could have been the black community's motto.[59]

The city's small black population posed no threat to the dominant position of the white majority. Blacks were more ignored than oppressed during these years. Their numbers climbed incrementally over time. In 1890 out of a total population of 23,000, 6.0 percent or fewer than 1,400 were African Americans, the smallest percentage of any major city in Texas at the time. In 1900 with the population approaching 27,000, that percentage had risen to 15.9 percent, or about 4,300 blacks. Ten years after that, with the population having soared to 73,000, the percentage was up to 18.1 percent or about 13,200 blacks. The percentage of blacks in the population stayed at about 18 percent through most of the twentieth century.[60]

The two races maintained a delicate social balance. For the white majority, blacks were good for just two things: hard labor and entertainment. The labor part was obvious as blacks did the hardest and dirtiest jobs. The entertainment part might be in the form of humorous "Uncle Remus"-style stories or touring minstrel shows. Or it might be in the ring. Long before Jack Johnson shocked the world by taking the heavyweight boxing title, white fighters were taking on black challengers in backwater rings around the country. In 1889 Fort Worth sporting man Luke Short tried to arrange a bout between bare-knuckles champ John L. Sullivan and a black man billed as "the Colored Champion of Australia." (Fighting an ordinary African American was not exotic-sounding enough.) The bout fell through reportedly because Sullivan refused to "fight with a negro," but there is no doubt it would have been a huge draw if Short could have pulled it off. One form of entertainment with the headliner a less-than-willing participant was public executions. In 1880 the second person executed legally in Fort Worth was Isham (or Isom) Capps, a black man charged with "assaulting" a white woman. The wonder is that he lived long enough to have a trial before being hanged. A white resident of the town in a letter to an Iowa friend mentioned the hanging, but did not seem the least moved by it.

> Well there is a negro going to be hanged tomorrow about 200 yards from our house, and I think I will see him if nothing happens. The wheat is all out in head, and the oats soon will be, and the corn looks nice, . . . and they are just planting cotton.[61]

There was a *modus viviendi* that allowed for some sharing of public spaces and public services. For instance, blacks could hold civic forums in both city hall and the courthouse so long as such meetings were cleared with the powers that be and did not conflict with white activities. Blacks also benefitted from the water and sewage systems, fire and police protection although not to the same extent that whites did. Most if not all blacks lived on properties that did not have municipal water and sewage connections. Besides, different levels of service made sense to whites because it was overwhelmingly their taxes that paid for these services.[62]

In what we call the "private sector" today, respectable black businesses like restaurants, barber shops, and general merchandise stores multiplied during the decades of the 1880s and 1890s. They tended to congregate on certain streets, principally East First, East Ninth, and Calhoun, often side-by-side with residential housing.

One of the big gaps in black social life was suitable places to hold large events. None of the black fraternal orders had meeting halls; they all met in rented spaces. Evans Hall and the Opera House, the city's two largest venues, were not available for blacks. That left the big churches like Mount Gilead Baptist, but sometimes the event was not compatible with a church or the church auditorium was already booked. At such times the sponsors had to find a white owner who would rent a venue to them. Germania Hall was one space that welcomed blacks for a price. Presumably, the ethnic German community was more open-minded than their fellow white citizens. Outdoor events were even more dicey. Since City Park was closed to blacks, that left only church grounds as gathering spots. With the black population growing steadily toward the end of the century, the shortage of suitable outdoor meeting spaces became a major problem, where "suitable" meant having a covered pavilion, public restrooms, and picnic grounds.[63]

The lack of a large public meeting place did not prevent a group of visionary black entrepreneurs from holding Texas' first Colored State Fair (CSF) in Fort Worth. The year was 1887, and the organizers needed to look no further for inspiration than the Colored People's World's Exposition in New Orleans two years earlier. Texas had put up a large exhibit in New Orleans, and now Bill McDonald and friends wanted to create something similar in Fort Worth. It would also be their riposte to the all-white Texas State Fair and Exposition, which started in Dallas in 1886. The annual state fair was the pride of white Texans. Blacks were barred except for one day of its run ("Colored Day"), so seven Fort Worth blacks formed the Colored State Fair Company to hold an event run by and for African Americans.[64]

Fort Worth was an easy choice because its black population was small but growing and it had excellent rail connections, a thriving economy, and peaceful race relations. The rail connections were especially important because they expected railroad companies to "contribute liberally" as they had done at New Orleans, starting with the Texas & Pacific, which had a major presence in Fort Worth. The directors received an enthusiastic response from both the black and white communities. One (white) banker was so taken by the idea that he offered to pay a $15,000 franchise fee for the right to collect all ticket revenues and grounds concessions. The directors chose as their leader a relatively unknown newcomer to the city, William M. McDonald. He turned out to be an excellent choice. They raised $25,000 through subscriptions and selected a spot on the north end of Samuels Ave. for the fair grounds. If they could not borrow the city park or set up on church grounds, they would create their own space. The site had no water, sewage, or gas connections, but otherwise it was a perfect spot, lying at the end of Fort Worth's silk-stocking street and near the cold springs that had long been a public gathering spot. The grounds would also be a short ride from the center of town.[65]

The Colored State Fair (CSF) opened on October 25, 1887, the first statewide event in Texas history put on by and for African Americans. The directors even got popular Texas Governor Lawrence Sul Ross to open the exposition. There is no known photograph showing what the fairgrounds looked like—whether there was one or several buildings or just tents, whether there was a big entrance with a big welcoming sign, or something more modest. We do know the CSF showcased a wide variety of Texas agricultural products and crafts like the Texas Spring Palace put on by Fort Worth two years later, only with everything produced by African Americans, including the entertainment. There was a track for horse racing, and a broad, grassy area for holding competitive military drills between militia companies from as far away as Arkansas. There are no attendance records for the five-day event to judge its success. The directors made one major misstep by attempting to go head-to-head with the Dallas State Fair, also held in October. That may be why the exposition finished in the red. Most Fort Worth blacks, it seemed, preferred to attend the Big Show in Dallas even if they got second-class treatment there. Promoters of the Dallas exposition responded to the Fort Worth challenge by creating a special "Colored Department" and making a strong pitch to black exhibitors to come to Dallas.[66]

While the CSF was not even a patch on Dallas' State Fair, it was lauded by white progressives for "advance[ing] the colored race morally and intellectually," which was no substitute for big crowds. As a commercial venture, the Fair was supposed to be about having fun, not uplifting either the morals or the IQ of the race. The 1887 Fair closed in the red. Critics accused the Fort Worth organizers of "bad management" and the local colored community of "non-cooperation." Backers debated whether to put all their eggs in the Dallas basket or "have a fair ground of our own, conducted and controlled by negro men, and thereby show the world the progress of our people in Texas." In the end, they decided on a second season for the CSF, but this one without Bill McDonald calling the shots and in Marshall instead of Fort Worth. They also decided to hold it in June instead of October. Before being pushed out, McDonald calculated the costs of a second season at $8,000, which was easily raised through subscriptions again. Marshall was delighted to have the Fair, and it was held there for six more years after the 1888 season. Fort Worth was represented at every fair by a hugely popular "colored brass band" that proved Fort Worth's black community had a wealth of musical talent and entrepreneurial spirit if not financial acumen. The CSF deserves a place in the history books if for no other reason than that it announced the arrival of a new force on the scene, William Madison McDonald.[67]

Building "Social Capital," Part 1

Sociologist Robert D. Putnam uses the concept of "social capital" to describe the importance of extensive social connections in creating a viable community; it is like financial capital, physical capital (buildings), and human capital (job skills). In Putnam's analysis, there are two kinds of social capital: bonding and bridging. Bonding is what occurs when individuals reach out to others within their same group, say a religious, age, or racial group. Bridging is what happens when members of one group make friends with persons who are not like themselves, for instance when blacks and whites find common ground. Early on, the only way blacks could rise was by building bridges to the white community. This is what Judge Charles C. Cummings and Henry Cavile did in 1875 to get the first black schools built.[68]

For Fort Worth's black community to truly succeed, they had to "bond" with each other in ways that went deeper than skin color, while continuing to build bridges to the majority white community. Creating social capital is no substitute for equality. Rather, it is an important step on the road toward full equality. It all starts with bonding. Black leaders were busy even before the end of the nineteenth century building new, inclusive institutions by reaching out to those with similar trades, interests, background, or religious beliefs to forge new organizations and political action groups. Many of these new organizations would fail and some would never get beyond the crawling stage, but they laid the groundwork for grander, more powerful organizations in the twentieth century.

The first manifestation of this bonding phenomenon was the black churches established during Reconstruction. Other organizations followed, some of them growing out of the churches and others having strong denominational ties. In the late 1890s a group of Fort Worth blacks formed the African-American Citizens' Conference (AACC) to promote black interests. The name they chose for themselves jumps off the page because at this date virtually every other black organization described itself as either "Colored" or "Negro." The AACC called themselves "African Americans," demonstrating that some blacks at least had a concept of themselves that combined both their nationality and their heritage. When this group was reported in the *Morning Register* in 1897 it was the first known use of the term "African American" in public print in Fort Worth.[69]

The only charter member of the AACC whose name has come down to us is Dave Black whose exact role is unclear but who was singled out by the white newspapers. At their organizational meeting on January 11, 1897, the group discussed various issues they planned to push, including both patronage-type concessions as well as more elevated measures for "the betterment of the colored race." Among practical objectives were getting a few black janitors hired to work in the city's schools and "at least one assistant janitor at the courthouse." But it was the group's higher goals that made them more than just another special interest group. They discussed shutting down the "colored gambling houses," calling out colored brethren who were trading "recognition of our race for small amounts of money," and most ambitious of all, running a "colored man" or "colored man's representative" from the Third Ward for city council. Since blacks were not even in the majority in the Third Ward, the best they could hope for would be a sympathetic white man ("a colored man's representative").[70]

Dave Black told a reporter they were merely at the discussion stage at that point but he injected a note of urgency when he added, "The colored people are fast losing ground in their present disorganized condition." Black and his fellow Fort Worth activists were probably in the black half of the Republican "black-and-tan" alliance, which was already dying as a political force at this date. Without enough votes to get African Americans elected to public office or enough economic power to influence policy, African Americans faced a bleak future. It would take years before blacks were organized enough to change the system.[71]

That same decade, members of the tiny black professional and middle classes of Fort Worth formed what they called the Colored Progressive Club (CPC), a combination chamber of commerce and political action group. Its modest headquarters was at Jones and Eighth streets among the "Negro tenements" and saloons until 1897 when it moved to Houston St. between Ninth and Tenth. Its membership included both men and women of color, making it truly "progressive" for its time. For more than twenty years, the CPC was the only full-time advocacy group claiming to speak for the black community. In 1915 it announced an agenda of three goals: 1) a black-owned newspaper; 2) a "social center for Negroes"; and 3) a public park "for negroes only." Years later, the CPC was superseded by other organizations such as the NAACP.[72]

Neither the AACC nor the CPC was any threat to white rule. Even their combined memberships—and it is likely that some men belonged to both groups—were exceedingly small because there was not much of a black middle class in Fort Worth and because many of those probably recognized the futility of fighting for a place at the table. A black man living in the tenements might work in a white-owned business such as the Congress Barber Shop (610 Main) where the city's lawyers and judges congregated, but he could not get his own hair cut or shoes shined there.[73] Occasionally, blacks had to venture into the white Fort Worth to find a particular service, such as a lawyer or photographer, and the Jim Crow system made allowances for such cross-over business. But there was never any doubt that Fort Worth was a racially segregated town and woe be unto anyone, white or black, who challenged that system.

Hell's Half-acre was where social "bridging" was most likely to occur because both races were seeking the same things. That is why one could find black bawds servicing white customers, black porters working in white saloons, and the occasional black cowboy on the street taking a break from driving a herd to Kansas. Even in the "Acre," however, there were rules. For instance, white men could patronize black prostitutes, but black customers never could hire white prostitutes. And black cowboys could work beside their white counterparts on the trail but had to patronize their own establishments when in town.

It was hard to create a vibrant community with certain professions and services completely lacking. What was lacking might be scarcely missed if not essential for daily life. For instance, there was not a single black professional photographer in Fort Worth whereas there were four or five white photographers working in the city at any given time from the 1880s on. Dressing up in one's Sunday best or even in one's working clothes was a way middle-class Americans preserved their family history. Those pictures also put a face on the community—the white community. If an African American wanted to have a photograph taken of himself and/or his family, he had to go see one of the white photographers in the white business district. The act of looking straight into the camera and posing proudly for a photograph granted a certain amount of dignity and immortality to the subject(s). Unfortunately, this little bit of dignity, this memento, was denied most African Americans.[74]

Far more serious was the lack of black lawyers, nurses, and homes for orphans. For instance, we don't know of a single trained black nurse or lawyer working in Fort Worth in the nineteenth century. We must assume therefore that the sick were looked after by friends or family, not professional nurses, and we know that those caught up in the justice system had to rely on court-appointed white lawyers or do without. Orphans' homes as charitable institutions operated by the well-off for society's outcasts don't seem to have existed either. We know there had to be black orphans and homeless children, yet we don't know who cared for them. White orphanages did not take in black children, so black orphans must have been placed in the care of good-hearted "aunties" and "uncles" who were not necessarily blood-related.

One Step Forward, Two Steps Back

Black progress often consisted of taking one step forward only to be knocked back two. Many of the gains of Reconstruction were taken away by Jim Crow rules, which came in toward the end of the century. Jim Crow segregation affected everything, including municipal services. Whites controlled the machinery of government, which included all the basic services: police, fire department, schools, and public health. City departments took care of whites first and blacks after that, if at all.

For example, the Public Health Department was created in 1881 in response to a major smallpox outbreak that spring. City fathers would probably not have concerned themselves with blacks if the outbreak that erupted in the black community had not threatened to spread to the white community. It began with a black man who lived behind one of the city's hotels and a little black girl who lived on Calhoun. Since quarantine and scrubbing were the only known defenses against contagious disease, the two victims and everyone living with them were removed to tents outside the city limits and their quarters thoroughly fumigated with camphor and pine tar, both believed to cleanse "bad air." Marshal Sam Farmer and Sheriff Walter Maddox became the de facto sanitation officers, assisted by the town's doctors. As other cases followed, the tent city was steadily enlarged until finally the city council made the decision to build a "pest house." As soon as the pest house opened, all white patients were moved into it while black cases continued to be quarantined in the tent city. Meanwhile, the town's doctors instituted a mass vaccination program among healthy blacks and whites alike. Not a word of protest came from the white community about the expense of vaccinating blacks because smallpox was a scourge that threatened the entire town regardless of race. Other emergency measures were also adopted. Yellow flags sprouted like spring flowers on shacks up and down Calhoun and Jones streets as well as on side streets. Like most diseases, the smallpox followed a vector; having started on one street it soon spread the length of the street. The epidemic had played itself out by early May 1881, but there would be other outbreaks in the future, and the pest house became a permanent fixture awaiting the next contagious outbreak.[75]

That came in August 1888 when smallpox struck again. As before, the outbreak started in the black community. When "certain negroes became ill," police moved quickly to remove them and "all their effects" to the pest house. The shacks where they lived were then burned. The epidemic became a legal matter when some infected bedding from the pest house was sold in town—to a white citizen. This compromised the quarantine and gave new life to the disease. White citizens ended up in the pest house alongside black citizens. Some of the white victims sued for damages because they had contracted the disease from the infected bedding. There is no record of how the suit was settled, but this latest smallpox outbreak eventually played itself out just like the earlier one. The lesson from public health crises like these was that the city only took notice of its black citizens when a contagious outbreak threatened to jump the racial divide.[76]

Photo 5. Administering the Sabine polio vaccine

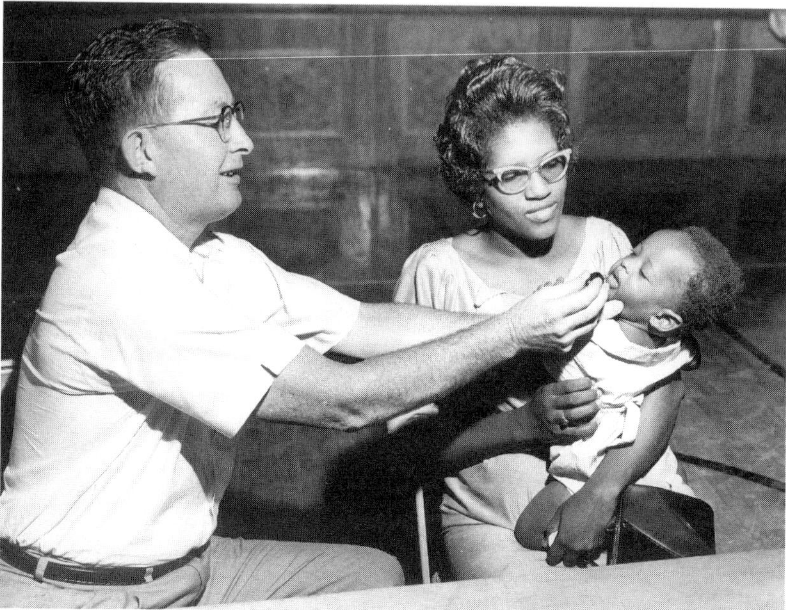

Blacks have always been slighted by the public health system although things had greatly improved by the time this photo was taken in the 1950s: a white doctor administering the vaccine to a black child. Courtesy of Tarrant County Black Historical & Genealogical Society.

Aside from being admitted to the pest house, the black community also won some uplifting concessions from the white majority, starting with their own park. It marked a signal moment in the city's history when in 1895 black residents got their own city park, named for Frederick Douglass, the first African American to achieve national recognition. The same year that Douglass died (1895), a trio of black Fort Worth businessmen led by Thomas Mason created Douglass Park by purchasing nearly six acres of river-bottom land just north of the bluff for the bargain-basement price of $90. At that time, Fort Worth had just one public playground, City Park (created in 1892), where citizens could picnic and hold large outdoor events, but it was off-limits to blacks. This was an issue in particular on June 19 ("Juneteenth") every year, which was the date that Texas blacks celebrated emancipation from slavery. Elsewhere across the South, blacks celebrated the Fourth of July as their "day of freedom" but not in Texas. First celebrated in 1866, June 19 was known as "Emancipation Day" until well into the twentieth century. As Emancipation Day or Juneteenth, its importance had grown every year since until it became the most important date on the black calendar. Since Fort Worth fathers were not willing to create a "negro park" *or* open City Park to African Americans, the black community took it upon itself to create their own park. Douglass Park was not really a public park since it had been purchased with private funds and maintained the same way. The Fort Worth Police Department did not even patrol it.[77]

In the years that followed Douglass Park went by a variety of names: the "North Side Park," the "Negro Park," or the "Negro Resort." They got the city to appoint a special officer to patrol the park at night, and over the years they developed it as they got the money, digging a well for fresh water, putting up a pavilion, and stringing a few electric lights. The main event held there for many years was the annual Juneteenth celebration, a two-day affair kicked off with a parade followed by speeches, games, and fireworks. Some years the parade that wound its way to Douglass Park was a mile long. One thing the participants never failed to do before all the baseball and barbecue was read Lincoln's Emancipation Proclamation out loud. Douglass Park became the social center of the black community and more than that, a safe ground from white tyranny. Eventually the land became too valuable for the black community to hang onto. First, the Magnolia Petroleum Company built a pipeline through it, then in 1925 the city sold it out from under its owners to Texas Electric Service Company to build a power station. Thereafter, the city opened up its public parks one day a year (Juneteenth) to blacks.[78]

Photo 6. Douglass Park

Named for Frederick Douglass, this was the first public park where African Americans could go in Fort Worth—at least until it was closed in 1920 or so. This photograph was turned into a postcard. Courtesy of Fort Worth collector Dalton Hoffman.

Other black parks followed Douglass Park, none of them as large or as nice. Sometime after 1899 a subscription drive generated the money to purchase Tyler Park, across the river and northwest of the bluff. In 1909 North Side blacks bought four acres at NE 28th and Old Azle Road for a park. It had picnic areas, ball diamonds, and playground equipment. One could start walking in the Trinity River bottoms at either the north or south city limits and reach all three parks without ever leaving the river bottoms because that was the only land the real estate brokers would sell to blacks.[79]

The second-class, unfunded parks are further proof that white residents did not consider blacks to be part of their community; they lived there and were subject to the same laws, but they were not part of the Fort Worth community. If you want more proof, consider the common white attitude toward "Emancipation Day," the most important date on the black calendar. They considered it simply an excuse for "negroes not to report for work tomorrow." The "elaborate celebrations" that attended the day were beneath disdain.[80]

Like social institutions, the criminal justice system was also stacked against blacks. The simple act of being accused by a white was proof of guilt. In this regard, things had not changed much since slavery. And vigilante action was favored over the legal formalities of a court trial. In 1880, several whites were brought to trial for attempting to lynch a black man accused of "assaulting" (a euphemism for rape) a white woman. *The Fort Worth Democrat* argued that any decent man would have done the same thing under the circumstances, asking rhetorically, "Could they do otherwise?" When the accused was cleared, the newspaper dismissed it as getting off on a technicality, and added that the exculpatory evidence was unknown at the time the men tried to lynch the accused. The following year, another black man was charged with raping another white woman. The day after his arrest he was tried, convicted, and sentenced to hang, and two days later he was stood up on a box with a noose around his neck and the box kicked out from under him. Before he could choke to death, however, a messenger ran up from the telegraph office to report that the governor had issued a stay of execution. The sheriff cut him down, and the *Democrat* subsequently editorialized that justice was only being temporarily delayed. These episodes show how much blacks lived on the edge, surviving only at the whim of the white majority.[81]

Yet another critical service blacks lacked was banking. Before the turn of the century, the black residents of Fort Worth could not get a business loan, finance a home, or create a savings account because all the banks were white banks. Fort Worth blacks would not get their own bank until 1909.

Hiram McGar—Businessman, sporting man, self-made man[82]

In the nineteenth century a sporting man (aka, sport) was a gentleman who made his living as a gambler, betting on anything that offered a chance to turn a profit. The difference between being a sport versus a garden-variety gambler was that a sport was both a gentleman and professional, a respected members of the community. For a black man, it was one of the few professions he could go into and prosper. The sporting life also provided an entrée into other, legitimate businesses. Hiram McGar was such a sporting-man-turned-entrepreneur, making him a more accessible role model for today's youth than an educator like I.M. Terrell or a physician like Riley Ransom.

Like most African Americans born into slavery, not much is known about McGar's early life. He was born December 12, 1863, to Hiram and Mary Shackleford McGar. Either one of the two was white or else Mary Shackleford had a deep, dark secret because years later, the Census described McGar as "mulatto." During Jim Crow times this could be both a stigma and an advantage in the black community. Fair-skinned blacks, especially if they had Caucasian features, rose to the top of the community even as they swept the circumstances of their birth under the carpet. Hiram McGar enjoyed extraordinary success as a businessman and sporting gentleman.

All we know about McGar's birthplace is that it was in east Texas. His name first appears in the public record is the 1870 Census as a sixteen-year-old living with his family in Walker County. As a young black man growing up in nineteenth century Texas, he had little if any formal schooling and probably got his first job as an agricultural worker, maybe a tenant-farmer.

He next appears as a "colored policeman" in Austin, Texas in 1897. Walking a beat every day in the "negro district," he saw how the real money was in the saloon business. Sometime before 1901 he relocated to Fort Worth and started a new life as co-owner of Watkins & McGar Saloon in the Acre. Four years later, he took on new partners at a new location, the Capitol Bar, also in the Acre. Two years later he struck out on his own, opening McGar's Saloon on E. Tenth. In 1912 he moved one block north and re-branded his establishment McGar's Pool Hall. He would continue to do business there for the next eight or nine years. It was here that he first got his name in the headlines when Tommy Lee murdered one of his customers, Walter Moore, in May 1913. Lee also shot a white policeman and three other persons, causing a white mob to try to lynch him. When that failed they turned their fury on the black business district, looting and burning stores and saloons, including McGar's place.

The combination of being well-spoken and having a good head for business opened doors for McGar in politics. At a time when blacks represented a majority of the Republican Party in Texas, he became state chairman, forging an alliance with William M. McDonald. McGar's political base was the Third Ward. The polling place for the Third Ward was McGar's saloon.

He remained a power in the state Republican Party until 1908 when the "Lily-whites" gained control. First he lost his place on the executive committee, then his seat at party conventions. Cast aside in politics, he found something else to invest his time and entrepreneurial skills in: baseball. McGar was no ballplayer; his interest was in the business side. Sometime around the turn of the century he organized the first African-American team in Fort Worth, part of the Lone Star Colored Baseball League. "McGar's Wonders," as dubbed them were as successful as every other enterprise he took up. They were League champions in 1909, attracting a large black *and* white following. Never content to do things halfway, he built the team a "grandstand" on some empty land one block west of North Main about a mile north of the Courthouse. Officially, it was McGar Park, but fans called it "McGar's ball yard." He may or may not have been the on-field manager, but he was definitely the team owner.

When the Lone Star League folded, McGar still owned both the Wonders and the stadium, and in 1913 he helped organize the Colored Baseball League of Texas and Oklahoma with the Wonders one of the six teams. McGar was the most experienced baseball man among the owners. In 1916 he was elected president of the League. A new league required a new name for the Wonders, so they became the Black Panthers, hoping to cash in on the popularity of the local white team, the Cats. McGar's team and his stadium may have been in the Negro Leagues, but that did not keep white fans from coming out to the games. The product was good and the stands were filled, but still something was wrong with the business model in Negro baseball. After the 1918 season, baseball ended at McGar's ball yard. The park was converted into a motorcycle race track.

Unwilling to give up, in 1919 McGar and his partners tried to resurrect black baseball in Texas. Six teams took the field for the 1919 season as the Texas Negro Baseball League, including the Fort Worth Black Panthers, who were now playing at Panther Park when the Cats weren't using it. The Texas Negro Baseball League folded after the 1927 season, a victim of economics and Jim Crow. One problem: when teams from Houston, Beaumont, and Wichita Falls came to town they had to stay overnight, which meant paying for food and lodging on top of transportation.

Meanwhile, McGar's principal business interest, the pool hall-saloon, was also in trouble. National Prohibition arrived in 1919, forcing saloon owners either to close down or operate illegally as "speakeasies." McGar took the legitimate route and converted his bar into Citizens' Drug Store, serving soda pop instead of beer and liquor. He kept the pool tables and continued to rent out rooms upstairs, a lucrative side-business in a town with no black hotel accommodations.

Little is known about Hiram McGar's private life. He married twice, the first time to a woman named Nancy whom he divorced in 1907, and the second time to Aggie Cohen of Fort Worth in 1909. Out of his first union came a son, Mannie McGar, who shot and killed a man in 1915 in a bar fight. Mannie did not do any time because no Fort Worth jury convicted a black man of killing another black man before 1946. It was another side of Jim Crow.

Hiram McGar died on December 13, 1930, and was interred in the Trinity section of Oakwood Cemetery. In retrospect, he was no saint, but he was not a bad man either. He was simply a businessman trying to make it in a world where the deck was stacked against his race.

Notes

1. Population statistics must be extrapolated from several unofficial sources. For Fort Worth's population in 1880, see *Dallas Herald*, July 1, 1880; for county population, see Paddock, *Fort Worth and the Texas Northwest*, Vol. 2, p. 834. For 1885 percentage, see *Fort Worth Telegram*, November 16, 1903; and for total city population see *"Federal Writers' Project,"*, Vol. 11, p. 4083. Blacks were often under-represented in federal census and local population counts because those who were counting were white and also because there were large numbers of transients in the black population. Tenth United States Federal Census (1880), Fort Worth, Tarrant County, TX, Microfilm Roll No. T9_1328 [hereafter U.S. Census, 1880].
2. Population statistics must be extrapolated from several unofficial sources. For 1880, see Paddock, *Fort Worth and the Texas Northwest*, Vol. 2, p. 834. Blacks were often under-represented in census counts both because census-takers were white and also because of the large transient population. Tenth United States Federal Census (1880), Fort Worth, Tarrant County, TX, Microfilm Roll No. T9_1328 [hereafter U.S. Census, 1880].
3. By the end of the decade the T&P would be part of the Missouri-Pacific system with its state headquarters in Marshall. There is a crying need for a detailed analysis of the 1880 U.S. census report and the city directories between 1880 and 1900 to get a better handle on the number of black residents in Fort Worth and what kinds of work they were engaged in. Unfortunately, there is no extant 1890 U.S. Census report because it burned up in a fire many years later. U.S. Census, 1880.
4. The Stag Saloon was in the 800 block of Main. Hill, "Trezevant," 107. For Stag Saloon, See Richard Selcer, *et al.*, *Legendary Watering Holes* (College Station: Texas A&M University Press, 2004), 271–72. On December 23, 1890, the black porter at the Bank Saloon had the misfortune of getting caught in the middle of a shooting affray between white gamblers Luke Short and Charlie Wright. He came out of it unscratched. *Fort Worth Gazette*, December 24, 1890.
5. For Pervis, see *Dallas Times-Herald*, July 9, 1890.
6. Geisel, *Historical Vignette*, 3–4.

7. The city was withering on the vine at this date because the railroad had stalled halfway between Dallas and Fort Worth. Many citizens were probably glad to have any kind of resident living in the corporate limits to keep Fort Worth from drying up and blowing away. *Fort Worth Democrat,* August 29, 1874. For the number of black "working girls" in the Acre, see *Dallas Morning News,* August 12, 1886.
8. *Fort Worth Daily Gazette,* July 29 and 30, 1887. See also "Federal Writers' Project," Vol. 9, p. 3503.
9. Madam C.J. Walker was the turn-of-the-century entrepreneur who made a fortune selling beauty and hair care products to African-American women. She earned the title "Madam" in a completely different line of work than Emeline Gooden! For Emeline's career, see *Fort Worth Gazette,* March 14 and November 21, 1887; March 5, December 6 and 7, 1888; and October 30, 1889. Mary Porter, another long-time Fort Worth madam, was a contemporary of Emeline Gooden. Mary bought a different type of house in 1905 and retired from the business. For Mary's story, see Richard F. Selcer, "Madam Mary Porter: Mary, Mary, Quite Contrary," *Fort Worth Characters* (Denton: University of North Texas Press, 2009), 204–219.
10. *Fort Worth Record,* October 10 and 11, 1917. Also cited in Harold Rich, *Fort Worth: Outpost, Cowtown, Boomtown* (Norman: University of Oklahoma Press, 2014), 196, hereafter Rich, *Fort Worth.*
11. *Fort Worth Weekly Gazette,* February 6, 1890. Reprinted in *Footprints* 48, no. 1 (February 2005): 8.
12. The 1882 *City Directory* provides more details: Trabue was a "faith doctor," and not included in the Directory's listing of practicing physicians. Fort Worth *Democrat,* March 15, 1882. Also cited in Rich, *Fort Worth,* 216, fnt. 6.
13. In 1887, the Knights of Labor collapsed as a national organization, discredited by a series of riots and railroad strikes across the country. For a history of the Knights of Labor movement, see Gerald N. Grob, *Workers and Utopia: A Study of Ideological Conflict in the American Labor Movement, 1865–1900* (Evanston, IL: Northwestern University Press, 1961); and Walter Licht, *Industrializing America: The Nineteenth Century* (Baltimore: The Johns Hopkins University Press, 1995). For Colored Knights in Fort Worth, see *Fort Worth Gazette,* December 9, 1885."We the Colored Citizens of Fort Worth" to "the Honorable Mayor and City Council," May 28, 1900, Records of the City of Fort Worth, Series I, Mayor and Council Proceedings, Box 1 (July 20, 1900), Fort Worth Library, Central

Branch, Local History, Genealogy, & Archives Unit, hereafter Mayor and Council Proceedings.

14. See "Colored Organizations" in *Fort Worth City Directory*, 1886–87. For background on specific groups, see "History of the Grand High Court Heroines of Jericho Prince Hall Affiliation—Texas Jurisdiction," http://grandhighcourthojtx.com/Past_Grand_Officers; and "United Brothers of Friendship and Sisters of the Mysterious Ten," http://nkaa.uky.edu/record.php?note_id=1510; *Fort Worth City Directory*, 1890; and W.H. Gibson, Sr., *History of the United Brothers of Friendship and Sisters of the Mysterious Ten* (Louisville, KY: Bradley & Gilbert, 1897); for The Seven Stars of Consolidation, Alwyn Barr, *The African Texans* (College Station: Texas A&M University Press, 2004), 32, hereafter Barr, *African Texans*; and "Wide Awakes" on Wikipedia.
15. Prince Hall Masonry came to Texas in 1876 with Lodge No. 1 in San Antonio. Alton G. Roundtree and Paul M. Bessel. *Out of the Shadows: Prince Hall Freemasonry in America, 200 Years of Endurance* (Forestville, MD: KLR Publishing, 2006). As recently as 2006, the two branches of freemasonry in Texas still did not recognize each other. Jay Reeves, "Segregation entrenched among Masons in South," *Fort Worth Star-Telegram*, October 24, 2006.
16. Lodge No. 20 means the Fort Worth lodge was the twentieth organized in the state, with San Antonio No. 1 in 1875. See "History of the Grand High Court Heroines of Jericho Prince Hall Affiliation—Texas Jurisdiction," http://grandhighcourthojtx.com/Past_Grand_Officers. Local lore says Prince Hall Masonry in Fort Worth owes its beginnings to William M. McDonald, but he did not live in Fort Worth in 1885 and the Proceedings clearly show that he had no role in founding the Fort Worth lodge. *Proceedings of the Most Worshipful Grand Lodge of Texas (Annual)*,1887-1929, Prince Hall Masonic Mosque, Fort Worth, Texas, Box 1, hereafter Prince Hall *Proceedings*. The *Proceedings* provide the best annual snapshot of the Prince Hall Masons in Texas, 1887–1929. For description of the building, see *Fort Worth Record and Register*, July 19, 1907, in "Federal Writers' Project," Vol. 36, p. 14017.
17. The address for the Prince Hall Mosque was 2214 East First. It also housed the offices of the Heroines of Jericho and Eastern Star women's auxiliaries. In later years it hosted concerts by Mahalia Jackson, Ray Charles, and B.B.King. But its greatest glory was hosting the annual state convention more often than any other lodge in Texas. Prince Hall *Proceedings*, June 18-21, 1889; and July 17-12, 1906, p. 19. Rebecca R. Sohmer,

"Fort Worth's Rock Island Bottom: A Social Geography of an African-American Neighborhood," Master of Arts thesis, Syracuse University, Syracuse, New York, 1997, pp. 63–64, hereafter Sohmer, "Rock Island Bottom."

18. Regarding size of membership, since no membership rolls are known to have survived, it is impossible to determine how much crossover there was among the various membership rolls. Information on the membership numbers and meeting places comes from "Colored Organizations," *Fort Worth City Directory*, 1886–87. For McDonald, see Barr, *African Texans*, 32. A.F.&A.M. (the white Masons) stood for Ancient Free & Accepted Masons. For city hall, see *Dallas Morning News*, July 3, 1906.
19. *Fort Worth Morning Register*, November 9, 1899.
20. U.S. Census, 1880.
21. *Fort Worth Star-Telegram*, May 7, 1909. For city's growth and location of railroad reservations, see Sanborn fire maps, 1889, 1893, and 1907, Dolph Briscoe Center for American History, The University of Texas at Austin (originals), or digitized versions on ProQuest Information and Learning at Environmental Data Resources website, www.erdnet.com.
22. "City services" quote and a complete description of the city's layout are found in the *Fort Worth City Directory*, 1890, pp. 37–38. *Fort Worth Telegram*, May 10, 1904; and July 22, 1905.
23. The real estate on what was originally known as Baptist Hill was bought up by white developer A.J. Chambers and developed as a blue-collar residential neighborhood before the end of the century. What the railroads started in the nineteenth century freeway construction completed in the middle of the twentieth century; the neighborhood became an island amidst a sea of railroad tracks and major roadways. See Lenora Rolla unpublished MS, Lenora Rolla Papers. *Dallas Morning News*, October 26, 1891; and October 17, 1897. *Fort Worth Morning Register*, November 25, 1901. For "the Hill" as a racially mixed neighborhood, see Sohmer, "Rock Island Bottom," 1–2.
24. This situation was not limited to Fort Worth. Examples can also be found in Dallas and other Western towns. Nor is it limited to the nineteenth century. *Dallas Morning News*, April 9, 1936.
25. *Fort Worth Star-Telegram*, March 29, 1915. The *Dallas Morning News* did a series of articles on "Housing Conditions in Texas," November–December 1911. This information came from No. 25 in the series, *Dallas Morning News*, December 13, 1911. The best explanation of the origins of the three names is: 1) Battercake Flats from identification of black domes-

tic life with "Aunt Jemima" character created by Quaker Oats to market pancake mix after 1889. The big, smiling "Mammy" was universally known by the turn of the century; 2) Yellow Row probably derives from "Yellow Negroes," a description for light-skinned blacks; and 3) the name Stick Town according to former residents came from the fact that when it rained, the clay-based muck of the area would stick stubbornly to the feet. For Stick Town, see Ken Hopkins, "Searching for Stick Town," vertical file in Local History, Archives, and Genealogy Unit, Central Branch, Fort Worth Library. The neighborhood centered on three streets that have been nearly wiped out by commercial development over the years: Armour, Swift, and Windmill.

26. For origins of the "state streets" (which started with Arizona Ave. on the west), see 1882 Fort Worth City Directory, p. 25.
27. For a general history of Stop Six, see Karen Rouse, "A Touch of Rural Amid Urban," *Fort Worth Star-Telegram,* May 16, 1999; and ibid., February 26, 1997. For "safe" quote, see Nadolyn Redmond Jones, "Stop Six: Greatness Faded But Residents Who Built It Won't Let It Be Forgotten," ibid. September 25, 2012.
28. The Bucket of Blood was at Calhoun and Twelfth. The Red Star's exact location is unknown today. Neither place made it into the city directory. For the Red Star, see *Fort Worth Daily Gazette,* November 21, 1887. For the Bucket of Blood, see Judge Irby Dunklin's recollections in *"Federal Writers' Project,"* Vol. 2, p. 526.
29. *Dallas Weekly Herald,* May 3, 1883.
30. *Fort Worth Daily Gazette,* April 1, 1887. Also cited in "Federal Writers' Project," Vol. 33, p. 13091. For Black Elephant, see undated clipping in vertical file, Hell's Half-acre, Fort Worth Library, Local History, Genealogy and Archives Unit.
31. The run of the *Fort Worth City Directory,* from 1877 to 1928 with a few missing numbers, is on microfiche at the Fort Worth Public Library, Central Branch, Local History, Archives and Genealogy Dept. For "dives," see *Dallas Herald,* April 2, 1885. For black prostitutes, see *Fort Worth Daily Gazette,* April 1, 1887. Also cited in "Federal Writers' Project," Vol. 33, p. 13091.
32. *Fort Worth Weekly Gazette,* April 24, 1890.
33. "Chronology of the Fort Worth Independent School District," compiled by Roy Housewright, archivist, Billy W. Sills Archives of the FWISD, hereafter "Chronology of the FWISD," Housewright. See also a history of early black schooling in Fort Worth is contained in the program for the

I.M. Terrell High School "All Student" Reunion of 1985. Tarrant County Black Historical & Genealogical Society Collections, Series II (Individual Collections), Box 1, File 4, Fort Worth Library, Central Branch, Local History, Genealogy, & Archives Unit, hereafter the TCBH&GS Collections.

34. For numbers of students and tax rate, see Paddock, *Fort Worth and Texas Northwest* 2, p. 834. For early history, see *Fort Worth City Directories*, 1882, 1883-84, 1885-86, 1886-87, and 1888-89. With the exception of that first year, the directories were published every two years. The 1888-89 *Directory* includes a brief history of the school system up to that date. See also "History of I.M. Terrell School," *Fort Worth Star-Telegram*, February 24, 2013. *Cf.* Oliver Knight, *Fort Worth: Outpost on the Trinity*, 2nd ed. (Norman: University of Oklahoma Press, 1990), 150–51, hereafter Knight, *Fort Worth*, which mentions only the "African Methodist Church" school. See also Rich, *Fort Worth*, 26; Fairley, "Terrell Was Early Black School Leader," *Fort Worth Star-Telegram*, February 20, 2002, which has a number of historical errors but gets the gist of the story right; and Gayle M. Hanson, "Isaiah Milligan Terrell," in *The Handbook of Texas Online*, www.tshaonline.org. Program of I.M. Terrell "All Student" Reunion of 1985, TCBH&GS, Series II (Individual Collections), Box 1, File 4. For pupil-teacher ratios, see *Fort Worth Gazette*, May 2, 1886; and Rich, *Fort Worth*, 26.

35. *Cf.* Knight, *Fort Worth*, 150–51, which mentions only a single black school, the "African Methodist Church." See also Fairley, "Terrell Was Early Black School Leader," *Fort Worth Star-Telegram*, February 20, 2002. For more on the segregated black schools, see Gayle Hanson, "Isaiah Milligan Terrell," in *The Handbook of Texas Online*, www.tshaonline.org; and O.K. Carter, "The History of an Old Quaker Endowment," *Fort Worth Star-Telegram*, July 31, 2007.

36. Program of I.M. Terrell "All Student" Reunion of 1985, TCBH&GS Collections, Series II (Individual Collections), Box 1, File 4. This was James Guinn's first school (misspelled in the newspapers and *City Directory* as "Guynn"). One other teacher was hired, Cornelia Shrieves ("Shrieves" in the Director, "Sheere" in the newspaper). *Fort Worth City Directory*, 1899-1900. *Fort Worth Morning Register*, August 5, 1901. A history of the school and its namesake was published on the occasion dedicating a historic marker. See *Fort Worth Star-Telegram*, November 4, 1988. For quotations and numbers of pupils, see *Fort Worth Morning Register*, September 1, 1901.

37. Fort Worth's Colored High School did not open until 1907, so it could not have produced a graduating class in 1893. The names of that first graduating class come from records of Tarrant County Black Historical & Genealogical Society.
38. Guinn died on July 11, 1917. Six days after his death in 1917, the Fort Worth School Board named the new school for black children at Rosedale and Louisiana in his honor. Texas Historical Marker application for the James E. Guinn School, Tarrant County Archives. *Fort Worth Star-Telegram*, November 4, 1988. When Guinn attended Prairie View, it was not the university it is today or even a college in the classical sense. It was equivalent to a high school with a curriculum devoted to training teachers (the "Normal" part) and industrial workers.
39. Jan L. Jones, *Renegades, Showmen and Angels* (Fort Worth: Texas Christian University Press, 2006), 285, hereafter Jones, *Renegades. Cf.* the *Fort Worth City Directory* for 1896-97 shows two private kindergartens for white children operating at W. 4th and Lamar and 213 W. Daggett Ave.
40. *Fort Worth Morning Register*, September 1, 1901.
41. For Griggs, see *Dallas Weekly Herald*, July 28, 1881; *Dallas Morning News*, November 13, 1898; and *Fort Worth Star-Telegram*, February 13, 1922..
42. There is some uncertainty about the exact sites where the congregation first met and the dates when they relocated. The earliest sites had no street names. A brief history of Mount Gilead is given in *Fort Worth Star-Telegram*, August 2, 1912 on the occasion of the upcoming move into a new building at Fifth and Grove. See also ibid., October 25, 1914. For an overview of Fort Worth's black churches, see "African-American Historic Places, Fort Worth, Texas," City of Fort Worth Planning Department, n.d., TCBH&GS Collections.
43. *Fort Worth City Directory*, 1883-84. *Fort Worth Star-Telegram*, May 14, 1922.
44. *Fort Worth City Directory*, 1890 and 1892-93.
45. *Fort Worth Democrat*, November 16, 1881 (cited in Rich, *Fort Worth*, p. 216, fnt. 6).
46. Griffin was dubbed "Sin Killer" by William Greene Sterett, publisher of the *Dallas Times*, sometime in about 1888. *Houston Daily Post*, January 11, 1896. *Dallas Morning News*, July 21, 1889. The 5,000 were reported at a September 17, 1896 service. If accurate, that number represented roughly one in 5 Fort Worthers! *Dallas Morning News*, May 6, 1894; December 5, 1895; September 13-18, 1896. Smith, "A Poor Pilgrim of Sorrow," 7–8.

For Griffin's vocal prowess, see *Fort Worth Morning Register*, September 17, 1897.

47. *Dallas Morning News*, August 24, 1889; May 6, 1894; and September 16, 1896. For theatricality and passing the hat, see *Dallas Morning News*, November 12, 1898.
48. Samuel P. Jones (1847–1906), the Methodist evangelist, and John Franklyn Norris (1877–1952), the Baptist preacher, were two of the most famous pulpit ministers of their time. For self-promotion, see *Dallas Morning* News, December 5, 1895; March 1, 1896. For "niggerology," see ibid., May 4, 1894 and September 16, 1896. *Fort Worth Morning Register*, September 17, 1897.
49. *Dallas Morning News*, December 4, 1902; January 19, 1903. *Fort Worth Star-Telegram*, February 1 and 4, 1903.
50. *Dallas Morning News*, March 4, August 19 and 21, and September 18, 1896. *Fort Worth Star-Telegram*, February 1, 1903; and January 20, 1908.
51. Griffin actually claimed to have a Doctor of Divinity degree! *Houston Daily Post*, January 11, 1896. *Dallas Morning News*, August 23, 1903. *Fort Worth Star-Telegram*, June 18, 1911.
52. For *The Enterprise*, see *Dallas Morning News*, March 28, 1886. The *FWS Globe* is mentioned in the *Fort Worth Daily Gazette*, January 5, 1889. For *The Item*, see *Fort Worth City Directory*, 1894–95, and advertisement in *Fort Worth Colored History and Directory*, 1909, in TCBH&GS Collections, Fort Worth Public Library, Central Branch, Archives, Local History, and Genealogy Unit, Box 1, File 2.
53. Griffin, better known as "Sin Killer" preached the same "pull-yourself-up-by-your-bootstraps" message as Frederick Douglass and Gooseneck Bill McDonald. For example, see *Dallas Morning News*, August 21, 1896. The *Baptist Star* was the organ of the black Baptist Church in Texas. Ibid., October 19, 1892. For press convention, see *Dallas Morning News*, August 15, 1899.
54. *Dallas Morning News*, September 11, 1898.
55. Jeanette Keith, *Rich Man's War, Poor Man's Fight* (Chapel Hill: University of North Carolina Press, 2004), 181, hereafter, Keith, *Rich Man's War*.
56. For *Chicago Defender*, see Roger Streitmatter, *Voices of Revolution: The Dissident Press in America* (New York: Columbia University Press, 2001), 141–158.
57. Editorial in *Atlanta Constitution*, reprinted in *Fort Worth Weekly Gazette*, September 12, 1889.

58. Pervis was visibly taken down a few pegs after being caught in perjury and facing time in prison. *Dallas Times-Herald*, July 9, 1890. For Smith, see *Fort Worth Register*, June 28, 1901.
59. For whatever reason, Bill Love is a forgotten figure in the history of Fort Worth's black community although the saloon man was a successful entrepreneur for years. He owned and operated the Trinity Saloon and lived at Thirteenth and Calhoun. He was fatally shot by an employee at his place of business on August 14, 1887. *Dallas Morning News*, August 16, 1887. For Gipson, see Allen (Sherrod), *Grace and Gumption*, 193. For Mason, see *Dallas Times-Herald*, July 9, 1890; and Fraternal Bank & Trust in the *Fort Worth City Directory*, 1912-13. Hazel Harvey Peace is quoted in *Fort Worth Star-Telegram*, March 13, 2005.
60. For 1890, see *Fort Worth Daily Gazette*, September 28, 1890. For 1900 and 1910 numbers, see "Federal Writers' Project," Vol. 11, p. 4083. For percentages, see Russell B. Ward, "Panther City Progressives," unpublished Master's thesis (1995), History Dept., Texas A&M University, College Station, TX., p. 16. See also *Fort Worth Colored City Directory*, 1906-07, Lenora Rolla Papers, hereafter cited as *Colored City Directory*.
61. Johnson was the first black heavyweight boxing champion (1908), and defended his title (1910) before losing it to the "Great White Hope," Jess Willard. For Sullivan fight, see *Dallas Morning News*, February 7, 1890. Capps' story is sketchy, mostly what was recalled years later by old-timers, so the details must be taken with a grain of salt. See Roberts, "Memories, p. 28. Letter from George Riddle to Edgar McCorkle, May 6, 1880 (handwritten), in collections of Dalton Hoffman of Fort Worth.
62. For use of city hall, see *Fort Worth Morning Register*, January 8, 1897.
63. For Germania Hall and other spaces, see Jones, *Renegades*, p. 285.
64. Sarah Gordon, *Passage to Union: How the Railroads Transformed American Life, 1829–1929* (Chicago: Ivan R. Dee, 1997), 181, hereafter Gordon, *Passage*.
65. The seven organizers were William M. McDonald, B.P. Johnson, J.D. Johnson, the Rev. T.W. Wilburn, S.W. Woodward, John W. Milledge, and Z.C. Brooks. W.O. Bundy, *Life of William Madison McDonald* (Fort Worth: Bunker Printing, 1925), 83. For State Fair, see Nancy Wiley, "State Fair of Texas, *New Handbook of Texas*; Gordon, *Passage*, 181.
66. The Fort Worth Fair was still being debated in the newspapers two years later. *Fort Worth Gazette*, February 18, 1889. See also *Dallas Herald*, October 29, 1887; and *Dallas Morning News*, September 22, 1887; February 5, October 1, and 3, 1888; October 11, 1892; and October 30, 1893. Reby

Cary, *How We Got Over! Second Update on a Backward Look: A History of Blacks in Fort Worth*, 2nd ed. (Fort Worth: privately printed, 2006), 3, hereafter Cary, *How We Got Over!*, 2nd ed.

67. *Fort Worth Gazette*, February 18, 1889; *Dallas Herald*, October 29, 1887; *Dallas Morning News*, February 5, October 1 and 3, 1888; October 11, 1892; and October 30, 1893. Charles Jackson, "Remembering 'Gooseneck Bill,'" *Fort Worth Star-Telegram*, February 12, 1984. Currently, Fort Worth author Jan L. Jones is writing the first full-length, scholarly biography of McDonald.
68. Robert D. Putnam, *Bowling Alone: The Collapse and Revival of American Community* (New York: Simon & Schuster, 2001). Peter Ling, "The Media Made Malcolm," *History Today* 62, no. 1 (January 2002): 50–51.
69. *Fort Worth Register*, January 8, 1897. The major Fort Worth newspapers of this era were still sprinkling terms like "darkey" and "nigger" in amongst more polite words. For example, see page 1 of the *Fort Worth Telegram*, October 2, 1907.
70. *Fort Worth Register*, January 8 and 9, 1897.
71. *Fort Worth Register*, January 9, 1897.
72. The CPC office in its second home was on the "Triangle block" between Ninth and Tenth near the location of the Carnegie Library, City Hall, and the Central Fire Station. A few years later it moved for the last time to 705 Grove. The leaders of the CPC in 1915 were J.P. Foster, Gabe Connors, Allen Ayres, Logan Smith D.H. Black, Louis Saunders, Vince Hardwick, and Louise Mosses. *Fort Worth Morning Register*, June 27, 1897; and July 7, 1901. *Fort Worth Star-Telegram*, March 15, 1915.
73. Example of the Congress Barber Shop specifically refers to Tommie Lee, who killed Police Officer John Ogletree and two others in a murderous rampage through the lower end of the city in 1913. When he was not gambling in the Acre, Lee worked at the Congress Barber Shop, hobnobbing with the white power-brokers of the Courthouse. For Lee's story, see Richard Selcer and Kevin Foster, *Written in Blood, Vol. 2* (Denton: UNT Press, 2011), 40–41, hereafter Selcer and Foster, *Written in Blood 2.*
74. An unforeseen result is that we lack a visual history of Fort Worth's black community from those early days. Scattered images of black Fort Worth residents exist, but the subjects are virtually never identified, nor is so much as a date provided. We are lucky if we can connect the photograph to Fort Worth.
75. Knight, *Fort Worth*, 140. For smallpox, see Joyce M. Williams, "Women in Fort Worth History," unpublished MS of talk presented June 5, 1999 at

the "Fort Worth 150" Symposium at Texas Christian University, vertical files, Fort Worth Public Library, Central Branch, Local History, Genealogy, & Archives Unit. For the official response to contemporary outbreaks of disease in racially divided Southern communities, see Keith, *Fever Season*, 51–53, 79–84, and 96–97.

76. *Dallas Morning News*, May 4, 1889.
77. June 19, 1865, was the date Union General Gordon Granger proclaimed the good news of emancipation in Texas. The term "Juneteenth" does not begin appearing in black newspapers until the 1920s. Prior to that, the term used by both whites and blacks was "Emancipation Day." See, for instance, *Dallas Morning News*, June 20, 1900; June 21, 1904; June 19, 1907, June 19, 1915, and January 17, 1918; and *Fort Worth Star-Telegram*, July 4, 1912. Bill Fairley, "Tarrant Chronicles," *Fort Worth Star-Telegram*, June 19, 2002. Through most of the twentieth century, its observance in Fort Worth was largely confined to Greenway, the city's official "Negro park." For the history of the holiday, see Teresa Paloma Acosta, "Juneteenth," *New Handbook of Texas*. Texas blacks also celebrated July 4th, only without the same reverence as Juneteenth. See for instance Harrison County blacks' planned celebration in 1919, datelined "Marshall, Texas." *Dallas Morning News*, June 24, 1919, p. 19. City Park was renamed Trinity Park in 1910. Susan Allen Kline, *Fort Worth Parks* (Charleston, SC: Arcadia Publishing, 2010), 10, 13. For the experience of other Southern cities creating black public parks and observing July 4th, see Keith, *Fever Season*, 202. For Douglas Park, see *Dallas Morning News*, January 17, 1918.
78. In the newspapers it was often misspelled "Douglas Park" by editors who had no idea who it had been named for. The last time Douglass Park appears in the public record is the 1924 *Fort Worth City Directory*, on microfiche, Fort Worth Public Library, Central Branch, Local History, Genealogy & Archives Unit. For the full history of Douglass Park, see Richard Selcer, "Historic Marker Application for Douglass and McGar Parks," vertical files, Fort Worth Public Library, ibid. For festivities, see *Dallas Morning News*, August 24, 1907; and July 12, 1912.
79. The North Side park was named Quality Grove Park after the nearby black residential neighborhood. "Federal Writers' Project" (microfiche), pp. 21388-89 and 30547. Note: By practice, blacks were not even allowed to buy land in Arlington. "From the Pasture to the Hill: A Community Heritage Celebration," Exhibition at Fielder House Museum, Arlington, June 27–Sept. 15, 1999.

80. *Dallas Morning News*, June 19, 1915.
81. *Fort Worth Democrat*, January 8 and 9, 1880; March 17, 18, 19, and 20, 1881. Also cited in Rich, *Fort Worth*, 10–11.
82. Sources: Max Hill, "Biography: Hiram McGar, Jr.," *Fort Worth Genealogical Society's Footprints* 47, no. 3 (August 2004). Selcer and Foster, *Written in Blood 2*, 58, 62. *Fort Worth City Directory*, 1901, 1905, 1907, 1912-13, 1914, 1916, 1919, on microfiche, Fort Worth Library, Central Branch, Local History, Genealogy, & Archives Unit. *Fort Worth Telegram* and *Star-Telegram*, February 21, 1907; April 25 and November 21, 1909; May 26, 1915; April 23, 1916. *Dallas Morning News*, August 27 and Dec. 13, 1902; June 30, 1904; August 2, 1907; May 13, 1908; and July 25, 1912. *Fort Worth Press*, April 30, 1947. Thirteenth United States Census (1910), Fort Worth, Ward 3, Tarrant County, Texas Microfilm Roll T624_1590. John Henry, "Texas Negro League Baseball, precursor for Dodgers' 1948 visit to Fort Worth," *Fort Worth Star-Telegram*, February 26, 2012. Mark Presswood, "Black Professional Baseball in Texas," online at www.texasalmanac.com/topics/history/black-professional-baseball-texas. www.negroleaguebaseball.com. For a map showing the location of Panther and McGar parks, ca. 1920, see Mark Presswood and Chris Holaday, *Baseball in Fort Worth* (Charleston, South Carolina: Arcadia Publishers, 2004), 105. The league cities in the Colored Baseball League, besides the Fort Worth, were Oklahoma City, Dallas, Waco, Mineral Wells, and Houston. *The Freeman* (newspaper), Indianapolis, IN, April 19, 1913.

Chapter 4

The World of Jim Crow

"Jim Crow" is arguably the most despised name in African American history, more than Jefferson Davis, or even "Uncle Tom." Derived from the name of a nineteenth-century, black-face minstrel performer, Jim Crow became shorthand for the entire system of racial segregation erected in the late nineteenth century—a vague, *ad hoc* collection of laws and conventions, ever-changing with the times. It was just as evil but more insidious than slavery because it paid lip service to equality when in reality it was just slavery by another name. Jim Crow's purpose was never to encourage equality, only the appearance of equality. Its real purpose was to keep the black minority separate *and* subservient.

Jim Crow denied blacks the basic benefits of American society: police and fire protection, representation in city government, even their own militia companies. From 1874 until 1952 Fort Worth had no black policemen on the regular force. Neither the volunteer fire companies nor the municipal fire department created in 1893 had black firemen. The first African American would not sit on the city council or school board until the 1960s, and in the late nineteenth century, Fort Worth had two local militia companies, both lily-white. Even finding a final resting place was challenging. There was no public burial ground for blacks in Tarrant County before 1889. Over the next few years privately donated properties, one adjacent to Oakwood Cemetery ("Old Trinity") and another in Haltom City ("New Trinity") became available. Only in 1911 did the city council take up the question of creating a black *public* cemetery, but the white outcry against locating it near any white neighborhood was so severe, the idea was tabled. In the meantime, death, like life, continued to be racially segregated. Old Trinity Cemetery had its own sexton, grave-diggers, and undertaker, and a fence separated it from Oakwood Cemetery.[1]

The adoption of Jim Crow practices accelerated toward the end of the nineteenth century. By that time the federal government and the Republican Party, the self-styled "party of Lincoln," had lost interest in the plight of the former slaves, and the growing numbers of blacks in the city's population coupled with their growing assertiveness began to challenge white supremacy for the first time.

By 1900 Fort Worth's population was 26,076, meaning it was still a neighborly small town scarcely noticed outside of Texas. In the next decade, however, the population exploded, nearly doubling to 50,000 in six years, then rising to 73,312 in the next four years after that—an increase of 175 percent over the 1900 population. The next two decades after 1910 saw impressive population growth of 45 percent and 53 pecent, respectively. In 1920 the city's population was approximately 106,500; by 1930 it was 163,447. That sort of growth was cause for celebration at the Chamber of Commerce, but all those newcomers shook up the comfortable, small-town atmosphere of Fort Worth.[2]

Photo 7. Old Trinity Cemetery

This cemetery was Fort Worth's historic black burial ground, adjacent to Oakwood Cemetery (for whites) but a wooden fence separated the two. The gateway into Trinity originally was on Grand Ave. Today the gateway is inside Oakwood. In the middle background is the tall obelisk that marks William "Gooseneck Bill" McDonald's grave. Most of the headstones in the section are gone, and many more graves are simply unmarked. Author's collections.

The population explosion included African Americans although their population did not grow as fast as the white population. In 1900, the black population was 4,146 (15.9 percent of the total population); in 1910 it was 13,269 (18.1 percent of the total population). By 1920 the black population had grown to 15,896 (14.9 percent), and by 1926, one black out-of-town visitor reported the "Negro population" to be 18,000. In 1930 the Census put it at 22,234 (13.6 percent). Clearly, while the population of the city as a whole was increasing, the percentage of the population that was black was trending downward. For its part, the Fort Worth Chamber of Commerce was either in denial or as the city's principal booster was only interested in selling the city as virtually an all-white community. In a slick publication put out in 1920, the Chamber claimed the population was "only 7.6% of Negroes," which it proudly compared to the 24.1 percent that was Dallas and 28.2 percent that was Houston. The following year the Chamber lowered the percentage to "less than 6%" in a shameless appeal to new business to locate in their fair city.[3]

Population numbers alone don't tell the full story. In sheer numbers alone, there were a lot more blacks on the streets than in the old days, and this by itself was alarming to many whites, percentages be damned. Absolute numbers aside, African Americans were still an insignificant segment of social and political life in Fort Worth, but because there were more African Americans on the streets, it is not surprising that open clashes between the races became more frequent and more violent as the twentieth century advanced.

All population statistics must be treated with care, not just because agencies like the Chamber of Commerce manipulated the numbers for their own reasons, but because many blacks could slip between the cracks. They were not counted during census enumerations because so many did not have fixed addresses and because they lived in areas that white census takers did not want to go, and in-between the decennial census counts it is impossible to know how many blacks lived in Fort Worth at any given time. The best we can do is comb through city directories from the nineteenth century when a "(c)" beside a name meant "colored," and we can glean additional information from the tax rolls, but even then we must extrapolate greatly. For odd years, we must grab onto whatever numbers we can find. For instance, a Dallas newspaper tells us that Dallas' black population in 1916 was 18,000 out of a total population of 100,000, and we know that Fort Worth's population was much smaller than Dallas'. The black population of the entire state of Texas in 1916 was only one million. What numbers like that help us understand is how easy it would be to dismiss a minority numbering fewer than 18,000 people.[4]

A snapshot of the city's black listings in the mid-1920s shows twenty-two churches, nine schools, sixteen doctors, one dentist, one lawyer, three newspapers, six drugstores, one bank, and one hospital. But something more significant was happening in the black community during these years that is not covered by the numbers. No longer were there just two Fort Worths, one black and one white; increasingly there were three—white, poor black, and middle-class black. The last-named was composed of educated and professional blacks represented by such luminaries as businessman William McDonald, author Lillian Horace, and educator Isaiah M. Terrell. Collectively they had achieved a level of sophistication and accomplishment that, skin color aside, gave them more in common with whites than poor blacks. The largest part of the black community, however, still consisted of those who worked as laborers and domestics or did not hold down any job at all.[5]

Belonging to the working-class did not make black people either anonymous or contemptible. On the contrary, the most humble could be respected, even beloved by whites. When Anderson Upshaw, Sr. died in 1901, he was described by the *Fort Worth Register* as "respected by both white and black" and a "tax payer." The former was high praise indeed for a man who had driven a dray for most of his working life, and being a tax payer certified him as a solid citizen. Upshaw's funeral was well-attended by members of both races. No one remembers him today because he was not an entrepreneur, entertainer or athlete, just a solid citizen.[6]

It was black professionals who held out hope for the future of their race. Before the turn of the century it was the rare black man who entered the professions. Black men who went into the ministry considered it a "calling," not necessarily something that required attending a seminary. Black doctors often got their training by apprenticing themselves to a practicing white doctor, or they had learned the basics of medicine as hospital stewards in the army. Black lawyers were practically unknown in the South. Fort Worth got its first black lawyer, A.J. McCauley, in 1905. His first professional call was on County Attorney Jefferson Davis McLean to whom he presented letters of reference "from many of the leading white citizens of the State." McLean reportedly accorded him proper professional respect. A second black lawyer, Charles Macbeth, opened a practice soon thereafter. There is no record of either man ever arguing a case in criminal court. Black educators like Isaiah M. Terrell and James E. Guinn likewise were exceptions. Having two men of such stature in the same town was practically unheard of. Almost by default, ministers and educators were the spokesmen of the rising black middle class.[7]

Achieving middle-class status was not the same as achieving the American Dream. As one scholar, Nell Painter, has pointed out, the hierarchy of Jim Crow racism involved a "clear ranking of classes, in which the word "white," absent a modifier, denoted a member of the upper class, while terms for African Americans like "negro" and "colored," unless otherwise modified, signified an impoverished worker. Painter says that any deviation from the standard classification of the time required further explanation, such as "poor white" or "middle-class negro."[8]

LIVING AND WORKING NEIGHBORHOODS

Race was more important than any other factor in determining where a person lived, trumping both wealth and social status. Not even being a member of the black middle class, whom Fort Worth author-publisher James Hamilton called "colored men of means," entitled an African American to live anywhere he wanted. Mixing the races was a taboo that kept blacks and whites in their own segregated neighborhoods. This was more than social convention; it was the law, and real estate agents made the most of it. In 1907 the West Fort Worth Land Company, promoting its new housing development west of town, the Factory Place Addition, ran this "Announcement!" in the newspaper:

> WE DO NOT SELL TO NEGROES, AND IT IS MADE A PART OF THE CONSIDERATION IN THE DEEDS GIVEN YOUR PURCHASERS, THAT THEY, TOO, MUST REFRAIN FROM SELLING, RENTING, OR LEASING TO A NEGRO.[9]

This was a reassurance to whites and a warning to blacks that no one could misunderstand. At this time Arlington Heights was still largely empty prairie, although because of Arlington Heights Country Club and Lake Como amusement park, it would soon be connected to downtown by a street car line. Developers who saw Arlington Heights as the city's next fashionable suburb believed property values would plummet if blacks were allowed to move in. To prevent that, they promised deed restrictions would remain in place even with next-generation sales, and as far as the record shows, those restrictions were not challenged in court. Arlington Heights remained exclusively white into the 1920s when Como became an African-American bridgehead on the west side.[10]

Real estate restrictions were part of the fabric of the city. A few years later when John and Henry King formed the Oakhurst Land Company and began developing the area between Riverside and the Trinity, they promoted it as a "sensibly restricted suburban residential district." Translation: It was closed to blacks.[11]

Part of Jim Crow thinking was the white delusion that blacks preferred to live with "their own kind" even if that meant living in tenement slums. In 1916 when a court case in St. Louis, Missouri, challenged race-based zoning restrictions, the *Fort Worth Star-Telegram* editorialized, "The Southern city is fortunate where self-respecting negroes are content to live among themselves and where the relations between the races are balanced by custom, without the need of legislation that is bound to be contested." The newspaper blamed "unscrupulous [white] real estate dealers" for "moving negro families into white neighborhoods." When the issue exploded in violence in Fort Worth two decades later, the finger of blame would again be pointed at white real estate agents. (see chap. 8)[12]

At the turn of the century, however, all was quiet in Fort Worth's residential neighborhoods. Most black Fort Worthers still resided on the east side of downtown, unless they lived in the Trinity River bottoms. The main eastside thoroughfares, Calhoun and Jones, had largely been turned over to African Americans. Neither street was paved or had utility connections, and there were no street signs at the cross-streets. Entire blocks of what were euphemistically called "negro tenements" stretched the length of both streets. The residential stretches mingled with small businesses and industrial properties to create an area treated by the city's white residents as a *zona rosa.* In 1902 the city council even took up a proposal to designate Calhoun a "reservation" where prostitution could be openly practiced, and place it "outside city jurisdiction." The term "segregated district" took on ironic meaning, defined by both race and wide-open vice. The proposal had become a "plan" by the time commission government arrived in 1907. Two years later the plan to turn Calhoun into a "reservation" was finally abandoned for good upon the vehement objections of property owners.[13]

That did not halt the steady decline of both streets. They were the last major downtown streets to be paved—with red bricks that were still in place in 1959 although not maintained. This was also the last area of downtown to be included in the city "fire limits," which meant that in the event of a fire the residents could not count on the Fort Worth Fire Department showing up. Long after the rest of downtown had been converted to brick and stone, Calhoun and Jones were still dotted with flimsy wooden structures, owned by absentee landlords, which "rented for a song." As the years passed, the area was converted to industrial use and trackage to serve the railroads. In 1920, B. B. Paddock said that "for thirty years property owners had been trying to make something out of Calhoun St., but had failed."[14]

Map 1. Map of Rock Island Bottom.

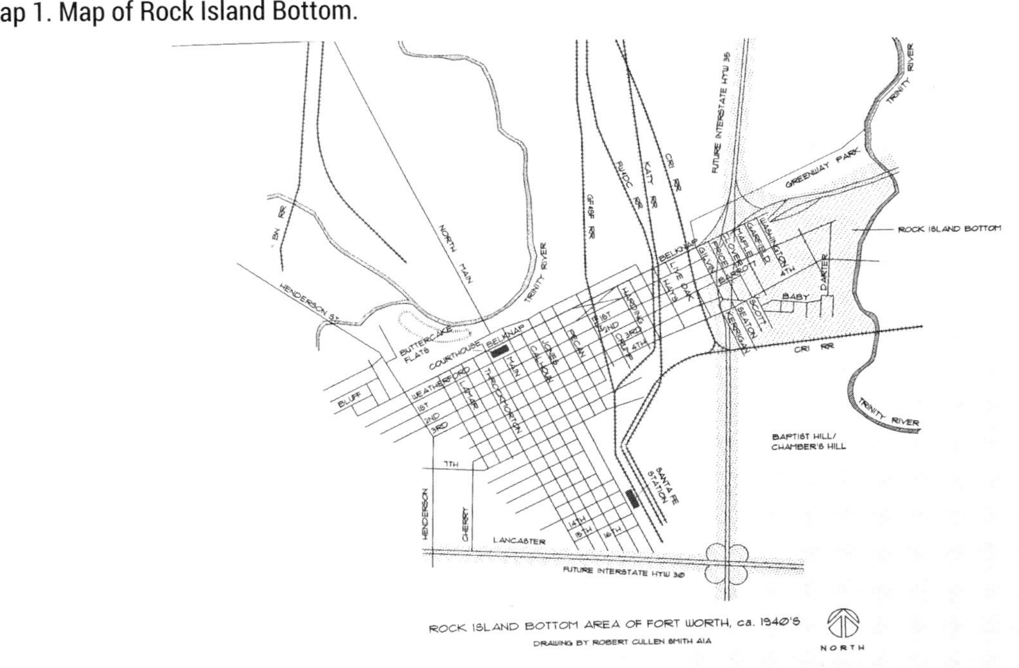

Courtesy of Robert Smith, Fort Worth architect.

River bottom communities started in the bend of the river just west of the courthouse and dotted the bottoms all the way around to the Riverside section. The largest of these were Battercake Flats on the west and Rock Island Bottom on the east, both of which dated from around the turn of the century. Battercake Flats lay north and west of the courthouse, running from Franklin Hill down to the confluence of the West and Clear forks. Its principal axis was Franklin St. which was really more of a track than an actual street. On the east side of the city was Rock Island Bottom, so named because it lay between the Chicago & Rock Island tracks on two sides and the Trinity River on the third. It was separated from the rest of the city to the south by Baptist Hill (aka, Chambers Hill). In between Battercake Flats and Rock Island Bottom were smaller collections of shacks that did not even rise to the status of being called "neighborhoods."

Those who lived in the bottom lands did not have to worry much about the authorities (tax collectors, health inspectors, police); all they had to worry about were the periodic floods that swept through. Whenever the Trinity overflowed its banks as it did in dramatic fashion in 1908, 1915, and 1922, residents of the bottom lands paid dearly for their choice of neighborhood. They were lucky if they lost only their "cabins" and "household effects" to the raging waters. Adding to their misery was the fact that they could not afford insurance to rebuild their lives. When flooding wiped out much of North Fort Worth in April 1908, the "lowland dwellers" of Stick Town just east of Samuels Ave. literally lost everything. White Fort Worthers were not unsympathetic. Private citizens and churches donated food and clothing while the city of North Fort Worth set up "commissaries" to feed the large numbers of homeless. Whites were so generous, in fact, that the pastor of the North Fort Worth Colored Church issued a "formal" thank-you from the pulpit for all that they had done. Swift and Armour also stepped up, promising work for "idle negroes." (The companies' motives were not entirely altruistic. Hiring black workers was a proven union-busting tactic.)[15]

But charity was not a long-term solution. Eight floods had already occurred before 1908, and in 1915 another historic deluge washed away residents and their homes. When engineers cut the levee near North Ninth (north side of the Trinity) to lower the flood waters, it was Battercake Flats that got hit the hardest. Compassionate white citizens sprang into action, providing generous emergency relief, but the cycle would repeat itself endlessly until those living in the shadow of the levees could be relocated to higher ground, which was unlikely to happen as long as no respectable neighborhood was willing to accept them. They were perpetual outcasts waiting for the next disaster to uproot their lives. Residents of the older neighborhood known as Little Africa, being out of the flood plain, were better off but only slightly.[16]

On the other end of the social and economic spectrum were the kind of black people W.E.B. DuBois called the "talented tenth." They were well represented in Fort Worth by the turn of the century in the form of a small but vibrant middle class. Fort Worth's James A. Hamilton characterized them as "progressive men and women" and observed that they were "engaged in every class of business from dish-washer to bank depositor." Their ranks included barbers, drugstore owners, physicians, teachers, saloon men, tailors, dry-goods dealers, pharmacists, grocery men, undertakers, and insurance salesmen. The elite were even in a position to send their sons off to college. Dr. William Davis sent his son to Wiley College, I.M. Terrell sent his to the University of Chicago. When the young men eventually returned home with degrees, they would be able to substantially contribute to the community. In the meantime, the black community was taking long strides in being able to stand on its own. As James Hamilton observed, "Anything a colored man wants can be found from members of his own race"—which happened to be the ideal of Jim Crow also—"separate but equal."[17]

Anything except a place to live. As some blacks began climbing the ladder of success they looked around for better housing. They longed to live where they had yards and municipal services instead of a patch of dirt, an outhouse, and a pump. It opened a wedge in the myth of racial solidarity when hard-working, respectable family men no longer wanted to live next door to the unemployed and those just one step away from jail. Nor was it progress to live in some white family's servants' quarters. On Sunday mornings they listened to preachers like the Rev. L.K. Williams of Mount Gilead Baptist Church preach on the benefits of "independence, self-respect, and self-help." "No man amounts to anything," declared Williams, "who depends upon other races to do his work." Blacks would have to pull themselves up by their own bootstraps. The message hit home. The *Register*, Fort Worth's most racially bigoted newspaper, conceded that the tenements were not "filled by bad negroes [only] by any means." Many residents, the newspaper admitted, were "colored men employed in good positions in the city." But as long as they lived in the tenements they would be tarred with the same brush just as if they had been part of the criminal class in Little Africa.[18]

It would take more than a philosophy of self-help, however, to break the cycle of poverty. Better housing was an important step. Black neighborhoods like the east side of downtown suffered from the ills of industrialization, neglect, and lack of zoning laws. This is why they had shotgun shacks right next to nice homes, and industrial properties mixed in with residential blocks. On top of everything else, no developer was willing to build the kind of residential "additions" for blacks that marked the growth of white suburbs. Neither the market nor the financing existed to attract investors. There was one more reason why there were no black housing developments: Even if a developer had been willing to build houses for blacks, the privately owned utility franchises (gas, electricity, water) would not have extended services to the area.[19]

Despite all the obstacles, some did manage to escape Little Africa and Battercake Flats, finding white home-owners in other neighborhoods willing to sell. Just before World War I, the first black families began moving into a previously all-white neighborhood on Crump St. on the Near South Side. Crump was just eight blocks east of Main but a million miles removed from most other white suburbs. It was a blue-collar neighborhood with less expensive houses. John Edward Martin, a white lawyer who had lived on Crump for more than a decade and who also owned two rent houses on the street, decided to move a few blocks south to Missouri Ave. As a descendant explained it years later, "The coloreds had begun to move closer. So he rented his three houses and moved." This is how Crump St. came to be Fort Worth's first transitional residential street. Martin was a pragmatist who had fought on the Confederate side in the Civil War, but when he came home he took off his uniform and never looked back, taking a job as a clerk with the Freedmen's Bureau. That made him a "scalawag" in the eyes of many of his peers.[20]

The leafy streets and nearness to town of the Near South Side continued to attract blacks looking for a better life in the years that followed, making it Fort Worth's first middle-class black neighborhood. The area stretched roughly from East Lancaster south to Rosedale and from South Main east to South Riverside Dr. In the early years, South Riverside Dr. and nearby streets such as E. Cannon, E. Leuda, E. Rosedale and E. Maddox were overwhelmingly white before transitioning into black neighborhoods. Eventually, the entire Near South Side became the black version of the city's white, silk-stocking neighborhoods, centered on E. Terrell and E. Humboldt and occupied by successful men such as Bill McDonald, Dr. George Flemmings, Dr. R.A. Ransom, banker William Coleman, and the Reverend A.W. Pryor. To have an appropriately upscale name, the area was dubbed "Terrell Heights," the first black neighborhood to have electricity, sewer lines, and sidewalks."[21]

The influx of black home-owners on the Near South Side provoked a furious reaction among white residents. The first black residents—denounced as "invaders"—brought only a sullen response that included warnings to go back where they came from and offers to buy them out "at a fair price." Some black newcomers took the money and ran, but more chose to remain, and they were soon joined by others.[22]

In 1925 sullenness turned into open violence. Black homes were dynamited, starting with 942 Maddox Ave. on the night of January 14–15. The blast demolished part of the house and hurled the resident out of her bed. Then on the night of March12–13, two blasts wrecked the houses at 937 and 941 E. Maddox Ave. but again no one was injured. For the next seven months quiet reigned on the Near South Side. In July, the Police Department announced that it would protect black residents of the area from "dynamiters and night riders," the latter reference being the first clue that the bombings might be connected to the Klan. All was quiet in the Seventh Ward until October when the bomber(s) struck twice in rapid succession on E. Leuda, the first time on the night of October 9–10 at A.L. Hunter's house, and then ten nights later at the house of C. Daniels. The residents were lucky in both instances because no one was injured, and the damage was relatively light. Police responded each time but turned up no clues and no suspects. The cases remained unsolved; the perpetrators got away with it. But instead of scaring off black home-owners, the bombings just accelerated the white exodus from the segregated neighborhood, putting more houses on the market at bargain prices.[23]

Life returned to normal for a few months. Then on the night of March 23, 1926, a black home at 1129 E. Cannon was dynamited. This time instead of being planted, the explosives were hurled from a passing car. As in the earlier cases, the damage was light and no one was injured, but it was only a matter of time before someone was seriously injured or worse. While the FWPD remained strangely silent, City Manager O.E. Carr threatened to take unspecified "drastic measures." The city put up a $300 reward for evidence leading to the apprehension of the bomber(s). Things quieted down for a few months again then the bomber(s) or like-minded friends struck again on the night of July 10, 1926, in the 1100 block of E. Cannon, one block north of E. Leuda. This time instead of leaving a bomb they posted typewritten warnings on the front door of every black home-owner on the block, warning them to move immediately or face more bombings. That was enough for the police to finally react pro-actively.

Chief Henry Lee assigned bicycle officers to patrol the neighborhood at night and issued orders to arrest anyone on the street who could not "give a good account of himself." But like earlier police follow-ups, this one produced no suspects and no clues. After the summer of 1926, the bomber(s) seem to have either lost interest or run out of dynamite. Terrell Heights remained quiet in the 1930s as whites continued to pack up and leave in a movement later known as "white flight."[24]

The rest of Fort Worth, or at least those who did not read *The Press* or the *Dallas Morning News*, may not have even been aware of what was happening on the Near South Side. The *Star-Telegram* did not cover the bombings. The *Dallas Morning News* did, but not simply for their newsworthiness. The editors sniffed that "terrorism has no place in Dallas" and expressed sympathy for the black home-owners under attack. The next wave of racial violence would hit Fort Worth in the 1940s, a few miles north of the Near South Side in the Riverside neighborhood.[25] (See Chap. 8)

The history of the Near South Side is a classic tale of a neighborhood in transition, having begun life as a white neighborhood. Not so the Booker T. Washington (BTW) Addition in North Fort Worth. It was the first purpose-built housing addition for "colored people" when it opened in 1907. It was an outgrowth of Swift and Armour packing plants, which brought in thousands of workers who had to have some place to live. The BTW Addition was located just east of the Cotton Belt and Frisco rail lines only a short walk from the packing houses. The advertising described it as "a beautiful tract of land" easily accessible by the street car line on North Main. It was also only a block or two from the river bottoms, which made it vulnerable to flooding, wild animals, and hoboes riding the rails. Still, it represented a big improvement over life in "Little Africa." W. N. McCaslin was the money man behind the development. He was white and a manager at Swift until he quit to enter the real estate business. In his new career the *Fort Worth Telegram* described him as one of the leading lights of North Fort Worth and a "hustler" in the positive meaning of that term. He had no partners in the BTW Addition; he was the "exclusive agent" (his words) of the city's first development "for negroes only." He was doing something no real estate developer, white or black, had ever attempted locally. The unserved market he hoped to serve were the relatively well-paid black employees of the two packing plants. He offered a hundred lots for $125 each at exceedingly generous terms—$10 down and $5 per month. A few days before he put them up for sale he predicted he would sell out in a matter of days—and he did.[26]

It was understood that the buyers would have to build their own house on the lot, which posed another challenge; building would mean taking out a loan, which if it came from a bank, would require having collateral and showing evidence of stable employment. A black Mason might have gone to his brother Masons for such a loan. For those who had no fraternal brothers, it was more problematical. One way or another, the financial commitment was substantial. Even a modest, framed house on the North Side at this date would have cost $1,600 to build—historically, more than most black men made in a lifetime. The appearance of contractors and lending institutions willing to invest in the black community marked a watershed in Fort Worth history.[27]

The BTW Addition cracked the door open. In the years that followed middle-class blacks created neighborhoods that they could call their own with a sense of pride. To whites they were "negro districts"; to blacks they were Quality Grove (on the far north side), Chambers Hill (east of town), and eventually Como (on the west side). Black neighborhood pride was a hedge against blacks trying to move into white neighborhoods.

Quality Grove's story is instructive. It began as just another white residential "addition" by Sam Rosen like Washington Heights or Rosen Heights. It was at the far end of North Main, connected to downtown by the Rosen Heights street car line. Rosen sub-divided the tract into 800 lots and opened a sales office, but then the majority of those who wanted to purchase lots were African-Americans. The influx of black property-owners scared away whites, ensuring a segregated neighborhood, and the police treated it that way, beginning with the North Fort Worth police and later the Fort Worth police. But the new residents were proud of their little community. In 1909 they raised $4,000 to build Shiloh Baptist Church, one of the surest signs of a family-oriented community. It was no slum like Battercake Flats or Little Africa; snug little houses with front porches were the norm. In 1919 there were still 160 "large lots" available, priced from $200 to $300 for "colored buyers." The terms were $1 down and $1 per week with no interest or taxes for two years. At those terms, those 160 lots were soon gone. By comparison, Rosen's plan for the white Rosen Heights Addition was to build houses on the lots and sell both as a package for $750 to $5,000. This also ensured a minimal standard for houses in the Addition, something he was not too concerned with in Quality Grove. Fort Worth Power & Light treated the area with the same disdain as the police, not extending service to Quality Grove until 1921. Sam Rosen was enlightened for his time. The one-time penniless Russian immigrant not only cheerfully sold to blacks, but he offered affordable terms and had a reputation for never foreclosing on a mortgage, no matter the color of the mortgage-holder.[28]

Following World War I a nice black residential area grew on the west side of Lake Como, a man-made lake created as part of a failed amusement park by the Arlington Heights Street Railway Company. In its formative years the neighborhood was populated mainly by the servants of wealthy white families who lived in Arlington Heights and River Crest. In 1922 Fort Worth annexed Como at the same time as the "Arlington Heights addition." By 1930 some 180 black families lived there, many of the breadwinners in those families still working as domestics for well-to-do white home-owners. As it did with Stop Six, Fort Worth grew out to Como. Black home-owners were safely above the Trinity River but lived with a similar flood threat. Lake Como had been created by damming a tributary of the Trinity. The earthen dam that held the lake threatened to collapse every time sustained rains fell.[29]

The residents of Como, Quality Grove, Chambers Hill, and Terrell Heights represented a new chapter in the history of black Fort Worth. The lives that blacks created for themselves in these neighborhoods were closer to the traditional American Dream than ever before. Becoming a home-owner has always been a central tenet of that Dream, and now a growing number of black men were in a position to grab hold of it.

By the end of the '20s, there were four black residential pockets: 1) due east of town on Grove, Harding, Elm, and Crump; 2) south of town between E. Leuda and E. Rosedale; 3) in far north Fort Worth; and 4) around Lake Como. Each of these insular neighborhoods had its own schools, churches, and identities.

Meanwhile, a thriving black business district had grown up along East Ninth to serve black residents. Starting at Main, all sorts of black-owned businesses stretched eastward for three or four blocks. The businesses included saloons, drug stores, barber shops, dry goods stores, and the offices of professionals (doctors, lawyers, insurance agents, etc.). The most impressive building on the street was the Fraternal Bank and Trust, which opened in 1912. The next year the *Star-Telegram* dubbed East Ninth a "negro colony," indicating both the density of businesses up and down the street as well as its insularity from the rest of downtown. Such a concentration of black businesses could also attract unwanted attention. The anti-black rioting of May 1913 targeted the Ninth St. businesses, resulting in considerable destruction. Unfortunately, most of the business owners did not have insurance, so rebuilding was a long and painful process.[30]

Education, the Ticket Out

One of the great paradoxes of Jim Crow was that segregated schools were simultaneously a bastion of racism and the ticket out of poverty and dependence. With their inferior facilities, under-funding, and poorly trained teachers, black schools turned out graduates who were not prepared to compete on equal terms with graduates of white schools, thus perpetuating the second-class status of African-Americans while maintaining the charade of equal education.

In 1901 a "mass meeting" of African Americans took place in Fort Worth to discuss issues of "education and race." The meeting did not produce any change in the existing system, but it produced a resolution asking for "better schoolhouses and longer [school] terms," and not white teachers but "the best teachers our race affords."[31]

The meeting focused on "industrial" schools because that was considered the most promising form of black education by both races. Black leaders talked not about book-learning but about equipping their people to earn a decent living and have a comfortable life, which would come from learning a trade. Conventional white wisdom was that "the Negro" was trainable but not educable, their solid record at Howard University and other black institutions of higher learning notwithstanding. Prairie View Normal *and Industrial* School was a monument to that sort of narrow thinking because its curriculum was vocational, and its faculty and administrators were white. The principal aim of "negro education" was not creating first-rate minds but training for menial, blue-color jobs. Fewer than one in six African Americans at this date saw the inside of a high school. The standard curriculum in white high schools included Latin, geology, geography, trigonometry, physics, chemistry, and biology, all of which were considered beyond their capabilities. The education of the overwhelming majority of black children stopped with the 3 Rs if it even went that far, which not only contributed to keeping them in perpetual dependency but also saved the money it would have taken to build and staff a black high school. Fort Worth did not build a colored high school until 1907. Even by Jim Crow standards, the city was overdue. Dallas already had a black high school. Even Cleburne had Booker T. Washington (Colored) High School (opened in 1904). And Fort Worth's Colored High School was built to serve not just Fort Worth but all of Tarrant County. It is not clear whether building just one high school for the entire county was an acknowledgment of the miniscule number of pupils it would serve or a reflection of the half-hearted commitment of the school board to educating black children beyond the primary grades.[32]

In the early twentieth century, Tarrant County was a hodge-podge of school districts large and small that included in addition to Fort Worth, the unincorporated communities of North Fort Worth, Marine, Polytechnic, Prairie Chapel, Washington Heights, and Riverside. Each of these areas had its own black residents and its own school board, taking the American ideal of local control of schools down to the neighborhood level. All of these school systems were eventually absorbed into Fort Worth's public school system when the communities they served were annexed. When that happened, their black and white pupils both became the responsibility of the Fort Worth school board, which had to scramble to take over operation of the new facilities and fit them into the budget. The Riverside public school system, for instance, operated quietly in the shadows of the Fort Worth system from 1905 until it was taken over in 1923. North Fort Worth, by comparison, was a special case because the opening of the Swift and Armour packing plants in 1903 caused the little community severe growing pains. All those new workers, managers, and new businesses caused a population spike the likes of which had not been seen locally since the railroad arrived in 1876. In 1904, North Fort Worth (incorporated since 1902) opened its first school for African-American children, the Yellow Row Colored School with just one teacher, Emma J. Guinn, wife of James E. Guinn, principal of Fort Worth's South Side Colored School. After enrollment reached sixty in 1905 they had to hire a second teacher. The North Fort Worth schools eventually reached critical mass when the district could no longer handle all the pupils enrolled, which was one of the factors that convinced North Fort Worth city fathers to welcome annexation by Fort Worth in 1909. After annexation, the Fort Worth school board renamed Yellow Row Colored School, and it became "North Fort Worth Colored School."[33]

Other surrounding districts operated their own schools long after there was no logical sense to having a fragmented system. All of these districts had one thing in common with Fort Worth's: they treated the education of black children as an after-thought, lower on the municipal agenda than stray dogs and overgrown lots. Fort Worth had thirteen public schools when the century began with at least one in every ward. Nos. 12 and 13 were designated "Colored" —one on the corner of Ninth and Pecan, the other in the 1200 block of Arizona Ave. The buildings told a tale. While the city invested $25,000 to build the first four white schoolhouses in 1883–84, and up to $20,000 each for later buildings, the two colored schools averaged about $8,000 to build, and that included the cost of acquiring the land they were built on. The construction differential reflected the thinking of city fathers about the importance of educating white versus black children. No. 13 School, which was eventually renamed Ninth Ward Elementary, was a two-room wooden building that was still being used decades later. The regular ward schools were expected to last for a decade or more; the colored schools, "poorly designed and inadequately constructed," were not replaced until they were on the verge of falling down.[34]

By 1909, thanks to growth and consolidation, there were six schools for African American children in what could be called Greater Fort Worth: Nos. 12 and 13 in Fort Worth proper, plus "colored schools" in Riverside, Marine, Polytechnic, and North Fort Worth. Before the end of the year the Polytechnic and North Fort Worth areas were annexed by Fort Worth. All the city's school buildings were in bad shape with the colored schools the worst of all, especially in regards to fire safety. At the South Side Colored School, the fire escape from the second floor ended eight feet above the ground. During fire drills pupils exiting from that floor either had to race down the stairs or jump the last eight feet. In March the secretary of the school board reported that all the colored schools were in shameful shape. A "strong wind," he warned bluntly, "would blow them down." The city commission, however, was more interested in cutting expenses than investing more money in dilapidated facilities. Commissioner George Mulkey proposed "cutting the negro school budget" to save money. It is not clear from the record whether he was proposing to cut it out entirely or just to the bare bones. He may have been eying municipal elections coming up in April, or perhaps he was hoping to show good stewardship of public money just before the council put a big school-construction bond issue before the voters.[35]

Even saving untold dollars by building on the cheap, the budget-conscious school board had another dilemma when it came to building colored schools. By tradition colored schools were staffed by colored teachers and a colored principal because no self-respecting white teacher or principal would accept assignment there. Not since the days of the Freedmen's Bureau had white teachers been placed in black classrooms, and that Yankee notion had ended with Reconstruction. So strong was this prohibition that when during the 1908 Texas Senate elections the challenger, Cone Johnson, proposed putting white teachers in "negro schools," incumbent J.W. Bailey gleefully dubbed him "Coon Johnson." The dearth of qualified black teachers, which Johnson's proposal would have addressed, was largely a product of the state's higher education system. Only at Prairie View State Normal Institute could an African-American resident of Texas get teaching certification in-state. Although that certification was inferior to a baccalaureate college degree, still it was an improvement over classroom teachers with no training. The problem was, Prairie View could not train nearly enough teachers to fill all the black classrooms.[36]

By 1909, most of the Fort Worth school district's facilities, some of which were twenty years old, were in dire need of replacement or major renovation. A related issue was how best to serve the city's black children. None of the "colored schools" had an auditorium or library. City fathers floated a $200,000 school-bond issue that included $75,000 for a new white high school and $40,000 for a "negro high school," the first in the city's history, replacing an older, all-grades building at East Twelfth and Steadman. The bond issue passed, and the city launched the biggest school-construction program since 1882. New colored elementary school houses went up on the North Side and in Polytechnic, dubbed "Colored School A" and "Colored School B," respectively, to distinguish them from the older colored schools with their numeric and street names. A $45,000 chunk of the bond money went toward purchasing land and constructing a new (white) Third Ward elementary on Chambers Hill. It was not just that the old building was old and dilapidated; the problem was that "the present school property is in the negro district and almost surrounded by negro residents," so a new school house with less objectionable neighbors was constructed at 1411 East Eighteenth and named for Andrew J. Chambers. It would be the last white school constructed on Chambers Hill. Because the black children of the Third Ward also needed something better, plans were announced to spend an unspecified amount of the bond money to construct a new "14-room negro [high] school" that would include the tenth through twelfth grades.[37]

The new Colored High School authorized in the 1909 bond issue was remarkable for several reasons. One was the amount of money spent on it—$5,000 for the land, another $40,000 for the building—a larger amount than the total spent to build all the colored schools in the city up to then. For that $40,000 black schoolchildren got the first all-brick "colored school" in Fort Worth, which the board pronounced "fire-proof." They were so proud of it they invited the legendary Booker T. Washington to come help dedicate the building as a guest of the city. At the time, Washington was the best-known and most respected black man in America. President Theodore Roosevelt counted him a friend and had even invited him to dinner at the White House. Unfortunately, the great man could not come to the dedication. The new high school's administration was placed in the hands of Isaiah M. Terrell. The board gave him nine teachers including a music teacher and eventually a P.E. teacher/coach. Music and athletics gave the school the first extracurricular program ever offered to the city's black children. The school had a library, stocked with hand-me-down books, but no science lab or playing fields.[38]

Fort Worth's black schoolchildren got their second brick schoolhouse in 1917. Not counting the high school, wooden buildings were still the norm at this date. However, the school board decided to spend the lavish sum of $25,000 to build a showplace school for black children, grades one through nine. The red-brick building at Louisiana Ave. and E. Rosedale had eleven classrooms on two floors and was on the same site as one of the early colored schools. The board broke with tradition by naming it for a person—James E. Guinn, the pioneering black teacher who had just died that same year. It was a perfect convergence of building and namesake. The James E. Guinn School educated the city's African-American children for the next sixty-three years.[39]

However, a couple of new brick buildings could not reverse decades of educational neglect. As long as the black community had to depend on the whims of a penurious white school board to provide teaching resources there was never going to be an educated black population. Black schools would always be stuck at the back of the line when it came to facilities, supplies, and staffing. For instance, when in 1904 the city began paying substitutes for the first time and hiring teachers for "special" programs (*e.g.*, music, drama, team sports), those perks were only for white schools. The city's black schools had to limp along with a single music teacher who divided her time between schools, and no paid substitutes for faculty. Black schools had no gymnasiums or play rooms. In 1923 by its own calculations, the city spent $60.03 per white pupil compared to only $28.23 per black pupil. By the end of the decade that amount had risen to $63.17 and $35.66, respectively. In the categories of "maintenance and operation" alone, the district spent $5.89 for white schools versus $3.00 for colored schools. The city's excuse for what the *Star-Telegram* called "the wretched state" of its black schools was that "many" of those schools had been "inherited" as a result of annexation in 1922, and annual school budgets in the years following had not caught up to the new demands.[40]

Some black schools were fortunate to find a benefactor. In 1907 when the one-room school serving the Marine black community was about to close for lack of money, the white Washington Heights school board took it over. If Washington Heights had not adopted it, the little school would have had to cease operations, either throwing its pupils onto the street or into the laps of the local black churches. Alternately, a generous benefactor could serve the same purpose. In 1911 the "patriotic, large-hearted" W. G. Turner of Fort Worth gave $1,000 to the cause of "manual training" for the city's African-American youth. Unfortunately, his gift was used as an excuse by budget hawks for not funding technical courses for black students.[41]

In many ways the Riverside school system was a microcosm of Fort Worth's system—a small black population that grew until it could no longer be ignored by the white majority, then a half-hearted commitment to its needs. The little rural settlement of Riverside, one-and-a-half miles from the Courthouse, traced its beginnings to 1891. Over the years a black community grew up in the area, on the south side of the Chicago, Rock Island & Pacific tracks. By 1903 it had its own church, Trinity Baptist, and in 1907 the (white) Riverside school board built a one-room, wood-framed "negro school" on 11th St. (later LaSalle). By 1911 the number of pupils had outgrown the building, so the school board committed to putting a two-room, brick schoolhouse on the same site. Erected at a cost of $2,000, this was the first brick schoolhouse for African Americans in Tarrant County if not all of north Texas, important not just as a historic site but also because detailed descriptions of the school by its pupils, grown up to be adults, exist today. Riverside Negro School grew from twenty-nine pupils the year it opened to seventy-nine pupils the year it was taken over by the Fort Worth school district. The building was divided into two overcrowded classrooms taught by two overworked teachers. For desks they used boards laid across wooden boxes. Instruction only went through grade six, and all ages were mixed together. Though the schoolhouse was sturdy red brick on the outside, inside the roof leaked and the walls and floor were covered with soot and coal dust from the single pot-bellied stove. Lacking indoor plumbing, pupils and teachers had to use two privies out back. After 1923 the building was designated "Colored School H" in the Fort Worth system. By the end of the 1920s the student population had once again outgrown the facility, and an official study recommended that temporary buildings be brought in until a new schoolhouse could be constructed or the existing one expanded.[42]

Though Fort Worth's black schoolchildren had inferior facilities, they had some outstanding teachers, starting with the two husband-wife pairs of Isaiah and Marcelite Terrell and James and Emma Guinn. Both I.M. Terrell and James E. Guinn rose through the teaching ranks, the former to oversee all Fort Worth colored schools as "superintendent" and the latter to be principal of the South Side Colored School (1900). Their wives displayed the same sort of commitment to black education. Marcelite Terrell worked alongside her husband for years. Emma Guinn never worked in the same school as her husband, but she carved out a respectable career of her own in education. Black teachers like the Terrells and Guinns had to be devoted to the work because the pay and the quality of what they were given to work with were so low. Too many graduates of Prairie View Normal and other historically black, teacher-training schools gave up and left for greener pastures just as their careers were getting started. S.E. Collins graduated from Prairie View Normal in 1901 and after three years trying to make a go of it as a teacher, gave up and took a job as a meat inspector for the federal government.[43]

The steady growth of the city's population added an average of a thousand more children to the school system every year. That number cannot be broken down by race, but the school-age population was growing across the board. Unfortunately, enrollment was not growing commensurately. From the time such records were kept, there was a significant gap between the numbers of black children enrolled versus the "census" of black children in Fort Worth. In the 1919–20 school year there was a difference of nearly a thousand.[44]

The Fort Worth district chose to focus on facilities, not enrollment. In 1920 the city built a new school for "North Side negroes," but other black schools had to make do with decrepit or temporary buildings. For the 1921–22 school year the South Side Colored School received "domestic science" and "manual training" equipment for the first time. This was the beginning of a vocational training program for black youths in Fort Worth, specifically, to train them for "domestic service jobs." In 1927, the school board appointed Lucille Bishop Smith teacher-coordinator over the vocational program. The fact that she was black gives an insight into how the board viewed vocational training—as a sideline of its main mission of educating white children. This was about the extent of the FWISD's commitment to non-traditional education until the creation of a full-fledged technical school decades later.[45]

By 1922 the city's school buildings were reaching the end of their life cycle; most were run-down and crowded. School board members toured all the schools and expressed shock at what they saw. The issues in the white schools were also present in the black schools in "aggravated form." For instance, the streets in front of the black schools were not paved and lacked sidewalks and gutters, and the land on which the buildings sat did not drain properly. The James E. Guinn School, a showplace for the district when it opened in 1917, had an overflow of 150 children crammed into shacks behind the building. Getting from the main building to the shacks in rainy weather required either wading through a sea of mud or, if the water was too high, using a flat-bottomed skiff that was kept tied up to the building for such times. Three years later, the newly created Fort Worth Independent School District took over all the city's schools. Writing about the "Negro schools" two years after that, one observer argued that neither the board of education nor the board of trustees was responsible for "all the worthless and wretched [Negro] school sites" that it had inherited.[46]

Photo 8. Black schoolboys' football team, 1920

They played for the "Colored High School," a fact reflected in their team logos. 1920 photo courtesy of Fort Worth collector Gregory Dow.

Photo 9. Black schoolboys' football team, 1920s

After 1921, they were the I.M. Terrell football team. Regardless of the name on the school, they had no practice field and little equipment. This 1926 photo from Dorothy Lasseter Doggett, "Survey of Fort Worth Independent School District" (1927 TCU Thesis), Courtesy of Special Collections, Mary Couts Burnett Library, Texas Christian University.

Schooling may have been the great black hope for little African-American children, but even that hope was qualified. Even black children who completed the primary and secondary grades had little hope of doing anything with their diplomas, in particular going on to higher education. Most young African Americans still faced a dim future of either domestic service or back-breaking agricultural labor. The conclusion was that all a high school diploma did was make its holder over-educated. In 1935, William McDonald pointed out that blacks who went off to college came home with a degree but no job prospects. They "await the call of employment and labor," he said, "but no call is heard." That was a searing indictment not just of society but of the state of black education.[47]

The only persons committed to the cause of higher education for African Americans, it seemed, were mission-minded churches and a handful of philanthropic organizations. Baptists, Presbyterians, and Disciples of Christ had long taken the lead among churches. In 1886, the Presbyterian Board of Missions for Freedmen established the first (and only) black girls' school in Texas, the Mary Allen Seminary. The (black) General Baptist Convention of Texas supported a broad range of good works in the state while the Negro Baptist Missionary and Educational Association focused its efforts specifically on schooling. The Christian Woman's Board of Missions was a part of the Disciples of Christ that included Mrs. Ida Van Zandt Jarvis of Fort Worth and her white friends. All three groups believed in "the possibilities and the worthiness of the Negro." All of these groups had one thing in common: they thought African Americans must be educated by whites. They also tried to soothe white fears by putting their schools in areas that already had a sizable black population. They knew the thought of "hordes of Negroes" descending on their communities would alarm white residents. That is why Jarvis Christian College, founded in 1912, was located on rural land in far east Texas even though most of its benefactors were Fort Worth residents, and why Mary Allen Seminary was located in Crockett, Texas.[48]

Both Jarvis and Mary Allen operated more like glorified high schools than genuine colleges because their students' schooling had not prepared them for the liberal arts curriculum. In 1924 the State Department of Education accredited Jarvis as a high school and took over the operation of Mary Allen. Closer to home, Fort Worth had the one colored high school, I.M. Terrell. After that, the nearest institutions of higher learning were Paul Quinn College in Waco (founded in 1877 by the African Methodist Episcopal Church) and Bishop College in Marshall (founded in 1881 by the Baptist Home Mission Society). Like Jarvis and Mary Allen, they scarcely qualified as colleges in the classical sense. Paul Quinn's original mission was to teach industrial skills to freedmen; only in later years was the curriculum expanded to include college-preparatory and college-level work. Bishop's priority was first and always religious training, not the liberal arts. Aside from religious instruction, most of the curriculum was high-school level. The Baptist Church treated the school as a religious mission. Naturally, its faculty and administration were all white. In 1907 the white president, Charles H. Maxson, told a black Fort Worth audience, "Bishop College is a school for the education of your people. . . to prepare [them] for better service for God and their race."[49]

Fort Worth's large black Baptist congregations, in particular those of Mount Gilead, Mount Pisgah, and St. James, took a strong interest in black education. They were determined to get a "negro college" for Fort Worth. In 1907 the Negro Baptist Missionary and Educational Association of Texas, led by their President Lacey K. Williams, launched a drive to accomplish that. At their national convention that year the association began trying to raise $20,000 to build a new school. Stymied on that front, they decided to move Hearne Academy (founded in 1881 in Hearne, Texas) to Fort Worth and rename it Fort Worth Industrial and Mechanical College. The idea was to create an "industrial school" modeled on Tuskegee Institute that would provide vocational training for "colored youth" (males) who did not have an affinity for academic subjects but still desired more out of life than farm work. White supporters believed a technical school, as it was also known, would teach practical job skills that would keep young black men from becoming beggars or worse, that old "ethical character" issue.[50]

The idea had the enthusiastic backing of two powerful black Fort Worth groups: pulpit ministers and Prince Hall Masons. They wanted to put it on empty land in Arlington Heights. Boosters collected $500 from the black community at the outset on the way to raising the full amount to build the school. Fort Worth Industrial and Mechanical College opened its doors seven months later only in the College Heights section of Fort Worth (the east side), not Arlington Heights where developers and well-heeled white residents had strongly objected to its placement. Despite the high-sounding name, the school's curriculum not surprisingly was limited to elementary and secondary instruction. When both attendance and funding languished, the college was forced to close its doors not long after opening. Otherwise, Fort Worth might have become home to one of the historically black colleges in Texas (*cf.* Waco, Prairie View, Marshall, and Dallas).[51]

Ironically, at a time when schooling for white kids was moving away from vocational training, black education was going headlong in the opposite direction. The Mary Allen Seminary in Crockett, Texas, tried to provide a liberal arts education for its students in its early years but finally yielded to criticism and converted the curriculum to vocational subjects such as cooking and dress-making. In 1917 Congress would pass the Smith-Hughes Act separating funding for vocational training from funding for high schools, meaning white high schools. Clearly, black children fell on the vocational side of that divide. Practically the only educational path open to them beyond the 3 Rs led to a life working on the factory floor. Vocational courses would not be re-integrated into the standard high school curriculum until the 1960s, not by chance coinciding with the end of Jim Crow.[52]

The dream of a handful of visionary black Fort Worth leaders of creating a technical school had been co-opted by a larger statewide movement to create such a school somewhere besides Fort Worth. The statewide movement was better funded and enjoyed the backing of a distinguished, racially mixed group of Texas business, political, and church leaders. Judging by contemporary newspaper reports, it seems many of the movement's white supporters were motivated as much by fear of the growing black criminal class as by pure altruism. Their fear was an updated version of the old slave-owners' fear of a mass slave uprising, only instead of malcontent slaves it would be black savages rampaging through the streets killing and looting. Job training and a strong dose of discipline, the logic went, would produce a docile, productive black working class safe from the allures of the saloon and the pool hall. All the money committed to the project came from private sources with the state as a silent partner. The resulting Texas Industrial School that opened near Hawkins, Texas in 1912 was soon absorbed into Jarvis Christian

College, but it gave new life to the dream of creating a technical school to serve the black communities of Dallas and Fort Worth.[53]

In 1914 a group of deep-pocketed Dallas philanthropists secured a charter from the legislature for the "Texas Normal Industrial Institute" whose purpose was "the establishment, maintenance, and support of an institution for the scientific, normal [*i.e.*, teacher training], and industrial training of colored youth, with authority to award diplomas and issue certificates." As its president explained in less orotund terms, the school was needed "so that our colored boys and girls may be prepared to serve in the home, field, and shop." Two years later the institute opened with an all-white board and faculty. It broke new ground, however, by admitting both girls and boys. The girls' side of the building was known as the Home-Makers' Industrial School for Negro Girls, and there was no shortage of applicants as soon as the word got around that tuition was covered. The educational options for young Dallas and Fort Worth blacks, post-high school, now included two vocational schools (at Dallas and Hawkins) in addition to Prairie View for those wishing to pursue academic studies.[54]

All of the high-flown talk of "educating the Negro" has to be put in the context of Jim Crow. At the end of the day, not even a degree from a prestigious white school like the University of Chicago counted for much if the degree-holder were black. One black Fort Worth resident who happened to be a graduate of the University of Chicago found that out first-hand. The University had a large enough alumni base in North Texas by World War I to form an alumni chapter. One of those alumni was Dr. Alexander Bismarck Terrell, son of Isaiah M. and Marcelite Terrell. Dr. Terrell had worked his way through medical school by waiting on tables. Back home in Fort Worth he established himself as a "physician of high standing." He had no reason to believe that the standards for admission to the UC alumni organization would be any different than admission to the university itself. He could not have been more wrong. Another Chicago alumnus living in the city at the time was Rabbi George Fox of Temple Beth-El, a classmate of Terrell who considered him "a fine young Negro" and a credit to the University. Yet when the Fort Worth alumni held their organizational meeting, Dr. Terrell was not invited to participate. When Fox asked why, the following exchange occurred:

Association Chairman: "He is a nigger isn't he?"

Fox: "Of course. Does the University of Chicago make distinctions between white and black alumni?"

Another alumnus [referring to the planned social activities]: "Would you want your wife to dance with a nigger?"

That put an end to the discussion. The meeting broke up, and no branch of the University of Chicago Alumni Association was formed in Fort Worth during all the years Fox lived here.[55]

Although their primary and secondary schools were second-class compared to white schools, blacks nonetheless took great pride in those schools. To have done otherwise would have been to resign themselves to inferiority as the status quo and, worse, accept the blame for failure since segregated schools were staffed and run by African Americans albeit under the oversight of white school boards. Blacks preferred to focus on I.M. Terrell and James E. Guinn rather than the one-room shacks that were the norm. This sort of willful blindness allowed black educators like E.L. Blackshear, the "principal" of Prairie View Normal and Industrial College, to say without irony, "Texas has the best negro school system of any state in the Union." Those sentiments were echoed by Rev. E.M. Griggs of Palestine who told the Negro Baptist Missionary and Educational Association convention in 1907, "There is not a state in the union which furnishes better facilities for education for our people." For African Americans, damning their schools would have meant damning the best chance they had of climbing up out of poverty and ignorance. Instead, those schools no matter how bad were held up to generations of black children as a source of community pride.[56]

Whites naturally went along with the charade. A history of the city's schools written by Howard W. Peak in 1922 recognized both I.M. Terrell and James E. Guinn for their enormous contributions to "negro education," while misspelling the latter's name as "Gwynn." Peak described the indomitable Terrell as "a credit [to] his entire race for his untiring efforts to disseminate knowledge and principles to those under his charge." Who needed good schools when one had "knowledge and principles"?[57]

The Black Church—The Community's One Foundation

The black church has always been the heart and soul of the black community. Typically there were more churches than any other institution except saloons in "colored town," and both followed the Biblical admonition to be fruitful and multiply. At the turn of the century the African-American faithful of Fort Worth could choose from twelve churches representing two denominations—four Methodist and eight Baptist—all on the east side of town. The four largest were Allen Chapel (African Methodist Episcopal), Morning Chapel (Methodist Episcopal), St. James Baptist Church, and Mount Gilead Baptist Church. The newest was Corinth Baptist Church in Riverside (Ennis and Park avenues). It was not until 1909—ten years after the Riverside Addition appeared on maps—that black Riverside residents got their own church. Before that they had to cross the river to attend Allen Chapel. Corinth Baptist Church showed the city's black population to be growing to the east and north.[58]

The churches were more than just houses of worship; they helped fill the void created by the absence of public parks, meeting halls, and family-entertainment venues. Most public gatherings used church auditoriums, which kept the buildings in use during the week as well as on Sundays. Allen Chapel and Mount Gilead in the early twentieth century had two of the largest auditoriums in town. The churches were also beacons of light in poor, black neighborhoods, pointing the way toward what Rev. Lacey K. Williams called, "the mental and moral uplift of our race."[59]

However, just outside their doors were hordes of evil-doers. Every black church had a nearby saloon or a crib, a problem long known to white churches on the south or Hell's Half-Acre end of town.[60] Black churches were also subject to the immutable laws of Jim Crow that governed every aspect of American life. None of the black Baptist congregations belonged to the Southern Baptist Association although they were acceptable Baptists by every measure except race. In 1909 when the Sunday School Committee of the Baptist Convention decided to conduct a canvass of Fort Worth residents to see who was going to Sunday School and who wasn't, the instructions to canvassers included the following: "If negroes occupy a house, take down the street and number and write 'negroes' across the card," suggesting that the committee did not follow up with black residents.[61]

It would take another century for the Tarrant Baptist Association to apologize for supporting slavery and Jim Crow, but through most of the twentieth century even Christian love had its limits. Black churches were forced to practice a kind of non-denominational ecumenicalism whereby black Methodists, Episcopalians, and Baptists had more in common with each other than with their denominational brethren.[62]

The most important name in black Baptist circles, perhaps the entire black religious community of Fort Worth, was the Rev. L.K. Williams. After graduating from Bishop College in 1905 and starting his ministry in Dallas, he accepted the pastorship of Mount Gilead Baptist Church in 1907, and his career took off. By 1913 he had grown Mount Gilead into the largest black church in the state and a powerhouse in the National Baptist Convention, U.S.A. His was arguably the most influential voice in the city's black community after Bill McDonald until 1916 when he was hired away by a Detroit church. Others who made their churches instruments of change were A.R. Griggs, J.H. Winn, and H.W. Jackson. A visiting preacher in 1907 said, "What [our] race will be depends largely on the leadership of the ministers."[63]

Photo 10. First Baptist Church preacher J. Frank Norris and unnamed man.

Norris poses in undated photo with unnamed man who was most definitely *not* a member of his congregation. They appear to be standing in front of the old neo-Gothic church building at 4th and Throckmorton, which means this was taken before 1932. A curious picture since Norris was no fan of African Americans. Courtesy of Laura and William Wynn of Fort Worth.

After the turn of the century, the city's black churches were on the rise, attracting new members, planting new congregations, and drawing up plans for magnificent new buildings. The oldest among them had outgrown their original buildings and were looking to build grand edifices on a par with their white brethren. In 1907, Mount Pisgah Baptist Church relocated to an impressive new building at Fifteenth and Crump. Five years later the membership of Allen Chapel replaced their existing building at First and Elm with a two-story, yellow-brick "temple" that could hold 1,300 worshippers at one time. It incorporated a three-quarter balcony, polished oak paneling, stained-glass windows, and a pipe organ in his design. But Allen Chapel did not hold the title of most majestic black church for long.[64]

That same year (1912), Mount Gilead Baptist Church launched a construction project to put every other black church in the city to shame. They drew up plans for a new $55,000 building at Fifth and Grove to replace the old wood-frame building at Thirteenth and Jones where they had worshiped since 1882. Upon completion of the new edifice, they simply closed up the old building and walked away, dropping their insurance policy in the process.[65]

The new building was more than just a combination sanctuary and Sunday-school classrooms; it included a day nursery for working mothers, a kindergarten, a "cooking department," reading room, a gymnasium, and even a swimming pool, which may have been the most remarkable feature of all. It was only the second swimming pool in Fort Worth after the Natatorium (Third and Commerce). Since blacks were not allowed to swim at the Natatorium, Mount Gilead offered the only place for African-Americans to swim in the city except for the Trinity River. This was just one of the things that made Mount Gilead a true community center besides being the largest black church in Texas.[66]

Mount Gilead's growth did not come without problems. When word got out that a black church was buying the property at Fifth and Grove, a delegation of white neighbors descended on city hall to protest blacks moving into their neighborhood; it did not matter that the newcomers were good Baptists, and this was a single church building, not a takeover. At the time no blacks lived within two blocks of the proposed site, and 1,500 moving in was plenty of cause for alarm. White representatives even approached church leaders offering to purchase the property at the same price they had paid for it. Mount Gilead stuck to its guns, however, and built the magnificent edifice they had planned. When the doors opened in 1913, none of their white neighbors were there to welcome them to the neighborhood.[67]

Unfortunately, the dreams of the black faithful encountered stormy waters. Many members of the Allen Chapel congregation lost their savings when the Provident Bank and Trust went under. Since the church was paying as it went, construction came to a halt. Rather than give up, they decided to pass the hat. According to church lore, a hundred members dug deep, even doing without Christmas gifts that year, to come up with the necessary $2,500 to continue the work. In the case of the Mount Gilead Church, the congregation took on a $33,000 mortgage that proved beyond the means of the 1,600 members to pay off out of regular collections. They ended up having to solicit donations from the white church-going community to help pay it off. The experiences of Allen Chapel and Mount Gilead taught the black community that it was impossible to keep up with the Joneses—or at least with J. Frank Norris whose mighty First Baptist Church (Fourth and Throckmorton) was a money machine that supported overseas missions, a seminary, a nice parsonage for the preacher, and a massive building project all at the same time.[68]

Other black churches were more inspired than scared by the Mount Gilead and Allen Chapel experiences. In 1922, Mount Zion Baptist Church moved into a new $60,000 building, inviting the Reverends S.E. Griggs from Memphis, Tennessee, and E.A. Wilson from Dallas to be the keynote speakers on "Dedication Sunday." That same year St. James Baptist added a $35,000 Sunday school annex onto its existing $110,000 building, the better to serve its 4,000+ members.[69]

The fact that all these churches were willing to take on major financial obligations and to eventually pay off their notes shows more than their faith in the Lord to provide; it shows the growing economic resources of the black community. When we think of Fort Worth "mega-churches" we usually think of J. Frank Norris' First Baptist Church, but Allen Chapel, Mount Gilead, and St. James were "mega-churches" for their time.

As the local roster of churches grew, so too did the diversity of the religious experience available to Fort Worth blacks. Until the World War I era, the only choice the faithful had was between the Methodists and Baptists. In 1914 the Presbyterians entered the mix when thirty-two congregants organized the Colored Cumberland Presbyterian Church of Fort Worth under the aegis of the Brazos River Presbytery. The congregation grew so rapidly that in just three years they were hosting the National [Negro] Sunday School Convention and General Assembly. Then in 1919 the Disciples of Christ opened an outpost in the black community when the first "Colored Christian [Church] congregation" was organized in Fort Worth.[70]

The remarkable growth in the black religious community brought state and national attention to the city. Baptists have always been fond of conventions, but black Baptists had never gathered in Fort Worth until 1898 when the Negro Baptist Missionary and Educational Association convened at the Mount Gilead church. More than 500 delegates came from all over the state, which was a new experience for Fort Worth's black church family. It was also something of a shock to white Fort Worth having so many black strangers in town. (They were put up mostly in private homes, ate covered-dish suppers, and stayed east of Rusk St.) The *Dallas Morning News* reassured its readers "The indications all point toward a . . . harmonious and peaceful gathering."[71]

The 1898 event was the beginning of a love feast between Baptist conventioneers and Fort Worth. Five years later the Educational Convocation of the General Baptist Convention of Texas assembled at the Mount Pisgah Church, and in 1907 the Negro Baptist Missionary and Educational Association of Texas held a two-day convention at Mount Gilead. In 1914 more than a thousand members of the Baptist General Convention of Texas descended on the city as guests of Mount Pisgah. Three years later 200 delegates of the Sunday School Chautauqua and Baptist Young People's Union came to Mount Pisgah. In 1921 it was 500 delegates of the General Baptist Convention of Texas meeting at Mount Gilead. The only other times this many African Americans got together in one place was for baseball games and Juneteenth celebrations. At a time when large political gatherings of African Americans were not possible, Baptist church conventions were a source of black pride. At the 1898 convention, attendees sang from the only church hymnal authored by an African American. Even something as small as that could be a source of great pride.[72]

Black churches were important because they filled many needs besides spiritual nourishment, such as the 3 R's. With public schooling for blacks unavailable before 1882 and extremely limited even after that, the school-church connection was very important. Between Sunday worship services church buildings could be turned into classrooms for neighborhood children. In 1894 the South Side Colored School rented space from Mount Zion Baptist Church (Rosedale and Louisiana). Twenty-five years later when Mount Zion built a magnificent new building (1101 Evans Ave.), they included an Educational Annex, and not just for holding Sunday School classes. Other churches no doubt were also committed to faith-based schooling, only their names did not make it into the history books. Once a grammar school system was in place, some churches turned their attention to higher education. At the Baptist Missionary and Educational Association convention in Fort Worth in 1907, a major item on the agenda was opening a black Christian college in Texas. Convention delegates heard the white president of Bishop College speak about "the education of your people." He told them the Baptist Home Mission Society annually spent $10,000 on "[secular] teaching alone." Another speaker on the program addressing the same theme stated that preachers and teachers were all in the same line of work.[73]

Black church construction also gave work to African-American architects and contractors long before anyone heard of "affirmative action." William Sidney Pittman, the son-in-law of Booker T. Washington, designed the Allen Chapel sanctuary in 1912, and George Powell was the contractor of record on the new St. James Baptist Church (1913–18). This is not even to count all the nameless black laborers who poured concrete, laid brick, and did roofing on these projects.[74]

The black church was a full-service institution, filling a variety of needs both spiritual and secular. The work went on seven days a week, and not just from the pulpit.

The Black Press, Part 2

Clubs and societies gave the black middle class a sense of worth; the black press celebrated those achievements. As the number of black Fort Worth residents who could read and write grew, a black press sprang up to cover black news and social activities (aside from crime, which the white press covered gleefully). The black-owned publications did not attempt to compete with the city's major dailies. Rather, they were niche publications like the labor and livestock journals. Most significant among the black entries in the newspaper field were Raymond L. "Pie" Melton's and John Quincy Miller's *Fort Worth Mind* and A.E. Harding's *Fort Worth Democrat* (not to be confused with B.B. Paddock's similarly named newspaper of the 1870s and '80s). Nothing is known of the short-lived *Fort Worth Democrat*, but *The Fort Worth Mind* was a shining light for five decades. Melton and Miller launched it in December 1932 as a spin-off of the *Dallas Express*. Modestly described by its owners as a "local news-sheet," circulation grew ten-fold in five years, from 500 to 5,000 subscribers. Melton was the driving force behind it, another one of those celebrated I.M. Terrell success stories. He went on to get a college degree at Morehouse College and came home to bring about change to his hometown. He was a one-man publishing machine. Not only was he co-founder of his little news-sheet, he was also advertising manager, circulation manager, and occasionally "paper boy," delivering papers out of the trunk of his car. For its part, the white establishment was not particularly impressed with *The Fort Worth Mind.* The *Dallas Morning News* sniffed that it was a "mild-mannered paper." Circulation never rose above 12,000, but that was still impressive for a strictly niche publication operating at a chronic deficit. More than that, it was the principal source of news for the black community until it ceased publication in 1986.[75]

A contemporary of the *Fort Worth Mind* was the *Fort Worth News*, which is not even a footnote in the history of the local black press. The *Fort Worth Eagle Eye*, the *Bronze Texan*, and the provocatively named *Torchlight Appeal* also came and went in the first half of the century. Together they live today only as vague memories in the black community and the occasional odd issue in private hands. The *Lake Como Monitor*, a weekly, was the last black newspaper of note to come along before the modern civil rights era. It was the personal project of W.H. Wilburn, owner-editor, who launched it as a neighborhood newsletter in 1940. The little four-page newspaper reflected the strength and solidarity of its neighborhood as well as the limitations of a black newspaper. In the 1950s, now known as the *Lake Como Weekly*, it led a successful fight to get a new elementary school in Como. However, even at its peak in 1960, the *Lake Como Weekly* had only 4,500 paid subscriptions. It finally folded in 1985.[76]

Only one black journal was home-grown, the short-lived magazine with the unwieldy name, *The White Man and the Negro*, published by "Professor" Phil R. Register from 1932 to 1933. He announced the purpose in its slogan: "to promote a better relation between the white and the black races." The magazine published pieces by Bill McDonald, William Coleman, Matthew Johns, and other notable members of Fort Worth's black community, but even at 15¢ an issue ($1.50 for a year's subscription) it was a luxury that most of its targeted market could do without.[77]

Phil Register, Pie Melton, and their friends did not give up easily. Not content to put out their little publications, in 1933 they launched an "Association of Colored Publishers" and announced a convention for November. Pre-registration was so small they did not even have to rent a meeting hall. They met in Register's offices on East Ninth. As far as the record shows, that was the first and last meeting of the Association of Colored Publishers.[78]

Black-owned publications were fighting an uphill battle against the white publishing establishment. Without the advertising revenue and readership of the large, white-owned dailies, they struggled to keep the presses running. Nonetheless, they were a potent symbol of success for the black community. They were the product of necessity as much as racial pride because white newspapers like the *Morning Register* and the *Star-Telegram* showed little interest in covering the black community except for vice and crime and the occasional human-interest story. This bias is evident in a set of scrapbooks assembled by the staff of the YWCA that followed the black community in the two major newspapers for two years (1944–46). The scrapbooks contain page after page of *Press* and *Star-Telegram* clippings, with a majority of the headlines starting with words like "Negro attack," "Negro assault," or "Negro trial." The scrapbooks were not intended to be a chronicle of black criminal activity, but such stories formed the majority of what the white dailies reported.[79]

For the most part, blacks were invisible to the big dailies, both as citizens and as consumers. In September 1901 the *Fort Worth Morning Register* reported on a construction accident at the Texas & Pacific station. Two men were seriously injured, one white, the other black. The newspaper described the injuries of the white man and gave his name. For the other victim, they simply said, "A negro man whose name was not learned was also hurt, but not so seriously."[80]

When not ignoring the black community completely, white newspapers used a tone that was either patronizing or demeaning. A couple of examples suffice to make the point: "Negro and Bear in Exciting Chase at Santa Fe Depot" read the headline in the *Fort Worth Star-Telegram* of October 15, 1910. As it turned out, the headline was more interesting than the story about a black porter at the station who coaxed the escaped animal back into its cage with a piece of fruit. As another example, the *Fort Worth Record* thought the best way to promote Negro League baseball in the 1920s was to advise its readers that the games "present an element of [black] comedy that keeps the crowd in an uproar." The talent on the field apparently was not sufficient to draw fans to the game. Aside from their obsessive focus on reporting black crimes, white newspapers did not treat blacks and whites equally. Black-on-black crime was only mentioned in the newspapers when it was particularly violent or bloody, whereas white crimes both large and small were always considered newsworthy. As late as 1946, the *Dallas Morning News* lumped together five homicides in the black community in a brief, one-column story. One of the newspaper's own columnists commented that such a story would "constitute a front-page crime wave" had the killings occurred in the white community.[81]

In 1920, the *Star-Telegram* attempted to build a bridge to the black community, but the thinking in the editorial offices was as clueless as ever. That March the newspaper proudly announced the hiring of Octavos Roy Cohen; his "famous negro stories" would appear in the paper twice a week. Although Cohen was as white as the rest of the *Star-Telegram* staff, the editors promised readers,

> Cohen knows the negro, the common everyday negro of the South and the sporty negro of the city. . . . He knows how to write about them; his stories ring true and his dialect is the real dialect of the Southern negro. . . . [They] contain gems of negro humor, tinctured with a little of the negro philosophy.[82]

Just as Joel Chandler Harris had the fictional "Uncle Remus" narrate his stories, Cohen created "Florian Slappey," described as "the Beau Brummel of the negro colony," to function as narrator in his columns. The *Star-Telegram* assured readers they would "roar" with laughter at Slappey's "delightful" stories. Octavos Roy Cohen and Florian Slappey were exhibits A and B why Fort Worth's black community needed their own newspapers.

Another problem was that black businesses did not advertise in the pages of the *Star-Telegram* or *Press.* Whether they were excluded by newspaper policy or simply saw no reason to advertise is not clear from the record. What is clear is that successful black-owned businesses like the Jim Hotel and Cooper Taxi Co. never appeared in either newspaper unless they were connected to some crime. The Jim Hotel, a fifty-room, first-class establishment at 413 E. Fifth, built and owned by Bill McDonald in the 1920s brought in nationally known entertainers to perform in its club room, but it might as well have been located on Mars as far as the readers of *The Press* and *Star-Telegram* knew.[83]

White news coverage of the black community was the velvet glove of Jim Crow—theoretically neutral but in reality perpetuating all the classic negative stereotypes. Northern-born members of the Fourth Estate could stumble badly when covering news stories in Southern states, whether it was the trial of a black man accused of a crime against a white person, or simply the protocols of Southern-style journalism. When newspaper titan William Randolph Hearst tried to break into the Fort Worth market in 1903 with the *Record,* his team of imported executives and reporters committed one embarrassing *faux pas* right out of the box. Hearst policy had always been to use the titles "Mr.," "Mrs.," or "Miss" plus the last name after first using the full name, irrespective of race. Locally owned newspapers like the *Register* and the *Star-Telegram* knew better; they followed the Southern tradition of referring to blacks by their *first names* after the initial citation, reserving the usual courtesy titles for whites only.[84]

Reporting local news involving blacks also involved a certain element of municipal rivalry between Dallas and Fort Worth. The two cities were so close together that the major dailies in each city maintained bureaus in the other city. They did not report events the same, however. In 1910 when a mob in Dallas dragged a black defendant out of a courtroom and lynched him, the *Fort Worth Star-Telegram* reported the story in its evening edition in all its lurid detail. The leading Dallas newspaper reported it a day later in far less lurid terms. In 1946 when a black residence on Fort Worth's Maddox St. was bombed, and in 1953 and 1956 when there were ugly racial incidents in the Riverside neighborhood, the leading Fort Worth newspaper virtually ignored the stories while the Dallas newspaper covered them extensively.[85]

Roy Wilkins as executive director of the NAACP once said, "Negro papers came into being as crusaders, and the minute they stop being crusaders and become chroniclers, they're done." Wilkins was not speaking specifically of the black press in Fort Worth, but it is true that none of them ever embraced the crusading ethos. They were content to chronicle the activities of church and community. Years later, the editor of the *Como Weekly* defiantly proclaimed, "We'll always have the Negro press; it will improve in time." But the history of Fort Worth's black press says otherwise.[86]

Medicine and Public Health

Perhaps the most despicable aspect of Jim Crow was the lack of access to good medical care. Unlike voting and most other civil rights, this was a matter of immediate life and death. Race-based medicine began with a couple of assumptions: first, that blacks were akin to draft animals, being somehow able to bear up under hard, physical work better than whites; and second, that some illnesses were "negro diseases," that is, confined mostly if not exclusively to the African-American population. Specifically, tuberculosis and syphilis were considered "negro diseases" despite all empirical evidence to the contrary. By contrast, yellow fever ("yellow jack") was considered a white-man's disease that blacks were virtually immune to. Even many African Americans believed these myths. Smallpox was not known particularly as a "Negro disease," but years after it had been practically wiped out in white communities it continued to plague the black population. This led some white doctors to associate the spread of the disease with race rather than germs and environmental conditions. In the spring of 1915, smallpox appeared three times in the county jail's "negro ward." The official response was to "segregate" infected prisoners and thoroughly fumigate the ward. One unforeseen consequence was that the backlash extended to the white legal system. Two district court judges refused to hear cases of black defendants, and one black defendant's court-appointed white lawyer asked the judge not to require him to meet with his client.[87]

The problem with Jim Crow medicine was not that there were no black physicians. Fort Worth could count more than forty practicing African-American physicians and dentists between 1887 and 1925 although not all at the same time. The earliest was Dr. William E. Davis who opened his practice in 1887 and was the only black physician in town until he was joined a few years later by Dr. John H. Connelly. The 1887 city directory describes Davis as a "physician and surgeon," which makes him all the more remarkable because the dual qualification means he attended medical school; he did not just apprentice himself to another doctor. He even had two telephone lines at a time when one was still considered a luxury.[88]

Then there was Dr. Alexander B. Terrell who was a graduate of Harvard Medical School. That singular accomplishment—some of his colleagues were still of the "old-country-doctor" variety—did not make him any more acceptable to his white members of the medical fraternity when he practiced in Fort Worth (1912–1917). He was not even accorded routine hospital privileges in the city's white hospitals. That is probably why Terrell departed Fort Worth for good in 1917, moving to California.

Black doctors and dentists simply were not part of the medical community as far as their white colleagues were concerned. They were not accepted in the Tarrant County Medical Society, nor did they have privileges in the white hospitals. The black equivalent of the hospital was the "private sanitarium," what we would call a clinic today. Physicians like Dr. William Davis who could perform surgery and treat a wide range of medical conditions, called their offices "sanitariums." Even with a few highly qualified physicians operating clinics, blacks still received second-class medical treatment—or worse.

In 1906 after Officer Sid Waller severely beat a black couple who would not quiet down, he had them hauled off to jail in the patrol wagon. The battered and bleeding pair was booked into jail and only then did anyone bother to summon a (black) doctor. By the time the doctor arrived, the black man was dead, so the doctor patched up the woman and departed. If this were nothing more than a statistical aberration it could be explained away, but this was standard operating procedure for injured black suspects in the custody of the Fort Worth Police Department. Three years later, G.D. Cosey, a black barkeep, was luckier. He got into a dispute with Officer Lee Tignor, who shot him. Tignor summoned the patrol wagon but at least had Cosey transported to a black medical clinic ("sanitarium") instead of to jail. Seriously injured blacks not in police custody could always go straight to a doctor, but it was a waste of time to try to go to one of the white hospitals first.[89]

In 1907, the City Directory bragged that Fort Worth was "the healthiest city in the state," but that was if one only considered the white population. The black community was always just one contagious case away from disaster. In the winter of 1911–12 the city was struck by a meningitis outbreak that the medical community was totally unprepared for. Meningitis had a survival rate of only 50 percent and was as feared in its day as polio or smallpox. Eighty-four cases were reported in January, thirty-three of whom died within a short time. City-County Hospital served as the headquarters for the medical response to the outbreak. All cases were directed there to be placed in an isolation ward, yet even in the midst of an epidemic, the hospital continued to strictly enforce segregation. Black physicians like Dr. Alexander B. Terrell treated black victims either in their offices or in the patients' homes. (Since there were no antibiotics at the time, "treatment" basically meant trying to alleviate the patient's suffering and monitoring their condition until either the fever broke or they died.) [90]

Out of professional courtesy more than anything else, Dr. Terrell regularly dropped by city hall to update officials on how cases in the black community were faring. During one of those visits, some members of the Tarrant County Medical Society (of which he was not a member because he was black) invited him to attend an emergency session of the society the next night. The invitation also extended to the rest of the city's black doctors. Up until that moment, more than two months into the outbreak, the black and white medical communities had not even been coordinating their response. For instance, in the fall city fathers had ordered the spraying of "germicide" on the streets of the business district and fumigation of infected homes. But two months later no one had any idea if the spraying had helped because records were not being kept of the epidemic's progress in the black community.[91]

This meningitis outbreak eventually passed, and life returned to normal for the people of Fort Worth, including the medical community. Black doctors resumed their regular practices dealing with cuts and scrapes and broken bones, and the Tarrant County Medical Society went back to its segregated ways. However, the meningitis outbreak was notable in the history of local race relations because one unnamed member of the white medical society had taken a stand:

> I believe the negro physicians should attend the meetings of the Society all the time. There are not enough of them to have an organization of their own, and it is just as important to the community [as a whole] that they have the information [white] physicians secure through the meetings, as other physicians do.[92]

Most black residents were not in the habit of seeing a doctor out of a combination of habit and not being able to pay for it. From slave days, blacks had treated themselves with folk remedies and practical measures. For instance, most black women delivered their own babies—with the help of a midwife if they were lucky. Officially, midwives had to be licensed by the State Board of Medical Examiners, but few bothered to apply for the license. In 1903, two black Fort Worth midwives applied for a license. No record exists of whether it was granted.[93]

Because few blacks ever visited a hospital, and the cost of building and running a fully staffed hospital was prohibitive, Fort Worth blacks did not get a hospital of their own until 1918. That was the year Dr. Riley Andrew Ransom relocated his Booker T. Washington Sanitarium from Gainesville. It was a milestone in the history of black medical care in Fort Worth.

They could not walk—or be carried—into a white hospital and expect the same level of treatment as a white person, but conventional wisdom that blacks were turned away from white Fort Worth hospitals is a myth. Any emergency patient was admitted to City-County Hospital regardless of race although they were segregated and either discharged or transferred as soon as possible. St. Joseph's Infirmary, the Catholic charity hospital run by the Sisters of Charity of the Incarnate Word, also admitted blacks—to the "Negro Ward" in the basement. Unofficially, black doctors, who weren't on staff, could treat patients in the segregated ward.[94]

Dr. Ransom's Sanitarium started out at 417 E. Fifth then moved into larger quarters at 509 Grove where it included, besides a twenty-bed ward, such modern facilities as a laboratory, a kitchen, and a nursing school. It set a new standard for black medical care, becoming the first black owned-and-operated clinic in Fort Worth to win accreditation from the American Medical Association, a big step up from the traditional sanitariums that doubled as hospitals. In 1925 it merged with the Negro Baptist Hospital, under which name it operated for the next three years. From 1928 until 1938 it was simply the Fort Worth Negro Hospital when the board changed the name to the Ethel Ransom Memorial Hospital in honor of Dr. Ransom's recently deceased wife. For all these years, Dr. Ransom was the crucial element in the hospital's credibility in both the black community and the medical community. His importance is reflected in the 1938 name change even though after 1925 daily operations were in the hands of Lula Williams, a sort of pioneering nurse-practitioner. The birth certificates of more than a few black Fort Worthers today show them being born at Ethel Ransom Memorial Hospital.[95]

Photo 11. "Fort Worth Negro Hospital"

The "Fort Worth Negro Hospital" and "Ransom Foundation," located at 1200 E. First in 1937, with Dr. R.A. Ransom, Sr. (far left) and some of the staff in front of the building. From 1937–38 *Negro Directory of Fort Worth*, courtesy of Scott and Linda Jo Barker of Fort Worth.

The hospital's connection to the Baptist Church in its early years gave it standing in the larger community. Dr. Ransom's Sanitarium had done good work, but it was still a one-man operation, a glorified clinic. The Baptists brought experience running hospitals, having operated one at 1400 Pennsylvania Ave. for many years before putting up the money for a facility to serve the black population. Henceforward, African Americans with serious medical problems had three options: the Negro Baptist Hospital, City-County, or the "Negro ward" at St. Joseph's. In 1928, the Baptist Church cut all ties with the hospital, and it became a privately owned and operated facility.[96]

In addition to old-fashioned sanitariums and the three hospitals, there was another option available to Fort Worth blacks needing medical care after 1920, at least for women: the Hope Home at 1510 West Peter Smith, operated by the Welfare Association of the Catholic Church under the guidance of Father Robert M. Nolan, pastor at St. Patrick's. Henceforward, all welfare services for "colored people" were centered here, marking Fort Worth's embrace of the settlement house movement that had been turned into a national phenomenon by Jane Addams during the Progressive era. While it offered the full range of "industrial, recreational, and social" services, its most valuable contribution may have been the medical care for the poorest members of the female gender. It was the nearest thing Fort Worth had to a maternity ward for black women giving birth. Father Nolan did not personally run the place; for that purpose he relied on "matrons," starting with Allie Washington, then later Amanda Irvine and Lula Williams. The hiring of women site administrators is important because at this date, most black babies were still delivered at home by a midwife such as Mary Keys Gipson or by a doctor making a house call; it was the lack of a well-equipped, well-staffed maternity ward, not just tradition or culture that kept home-birthing the norm in the black community long after white mothers had started delivering in hospitals. With the accreditation of the Fort Worth Negro Hospital, the Hope Home got out of the baby-delivering business, leaving that job to medical professionals in the future.[97]

The lack of quality care under the traditional system of private (*i.e.*, segregated) medicine explains why blacks were early supporters of national health care, or what critics would call "socialized medicine." In 1940 the National Negro Medical Association went on record favoring a "public health program with a theme of socialized medicine." Unfortunately, the AMA stood squarely against it, even though white doctors attending the 1940 convention in Houston expressed support. In the years that followed, being black and favoring a communist "plot" doomed any chance of getting better health care in the black community than the existing private system could offer. Not until the Affordable Health Care Act in 2010 did the situation improve. Fort Worth's segregated medical system during the city's first century is Exhibit A in the case for government oversight of medical care, just like the government long ago assumed oversight of voting, schools, and the workplace.[98]

Justice for Some

Like everything else, the justice system was stacked against African Americans. To begin with, otherwise innocent acts were made a crime and with serious consequences. In 1911 a black man and a white woman traveling together stopped over at the T&P passenger station. When word got around that they were a couple, an angry mob gathered, and police had to rescue them. It could just as easily have been members of the police leading the mob. And it was not just the police who were racist; the entire judicial system was in hostile white hands, including judges, prosecutors, and juries. Not a single member of the Fort Worth Bar Association was black. When young Hazel Harvey (Peace) was growing up in the 1920s her first ambition was to be a lawyer, but she quickly realized the hopelessness of that dream. "There was only one Negro lawyer in Fort Worth," she recalled years later, "and he was riding a bicycle, and I didn't want to ride a bicycle."[99]

African Americans seldom appeared in civil court because they were not used to settling their disputes with lawyers if they even had the money to hire counsel. As a rule they also did not possess the kind of valuable property that was litigated in the courts. In 1908 when a black woman claimed to have been cheated by her dress-maker, she did not hire a lawyer but instead complained to the nearest policeman to get her 50¢ back. He laughed off her complaint.[100]

Things were worse in criminal court. When blacks were caught up in criminal investigations, guilt was usually assumed from the outset. Most, therefore, lived in fear of even being accused by a white person. In 1902 Fort Worth officers stopped a couple of railroad employees on the street, one white and the other black, and began interrogating them. They searched them roughly before letting them go. The white man went straight to city hall and complained; the black man disappeared because complaining was likely to bring him more trouble rather than an apology.[101]

Then there was the case of Lucy Jane Johnson. Lucy was a graduate of the city's colored schools, described as "a colored damsel of high degree," working as a "washer woman" in 1897. When she delivered a load of laundry to a "Mr. and Mrs. Thomas" and demanded payment, they refused to pay the full amount of the bill. When she tried to keep the laundry, a "scuffle" broke out, two against one, that Lucy got the worst of. Both parties swore out a complaint in city court (aka, police court) and appeared before Judge James H. Jackson. Lucy charged the Thomases with assault and battery and asked for payment. The Thomases accused her of being "very impertinent" and "using language calculated to break the peace." Judge Jackson dismissed the case, and the *Register* reported Lucy "went home none the worse for wear."[102]

Lucy at least got her day in court. Typically, African Americans did not enjoy even the most basic procedural protections. Being stopped and questioned on the street without cause was a minor example. In what may be the earliest example of "driving while black," four Dallas African Americans motored over to Fort Worth in 1911 on a lark. They were stopped twice in twenty minutes by Fort Worth officers who assumed the car was stolen. Still, they got off lucky because they were allowed to go their way. In 1910 Police Chief James Maddox told a convention of the International Chiefs of Police Association that if a "good clout" with a strap was necessary to make a "negro prisoner" quit lying, he would not hesitate to use the strap.

Even if he got his day in court, a black suspect was lucky if the white judge appointed a (white) lawyer to represent him. Too many times black defendants were not even afforded that courtesy because judges exercised their own discretion in deciding whether a defendant needed or deserved legal counsel.[103] The best hope for a black defendant accused of a serious crime in Fort Worth was to land in the courtroom of Judge James Swayne. During his many years in legal practice and on the bench (Seventeenth District Court), Swayne was known as a scrupulously fair man, some even said a "negro lover." He declared during one case, "Justice should be done [this] unfortunate Negro who, if he had been a white man, would never have been indicted in the first place." Swayne protected the interests of two of the most execrable criminals in Fort Worth history, cop-killers Jim Toots and Tommy Lee, both of whom were black. And in the aftermath of the biggest racial upheaval in Fort Worth history, the 1913 race riot that saw a white mob torch black homes and businesses while police and firemen stood aside, Swayne said, "The Negroes of Fort Worth and their property are entitled to as much protection as the white people and theirs." He even went so far as to argue that the city should provide financial restitution to black property owners. No one was ever prosecuted for the riot, but Judge Swayne did more than anyone else to try to bring the perpetrators to justice.[104]

When an African American was prosecuted, more often than not it was for a crime against a white person. In fact, if there was a black person in the vicinity and no other suspect, he or she was inevitably the prime suspect. That is what happened in 1906 when Mrs. A.B. Wharton's jewels disappeared from her house in broad daylight—while she was at home. Police had no clues and no likely suspects so they arrested the white family maid and the black butler. Sam Dunn, the butler, had been a faithful family retainer for years, but that did not keep him from being a prime suspect. He was finally released, with no apologies, when police decided to concentrate on the maid, but his chances of future employment in the households of Fort Worth society after that were practically nil.[105] Still, Sam Dunn was lucky. Most black suspects in high-profile cases did not get off so easily.

Black-on-black crime was a different story. Typically, the police did not put themselves out trying to solve crimes confined to black people. In 1908 when Miles Hill, an African-American resident of the North Side, was burglarized, he complained to the North Fort Worth Police Department. The only action they took was to request the Fort Worth police to be on the lookout for the stolen items. They did not make a report or question anyone. Even violent crime was treated differently by a Jim Crow police department. The official report might simply say, "Somebody shot a negro"—no name and no details. Any subsequent investigation was half-hearted. The police tended to be jaded about knifings and shootings in the Third Ward because they occurred so frequently in that part of town, but there was another reason the area was treated as a combat zone. There was a large black population, and white police officers got little cooperation when trying to investigate black-on-black crime. The days when a Hagar Tucker could serve as a liaison between white authorities and the black community were a thing of the past.[106] (see Chap. 2)

Black-on-black crime raised another Jim Crow paradox. As one observer noted, "A Negro can kill a Negro and be pretty sure of a light sentence at the hands of a [white] jury." He added paradoxically, "As things are, a Negro killer of a Negro stands sometimes a better chance than the white killer of a Negro." Circumstantial evidence supports that conclusion. In 1915, Mannie McGar, a black bar porter and son of Hiram McGar, shot and killed Bennie Lewis, another black porter. McGar was arrested and jailed without bond. He was never indicted, however. The prosecutor chose not to take the case to the grand jury. Black leaders complained about the inequity of the system, and the *Dallas Morning News* claimed, citing unidentified persons, "The better class of Negro citizens. . . want the Negro slayer of a Negro victim to get the same kind of justice that the Negro slayer of a white victim gets." That statement flies in the face of the idea of "black solidarity," but goes along with the story of "one conspicuous negro" who was part of a white mob that lynched a black man accused of raping a white, three-year-old girl in Dallas in 1910. His presence presumably demonstrated the fairness of mob action.[107]

Black citizens often got their first introduction to the criminal justice system when they were "braced" by a white officer, which is the Old West term for "stopping and frisking," only bracing tended to be a lot more brutal, up to and including cold-cocking the suspect. The most blatantly racist cops on the FWPD were brothers Sid and Lee Waller, around the turn of the century. Sid's nickname, which he wore proudly, was "Nigger Killer" because of his record of shooting first and asking questions later. After the turn of the century, the department had a detective whose sole duty was "working among the negroes," thereby removing the need to employ black officers. Although Fort Worth did not hire another black officer after Hagar Tucker for eighty years, city fathers paid lip service to diversity by appointing black "special officers" to work as glorified park police and saloon bouncers. In 1886 when rumors circulated that someone intended to blow up the Colored Methodist Church, the department hired an additional special officer as night watchman. Five years later when an unnamed black man applied to the city council to be a "sanitary officer" (part of the police department), white officers turned out at the next council meeting in force. They addressed the council in what one newspaper called "plain terms," declaring there was "no law that could compel them to work with a nigger." The council shelved the application.[108]

When a black man applied for a special officer's commission, the reaction could depend on where he was assigned. If said officer would be nothing more than a bouncer or doing some other duty that white officers turned up their noses at, the hiring sailed through without a hitch. Edward Loving in 1896, Dick Burns in 1897, and Jeff Daggett in 1906 were all hired to patrol Douglass Park, the city's only public park for blacks, because white cops did not want to patrol there. Henry Davis held a special officer's commission (1910) and split his time between police work and his duties as a porter at city hall. In the former capacity, he was expected to ride herd on any of "his people" who had business with the city. The two jobs were not incompatible in white thinking. None of these men were regular policemen, and most at one time or another did double-duty as janitors. As officers, it was always understood that they had no authority over white people. Jeff Daggett apparently did not understand this part of the job when he put on the badge. In 1909 he was severely beaten when he tried to stop and question two suspicious-looking white men in Douglass Park late one night. Henry Davis, on the other hand, knew his place. The *Star-Telegram* dubbed him "guardian of the peace" in the park. He had his own issues, however, when it came to the social order. In 1916 Davis pushed city fathers to officially recognize Juneteenth as a "special occasion" for the black community. No one had ever made such a request before, and not surprisingly it was turned down.[109]

For all the limitations attached to being a special officer, the position still carried a certain prestige in the black community. Edward Loving, who patrolled Douglass Park, was a confidante of both Hiram McGar and Thomas Mason, elite members of the black community and power-brokers in the Republican Party. He may have been just a lowly park officer to whites, but in the black community he was a respected figure who held the position of "Worshipful Master" in the local Masonic lodge.[110]

Jeff Daggett, perhaps because he had one foot in the white community and one foot in the black community, was appointed a special officer at a black nightclub in 1917. The job should have been an easy paycheck for the burly Daggett, but it got complicated on the night of October 17 when Tarrant County Detective Ben LeGett showed up demanding entrance. Daggett made the mistake of trying to keep him out and was severely beaten for it. A few days later he went down to the courthouse to file a complaint against LeGett, which ended when the Detective ambushed him in the elevator and shot him to death.

Jack Palmer was another black man who did not understand the unwritten rules of Jim Crow. His mistake was entertaining the delusion that he could be the equal of the white cops he saw walking their beat in his North Fort Worth neighborhood. He made a nuisance of himself around police headquarters seeking a job on the force. The cops considered him a "good negro," but that was not enough to get him a badge. On the contrary, they made fun of him as "Officer Jack," telling him if he saw any crimes just to arrest the lawbreaker and bring him on down to the station house. Jack missed the joke, and tried to make a citizen's arrest. He was shot and killed. Everyone in the department felt badly, but not enough to change their attitude about black policemen.[111]

In one of those strange contradictions of Jim Crow, the judicial system could also show compassion to black residents, so long as it did not threaten the status quo. In 1885 a street car on lower Main ran over and killed the six-year-old child of Mr. and Mrs. Allen Howard, a black couple. The parents filed suit against the Fort Worth Street Railway Company for $25,000, and in the subsequent jury trial the all-white jury found for the plaintiffs. However, in another sign of how Jim Crow worked, the jury placed only a $500 value on the boy's life, much less than the payout would have been for a white boy.[112]

Prosecutors were no friends to the black man. In 1902 the black porter at "one of the resorts in the Acre" was assaulted by a white customer and badly beaten. The unnamed porter, described in the newspaper as a "faithful negro," was popular with the bar's regular clientele who did not like to see "*their* Negro" mistreated. Based on their testimony, police arrested Sam Shrowder and charged him with aggravated assault. However, the case ran out of steam before it ever got to court because the county attorney refused to prosecute it. Even when cases got to court, judges often disposed of them informally, sometimes with nothing more than a stern lecture to the black defendant.[113]

White police were notoriously unsympathetic, and it did not matter whether they wore a Fort Worth uniform, North Fort Worth uniform, or Niles City uniform; they were all part of the same law enforcement culture. Things got worse, if that were possible, after 1915. That was the year FWPD officers resurrected the Ku Klux Klan, which had not been active in Fort Worth for forty years. By the end of the decade law enforcement had become a bastion of the reborn Klan. Membership in the Klan was practically prerequisite to be a member of either the police or sheriff's department. In 1921, the city's last lynch victim, Fred Rouse, got a taste of white vigilante justice. Hired as a strikebreaker by Swift & Co., he was confronted by white strikers while leaving work, pulled a pistol and shot two of them. The crowd beat him savagely enough to send him to the hospital. His life was saved by the intervention of the Niles City police who threw him into the back of an "express wagon" and took him to City-County Hospital. Even there he was still not safe. Five nights later a group of more than thirty "unmasked men," including two later identified as policemen, whisked him out of bed under the noses of the hospital staff and drove him out to Samuels Ave. There they strung him up to a hackberry tree and riddled his body with bullets. Both the police and sheriff's department promised a thorough investigation, but no one was ever prosecuted for the brazen killing. Fred Rouse was not just the last man lynched in Fort Worth, he was the *only* black man lynched in the city's history, a sad claim to fame.[114]

The police showed their contempt for blacks in more subtle ways, too, such as leading tours through the "Little Africa" section. Since most whites did not know any blacks, they regarded African Americans with the same curiosity as exotic animals in the zoo. A few beat cops ran a nice, little side-business taking bohemian types on guided tours through Little Africa.

For a black man arrested on the street, the trip to jail could be dangerous to his health. Officers had no compunction about working them over on the way. Once at the jail, the accused got his second lesson in the criminal justice system. Accommodations in the city jail (the basement of city hall) were extremely limited, so blacks and whites were confined together.

In the more spacious county jail, prisoners were assigned according to race and gender unless a white prisoner "misbehaved." Then he was put in the "negro cell" until he learned his lesson. A black prisoner who misbehaved was put in chains, and this was the practice until well into the twentieth century.[115]

Once in custody, black defendants were assumed to be guilty based on the logic that if they weren't guilty they would not have been accused. If their crime was against a white person they could expect the worst, if they even made it to court, which was hardly a sure thing. Sometimes they did not even make it to jail, or if they did they arrived more dead than alive. This kind of extracurricular brutality was justified by claiming the black victim had been defiant or resisted arrest. [116]

Lynching was a very real threat to every black man. Between 1882 and 1927, there were 370 known lynchings of African Americans in Texas. Most took place in rural communities where few blacks resided and justice was swift if not always legal. News of a lynching traveled fast. Just in October 1903, Fort Worth citizens could read about four lynchings of black men, two of them in Texas. Mob justice made good reading, and the more sensational the better. In 1915 a white mob in Temple, Texas, burned Will Stanley, a black man, alive, and the story was splashed across Fort Worth and Dallas newspapers within twenty-four hours. Fort Worth's black community did not even have to read the newspaper to be aware of what happened to black men who violated white laws *or* white ideas of right and wrong.[117]

Not even proper deference and law-abiding behavior could guarantee safety. The black community was always just one incident away from mob action. The threat was even the subject of sermons in black churches. In 1914 Mount Gilead Baptist's L.K. Williams appealed from the pulpit "to the white people of this country . . . to protect life and property and to put down lynching." He went on to draw a direct connection between the frequency of mob action in the South and the wholesale flight of blacks from the region.[118]

In misdemeanor cases the courts typically handed down jail time instead of fines so that black defendants could be assigned to the county farm or a work camp, which meant hard labor. Black women, even those convicted of trifling offenses, received the same sort of treatment. At the county jail, where white and black prisoners were separated, if there were twenty black prisoners and one white, the black prisoners were crammed into one cell while the white prisoner got a cell all to himself. It galled some officials that black female prisoners got to sit around all day "living it up" at the county's expense. They considered a bed, a roof over their heads, and two square meals a day living it up. In 1907 the county jailer proposed putting black female prisoners to "hard labor" on the work farm to earn their keep "instead of being a charge upon the county." Everyone except the county judge thought it a grand idea, and he only rejected it because at any given time there were not enough black female prisoners to justify hiring the additional guards to oversee them while they worked.[119]

Down the street at the city jail where whites and blacks were routinely locked up together, this violation of Jim Crow protocols did not arouse comment only because polite white society was generally unaware of it, at least before 1902. That was the year Progressive penal reformers launched a big drive to improve the horrible conditions in the jail. Near the top of the list of issues was "confining white and colored women" together in the same cell.[120]

The criminal justice system was more than just lockups. Black faces were never seen in a courtroom except as defendants. For many years, state law prohibited blacks from testifying against whites or sitting on juries. The prohibition against testifying had only recently been removed when Baptist preacher J. Frank Norris was put on trial for arson and perjury in 1912. The defense called John Lloyd Cooper, an African American who lived at the rear of First Baptist Church. His responses on the stand provoked so much mirth, Judge Tom Simmons warned those in the courtroom to cease their "demonstration." And both defense counsel and prosecution addressed the witness condescendingly as "John," not "Mr. Cooper."[121]

The mental health system was yet another black hole that could swallow up African Americans. Once they were ruled insane by a judge or jury they were locked up, and not in nice private sanitariums. If it were a civil commitment, they were lodged in the county jail until they were deemed fit to be released or could be transferred to one of the state hospitals. The nicer alternatives, private institutionalization or being placed in the care of family, were not really options for blacks. Incarceration in one of the state asylums, as bad as those were, was still preferable to the county jail, but as the *Star-Telegram* summed up the situation in 1907, there was simply "no room for them [blacks] in state institutions." (There was not enough room for white patients either.) In July of that year, the Tarrant County jailer reported three "colored lunatics" in his care. Two had been there three years with no expectation of being released any time soon and little likelihood of space opening up for them in one of the state institutions. The nearest, Terrell State Hospital for the Insane, had a backlog of 130 applications for "negro insane" from counties in north Texas, and as the director explained, "There are no accommodations for them, and probably will not be for some time." Translation: the existing state asylums were not accepting black commitments. The *Star-Telegram* called the situation "inhuman and cruel" and urged the legislature to do something about it. The legislature did nothing for three years, the explanation being that the budget "deficit" tied their hands.[122]

Finally, in 1910 the legislature appropriated funds to build a "negro ward" at the state asylum in Austin to house 100 patients, far fewer than were being held in county jails across the state. Still, Governor Thomas Mitchell Campbell announced proudly that counties all over the state would be able to "remove negro insane" from their jails. In September the new "negro ward" opened, only to be overwhelmed before the year was out with requests from sheriffs all over the state to transfer their black "lunatic" prisoners. One of those sheriffs hoping to clean out his jail was Tarrant County's O.M. Sweet.[123]

Nine years later Tarrant County had a different sheriff and a new, modern jail, but the same old problems. In the summer of 1919, Sheriff Sterling Clark had in his jail a black inmate, Anna Smith, who had been there for more than two years. On the few occasions she was allowed out of her cell she became "a raving maniac" despite the fact, as Sheriff Clark explained, "She was reared under the patronage of one of the wealthy families of Fort Worth and educated. . . . She speaks perfect English and is very quiet and docile" most of the time. Clark said he had begged the state's three "asylums" to accept her, but they all turned him down. Not until a new state asylum opened at Rusk in September 1919 was Anna Smith finally transferred to an institution where at least they were trained to deal with unfortunates like her. What happened to her ultimately is unknown, but Anna's case typifies how black mental patients were handled under Jim Crow. There was not even any attempt to maintain the pretense of "separate but equal." [124]

Anna Smith was a civil commitment. In cases of the criminally insane who also happened to be black there were no options, no choices. The decision on what to do with them was easy; they were shipped off to Huntsville penitentiary where they were segregated from the general population, being basically consigned to solitary confinement for life although they had broken none of the prison's rules. That was the only way to protect them from harm at the hands of the other inmates or from harming other inmates.

Another social problem that blurred the lines between the criminal justice and public health systems was the drug epidemic. It seemed to come out of nowhere around the turn of the century, taking the authorities by surprise. Fort Worth police had dealt with laudanum addicts and morphine suicides among the city's "working girls" for years, but this new epidemic had a frightening racial element to it. It was conventional wisdom that cocaine drove black men into a frenzy making them sexual predators and giving them superhuman strength. If the supply was not cut off they would become raging beasts. Any black who turned violent or killed indiscriminately was referred to by newspaper reports as "crazed," "half-crazed," or "demented." By the same token, any black man committing a particularly heinous crime was often said to have "run amuck."[125]

Opium also became a much bigger cause for concern after the turn of the century because it, too, produced subhuman "drug fiends." Some authorities made no distinction between opium and cocaine when it came to breaking down traditional morality. Said Sgt. Bill McCain, the FWPD's drug expert, "[Opium] gets 'em as quickly as cocaine." But for most whites, cocaine was the bigger threat to civilized society because of its effect on blacks. (Opium was considered a "Chinese problem.") The newspapers after 1900 were full of horrific stories of cocaine users *and* dealers in the black community. As far as the press was concerned, this was a "negro epidemic."[126]

Cocaine was a double curse for blacks. At 10¢ a hit it was legal and so cheap that even the poorest could afford it, plus the authorities targeted blacks as the biggest dealers and the most wanton users. Before federal legislation criminalized cocaine in 1913, anyone could go into a pharmacy and purchase it over the counter, no questions asked. Under state law it was only a crime to sell it to children. A Tarrant County grand jury in 1911 blamed black dealers for "peddling cocaine among school boys" in the city. The police, who were unfamiliar with the drug underworld, could not decide if blacks were just "runners" for white dealers or were running their own operations. Police Captain John Connelley leaned toward the former but justified the lack of arrests by saying "negro runners" were hard to nab because they were so sneaky and fast. And the problem was bigger than schoolboys; white family men were also buying the stuff from black pushers. According to Connelley, they could be found on street corners and back alleys in the Acre selling their vile product.[127]

To be sure, drug-dealing had a certain allure. It provided new entrepreneurial opportunities for a black underclass locked out of the white community when it came to legitimate business. And drug-dealing was not only highly profitable but color-blind! At the trial of a couple of white Fort Worth pharmacists in 1913 charged with selling cocaine in violation of the Harrison Act, a black witness testified that he was able to buy it easily at their east side pharmacy.[128]

Then there was Bertha Wallace, an African-American resident of the Acre, also the first entrepreneur of her race *and* gender in Fort Worth, who set herself up as a drug-dealer—at least until police nabbed her in 1915. Although no role model, Wallace was well on her way to becoming the next Madam C.J. Walker because she identified her market and satisfied a demand in the black community—only it was drugs instead of hair-care products. Wallace continued to do business even behind bars. She was caught trying to slip some of her product into the Tarrant County Jail.[129]

Bertha Wallace could not have done so well without black customers, a fact the white press picked up on immediately. The same muck-raking journalists who wrote about black madams and black drug-dealers found plenty of black "coke fiends" and "coke hotels" in the lower portion of the city, specifically between Fourteenth and Fifteenth streets. One exposé by an unnamed reporter described how he forced his way into a "negro cabin" in the Acre looking for coke addicts. White muckrakers found plenty of material for their exposés in the underworld known as the Acre. Users included "big, black bucks" and hard-working washer-women. One *Dallas Morning News* story described an "enormous underground traffic. . . [where] any negro who can scrape together a few cents can get a supply whenever he wishes it." The over-heated reports fed the new stereotype of the deranged black driven mad by "excessive use of cocaine." Identifying the cocaine problem with blacks relieved the authorities from having to deal with the bigger problems of drug availability, white addiction, and treatment of the problem. It was easier just to lock up blacks and throw away the key.[130]

Ironically, the drug epidemic created common ground for blacks and whites. Police reports revealed that the two races were teaming up to distribute illegal drugs. White druggists cheerfully sold to black users and vice versa; black "runners" worked for white drug lords; and blacks and white pushers divided up the turf. Exhibit A in this unseemly racial alliance was W.L. Avery and J.D. Williams. In 1914 police arrested the pair for operating a "coke house" in the Acre. Avery was white and Williams was black.[131]

The passage of the first federal anti-drug law in 1913, the Harrison Act, provided an unexpected benefit to Southern law enforcement. Now any black person arrested on drug charges could be turned over to United States officers for prosecution, and upon conviction they were incarcerated in federal prison. State and local officials could thus wash their hands of one booming form of crime.

The arrival of national Prohibition in 1919 diverted some attention from the drug problem. Bootlegging and making moonshine now joined the list of highly profitable criminal enterprises. Blacks were no more likely to be bootleggers and moonshiners than they were drug-dealers, but judging from the newspapers they were a lot more likely to be nabbed by the police. Going down to the south end of town and purchasing a little moonshine whiskey from a black street dealer was a popular way for white gentlemen to get their hooch. In January 1919 Fort Worth police and federal agents nabbed a gang of "professional negroes" running a sophisticated bootlegging operation that stretched from Monroe, Louisiana, through Fort Worth and all the way to Waco. A black undertaker in Monroe would get a death certificate from a black physician that allowed him to ship a "body" to Fort Worth or some other spot in Texas. Then instead of a corpse, he would fill the coffin with moonshine. It was apparently a sweet operation until uncovered by the authorities. The operation's best customers, it turned out, were not blacks, but whites who could afford to pay top dollar for premium Louisiana moonshine. This is a prime example of how black and white society collaborated in the criminal underworld even while maintaining the façade of Jim Crow segregation.[132]

Politics

Like all other aspects of life under Jim Crow—medical care, social services, and the justice system—politics was tightly controlled by whites. Blacks had been able to vote in general elections since 1870 (thanks to the 15th Amendment to the Constitution), but after 1876 there was only one political party that mattered in Texas, the Democratic Party, and elections were won or lost in the party primary, not the general election. Whoever won the Democratic primary was practically guaranteed to win the general election, and the Democratic primaries were lily-white by law after 1905. In 1902, the state legislature had also made paying a poll tax mandatory to vote, which had the effect of keeping poor blacks who might vote Republican away from the polls at general elections.[133]

After the turn of the century, President Theodore Roosevelt attempted to create a "black-and-tan" alliance inside the party of Abraham Lincoln, but practically the only blacks to actually benefit were a few community leaders like Bill McDonald, R.L. Griffin, and Hiram McGar whom, it was believed, could get out the black vote for the Grand Old Party come election time. What the white Republican leadership did not realize was that too many obstacles had been erected to keep blacks away from the polls no matter what party they identified with. Furthermore, the black vote was not monolithic any more than the white vote was, nor could one or two men mobilize it by snapping their fingers.

The Republican Party in Texas was so marginalized that its leaders jumped on the Jim Crow bandwagon in an effort to appeal to more white voters. At a meeting in Dallas in October 1919 they voted to expel blacks en masse from the state organization. Said the party chairman,

> We have made a start to enlist greater support by eliminating the negro from active participation in our councils and activity. I

> believe the negro influence to have been a most detrimental one to the party and am glad we have at last taken a stand as a white man's organization.[134]

Thus in one fell swoop Republican leaders ended the "black-and-tan" experiment in state politics, consigning men like Bill McDonald, R.L. Griffin, and Hiram McGar to the sidelines. They would never again have a voice in the party they had grown up in. The following year the Republican National Committee had something to say about this when they met in San Antonio for the national convention. They flatly refused to seat the "Lily White" Texas delegation, which included Fort Worth's J.H. Mumbower, a spokesman for the Lily Whites. Unbowed, Mumbower told the hometown paper that, "Under black leadership, the Republican party in Texas had no future. . . The negro must get off the rostrum and sit in the gallery. . . . The scepter of rulership must be in the hands of white men." He went on to say that anyone attempting to "eliminate the color line" was a "party outlaw and will be treated as such."[135]

The Republican action changed the rules of the game but did not change the political balance of power in the state. Democrats continued to rule and were as determined as their Republican brethren to keep blacks at arms' length. A state law passed by the Democratic-dominated legislature in 1923 stated that "in no event shall a Negro be eligible to participate in a Democratic primary election in the State of Texas," underscoring the seriousness with which white legislators took the matter by adding, "Should a Negro vote in a Democratic primary election, such a ballot shall be void and election officials shall not count the same." They could not have made it any plainer. Following a court challenge, the law was repealed in 1927, only to be replaced with another saying the same thing in different language: "Every political party in this State through its State Executive Committee [shall be the judge of] the qualifications of its own members." That law passed judicial scrutiny.[136]

When it came to the "Negro vote" in general elections, both parties welcomed the vote of any black man who could navigate all the obstacles to voting. J.H. Mumbower told the *Star-Telegram*, "We welcome . . . every good citizen who will vote our ticket." It did not really matter which party held the "scepter of rulership" in Texas; blacks were only permitted to exercise the franchise when their vote could be leveraged for some political advantage. As Hannah Mullins, an interviewee for the Works Progress Administration (WPA) "Slave Narratives" in 1937 recalled,

> The only time whites like black folks. . . is votin' time. The whites say, "You vote like we tells you and things go all right for you."[137]

Exclusion from the ranks of the two state party organizations did not mean that blacks dropped out of politics altogether or meekly accepted the status quo. They redoubled their efforts on the local level. Some black residents of Fort Worth were braver or more assertive than others. In 1897 a group of black leaders calling themselves the Afro-American Citizens' Conference met to discuss running a "colored man's representative" from the Third Ward for city council. (That was the ward where the majority of the city's black population lived.) They held their meeting in city hall, which in spite of Jim Crow, was a center of black public life, whether it was revivals on the lawn or meetings in the auditorium. In the end, nothing came of the proposal because whites were still a majority in the Third Ward and even if they had not been, blacks could not translate their numbers into political power at this date.[138]

The Progressive movement of the early twentieth century did not significantly benefit African Americans despite the creation of the National Association for the Advancement of Colored People in 1909 as one of the era's signal accomplishments. Blacks could wear the label "progressive" just like whites—W.E.B. DuBois was their hero—and when President Roosevelt came to town in April 1905 both races turned out to see Progressivism's best-known champion. The president was guest of honor in a parade through downtown, and stationed on the parade route was a choir of 600 black schoolchildren who serenaded him with the "Star-Spangled Banner." Roosevelt seemed genuinely touched when one of them "ran from the crowd. . . and thrust a bouquet" into his hands.

Afterwards, while the president and his hosts continued their festivities, the children returned to their segregated schoolhouses. In the same spirit of progressivism, inspired by the examples of colleges like Paul Quinn and Wiley, Fort Worth black leaders in 1909 secured a site six miles west of town to build their own "colored college." The dream was never realized, but had it been built it might have become one of the seven historically black colleges in Texas today. [139]

Personal safety came before voting rights, economic opportunity, and all other goals of the black community. While Fort Worth's dominant white community was more tolerant than many across the South, blacks still had to be careful not to provoke the authorities, meaning specifically the police. In 1892, a black sporting man, Jim Burris (aka, Jim Toots), had a confrontation on the street with Officer Lee Waller over a woman. Waller knocked him down and even shot at him when he jumped up and ran off. Both men rounded up their pals and went looking for each other that same night. They found each other, and in the ensuing shoot-out Waller was killed. The police department and a mob of white vigilantes were incensed, tearing the black district apart looking for Burris. More killing was narrowly avoided as black residents locked themselves indoors and prayed. Eventually, Burris was brought to justice and sentenced to life in the penitentiary, but the episode illustrated how fragile a thread black peace and safety dangled by. In October 1906, with the Burris episode and similar cases in mind, Texas black leaders met in Fort Worth to organize the Negro Protection Congress of Texas (NPCT). The founders were careful to emphasize that they were strictly a "benevolent" organization with no political or religious agenda.[140]

The gradual breakdown of Jim Crow politics came in small, baby steps. In 1925 Fort Worth adopted a form of municipal civil service to take political patronage out of some city jobs, namely positions in the fire and police departments. Theoretically, henceforward, employment would be based on an applicant's score on a color-blind, non-partisan test. But city jobs were still white men's jobs (and a few women) for the next two-and-a-half decades. Blacks were simply prohibited from taking the tests. It was not until the 1950s that those civil service tests became an entry into a job with the city, starting with the police, fire, and park departments.[141]

Transportation

It was in this era that what we think of as Jim Crow rules were introduced for the first time in local transportation, meaning city street cars. Fort Worth had possessed a street car line since 1877, expanding in the years that followed until it became a system that consisted of multiple short, privately owned lines crisscrossing the city. The main line on Main St. was electrified in 1890 and the network grew outward as new lines were built to the suburbs, but all the lines were always privately owned (franchises). By 1905 most of the system had been consolidated under the umbrella of the Northern Texas Traction Company (NTTC) with its headquarters in the Jett Building on the corner of Third and Main.[142]

That was the year the city stepped in to set riding rules. Heretofore, there had been no rules; anybody could ride, standing or sitting, and jump off whenever they wished. But sentiment had been building for several years to segregate the cars. In the spring of 1905 several petitions from white citizens were taken up by the city council. The Judiciary Committee did a feasibility study which included asking the NTTC to determine "the percentage of negroes" riding the cars, and reported to the full council in July. Out of the resulting discussion came City Ordinance No. 944 in October requiring "the separation of white and negro passengers on the street cars of the city of Fort Worth." A press release offered this explanation: "The indiscriminate seating and co-mingling of white and negro passengers on street cars causes affrays [and] disturbances of the peace, and makes travel thereon unsafe and insecure." Henceforward, every street car operator in the city would have to separate passengers by race with white riders filling up the seats from the front and black riders from the back. In the event of a full car blacks would have to give up their seats and either ride in the back standing or get off and catch another car. The ordinance included fines of $5 to $25 for violators, whether riders or conductors, for not enforcing the law. The ordinance was enacted without the signature of Mayor Thomas Powell under an obscure provision of the city charter. Why Powell did not sign off on it is unknown. Two additional curiosities related to the ordinance were: 1) the exact definition of the term "negro" was referred to state law, thereby avoiding the touchy legal issue of determining how to apply it to persons of mixed race; and 2) exceptions were allowed for white passengers traveling with black nurses and white officers transporting black prisoners.[143]

A new chapter had opened in the local history of Jim Crow, and not just in Fort Worth. That same year, Dallas adopted "separate seating" on street cars. The surprising thing is not that such ordinances were passed at this time but why city fathers had not seen it as a problem in all the previous years. Henceforward, on street cars first and later on city buses, wooden plaques were placed on one of the seat backs, with "Whites" on one side and "Colored" on the other. The signs could be moved forward or back depending on "whether African Americans were filling up the back seats or whites the front seats."[144]

That Was Entertainment

Black entertainment was both a reminder of blacks' second-class status and a bridge between the black and white communities. All large public events like the annual Fat Stock Show, the State Fair (Dallas), and the Texas Spring Palace set aside special "Colored Days," which was more about cashing in on the black market than serving the principle of equality. Naturally, whites could attend on Colored Day, but the same privilege did not extend to blacks on other days Another reminder of second-class status was the chronic shortage of public space. Black groups had to beg for borrowed spaces or meet in churches. Things got a little better after 1907 when the Prince Hall Masonic Lodge opened on East Ninth. The meeting room on the second floor was available to rent for a modest sum. The Masons would come through even better in 1924 when they built a "Grand Lodge Mosque" on East First that could accommodate 3,000 people. Thanks to the Prince Hall Masons, no longer did Fort Worth blacks have to go begging for meeting space.

While the white community looked down on black social gatherings, they loved black entertainers. For years, one of the most popular local entertainments was the annual "Old Fiddlers' Contest" sponsored by the Julia Jackson Chapter of the United Daughters of the Confederacy to raise money for aging Confederate veterans. At the 1901 contest, the high point of the show was some "Old-time Darkey music" performed by a couple of talented African-American fiddlers, Sam Green of Tarrant County and Ran Vesey of Decatur. The newspaper the next day described the two contestants, who were competing for a nice prize, as "the best old darkey fiddlers" around; Sam was a "good-looking mulatto," while Ran was a "pitch-black 'old-timer' who says he is 72 years old." When the pair got down to some serious fiddling, the audience whooped and hollered, enjoying it even more than they did the earlier white contestants. The audience included both ladies and gentlemen, so this was not some crude, boys-night-out.[145]

Old-style minstrel shows really brought out a white crowd. The performers could be either white performers in black face or even black performers, but either way, they sang and danced in highly stylized fashion to the delight of white audiences. The leading impresario of such shows at the turn of the century was Al G. Field, a Pennsylvania-born white man who started a traveling minstrel company in 1886 and was still on the road forty years later. The act went through several permutations, one of which, the Al G. Field Real Negro Minstrels, consisted of what the advertising called, "40 genuine Southern negroes, representatives of Darkest America." They performed old-style plantation songs with "real Negro eccentricities" to the delight of white audiences across the country.[146]

Field brought his troupe to Fort Worth many times, appearing at Byers' (aka Greenwall's) Opera House, and in the Chamber of Commerce auditorium. For his Fort Worth appearances he used only white actors in black face out of deference to local sensibilities until 1903 when he brought along a black man, John Blackford, who was billed as "the crack colored comedian in the country." White ticket-buyers were assured, "There is nothing coarse or ribald in Blackford's work." Playing to white audiences, the Field minstrel troupe always sold out the house wherever they played. They played Fort Worth every year for more than two decades, during which visits the black community said nothing publicly even as well-heeled white audiences laughed uproariously. The company also played Dallas whenever they came through the area, and during their 1907 appearance, they were followed on the stage of Dallas' Majestic Theater by a performance of Thomas Dixon's *The Clansman*, a dramatization of the novel that became the basis for D.W. Griffith's *Birth of a Nation* film classic eight years later.[147]

Polk Miller, considered by some to be "the best living interpreter" of Southern black culture in his day, sang and played banjo and told dialect stories. The Sons of Confederate Veterans and United Daughters of the Confederacy brought him to Fort Worth to perform on several occasions, and he never failed to pack the city hall auditorium. Miller, of course was white.[148]

Miller and Field were so popular, they inspired local imitators. The Fort Worth Police Benevolent Association began putting on an annual, black-face minstrel show as a fund-raising event until well into the 1920s. White cops adopted what the newspaper called "appropriate darky dialect," although method actors they were not. The talent level was not up to Field's troupe, and the performances did not even measure up to what appeared on the I.M. Terrell High School stage. But supposedly the cause was a good one (retired and disabled police officers), and it was all in good fun. The same folks who turned out en masse to support

Ku Klux Klan parades through downtown in the 1920s had no trouble supporting black-face minstrel shows.[149]

Well-heeled white Fort Worth audiences did not see an African American on stage in a serious drama until 1909 when *The Gentleman from Mississippi* played Greenwall's Opera House that fall. To add a "natural element" to this extremely popular play, the producers used black actors "for the parts of negro servants." The fact that they had speaking parts is attested by the theater critic of the *Star-Telegram* who called it "a decided relief. . . to a Southern audience to see the [servants'] parts thus taken instead of being caricatured by an actor with a Manhattan accent." All told, it was a "novel stage experience" for a Fort Worth audience. Unfortunately, that audience was all white; blacks could only read about it in the newspaper.[150]

Jim Crow segregation was not a hard, fast line when it came to entertainment because whites could appreciate black talent, in particular musical and athletic talent (so long as the latter did not compete in the ring or on the field against white athletes). Black minstrel troupes, ragtime-piano players, and child performers were especially popular with white audiences. Black musical talent was held in such high regard, teachers and performers often wore the handle "Professor," which was an honorary title, not a degreed title. Fort Worth had at least two well-known black professors of music, Phil R. Register, who ran a popular music store and school on the east side, and W.M. Nix, who taught piano to black students and tuned pianos for a white clientele.[151]

Boxing and baseball were two sports that appealed across racial lines. In March 1919 Fort Worth promoters arranged a "battle royal" in the ring between "some of the best negro sluggers" in town. The *Star-Telegram* trumpeted the event as a fund-raiser for a Theodore Roosevelt memorial. (The former president had just died.) We can be certain the promoters were not staging the event for black fight fans. The same can be said of black actors and musicians. The performers on the stage might be black, but it was the faces on the other side of the footlights that told the real story. Not only were audiences white, but all the major venues and booking agencies were also owned by whites. Jim Crow entertainment was a one-way street.[152]

Most black stage performers that white Fort Worth audiences saw were not professionals; they were local talent. They were high school students, their teachers, and church choirs. The performances relied heavily on black stereotypes with jigs, plantation songs, and spirituals filling most programs. Marcelite Terrell, who taught alongside her husband, Isaiah M. Terrell, was the black music teacher in the public schools for many years. She staged the first public performance of her students' talents in 1885, billed as an evening of black "comedies and songs." The show was a big hit with the white audience, and she continued to stage similar events. In 1906 she pulled out all the stops, putting on a cantata in the city hall auditorium using all local talent. Her musical programs were such a success, the school board appointed her "Supervisor of Music" when the Colored High School opened in 1907. It was the only other titled position at the school besides her husband's ("principal").[153]

Music was not the only diversion available to blacks during Jim Crow. Sports was another way to forget one's troubles. Over the decades "sports" had come to be more than a euphemism for gentlemen gamblers; it meant mass-appeal athletic contests. And black entrepreneurs early recognized that sporting events were entertainment. Years before Negro League Baseball appeared, the Rev. J.L. Griffin was bringing along a Dallas "colored" baseball team on his revival tours through north Texas. Griffin preached, and his boys played the local team in a friendly nine-inning contest. His revivals were always big events.[154]

The most popular organized sport was baseball, which may have been as all-American as apple pie, but was still subject to Jim Crow rules. The Negro Leagues, which arose during this era, brought joy and a sense of pride to African Americans on every social level. Texas was a hotbed of Negro League baseball right from the beginning, and Fort Worth was one of the principal stops on the circuit. The Black Wonders, who began as the Yellow Jackets, were Fort Worth's team of home-grown players, and had a strong fan base. Baseball historians have tended to focus on the 1920s and '30s as the heyday of black baseball in Texas, but the foundation for those golden years was laid more than a decade before. Tyler-born Louis Santop, the first great African-American home-run hitter, began his playing career in 1909 with the Black Wonders. The team did not have nice uniforms or a nice ballpark, but they had talent and a loyal following. In 1910 a traveling black all-star team played the local boys before a crowd of more than 3,000 fans that included both black and white fans.[155]

When white, minor-league baseball took off in Fort Worth in the 1920s, black baseball hitched its star to the white game as both a business and sporting enterprise. The white Fort Worth Panthers (aka, the "Cats") won six consecutive Texas League championships, and the team's owners built a suitable new park on North Main in 1926. Three years later it was renamed LaGrave Field in honor of the man who had brought winning baseball to the city. The ballpark was one of the finest in the minor leagues with bleachers seating more than 10,000. When the Cats were not playing at home, Will Stripling and Paul LaGrave let the Negro Baseball League use it for their games. In another example of cross-over marketing, sometimes the Cats booked black bands to entertain the fans. Sam Leach, a local black entrepreneur, arranged the bookings. Since the stands were filled with white fans, the only way a black man could get into the park was as part of the entertainment. During the Depression when the money was no longer rolling in and the Cats were losing more games than they were winning, both black and white minor-league baseball declined, but they left behind a legacy of excellence and a slew of legends.[156]

JEFF DAGGETT—CAUGHT BETWEEN TWO WORLDS[157]

Jeff Daggett was the anti-Hiram McGar. Both men were mulatto, but Daggett spent his adult life angry, breaking the law, picking fights, defying authority. As was usually the case in mulatto unions, his mother was a slave and his father was a member of the master's family. He was born in 1864 to Matilda Smith and Ephraim "Bud" Daggett on the Daggett plantation in Tarrant County. His paternal grandfather was Captain Ephraim M. Daggett, remembered in history as the "Father of Fort Worth." Bud was the only son of Captain Daggett and Pheniba Strauss Daggett. His mother died when he was very young. His father remarried, but Bud was raised by a beloved black mammy. With Captain Daggett away quite often on business, Bud by default became the man of the house. Matilda's place in the household is unknown, but after emancipation she stayed on with the family as both a servant and more than a servant.

Bud Daggett played no role in raising his mulatto son. His own father, the Captain, wrote Bud completely out of his will for reasons that are not clear, perhaps related to the fact that Bud was a notorious hell-raiser. Jeff was also an outcast, but not for anything he did growing up. Unlike many mulattos, he could not pass for white; his features and complexion were very clearly African-American. He lived in the servants' quarters, and his only family was his mother. When it came time to go out on his own, the only thing he took with him from his father was his last name. Around town, everyone knew that Jeff was the offspring of the Daggett clan, but nobody spoke of it publicly. Jeff's conflicted feelings on the subject can be seen in the fact that for the rest of his life, he used both "Daggett" and "Smith" as last names, never settling on one or the other. If he ever needed reminding what he was, he had only to roll up his sleeve and see tattooed on one burly arm, "J.D.S." for Jefferson Daggett Smith.

Jeff was a fireplug of a man, 5-feet 3-inches tall and weighing 174 pounds. The chip he carried around on his shoulder added a few more pounds. He spent his time in Hell's Half-acre gambling, drinking, and brawling with all comers. He laid out more than a few men with his fists, and he lost a few fights, too. The police knew him well, and he was quite familiar with the inside of the jail, doing time for disturbing the peace, petty theft, and aggravated assault. The *Dallas Morning News* in 1889 called him a "Third Ward celebrity" (Third Ward was another name for the Acre). He preferred to think of himself as a "sporting man," because gambling was his vocation. Jeff was lacking in formal education, but he had a good head on his shoulders. He could also be charming when he desired.

The Daggett plantation was his home until 1883 when the Captain died. Jeff moved out and at nineteen he was on his own. He married a mulatto woman named Hester, and they set up house in "Irish Town," the black section on the eastern edge of the Acre. They had three children, all of whom died or left town by 1910.

As a father and husband, Jeff did not win any awards, but he became more respectable, opening a gambling joint in the Acre where he was both the owner and bouncer. The tools of his trade, besides cards and dice, included a blackjack and a .45 caliber pistol. On the side he worked for the police as an informant, fingering pickpockets and "Wanted" men among the Acre's colorful population. Being a "snitch" helped protect his own shady operation from police harassment.

Neither his family name nor police connections could protect him in 1889 when he shot and killed Dick Vann, a rival gambler described as "half Comanche and half Negro." He was indicted for second-degree murder. To their credit, his white family hired a good (white) lawyer to defend him. He fought the charges through the courts until 1892 when he ran out of appeals and was sentenced to the state penitentiary for ten years. He was paroled after two years and returned to Fort Worth where he reinvented himself for the third time. Hester had waited for him and apparently the time in prison had changed him for the better. He found his niche as a Republican Party stalwart and community activist in the Third Ward. He put the gambler's life behind him and found honest if less remunerative employment as a "porter" and private security guard ("special officer"). The latter gave him the right to wear a badge and carry a gun although technically he was not a policeman. Once when he tried to question two white men, they severely beat him, and when the police showed up they beat him again for having the temerity to accost white men. When the police department revoked his special officer's commission, he went back to what he knew best, the saloon business.

This saloonman-turned-janitor-turned-saloonman still had politics. Jeff attended the 1904 Republican county convention as representative of the Third Ward. His family name did not hurt when it came to rubbing shoulders with the party's white power-brokers, but any future he might have had in politics dried up after the lily-whites seized control of the Republican party in Texas.

By 1917 Jeff had acquired another special officer's commission to work as an "out-guard" (bouncer) at a black saloon in Irish Town. On Saturday night, October 20, Tarrant County Detective Ben LeGett tried to push his way past Daggett. When Daggett resisted, LeGett pistol-whipped him. Jeff did not know what hit him, and by the time he came to, his assailant was gone. He huffed and puffed for a few days, then on October 23 he went down to the courthouse to file a formal complaint. For once in his life he was following the rules. The good, old boys around the courthouse looked askance at the black man wandering the halls looking for someone to hear his complaint. Ben LeGett was also in the building that day and heard that Jeff was trying to make trouble for him. He cornered Daggett in the elevator on the first floor, and without saying a word, pulled out a pistol and pumped three bullets into him. Jeff was unarmed and died where he stood. They carried his body downstairs where a justice of the peace conducted a perfunctory inquest before releasing LeGett on a $1,000 bond. Two days later, Jeff Daggett was laid to rest in the Trinity section of Oakwood Cemetery.

Public opinion was overwhelmingly on LeGett's side. The newspapers characterized the victim as a brawler and a bully who had killed at least two or three men. At the trial in November 1918, LeGett's lawyers showed that Jeff had publicly threatened their client, which under Texas law justified LeGett shooting Daggett, whether the latter was armed or not. The prosecution did not put up much of a fight. The trial lasted just one day, and the all-white jury brought back the expected verdict of "not guilty."

Jeff Daggett was a sad man who got a raw deal at birth and spent the rest of his life making it worse. To his credit, he took on the world on its terms and never asked for anything. He was resourceful enough to carve out a niche in the rough-and-tumble worlds of politics **and** the saloon business, yet his self-destructive behavior set him on a path to destruction. Under different circumstances, Jefferson Daggett might have been a successful sporting gentleman and ward heeler, but there was no place for a black man with a large chip on his shoulder in turn-of-the-century Fort Worth.

Notes

1. The black community's "undertaker/embalmer/funeral director" for many years was all in the hands of Robert C. Houston, Jr. The lack of support structure explains why today there are no burial records for either Old Trinity or New Trinity cemeteries, and only the sketchiest idea of who's buried where. The only surviving burial records belong to Baker Funeral Home (black). For Houston, see *Colored City Directory.* For New Trinity Cemetery, see historic marker, 4001 NE 28th St., Haltom City. For public cemetery debate, see Mayor and Council Proceedings, Box 5 (May 30, 1911), and Box 10 (May 12, 1914).
2. Fourteenth and Fifteenth United States Federal Censuses (1920 and 1930), Fort Worth, Tarrant County, Texas, on microfilm.
3. Fort Worth's population explosion during these years is reviewed in *Fort Worth: 1849–1949, 100 Years of Progress* (Fort Worth: Chamber of Commerce, 1949), 21. For black figures, see Lady George Munchus-Forde, "History of the Negro in Fort Worth—Syllabus for a High School Course" (M.A. Thesis, Education Dept., Fisk University, Nashville, TN., 1941), p. 38. In 1907, James A. Hamilton calculated that "about one-sixth" of the total population of "over 50,000" was "colored." Hamilton, *History and Directory,* 34. D. N. McCutcheon was the 1926 visitor in a letter to his wife in Detroit. Author's collections. For Chamber of Commerce figures, see "Fort Worth and the Billion-Dollar Circle: Cotton, Cattle, Grain, Oil," Fort Worth Chamber of Commerce publication, May 1920, in collections of Dalton Hoffman of Fort Worth. For 6 percent, see *Fort Worth Star-Telegram,* May 29, 1921.
4. Figures for Dallas and Texas come from *Dallas Morning News,* February 18, 1916. Fort Worth's total population in 1910 was 73,312, rising to 106,874 by 1920. Paddock, *Fort Worth and Texas Northwest,* Vol. 2, p. 835.
5. Source for snapshot numbers is letter of D.N. McCutcheon to wife, September 8, 1926. (McCutcheon was in town for a convention.) The white city directories of the day are unreliable for information on black residents and businesses. Author's collections.
6. Ward, "Panther City Progressives," 16; *Fort Worth Morning Register,* September 13, 1901.
7. For McCauley, see *Fort Worth Morning Record,* March 25, 1907. For Macbeth, see Hamilton, *History and Directory,* 39.

8. Nell Irvin Painter, *Southern History across the Color Line* (Chapel Hill: University of North Carolina Press, 2002), 113.
9. Hamilton, *History and Directory*, 40; *Fort Worth Telegram*, March 3, 1907 (advertisement on p. 5).
10. Richard Selcer, "When Streetcars Roamed Fort Worth," *Fort Worth Magazine* 15, no. 12 (December 2012): 58–93; and Jan Batts, "On the Shores of Lake Como," ibid.,Vol. 9, no. 8 (August 2006): 110.
11. Libby Willis, "History of the Oakhurst Neighborhood, Fort Worth, Texas," unpublished address, 2006, in author's files.
12. *Fort Worth Star-Telegram*, May 6, 1916.
13. *Fort Worth Star-Telegram*, January 21 and May 3, 1901; February 1, 1920; Rich, *Fort Worth*, 101.
14. *Fort Worth Star-Telegram*, October 16, 1919. For changes in city fire limits, see *Fort Worth Telegram*, July 22, 1905. In 1959 the bricks on Calhoun were finally pulled up and the street was paved over with asphalt, but this was only done after the street had become an embarrassment to the city. *Fort Worth Press*, October 30, 1959. For Paddock, see *Fort Worth Star-Telegram*, January 14, 1920.
15. Stick Town cannot be pinpointed, but it was in the river bottoms northeast of the North Side community. Sohmer, "Rock Island Bottom," 1–2. For 1908 flood, see *Fort Worth Telegram*, April 18, 20, and 21, 1908. For impact of flooding and photographs, see Bob Ray Sanders, *Calvin Littlejohn: Portrait of a Community in Black and White* (Fort Worth: TCU Press, 2009), 80–83, henceforward, Sanders, *Calvin Littlejohn*.
16. For 1915 flood, see *Fort Worth Star-Telegram*, June 14, 1915.
17. Hamilton, *History and Directory*, 34, 40.
18. For Williams, see *Fort Worth Telegram*, October 17, 1907; *Fort Worth Morning Register*, November 25, 1911.
19. For the chronic ills of black neighborhoods, see "Mosier Valley Study," 1. For the problem with getting the utilities to serve a black neighborhood, see the example of Quality Grove as late as 1920. *Fort Worth Star-Telegram*, August 31, 1920.
20. Martin died in 1914. This information comes from the John Edward Martin Papers, Tarrant County Archives. The area where Martin and his family lived on Crump St. was later purchased for the Butler Housing Project, and is today underneath the North-South Freeway (I-35). A "scalawag" in Southern vernacular was any Southerner after the Civil War who cooperated with the hated Yankee carpetbaggers.

21. Flemmings lived at 1233 E. Humboldt, Ransom at 1115 E. Terrell, Coleman at 1064 E. Humboldt, and Pryor at 1064 E. Humboldt. See Fort Worth City Directories. Hamilton, *History and Directory*, 40; *Dallas Morning News*, March 14, 1925.
22. *Dallas Morning News*, March 14, 1925.
23. *Fort Worth Press*, July 10, and October 10 and 20, 1925; *Dallas Morning News*, October 11, 1925.
24. *Dallas Morning News*, October 11, 1925; March 25 and July 12, 1926.
25. Reporting on the Fort Worth bombings of 1925–26 was scant; they were covered by the *Fort Worth Press* but not the *Star-Telegram*, and by the *Dallas Morning News*, which always seemed to take delight in reporting the darker side of Fort Worth. The big story in the newspapers on the same the day as the October 10 bombing was the opening of the State Fair in Dallas. *Fort Worth Press*, October 10, 1925.
26. Fort Worth Telegram, May 26 and August 30, 1907.
27. For cost to build a house, see "Rosen Heights" section in "Suburban News" column of *Fort Worth Telegram*, July 27, 1906.
28. J'Nell Pate, *North of the River* (Fort Worth: Texas Christian University Press, 1994), 38, 40-47. Bill Fairley, "From Russia to Cowtown," *Fort Worth Star-Telegram*, July 30, 1997; *Fort Worth Telegram*, January 4 and October 17, 1907; *Fort Worth Star-Telegram*, August 23, 1909; May 12, 1914; August 3, 1919 (advertisement, p. 9); January 15 and August 31, 1920. The advertising was pitched to "colored people."
29. Jan Batts, "On the Shores of Lake Como," *Fort Worth Magazine* 9, no. 8 (August 2006): 110; *Dallas Morning News*, April 25, 1908.
30. *Fort Worth Star-Telegram*, May 17, 1913; Hamilton, *History and Directory*, 38. For riot, see Selcer and Foster, *Written in Blood 2*, 39–87.
31. No details exist of this meeting to know how many attended or who they were. *Dallas Morning News*, April 18, 1901.
32. Fort Worth's Colored High School first appears in the 1907–08 *City Directory*. Its progress thereafter, including changes in name and location, can be followed through the city directories. Thomas Hine, *The Rise and Fall of the American Teenager* (New York: Avon Books, 1999), 198. For "character," see Doggett, "Survey," 112.
33. Until 1909, Riverside Colored School was on Park Ave. one block south of Ennis; Marine was two blocks east of Grunewald Park; Washington Heights was on Refugio Ave. (North Fort Worth); and Prairie Chapel was on South Johns, four blocks west of 12th Ave. *Fort Worth City Directory*, 1902-03, 1904-05, 1905-06, 1907-08, and 1909-10. *Fort Worth Telegram*,

April 17, 1906. The *Fort Worth Telegram* of October 17, 1907 incorrectly calls the Yellow Row School "Quality Grove." For Riverside in particular, see Susan Allen Kline, application for historic marker for Riverside [Colored] School, 1999, Sec. 8, pp. 11-17, Billy W. Sills Center for Archives, Fort Worth Independent School District, Fort Worth, TX, hereafter cited as Kline, marker application.

34. For comparative cost of buildings, see *Fort Worth City Directory*, 1888–89 ("History of the Fort Worth school system"); and "Chronology of the FWISD," Housewright. For Ninth Ward Elementary, see interview with Regina Farr Ross in Bob Ray Sanders, "Fourth of July Very Special for One FW Woman," *Fort Worth Star-Telegram*, July 2, 2014. For "design," see Doggett, "Survey," 24.
35. *Fort Worth Star-Telegram*, March 19, 1908 and March 23, 1909.
36. Teacher-training institutes were called "normal schools" and considered a step below degree-granting colleges. Hamilton, *History and Directory*, 42. Dana Goldstein, *The Teacher Wars* (New York: Doubleday, 2014), 24–25, hereafter, Goldstein, *Teacher Wars*. Cone Johnson lost the election although his radical teachers' proposal was not the only reason. *Dallas Morning News*, April 17, 1908.
37. Doggett, "Survey," 31–32. *Fort Worth Star-Telegram*, March 23, June 19, and December 12, 1909. In 1938 I.M. Terrell High School would move into the Chambers Hill/East Eighteenth St. building with a little help from the Works Progress Administration to enlarge and remodel it.
38. Mrs. I.M. Terrell was the school's "supervisor of music" See *Fort Worth City Directory*, 1907–08. For Washington, see *Fort Worth Star-Telegram*, December 12, 1909. Program of I.M. Terrell High School "All Student" Reunion of 1985, TCBH&GS, Series II (Individual Collections), Box 1, File 4.
39. Guinn Elementary was the largest black school in the segregated Fort Worth school system in 1930. A Texas State historical marker was dedicated at the James E. Guinn School on October 12, 1986. For the history of the school and the ceremony, see marker application, Tarrant County Archives and *Fort Worth Star-Telegram*, November 4, 1988.
40. Kline, marker application, p. 15. "De-segregation of Fort Worth Schools," undated 1920s newspaper clipping in vertical files at Billy W. Sills Center for Archives, Fort Worth Independent School District (FWISD), 2720 Cullen St., Fort Worth, TX, hereafter Billy W. Sills Archives. I.M. Terrell was the first black school to have a gym. It was added as part of the remodeling in 1937 to the Chambers Hill building. Bill Fairley, "Tar-

rant Chronicles," *Fort Worth Star-Telegram*, February 24, 1999. In 1927, an expose of the FWISD revealed that neither of the brick "colored schools" was really fire-proof. Doggett, "Survey," 43.

41. *Fort Worth Telegram*, October 17, 1907. For Turner, see letter of School Board President George C. Clarke to Superintendent Alexander Hogg, *Fort Worth Star-Telegram*, February 19, 1911.
42. For church, see *Fort Worth Star-Telegram*, December 22, 2014. For school, see Kline, marker application, pp. 11-15; and *Fort Worth Star-Telegram*, December 17, 1911 and March 10, 1912. The Riverside Colored School building still stands today (2015), one block off Sylvania at 2629 LaSalle. Since 1999 it has been protected by a National Historic Marker. The original building is still recognizable, including the 1911 cornerstone, despite heavy remodeling over the years to bring it up to code. It is currently owned by the Corinth Baptist Church. Note: school districts used different nomenclature arbitrarily to designate their African-American schools as either "Colored" or "Negro." Riverside used "Negro"; Fort Worth used "Colored."
43. Hamilton, *History and Directory*, 42.
44. Doggett, "Survey," 3.
45. For Smith, see *Fort Worth Star-Telegram*, December 22, 2014. Technical High School (now Green B. Trinble Technical High School) at 1003 W. Cannon opened in 1955. Ibid., August 6, 1921.
46. *Fort Worth Star-Telegram*, November 25, 1922; Doggett, "Survey," 7.
47. Bill McDonald, "Address to Our Youth" (editorial), *Fort Worth Eagle Eye*, August 17, 1935. Cited in Sohmer, "Rock Island Bottom," 53.
48. For Presbyterians, see Ruthe Winegarten and Janet G. Humphrey, *Black Texas Women: 150 Years of Trial and Triumph* (Austin: University of Texas Press, 1995), 85–86, hereafter Winegarten and Humphrey, *150 Years*. For Baptists, see Michael R. Heintze, *Private Black Colleges in Texas, 1865–1954* (College Station: Texas A&M University Press, 1985), 39-40, hereafter Heintze, *Private Black Colleges*. For Jarvis, see Colby D. Hall, *History of Texas Christian University* (Fort Worth: TCU Press, 2014), 346–47. The 465-acre tract for Jarvis was donated by Mrs. Ida Van Zandt Jarvis.
49. For Paul Quinn, see Douglas Hales, "Paul Quinn College," *New Handbook of Texas*. Bishop's President Maxson was white. *Fort Worth Telegram*, October 17, 1907. For white faculty at historically black colleges, see John Egerton, *Speak Now against the Day* (New York: Alfred A. Knopf, 1994), 130. See also Heintze, *Private Black Colleges*.

50. Heintze, *Private Black Colleges*, 40. For "negro college" in Fort Worth, see *Fort Worth Telegram*, October 15, 1907.
51. *Fort Worth Star-Telegram*, April 4 and November 11, 1909. Ironically, the Como section of Arlington Heights a little more than ten years later became an all-black neighborhood which would have rolled out the red carpet for a Negro Industrial College.
52. For the Mary Allen Seminary, see Winegarten and Humphrey, *150 Years*, 85–86.
53. Mrs. J.J. Jarvis was one of the largest contributors and a driving force in the creation of Jarvis Institute, which is what it was known as before it became Jarvis Christian College. *Fort Worth Star-Telegram*, January 19 and March 9, 1913. *Dallas Morning News*, June 8 and 22, 1913.
54. *Dallas Morning News*, September 13, 1914. *Fort Worth Star-Telegram*, February 18 and 25, 1916. For Home Makers' Industrial School, see ibid., October 13, 1918.
55. This is the raw version of the story that appears in Fox's draft MS of his memoirs. The cleaned-up version is told in George Fox, "End of an Era," in Stanley F. Chyet, ed., *Lives and Voices: A Collection of American Jewish Memoirs* (Philadelphia, PA.: Jewish Publication Society, 1972), 281–82, hereafter Fox, "End of an Era." Also in the published version, the black physician is not named, but the draft version reveals his identity as Dr. Alexander B. Terrell. The unpublished draft is in the archives of the Beth-El Congregation, Fort Worth, TX. After graduating from the University of Chicago, Terrell went on to Harvard medical school where he graduated in 1910, the only Fort Worth physician of his era to get his medical degree from the nation's premier medical school. Eventually Terrell found Jim Crow Fort Worth intolerable and moved to California.
56. *Fort Worth Telegram*, October 18, 1907. Fort *Worth Star-Telegram*, October 17, 1914.
57. *Fort Worth Star-Telegram*, August 13, 1922.
58. The Corinth Baptist Church first appears in the 1909–1910 *Fort Worth City Directory*.
59. *Fort Worth Star-Telegram*, February 17, 1991. For Williams, see *Dallas Morning News*, April 30, 1907.
60. St. Patrick's Catholic Church on the south end of town had dealt with the same problem ever since opening its doors in 1892. Those doors looked straight down Eleventh St. to a brothel just two blocks away. See Richard Selcer, *Hell's Half-Acre* (Fort Worth: Texas Christian University Press, 1991), 133-34, hereafter Selcer, *Hell's Half-Acre*. Cribs were tiny, one-

room brothels where the lowest of the low did business on the quick and dirty.

61. *Fort Worth Star-Telegram*, March 24, 1909.
62. Bob Ray Sanders, "Churches Recall History, Faith," *Fort Worth Star-Telegram*, August 14, 2002; "Tarrant Baptists Apologize for Slavery," ibid., January 1, 2004.
63. Quote is by Rev. J.B. Pius of Austin. *Fort Worth Telegram*, October 17, 1907. *Fort Worth Star-Telegram*, August 2, 1912. Jackson was the dean of Fort Worth's black pastors, leading Mount Pisgah for more than 20 years. *Dallas Morning News*, April 30, 1907. Williams information comes from D.N. McCutcheon letter to wife, September 8, 1926. Author's collections.
64. *Fort Worth Star-Telegram*, February 17, 1991.
65. The building sat empty for two years before burning down in 1914, the victim of arson. *Fort Worth Star-Telegram*, August 2, 1912 and October 25, 1914.
66. The Natatorium was a public bath and swimming facility from 1890 until it was torn down in the 1920s. Mike Nichols, *Lost Fort Worth* (Charleston, SC: The History Press, 2014), 113–15.
67. *Fort Worth Star-Telegram*, February 16 and 18, 1910; August 3, 1913.
68. *Fort Worth Star-Telegram*, February 17, 1991; and August 3, 1913. For bank failure, see *Dallas Morning News*, February 18, 1912.
69. For Mount Zion, see *Fort Worth Star-Telegram*, February 13, 1922. For St. James, see ibid., October 23, 1922.
70. *Fort Worth Star-Telegram*, April 20, 1914; May 13, 1917; and October 5, 1919.
71. *Dallas Morning News*, October 12, 1898.
72. The hymnal was *Celestial Showers* by William Roseborough of Texarkana. *Dallas Morning News*, October 12, 1898. For other conventions, see *Fort Worth Star-Telegram*, March 8, 1914; June 1, 1917; and October 12, 1921.
73. For Mount Zion, see Carol Roark, ed., *Fort Worth and Tarrant County: An Historical Guide* (Fort Worth: TCU Press, 2003), 84, 93-94, hereafter Roark, *Historical Guide*. For BME convention, see *Fort Worth Telegram*, October 17, 1907.
74. Roark, *Historical Guide*, 32–33.
75. For *Fort Worth Mind*, see J. H. Smith, *Negro Directory of Fort Worth*, 1937–1938, p. 22, hereafter cited as Smith, *Negro Directory*. The *Fort Worth Mind* was the city's only black newspaper from 1932 to 1940. Calvin Littlejohn was the staff photographer as an independent contractor, not salaried

staff. See Littlejohn's obituary, *Fort Worth Star-Telegram*, September 9, 1993. For Littlejohn's work, see Sanders, *Calvin Littlejohn*.

76. For the *Baptist Star*, see *Fort Worth Star-Telegram*, March 15, 1915. For *Fort Worth Mind* and *Fort Worth News*, see Lenora Rolla, unpublished MS, Lenora Rolla Papers. For other black newspapers, see Bill Fairley, "Tarrant Chronicles," *Fort Worth Star-Telegram*, February 3, 1999; and Sohmer, "Rock Island Bottom," 63. For a brief history of local "Negro Newspapers," see also *Dallas Morning News*, April 2, 1967.
77. Phil Register was called "Professor" for his musical talents. *The White Man and The Negro* 1, no. 7 (September 1932) is one of three surviving issues in the personal collections of Fort Worth's Dalton Hoffman. For "colored publishers," see ibid., vol. 2, no. 4 (June 1933): 269–70. See also Paula Oates, ed. *Celebrating 150 Years: The Pictorial History of Fort Worth, Texas* (Fort Worth: Landmark Publishing, 1999), 51, hereafter, Oates, *Celebrating 150* Years.
78. *The White Man and The Negro* 2, no. 4 (June 1933): 269–70.
79. For scrapbook, see Diana Roach, "Scrapbooks," March 1, 1944–late 1946, collected by staff members of the Fort Worth YWCA. Tarrant County Black Historical & Genealogical Society. Roach was one of the YWCA staff members who put them together.
80. *Fort Worth Morning Register*, September 18, 1901.
81. *Fort Worth Record*, n.d., quoted in John Henry, "Fort Worth Negro Baseball League. . . ," *Fort Worth Star-Telegram*, February 26, 2012. For Dallas homicides, see Lynn W. Landrum, "They Want Protection," *Dallas Morning News*, June 24, 1946.
82. *Fort Worth Star-Telegram*, March 29, 1920.
83. The three-story Jim Hotel was named for McDonald's second wife, Jimmie. McDonald sold it in 1934, and it closed for good in 1962. Despite the presence of the Jim Hotel, the city's black community still preferred to put up distinguished visitors who came to town in private homes in the Jim Crow era. Cheryl L. Simon, "Jim Hotel," *Handbook of Texas Online* (www.tshaonline.org/handbook/online/articles). Christopher Evans, "The Hot Spot—Fort Worth's Jim Hotel. . . ," *Fort Worth Star-Telegram*, June 30, 1991.
84. The Hearst newspaper's insensitivity to Southern newspaper protocol is discussed in Samuel E. Kinch, Jr., "Amon Carter: Publisher-Salesman," Thesis presented to the Faculty of the Graduate School of The University of Texas. . . for the Degree of Master of Journalism (Austin: University of Texas, 1965), 37, 43–44, hereafter Kinch, "Amon Carter." A *Star-Telegram*

editor many years later stated that this was one of the things that helped kill off the *Record* in 1925.

85. For 1910 hanging of Allen Brooks, see *Fort Worth Star-Telegram*, March 3, 1910. *Cf. Dallas Morning News*, March 4, 1910. The Maddox St. bombing of Feb. 28, 1946, was not reported in the *Fort Worth Star-Telegram* although it was carried in the *Fort Worth Press*. For the case of Lawrence Peters in 1953, see *Dallas Morning News*, November 3, 5, and 6, 1953. For the case of Lloyd Austin, see ibid., September 3, 4, 1956.
86. *Dallas Morning News*, April 2, 1967.
87. For attitudes toward yellow fever see Keith, *Fever*, 61, 79, 84, 96. For Fort Worth and smallpox, see *Dallas Morning News*, May 7, 1918, and *Fort Worth Star-Telegram*, May 27, 1915.
88. For a fuller accounting of black physicians in Fort Worth, 1887 to 1925, see website www.fortworthafricanamericandoctors.wordpress.com. Most of the information was assembled by pioneering Fort Worth genealogist and librarian Shirley Apley. On May 5, 2012, Apley presented "Hidden in History: African-American Doctors in Fort Worth, 1887–1925" in the Tandy Lecture Series at the Fort Worth Library.
89. The exception was St. Joseph's (Catholic) Infirmary (hospital) which treated black patients in the basement "Negro ward." For Waller, see *Dallas Morning News*, May 27, 1906. For Tignor and Cosey, see *Fort Worth Telegram*, January 11, 1909.
90. *Fort Worth City Directory*, 1907. For a discussion of the meningitis epidemic in Fort Worth, see Selcer and Foster, *Written in Blood 2*, 27–30.
91. *Fort Worth Star-Telegram*, January 22, 1912.
92. Quote comes from *Fort Worth Star-Telegram*, January 22, 1912. When the next meningitis outbreak struck in 1918, it was not as widespread and the public's attention was focused on the war in Europe, so it caused barely a ripple even though people still died. Hollace Ava Weiner, *Jewish Stars in Texas* (College Station: Texas A&M University Press, 1999), 94, hereafter Weiner, *Jewish Stars*.
93. *Fort Worth Telegram*, October 13, 1903.
94. For emergency cases, see George Harris who fell from the Fort Worth & Denver trestle over East 7th in 1915 and was taken to City-County in an ambulance. *Fort Worth Star-Telegram*, November 7, 1915. Other examples turn up occasionally in the old newspapers which refute the myth of no admission. Later, City-County was renamed John Peter Smith Hospital. The Texas Medical Association did not admit black doctors until 1955, so technically St. Joseph's could not extend privileges to them, but the

hospital allowed them to work unofficially in the "Negro ward." There is no record of when St. Joseph's set up this ward, but Dallas' Parkland Hospital established that city's first "Negro ward"—in the basement—in 1915. *Dallas Morning News*, June 30, 1915.

95. For "sanitariums," see, for instance, *Dallas Morning News*, April 4, 1912, which identifies the Negro "hospital" there as St. Paul's Sanitarium. For Dr. Ransom, see Gayle Hanson, "Riley Andrew Ransom, Sr., 1886-1951," www.blackpast.org , hereafter, Hanson, "Ransom"; Mike Nichols, *Lost Fort Worth* (Charleston, SC: History Press, 2014), 77–78; and Bob Ray Sanders, "A Pioneering Black Doctor in Fort Worth," *Fort Worth Star-Telegram*, December 6, 2011. For an overview of Fort Worth's *white* medical history, see Ann Arnold, *A History of the Fort Worth Medical Community* (Arlington, TX: Landa Press, 2002). Bob Ray Sanders, "Station Mural," *Fort Worth Star-Telegram*, February 24, 2002.
96. For the progression of black medical treatment in the city, see *Fort Worth City Directory*, 1920-1929, on microfiche and in book form (1929) at Fort Worth Public Library, Central Branch, Local History, Genealogy, & Archives Unit; and Hanson, "Ransom." For Dr. Brooks, see *Fort Worth Star-Telegram*, September 30, 2002; and March 4, 2003 (obituary).
97. For the chronology of the Hope Training Home, see *Fort Worth City Directory*, 1920-1929, on microfiche or in book form (1929) at Fort Worth Public Library, Central Branch, Local History, Genealogy, & Archives Unit. For description of same, see "Fort Worth Welfare Association" advertisement in *Fort Worth Star-Telegram*, May 29, 1921. For a general history of the settlement house movement, see Allen F. Davis, *Spearheads for Reform: The Social Settlements and the Progressive Movement, 1890-1914* (New Brunswick, New Jersey: Rutgers University Press, 1966, rev. ed.). Gipson got her nursing certification in 1907 and thereafter divided her time between mid-wifing and working for white doctors like Elias J. Beall. Allen (Sherrod), *Grace and Gumption*, 193–94.
98. *Dallas Morning News*, August 15, 1940.
99. For black and white couple, see *Fort Worth Star-Telegram*, October 6, 1911. For Hazel Harvey [Peace], see *ibid.*, May 23, 1977; and *Dallas Morning News* (obituary), June 15, 2008.
100. *Fort Worth Telegram*, December 24, 1908.
101. Both officers were suspended by the police committee, but their suspensions were overturned by the full council. *Fort Worth Mail-Telegram*, July 2, 1902.
102. *Fort Worth Register*, April 16, 1897.

103. For auto arrest, see *Fort Worth Star-Telegram*, April 14, 1911. For Maddox, see ibid., March 11, 1910.
104. For Swayne, see Richard Selcer, "James W. Swayne: Straight-arrow Judge," *Fort Worth Characters* (Denton: University of North Texas Press, 2009), 230–31; and for race riot in particular, see Selcer and Foster, *Written in Blood 2*, 69–82.
105. *Fort Worth Telegram*, December 21, 1906.
106. For Hill, see *Fort Worth Telegram*, December 24, 1908. For "somebody," see *Dallas Morning News*, August 25, 1909.
107. Lynn W. Landrum, "They Want Protection," *Dallas Morning News*, June 24, 1946. For McGar, see *Fort Worth Star-Telegram*, May 26, 1915. For lynching, see ibid., March 4, 1910.
108. For the Wallers, see Richard Selcer and Kevin Foster, *Written in Blood*, vol. 1 (Denton: UNT Press, 2010), 133–171, hereafter Selcer and Foster, *Written in Blood 1*. For detective, see *Fort Worth Press*, October 16, 1925. Special officers were the equivalent of today's private security. They were commissioned officers but were paid by their private employer. *Dallas Morning News*, June 4, 1886; and August 13, 1891.
109. For Daggett, see *Fort Worth Star-Telegram*, July 6, 1909. For Davis, see ibid., June 20, 1914; September 14, 1915; and June 19, 1916.
110. For Loving, see *Dallas Morning News*, May 20, 1896; and Prince Hall *Proceedings*, August 18, 1900, p. 73. For power-brokers, see *Fort Worth Mail-Telegram*, September 4, 1902.
111. *Fort Worth Star-Telegram*, December 26, 1908.
112. *Dallas Morning News*, December 2, 1885.
113. For 1902 case, see *Fort Worth Mail-Telegram*, September 23, 1902. For informal, see *Fort Worth Telegram*, April 24, 1908.
114. For Fred Rouse, see *Fort Worth Star-Telegram*, December 11 and 12, 1921; and February 9 and 13, 1922; and Tim Madigan, "Lynching on Northeast 12th ," Part 4 in a 7-part series, "The Color of Hate," ibid., October 9, 2002.
115. *Dallas Morning News*, October 5, 1891.
116. Newspaper reports of black suspects defiantly declaring their guilt, even saying that they wanted to kill/rape more whites, were so common in the old days as to suggest that either a lot of black men had a death wish, or else the reports were yellow journalism, made up to incite white passions. The fact that such reports often coincided with a lynching points toward the latter. A defiant "Negro" murderer/rapist deserved what he got! *Dallas Morning News*, November 9, 1887.

117. Lynchings were rare in urban communities with large black populations. Statistics come from Walter White, *Rope and Faggot* (New York: Alfred A. Knopf, 1929), 258, hereafter White, *Rope and Faggot.* For October lynchings, see *Fort Worth Telegram,* October 2, 16, 22, and 28, 1903. For Stanley, see *Fort Worth Star-Telegram,* July 31, 1915.
118. Rouse was lynched on December 6. The other two victims that same year were Alexander Winn in Decatur (August 15) and Wyllie McNeely in Leesburg (October 10). White, *Rope and Faggot,* 258. The only other lynch victim in Fort Worth history was Tom Vickery (white) for killing an officer in 1920. For Williams, see *Fort Worth Star-Telegram,* October 17, 1914. The white explanation for the "exodus" was that blacks were leaving "the land" for the city, not fleeing the South altogether.
119. *Dallas Morning News,* February 28, 1913; *Fort Worth Telegram,* June 27, 1907.
120. *Fort Worth Morning Register,* April 14, 1902.
121. *Fort Worth Star-Telegram,* April 13, 1912.
122. *Fort Worth Star-telegram,* May 14, 1910.
123. *Fort Worth Star-Telegram,* May 14, 1910.
124. *Fort Worth Telegram,* April 24, August 3, September 19 and 24, 1907; *Fort Worth Star-Telegram,* June 13 and September 15, 1919.
125. David F. Musto, *The American Disease* (New York: Oxford University Press, 1999), 5–7, hereafter Musto, *American Disease*; Graeme Donald, *They Got It Wrong: Science* (New York: Reader's Digest, 2013), 111. For formulaic reporting of what cocaine did to blacks, see *Fort Worth Telegram,* December 6 and August 24, 1907; and *Dallas Morning News,* August 25, 1909. For targeting black dealers, see ibid., September 27, 1911.
126. For opium, see Musto, *American Disease,* 5–6. For quote, see *Fort Worth Star-Telegram,* December 23, 1914.
127. *Fort Worth Star-Telegram,* September 16 and 18, 1911; October 28, 1911; July 29, 1914. For cost and availability of cocaine, see *Fort Worth Morning Register,* November 25, 1901.
128. *Fort Worth Star-Telegram,* November 28, 1915.
129. *Fort Worth Star-Telegram,* June 19, 1915.
130. *Fort Worth Morning Register,* March 13 and November 25, 1901. *Fort Worth Telegram,* July 21, 1906. *Fort Worth Star-Telegram,* October 28, 1911. *Dallas Morning News,* September 21, 1914.
131. *Fort Worth Morning Register,* November 25, 1901. *Fort Worth Star-Telegram,* July 29, 1914.

132. *Dallas Express*, January 11, 1919.
133. White primaries remained in effect in Texas until 1944 and the poll tax until 1966 when they were struck down respectively by the Supreme Court. Rupert N. Richardson, et al., *Texas: The Lone Star State,* 4th ed. (Englewood Cliffs, NJ: Prentice-Hall, 1981), 348–49.
134. *Fort Worth Star-Telegram*, October 19, 1919.
135. *Fort Worth Star-Telegram*, June 6, 1920.
136. V.O. Key, Jr., *Southern Politics in State and Nation* (New York: Alfred A. Knopf, 1950), 621–22, hereafter Key, *Southern Politics.*
137. For Mumbower, see *Fort Worth Star-Telegram*, June 6, 1920. For Mullins, see Bill Fairley, "Ex-slave recalls good children," one of a series of articles for Black History Month in Fairley's regular column in the *Fort Worth Star-Telegram*, February 26, 1997. (The dialect spelling is taken directly from the interview in the "Federal Writers' Project.")
138. *Fort Worth Morning Register*, January 8, 1897. Some Texas counties, *e.g.*, Tarrant, held whites-only primaries as early as the 1890s. The Democratic Party embraced the practice in practically every county by 1904. In 1923 the legislature wrote it into law, which had to be rewritten in 1927 to get around a hostile Supreme Court. Fort Worth consistently defied the courts and the NAACP in resisting black suffrage. For white primaries in Fort Worth, see *Fort Worth Star-Telegram*, November 17, 1910. For general discussion of the white primary in Texas, see Alwyn Barr, *Black Texans: A History of African Americans in Texas, 1528–1995*, 2nd ed.(Norman: University of Oklahoma Press, 1996), 79, 134–36, hereafter Barr, *Black Texans*; and Darlene Clark Hine, *Black Victory: The Rise and Fall of the White Primary in Texas* (Columbia: University of Missouri Press, 2003).
139. *Fort Worth Morning Register*, June 27, 1897. For Roosevelt's visit, see *Fort Worth Record*, April 9, 1905, and Fort Worth Telegram, April 8, 1905. For colored college, see TCBH&GS Collections, ibid., pp. 94-96. The land was donated by the Arlington Heights Realty Company. Texas' historically black colleges/universities today are Huston-Tillotson University, Jarvis Christian College, Paul Quinn College, Prairie View A&M University, Texas College, Texas Southern University, and Wiley College.
140. For Burris' story, see Richard Selcer and Kevin Foster, *Written in Blood 1,* 133–171. For the NPCT, see TCBH&GS Collections, Series III, Box 1, File 2, p. 90.
141. Even in the 1950s civil service exams were still given to whites and blacks on different dates and in different locations. Whites took their

exams at city hall; blacks took theirs in the old Post Office building. *Fort Worth Press*, February 24, 1948; and June 5, 1953.

142. Richard Selcer, "When Street Cars Roamed Fort Worth," *Fort Worth Magazine* 15, no. 12 (December 2012): 58–63.
143. Ordinance No. 944 was passed October 2, 1905 and signed by City Secretary John T. Montgomery, going into effect immediately. It was published as a "Legal Notice" in the *Fort Worth Telegram*, October 11, 1905. See also *Fort Worth Telegram*, July 22, 1905; and *Dallas Morning News*, July 8, 1905.
144. For Dallas, see *Dallas Morning News*, September 15, 1905. For seating designation, see Bill Fairley, "Tarrant Chronicles," *Fort Worth Star-Telegram*, March 10, 1999. Fort Worth Klan membership in the 1920s was roughly 6,500 while Dallas' was roughly 16,000. In 1922, Fort Worth was Texas headquarters for the Klan. That was the same year 5,000 Klan members paraded through the city in full regalia. Kenneth T. Jackson, *The Ku Klux Klan in the City, 1915–1930* (Chicago: Ivan R. Dee, 1992), 84, 239. *Fort Worth Star-Telegram*, October 30, 1949 (Special Centennial Edition), p. 38 "Commerce" section.
145. *Fort Worth Morning Register*, April 13, 1901.
146. Lynn Abbott and Doug Seroff, *Out of Sight: The Rise of African-American Popular Music, 1889–1895* (Jackson: University Press of Mississippi, 2009), 332–335. Field enjoyed telling the story how in his early years after countless performances in black face, he once stayed at the home of a Southern friend. The friend's black cook knew Field only by his public persona and based on that prepared dinner for him in the kitchen because she thought he was actually black. *Fort Worth Star-Telegram*, November 11, 1920. For Field's background, see ibid., November 10, 1909.
147. *Fort Worth Morning Register*, November 8, 1901. *Fort Worth Star-Telegram*, November 10, 1909. *Dallas Morning News*, November 7, 1907. For a sampling of Field's many visits to the area, see *Fort Worth Register*, November 3, 1900; November 5, 7, and 8, 1901; *Fort Worth Telegram/Star-Telegram*, November 2, 1903; November 7, 1906; November 7 and 10, 1909; November 11, 1920; November 12, 1922; and *Dallas Morning News*, October 29, 1905; November 7, 1907; November 10, 1922
148. Miller was unique in that he didn't just interpret black music; he recorded the first inter-racial recording in American history with a black vocal quartet in 1909, recorded by Thomas Edison's engineers. *Fort Worth Telegram*, October 30 and 31, and November 2, 1903.

"The Story and Music of Polk Miller and the Old South Quartette," www.polkmiller.com.

149. *Fort Worth Star-Telegram*, January 6, 1914.
150. *Fort Worth Star-Telegram*, November 6, 1909.
151. Neither Prof. Register nor Prof. Nix confined himself to music. Register also published a magazine and Nix repaired watches. *The White Man and the Negro* (magazine) 1, no. 7 (September 1932), inside front cover and advertisements.
152. For "sluggers," see *Fort Worth Star-Telegram*, March 8, 1919. For stage, see Jones, *Renegades*, 283–89.
153. Jones, *Renegades*, 285; *Fort Worth City Directory*, 1885–86 and 1907–08.
154. *Fort Worth Gazette*, June 29, 1891.
155. Jeff Guinn, *When Panthers Roared* (Fort Worth: Texas Christian University Press, 1999), 26, hereafter, Guinn, *Panthers*. Rob Fink, *Playing in the Shadows* (Lubbock: Texas Tech University Press, 2010), 10, 37, 49-50, hereafter, Fink, *Playing*.
156. Guinn, *Panthers*, 22–26, 44–45, and 108; *Dallas Morning News*, July 5, 1940; Fink, *Playing*, 89, 91–93.
157. Source: Richard Selcer, chapter 7 of *Fort Worth Characters* (Denton: University of North Texas Press, 2009), 131–148.

Chapter 5

World War I: Jim Crow Comes Marching Home

When the United States entered "the Great War" in 1917, President Woodrow Wilson called on the American people to rally 'round the flag and "make the world safe for democracy," without reference to race or creed. This stirring call did not resonate equally with African Americans and whites. W.E.B. DuBois, one of the founders of the National Association for the Advancement of Colored People, told his people, "We the colored race have no ordinary interest in the outcome" of this war. Still, he advised them to forget their "special grievances and close ranks shoulder to shoulder with our white fellow citizens." In 1917 the U.S. Army had four all-black regiments numbering 10,000 men in all (with no black commissioned officers). Another 10,000 African Americans served in Negro National Guard units. All of them were liable to being called up and shipped out to the Western Front despite the fact that the high command had long-standing reservations about the black man's fitness for combat. Their intelligence, initiative, and vigor were all suspect. White officers like Col. William Pitcher of the 27th Infantry Regiment did not believe the U.S. Army should even be trying to make soldiers out of African Americans because "they are not up to the challenge."[1]

When Congress enacted conscription in May 1917, it pulled in thousands of men, both black and white, but not equally. The original bill made no exception for race, which sparked an intense debate in Congress. Representative Julius Kahn of California assured his colleagues that blacks would be "called to arms exactly the same as white citizens" but would train "in separate units." That did not placate Southern Congressmen who vehemently opposed drafting blacks under any conditions. One warned, "This would accomplish the very thing which the South has always fought against—the placing of arms in the hands of a large number of Negroes and the training of them to work together in organized units." The issue was smoothed over by allowing local draft boards complete autonomy in filling their assigned quotas. As one critic observed later, "A draft board is more autonomous than a jury. . . handing down verdicts on the thousands of cases brought before it." Local draft boards weighed race, family connections, and half a dozen other arbitrary factors in deciding who to call up and who to grant a "deferment" to. They red-flagged race by putting the notation "white" or "colored" beside the name of every man certified for service. The War Department also set a total quota for enlisting blacks—which was met and exceeded in the first week of the war by volunteers. Blacks not swept up in the patriotic fervor or looking for adventure were another matter, however. Registration for the draft was slow in the black community; reporting for induction was even more of a problem. The cause of the problem was where opinions differed. Two Southern governors attributed it to "the general illiteracy of that race and their roving disposition, and not due to lack of patriotism or intention to evade the draft on their part."[2]

Photo 12. Corry Bates Emory, 1917

Corry Bates Emory of Dallas in his U.S. Army uniform. After the war he came home to work as a janitor. Courtesy of Emerson Emory Papers, Special Collections, University of Texas at Arlington Library, Arlington, TX.

Perhaps the appeal to black patriotism was not well served by assigning the overwhelming majority of black recruits to labor battalions, not combat arms. African Americans were not asked to fight; they were *ordered* to clean and dig and cook. And that is how thousands of black soldiers came to be at Camp Bowie. A decade into the twentieth century, Fort Worth was still an overwhelmingly white community that tolerated its black minority because they were practically invisible. The 1910 census showed fewer than one in eight residents of the city was black, far short of the critical mass found in other Deep South communities that could provoke repression and violence. Fort Worth whites were not prepared in 1917 for the arrival of 3,000 black males even if they were guests of Uncle Sam. The city's historic racial balance was shattered. [3]

You might say city fathers asked for it. Even as the debate over conscription was raging in Congress in April 1917, they went knocking on doors seeking one of the sixteen training camps the Army planned to build. They got their wish and happily prepared to receive the thousands of enlistees and millions of dollars that Uncle Sam was about to send their way. What they were not prepared for was that 3,000 of those recruits would be black. In August, War Department officials decided that black and white recruits would train at the same camps albeit segregated in their "organizations" and living arrangements. In other words, black labor battalions would not train, eat, or sleep beside white combat battalions.[4]

Meanwhile, in July construction of Camp Bowie got underway on a site three miles west of town on the Arlington Heights. It sprawled over 2,186 acres with boundaries roughly corresponding to present-day University Drive on the east, Merrick St. on the west, White Settlement Road on the north, and Vickery Blvd. on the south. It was built for a population of 27,000, but the hasty construction made no allowance for segregated living quarters and training facilities as promised in the Selective Service Act. The Camp was connected to downtown Fort Worth by Arlington Heights Blvd. and a street car line that ran right to the front gate. The first 450 recruits arrived on July 26, members of the First

Texas Cavalry mostly hailing from Amarillo, Corsicana, Houston, and San Antonio. The only black faces to be seen that summer were part of the 3,500-strong construction crew hired locally. White Southerners were used to seeing black faces mixed in with white faces in construction crews on big projects.[5]

The first black recruits did not arrive until the fall of 1918. Between then and the summer of 1919 when the camp was deactivated, their presence caused a culture shock the likes of which had never before been seen in Fort Worth. Rumors of their coming began circulating in early September. The decision to put black and white recruits together at Camp Bowie was made by some War Department bureaucrat in Washington, D.C. who probably had no idea how momentous that decision was. On September 9 the *Star-Telegram* felt obliged to reassure its readers, "It is not expected that the War Department will train men of both races at the same camp." Six days later, citing an "Associated Press dispatch," the newspaper had to eat those words, advising its readers that "no more than 300 Negroes" were on the way to Camp Bowie. About two weeks later the first thousand black recruits arrived by train. They climbed onto trucks for the ride out to Camp Bowie to join the 10,000 white members of the 36th Division already training. White Fort Worthers at the Texas & Pacific station simply stood and gaped as their sergeants herded them through the station. The men were mostly from rural areas of Texas and Oklahoma, but some were from Ennis, Waxahachie, and Dallas. White citizens had never seen that many black men together in one place at the same time.[6]

The first trucks began unloading at the gate at 9:00 a.m. on September 26. As another in a long string of concessions to Southern sensibilities, draft boards were not supposed to send white and black soldiers together out of fear of an incident enroute, but both blacks and whites were in the first load of recruits that day. They all received a warm welcome from white recruits lining the road outside the gate. The *Star-Telegram* reported with an almost audible sigh of relief, "The darkies shouted back just as lustily." Then they lined up and marched through the gate to their home for the next six weeks or more.[7]

The 36th Division they were going to train with was something of a "rainbow division." In addition to whites and blacks, it also contained 600 Native Americans representing seventeen different tribes. The 36th was more "Native" than any other division in the Army, which explains the arrowhead patch worn by its members. Unlike blacks, Native American recruits trained and lived with whites. The Commissioner of Indian Affairs, who visited Camp Bowie twice before the 36th shipped out for France in 1918, reported morale high, accommodations satisfactory, and no friction with the locals.[8]

Things were not so rosy for the African-American recruits. From the beginning they were treated as second-class soldiers. Unlike black recruits assigned to Houston's Camp Logan (the other training camp in Texas for blacks), all African Americans sent to Camp Bowie were slotted for labor battalions. None would join black infantry regiments, not those already in existence or those being raised currently (the 349th, 350th, 351st, 367th, 368th,, 369th , 370th, and 807th). None of the black men who entered Camp Bowie's gates ever actually got the honor of *fighting* for their country; they learned to march and salute, but when their training was finished they were not allowed to carry anything more lethal than a pick and shovel. That was a distinction lost on nervous white citizens. They imagine thousands of *armed* black men on the Arlington Heights. It was hardly reassuring that they would be commanded by white officers, namely Captains Ross Lillard and James Berry. The tradition of white officers leading black troops went back to the Civil War, but even at this date any white officer who did so was known to his fellow officers as a "Negro lover." Lillard and Berry faced the usual razzing from their fellows, but they performed their duties at Camp Bowie with distinction and were rewarded for it. Before the end of the year both were reassigned to the "Negro provisional division," a combat division training on the east coast.[9]

The first stop for newly arrived recruits was the Personnel Office where they traded in their civilian duds for army issue. Then it was off to the camp hospital for medical exams and shots. The biggest fears army doctors had that fall were Spanish flu, eye infections, and venereal disease in that order. After their physicals, recruits got their first army haircuts and received their "preliminary classification." The latter was easy because all were being assigned to either a labor battalion or some vague classification known as "limited service." The former meant constructing roads and barracks, laying out firing ranges, digging latrines, baking bread, and countless other menial jobs that were necessary to support the fighting men. Limited service included working as hospital orderlies, clerical staff, and musicians. Among the latter was Marcus Fisher of Cass County, Texas, who was a virtuoso with the violin, mandolin, guitar, and slide trombone. The army singled out Fisher to create "a good jazz band for Camp Bowie." Many of the new recruits were looking forward to army life as a relief from picking cotton and doing other hard, physical labor that they had to do back home. However, if they imagined army service as a life of leisure, drill sergeants quickly disabused them of the idea. Their rude awakening began when processing officers collected all the musical instruments, dice, lucky charms, and blank postcards they had arrived with. The white doctors marveled at some of the physical specimens they saw, such as Rolo Harris, a piano mover from Houston. In their expert medical opinion, he was "as nearly perfect physically" as any man, white or black, they had ever seen. In civilian life most white doctors had never examined a black person. Now they had a chance to poke and prod thousands of them and see how they measured up to white men. It was all quite exhilarating in the spirit of medical inquiry.[10]

New recruits had to spend their first two weeks in "detention camp" to be sure they did not have any contagious diseases *and* to introduce them to army life. During this initiation phase the men lived in tents, but at least they could look forward to moving into better accommodations (barracks) afterwards—all but the black soldiers, most of whom would live in tents for the duration of their stay at Camp Bowie. Even the first wave of black recruits were not permitted to get too comfortable because when a group of white recruits arrived in mid-October, the black troops were relocated to another tent camp on a more distant section of the post.[11]

Culture shock came early for black recruits. Upon being introduced to showers, they were "very reluctant" to get under the hot spray, thinking it might be dangerous. That was just one of many new experiences they faced. Another shock came when some of their families showed up at the front gate in the early weeks expecting to visit their men. Captain Cleveland Sammons went to the gate and explained that recruits were not permitted to have visitors until they completed basic training (two weeks). Training officers have always felt contempt for raw recruits, but white commanders at Camp Bowie found plenty to laugh about, too. As the new arrivals were being processed some officers noted how many "Abraham Lincolns," "George Washingtons," "Thomas Jeffersons," "Ciceros," and "Caesars" there were. The dietary habits of the black recruits also became an issue. The "nutrition officer" at first did not understand why the black recruits were not eating all the good white bread prepared by the camp's bakers. It took him about a week to figure it out. "When left to his own devices," he reported to the camp commander, "the negro eats cornbread and salt meat or in lieu of that, sweet meats [liver, heart, gizzard]." He was informed by his mess sergeants, "Negroes do not like to eat white bread because the crust scratches their throats." After that, commissary supply officers adjusted their menus, and the Army got on with the business of turning farm boys into soldiers. [12]

These were just some of the countless adjustments large and small the two races had to make in order to serve in the same army. Of course, the U.S. Army had done this before during both the Civil War and Spanish-American War, but not on such a massive scale. And unfortunately, everything learned in those earlier wars had been forgotten during the years of peace. The service's institutional memory did not put a high priority on such things.

The culture shocks kept coming. Most white residents of Fort Worth felt as if invaders from Mars had landed on Arlington Heights. It did not help that the arrival of thousands of black men coincided with an outbreak of influenza in Fort Worth in the fall of 1918, part of a worldwide pandemic that would ultimately claim up to fifty million lives. The recruits who arrived in August and September may have unknowingly brought the flu to Fort Worth with them; there is no way of telling. Rural farm boys, many of whom had never been more than a few miles from home, were particularly vulnerable to the lethal virus. They came from all over the Southwest and rode on public transportation to Fort Worth. Black recruits were the most vulnerable of all because as civilians most had slipped between the cracks of the medical system, and once in the army they received second-class medical treatment. On October 5, influenza claimed its first Camp Bowie victim, a black soldier named Louis Warren. Hundreds more soldiers, white as well as black, would die before the epidemic ran its course in Fort Worth.[13]

The army's medical screening process for new recruits did not occur until their first day in camp. It was a particular shock to men who never been examined by a doctor or dentist before. Camp Bowie doctors found that an unusually large number of black recruits arrived with untreated conditions, including VD and rotten teeth. They got a one-way ticket back home. Hundreds did not even unpack before being discharged due to "physical defects," the army's catch-all category for chronic conditions. The army wanted only the healthiest specimens of manhood.

The Camp's (white) doctors implemented "extra sanitary measures" for black troops, ordering their white officers to see that the measures were "properly executed." When black soldiers began to come down sick anyway and reported to the hospital there were surprises on both sides. Said Lt.-Col. L.H. Hanson, the hospital commandant, "Some of them don't understand at all that they are sick and must be treated in this fashion for they never saw sick men so handled before." It was a novel experience to lie in bed all day in pajamas while white folks catered to them, even bringing them their meals. The lieutenant colonel was as unprepared as his patients for the experience. One thing he found almost comical was that his black patients believed the doctors and nurses wore sanitary masks because they were Klan members.[14]

Even apart from their first introduction to army-style medicine, military life was a shock with its highly structured system of ranks and endless protocols. Some recruits referred to every white man as "Cap" or "Boss" regardless of rank, a form of deference likely instilled by stretches in jail or on a chain gang by some soldiers. Recruits had to be taught how to salute, use proper forms of address, and perform their duties with pride. These were things Jim Crow had never taught.[15]

The Selective Service Act of 1917 recognized just two exceptions to conscription, "dependency or conscientious objection." The former covered men who were the sole support of their families. The latter covered men who belonged to a church philosophically opposed to war. The most famous was Tennessee's soon-to-be famous Alvin York, who was white. For black recruits, however, conscientious objector status was not really an option. Among those who came through Camp Bowie were twenty men who had been preachers before Uncle Sam called. After two weeks, the report on them was that they were "the life of the camp and good disciplinarians as well." All except one had apparently dropped their claim to be conscientious objectors. The lone holdout must have stuck to his guns because his case was still under consideration. The *Dallas Morning News* reported he was "the only negro claiming CO status."[16]

By the middle of October the first wave of black recruits had moved out of detention camp, but had not yet been assigned to a labor battalion. In the meantime, they had to be kept busy, and the Army was good at keeping men busy. One large group was divided into small squads to "police the various quarters" in the camp. Another was detailed to the mess halls on "kitchen police" duty, thereby relieving white soldiers of something soldiers have despised as long as there have been armies. Overall, black soldiers got good marks. Their white officers reported they "seem to be happy with their surroundings and well-pleased with army life." Since these black soldiers would never see combat, they received only the rudiments of basic training. Still, to fill the time they spent "several hours" a day learning the infantry manual. Drills were simplified because it was felt they could not handle all the complexities of the manual. After two months the most promising black recruits were organized into a "development battalion" to make them real soldiers who could be sent into combat. In the end, however, none of Camp Bowie's black soldiers ever saw combat in World War I.[17]

National conscription was the law of the land for two years, and had a wealth of problems unrelated to training. Drafting American boys to fight a "patriotic war" raised the sticky question of how to handle "draft evaders" (aka, "slackers" or "draft resisters"). This was the first generation of Americans to face conscription since the Civil War, and not every young man fancied himself a "real, live nephew of his Uncle Sam," as the George M. Cohan song of the period said. For blacks in particular, military service was completely new because they had not been raised on equal parts mother's milk and flag-waving. Then there were the practical problems. Since most blacks had not been born in hospitals and record-keeping in the South was very sketchy anyway, they lacked birth certificates, so it was impossible to determine if they were subject to the draft (21 to 30 years old). Many did not have a regular mailing address where draft notices could be mailed, or they could not read the notice even if it found them. When brought in by the sheriff, more than a few "draft evaders" could truthfully claim to be "ignorant" of the law or say they never received their notice. Even the importance of the 1917 draft card, which they were supposed to carry on their person, was lost on them for the simple reason that it was the first official piece of personal identification they had ever received. This was an era before driver's licenses and social-security cards, and since blacks were largely disfranchised, they did not have voting registrations. They were anonymous, and on top of all that, not having money or IDs they had never acquired the habit of carrying a wallet.[18]

An added incentive to rounding up draft evaders was the $50 reward offered by Uncle Sam for every one brought in. For some reason, the reward produced more black draft evaders than white in Southern states. Army officials said the problem was mostly confined to blacks, a claim supported by conventional wisdom which said whites were by nature more patriotic and more manly. A supposed lack of strong patriotic feelings went along with a general lack of soldierly qualities, so whenever the army snared a draft evader, it had the option of either locking him up or inducting him anyway and doling out punishment during training. It all sort of depended on the draft evader's attitude; a contrite attitude went a long way toward ameliorating the crime. Once in training, one thing was just the same as in civilian life: being ordered around by white men. A lifetime of taking orders carried over into their new life in uniform. Authorities at Camp Bowie reported no "strenuous objections . . . among the negroes" to army routine.[19]

Handling the few African-American recruits who ran afoul of army rules and regulations posed another dilemma. Training camps like Camp Bowie could conduct minor court martial proceedings, but were not set up to handle big cases, much less long-term incarceration. The usual solution was to move the problem soldier to one of the posts with penal facilities, specifically Fort Leavenworth (Kansas) or Fort Sam Houston (San Antonio). When Camp Bowie's adjutant had to transport a pair of prisoners, one black and one white, to Fort Leavenworth in September 1918 he decided that "military necessity" took precedence over contrary state law about traveling in the same railroad car and sent them together with a white guard detail on the next train out of Fort Worth. The identities of the prisoners and what they were charged with is unknown. What is known is that at this date the first convoy of black inductees had not yet arrived at Camp Bowie. The attitude of railroad officials in Fort Worth to this flouting of Jim Crow convention is not reported so perhaps they made an exception. It was a different matter fifteen months later when two black sergeants escorting a white deserter came through town on the way to Jefferson Barracks, St. Louis. Fort Worth police detained all three, and a white crowd gathered at the Texas & Pacific station threatening trouble. The commandant at Camp Bowie quickly replaced the black guards with a white escort, and the journey resumed. It was another example of how Camp Bowie challenged traditional Jim Crow attitudes.[20]

Although Camp Bowie was federal property and therefore presumably immune to regional prejudices, the U.S. Army respected local Jim Crow attitudes. Black and white trainees at the camp, besides being quartered apart, trained separately, ate separately, worshipped separately, and had their own entertainments. The black troops were the objects of much curiosity. They often gathered outside their tents at night and put on "minstrel and vaudeville" shows which they called "showdowns." White troops who were not on duty came around to enjoy these impromptu shows, which fostered more fraternization among the races than would have occurred in normal civilian life. For more organized entertainments, the all-white YMCA allowed the use of their "recreational hall" as the only covered venue blacks could use. On November 5, 1918, black troops put on a "big sing-along" in the hall, and an estimated 2,000 men jammed into the building either as performers or part of the audience. It was such a big event, Camp officials issued a press release to the *Star-Telegram* calling it, "the first event of this kind at Camp Bowie and among the first ever staged in the Southern Department [of the U.S. Army]." Quarantine measures for the influenza epidemic were even relaxed so that town residents could attend. In another show a few weeks later, 400 black singing soldiers put on a program of traditional "Negro spirituals" and "plantation songs." The black men may have been indifferent soldiers, but they were wonderful entertainers. The paradox was not lost on officials. The YMCA music director who organized the event played little part in putting the program together. He was more than a little puzzled that "the Negroes just couldn't seem to grasp the mysteries of chorus singing" and shook his head that they even had difficulty with patriotic songs. He simply could not understand why any red-blooded American would be unfamiliar with the patriotic standards he had grown up with.

When Thanksgiving came, the black troops were back in the spotlight, putting on a "big athletic meet" with boxing, wrestling, and foot races. The YMCA hall was the venue again, and as before, a white audience came out and enjoyed the show as much as the blacks. Less than two weeks later, famous evangelist Billy Sunday, a late convert to wartime patriotism, came to town to hold a revival "for Negroes only" at Camp Bowie. African-American residents of the town were also invited. The event was too big for the YMCA hall at the camp, so the city, always willing to oblige the army, let Sunday use the North Side Coliseum.[21]

What all the various social activities show is that there was no shortage of entertainment for Camp Bowie's black troops and that white troops were always welcome. But the two races could not train or live together. That was just the way it was in the Jim Crow army.

And for anyone who did not understand the facts of segregated life, there was the performance of Miss Fritzi Schiff, a popular Fort Worth song bird of the day. In October 1918 she gave a concert at the camp for the latest bunch of white inductees, capping her performance with a "negro melody," which the crowd cheered appreciatively. The audience of 5,000 officers and men did not include a single black face.[22]

Once out of the detention phase, all trainees, blacks as well as whites, were allowed to apply for twenty-four-hour and weekend passes into town. All soldiers were warned against the Acre, but black soldiers had to be particularly careful where they went after getting off the street car. They were welcome in town but only as long as they confined themselves to "their own" neighborhoods and businesses. To help insure that there were no racial incidents, city fathers set up segregated recreation facilities for black soldiers, using "respectable young negro women" as "hostesses." Being soldiers, many of the men bypassed the official places and headed for the east side of Hell's Half-acre where they found a different kind of entertainment.[23]

During the ten months that black troops were at Camp Bowie, not a single racial incident was reported in town. The definition of "incident" does not include "misunderstandings" between white, Southern-born soldiers and black residents. In May 1918, one well-dressed black woman who worked for a state legislator was accosted by white soldiers as she walked through the city park. They assumed she was "available." More serious incidents were avoided because blacks, whether out of fear or prudence, stayed in their part of town, continued to ride in the back of street cars, and did not get crossways with the all-white police or MPs.[24]

This is all the more remarkable considering what happened at Houston in August 1917 involving troops of the black 24th Infantry Regiment and white townspeople. On the night of August 23, 1917, a white police officer, Lee Sparks, severely beat two members of the 24th for no reason. Other members of the regiment were outraged and armed themselves. More than a hundred marched into town from Camp Logan seeking revenge. On the way into town they killed sixteen and wounded a dozen more people who were guilty of nothing more than being white. The Houston police turned out in force, and a gun battle erupted on the city's streets. The soldiers finally returned to camp and order was restored. As punishment, the Army transferred the entire 24th to Columbus, New Mexico, and brought charges of mutiny and murder against thirteen men identified as ringleaders of what was being called "the Houston riot," moving them to Fort Sam Houston for trial.[25]

The fallout reached as far as Camp Bowie where Major H.S. Grier, inspector general, was assigned by the army to be defense counsel of the Houston thirteen. Grier had previously served with the 24th and was known as a conscientious and fair-minded officer. The mutineers' gain was Camp Bowie's loss, but not even Grier could get a fair trial for his clients. Their courts martial lasted three months, at the end of which, all thirteen defendants were found guilty and hanged. For the remainder of the war, black troops at Camp Bowie as elsewhere lived under a cloud of white distrust. The army itself was not quite sure how to handle the mixed racial populations at its two Texas camps (Fort Logan and Camp Bowie). Secretary of War Newton Baker, called them the most "deplorable" camps in the entire system. One cannot help but conclude that there was a connection between their racial makeup and his considered opinion. A different opinion came from Dr. Charles Satchell Morris, a leader of the Freedmen Baptist Association who visited Camp Logan in March 1918. He said he was inspired by "the spirit of patriotism and loyalty exhibited by our boys," and felt assured that when the opportunity presented itself, "They would give a good account of themselves." For Camp Bowie blacks, that "opportunity" (i.e., to see combat) never presented itself.[26]

Camp Logan was not the first time black troops in Texas had been involved in a racial incident. Another incident had occurred in August 1906, and it, too, echoed in Fort Worth. The 906 incident was sparked by a shooting on the streets of Brownsville. The town's white citizens blamed members of the black 25th Infantry stationed at nearby Camp Brown. Despite the flimsiest of evidence, the charge stuck and President Theodore Roosevelt in November ordered dishonorable discharges for 167 men. Fort Worth got involved when three other companies of the 25th stationed at Fort Bliss, Texas, were ordered to proceed to Fort Reno, Oklahoma, a month later. They had to change trains in Fort Worth, and the army was concerned that there would be another incident involving troops of the disgraced regiment. To avoid any problems, the army arranged to get the soldiers in and out of Fort Worth as quickly and quietly as possible. They traveled in segregated cars, and when they arrived in Fort Worth the train to take them on to Fort Reno already had steam up. The soldiers' cars only had to be uncoupled and then re-coupled to the waiting engine. There would be no layover or sight-seeing in Fort Worth. Most citizens did not even know they were in town.[27]

Now, in the fall of 1917 white residents of the city stayed abreast of the latest events in Houston through newspapers and letters from friends there. One unnamed Texas newspaper declared, "The fact is that negro troops cannot safely be quartered in a Southern community," and called the War Department's posting "experiment" a failure. The state legislature chimed in, with members of the Senate passing a resolution to the effect that black soldiers in Texas communities were "a serious menace to the safety and welfare of white citizens," and calling on the state's congressional delegation in Washington to get all black soldiers removed. Even a black newspaper, the *New York Age*, seemed to agree, editorializing that "quartering Negro troops in the South is equivalent to sending them into the enemy's country with the difference that they are forbidden to exercise the right of self-protection." Black troops were still posted to Camp Bowie a year later, but the War Department took precautions to prevent another Houston incident.[28]

The Houston incident was the main reason Fort Worth was placed under martial law in 1918. Uniformed MPs set up an office downtown and patrolled the city's streets. Fort Worth was potentially another racial flash point like Houston, and the army was determined that was not going to happen. For blacks, events at Houston served as a reminder that not even being in a U.S. army uniform and presumably under the protection of the federal government could protect blacks from racial violence. It had only been four years since Fort Worth experienced its own race riot, and a black man would be gunned down in the middle of the Tarrant County Courthouse in October 1917. It is no surprise that Fort Worth had a case of "race nerves." The city was just one misstep away from being another Houston. [29]

The war ended before most of Camp Bowie's black soldiers could be shipped off to the front. Most of those who did go to France went with the 435th Reserve Labor Battalion. Although they trained at Camp Bowie, the members of the 435th did not get the honor of participating in the big parade through town for the 36th "Panther" Division on April 11, 1918. Instead, they were shipped out quietly, without patriotic fanfare. The black troops who remained at Camp Bowie finally got to "march in review" on the parade ground that fall. The public was not invited.[30]

Rare was the black soldier who got to do anything for Uncle Sam other than heavy labor. The first to break the mold at Camp Bowie was Dave Alex of Ennis, Texas, who in October 1918 was assigned to the camp hospital to assist in administering typhoid shots to black recruits. In effect, the army made him a member of the camp medical staff. It was extraordinary enough to cause a Dallas newspaper to comment.[31]

Even rarer still was a letter home from a black Fort Worth soldier who made it to Europe. Only one such letter is known to exist, written by Pvt. Harrison Brister to his parents and dated May 12, 1918. He had sailed for France from New York on December 5 and spent Christmas on the Western Front. Brister described himself as "a sharp shutter [*sic*]," but little else is known about him. For some reason his letter to his folks came back to Camp Bowie where the Assistant Division Adjutant, Maj. J.R. McDowell, opened it and shared the contents with the *Star-Telegram*. Brister's letter is reproduced here just as it was written, including the misspellings and grammatical mistakes:

> Helo, my Dear Mother and farther. how er you all to night. I am well and I hope when thease few lines has reached your hands I hope that it fine you all well and darning well. tell John helo. tell all the Boys helo. an Rosa helo. tell all the girls helo. tell al they boys they outer to be a Man lik me. stand up and be a man. Come over an take part with us in France. I has crossed the sea it is thirty hundred miles across we wear sixteen Days and Nights crossing the Deep Blue Sea. the armey is all rite. I like the army fine. tell John that war is hell. But I am a Brave man. I am a solger in the armey. I will be home sometime I don't know when. But it is not going to be veary long I don't think. . . . Mother Don't wore about me Ma far I am all rite. Pray for Me that I Mite hold out until the end. [32]

The newspaper reported with no sense of irony that the letter had been read "with many a chuckle at headquarters," adding that Private Brister had "the right stuff."[33]

Outside the army, other African Americans did their part for the war effort, going to work in war industries or buying "Liberty" bonds if they were financially secure. It was at one of those war-bond drives in Fort Worth that the contradiction between fighting for liberty and democracy on the Western Front versus living under Jim Crow back home was underscored. The person pointing out the contradiction was Rabbi George Fox of Temple Beth-El. Fox had been one of the top fund-raisers in the local drive as a member of Fort Worth's "Liberty Bond committee," so he was invited to a luncheon at a downtown hotel to hear financial reports and map out strategy for the bond drive. On the way into the dining room he was disturbed to see black leaders who were on the program seated in a side waiting room. The organizers informed him that the "chairman of the Negro Division" would be summoned at the appropriate time to give his report but until then he had to wait with his kind. What happened next is best described in Fox's own words:

> When I asked why they were not with us, I was told that Negroes and whites do not eat together at affairs of this sort. I arose and requested permission to ask a question. . . . whether the Liberty Drive was an American enterprise for all Americans [and] whether there would be any distinction in the monies raised as to color or race. . . . All those who worked on the Liberty Bond drive had the same United States at heart. . . . Was it in the spirit of true Americanism to make a distinction between white and colored Americans as long as they worked together for the welfare of our country? I then stated that so far as I was concerned I would not participate in the meeting if the black Americans were not permitted to come in. There was a hush and subdued excitement, but they [the blacks] were invited in, and a real Liberty Bond celebration was held.[34]

As a member of a minority that had experienced oppression and prejudice for much of its history, Fox was particularly qualified to lecture his fellow citizens on right and wrong, which may be why they listened to him that day. His opinions on Abraham Lincoln, African Americans, and the Ku Klux Klan also coincided with blacks' opinions. Fox writes in his memoirs years later about "how strong was the [racial] prejudice against Negroes" in Fort Worth, and he was proud of the stand he had taken.[35]

When the 1918 global influenza epidemic struck Fort Worth in September, not even the worst medical crisis in the city's history could shake the Jim Crow mindset. Representatives of the U.S. Public Health Service and the city's medical community at first were in agreement that this was just another outbreak of "old-style la grippe." That announcement at the end of September ignored nearly 1,000 reported cases already in the Camp Bowie hospital. Within a week those same doctors had changed their tune; now they were calling it an "epidemic." The number of suspected Camp Bowie cases rose to 1,400, three hundred of whom were black. And this is where Jim Crow reared its ugly head.[36]

The first reports of the African-American cases took a facetious tone. The camp doctors said "the negroes" believed being placed in the hospital under quarantine was all part of their army training. Those who were not yet in the base hospital expected to be sent there soon, and those who were already patients were regarded by the medical staff as near-aliens. The lieutenant colonel commanding, a veteran army doctor, told the *Star-Telegram*, "The negroes are totally different from any patients ever placed in the institution." As he explained it, they did not understand the process of diagnosing or treating disease because they had never before experienced it. The first week in October was the worst week. All schools and public amusements in the city were closed, and the entire camp was quarantined. But the only death among 2,000 patients admitted to the camp hospital with flu-like symptoms that week was black. During the second week there were seven more deaths at the camp hospital, six of them black. The only one of the seven whose background information was announced (hometown, unit, etc.) was the white soldier. The other six only had their names printed and "home" was apparently the detention camp. The worst of the flu epidemic had passed before the end of the month leaving a death count of 219, but the disease lingered on through the winter.[37]

The response of the white medical community, both U.S. government doctors and private physicians, was shamefully racist. Nothing had really changed since the smallpox outbreaks of the 1880s. Public health measures were still for whites. Not a single black doctor in 1918 was included in all the conferences and planning sessions for combating the flu. Dallas at least appointed a black nurse to "work among negro patients." There is no record that Fort Worth fathers even took that step. The black community had to depend on the ministering angels of the (white) Fort Worth Relief Association (FWRA), a charitable organization whose nurses visited patients at home. While the Camp Bowie hospital quarantined those diagnosed with flu in the same wards regardless of race, the city's white hospitals still could not bring themselves to admit black patients, not even those with flu symptoms. They were directed to their own doctors and clinics or told to go home and wait for one of the nurses of the FWRA.[38]

Meanwhile at Camp Bowie, black recruits continued to live in their "detention camp" tents during the worst of the epidemic and through the winter of 1918–19. Not surprisingly perhaps, blacks constituted "the greatest number of patients" admitted to the camp hospital even though their numbers in the total camp population were far smaller than whites'. About the only adjustment made for black recruits was to go easy on their training until most of those in the hospital had been declared "fit for duty" and discharged. Those soldiers who died, regardless of color, were put in a pine box and shipped home.[39]

Because it was wartime and they did not know if they would be shipped overseas, more than a few black soldiers at Camp Bowie bought what the agents called "war risk insurance." Historically, African Americans had never been players in the insurance market because most did not own enough property to make property insurance worthwhile, and life insurance was a luxury they could not afford. That was something else the war changed; the camp insurance officer, Lieutenant A.L. Gustafson, did a brisk business among black soldiers. A month after arriving in camp, most black soldiers had taken out life insurance, many signing up for the full amount of $10,000.[40]

Fort Worthers greeted the news of the Armistice on November 11, 1918, with joy. The war was virtually over. City fathers hurriedly put together a big parade through the city, starting at 4:00 that same afternoon. It was organized into five successive "divisions," each led by a "field marshal." At the tail end of the parade, behind the Students' Division, was the "Colored Division" for black Fort Worthers. It was the first time in Fort Worth history blacks had ever marched in a city-wide parade.[41]

When demobilization got underway in 1919, the black troops who had trained at Camp Bowie were among the thousands that returned to be discharged. The 471 men and officers of the (black) 317th Regiment, 92nd Division, were processed in March. This was the only "all-negro" division that had served in France. Not all black soldiers who were processed through Camp Bowie had trained there. Another black unit to be discharged in Fort Worth was the 435th Labor Battalion. The two companies who came through together got a big send-off from the city's black community on April 21, 1919. Black churches and organizations put together a parade through downtown capped off by speeches at the Chamber of Commerce auditorium. Unlike the newspaper's indifferent coverage of black soldiers at Camp Bowie during the war, the *Star-Telegram* covered their departure in detail. Not every black soldier who reported to Camp Bowie after the war went home. When the army needed soldiers for "border service" on the Rio Grande, they persuaded forty-five of those same soldiers to re-enlist. On July 10, 1919, Camp Bowie closed for good.[42]

The opening of Camp Bowie in 1917 represents a milestone in the history of black Fort Worth albeit not because, as one source incorrectly states, it "displaced [so] many blacks who had been living" on the western edge of town. Truth be told, in 1917 the western edge of town was largely empty except for the star-crossed Arlington Heights and Lake Como developments. No, the years 1917–1919 are important in the history of black Fort Worth because the presence of thousands of African Americans training alongside white recruits at Camp Bowie forced the city's white residents to confront their deepest fears. When they were not murdered in their beds or overrun by hordes of armed black men, they had to reassess some of the mythology of Jim Crow.[43]

It is virtually impossible to identify any Fort Worth blacks by name who served In World War I *and* did their basic training at Camp Bowie. The absence of a local black veterans' organization in the 1920s and '30s suggests that the city did not contribute a significant number of blacks to the army. Those blacks who demobilized at Camp Bowie in 1919 did not stick around but went back to their homes elsewhere. Life in Fort Worth quickly returned to "normalcy" as President Warren G. Harding put it—the familiar routines and long-standing race relations that had been interrupted by the war.[44]

A postscript to the Camp Bowie experience was added by the 100th Infantry Division of the U.S. Army after World War II. This all-white division had been mobilized in July 1918 to replace the 36th Division at Camp Bowie when the latter left for Europe. One year later the 100th was demobilized without ever seeing combat. Reconstituted during World War II, it survived the end of the war to become one of the army's first racially integrated divisions in 1948. Thus Camp Bowie's central role in black history came full circle.[45]

Photo 13. 1918 parade

When the soldiers of Camp Bowie marched through downtown Fort Worth on April 11, 1918, there were no members of the black labor battalions in the parade. This was an all-white parade that sent "the boys" off to the Western Front in World War I. Photographed by John Swartz. Author's collections.

Notes

1. James Haskins, *Black Music in America* (New York: HarperCollins, 1987), 53, hereafter Haskins, *Black Music*. For DuBois quote, see "Close Ranks," *Crisis*, July 1918, p. 111. For Pitcher, see "Brownsville, Texas Riot of 1906," Walter C. Rucker, Jr. and James N. Upton, eds. *Encyclopedia of American Race Riots*, vol. 1 (Westport, CT: Greenwood Press, 2006), 80.
2. Racial concerns did not affect the U.S. Navy or Marine Corps because the former relegated all African Americans to duty either as cooks or stewards, and the latter did not accept blacks at all. Under this act and its subsequent amendments some twenty-four million were registered and almost three million drafted into military service. Rawn James, Jr., *The Double V* (New York: Bloomsbury Press, 2013), 27–30, hereafter James, *Double V*. Quotes come from "Pleads for Fair Play for Colored Soldiers," *Baltimore Afro-American*, September 15, 1917. The governors of Georgia and Arkansas, quoted in Keith, *Rich Man's War*, 179–80. For draft boards, see Maury Klein, *A Call to Arms* (New York: Bloomsbury Press, 2013), 691, hereafter Klein, *Call to Arms*.
3. Getting an accurate count of the black population in the early twentieth century was still very "iffy." According to one source, the approximate number of Fort Worth black residents was 13,000, as opposed to 60,000 whites. A more realistic number is 7,000 blacks vs. 66,000 whites in 1910. See "Federal Writers' Project," Consolidated Chronology, 1889-1923, Vol. 2, pp. 7778-79.
4. Combat battalions included infantry, artillery, cavalry, and engineering. Labor battalions would serve in rear areas. Pate, *Arsenal of Defense*, 40; James, *Double V*, 28–29.
5. Pate, *Arsenal*, 40–41.
6. *Fort Worth Star-Telegram*, September 9, 15, 25, and 26, 1918. One authoritative history of blacks in the U.S. military says "a paltry 4,000" (total) African Americans were enrolled in the U.S. Army during World War I, which must count only those enrolled in combat units. Gerald Astor, *The Right to Fight* (Cambridge, MA: Da Capo Press, 1998), 140.
7. *Fort Worth Star-Telegram*, September 25 and 26, 1918.
8. The 42nd Infantry Division, activated in 1917, was actually known as the Rainbow Division. Pate, *Arsenal*, 45.

9. The 24th (Colored) Infantry trained at Camp Logan. For "negro lovers" see James, *Double V*, 48. *Fort Worth Star-Telegram*, September 25, 1918. *Dallas Morning News*, December 25, 1917. For non-combat status of Camp Bowie's black recruits, see ibid., October 21, 1918. Curiously, the Dallas newspaper gave much more coverage to black troops training at Camp Bowie than the Fort Worth newspapers.
10. In some other camps, black troops were also assigned to guard battalions, but not at Camp Bowie. *Fort Worth Star-Telegram*, September 25, 26, 27; and October 9, 1918. *Dallas Morning News*, September 26, 1918. For Fisher, see ibid., September 25, 1918. For medical concerns of camp doctors, see Rich, *Fort Worth*, 195–96.
11. *Fort Worth Star-Telegram*, October 15, 1918. For blacks' otherwise permanent assignment to their first home even after their two-week detention was up, see ibid., October 19, 1918.
12. *Fort Worth Star-Telegram*, September 23, 25, and 27; November 24, 1918.
13. *Fort Worth Star-Telegram*, October 6, 1918. Bud Kennedy, "DFW Walloped in 1918 Pandemic," ibid., October 15, 2014.
14. *Fort Worth Star-Telegram*, September 25 and October 4, 1918. *Dallas Morning News*, October 1 and 3, 1918.
15. *Fort Worth Star-Telegram*, October 4 and 17, 1918.
16. *Fort Worth Star-Telegram*, October 13, 1918. *Dallas Morning News*, October 24, 1918.
17. *Dallas Morning News*, October 18 and 19, 1918.
18. For a discussion of the problems of black conscription in World War I, see Keith, *Rich Man's War*, 111 *ff.*
19. *Fort Worth Star-Telegram*, July 30, 1918. *Dallas Morning News*, July 19, 1918. Typical of black draft evaders was Richard Daniels of south Dallas. When he failed to show up for his physical examination in August 1917, MPs picked him up. The chairman of his draft board "arranged" for him to be inducted and sent immediately to Camp Bowie. *Dallas Morning News*, February 22, 1918.
20. *Fort Worth Star-Telegram*, September 13, 1918; and December 29, 1919.
21. *Dallas Morning News*, October 4 and November 5, 1918. *Fort Worth Star-Telegram*, November 24 and 27, 1918. For Billy Sunday, see ibid., November 28, 1918. Sunday was in town for a full week, preaching to whites-only audiences on December 1 and 6.
22. *Dallas Morning News*, October 6, 1918.
23. *Dallas Morning News*, October 4, 1918.
24. *Fort Worth Star-Telegram*, May 13, 1918.

25. James, *Double V*, 31–34. Meirion and Susie Harries, *The Last Days of Innocence* (New York: Random House, 1997), 107–109, hereafter Harries, *Last Days*. For local reporting on the affair, see *Fort Worth Star-Telegram*, October 19 and 20, 1917.
26. James, *Double V*, 34; Harries, *Last Days*, 109. For Grier, see *Fort Worth Star-Telegram*, February 8, 1918. For "deplorable," see *Fort Worth Star-Telegram*, February 15, 1918. For Morris, see Louis F. Aulbach, Linda Gorski, and Robbie Martin, *Camp Logan, Houston, Texas, 1917–1919* (Houston: Louis F. Aulbach, 2014), 27.
27. For "Brownsville Incident," see John D. Weaver, *The Brownsville Raid* (New York: W.W. Norton, 1970); and E.L. Bute and H.P. Harmer, *The Black Handbook* (London, U.K.: Cassell, 1997), 77. For Roosevelt's role, see John Allen Gable, *The Bull Moose Years: Theodore Roosevelt and the Progressive Party* (Port Washington, NY: Kennikat Press, 1978), 61–62. For train, see *Fort Worth Telegram*, December 5, 1906.
28. Quoted in James, *Double V*, 34–45.
29. Harries, *Last Days*, 107–109.; *Fort Worth Star-Telegram*, February 8, 1918. The black man gunned down in the Courthouse was Jeff Daggett (October 23, 1917). For Daggett's story, see Richard Selcer, chapter 7 of *Fort Worth Characters* (Denton: University of North Texas Press, 2009), 131–148.
30. *Fort Worth Star-Telegram*, October 17, 1918.
31. *Dallas Morning News*, October 3, 1918.
32. Brister's letter is reproduced in full in the *Fort Worth Star-Telegram*, July 8, 1918.
33. *Fort Worth Star-Telegram*, July 8, 1918. For additional coverage of Camp Bowie's black recruits in Fort Worth's number one newspaper, see *Fort Worth Star-Telegram*, September 9, November 5, and December 15, 1918; and July 3, 1919.
34. This particular version comes from Rabbi Fox's unpublished MS, Beth-El Congregation archives, Fort Worth, TX., p. 4. See published version in Fox, "End of an Era," 281-82. Also cited in Weiner, *Jewish Stars*, 92–93.
35. For a good overview of Fox's views on the Klan, racial prejudice, etc., see Chap. 5, "Cowtown's Front-Page Rabbi," in Weiner, *Jewish Stars*, 80-101. Quotation comes from unpublished Fox MS, ibid., p. 4.
36. *Fort Worth Star-Telegram*, September 29 and 30, 1918. *Dallas Morning News*, October 3, 1918.
37. The first black soldier to die was Pvt. Louis Warren. The report does not mention funeral arrangements for him. None of the six in the second

week were Fort Worth residents. The medical community distinguished between deaths attributed to influenza and those attributed to pneumonia. *Fort Worth Star-Telegram*, October 4, 8, and 18, 1918. For Lt.-Col L.H. Hanson, see *ibid.*, September 25 and October 4, 1918. For October deaths, see *Fort Worth Star-Telegram*, October 15, 1918; and *Dallas Morning News*, October 27, 1918.

38. *Fort Worth Star-Telegram*, September 25, October 4, December 6, 1918; and March 13, 1919. For "negro nurse," see *Dallas Morning News*, October 21, 1918.
39. *Dallas Morning News*, October 3 and 9, 1918. *Fort Worth Star-Telegram*, October 17, 1918.
40. It sounds like a big racket since the Camp's African Americans, restricted to labor battalions, were never going to see combat. *Dallas Morning News*, October 9, 1918.
41. This was a civilian, not an Army event; it did not include soldiers from Camp Bowie. *Fort Worth Star-Telegram*, November 11, 1918.
42. Note: Even "all-negro" divisions had white commissioned officers. *Fort Worth Star-Telegram*, March 14 and 22, 1919. *Dallas Morning News*, July 3, 1919.
43. For "displaced," see Geisel, *Historical Vignette*, 4.
44. There are no records of who trained at Camp Bowie, 1917–18, only the rolls of the 36th Infantry Division. Research into the rolls of the various labor battalions has never been done.
45. Jim Atkinson and Judy Wood, *Fort Worth's Huge Deal* (Fort Worth: Self-published, 2010), 156–163. "The Story of the Century: The Story of the 100th Infantry Division," www.lonesentry.com; and "The 100th Infantry Division Association," www.100thww2.org/.

Chapter 6

Jim Crow Rules!

Camp Bowie, which brought a small army of black men to Fort Worth without a single racial incident, was the biggest thing that had happened to the local African-American community since emancipation. Sadly, it did not produce any real progress on the long road toward equality. It was an aberration, compliments of Uncle Sam. The black soldiers who trained at Camp Bowie could not break down the walls of Jim Crow or capture the castle in a single determined rush. The ultimate victory would have to be won one small victory at a time.

As African-American numbers grew in the twentieth century, so too did the number of social and professional groups representing their interests. The combination of greater numbers and more assertiveness provoked white resistance that was reflected in vague talk of a "race problem" in the newspapers. There was no race problem but that was all it took for Jim Crow to clamp down tighter as the twentieth century advanced. Yet there was this silver lining: the creation of numerous organizations and institutions in the black community that advanced the cause of equality.

BUILDING "SOCIAL CAPITAL," PART 2

It was in unity that African Americans found the strength to resist racial oppression. The process of socialization (building "social capital") that had begun toward the end of the nineteenth century gained momentum in the twentieth century. (See Chap. 3) In 1900, J.W. McKinney, Grand Master of the Texas branch of Prince Hall Masons, speaking to a convention of black Masons at Galveston, deplored the lack of racial unity: "Never was there greater want of unity of action among men," he said, "than there is among our race today." That message must have resonated outside the meeting hall because things began to change rapidly in the years that followed. A flurry of organizations appeared in the black community that mirrored the white community.[1]

Whites had always had their fraternal groups, social clubs, and the like; it was only natural for African Americans to want the same thing. Fraternal orders such as the Masons ranked only slightly behind the church as centers of community life and mutual aid societies. The Rev. C.A. Harris at the same Galveston convention cited above told attendees, "Fraternal orders are national blessings. They promote thrift, economy, sobriety, without freezing the soul into selfishness." They also represented an important rung in the long upward climb from slavery.[2]

Although the list is practically endless, some groups stand out. For instance, black business owners formed the Colored Business Men's League; black teachers formed the Texas Colored Teachers Association; black newspaper publishers, the Colored Press Association of Texas; black golfers, the Negro Golf Association; black doctors, dentists, and pharmacists, the Lone Star State Medical, Dental and Pharmaceutical Association (*cf.* the National Negro Medical Assoc.); black nurses, the Association of Colored Graduate Nurses; black church-goers, the Friendship Sunday School Convention; black social activists, the Colored YMCA and YWCA, Colored Women's Christian Temperance Union (CWCTU), and Southern Negro Anti-Saloon Congress. Some of these groups were national; others existed only on the state or local. But they all represented the same thing:

black pride of accomplishment. They were the hallmark of a civilized society as well as potent symbols of the good life showing that African Americans were no longer just getting by; they were "movin' on up" as the television program *The Jeffersons* put it so many years later. And Fort Worth blacks took a back seat to no one. Fort Worth's "Colored YMCA," established as its own branch in1919, was the first African-American branch in Texas admitted to the National Council of YMCAs.[3]

Organizations like these represented a giant step on the road to equality, but they still had to fit within the familiar bounds of Jim Crow society. The Colored YMCA of Fort Worth, although established in 1903, was not accepted into the metropolitan (read that white) organization until 1919. When the (black) Lone Star State Medical, Dental and Pharmaceutical Association held its convention in Fort Worth in 1930, they had to use the auditorium of Mount Gilead Baptist Church because they could not rent space in a white meeting hall. And being unwelcome in the city's larger restaurants, they had all their meals prepared by the ladies of the church. (At least the all-white Tarrant County Medical Society graciously co-hosted the convention.) Black tennis players in Fort Worth had no sponsoring organization or even decent courts to play on. The first black tennis tournament in Fort Worth (1931) was held on the cracked, uneven asphalt courts of Greenway Park because the nicer country-club facilities were off-limits. Nor did the winners receive any prize money or recognition in the major newspapers.[4]

Two of the best examples of "social bonding" appeared around the turn of the century. The Colored Progressive Club (CPC), organized by the city's black elite sometime in the 1890s, promoted entrepreneurial opportunities and political involvement. The members were up-and-comers excluded from the Board of Trade (antecedent of the Chamber of Commerce) and other white civic organizations. The CPC was an agency for black professionals, not an advocacy group for all African Americans. In 1908 the city's black business community joined a statewide movement to create the Texas Negro Business League (TNBL). Leading the Fort Worth contingent to the first organizational meeting at Prairie View College that July were Isaiah M. Terrell and Dr. Jack Moseley. The following year the group met in Waco, and again Fort Worth was well-represented. One of the topics on the Waco program was "What Can Negro Business Men Do to Capture the Trade of Their Race?" Attendees at the conference must not have been able to come up with a good answer because the TNBL folded within a few years. In its place, black businessmen in different cities, working independently, formed their own organizations. One of the first was the Dallas Negro Chamber of Commerce (1926). Fort Worth's black businessmen were much slower to organize. They tried unsuccessfully to establish a Black Chamber of Commerce in 1936 before a second try produced the Metropolitan Black Chamber of Commerce in 1979.[5]

Despite the lack of organizational unity, the black community was not lacking in entrepreneurial spirit. In 1909, they opened the city's first black-owned-and-operated bank, Provident Bank and Trust. That was just one year after the idea of establishing black-owned banks was raised at the first meeting of the Texas Negro Business League. It took a year to raise the necessary capital ($50,000) but the growing black middle class who bought shares in the bank saw it as more than just another financial institution; it would be a symbol of their independence from the white community. In a practical sense, it would also be the wellspring for nurturing the growth of the black businesses and building black housing. The bank was practically an arm of the Prince Hall Masons. It principal investors and most of its initial depositors were Masons who also provided both the president of the bank, R.C. Houston, Jr., and its board of directors. Tom Mason and Bill McDonald, two pillars of the business community, sat on the board. The bank was even located in the Prince Hall Masonic Temple on East Ninth. There is no way of knowing how many business loans or home mortgages the bank backed, but it was a source of pride in the black community. At least until 1912 when it went into receivership. Poor management and weak deposits were to blame. At the time it folded, it held only $20,000 in deposits. Its loss was both a financial and symbolic loss to the black community.[6]

The optimistic spirit of Progressivism still burned brightly in the black community, and not just among the tiny business fraternity. Around 1910, a group of prominent public men formed the Fort Worth Negro Civic League. The leadership, a mix of educators, ministers, and businessmen, included some distinguished names: Professor G.T. Gray, William M. McDonald, W.H. Harvey, Nathan Johnson, F.T. Perkins, and the Rev. M.L. Smith. They met at the Morning Chapel Methodist Episcopal Church at Twelfth and Crump, demonstrating yet again how important the black church was, not just in religious matters but in all community activities.[7]

The higher up the social scale one went, the more important professional groups like the Fort Worth Negro Business League and Fort Worth Negro Civic League became. But social and fraternal groups were right up there with them. A few years after the Prince Hall Masons established their lodge in Fort Worth, the Grand United Order of Odd Fellows (G.U.O.O.F.) followed. The G.U.O.O.F. was the "Colored" branch of the Independent Order of Odd Fellows (I.O.O.F.), which traced its roots back to England and had had a presence in Texas since 1838. Like its white counterpart, it was a middle-class, service-oriented organization that focused its efforts on "cooperative and industrial work," including operating grocery stores, savings banks, employment services, and orphanages for its members. In 1901 and again in 1913 the Fort Worth lodge hosted the annual state convention. Since there was no conflict between the mission or the rituals of the two organizations, many men were members of both. The Masons even allowed the Odd Fellows to use their building for meetings until the latter could build their own meeting hall. Their brethren in white I.O.O.F. were not nearly as gracious.[8]

The attitude of white Fort Worth toward black social and service organizations was less than supportive. In 1913, the *Star-Telegram* called "negro social clubs" a "disgrace to the city" after a reporter visited several on a Sunday night and saw "the tango, the bunny hug, and similar dances in full swing." When the Colored Odd Fellows came to Fort Worth two months later for a convention, Mayor R.F. Milam initially welcomed the visitors, saying he was "honored" to have them in his city. The white backlash that followed brought a quick retraction from Hizzoner, and left the delegates suddenly feeling considerably less than welcome.[9]

Where the men led, African-American women followed. Two years after the Prince Hall Masons opened for business in Fort Worth, their spouses formed a women's auxiliary, the very first African-American women's organization in the city's history. They were part of an umbrella group known as the Heroines of Jericho, organized into "courts" which, like their male brethren, belonged to the Grand Lodge of Texas. The Fort Worth Heroines were just the eighth court organized in the state after the first in 1875. Two years after the Heroines, a rival Masonic women's auxiliary, the Order of Eastern Star, organized a Fort Worth chapter. Perhaps most remarkable is that there were enough Masonic wives to form two separate groups. In 1906 the Texas Heroines of Jericho relocated their state headquarters to Fort Worth, headquartering in the Prince Hall Temple at Ninth and Jones. The move demonstrated the drive and initiative of the city's black middle-class women. The wives of Fort Worth's white Masons did not organize until 1894, seven years after the Heroines of Jericho.[10]

The Heroines of Jericho and the Order of Eastern Star were just the start for women of the black middle class. If the city's grand dames would not allow them into the Fort Worth Woman's Club (neé, the Woman's Wednesday Club, 1889) or the Fort Worth Library Association (1892) or the Fort Worth Young Women's Association (1907), then they would form their own organizations. Equal parts feminism, racial pride, and social climbing, this phenomenon reached its pinnacle with the "coming out" of prominent young women of high society or "debutantes." Annual debutante balls were a long-standing tradition in white society in the Deep South. Since wealthy white families had their Steeplechase and Assembly balls, black social elites had their equivalents in the Ambassador and (Colored) Fort Worth Assembly balls. All up and down the social scale were similar organizations. White colleges had Greek sororities and fraternities; so did black colleges. White children had scouting (Boy Scouts, Girl Scouts); so did black children. The average African American of the time would have been unlikely to belong to one of these organizations, but they were nonetheless potent symbols of achieving the American Dream. Booker T. Washington's story, chronicled in *Up from Slavery*, was only the beginning; it was how far *up* that mattered. The difference between the two worlds was illustrated by the Negro Boy Scouts. By the 1940s there were more than a hundred in the Fort Worth troop. The problem was they could not find a suitable site for their campouts. White Boy Scouts never had that problem.[11]

Other social groupings represented a less exclusive segment of the black community. William Trezevant, Jr. who had worked in saloons his entire adult life, opened a "negro social club" in 1913. It was in the rapidly developing Near South Side, on Rosedale near the Frisco tracks. Three years later he upgraded both the name and the location of the place by moving it upstairs over 1120 Harding and renaming it the Colored Country Club. He moved again in 1926 to rooms over 907 Jones where he operated until the space was turned into an annex of the Delray Hotel in 1931. Trezevant's place was more than just a saloon; it was an upscale gathering place for the city's growing black middle class. Even the name he gave it in 1916, "country club," made a statement that blacks had arrived.[12]

Photo 14. Fort Worth Debutantes

Fort Worth Ambassador Debutantes, 1962. The Assembly and Ambassador debs were part of the shadow society erected by African Americans during Jim Crow. The young ladies were presented at formal "coming out" parties every spring, just like their white counterparts. Courtesy of Tarrant County Black Historical & Genealogical Society.

Most black social organizations were an extension of their white counterparts, serving the same needs and even working together sometimes. Not so with military veterans. White sons of the Old South had the Confederate Veterans (CV) organization to honor their Civil War service and represent them for many years after Appomattox. In 1889 a group of Fort Worth Confederate veterans formed the R.E. Lee Camp of the CV, counting among their members such distinguished community leaders as C.C. Cummings, K.M. Van Zandt, R.E. Beckham, B.B. Paddock, and William P. McLean, some of them widely known as friends of the black man. (See Chap. 2) The elderly veterans did more than just meet together to reminisce; they exerted a disproportionate influence in social and political affairs, presiding over the courts and running the leading newspaper and banks. They held their meetings in the courthouse and considered emancipation the worst thing that had ever happened to the country. In 1915 their offspring organized the Sons of Confederate Veterans (SCV) to perpetuate the same unreconstructed view of history. [13] Black veterans had no such organizations to honor their service in the Civil War or any other conflict in the nineteenth century. The local chapter of the Grand Army of the Republic (GAR) for Union veterans was as white as the CV organization.

While some African Americans were organizing, the overwhelming majority remained stuck in poverty and ignorance, provoking a certain amount of jealousy and resentment toward those who managed to break out of the ghetto. Not every African American applauded "brothers" like Bill McDonald, Thomas Mason, and Hiram McGar for achieving the good life. The contemptuous slang term "bougie" (pronounced "boojie," from bourgeois) was coined in the black community to describe those with social pretentions. African American social divisions were also reflected in the debate over the aesthetics of skin color (black, brown, or "yellow") and straight vs. curly hair. Publicly they may have presented a united front, but behind the scenes such issues divided the black community deeply.[14]

Climbing the Ladder of Success

In Jim Crow days, the definition of a "good job" was different in the black community than in the white community. Lacking education and equal opportunity, few African Americans could aspire to a white-collar job. The gold standard of middle-class employment was getting on as a Pullman porter with one of the railroads. The sleeping coaches manufactured and operated by the Pullman Palace Car Company of Chicago were used on all the long-distance routes. Every Pullman car was staffed by a uniformed African-American attendant who took care of the needs of white passengers during the day and had their sleeping berths ready at bed time. Pullman porters represented perhaps the highest evolution of domestic service. "Porter" became practically shorthand for African-American employees who did general janitorial work around a white-owned business. In contrast to their exalted image, Pullman porters worked long hours for low wages and no benefits, had to pay for their uniforms and food out of pocket, and were strictly prohibited from mixing with white passengers. But the job had its perks. They got to travel, were treated kindly by most customers, could earn generous tips, and were lords of their domain, at least for the duration of the train trip. Being a Pullman porter did not guarantee respect away from work, however. Off duty, they were just another black man liable to be bullied or forced to step aside by whites. Not even their personal safety was assured. In 1907, Pullman Porter G.B. Ballard was inside his car in the T&P rail yards cleaning it when he was shot and killed. The shooter was not some thief or hobo but Policeman James Kidwell Yates. "Kid" Yates was a well-known hot-head and all-around "bad man," but he was never prosecuted. When other officers arrived on the scene, they found Ballard dead "with an open knife clutched in his hand." Yates called it self-defense.[15]

Though Pullman porters were in point of fact glorified butlers, they did constitute the largest single job category of African-American men not engaged in manual labor, numbering more than 20,000 by the early twentieth century. The job carried an enormous amount of respect in the black community as an entry into the middle class. Members of the group would also play a crucial role in the modern century civil rights movement. They were the first African-American workers to successfully unionize—the Brotherhood of Sleeping Car Porters (founded 1925, recognized 1937). They also served an important function in the black community as a grapevine for transmitting the latest black news and information about consumer products to distant corners of the nation.[16]

Second in prestige only to being a Pullman porter among working-class African Americans was working for the federal government, more specifically the U.S. Post Office. The job paid decent wages, came with a degree of security unknown in other work, and was open to anyone who passed the civil service exam. They were hired as both mail clerks and letter carriers, although the latter only worked in black neighborhoods. Edward D. "Dan" Oliver was a railway postal clerk, which meant he rode in the mail car sorting the mail enroute between cities. William C. Anderson had a mail route in Fort Worth's black neighborhoods. The additional appeal of jobs with the Post Office, besides the regular paycheck, was that employees got to wear uniforms and were on a career ladder, both of which were highly unusual for black men during the Jim Crow era. Anderson started out as a "substitute carrier," then got a regular route and achieved the status of "old-timer" by the time he retired in 1901. Interviewed by the *Fort Worth Register*, he said he was proud to have been a "colored letter carrier" for all those years. Another job in federal service, albeit less prestigious than working for the Post Office, was janitor in the federal building.[17]

After Pullman porters and postal workers, the most desirable blue-collar jobs were in domestic service, specifically, porters, waiters, elevator operators, and chauffeurs after the number of cars on the street multiplied. Practically every saloon and business in town had one or more black porters. We would call them janitors or maintenance men today. They worked in the shadows, sweeping floors, emptying spittoons, polishing brass work, doing the myriad little jobs it took to keep a place spruced up for the public. The only time they got any recognition was when they did something criminal or something laughable, such as when the porter at the Crown Saloon lit a match to see how much whiskey was in the bottom of an open barrel—and nearly destroyed the place when the fumes ignited.[18]

Jim Warren was another one of those faithful, hard-working domestics, only he had genuine talent as a cook. Warren was already white-haired in 1901 when he was hired to run the kitchen at the Tarrant County Jail. It was a good, steady-paying job, and the clientele was not too discriminating. The county contracted food service for prisoners, so he did not actually work for the county, but he still reported seven days a week to the old jail on Belknap. He liked to say he had visited "almost every country on the globe," so his education came from life, not books, but all the inmates cared about was his wizardry whipping up fresh-made biscuits, gravy, and gingerbread on a budget of 40¢ per day per prisoner. He sometimes dipped into his own pocket to supplement the meager food allowance the county gave him. He fed the men and women in county lockup for more than a decade, and was so beloved by them that they called him "Chef."[19]

But the most fortunate domestics were those who caught on with a wealthy family or an exclusive private club. Photographs of family gatherings and social events at country clubs like River Crest often show black faces in the background either going about their duties or sometimes as part of the family group. Domestic service could last decades, and it came with the sort of perks men like Jim Warren never saw, such as Christmas bonuses and even in some cases living quarters. What it did not come with was a medical plan or retirement pension. But domestic service easily beat tenant farming and day labor as a way to earn a living wage.

Job opportunities for the average African-American male expanded dramatically after industry came to town. No longer did a black man have to settle for a job in agriculture or as a janitor. The manufacturing sector expanded with the opening of the Texas Brewing Company in 1891. Blacks could get jobs working in the warehouse, in the stable, on the loading dock, and make higher wages than they could picking cotton. The Texas Brewing Company was the biggest industry in town until the arrival of Swift and Armour meat-packing plants in 1902. The "help wanted" signs went up not just at the plants but in the adjacent stockyards where a man who could handle cattle was prized regardless of his skin color. The jobs on the slaughter-house floor at the packing plants were nasty but paid decent wages. Sam Jones Washington worked on a farm before taking a job at one of the packing plants. And the packing plants opened up other job opportunities. S.E. Collins went to work there in 1904 as a government meat inspector working for Uncle Sam. The new industrial jobs were racially segregated, but that did not pose any problems until a company tried to use cheap black labor to break a strike by white workers. This is what happened at Swift and Armour in 1921.[20] (See Rouse's story in Chap. 4.)

Swift and Armour were followed by Texas Steel, which built a plant on far south Hemphill and began hiring blacks in 1907. Trinity Valley Iron & Steel, which opened in 1924, also welcomed blacks, and before the end of the decade Northern Texas Traction Company (NTTC) had black conductors and motormen on its cars. Unlike the steel mills and packing plants, NTTC jobs did not require a man to risk life and limb every day. This fact alone made the NTTC one of the most progressive employers in the city. After Pullman porter and federal government jobs, NTTC jobs were the best route out of poverty for an uneducated black man. The problem with jobs in manufacturing was that they held little or no promise of advancement out of the blue-collar sector. Still, they represented progress from agricultural jobs.[21]

Although most of the rising black middle class worked for white bosses, there were some notable exceptions. One shining example of individual entrepreneurship was E.C. Gray, who was in the grocery business at 315 E. Ninth when he had a flash of inspiration. He owned one of the very few if not the only automobile in the black community and saw an opportunity to make it pay. There were 130 privately owned taxis or "jitneys" in Fort Worth, none of them operated by an African American. Blacks who wanted to get around town had to go by street car, horsepower, or walk. In January 1915, Gray went down to the police department, which handled such things, and got a license to operate a jitney "exclusively for negroes." Perhaps with an appreciation for irony, Gray called his jitney service "Jim Crow." Even the *Star-Telegram*, which did not normally notice black accomplishments, reported the story admiringly.[22]

About that same time, Levi Cooper and family were moving to Fort Worth from Hearne, Texas, where he had owned a store. He put all his savings into buying a used Model-T Ford, and started the Cooper Rent-a-Cab company in 1917. A few years later he had enough to buy a "fleet" of four brand-new Dodge sedans. In the meantime, his brother Oscar established the Snappy Cab Company as a friendly competitor. One of the things the Cooper brothers and E.C. Gray had to contend with was a city ordinance that said they could not transport white passengers. Business thrived anyway.[23]

Another would-be black entrepreneur did not fare so wall. George Hall had the idea of doing door-to-door sales by blowing a "postman's whistle" to bring people out of their houses, then once he got them on the street he tried to sell them postcards and "other trinkets." His brainstorm got him arrested for vagrancy. Then it was discovered that he was wearing a button on his lapel with the letters "U.B.U." on it. No one really knew what it stood for, but someone at the jail thought it stood for "United Burglars' Union," which really put him in hot water. Being black and without a lawyer he was lucky to get off with a fine in J.P. Court.[24]

Black entrepreneurs were rare not because blacks lacked imagination or ambition—George Hall had been quite imaginative and quick-thinking—but for reasons beyond their control. The black buying public was quite small (less than 10 percent of the city's population), and black entrepreneurs could not get start-up loans from white-owned banks (every bank in the city except one). Still, by 1903 there were enough entrepreneurial types to organize a Fort Worth chapter of the Colored Business Men's League (CBML) and apply for a charter from the national organization. They were just the third group to secure such a charter. One of their success stories was Marcus F. Wilson. In 1909 Wilson advertised his buggy shop as the only black-owned buggy shop in all of Texas. He did a little bit of everything—custom-building, repairing, decorating, renting and selling. If it was related to buggies, he did it. That same year saw W. B. Taylor and J. A. Thomas split the black barbering business in the city between their shops. In 1934, when G. B. Grimble and Calvin Littlejohn opened a photography studio, they became the city's first black professionals in their field. Entrepreneurs like Wilson and the rest were tolerated by the white business community because they did not take away business from white shops. For instance, the only black person likely to be seen in a white barber shop was the porter sweeping up the hair clippings.[25]

Business opportunity was defined differently in the black community. Fort Worth's first black business district grew up on the south end of town in the shadow of Hell's Half-acre. A residential area could spring up anywhere there was a bit of land unoccupied by whites, but business needed to be close to the heart of the city, accessible by street car and commercial delivery vehicles. Starting in the late 1880s, East Ninth Street fit all these requirements; it was separated from the white business district but still close in to town. Business districts tend to create their own synergy with new businesses feeding off the customer base of established businesses nearby. Thus it was on East Ninth. A little bit of everything lined the street: dry-goods merchants, clothing stores, green grocers, eating joints, saloons, variety theaters, a bank, the Masonic Temple. Black customers could walk over from nearby tenements or walk into town from outlying neighborhoods. These were the only places of business that blacks could patronize, which gave their proprietors a kind of monopoly. Most black businesses never made it into the city directory because both the publishers and clientele of the directory were white. Over the years the city's modest black business district expanded onto lower Rusk (Commerce after 1911) and Calhoun and Jones streets until it reached its natural limits, which had nothing to do with the size of the population and everything to do with the boundaries imposed by Jim Crow. East of Jones were railroad tracks while to the west Main St. was off-limits because it was the main thoroughfare from the T&P passenger station to the public square. It was, as one city official put it in

1911, "public policy" that "Negro businesses" must be strictly segregated. When this rule was flouted in 1911, the resulting white outrage produced the biggest disturbance on the city's streets since the 1886 railroad strike. The Dixie Theater Riot showed Jim Crow at its ugliest.[26]

If the black businessman had a tough time, that was nothing compared to what black women experienced trying to break out of traditional roles. Educated and ambitious women like Hazel Harvey (Peace), Lenora Butler (Rolla), and Dionne Bagsby had little hope of having a career because being black *and* a woman was a double whammy. Bagsby's musical talents seemed to point her toward a singing career, which did not require book-learning, but her parents pushed her to get a first-rate education, which opened the door to a teaching career. For black women who were not inclined toward performing or teaching, about the only career open was the beauty industry, i.e., in a beauty parlor. Madam C. J. Walker showed the way by becoming the first black female millionaire in the United States. Fort Worth had a handful of black-owned beauty parlors, and perhaps equally important, black beauticians were hired by the owners of white beauty parlors, thus giving them not only a regular paycheck but also contacts in white society. The relationships forged between white matrons and their black maids and beauticians would eventually help break down the walls of Jim Crow, perhaps as much as street protests and political action. And Fort Worth's own Lucille Bishop Smith, who got her start as a seamstress and cook for privileged white clients, became a nationally known authority on commercial food preparation and author of cookbooks. Today she is credited as "the first African-American businesswoman in Texas," although that claim is based more on lack of historical records than any actual records.[27]

Photo 15. Beauty Salon

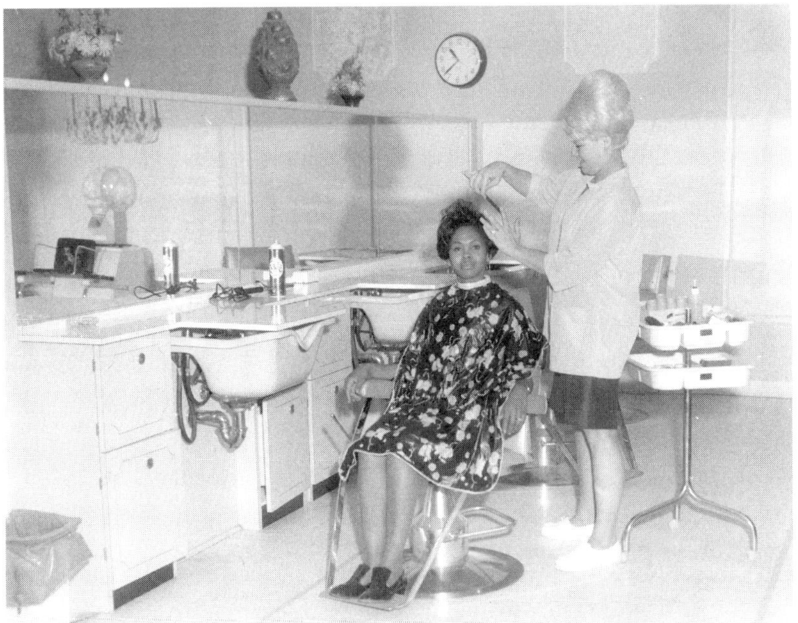

The Carol Brent Beauty Salon represents one of the very few careers open to black women outside the home, the beauty trade. What is unusual about this photo is the color of the customer and the color of the beautician, reversed from what one would expect. Courtesy of Tarrant County Black Historical & Genealogical Society.

The business segment of the black community became an unintentional beneficiary of Jim Crow—a dualistic world of black and white businesses meeting the same demand only on different sides of the color line. E.C. Gray did not start his jitney service simply because he saw a chance to turn a profit but because white taxis would not pick up black fares. Under Jim Crow every aspect of life in the white community had to be duplicated in the black communit—the good as well as the bad. From 1884 until 1913, the city had a White Elephant Saloon that was one of the premier "fancy saloons" in all of the Southwest. The year after the White Elephant opened, West Mayweather, a black saloon man, opened the Black Elephant on the opposite end of Main. Far from having any pretensions of being a fancy saloon, it was described inelegantly in the *Fort Worth Gazette* as "a notorious coon dive." But like its white counterpart, it was a thriving operation. The door between the worlds of the White Elephant and the Black Elephant clientele swung only one way: whites could patronize the Black Elephant but never vice versa. The only black faces seen at the White Elephant were the porters and shoe-shine boys. Not even the size of a black man's bankroll or being a member of the sporting fraternity got him admitted to that uptown joint.[28]

Meanwhile, Fort Worth's well-heeled black community conducted their affairs as if the ugly world of Jim Crow did not exist. Acknowledging that it did would have forced them to accept their second-class status no matter how well-spoken or how educated. They accommodated themselves to the Jim Crow system by creating an insulated social sphere, not antagonizing the white majority, and especially not bringing the wrath of the police down on their heads.

The city's most distinguished African American in the first half of the twentieth century was William M. "Gooseneck Bill" McDonald, who built a financial and real-estate empire in the "negro quarter" that included a bank, a pharmacy, and a hotel. He refused to be defined by his skin color, and before he was done Bill McDonald was bigger than his hometown, a nationally known figure much like his predecessors, Frederick Douglass and Booker T. Washington.

Men like E.C. Gray, William McDonald, and even West Mayweather were the kind of entrepreneurs that Booker T. Washington believed could lift the black race onto their shoulders. But blacks were pulled in two different directions by competing voices among their own leaders. On the one side were "accommodationists" like Booker T. Washington who believed blacks should accept the social and political status quo while establishing themselves as an economic force. Squarely in this camp was Bill McDonald. In 1900 he told the assembled membership of the Prince Hall Masons,

> There is no good reason why Negro Masons should crave recognition from white Masons. The very laws of God recognize the rules of caste, and while Negro Masons may contend for equal rights before the laws of their county, it is insanity grown to weeks [*sic*] to contend for equality in social, religious, and civic societies.[29]

Accommodationists even went so far as to publicly denounce those who dared to speak out against racism and the rule of lynch law in the South. On the other side were those like W.E.B. DuBois who argued for equality in all things and equality now. Somewhere in the middle were men like Fort Worth preachers L.K. Williams and Prince Jones. The latter told a gathering of black Baptists in 1907 that "Negro independence" must be based on "self-respect and self-help," not white legislation and court rulings. "No man," he said, "amounts to anything who depends upon other races to do his work." Williams echoed similar sentiments when he told the same audience, "He who would have anything in this world must earn it, and this applies to the negro as much as to other people."[30]

Role models on the national stage were few and far between for African Americans. One was boxer Jack Johnson, known as the "Galveston Giant," who won the heavyweight championship of the world against (white) James J. Jeffries on July 4, 1910. Johnson was the first black boxer to win the title, and wild celebration among African Americans all over the country followed. Johnson was instantly elevated to celebrity status, receiving more press coverage than all other black national figures combined. A film made of the bout proved a bigger draw than any other film in cinematic history before *Birth of a Nation* (1915). In Fort Worth, the city commission would not even allow the film to be shown because of the incendiary subject matter—a black man thrashing a white man in the ring. Yet white fight fans who would never countenance a black champ taking the heavyweight boxing title would jam-pack black fight clubs to bet on brawlers like Dallas' "Li'l Dynamite" and other "dusky ring artists."[31]

Johnson's victory over Jeffries produced two very different reactions in Fort Worth's black community. On the one hand, people on the street celebrated the triumph of one of their own; on the other hand, black ministers like Mount Gilead's L.K. Williams added their voices to Mayor W.D. Davis', denouncing Johnson from the pulpit. It was one of those rare times when black and white leaders were in complete agreement—a black man who made a living beating up white men was not a good example for the black community.[32]

William M. McDonald was not only a better role model than Jack Johnson, but also the best-known member of Fort Worth's small black elite. His personal wealth exceeded that of more than 95 percent of white residents. The difference was that McDonald and his few well-heeled, black peers could not spend their wealth freely because they were still shackled by the invisible chains of Jim Crow. But not even Jim Crow could keep them down completely. Some members of the black elite took their families to Europe on vacation, something the majority of whites could not afford to do. And more than a few black teachers at I.M. Terrell held advanced university degrees in contrast to their peers at white high schools who were graduates of "normal" schools. Black teachers had little or no hope of attaining jobs in the college ranks regardless of their level of education because the majority of colleges and universities did not hire black faculty. They had to content themselves with raising up the next generation of black leaders—the "talented tenth"—at schools like I.M. Terrell.[33]

One of the benefits of being the only colored high school for miles around and having the pick of black teachers was the quality of education at I. M. Terrell. It produced many if not the majority of the black middle class in Fort Worth, and its alumni broke the color barrier in city and county government and made their mark on local culture thanks to launching groups like the Colored Women's [Literary] Club. Defying white expectations for black high-school students, I.M. Terrell was a college-preparatory school. Its graduates went on to become community leaders, and more than a few cast giant shadows—e.g., Lenora Rolla, Hazel Harvey Peace, Reby Cary, James Cash, Walter Beatrice Barbour, and Ornette Coleman. It was a training ground for talent and a place that instilled an indomitable "can-do" spirit in its students. But Terrell was also an insular, privileged world that nurtured high expectations only to have those expectations rudely shattered when graduates encountered the outside world.[34]

Social Services

One yawning empty space in the black community during the Jim Crow years was the lack of social services for those who had been knocked down by life or were victims of natural disaster. The biggest relief organizations of the day all had a blind spot when it came to the black community. The American Red Cross, founded in 1881, did not swing into action when disaster struck a black community as it did when disaster struck a white community. The YMCA, which came to town in 1890 to battle the evils of the Industrial Revolution, and the Salvation Army, which set up shop in 1900 to "work among the poor," both confined their activities to the white community, too. The same was true of the Knights of Columbus, the service branch of the Catholic Church, and the Union Gospel Mission. All of these organizations did good work, particularly during the times when the Trinity River flooded, but their outreach extended only so far as the white neighborhoods. The ladies of the Fort Worth Woman's Club did some service activities in the black community according to their records but on a very limited basis.[35]

During World War I, when the town's black population exploded overnight due to the influx of black trainees at Camp Bowie and wartime jobs in the civilian sector, a "negro welfare association" was created under the auspices of the Fort Worth Relief Association (FWRA). J.B. Rawlings, the secretary of the association, brought together black ministers, physicians, and school principals to come up with a plan. However, the war ended before anything could be accomplished.[36]

The FWRA reinvented itself as the Fort Worth Welfare Association after the war and finally did something for the black community. In 1920 they spent $4,000 on "negro welfare work" as opposed to $22,000 on "social services and relief" for whites. Mrs. Mary A. Drake (white) took charge of welfare work "among negroes" and performed nobly. That same year the association bought a residence on West Peter Smith for "delinquent negro girls," dubbing it "Hope Home." The girls placed there were called "inmates," and a laundry was installed on site to teach them the skills they would need to get jobs as "wash women" when they were released. While Mrs. Drake oversaw the operation, the money to create Hope Home had all been raised in the black community.[37]

Mostly the black community had to draw on its own limited resources. Organized benevolence started with the black church but also included the Prince Hall Masons after 1885. Masonic dues supported a "Relief Association," and part of their mission statement said, "Charity is the foundation of our sacred edifice." Their treasury could help out the occasional widow or orphan, but there was no way they could mount a major relief effort in the event of a natural disaster. In normal times, white Masons (the Ancient Free & Accepted Masons) offered some help to their black brethren. Their women's auxiliary, the Order of Eastern Star, supported a black orphanage "in the shadow of the Tarrant County courthouse." The Eastern Star ladies assessed themselves 10¢ per month to fund relief efforts. They made their first payout in 1901—$50 to the widow of a recently deceased member. This sort of bonding is what sociologist Robert Putnam had in mind when he talked about building a viable community.[38]

A few years later, the Negro Welfare Council was created under the auspices of the National Urban League, a civil rights pioneering organization founded in 1910. The council's stated purpose was to provide relief for "poor negroes who have no other source of aid." The local chapter met at Allen Chapel.[39]

When bigger problems than caring for the occasional widow or orphan came along, "social bridging" was necessary, i.e., reaching out to the white community for help. Black residents of the city came to depend on the Fort Worth Relief (meaning welfare) Association to provide social services that were beyond the limited resources of the black community alone. The association dispatched nurses and social workers into black neighborhoods and those populated by Mexican nationals, and also operated summer camps for the city's poorest children, with everything free including medical care.[40]

Fort Worth's black community lived in the shadows for a lot of reasons, but definitely one of the things that marked them as second-class citizens was the lack of a safety net. Social services for blacks were almost entirely a matter of private charity.

A "Race Problem"?

The 1905 street car ordinance (see Chap. 4) was one early sign that white Fort Worth thought it had a "race problem," also known in less polite circles as a "negro problem." In the late nineteenth and early twentieth centuries those terms were shorthand for the alarm whites felt over the growing black population and all that it meant—specifically, the need for more jobs, more housing, and more schools. It did not matter that blacks were not increasing their percentage of the population; it only mattered that their absolute numbers were growing, making them less invisible than they had been when they were a miniscule part of the larger population. Most tax-payers were unwilling to spend public funds to provide the same services for blacks as for whites, especially since most blacks did not pay taxes. When whites looked around "their" city, they saw blacks opening up businesses, pushing neighborhood boundaries, and flexing their political muscle, and they did not like it. Ironically, some African Americans also spoke of a "race problem," but what they meant was the difference between rising black expectations and legitimate rights versus the reality of Jim Crow—the other side of the problem.[41]

And it was not just major cities like Fort Worth and Dallas where whites felt threatened. Small towns like Graham, eighty-eight miles northwest of Fort Worth, also felt the ground shifting beneath them. In 1902 Graham residents put up a virtual "keep out" sign:

> We have never had the negro to any extent, nor do we want him. They will not be encouraged to come here, and will find no employment nor inducement to remain if they do come.[42]

Decent white folks would never think of joining a lynch mob, but they might secretly cheer on such a mob if it could keep the streets safe for white folks and put insolent blacks in their place. Even whites who considered themselves Progressive could be so blinded by in-grained racism that they could not see their own bigotry. One white business owner in Fort Worth wrote a letter to the *Star-Telegram* deploring mob violence, but he qualified his condemnation by asserting, "I have never yet turned a worthy white man away and given work to a negro, which I have observed done often in this city."[43]

Fort Worth blacks never lived under a cloud of fear, but they did not need the wire services to follow events in other communities; word traveled fast when the news was of a lynching. In 1893, Henry Smith, a black resident of Paris, Texas, accused of rape and murder, was tortured and burned to death by a white mob. In 1910 there were more acts of racial violence in the news. In March, a Dallas mob numbering more than a hundred stormed the courthouse and threw Allen Brooks out of a second-story window, then strung him up. Four months later came the "Slocum race war" (aka, "Slocum Massacre") in east Texas that left eight persons dead near the town of Slocum in Anderson County, all of them black. Most of the victims were unarmed and had been shot in the back. Even Anderson County's white sheriff, W.H. Black, said they had been "hunted down like sheep." The *Fort Worth Star-Telegram* attributed the origins of the affair to a "negro plot" to burn out whites, reassuring its white readers, "[Fort Worth] negroes are all quiet and threaten no disturbance." In none of the three cases was anyone ever brought to justice. In the Slocum case, seven white men were indicted for the "wholesale slaughter of negroes," but none were prosecuted. In the Brooks lynching, a grand jury was charged with investigating it, but even before the grand jury began its deliberations, the *Star-Telegram* reported, "It is not thought any bills will be returned."[44]

Word of these atrocities spread from town to town. The lynching of Allen Brooks was being talked about in Shreveport, Louisiana's black community the same day it occurred. The events in Anderson County were reported in Fort Worth newspapers the next day. The local African-American population had good reason to be alarmed even if, after the Brooks lynching, the *Star-Telegram* pronounced all "Negro prisoners" in the Tarrant County jail perfectly safe. The truth was something else. The black community was only a single incident away from what had happened in Paris, Dallas, and Slocum.[45]

Such an incident came just seven months after the Slocum Massacre, provoked by an innocent business deal. The Dixie motion picture theater at Eleventh and Main was an unremarkable movie house before February 1911, not even pulling in enough business to pay the bills. But it was a *white* theater, and that made all the difference. The surrounding disreputable area (the "Acre") discouraged whites from patronizing the place when there were nicer theaters uptown. The white owner, William Evans, faced foreclosure if he did not do something drastic, so when the theater opened on Monday, February 27, a big sign out front announced "For Colored Only," and a black girl occupied the ticket booth. The word quickly spread up and down Main St., and every white ticket-taker at the other theaters walked off the job in protest at having to share their street with an establishment catering to black customers. That evening when a group of men and boys gathered on the nearby street corner, a concerned citizen summoned the police. Detectives came and warned Evans not to open, but the mob was not placated. Somebody hurled a brick through the Dixie's ornate glass front window, and the crowd was talking about storming the place. Evans, his brother, and two detectives were inside, and the black staff all fled out the back door. Evans finally sent a white employee outside to try to reason with the mob. The message carried by the man was conciliatory, even pleading:

> Mr. Evans asks you not to do any damage. He is sincerely sorry that he has opened this negro show and promises you on his word of honor that he will never make the mistake again. He asks your pardon. [46]

Both police and special officers were now on the scene although they were not sure what to do; none of them had ever faced a riot before, nor did they have any training in dealing with one. The mob, now swelled to a thousand or more, milled around blocking the street, also uncertain what to do next until they spotted a black man approaching on Main St. They chased him down and beat him severely. Then someone smashed a music store window and grabbed a guitar. Waving it over his head he led the mob in pursuit of another black victim whom he bashed over the head with it after they caught him. As mobs go, this was not a murderous mob; they were just having good, old-boy fun. Someone else grabbed the broken guitar, and it became their battle flag leading them into action. They set off down Ninth St. smashing windows and kicking in doors of black businesses and the Masonic Temple, a highly visible status symbol of the black community. The mob was on the rampage now, looking for new targets. Meanwhile, back at the police station, Night Captain Tom Blanton called out every available officer and raced to the scene in person with Mayor W.D. Davis in his personal automobile. Along the way they picked up two terrified blacks and hid them on the floorboard until they could get them home safely.

It was a good thing because not even what the newspapers patronizingly called "innocent negroes" were safe. Members of the "Negro Methodist Episcopal Church" (i.e., Allen Chapel) on their way to evening services were attacked and sent on their way beaten and bloody. Pastor M.L. Smith was manhandled by the mob and "everything in his pockets taken."[47]

The mob went back up Ninth St. and caught their breath on the lawn in front of city hall before moving uptown to Byers' Opera House at Seventh and Commerce. There they made so much noise, the performance had to be halted. The well-heeled audience stayed where they were, afraid to come outside. The streets were now filled not just with the mob but with the curious watching to see what the mob would do next. Someone on the sidelines hurled a couple of bricks *at* the mob who responded in kind. It was no longer just a race riot; it had become a free-for-all. Police and Fire Commissioner George Mulkey would state later that trying to stop that mob "was like trying to stem the rapids of Niagara."[48]

Meanwhile, Captain Blanton and Mayor Davis had caught up with the mob. Blanton pleaded with them to go home, promising no legal action would be taken if they would just get off the streets. Instead, they started moving again, back toward Main St. on the hunt for more blacks. It was nearly 11:00 p.m. now, and Commissioner Mulkey ordered the fire chief to call out his men and be prepared to turn the fire hoses on the mob if they did not disperse. The chief demurred, arguing that his men were unarmed firemen. "If there is a fire we will get there and won't let anyone stop us, but I don't think the men should be ordered out to turn water on people." The police and sheriff's department were right there with the fire department in acting craven that night or worse. It was rumored afterwards that the police may have been complicit, "encouraging the rowdies" in their destructive rampage, and Sheriff William Rea did not even put in an appearance on the streets all night. As he later explained, he was "at home. . . and the disturbance was over before I learned of it." While the sheriff slept, Rome burned.[49]

Eventually, the mob ran out of steam and headed for home of its own volition, perhaps persuaded by the fact that every black person in Fort Worth was behind locked doors. Luckily, there had been no deaths or serious injuries although there was plenty of destruction to clean up. The next morning Judge Tom Simmons of the Sixty-seventh District Court said everyone should be thankful that "no more damage was done." He went on to offer the unsolicited opinion that the problem with mobs was that they did not know when to stop. They had "closed up the picture show," he said, but then not satisfied, they "began to hunt down negroes indiscriminately." The judge differentiated between proper mob business and excessive mob activities.[50]

The leadership of the FWPD presented a united front when interviewed by the press. Commissioner Mulkey said that the police had "done their best." Chief June Polk concurred, telling the newspaper, "I think the men faithfully protected the negroes." The *Star-Telegram* was also on board, reporting that no lives had been lost although "several negroes *are reported* [emphasis added] seriously wounded."[51]

Rather than admit there had even been a race riot, Mayor W.D. Davis went into full damage-control Wednesday morning. He attributed all the trouble to delinquent "young boys and children," and declared the responsibility rested with their parents. The police had not resorted to force to disperse the mob because they were afraid of hurting children. The mayor also said that it was purely coincidence that a black man had been killed that same night in a "private establishment" in another part of the city. He was adamant that Fort Worth not be "branded as a city in which a negro was mobbed and killed." He concluded his statement to the press with this: "We owe a duty to the city to preserve its reputation and we are going to do it." In that regard, the timing of the riot could not have been worse. The Southwestern Fat Stock Show opened in a week, and it was one of the biggest yearly events on the municipal calendar. With thousands of out-of-town visitors coming to Fort Worth, nobody wanted the main thing on their mind to be a race riot. And there was the greater fear that some of those anticipated thousands might stay home this year.[52]

Every citizen did not agree. One letter-writer to the *Star-Telegram* called the police "a disgrace" to the city hastening to add he was no "nigger lover." He pointed out accurately that a "mob of boy ruffians and saloon loafers" had "terrorized negroes and damaged and destroyed property," but he was most concerned that their actions had endangered *white* men, women, and children on the streets. He blamed not the parents of the delinquent boys, but the police for not reining them in. So this is what the story came down to: the real problem was either bad parents or a bunch of hooligans endangering respectable white folks. There was no other way to look at it.[53]

An anonymous voice of reason attempted to put the riot in perspective: "Whether we like negroes or not, we have them in Fort Worth. They are an economic necessity and the industries of the town would be seriously embarrassed by their absence." The writer suggested that the authorities deal sternly with the "mob spirit" wherever and whenever it appeared to preserve the good name and assure the economic future of the city.[54]

Black movie-goers would not get their own downtown theater until 1941 when Mays C. Maxwell opened the Ritz Theater at 909 Calhoun. He shrewdly latched onto the "Ritz" name because it had a long history as a theater venue, and not just in Fort Worth. Here, a white vaudeville house under that name had opened in 1924 at the southwest corner of Tenth and Commerce. It changed owners, names, and even purpose over the next six years on the way to becoming a movie house under the name New Liberty Theater in 1930. Maxwell resurrected the original name a decade later for his movie house. For ten cents' admission in the beginning, black kids who lived on the east side could walk to the Ritz and see Hollywood movies like *Cabin in the Sky* (1943) and long-since-forgotten, low-budget, black-produced films. The Ritz remained in the Maxwell family until they gave up the fight and closed it in 1948. Over the years the major white-owned theaters downtown—the Hollywood, Worth, Palace, and Majestic—had consistently opposed the opening of black theaters because the places took business away from the white theaters that otherwise had a monopoly on both black and white business. If blacks wanted to enjoy the great American experience of seeing a movie, they had to sit in segregated balconies. It became increasingly harder to maintain that monopoly, however, as the city's black population grew and black-owned businesses could make a respectable profit even under the restrictions imposed by Jim Crow. But it was a two-edged sword.[55]

At the end of the day, racial solidarity trumped law and order. District Judge James Swayne, a paragon of racial enlightenment on the bench, declared, "I have no sympathy with the white man who opens a negro picture show on Main Street, nor with the men who rent their buildings for such purposes." But he also admitted, "The negroes who attended the show were not to blame, and the attacks upon innocent negroes was an outrage that should be atoned if possible." He ordered a grand jury to "make a full investigation" and if laws were broken to charge the guilty regardless of whether they were white or black.[56]

Two weeks after the riot, Swayne's grand jury submitted its report. The all-white jurors did not achieve any breakthroughs when it came to either identifying the perpetrators or pinpointing the causes of the disturbance. While admitting there had been a "race riot," they indicted no one and did not even rap the police on the knuckles for their meek response. Nobody would ever appear before Judge Swayne's bench to answer for the events of February 27. In the end, the only action the city took was to purchase a "fully equipped riot car" so that if such a disturbance should ever occur again, the police would be ready. The deeper causes of the riot were not so easily addressed. Of course, in the event another race riot erupted, there was no telling which side the department's juggernaut would be used against, the rioters or the victims.[57]

And there race relations stood until 1913 when another incident exploded into a full-blown race riot. On May 15, Tom Lee Young (aka, Tommie Lee), a young black man well-known to police, took a twelve-gauge shotgun and went on a killing spree through the Acre. By the time it ended in a railroad culvert half an hour later, he had killed two men and severely wounded four others. Two of his victims were white, including Police Officer Johan Ogletree. Police Chief O.R. Montgomery single-handedly arrested Lee and turned him over to Sheriff William Rea who locked him up in the county jail on Belknap. It was not long before

Rea could look out his window and see a white mob gathering on the lawn and street in front of the jail. Along with Chief Montgomery, they prepared the jail for a siege, and Montgomery sent word to the black business district on the south end of town to close up and go home. As evening descended, the mob in front of the jail grew bolder, demanding that Tommie Lee be turned over to them. By the time darkness fell, their numbers had swelled to at least 2,000, most of them well-lubricated and spoiling for a necktie party. They stormed the jail, and after being turned back went looking for easier targets. They found a street car on East Belknap carrying several black passengers, flipped it over, and dragged out the passengers. After beating them senseless, the mob headed down Commerce toward what the newspapers called "Negro Town" to do a little "Negro bashing."[58]

There was a sense of déjà vu, but this time it was worse than the Dixie Theater riot. The first places the mob hit were saloons to get more liquor. Then they hit the Fraternal Bank and Trust before moving on to the "tenements" on Jones St. Not content to break windows and kick in doors, they set fires along the way and assaulted any black person still out on the street. From Seventh down to Eleventh and from Main over to Jones, they wreaked havoc across twelve square blocks. No black business or residence was safe. For over an hour they ran wild. The mob did not disperse until Chief Montgomery showed up with a scratch riot squad of police and began clearing the streets. By midnight peace had once more descended on the south end of town. Only then did the Fire Department show up and put out the fires. The jail was not secured until state militia troops were mobilized by the governor and took up positions around the jail.[59]

In the aftermath of the riot, estimates of the property damage ranged from $8,000 to $14,500. Nobody really knew because few if any black storekeepers or residents had insurance. Who could afford it? There was some talk of passing the hat among the white business community and collecting money to rebuild, but nothing came of it. The *Fort Worth*

Record spoke for a lot of citizens when it labeled the destruction simple "malicious mischief." The *Star-Telegram* called it what it was—a "race riot." Fortunately, no one had been killed, and everyone was thankful for that. Judge James Swayne convened another grand jury and promised indictments, but in the end not a single person was ever charged with arson, assault, or even vandalism. Fifteen rioters identified by officers that night were hauled into Judge T.J. Maben's justice of the peace court and charged with "disturbing the peace," or Judge Hugh Bardin's municipal court and charged with "public drunkenness." All but two paid their minimal fines and were released; the other three claimed indigence and were ordered to work off their fines on county road gangs.[60]

The cause of all this uproar was indicted for murder of the black man, not the white officer or any of the other white victims. Lee was tried in Judge James Swayne's court in July. After two days of testimony the all-white jury took just ten minutes to find Tommie Lee guilty and sentence him to hang. A long, drawn-out series of appeals followed that got the verdict overturned, and he was eventually sentenced to life in prison.[61]

Fort Worth never experienced another race riot after the 1913 Tommie Lee-related rampage, and over the decades that followed forgot that it had *ever* experienced such a thing. No history of the city published before 2004 even mentioned that the city had experienced such a domestic disturbance for obvious reasons: neither blacks nor whites wanted to recall the bad, old days. When a series of race riots wracked the country in the late 1960s, Fort Worth held itself up as a paradigm of peaceful race relations throughout its history. Any reference to two race riots in two years (1911 and 1913) would have sullied that image.[62]

The white community may have moved on after 1913, but the black community could not forget how precarious their existence was. They were never more than a single incident away from mob action. In the spring and summer of 1919, racial violence erupted all over the country—in Charleston, South Carolina (May); Chicago, Illinois, Houston and Port Arthur, Texas (July); New York and Omaha, Nebraska (September). The violence was not even clear across the state; it was as close as Longview, Texas, just 160 miles east of Fort Worth. On July 10 a race riot erupted there when a white mob attempted to seize a black school teacher accused of writing a newspaper article that "attacked the character" of a local white "lady." He retreated to the house of a local black doctor, and the two of them held off the mob that had turned its fury on the black section of town. Before it was all over a week later, four white men were wounded, one black man was dead and another two had fled the state, the black section of Longview had been torched, and the city was under martial law. For Fort Worth blacks two lessons were clear: 1) They were never far removed from mob violence; and 2) The white majority did not take kindly to blacks standing up for themselves.[63]

The Big Paradox of Jim Crow

Racist whites were not all evil, torch-waving rioters. On the contrary, they were mostly decent folks who had grown up in a segregated society with ccrtain ideas instilled since childhood. As adults, they wrapped themselves in the cloak of pseudo-science, paternalism, and mannered politeness. The language of Jim Crow reflected this reality. In polite circles African-American women were usually referred to as "colored" while men were "negroes." It was a subtle distinction that spoke volumes, implying that the women were harmless while the men were something else, perhaps even by nature dangerous. It was the politically correct etiquette of the day.[64]

Photo 16. Manet Harrison

Manet Harrison was a true Fort Worth success story. A musical prodigy and graduate of the Colored High School, she married Stephen Fowler in 1915 and founded the Mwalimu School of African Art and Music. They moved to New York City in 1932, and her school became part of the legendary Harlem Renaissance. Here Manet is in her wedding dress. Courtesy of Scott and Linda Jo Barker Collection.

Most whites did not know any blacks except menials. They loved black dialect stories and jokes told at black expense and saw nothing wrong with passing them down from one generation to the next. In 1897 at a gathering of the Young Peoples' Union of St. Paul's M.E. Church, the pastor, Dr. McGaha, told the story about a coroner's jury that "sat upon" a dead black man and a dead fish, both of which had washed ashore at the same place. The jurors' verdict came out like this: "We the jury find that this fish and this negro came to their death at the hands of a gig in one and a rope around the neck of the other, but we are unable to determine whether the nigger went a-fishing or the fish went a-niggering." The newspaper reported appreciative laughter in the audience.[65]

Whites who employed a maid or yard man considered them not so much people to be feared as objects of condescension or perhaps ridicule. Old-timers like William B. Tucker and Samuel B. "Burk" Burnett who had grown up in the Old South still held to the social conventions of their youth. When Burk Burnett died in 1922, a provision in his will allotted $30 per month to long-time servant, Oak Owens (aka, "Coley") for the rest of his life. Such a noble gesture did not violate the conventions of Jim Crow.[66]

There was an element of paternalism attached to such generosity, but small kindnesses aside, there was always a line that could not be crossed. Racism was part of the culture reflected in the language of the time. For instance, the term "maroon" was applied to a certain subset of African Americans. It had a long history going back to colonial times as a West Indian term of Spanish origins to describe runaway slaves. But when used by Southern whites like Burk Burnett and William Tucker it meant any black person who was "uppity" or independent-minded.[67]

On a few notable occasions during this era, blacks and whites managed to find common cause. The first significant occasion was the Great Railroad Strike of 1886. It started among workers on the Missouri-Pacific line at their hub in Marshall, Texas. The strife moved west to Dallas and Fort Worth following the Texas & Pacific tracks. Fort Worth at the time was a working-class town that had a lot of sympathy for the strikers. When the company brought in strike-breakers and hired guns to protect its property, local workers put aside racial differences in favor of labor solidarity. On April 3, a crowd of about 800 men, both blacks and whites, gathered at the Dallas T&P depot to vent their anger. When they did not get the company's attention, workers on the west side of the Trinity decided to take stronger action. The violence that followed was not about race, but if the company had brought in black strike-breakers, it would have been. That was the experience in other strikes.[68]

Other notable examples of cooperation were the smallpox outbreaks of the 1880s and the meningitis outbreak of 1912 when defeating the disease trumped all other issues. Then there was World War I when national interests brought blacks and whites together *en masse* at Camp Bowie. On such occasions, when their mutual interests outweighed racial differences, blacks and whites could join together against a common enemy. The lamb was not ready to lie with the lion yet, but these were truly steps toward becoming one nation.[69]

The military establishment played a quiet role in growing Fort Worth's black community and integrating it into the general population. In 1892 the city hosted a remarkable, three-day reunion of Civil War veterans, but not the sort of old-timers who would have broken bread with members of the Confederate Veterans organization. These were former members of the U.S. Colored Troops, who had settled in the South after being mustered out in 1865. The choice of Fort Worth as a reunion site is curious because there were few public facilities black visitors could use. Still, the local black community welcomed them. The white community paid them little or no attention.[70]

At this time there was no active black military presence in Fort Worth. The two companies of the state militia that called Fort Worth home, the Fort Worth Fencibles and the Bovinian Rangers, were all-white. Although there were four "colored militia" companies in Texas at the time—the Excelsior Guards of San Antonio, the Ireland Rifles of Seguin, the Brazos

Light Guards of Bryan, and the Capital City Guards of Austin—no Fort Worth citizen would have seen any black soldiers marching and drilling in Fort Worth—at least not until 1918.[71] (see Chap. 6)

The biggest paradox of the Jim Crow era is that it gave us I.M. Terrell High School and a vibrant black business district, but at a terrible price to both races. On the one hand, Jim Crow was demeaning, putting an entire race in a permanent state of inferiority and forcing them to live under the ever-present threat of vigilante action. On the other hand, Jim Crow also gave us kindly white patrons who during tough times could be a god-send for a people like Clabe Thompson. Thompson was a poor black man so crippled from a construction accident that he could no longer work. In the days before workman's compensation for black *or* white workers, Thompson's former employer provided a large house where he could live and take in boarders plus a dollar a week in spending money. So far as is known, there were no strings attached, nor did the employer seek notoriety for his altruism.[72]

But the bad far outweighed the good no matter how many white Good Samaritans stepped up. One of the last of those Good Samaritans of the Jim Crow era was Amon Carter, "Mr. Fort Worth" to his many admirers. Carter dug into his own pocket to buy Lake Como and the surrounding property from A.J. Duncan to create a "public park for Negroes." And when he died he left money in his will for the black woman who had served his family loyally for so many years; it was only $250 out of an $800,000 bequest he left to friends, family, and associates, but it showed that the great man had not forgotten the hired help.[73]

Everyone applauded Carter's generosity for adding to the city's string of a dozen or more public parks. But it was always understood that white interests had first call on any property, public or private. That is what happened with Douglass Park, the city's first park for blacks. Although privately owned, it was considered a city park because it was open to the general public. When the property was desired by Texas Electric Service Company in the 1920s, it was appropriated "for the good of the community," meaning the white majority. Likewise, in 1906, the East Ninth Street Colored School, the city's only free public school for blacks at the time, was forced to relocate because the Fort Worth & Denver Railroad needed the land it sat on.[74]

Jim Crow was neither monolithic nor rational. Residential property, public schools, even the county jail were all notably segregated by race. Yet before 1931, the T&P train station was not. It had just one waiting room for all passengers, and black passengers could even eat at the lunch counter. The experiences of the Reverend J.L. Griffin in 1892 and black soldiers coming through the city during World War I prove as much. That does not mean African Americans were welcome to spend time in the place, only that there was no law prohibiting them from sitting or dining there. That would change when the 1931 station opened.[75] (see chap. 7)

The Jim Crow era spawned its share of myths and misconceptions besides the foundation mythology of racial inferiority. One of the most pernicious was that black men were over-sexed and posed a continuous threat to white women. A closely related myth was that they became ravening beasts when full of whiskey or cocaine. Less known is a piece of folk wisdom that appeared around the turn of the century that the black race was dying out, analogous to the myth of the "Vanishing Indian" that was popular around this same time. What might be called the "Vanishing Negro" myth may have been nothing more than wishful thinking on the part of some whites, but it claimed to be based on scientific research showing shorter life spans and a plummeting birth rate among blacks. That trend was supposedly aggravated by lack of maternal instinct among black women. "Negro women are very poor mothers," it was said, "careless and unintelligent." The population decline was also attributed to the combined effects of whiskey, cocaine, and venereal disease. Of course, there was no empirical evidence for any of this, but that did not keep it from being circulated in national publications. Some of those reports were picked up by local newspapers such as the *Dallas Morning News* and *Fort Worth Morning Register.* Negative racist myths coincided with the rise of the eugenics movement in this country, which believed in racial ordering and selective breeding to preserve the "vitality" of the nation. Otherwise well-educated and enlightened whites such as Theodore Roosevelt, Oliver Wendell Holmes, and Margaret Sanger were true believers in eugenics theory.[76]

Calvin Littlejohn—Man with a camera[77]

> I started farming at 11 years old. I lived on a farm at Cotton Plant, Arkansas. When I was 12 or 13, I got in an agricultural program. I was in it three years. The first year I grew watermelons and did good. The second year I had cotton and did pretty good. The third year I grew peanuts and had a bumper crop.

Thus began the career of the man who eventually became one of the pre-eminent professional photographers of Texas. Like most other African Americans of his generation he did not have a choice of careers when he started out.

He was born in Cotton Plant, Arkansas, to Henry and Ira Littlejohn on August 1, 1909. His parents had endured slavery, but they owned their homestead free and clear by the time he was born. Calvin attended high school, but that did not hold as much promise for the future as the agricultural program he enrolled in. He farmed part of his father's land and made enough money to pay for a correspondence course in commercial art. He applied himself and became adept in all the major mediums: fashion drawing, landscape, portraiture, color separation, printing, and photography. He had found his calling. Still, he never forgot his love of the soil and what it could produce. Many years later he kept a greenhouse behind his Fort Worth home.

He was bitten by the photography bug. He bought a cheap box camera and began taking pictures. The world beyond Cotton Plant, Arkansas beckoned. He moved to Little Rock and enrolled in Philander Smith College where he studied until his money ran out and he was forced to drop out of school. He landed in Fort Worth in 1934 where he took a job teaching art at the Adult Industrial School for blacks. When G.B. Grimble opened the first black photography studio that same year, Littlejohn went to work for him. The experience was good, but the pay was small. Forced to find other ways to make ends meet, he worked as a short-order cook then as a janitor at Montgomery Ward's Department Store. Meanwhile he spent every spare moment and every penny on correspondence courses from the University of Texas, Wiley College, and Texas Southern University. He had hopes of going out on his own some day as a photographer. He married Agnes Anderson of Fort Worth in 1941, but the timing could not have been worse: World War II came along just a few months later.

He was drafted into the Army, but it was not all bad news. He was assigned to the photography section, specifically "visual education duties" at the Engineers Training Center at Fort Leonard Wood, Missouri. He also set up the Human Relations office for black soldiers, which became a model for the wartime U.S. Army. He revealed a talent for writing and producing stage shows. He finished the war at Fort Leonard Wood because he was too valuable to stick a rifle in his hands and ship him out. When the war ended, he mustered out and returned to Fort Worth. He liked to be his own boss, and his talent allowed him to freelance as a professional photographer. He soon earned a reputation as the go-to photographer in the black community, whether it was doing the I.M. Terrell Annual every year, photographing weddings, or supplying pictures to the *Lake Como Weekly*. The word spread, and he was the first person called to click pictures of big musical performers and other celebrities who came through town with his Speed Graphic box camera. His photographs appeared in publications far from Fort Worth, including the *Black Dispatch* out of Oklahoma City and *The Chicago Defender*.

He founded his own news magazine (*Spot*) chronicling Fort Worth's black community, but it took him away from what he loved most, so focused exclusively on photography. Many big events a black photographer was not invited to, such as the visits of Presidents Truman, Kennedy, and Carter to Fort Worth, but he showed up anyway and took pictures on his own dime. His greatest legacy, however, was recording five decades of African-American life in Fort Worth, mostly from his little studio on Harvey St. He was more than just a photographer. He was an entrepreneur and inventor who was the official photographer for every black school in the FWISD system, and who patented an anti-car-theft device.

And as a photographer he was more than a technician. He used his camera to break down social barriers. In 1951 he became the first African American to attend the convention of the Southwestern Photographers' Association. The first day he had to use the freight elevator or back stairs at the Hotel Texas to attend the sessions. He protested to the hotel's manager, and after that he entered through the front door. He was also the first African American to work as a staff photographer for the *Fort Worth Star-Telegram*. In 1984 he was honored by the Tarrant County Black Historical & Genealogical Society as the oldest black photographer in the state if not the country.

He was active in his church and community. He was a member of the Evans Ave. Business Association that helped revitalize his Near South Side neighborhood. He served on the board of trustees of Allen Chapel AME Church and added his voice to the choir on Sundays. He also took on the job of "historical curator" for the 114-year-old church.

The end came on Monday, September 6, 1993, in his eighty-fourth year. He had been suffering from chest pains and went to the hospital Sunday night. He died there at five o'clock the next morning. He was blessed in being recognized for his accomplishments while still alive, and there was no chance he would be forgotten. His papers went to the Fort Worth Public Library, and his collection of photographs went to the Dolph Briscoe Center for American History at the University of Texas at Austin.

For more than half a century, Calvin Littlejohn was "the Man with the Camera" at practically every African-American event in Fort Worth, creating a priceless chronicle of a community that white photographers virtually ignored. When Fort Worth dedicated a memorial on Evans Ave. in 2004 to thirty-five black leaders in the city's history, Calvin Littlejohn was among them. More than just a photographer, he was an inspiration. His life was summed up in his simple philosophy: "First thing, you make up your mind that you need something, then you find out what you need to do to get it."

WILLIAM MADISON MCDONALD—A MAN OF WEALTH AND POWER [78]

One of the richest men in Texas, perhaps even the first black millionaire in America, William McDonald is hands-down the most notable African American in Fort Worth history. His is the only name most white Fort Worthers can name. His importance in Fort Worth history derives not just from his immense wealth, but from the business empire he built and the power he wielded in the Republican Party. He was also an apostle of the self-help philosophy and a visionary at a time when most men of color were just trying to survive.

He was born in Kaufman County, Texas on June 22, 1866. His father had been a slave, his mother a free woman, and had the Civil War not ended the way it did, Bill McDonald would have faced a life of servitude himself. Instead he attended Roger Williams College in Nashville, Tennessee, before dropping out and coming to Texas to follow a different path to the good life. He taught school for six years then entered politics, allying himself with railroad baron E.H.R. Green as a living example of the Republican "black-and-tan" alliance in Texas. Newspaperman William Greene Sterett of the *Dallas Morning News* gave him the name "Gooseneck Bill" in 1896 while reporting his attendance at the Republican national convention in St. Louis, saying, "There is a colored man here from Kaufman, Texas by the name of McDonald; he has an Irish [last] name, but is a kind of goose-necked Negro, evidently smart as a whip." The name stuck and followed him the rest of his life although it could also be argued it was a demeaning nickname for someone who wanted to rub shoulders with the elite.

After landing in Fort Worth, he went to work for D. Schwartz & Co. until they went broke in 1887. He looked around and found the kind of grandiose project he thrived on: the Texas Colored State Fair Association. He seized the reins in organizing their first fair in Fort Worth that same year. The following year his colleagues elected him president of the association. At the time he was living in Terrell, Texas. His permanent move to Fort Worth in 1908 coincides with his rapid ascent in wealth and influence.

McDonald took to politics like a goose to water. He was an eloquent platform speaker admired by both races. As his mentor E.H. Green's career soared so did McDonald's, at least until 1912 when segregationists captured control of the Republican Party. Democrat Woodrow Wilson's election to the presidency that same year was another blow to his political ambitions, yet his influence in Texas politics is undeniable. He helped deliver the black vote to the Republican Party in every presidential election between 1896 and 1912. Unfortunately, he also had an unfortunate penchant for backing the wrong presidential candidate. He missed with William Howard Taft (1912), Leonard Wood (1920), Al Smith (1928), and Thomas Dewey (1944). Eventually the Republican Party sidelined him.

His business career was more successful than his political career. He created the Fraternal Bank and Trust in Fort Worth, parlaying his statewide Masonic connections into a solid financial institution. The Prince Hall Masonic Temple was on the second floor of the bank. He also built the McDonald Building a few doors down the street, renting out space to dentists, doctors, insurance companies, and the Baptist General

Convention of Texas. Twice (1911 and 1913) his properties were heavily damaged by white mobs, but he rebuilt each time.

McDonald was a chameleon who moved as easily in white power circles as in black, although he was never comfortable as a spokesman for the black community. He was no civil rights activist, no champion of the masses. He lived large, and his wealth and business connections made it impossible for the white power brokers to ignore his people. Occasionally he did use his influence, such as in 1949 when he was instrumental in bringing civil rights firebrand Adam Clayton Powell to Fort Worth. And his legacy nearly a decade after his death influenced Martin Luther King, Jr.'s decision to come to Fort Worth in 1959.

In his personal life he made one bad choice after another. He married five times, the last time to a woman fifty years his junior. He fathered one child, a son who did not survive long enough to follow in his father's footsteps. When McDonald died at the age of eighty-four he expected to be laid to rest beside his son whom he had interred in 1918 beneath a towering granite obelisk in Fort Worth's Trinity cemetery. It was the largest, most magnificent monument in the "colored" section of Oakwood Cemetery, and typical McDonald—grand and expensive. After a well-attended funeral service at Mount Pisgah Baptist Church, his widow had him buried in the family plot he had purchased, but not under an appropriate marker. On the contrary, his grave is not marked, and even its exact location is open to question.

In 1949, *Ebony Magazine* crowned him "probably the richest Negro in America," describing him as a "multi-millionaire." That claim is unprovable and highly unlikely unless you place a top-dollar value on all his property holdings. Upon his death a year later, the same magazine recalculated his estate at "more than $100,000," again without offering any supporting evidence. Regardless, the reports of his wealth in a national publication were a sign of his status. For a black man to be dubbed a "financier," and enjoy a "fabulous career" as McDonald did, amounted to the kind of bragging rights African Americans seldom enjoyed in his day. The American Dream was alive and well for people of color in the person of Bill McDonald.

If bling were the measure of a man's success, William McDonald was a smashing success, dying in a fine house with all the trappings of great wealth, including diamonds, oil paintings, and a full-time nurse. When asked on his death bed if he thought "conditions of the Negro have improved," he would only say, "They have in my lifetime." Conditions had improved in Fort Worth at least partly due to his influence. In 1944 the Metropolitan Fort Worth YMCA opened a "colored branch," naming it in his honor, and a suburban branch still carries his name today. The black community, which he had held at arms' length when alive, has embraced his larger-than-life legend without question. It is said, for instance, that the Fraternal Bank & Trust saved insolvent white banks during the Depression, another unprovable claim. His legend rests on his remarkable personal success. He was proof positive that a black man could make it on his own terms in white society. For his own people, however, he was a stern father figure, always preaching a tough-love message: "If you want stores, go establish such stores; if you wish for black editors, go and establish a black newspaper; if you want to manage great business concerns and great enterprises, go establish them." He had little sympathy for those who could not keep up.

NOTES

1. Annual address of the Grand Master to the Twenty-fifth annual "Communication" of the Most Worshipful Grand Lodge of Texas, Prince Hall *Proceedings*, August 14–18, 1900, Box 1, p. 16, Archives, Grand Lodge of Texas, Fort Worth.
2. Prince Hall *Proceedings*, August 18, 1900, p. 73.
3. The Colored Business Men's League in 1903 received just the third charter in the country from the National Business Men's League of New York City, Booker T. Washington, President. Ben Standifer, "The Black Business District, 1900–1940, Term paper, TCU History Course No. 3970, Fall term 1998, p. 2. The Texas Colored Teachers Association, also known as The Teachers State Association of Texas, was founded in 1884. www.tshaonline.org. For black newspaper publishers, see *Dallas Morning News*, August 15, 1899. The Texas black golfers' organization pre-dated by many years the National Negro Golf Association, founded in Lebanon, PA in October 1965. See www.nnga.us/history.html. For the Fort Worth Negro Golf Association, see Ramona M. Harriet, *A Missing Link: The Journey of African Americans in Golf*, 2nd ed. (Floriday: Privately Printed, 2013), 58–60, hereafter Harriet, *Missing Link*. For Lone Star State M, D, & P Assoc., see *Dallas Morning News*, June 12, 1930. This was separate from the National Negro Medical Association, founded November 26, 1895, which became the National Medical Association in 1900. See www.aaregistry.org. For Friendship Sunday School Convention, see *Fort Worth Telegram*, October 1, 1903. The Negro YMCA opened in 1903; the Negro YWCA in 1919. See "History of YMCA of Metropolitan Fort Worth," www.ymcafw.org/About-YMCA/YMCA-History; "YMCA Colored Branch" in Smith, *Negro Directory*, 2; and Laurene Sharpe, comp., *One Hundred Years of the Black Man in Fort Worth*, vol. 1 (Fort Worth: privately printed, 1973), hereafter Sharpe, *One Hundred Years*. The CWCTU was organized in 1906 by members of the Quality Grove Church. See *Fort Worth Telegram*, July 27, 1906. For black nurses, see Allen (Sherrod), *Grace and Gumption*, 194. The Anti-Saloon Congress was organized in 1909 in Atlanta, GA. *Dallas Morning News*, March 4, 1909.
4. For YMCA, see "History of YMCA of Metropolitan Fort Worth," www.ymcafw.org/About-YMCA/YMCA-History. For convention, see

Dallas Morning News, June 12, 1930. For tennis tournament, see *Fort Worth Press*, August 7, 1931.

5. For Colored Progressive Club, see for instance, *Fort Worth Register*, January 22, 1897. The Board of Trade (1882–1912) changed its name to the Chamber of Commerce. See "Fort Worth Chamber of Commerce 125th Anniversary," *Fort Worth Star-Telegram*, September 24, 2007. *Dallas Morning News*, July 6, 1908; July 7, 1909; and February 17, 1945. For 1936 black Chamber of Commerce, see The *Fort Worth Mind*, June 6, 1936, collections of Fort Worth Library, Central Branch, Local History, Genealogy, and Archives Unit. Also cited in Fairley, "Tarrant Chronicles," *Fort Worth Star-Telegram*, February 3, 1999. For a brief history of the present black Chamber of Commerce, see "The Fort Worth Metropolitan Black Chamber of Commerce," in Oates, *Celebrating 150 Years*, 50.
6. Houston was no banker; his chief qualification to be president of the bank besides being a Mason was being secretary and treasurer of the Trinity (Negro) Cemetery Company. Another problem was that the bank was a privately held bank. When it went under, the directors were asked to pay off the depositors out of their own pockets. See *Dallas Morning News*, July 6, 1908; July 7, 1909; and February 18, 1912; and the "Cowtown to Nowtown" section in *Fort Worth Press*, February 25, 1973. Information on R.C. Houston, Jr. comes from Mike Cochran, "One City, Two Downtowns (Part 1)," on website www.hometownbyhandlebar.com.
7. *The Freeman* (newspaper), Indianapolis, IN, April 19, 1913.
8. *Dallas Morning News*, August 11, 1900; August 2, 1907. *Fort Worth Telegram*, September 19, 1905; August 5 and 6, 1908.
9. *Fort Worth Star-Telegram*, June 23 and August 6, 1913.
10. The Heroines of Jericho were organized in Texas in 1875 and officially recognized by the Grand Lodge Free and Accepted Masons in 1886. The group was under the authority of a "Grand Joshua" of the State of Texas. In 1892, William M. "Gooseneck Bill" McDonald was elected Grand Joshua of Texas. Starting in 1889 the Heroines of Jericho and the Order of Eastern Star fought it out to be the sole female auxiliary of Prince Hall Masonry in Texas with the Eastern Star eventually winning out. Both groups still exist today. See "History of the Grand High Court Heroines of Jericho Prince Hall Affiliation – Texas Jurisdiction," http://grandhighcourthojtx.com/Past_Grand_Officers; and for Fort Worth, see "Colored Organizations" in *Fort Worth City Directory*, 1890 and 1907.
11. Curiously, although the Texas Federation of Women's Clubs did not admit blacks, the state organization had an "interracial committee,"

which was known on occasion to invite a member of the Negro Women's Clubs to address them. *Dallas Morning News*, October 13, 1931. For Fort Worth Woman's Club, see Richard F. Selcer, *Fort Worth, A Texas Original!* (Austin: Texas State Historical Association, 2004), 50–52. For scouts, see "Camp Site Sought for Negro Boy Scouts," *Fort Worth Star-Telegram*, March 6, 1944.

12. Max Hill, "William Trezevant, Jr.," *Fort Worth Genealogical Society's Footprints* 47, no. 3 (August 2004): 107.
13. Ten men organized the R.E. Lee Camp of the Confederate Veterans on October 16, 1889. *Fort Worth Gazette*, April 29, 1891. *Fort Worth Telegram*, January 10, 1909. *Fort Worth Star-Telegram*, March 15, 1915.
14. The story of the social and economic divisions within the modern black community is related by Lawrence Otis Graham, *Our Kind of People: Inside America's Black Upper Class* (New York: HarperCollins, 1999), although when the book came out it provoked a fire-storm among both scholars and the general public. See Jack E. White, "Bougie Like Me," *Time Magazine*, March 15, 1999, and Graham's response in "Letters to the Editor," ibid., April 5, 1999; also "Letters to the Editor" in *U.S. News & World Report*, April 22, 1999, p. BC-20. For "yellow negroes," see for instance newspaper reports such as *Dallas Morning News*, December 17, 1891.
15. Typically, Pullman porters worked 400 hours per month and earned more in tips than in salary. "The Evolution and History of the Union," A. Philip Randolph Pullman Porter Museum, www.aphiliprandolphmuseum.com/evo_history4.html. For a history of black porters, see Larry Tye, *Rising from the Rails: Pullman Porters and the Making of the Black Middle Class* (New York: Henry Holt and Co., 2004). For abuse, see unnamed "train porter" braced on the street by a pair of white Fort Worth officers in 1902. *Fort Worth Mail-Telegram*, July 2, 1902. For Ballard and Yates, see *Fort Worth Star-Telegram*, September 29, 1917.
16. "The Evolution and History of the Union," A. Philip Randolph Pullman Porter Museum, www.aphiliprandolphmuseum.com/evo_history4.html.
17. Hamilton, *History and Directory*, 42–43. For Oliver, see Geisel, *Historical Vignette*, 3, and 1902-03 *City Directory*. For Anderson, see *Fort Worth Morning Register*, September 18, 1901. He only appears in two city directories, 1899-1900 and 1901-1902, which not unusual for a black person, regardless of how long they had lived in the city. Anderson's story of working for the Post Office was rare if not unique. When World-War-

II vet Milton F. Johnson started carrying the mail in Fort Worth in 1951, he was the only black carrier in the system. Bob Ray Sanders tells his story in "Fort Worth's First Black Postman," *Fort Worth Star-Telegram*, August 1, 2012.

18. *Fort Worth Star-Telegram*, July 3, 1902.
19. On the occasion of his retirement, the *Star-Telegram* did a special piece on Warren in 1912. *Fort Worth Star-Telegram*, December 29, 1912.
20. For Washington's story, see T. Lindsay Baker, "Remembrances: Black Cowboy Life in Texas," in *Black Cowboys of Texas*, ed. Sara R. Massey (College Station: Texas A&M University Press, 2000), 23–24. For Collins, see Hamilton, *History and Directory*, 42.
21. For various job opportunities, see *Fort Worth Colored History and Directory* (1909) in TCBH&GS Collections, Series III, Box 1, File 2; and ibid., Box 1, File 21 ("Negro Progress"), p. 27. For NTTC, see *Traction News* (Newsletter of the Northern Texas Traction Company), May 1929, p. 15, Fort Worth Library Archives.
22. The story appeared on the back page (p. 11) of the *Fort Worth Star-Telegram*, January 20, 1915.
23. Christopher Evans, "A Drive through History—Two African-American Brothers. . . ," *Fort Worth Star-Telegram*, March 14, 1993.
24. *Fort Worth Telegram*, December 13, 1907.
25. For Fort Worth CBML, see TCBH&GS Collections, Series III, Box 1, File 2, p. 86. For Wilson, Taylor, and Thomas, see *Fort Worth Colored History and Directory* (1909), TCBH&GS Collections. For Grimble and Littlejohn, see Sanders, *Calvin Littlejohn*, Foreword.
26. For Calhoun and Jones, see *Fort Worth Star-Telegram*, October 16, 1919. For "public policy," see "Seventeenth District Court Judge James Swayne," ibid., March 6, 1911.
27. The story of the black beauty industry in Texas from World War I through the 1960s is told in Julia Kirk Blackwelder, *Styling Jim Crow* (College Station: Texas A&M University Press, 2003). Madam C.J.Walker (1867–1919), born Sarah Breedlove, single-handedly created the black cosmetics industry starting in 1905. Beverly Lowry, *Her Dreams of Dreams* (New York: Alfred A. Knopf, 2003). For Dionne Bagsby, see "The Legacy of Dionne Bagsby," *Fort Worth Star-Telegram*, April 2, 2005. The claims for Lucille Smith also ignore the presence of successful black madams like Lottie Freeman and Emeline Gooden in Fort Worth. Selcer, *Hell's Half-Acre*, 140, 144. Perhaps Smith should be called Texas' first

legitimate black businesswoman. For Smith's accomplishments, see *Fort Worth Star-Telegram*, December 22, 2014.

28. For the White Elephant, see Richard Selcer, "The White Elephant: Fort Worth's Saloon *Par Excellence*," *Legendary Watering Holes* (College Station: Texas A&M University Press, 2004), 227–289. For Black Elephant, see *Fort Worth Gazette*, June 25, 1885; and *Fort Worth Record*, Dec. 30, 1906.
29. Prince Hall *Proceedings*, August 18, 1900, pp. 113-14.
30. For Jones and Williams, see *Fort Worth Telegram*, October 17, 1907.
31. For Johnson, see *Fort Worth Star-Telegram*, July 5, 1910. Black "boxing clubs" existed in the shadows in both Dallas and Fort Worth for years. Usually the audiences were "equally divided between blacks and whites." *Dallas Morning News*, August 29, 1926.
32. The fact that Johnson consorted with white women—he married three—did not help. For Johnson's full story, see Theresa Runstedtler, *Jack Johnson, Rebel Sojourner: Boxing in the Shadow of the Global Color Line* (Berkeley: University of California Press, 2012); and Ocania Chalk, *Pioneers of Black Sport* (New York: Dodd, Mead, 1975). For Fort Worth reactions, see *Fort Worth Star-Telegram*, July 11, 1910.
33. "Trips to Europe" comes from "Hidden in history: African-American Doctors in Fort Worth," a talk by Shirley Apley, former Fort Worth librarian and archivist, at the Fort Worth Central Library on May 5, 2012.
34. The stories of Rolla, Peace, Cary, Cash, and Coleman are told elsewhere in the text.
35. For Salvation Army, see *Fort Worth Morning Register*, March 3, 1902. General William Booth, the founder, even visited Fort Worth in 1902 to encourage the troops. Ibid., July 12, 1901; January 15, 1902. For YMCA, see *Fort Worth Star-Telegram*, June 10, 1009.
36. *Fort Worth Star-Telegram*, June 28, 1918.
37. Drake was honored by the Federated Missionary Society of Fort Worth for her efforts. *Fort Worth Star-Telegram*, July 23, September 26, October 28 and 31, and November 4, 1920.
38. "Divisional headquarters" of the local Salvation Army was in Dallas and served both Fort Worth and Dallas. *Fort Worth Morning Register*, September 18, 1901. For the Masons, see *Proceedings of the Twelfth Annual Communication of the Most Worshipful Grand Lodge of Texas*, 1887, p. 7. The AF&AM Order in the form of Lodge No. 148 arrived in Fort Worth in 1855. For Eastern Star orphanage, see *Souvenir Book*, [Prince Hall] *Masonic Golden Jubilee, 1875-1925* (Fort Worth: privately printed, 1925).

39. *Fort Worth Star-Telegram*, April 20, 1944. Before 1920, the National Urban League was known as the Committee of Urban Conditions among Negroes.
40. For the long-forgotten Fort Worth Relief Association, see *Fort Worth Star-Telegram*, May 25 and August 3, 1919. The only serious outreach these organizations had for blacks was at Camp Bowie during World War I when all maintained full-time offices at the camp to provide entertainment and social services to the thousands of black recruits, easing their adjustment to army life.
41. After the Civil War, Southern whites spoke obliquely of the "Negro Question," meaning what to do with four million freed slaves. The term continued to pop up occasionally in polite conversation and political discussions for many years, always among whites. After the turn of the century, whites increasingly spoke of the "Negro Problem" or "Race Problem." For "Question," see Lubbock, *Six Decades*, 463; *Fort Worth Daily Gazette*, January 5, 1889; and *Fort Worth Telegram*, October 6, 1903. *Cf.* "Seventeen Texas Sheriffs to Help Avert Lynchings," *Dallas Morning News*, December 9, 1934. For "Race Problem," see ibid., December 1, 1898.
42. *Fort Worth Morning Register*, February 20, 1902.
43. *Fort Worth Star-Telegram*, March 1, 1911.
44. For the Smith lynching, see Reed Karaim, "Vigilante Justice," *American History Magazine* 46, no. 6 (Feb. 2012): 51, 53. For Brooks lynching, see *Fort Worth Star-Telegram*, March 3 and 7, 1910; and *Dallas Morning News*, March 4, 1910. For the "Slocum Massacre" or "Slocum race riot," see *Fort Worth Star-Telegram*, July 30 and 31, August 18, 1910; March 14, 1911; and March 31, 2011; and *Dallas Morning News*, August 1, 1910. Initial reports out of Anderson County were that as many as eighteen blacks had been killed. In 2011, state legislators passed a resolution formally acknowledging the racial atrocity that has been swept under the rug for more than a century.
45. *Fort Worth Star-Telegram*, March 7, 1910.
46. The story here and in the paragraphs following unless otherwise indicated, comes from *Fort Worth Star-Telegram*, February 28, 1911.
47. By "innocent negroes," the newspapers meant blacks who had not violated some tenet of Jim Crow or provoked the mob in some other way, i.e., "respectable" blacks minding their own business. *Fort Worth Star-Telegram*, February 28, 1911.
48. *Fort Worth Star-Telegram*, February 28, 1911.

49. Whether Blanton's promise of amnesty was sincerely meant or just a stratagem to gain control of the situation is impossible to say. For police, see *Fort Worth Star-Telegram,* March 6 and 11, 1911. For sheriff, see ibid., February 28, 1911.
50. *Fort Worth Star-Telegram,* February 28, 1911.
51. *Fort Worth Star-Telegram,* February 28, 1911.
52. *Fort Worth Star-Telegram,* March 1 and March 6, 1911.
53. *Fort Worth Star-Telegram,* March 1, 1911.
54. *Fort Worth Star-Telegram,* March 6, 1911.
55. For story of white Ritz Theater, see Jones, *Renegades,* 137–38. Additional material supplied by Jones via email, August 28, 2013. For story of black Ritz Theater, see Cary, *How We Got Over!* 2nd ed., 56–57. Cary talks about growing up "during the Great Depression" and going to the Ritz Theater although he calls the owner "Charles Maxwell" [*sic*].
56. *Fort Worth Star-Telegram,* March 6, 1911.
57. *Fort Worth Star-Telegram,* March 4 and 11, 1911
58. One newspaper came right out and called Tommie Lee a "bad nigger." Note also the feminization of his name, "Tommie Lee," not Tom or Tom Lee. This was normal in white newspaper reports about black persons. *Fort Worth Record,* January 4, 1912. For the full story of Tommie Lee's killing spree and the related race riot of 1913, see Selcer and Foster, *Written in Blood 2,* 39–87.
59. Selcer and Foster, *Written in Blood 2,* 39-87.
60. *Fort Worth Record,* May 17, 1913. *Fort Worth Telegram,* May 16, 1913.
61. Tom Lee Young was the first black man in Fort Worth sentenced to death for the murder of another black man. Young had no fans in the black community either. When the final verdict came down—life in prison—black Fort Worthers could only shake their heads over a judicial system that placed so little value on the life of a black victim. It was never explained why the state chose to prosecute the murder of the black victim, not the white officer. We can only speculate. *Fort Worth Star-Telegram,* March 9, 1914.
62. For the first mention of Fort Worth's riotous past, see Richard F. Selcer, *Fort Worth, A Texas Original!* (Austin: Texas State Historical Association, 2004), 27, 73.
63. The full story of the riot is told in the newspapers: *Fort Worth Star-Telegram,* July 11–23, 1919; and *Dallas Morning News,* July 11–23, 1919. *Cf.* Lewis, *Harlem,* 18–19. Lewis focuses on socio-economic issues rather than the newspaper story and says five were killed. See also Arthur I.

Waskow, *From Race Riot to Sit-in: 1919 and the 1960s* (Garden City, NY: Anchor Books, 1966), 16–17.

64. See, for instance, Fort Worth Chief of Police A.E. Dowell to City Manager Dudley L. Lewis, March 30, 1938, Mayor & Council Proceedings, Box 1, File 4, 1938 Proceedings.
65. *Dallas Morning News*, October 17, 1897.
66. For Burnett, see relevant provisions in his will in *Fort Worth Star-Telegram*, July 5, 1922.
67. For a discussion of the origins and meaning of "maroon," see Philip Morgan, *Slave Counterpoint: Black Culture in the Eighteenth-Century Chesapeake and Lowcountry* (Williamsburg, VA: Omohundro Institute of Early American History and Culture, 1998).
68. For the 1886 strike, see Selcer and Foster, *Written in Blood 1*, 88–105; and *Dallas Morning News*, April 4, 1886. For the effect of hiring black strike-breakers to replace white strikers, see the case of Fred Rouse, Chap. 4.
69. In the 1922 strike at the Swift and Armour plants on the North Side of Fort Worth, this is indeed what happened, which resulted in the last lynching of a black man, Fred Rouse, in Fort Worth history.
70. *Dallas Morning News*, June 18, 1892.
71. *Dallas Morning News*, August 24, 1942.
72. *Fort Worth Telegram*, July 21, 1906.
73. Kinch, "Amon Carter," 118–120.
74. *Fort Worth Press*, October 30, 1952. For Douglass Park, see Richard Selcer, Texas Historical Commission Historic Marker Application for Douglass and McGar Parks, 2010, Tarrant County Archives. For East Ninth St. Colored School, see Gayle W. Hanson, "Isaiah Milligan Terrell," *Handbook of Texas Online*, website of the Texas State Historical Association. Three years after having to move, the school moved into a new building thanks to a belated bond election passed by voters. For Como, see Delbert Willis, "Moonlight and Rowboats," *Fort Worth Press*, June 6, 1953.
75. Fort Worth had three T&P stations before 1931, the 1876 station, the 1899 station, and the 1905 station built after the 1904 fire that destroyed the second station. For earlier practices, see *Fort Worth Gazette*, October 24, 1892; and *Fort Worth Star-Telegram*, January 9, 1917. For 1931 station, see Roark, *Historical Guide*, 41–42, hereafter Roark, *Fort Worth and Tarrant County*.
76. For myth of black sexuality, see reports of attacks on white women in *Fort Worth Daily Democrat*, November 30, 1879. Also described as "black sexual potency" in Amilcar Shabazz, *Advancing Democracy in*

Texas (Chapel Hill: University of North Carolina Press, 2004), 147, hereafter Shabazz, *Advancing Democracy*. The eugenics movement was supported by such worthies as Theodore Roosevelt (1858–1919), the 26th President of the United States, Supreme Court Justice Oliver Wendell Holmes (1809-1894), and social reformer and women's rights activist Margaret Sanger (1883–1966). *Metropolitan Magazine*, a national magazine carried the "Vanishing Negro" story (n.d., 1913), and it was reported locally by the *Dallas Morning News*, October 25, 1907. For example of whiskey- and cocaine-fueled blacks, see *Dallas Morning News*, August 25, 1909.

77. Sources: Sanders, *Calvin Littlejohn. Fort Worth Star-Telegram*, June 27, 1980 (PM ed.); April 3, 1992; Obituary, September 9, 1993; and October 22, 2009. "Calvin Littlejohn" in vertical files, Fort Worth Public Library, Central Branch, Local History, Genealogy, & Archives Unit. *Tarrant County Black Historical & Genealogical Society Newsletter*, Sept.–Oct., 1984, pp. 152-157. Late in life, Littlejohn won awards for his "urban gardening" project from Neighborhoods U.S.A., Inc. and Fort Worth Clean City, Inc., "Near Southwest News," vertical files, Fort Worth Public Library, Central Branch, Local History, Genealogy, & Archives Unit.
78. Sources: Bruce A. Glassrud, "William M. McDonald: Business and Fraternal Leader," in Alwyn Barr and Robert A. Calvert, eds., *Black Leaders: Texans for Their Times* (Austin: Texas State Historical Association, 1981), 87. Mary McLeod Bethune, "The Richest Negroes in America," *Ebony Magazine* (April 1949), p. 13; (Sept. 1949), p. 55; and "Death Comes to the World's Richest Negro," no author, *Ebony Magazine* (October 1950), pp. 66-70. William Oliver Bundy, *Life of William Madison McDonald* (Fort Worth: Bunker Printing & Book Co., 1925), p. 292. Jack Gordon's column, *Fort Worth Press*, March 23, 1949. "Legacy of Early Black Banker Recalled," *Fort Worth Star-Telegram*, December 31, 1999. Matthew Johns, "What I Know and Think of Gooseneck Bill," *The White Man and The Negro* 2, no. 4 (June 1933): 96, 105. Obituary, *Dallas Morning News*, July 6, 1950. The story of how McDonald got his famous nickname has been told many times, not always the same way. See Reby Cary, *How We Got Over!*, 2nd ed., 3–4; *cf. Fort Worth Star-Telegram*, July 6, 1950 (AM ed.).

Chapter 7

The Depression

Or, Old Man Trinity Just Keeps on Rollin' Along

The stock market crash of 1929 did not have an immediate impact on the black community, but the Great Depression that followed within a year had an enormous impact on all areas of black life. In 1936 Universal Pictures released the definitive version of the musical *Show Boat* with black actor-singer Paul Robeson pouring his heart out singing the world-weary "Old Man River." That heart-wrenching number not only became Robeson's signature song, it also went on to become the first anthem of the modern civil rights movement, expressing all the bitterness and resignation felt by African Americans at the height of Jim Crow, which coincided with the depths of the Great Depression.[1]

The song talks about how no matter what blacks do nothing ever seems to change—"Old Man River just keeps on rollin' along." This was the way life in these United States looked to African Americans in the 1930s. The Depression was hard on everyone regardless of race, but it seemed to weigh especially hard on minorities.

The poorest of blacks could not sink any further. It was the black business community that had the props knocked out from under it. Barely getting by in the best of times and dependant on a tiny fraction of the population to turn a profit, black businesses failed right and left, starting with black-owned banks, which did not have the reserves to ride out an economic downturn. Only two black-owned banks in all of Texas survived the decade. One was Bill McDonald's Fraternal Bank and Trust. [2]

As for the average black working man, he too was a victim. Historically, when the job market tightens, marginal workers lose their jobs first. And no group in the 1930s was more marginal than blacks. Without unions to protect their jobs, and without the education and skills to switch jobs, they were completely vulnerable. In Texas, unemployment among African Americans topped 8 percent by 1933.[3]

In 1930 with a population of 163,447, Fort Worth was the third largest city in the state after Dallas and Houston. Of that number, 29,171 or almost 18 percent were black—still not enough to make a difference at the polls, but too many to be completely ignored. Dallas and Houston had more than twice as many blacks as Fort Worth, which helps explain why the black community in those two cities was more out-spoken and wielded more influence at city hall.[4]

At the beginning of the decade, there was no New Deal and no safety net for Americans who had lost everything. No one was expecting a decade-long depression, so help for those affected took the usual forms. Whites looked to family first, then private charity and local government. For blacks, the first stop was their church, then the black branches of the YMCA and YWCA, and then nothing. As Dr. J. H. Black of the Texas Commission on Inter-racial Cooperation (TCIC) stated, "These two organizations are manned by men and women of the [Negro] race, built to serve their own particular needs and dedicated to their own service." But the black branches of the YMCA and YWCA were at the end of the charitable pipeline into the white community and therefore had little to offer. The black churches were not much better off. No church or private charity was equipped to handle the massive problems caused by the Great Depression.[5]

If proof were needed that Jim Crow reigned supreme in Fort Worth, it was only necessary to look to the two biggest local construction projects of the decade, the Texas & Pacific terminal and the Will Rogers Memorial Complex. Both were designed by architect *wunderkind* Wyatt C. Hedrick who drew up the designs but had no say in who used the buildings. The T&P terminal, in the popular art-deco style of the era, was constructed in 1931 to replace the 1905 passenger station. Will Rogers Auditorium, constructed between 1936 and 1937 as part of the sprawling Will Rogers Memorial Complex, was built as Public Works Administration Project No. Tex1342R. It is still the largest public venue ever constructed in Fort Worth. Hundreds of construction laborers were needed on both projects, and African Americans worked on both, doing the dirtiest, hardest jobs such as manhandling steel and pouring asphalt. On the Will Rogers project, they were paid 75¢ an hour while their white supervisors made $1 an hour—both of which were lower than union wages.[6]

Both the T&P terminal and Will Rogers were built to be public venues, but that did not mean the races could mix at either place. The train station design included a separate window for blacks to buy their tickets and a smaller "Negro entrance" just west of the main entrance, which led to a "Negro waiting room." The auditorium likewise had a smaller entrance on the (east) side for blacks which led up to the balcony. This was the area designated for them during any public event where the audience was mixed. It would remain the city's principal public auditorium until the Convention Center was built in 1965. Years later architect Martin Growald in a newspaper interview called the Auditorium "a monument to segregation." Black groups were allowed to rent the space only as long as no white group requested it on the same datc. In July 1937, the National Association of Colored Women (NACW) held its biennial meeting there, drawing more than 300 women from all over the country with their inspirational motto, "Lifting as We Climb."[7]

GETTING ORGANIZED

For blacks living through the 1920s and 1930s, the 1920s (the "Roaring 20s") were not that good, and the 1930s (the Great Depression) were a double disaster. They survived not just by relying on each other, but by organizing. In a historic address at the Philadelphia Sesquicentennial Exposition in 1926, socialist and labor organizer A. Philip Randolph preached the gospel of collective action: Blacks must organize if they were to break the bonds of racial oppression. That message resonated in the years that followed. Mrs. Jessie Daniel Ames, one of the founders of the Commission on Inter-racial Cooperation, told a black Fort Worth audience in 1931 they would have to "work for race unification and avoid factionalism within their race." She warned that they could not expect help from whites. Seven years later, Dr. Edwin Elliott, regional chairman of the Federal Labor Relations Board, reinforced the first half of her message when he told a Dallas audience that blacks could help themselves in two ways: The first was "organization of various kinds"; the second was "legislation sponsored by white friends who believe in democracy." By that time, nine years into the Depression, new black organizations had sprung up to lead the fight for racial equality, not just in the political arena but also on the job and in the social sphere, and some older organizations had gotten a new lease on life.[8]

Among the new organizations were black veterans of the Great War who had only gotten around to organizing in 1937, long after white veterans. Blacks veterans of the "American Expeditionary Force" had been excluded from the American Legion when it was formed in 1919. In response, they formed the Colored War Veterans of America (CWVA). But that group had languished from lack of broad support in the black community and lack of respect in the white community. No white veterans' group would associate with them. It was not until 1937 that black veterans in Texas organized a "department" of the CWVA, encouraged by a War Department that was anxious to fan the flames of African-American patriotism with another war looming on the horizon. The

Texas vets held their first encampment at Austin in 1941 just months before Pearl Harbor. After the U.S. entered World War II they held a second encampment on July 4, 1942, in Fort Worth. They decided to stay on the sideline as America embarked on another great patriotic war. The CWVA never thrived because black veterans of World War I were few in number and scattered all over the country, plus they never received the same kind of official support as the (white) Veterans of Foreign Wars and American Legion. The CWVA was also unable to channel black patriotism in World War II as its sister organizations did with white patriotism. There is no record of a black veterans' parade or other demonstration of patriotism in Fort Worth or any other city in Texas.[9]

An African-American group with a happier story was the National Association of Colored Women's Clubs (NACWC). Originally founded in Washington, D.C. in 1896 by the merger of several women's groups, it had a political agenda as opposed to the purely social agenda of the Federation of Negro Women's Clubs (aka, the Federation of Colored Women's Clubs). Though the latter largely confined itself to hosting teas, art exhibitions, and lectures, the two groups were often confused in the popular press. The NACWC had as its purpose advancing black civil rights in general and repudiating demeaning white racist ideas about black women specifically. National membership reached 300,000 by 1918, but it seems to have had a very small presence locally, at least until the Depression. The closest organization to get press coverage was the "Home-Makers' Industrial School for Negro Women," which held a "Chautauqua" tent meeting in Dallas in 1921 highlighted by a "barbecue and watermelon feast."[10]

The problem with both groups was that their membership consisted of a small number of professional and middle-class women who had a heightened social conscience and the wherewithal to pay dues and travel to conventions. Those two things excluded the overwhelming majority of black women stuck on the lower end of the socio-economic scale. Though weak in numbers, however, these organizations projected a more positive image of black women than the traditional "Aunt Jemima" stereotype.

Whereas in decades past, Fort Worth blacks had largely confined themselves to bonding in fraternal and religious groups, in the 1930s they began forming advocacy and political action groups. For those involved there was a thrilling sense of the possible, of accomplishing great things that had never before been done. In July 1937 the Federation of Colored Women's Clubs held its national convention in Fort Worth. The organization dated from 1901, but this was the first time the ladies had held their national convention in the South. Representatives from every state attended, and Fort Worth was a gracious host. The activities were split between Mount Gilead Baptist Church and Will Rogers Memorial Auditorium. The latter had only been open for a year, and this was the first black gathering to use the facility. Tellingly, neither of the major Fort Worth dailies covered the event.[11]

A group that was rejuvenated in the 1930s was the North Texas Colored Teachers' Association, organized in 1899. After an early emphasis on "industrial education," the group found its voice in the thirties. They began speaking not just to each other, but to the white community, decrying the deplorable state of "Negro education" in the nation. They found a particularly sympathetic audience for this message at I. M. Terrell High School.[12]

On the labor front African Americans also took direct action. They had always been excluded from the American Federation of Labor, not just because of race but also because the overwhelming majority of blacks were unskilled laborers and the AFL was for skilled workers only. In 1901 Fort Worth's Colored Progressive Club tried to organize the "colored labor force" without any success. Their numbers were too few, and they had no financial resources. Nationally, a handful of black labor unions struggled to represent their interests, among them hod carriers, freight handlers, and dining car workers. In a country still fearful of communist subversion, black labor organizers operated at a greater disadvantage even than white organizers. Black workers in construction, for instance, when they could find work, were typically paid at half the rate of white workers. For that reason alone, "cheap negro labor" was despised by white workers. Another problem was that a lot of heavy construction jobs in the South, the only kind that most black men could get, often went to convict labor. Most Texas roads were built and most cotton was picked by black convict labor contracted out to white employers. With jails and prisons full of black inmates, it was nearly impossible for a free black man to get even a low-level construction job.[13]

The public's fear of communist influence in the labor movement was palpable. When two African-American cotton pickers at Fort Worth reported that they had been approached by a "communist agitator" warning them to quit working or else, the police launched an investigation. They found no agitators, communist or otherwise.[14]

By the 1930s, the nation's most powerful black labor union, indeed the only black labor union with a track record of success, was the Brotherhood of Sleeping Car Porters (BSCP), led by the same A. Philip Randolph who gave the historic address at Philadelphia in 1926. The BSCP enjoyed a good working relationship with the American Federation of Labor; they were allies not rivals because the union confined its organizing to black train porters. They were also the backbone of the black middle class in many cities, living in the nicest homes in the nicest homes. An unscientific survey of young black men in 1918 revealed that when asked what kind of job they wanted, two-thirds said they wanted to be Pullman porters. For the average urban black man with a high-school education or less, it was the ticket to a better life. During the Depression, a train porter could make $50 a month. It was not for every black man, however. A member of the U.S. Employment Bureau observed that farm boys with no education had "no possible chance to be a porter."[15]

Even Pullman porters who achieved The Dream were just another black man as far as white residents were concerned. It was when blacks started acting middle class that trouble followed, as one Dallas Pullman porter discovered when he tried to move into a white neighborhood in 1932. His house was bombed. The city bought him out, and he moved to a black neighborhood. The lesson was clear on both sides of the Trinity: members of the Brotherhood of Pullman Porters were no more welcome than the lowliest industrial laborer, which is not to say that Fort Worth was anti-labor.[16]

Fort Worth had always been a strong labor town going back to the 1880s and the Knights of Labor. On Labor Day typically, Fort Worth workers always held a big celebration in the city's parks, kicking off the day with a parade through downtown. The 1936 parade saw the biggest turnout in the city's history—30,000 people including contingents from Dallas and other surrounding communities. None of the celebrants, however, were African American for two reasons: blacks were barred from membership in most unions, and the public parks were off-limits to them. If black workers wanted to celebrate Labor Day they had to do it in Greenway Park or a church, and the festivities, no matter how elaborate, were not covered in either of the city's major newspapers. In Dallas, the Pullman Porters' Union celebrated Labor Day at Wahoo Park with a barbeque and picnic.[17]

In the spring of 1934, the outlook for labor organizing in Fort Worth had never looked more promising. With the encouragement of the Roosevelt administration, black activists had launched an ambitious campaign to create a "Negro union" at each of the major industrial plants. They kicked off the drive with an open meeting on the night of April 15. In attendance, besides Bill McDonald, were representatives from most of the white trades unions who came to lend moral support. McDonald, the keynote speaker, urged his audience to organize new unions and invigorate existing ones. Thus inspired, activists had big plans. After organizing black industrial workers, they aimed to target black musicians who constituted a sizable segment of the professional black community since Fort Worth was part of the so-called "chitlin' circuit." In the end, nothing came of all this union talk, one reason being that there was no way to organize mass demonstrations of black workers without arousing the worst fears of the white community—communist subversion and race war.[18]

Local civil rights organizers fared only slightly better than union organizers in this era. A Fort Worth chapter of the National Association for the Advancement of Colored People (NAACP) had existed in the city since 1918 although it had kept a low profile under the watchful eye of the Klan. The white Texas Commission on Inter-racial Cooperation (TCIC) mostly carried black hopes in the Lone Star State. It was a mild-mannered, non-confrontational group that tried to work within the rules of Jim Crow. The national CIC had been founded by white liberals in Atlanta in 1919; it incorporated in 1929 by which time it had more than 800 local chapters, including one in Texas founded in 1922. In 1929 the group was forced to cut back dramatically on field operations because funding had dried up due to the deepening Depression. The bad economy and the social climate in Texas made the TCIC practically toothless. Even at its most assertive, it was not so much an advocate of racial equality as a voice against lynching and mob violence. (It also spoke out for greater access to public education.)[19]

The NAACP eventually supplanted the CIC in Texas because the former spoke with the authentic voice of the African American; it was not a paternalistic white-run organization pushing an accommodationist agenda. Dr. George D. Flemmings was elected president of a reinvigorated Fort Worth NAACP in 1938 and held that post for the next twenty years. No matter what the history books say, Fort Worth blacks date the beginning of the city's NAACP from Dr. Flemmings' presidency. What influence the TCIC continued to wield came from the personal stature of its white leadership, not the mass of African Americans it claimed to represent.[20]

In Fort Worth at least the TCIC carried a lot more weight than the NAACP. The state organization held its annual convention in Fort Worth in 1931. The site of the convention was J. Frank Norris' First Baptist Church, which many considered to be the religious heart of the city. By throwing open the doors of his sanctuary the controversial pastor may have been trying to make up for openly supporting the Klan previously. Some members of his flock were shocked at the mixing of the races in the House of the Lord, but they could hardly have disagreed with what they heard from the pulpit. The keynote speaker, Mrs. Jessie Daniel Ames, hammered on the themes of unity and self-help (see above). While well-intentioned, the 1931 convention was hardly representative of the black community. What it really represented were the hopes and dreams of a small band of activists. For the mass of working blacks, it did not put food on the table or a roof over their heads. As a civil rights event it barely stirred a ripple.[21]

The TCIC continued to hold annual conventions for the rest of the decade. In 1934 they were back in Fort Worth, this time at First Christian Church which proved just as gracious a host as the Baptists had been. The organization's 1934 agenda included "controlling tuberculosis and other [killer] diseases among Negroes" as well as the usual concerns about "Negro education." They also took up a more incendiary issue, lynching, by holding a joint convention with the Association of Southern Women for the Prevention of Lynching (ASWPL). That swelled attendance at the convention to 4,000. Jessie Daniel Ames was back for an encore as the keynote speaker. She assured her audience, "It is not a Southern tradition to discriminate against Negroes," and reportedly no one fell out of their pew. She appealed to all Texas peace officers, represented at the convention by seventeen members of the Texas Sheriffs' Association, to join the TCIC in working to put an end to lynching. The convention may have been in Fort Worth, but the only Fort Worth resident on the program was Dr. W.A. Barnwell (who was white).[22]

The TCIC returned to Fort Worth in 1938, again holding their convention at First Christian Church. They had another full agenda but could point to very little progress after a decade of activism unless you count the decline in reported lynchings. How much credit they could take for that is questionable. With just 300 in attendance in 1938, the numbers were down significantly from their previous visit to the city, an indication that the organization was in decline. As usual, all the principal speakers were white although they represented a diversity of interests—church, business, and civic groups. This was the last time the TCIC met in Fort Worth. When the modern civil rights movement burst onto the national scene in the 1950s, it would be led by African-Americans organized in groups like the NAACP, the Congress of Racial Equality (CORE), and the Southern Christian Leadership Conference (SCLC).[23]

Shut out of the white city government, black leaders like George D. Flemmings and R.L. Melton created a shadow government with offices representing the same functions as the white municipal structure, including a "bronze mayor," a city manager, and fourteen councilmen. They had absolutely no power, but they were a proud statement that African Americans were also a part of the population like whites even if they were excluded from the power structure.[24]

On the street, blacks found a more urgent cause to rally around than a lot of windy civil rights rhetoric—a movie theater. In 1932 a new black movie theater was announced in a formerly all-white neighborhood. The first round of this battle had been fought in 1911 with the Dixie Theater, resulting in a full-blown race riot. (See Chap. 4) Now twenty-one years later it was another theater in another part of town, but the issue was the same: blacks having a theater of their own outside the historic boundaries of the black section of town. The M.C. Embry Amusement Company planned to open the theater on Evans Ave. (the Near South Side district), which by this date had become predominately black. That fact did not prevent the remaining white residents from raising a storm of protest. A petition signed by 125 of them was delivered to the city council and they sent representatives to a council meeting. The city manager and city attorney took turns explaining that there was nothing they could do; it was all legal. Councilman William Monnig, the department store magnate, spoke in support of the petition arguing that the theater would be a bad influence on the neighborhood. The council arranged a compromise behind closed doors with the Embry Company to delay the opening for a week, giving passions time to cool off. The theater opened, giving Jim Crow a rare defeat locally.[25]

There were several significant differences between the Evans theater dust-up and the Dixie Theater riot of 1911: First, the Near South Side was not the downtown business district; it was a largely black residential neighborhood. Second, black residents of the area were no longer the helpless victims of white fury. When the situation turned ugly they formed an armed neighborhood watch to patrol the construction site at night. Last, the situation did not escalate into a riot; passions were vented at the city council meeting, not on the street. One thing did remain the same from 1911 to 1931: the Fort Worth police were nowhere to be seen during both affairs. Even if the department had wanted to try to defuse things on Evans Ave., it had no credibility with black residents in the neighborhood. That fact came out when one council member asked the city manager if the police department had any black officers it could assign to the neighborhood. The answer was "no."[26]

Even without confrontations, there were still plenty of areas for activists to address, starting with medical care. The breakdown of society during the Depression caused a corresponding rise in public health issues across the population, in particular tuberculosis. Blacks were already considered predisposed toward tuberculosis (TB), so the authorities kept a vigilant eye on its occurrence in the black community. In 1931 there were 7,600 recorded cases, and doctors considered those just the tip of the iceberg. Yet, Texas did not have a single TB sanitarium for blacks. The only place a black man with TB could get treated was Huntsville penitentiary, but only if he were an inmate. Rampant TB among the black population was both a public health and an economic crisis that one official estimated cost the state $2,000,000 a year in medical costs and lost productivity. As a public health crisis, it could not be confined to the black community because more than a few sufferers worked for whites as maids, cooks, and servants. The TCIC appealed to the "self-interests of white families" in getting the state to build a TB facility for blacks. As usual, the cash-strapped legislature chose to study the problem rather than take action. Meanwhile, in March 1938 the Fort Worth City Council proclaimed an "early diagnosis campaign. . . to insure a more healthful and happy city." Nothing was said in the proclamation about race, but the same old Jim Crow rules still applied.[27]

Education was another issue demanding organization and active lobbying if things were ever going to improve. In addition to the familiar call for more and better "negro schools," new causes gained traction in the 1930s, such as a "training school" for delinquent black girls to keep them out of prison, and professional schools to train black doctors, lawyers, and teachers. At this time, there was not a single medical or law school in Texas for blacks, and only one "normal school" (Prairie View) for teachers. By one estimate, there were 25,000 black students in the state in 1938 who could not go to school because there were not enough teachers. And would-be doctors and lawyers had to go out of state to complete their education. Too many of those never came back. This meant that many black patients were dependent on the professionalism of white doctors and hospitals, and most black defendants had to depend on white public defenders to represent them. In 1938, the legislature took up the issue of professional training for African Americans in law and medicine. In the absence of viable options in-state, the next best thing was public funding to "send eligible members of the negro race to out-of-state institutions so that Texas may be served better when these citizens return to bring economic, health and social uplift to their brothers." After a lengthy discussion, the legislators voted to provide scholarships for black students to study out of state.[28]

The New Deal Comes to Fort Worth

The Roosevelt administration that came into office in 1933 was the best thing that had happened to the nation's black population in many years. It was as much self-interest as altruism. A segment of the "Roosevelt

Coalition" that helped keep the White House in Democratic hands for most of the next three decades was the black vote, concentrated mostly in the South. But FDR had to be careful not to alienate the white Southern wing of the party. This proved an especially delicate balancing act in Texas where Jim Crow still reigned supreme.

Blacks could not even exercise the right to vote in party primaries, which in these years is where Texas elections were really decided as opposed to general elections. The Democratic Party still barred black voters from participating in primary elections, and Tarrant County endorsed the practice in law. An early lawsuit challenging the law was tied up for years in federal court, effectively killing the case before it could even get a fair hearing. The law was not overturned until 1944 when the U.S. Supreme Court case Smith vs. Allwright struck down white primaries in Texas.[29]

Blacks could not sit on the bench, serve in juries, or sit at the prosecutor's table in Tarrant County. It was only in 1937 that the first black man was called for a grand jury panel. In this case the man was ruled ineligible because he had not paid his poll tax. Eighteen months later, another black man, Watson Barton, was put on a grand jury panel in Judge Willis McGregor's Criminal District Court, but only at the judge's specific request. The judge was responding to recent federal court decisions that a black defendant could not receive a fair trial if blacks were not represented on the grand jury panel. But even this little progress did nothing to change the make-up of local courts since being on a grand jury panel did not mean one would actually be picked to sit on a grand jury, much less a trial jury. Justice, like party primaries, was still lily-white in Tarrant County.[30]

The Democratic Party had a virtual lock on both state and local political offices in Texas during these years. The Republican Party typically tried to make just a respectable showing. In 1944 when FDR ran for a fourth term, the Democratic state organization was led by state senator Tom Tyson. During the one-sided campaign Tyson blasted his Republican opponents for trying to pry blacks away from Roosevelt. "The Republicans have attempted to create disunity among the Democrats on racial disunity, [but] I am not so concerned about Negroes as I am about political white trash." Fort Worth blacks supported Roosevelt in 1944 (and Truman in 1948) but their support did not count for much.[31]

Local black leaders decided to take their fight to Washington. Enlisting the federal government as an ally would have been inconceivable in the 1920s when the Republican Party and the KKK were riding high, but the Roosevelt administration held out real hope. After 1933 New Dealers from various agencies came to north Texas to offer their assistance organizing labor and civil rights actions. In 1934, Holman Swor, U. S. Employment service director, addressed a meeting of black union organizers in Fort Worth. He could offer nothing but encouraging words and moral support, but that was more than any previous visitor from Washington had offered. In 1937 Dr. Roscoe C. Brown of the U.S. Health Service came to town and addressed a gathering at I.M. Terrell High School. Brown himself was white, but he was over the Health Service's "work for Negroes" initiative. He spoke on "fitting the curriculum of negro schools to the pupil and to community needs." The parade of New Deal bureaucrats who came through Fort Worth in the 1930s showed that the federal government for the first time seemed to be aware that African Americans even existed as anything but a "Problem."[32]

While leery of Washington's interference in local matters, Fort Worth leaders were not above tapping the cash cow that was the New Deal for major projects. For the school board this meant applying to the U.S. Public Works Commission in 1933 to build a much-needed, second "negro high school." Black leaders asked the board to purchase ten acres "somewhere on the [Near] South Side" for the school, but Bill McDonald dismissed that idea out of hand. "Nowhere in the confines of the city," he wrote, "can ten acres be purchased for the exclusive use of Negroes." In the end, the city used federal money to expand and upgrade the existing high school on Chambers Hill (I.M. Terrell).[33]

Of all the New Deal's famous "alphabet agencies," perhaps the National Labor Relations Board (NLRB), created by executive act in 1933, took the greatest interest in helping the black man. In 1938, Dr. Edwin A. Elliott, the NLRB's Southwest Regional Director, spoke at the annual convention of the TCIC in Fort Worth. His topic was "The Economic and Labor Adjustment of the Negro." The fact that he even chose this topic to address the all-white audience is notable, but Elliott was something of a civil rights crusader.[34]

The New Deal helped focus national attention on the plight of the poor and disadvantaged. The United States Housing Authority (USHA) in Washington, D.C. sent out a directive to all of its local agencies to investigate housing conditions among poor Americans. The results demonstrated conclusively that blacks (and Hispanics) were the poorest of the poor. The report of the Fort Worth Housing Authority stated that "at least 30,000 [Fort Worth] citizens" lived in "decrepit, disease-breeding homes." A significant number of those homes were what were euphemistically known as "shotgun shacks" or "railroad houses." The former name came from the fact that you could fire a shotgun through the front door and it would go straight out the back door. The latter name came from the fact that they were long and narrow like railroad cars and tended to be found along railroad tracks. The typical shotgun house (or shack) might be only twelve feet wide and twenty-four feet deep, allowing space for just three 8 by 12-foot rooms, one behind the other. As many as eight could be crammed into the length of a single block. They were built of the cheapest materials, and often sat up on pilings instead of foundations. Typically, they lacked electricity and indoor plumbing but might have a front porch that was the coolest place in the house in the heat of summer. Shotgun houses were familiar sights on the edge of many Southern towns. In Fort Worth they were clustered below the Bewley and Ralston Purina flour mills, around Chambers Hill, and in the Rock Island Bottom. By the 1920s shotgun houses had become "symbols of poverty," a fact recognized by the USHA a decade later. Replacing them became a prime objective of the New Deal housing policy.[35]

Photo 17. Shotgun houses, 1939

Row of newly constructed shotgun houses, showing their unique construction. Unidentified Fort Worth location. Note unpaved streets. Courtesy of Genealogy, Local History, and Archives Unit, Fort Worth Library, Fort Worth Planning Dept., RG 18, Series III, Box 1.

USHA directives instructed its local agencies to provide "more and better homes" for "whites [*sic*], Hispanics, and Negroes," although they were a little vague on just what form those homes should take. City fathers were enchanted by the prospect of "free money," poor blacks were reeled in by the promise of well-built, tax-free residences, and contractors were mesmerized by the prospect of fat construction contracts at a time when business was scarce. And while nobody said as much, bigots recognized another benefit of public housing projects: They made it easier to segregate minorities into well-defined areas—ghettoes without the stigma.[36]

The best kind of public housing the New Dealers came up with was brick apartment buildings clustered together, creating instant neighborhoods complete with playgrounds and community centers. The U.S. Public Housing Authority called it "slum clearance," and that description certainly fit Fort Worth. The two areas where housing projects were to be placed were covered by block after block of what can only be generously described as slum housing—a jumble of shacks sitting up on rock pilings opening onto dirt alleyways, populated by the city's poorest. They were not even up to the standards of shotgun houses.[37]

Photo 18a. Before image of Franklin Hill

Before construction of the Ripley Arnold Project, when it was a slum quarter.

Photo 18b. Afterwards when it was public housing

"Ripley Arnold" represented an enormous improvement on the original site, but ironically came to be regarded as just as bad an eyesore in later years. Courtesy of Genealogy, Local History, and Archives Unit, Fort Worth Library, Fort Worth Planning Dept., RG 18, Series III, Box 1.

Master plans for the projects were drawn up in Washington, D.C. to be adapted to local sites by locally hired contractors. In 1939 the first bids were let in Fort Worth for three "low-cost housing projects," one for whites, another for "Negroes," and the third for Hispanics. In the end, plans were scaled back to just two, one for blacks (the H.H. Butler project) and the other for whites (the Ripley Arnold Project). The area "northwest of the 1917 Criminal Courts Building" was cleared for thirty-one buildings in the Ripley Arnold unit, and Chambers Hill east of town was cleared for the same number in the Butler unit. The city council selected Chambers Hill for the Butler unit because, although the area had begun as a white neighborhood, by the 1920s it had been taken over by poor blacks, and therefore no longer considered fit for whites. A total of $737,840 was budgeted by the U.S. Public Works Administration for Butler with construction to be completed in 400 days. J.E. Morgan & Sons, the contractor, missed the deadline but had the buildings ready to move into by early 1941, sans landscaping, paved streets, or street lighting. "Urban renewal" had come to Fort Worth![38]

Although the projects were built and maintained by the federal government, they were managed by the Fort Worth Housing Authority. To move into the projects, a family had to apply to the Authority and show they were living in "overcrowded, unsanitary or bad housing conditions generally." Butler represented a quantum leap over existing housing, not just in the Chambers Hill area but for most Fort Worth blacks. Each apartment had electric lights, running water, a water heater, and indoor plumbing. The buildings eventually were surrounded by grassy areas, connected by sidewalks, and reached by paved streets. Despite all those amenities, however, they still represented segregated housing on marginal property. The Ripley Arnold Project backed up to the Trinity River bottoms. The Butler project was safely above the flood plain, but cut off from the heart of the city, described by one resident as "an island away from everyone else." Like other public housing projects, they were handed over to the city, but that did not obligate the city to keep them up. The attitude of officials seemed to be that the residents would keep up the property the same way white, middle-class residents did their neighborhoods. In 1942, one federal official said, "We hope *and believe* that the occupants of the units will respond positively to their better surroundings." (emphasis in original). Instead, "the Projects" suffered greatly from lack of maintenance. The Butler Housing Project still stands today—hemmed in on three sides by freeways—and still a monument to racial segregation. Butler also faces an uncertain future because the current thinking is to disperse low-income residents throughout the city rather than concentrate them in "projects."[39]

Even in its heyday, the Butler project was a mixed blessing. It did indeed clear out a major slum and provide better housing for scores of black families, but clearing the site also uprooted an entire neighborhood, displacing long-time residents who had sub-standard housing but also a sense of community. Not all of those uprooted residents got into the new project. To compensate those who were thrown on the street, Uncle Sam provided a financial pay-out, which did not solve the problem of where they were going to live henceforward. In the end, the housing projects created a ripple effect in the market that hurt a lot of ordinary people. As one Dallas writer said, speaking of his own city, "Everybody connected with the housing projects meant well, but when you squeeze hundreds of Negroes out of their homes *THEY HAVE TO GO SOMEWHERE.*" This would not be the last time Fort Worth blacks living on the east side of town were dispossessed by a massive federal project.[40]

In Dallas when hundreds of minorities were displaced by five public housing projects they poured into white neighborhoods, principally in the Oak Cliff section, creating a racial firestorm the likes of which had not been seen before in the city. By contrast, in Fort Worth the displaced were mostly absorbed into other black neighborhoods, lessening the impact of the dislocations and avoiding civil disturbance.[41]

Mostly absorbed does not mean entirely. The disruption caused by the Butler Housing Project may have had something to do with what happened in Polytechnic in 1939. Poly as it was known was as white as any neighborhood in Fort Worth in the beginning. In 1915 E. Rosedale, the area's principal residential thoroughfare, counted 540 homes, only one of those occupied by an African-American family, which does not seem to have been an issue for the white majority. But the status quo was challenged in 1939 when Otis Flake, an African American, bought the house at 940 E. Annie. The white real estate agent who brokered the deal assured him there would be no trouble. He was either lying or had not really consulted white neighbors because those neighbors erupted in fury when the word got around. Things came to a head on Saturday night, June 17. What one newspaper described as "a group of protestors" numbering at least a hundred gathered on Flake's lawn, and they were not there to welcome him to the neighborhood. The police showed up and half-heartedly attempted to disperse the mob which finally left without doing any damage. Things were quiet on Sunday, but the mob returned Monday night, on a date coinciding with Juneteenth. This time their numbers were about 500 men, women, and children. While they were working themselves up into a lather, Flake and his family fled. The mob then stormed the empty house, carrying out furniture and family possessions and hurling them into the street. Not content to "smash" the house and drive out the owner, the crowd attacked a black man who happened to be walking home from the store and beat him badly enough to put him in the hospital. The police had been on the scene since nine o'clock in the morning but did nothing until the mob started smashing the house. Then they called in reinforcements, which consisted of ten police cars full of officers plus additional men from the Department of Public Safety and the Sheriff's Department. Still, they did not attempt to halt the destruction being inflicted on Flake's house by what the next day's *Star-Telegram* called "the raiders." The newspaper did quote a police department spokesman who said officers were not able to "get mobilized" before the mob did its dirty work. The police did, however, "remain at the scene" after the mob left to "watch over" what was left of the house for the rest of the night.[42]

Otis Flake did not return, and his white neighbors celebrated their victory. The next day, of the city's two major newspapers only the *Star-Telegram* reported what had happened on East Annie St. Both the *Star-Telegram* and *The Press* preferred to focus on Juneteenth festivities rather than the ugliness of the previous night. The *Dallas Morning News* reported what happened in more detail although carefully so as not to alienate the newspaper's white readers on the west side of the Trinity.[43]

After vanquishing Otis Flake, white East-Side home-owners took precautionary measures to keep out future block-busters. At the

Wednesday night meeting of the city council, they showed up in force to support a proposed zoning ordinance that would permanently "restrict" some neighborhoods, like their own, to "white citizens." Even the City Attorney Mack Taylor supported their demand. But for a variety of reasons the zoning ordinance did not pass. Still, the message had been sent. It would be another two decades before the Poly neighborhood was integrated. In the meantime the Butler Project eased some of the pressure on local housing that created neighborhood face-offs like what happened in Poly.[44]

Another New Deal initiative, which benefitted African Americans and historians both, was the Works Progress Administration's (WPA's) project to interview as many surviving slaves as possible. It was part of what was called the "Slave Narratives" gathered by the "Federal Writers' Project." More than 2,300 first-person accounts of former slaves were collected nationwide between 1936 and 1938 and microfilmed in 1941. The "Texas Narratives" comprise one volume numbering 1,143 pages. Some of the elderly persons interviewed had lived in Tarrant County, and their recollections fill in a huge gap in the historical record. The Project has been called "one of the most enduring and noteworthy achievements of the WPA."[45]

The interviewees whose stories are contained in the "Slaves Narratives" were a direct link to the past for Fort Worth's black community, even if the "Federal Writers' Project" itself was a white initiative. What was important was preserving the oral history. The subjects were at the end of their lives, their bodies frail and their memories failing, but they were living reminders of how far blacks had come in the 60-plus years since emancipation. Fifty-five of those old-timers who were living in Fort Worth at the time were honored as part of the Juneteenth celebration in 1939. The oldest, Lucinda "Lucy" Clayton, was 105 years old, and the youngest guest of honor was seventy-four. The group performed a selection of "spirituals and old plantation songs" that evening at the

"Negro [Masonic] Mosque," bringing back memories of the old days for a mixed audience of blacks and whites.[46]

Yet another reminder of the old days was the recognition of Lucinda's white benefactor, Richard Stockton, a local building contractor who had built her a "modern home" on Avenue B in her dotage, although she had never been a slave of the Stockton family. Richard Stockton was just a kindly benefactor.[47]

Lucinda and her contemporaries were as much a part of black mythology as of American history. Theirs was a tale of suffering and heroic survival that could inspire later generations. To their number we can add John Hickman, a black resident of Texas who belonged to a Confederate officer at the end of the Civil War when he began a new life as a cowboy. He eventually settled in White Settlement and lived long enough to become a local celebrity. In 1911 he was interviewed by the *Fort Worth Record.* In 1930 when he claimed to be 110 years old, he was honored at the State Fair in Dallas. Among his impossible-to-verify claims, he said he was the first slave brought to Texas, that he retrieved Jim Bowie's body from the Alamo, met Sam Houston, was present at Robert E. Lee's surrender at Appomattox, fought Comanche Indians, rode with Billy the Kid, and punched cows for legendary cattleman John Chisum. When he died in 1931, even the local chapter of the United Daughters of the Confederacy paid their respects. The stories of old-timers like John Hickman gave blacks a place of distinction in American history. They had been more than slaves; they had been witnesses to history, and therefore worthy of respect by whites as well as blacks.[48]

"AIN'T WE GOT FUN"

During the Depression, entertainment blurred the lines between races more than even before. The black entertainment spectrum covered everything from legitimate theater to anything-goes nightclubs. In 1938 the Grand Theater opened on the Near South Side at Fabons and

E. Rosedale. It alternated white movies with live, black performers, sometimes on the same night. In June 1938, Louise Beavers, the "noted negro [film] actress," appeared at the Grand. Fort Worth was a long way from Hollywood, but she stayed over for four nights. Jack Gordon, the *Fort Worth Press* entertainment columnist, said cryptically, "Only members of her own race can see her." The rule was, white patrons were always welcome at black performances, and Beavers was a genuine Hollywood celebrity.[49]

One often-overlooked aspect of Jim Crow is that many whites wanted to see the big-name black performers when they came through the area. Black performers like big-band leader Cab Calloway ("the Hi-De-Hi King of Jazz") or singer Dorothy Maynor could pack a house with white fans. On April 29, 1933, Calloway and his Cotton Club Orchestra played the Worth Theater before an all-white audience. They played three more nights in Fort Worth, including one dance for whites and one for blacks, before moving on to a six-night stand in Dallas.[50]

When cross-over performers like Calloway and Maynor played for a black event, whites still showed up, but expected to be seated in their own section of the room. They were. Promoters routinely advertised "special accommodations. . . for white people wishing to attend." Naturally, those accommodations were the best seats in the house.[51]

Even ticket sales for mixed-audience events were handled differently for the two races. When the Golden Gate Quartet, a black group, was booked into Will Rogers Auditorium in June 1944, they were heavily promoted in the city's two major newspapers. Ticket prices ranged from 80¢ to $1.80 for all comers, but whites could buy their tickets at Fakes & Co. Furniture Store while blacks had to go to the Greenleaf Café. And the racism did not stop at ticket sales and Will Rogers seating. The Golden Gate Quartet was an early version of the 1950s doo-wop style that had a more ethnic sound than the better-known Ink Spots and Mills Brothers (both also black). After the Quartet's performance on June 25, reviewer E. Clyde Whitlock of the *Fort Worth Star-Telegram* had this to say about the show: "Their performance violated every principle of music as an art. . . . This style of musical effort will not have to go far to be back in the jungle." Their act was not even music; it was "musical effort."[52]

At the end of the decade the great African-American contralto Marian Anderson performed in Fort Worth. While her voice was peerless, her race and political activism had heretofore kept her mostly north of the Mason-Dixon Line. She was not the first internationally famous African-American singer to perform in Fort Worth. In 1919, Madam Calloway-Byron, "the well-known negro soprano of Chicago," appeared at the City Hall auditorium. She was brought to town by a group of "prominent white [Dallas] club women" to perform for an all-white audience although it was in a good cause.[53]

Now, twenty years later, on March 19, 1939, Marian Anderson was in town as the guest of the all-white Fort Worth Civic Music Association, a group organized in 1931 by merchant W.C. Stripling and some of his wealthy friends. Unlike the Dallas club women, they took the risky move of opening the audience to blacks and whites both and using the city's premier venue, Will Rogers Auditorium. The records are not clear, but Anderson seems to have performed twice that day, first at Mount Gilead Baptist Church then that evening at Will Rogers. The great opera diva's appearance at the "Municipal Auditorium," while notable, was hardly a social revolution; whites got the seats on the main floor while blacks took their usual place in the balcony.[54]

Another reason Anderson did not make many appearances in Southern cities: she could not stay in the first-class hotels. The record is not clear but in Fort Worth she either stayed in the Jim Hotel (413 East Fifth) or else in a private home, arriving at Will Rogers just in time to prepare for her performance. What followed was a quiet evening of music, but less than a month later Anderson's appearance in Washington, D.C. stirred up a political firestorm. The Daughters of the American Revolution refused her permission to perform in Constitution Hall, whereupon Eleanor Roosevelt intervened and got the event moved to the steps of the Lincoln

Memorial where 75,000 saw it and millions more tuned in on the radio. Anderson became a national celebrity to millions of Americans who otherwise would never have taken any interest in classical music At the time of her first appearance in Fort Worth her reputation was largely confined to classical music devotees. One might expect that regardless of her remarkable talent, her race would have been as off-putting to white Fort Worth sophisticates as to the strait-laced ladies of the Washington DAR. Yet, here she performed before a mixed audience in a public venue without a hint of protest or demonstration. Truly, Cowtown was making progress.[55]

Anderson must have been a hit because she came back to Fort Worth in January 1941, again as the guest of the Civic Music Association. Before another packed house at Will Rogers she sang a variety of opera arias, "art songs," and baroque pieces, finishing with several "Negro folk songs," which was expected by white audiences who otherwise got few opportunities to hear authentic African-American folk songs performed by a black artist. Anderson, a classically trained opera star, always included some of the old songs in her performances out of a mixture of racial pride and audience demand. Those black artists who performed jazz, ragtime, or blues exclusively were not invited to perform by high-brow groups like Fort Worth's Civic Music Association. Those kinds of music were too black for staid white audiences. White Fort Worthers would have to wait until after World War II to hear live performances of what *Billboard* magazine called "race music."[56]

Anderson's visits to Fort Worth, and those of other black celebrities like Jesse Owens, the 1936 Olympic gold medalist, and Joe Louis, the heavyweight boxing champion, were more than just public appearances; they were testimonials to black progress and a chance to reconnect with their roots instead of just being show ponies for white promoters and agents. Anderson, the grand dame of the concert stage, arrived in town for her concert dates early so that she could visit informally with "her people" in their homes. In 1941 she spent the morning before her performance at the home of Dr. J.M. Burnett on East Terrell. Fifteen years later, when Joe Louis visited Fort Worth, he ate lunch with faculty and staff at I.M. Terrell High School. Both Anderson and Jesse Owens were interviewed by Lenora Rolla, an activist in the black community who picked up the occasional assignment with a local black newspaper.[57]

Night life for the city's African Americans in the 1930s and '40s thrived in segregated clubs like the College Inn. This high-brow-sounding establishment was in the lobby of the Jim Hotel at 413 E. Fifth St. Purchased with the hotel by Levi and Oscar Cooper from Bill McDonald in 1934, it quickly earned a reputation as the finest jazz and blues venue in the city. The legendary Aaron "T-Bone" Walker headed up the house band. On any given night, a mixed audience of whites and blacks could enjoy the sounds of musical celebrities like Louis Armstrong, Fats Waller, or the Original Ink Spots among others. And after the club closed at night, the musicians "jammed" into the early morning hours. The Jim Hotel continued to be the place to go for "real jazz" into the 1950s when it began a precipitous decline along with the rest of the neighborhood around Calhoun and Jones.[58]

The hottest black night spot in Fort Worth was the Egypt Club, which opened in 1929. The owner, J.C. Kennard, was an in-law of Bill McDonald and was known as "the Professor" because his day job was teaching at the Texas College of Embalming. But Kennard had bigger ambitions: establishing a chain of variety theaters on the "chitlin' circuit" in Texas, Oklahoma, Arkansas, and Louisiana. ("Chitlin' circuit" was the slang term for the chain of black-owned venues that stretched across the country favored by African Americans. Clubs on the circuit booked the big-name black talent as well as rising artists and girly shows.) The Egypt Club was big enough to be written up in the nation's leading black newspaper, *The Defender* out of Chicago. Kennard also imported talent from the "Windy City," such as Emma Wharton, the "shapely bronze hip queen" who played three months at the Egypt in 1937.[59]

The same Oriental mystique represented by the Egypt Club also attached to Pat's Araby Club at 5925 E. Rosedale, which became a fixture on the local night-club scene years later. The owner changed the name from the Penguin Club in addition to doubling the size and redecorating the place. The decorator was Darcy Keely, also known for creating Los Angeles' famous Cocoanut Grove lounge. As Pat's Araby Club the place was a high-class dance club whose Oriental motif included red carpets, gold ceiling, and a red-striped canopy over the bandstand. The legendary Ray Sharpe fronted the house band. Opening night was on December 2, 1960, and it remained a hot night spot the rest of the decade, bringing in nationally known acts such as the Coasters and Z.Z. Hall. It aimed at a broad audience with an admission price of $2.75 a person. The club's East Rosedale location and majority black patronage scared away most whites, but those who appreciated good music and a good time found Pat's Araby Club.[60]

Photo 19. Pat's Araby Club

Pat's Araby Club with owner Furman Alexander and hostess. A popular nightclub for Fort Worth blacks in 1940s and '50s. Courtesy of Tarrant County Black Historical & Genealogical Society.

Another popular black night spot of the 1930s and World War II was the Dixie Tavern on East Third, which attracted a different sort of crowd than the Egypt club. Besides its regular black customers, the Dixie Tavern attracted "three or four tables" of whites every night to see the "hotcha floor show." A shooting in the place in 1934 brought unwanted police attention and nearly got the place shut down, but it survived. In November 1935 the Dixie Tavern brought in a top-drawer floor show from Harlem for two weeks that brought the white audiences back.

The question of policing the black night clubs and dance halls caused some debate at city hall. The police force, of course, was all-white, so one suggestion was to hire "special policemen" to "supervise" the black venues. The idea did not get very far because the chief of police refused to even consider integrating the police force, so black night spots continued to operate in the shadows, policing themselves and trying to keep a low profile.[61]

Anything but a low profile was the black presence at the Texas Centennial Exposition in 1936. It was a unique event on several levels: a giant extravaganza marking the 100th anniversary of Texas' independence from Mexico, a prime example of Dallas-Fort Worth rivalry, and the biggest thing on the local scene since the Texas Spring Palace (1889–90). The crowds would be huge, and the nation's eyes would be upon the state. It was an opportunity for many groups and organizations to make a public statement. The (white) organizers saw it as "an important milestone in the mutual interests of the two races that must always live side by side." For the state's black community, it offered a golden opportunity to lay claim to at least a part of Texas history *and* gain a little recognition in their fight for acceptance. The Centennial commission planned events all over the state, but the main show was in Dallas. The Exposition adhered to Jim Crow conventions, which meant designating one date as "Negro Day" during the exhibition's run (June 6–November 29). Naturally, it coincided with Juneteenth, which for that one day was given the name, "Emancipation Jubilee." Overseeing the day was Sam W. Houston, the white Director of Negro Relations at the Centennial. African Americans turned out in force for their big day at the fair, 67,000 strong by official count. It was the single biggest day of the Exposition in terms of gate receipts. Special chartered railroad cars and buses brought in blacks from all over Texas and beyond, including many from Fort Worth. General admission was 40¢ and admitted fair-goers to a series of special "negro events" conceived by Sam Houston and his staff "to please the negroes." The biggest star to perform was nationally known black band leader Cab Calloway with his orchestra. The all-white National Folk Festival turned over the amphitheater to Calloway for that one night. It was obvious that whites planned the program because it featured "negro singing games," "old negro hymns," and an old-fashioned "cake walk" reminiscent of nineteenth-century minstrel shows. For every event on Negro Day (a "bathing beauty review," boxing matches, etc.) there was one section reserved for whites. Most black visitors brought their own food and drink because the regular vendors at the fair either would not sell to them or else charged outrageous prices. Fort Worth blacks were also there as performers in the form of an unnamed church choir (Mount Gilead's?) that sang "spirituals" and "singing games" in the Cotton Bowl stadium.[62]

The white organizers of the Centennial Exposition, who could count gate receipts, planned a second Negro Day in August and a third in October, which were also well-attended. Special trains again brought black fair-goers into town from all over Texas plus Oklahoma and Louisiana. The program for the August date included sermons by distinguished black preachers—part of what the *Dallas Morning News* called "all church day for the Negroes." After being properly churched, black fair-goers could stay and hear popular bands perform the latest sounds or see *Macbeth* performed with an all-black cast. Among the preachers on the all-church program was Dr. T.S. Boone of Fort Worth's Mount Gilead Baptist Church. More than a few Fort Worth brethren made the journey to Dallas to hear him.[63]

For most black visitors to the Exposition, their proudest moment had to be going through the Hall of Negro Life. This magnificent building was supposed to recognize accomplishments in the arts, economy, and education, although ironically, blacks could only get into the grounds to see it on Juneteenth. It also had the only "colored restrooms" on the grounds. Despite not feeling really welcome, blacks from all over north Texas flocked to the 1936 Fair in record numbers.[64]

Meanwhile, miffed at being passed over for the Centennial's big showcase in favor of Dallas, Fort Worth put on its own extravaganza, dubbing it the "Frontier Exposition" and proclaiming, "For education go to Dallas; for entertainment come to Fort Worth!" The Fort Worth event was staged on twenty-three acres of empty land at the intersection of

Lancaster and University, from July through November 1936 in direct competition with the Dallas exhibition. Fort Worth had Wild West shows, musical revues, Indian villages, big-band performances, and even a girly show. What it did not have was African Americans. When the Frontier Exposition opened on July 18, 1936, the only blacks to be seen were the 250 waiters working the Casa Mañana dinner theater, a boost to black employment if not black pride. Unlike Dallas, the Frontier Exposition had no "Negro Hall" and no "Negro Day" on the calendar. The Jim Crow policy was loosened after gate receipts fell off. The exhibition's management quickly huddled and decided to admit blacks to two daily shows, the "Last Frontier" (a pioneer-themed pageant), and "Jumbo" (a circus). One scholar estimates attendance jumped by 35,000 to 40,000 over the run of the exhibition as a result, but dismisses the jump as "Joe Louis gate hypo," shorthand for the surge in black pride that followed the "Brown Bomber's" amazing rise to the top of the boxing ranks from 1935–1937. Some things did not change: 1) Paying black customers still had to enter the grounds through side gates and sit in segregated seating; and 2) They were still barred from the Pioneer Palace, Casa Mañana, and midway sections.[65]

Reacting to the segregated Frontier Centennial exposition, Fort Worth's black community decided to hold its own exhibition based on the theme "A Century of Negro Progress." It was an ambitious undertaking that Dallas' larger black community had not attempted, but that did not deter them. The site they selected was Lake Como, a scenic setting surrounded by a black middle-class population that would hopefully turn out to support it and not be intimidating to potential white exposition attendees. It was also the only possible site with the cleared land, utilities connections, and public transportation access for such an enterprise. The Negro Centennial exposition opened on June 17 with high hopes and little else. Both the financial entertainment bookings were so modest that it fizzled. With competition from "Negro Day" in Dallas and two shows thrown open to African-Americans at the Frontier Centennial, there was not much reason to support the Lake Como event aside from racial solidarity. In the end, it was a footnote in the black effort to emulate the best of white society.[66]

In the meantime, life went on. The following year, the Dallas State Fair was reborn as the Greater Texas & Pan-American Exposition. Consistent with Jim Crow traditions, a "Negro Day" was scheduled for October 18. Gate receipts showed 42,287 fair-goers came out that day, a number which included numbers of black Fort Worth who came over by automobile. That was a historic change from previous State Fairs when most had to come by train or interurban. The automobile had become a significant part of the transportation options for African Americans. In addition, the I.M. Terrell school band performed at the 1937 Fair. Among other popular attractions on "Negro Day" were a couple of college football games in the Cotton Bowl and the "Road to Rio" show, which had separate seating for whites and blacks. Organizers also thoughtfully provided "all-Negro peep shows," which were a different form of education. As on previous occasions, "Negro Day" was proved one of the biggest days in the Fair's run.[67]

Whether they came by automobile or train, Fort Worth blacks could be counted on to support major entertainment events in Dallas. The I.M. Terrell band and such church choirs as that of Mount Gilead Baptist made multiple appearances at the State Fair over the years. Other events also brought out Fort Worth talent. In January 1939, several black Fort Worth couples competed in a jitterbug dance contest that for a few hours took participants' minds off the Great Depression. As usual, the contest brought out a white audience that could appreciate black talent and did not make Jim Crow distinctions.[68]

Athletics was another area of public life where the lines of Jim Crow blurred. With an infusion of New Deal money, the city built Farrington (football) Field in 1939, right across the street from Casa Mañana and the Will Rogers Complex. Seating 19,450, it was the premier playing field for the city's high schools during the fall. When not being used by white FWISD schools, it was available to I.M. Terrell. In fact, it was rented to all comers willing to pay, including the Southwestern Athletic Conference of black colleges in Texas, Oklahoma, Arkansas, and Louisiana (*cf.* Southwest Conference, 1914–1996). Much like how the Cotton Bowl in Dallas became home to the annual fall classic between the University of Oklahoma and the University of Texas in later years, Farrington Field was a convenient neutral ground for members of the Southwestern Athletic Conference. In 1939, the Bishop College Tigers of Marshall, Texas, played the Langston University Tigers of Langston, Oklahoma. The city really rolled out the red carpet for the two teams, considered two of the outstanding "Negro squads" in the country at the time and both of them undefeated. Fans poured into town from Oklahoma and east Texas for the Saturday night, October 21 contest. The game was preceded by a big parade that afternoon, organized by and composed entirely of African Americans. But that did not mean white fans were turned away from the game. A special section at Farrington Field was filled that night with white fans cheering on the Texas boys.[69]

All the Fort Worth arrangements were made by an ad hoc committee composed of W.F. Bledsoe, Jr., Dr. George D. Flemmings, and the local Bishop College alumni chapter. The parade, the official reception, and the game all came off without a hitch, demonstrating for any skeptics among whites that blacks could organize and underwrite a major public event without passing the hat around the white community.

Daily Life in Depression-Era Fort Worth

Black Fort Worth residents rode out the Depression mostly hunkered down in their own insulated community. A new black business district had grown up in the E. Rosedale-Terrell corridor, competing with older businesses on Jones and Calhoun downtown. The Jones-Calhoun corridor had already lost most of its residential population. As early as 1927 one observer predicted, "It is probable that in time the Negro residential district in the downtown section will be abandoned, and its place taken by white and Negro industrial enterprises." Warehouses and industrial properties were already pushing out retail activity, and that process accelerated in the next few years.[70]

What might be called "black flight" took the African-American population farther away from downtown, looking for nice neighborhoods to live in just like whites. Black suburbanites still had to be able to get back and forth between those neighborhoods and downtown, and unlike whites, most of them depended on public transportation. In 1938 they lost ground on that front when the last street cars were taken out of service, to be replaced by public buses, which were supposed to serve all the same areas. Though the change-over hit black suburbs harder than white, this was no racially motivated conspiracy. The reasons were simple economics: street car lines had been losing money for years, and with automobile and bus manufacturers aggressively pushing their vehicles, the city made the decision to pull up the last street car tracks —the Riverside line that ran out East Fourth. Most black citizens did not own cars, so they had to depend on public transportation. Many Como residents, for instance, had used the Arlington Heights line to get to their jobs and to downtown businesses. The fact that blacks were the principal riders of street cars in later years simply made it easier to shut down the last lines. But the buses did not run as frequently, nor in the beginning did they serve every neighborhood served by the old street car lines. Buses, however, like public housing, were supposed to be a great leap forward.[71]

Some things remained the same. Blacks were still far more likely to get their names in the newspaper for breaking the law than for some notable civic or personal achievement. About the only other time a black person got his name in the newspaper was when he died, and even then there were no guarantees if it were an unremarkable death. Crime was always news, and the more lurid the better. One of the biggest crime stories of the decade concerned the robbery of the First State Bank of Polytechnic by three black men who were set up by a rogue Fort Worth cop. First he recruited them and planned the job, then he betrayed them to the police and helped shoot them down when they tried to make their get-away. The whole thing climaxed in a big shootout on East Rosedale just a little after high noon. Detective John Alsup's objective was to collect the $10,000 reward offered by the state bankers' association for any bank robber killed in the act. Alsup was found out and went to prison, but what shocked Fort Worth citizens more than the idea of a bad cop was a trio of black men having the temerity to try to pull a bank job in broad daylight. [72]

Anytime the police showed up, blacks were at a disadvantage because the boys in blue were always there to defend white interests. In 1932 when there was a threat of racial trouble in Terrell Heights over the new black theater, the city council met in special session to discuss the best way to handle the situation. When one council member innocently asked City Manager G.D. Fairtrace whether the city had any "negro policeman" who could calm black residents, the answer was no. That was enough for the council. They decided to send in the police in force to separate the two sides and, by inference, keep a lid on black anger.[73]

The *Fort Worth Star-Telegram* did not cover the Terrell Heights troubles, only *The Press*, and then only perfunctorily. Both newspapers wanted to uphold the good name of the city, so whenever it came to the black community there was almost a code of silence. Most Fort Worthers had to read about what was happening there in one of the Dallas newspapers, the *Times-Herald* or *Dallas Morning News*. The leading Fort Worth daily, Amon G. Carter's *Star-Telegram*, studiously ignored black news except for crime. For instance, it did not report on the meetings of the TCIC in Fort Worth in 1931, 1934, or 1938, and since Carter called all the shots at his newspaper, one is forced to conclude that this was his editorial policy.

But no matter how back things got during the Depression, Fort Worth blacks could always look upward—to heaven and to the high school on Chambers Hill. The church remained the rock of the black community, offering both aid and inspiration to those laid low. The African-American church gave the faithful a new celebrity, Hattie M. Crooms, the most dynamic black preacher on the local scene since Sin Killer Griffin was stirring things up before the turn of the century. Like Griffin, Crooms was a Baptist, and like Griffin her flock was not limited to her denomination. She was a "brilliant and electrifying young evangelist" who toured nationally. At a time when women evangelists were a rarity, especially in the Bible Belt, Crooms was the black Aimee Semple McPherson. In 1938 she drew national attention by accusing Fort Worth ministers of "cowardice" for not speaking up after the grand jury refused to indict a white man accused of raping a black woman. In her spare time, Ms. Crooms also wrote a column for the *Fort Worth Mind*.[74]

Sitting just a little below heaven was the school on Chambers Hill. I.M. Terrell was more than a high school: it was a monument to black accomplishment. For countless students who passed through its doors, it was the ticket out of poverty and ignorance. For its faculty, it was an honorable place of employment. Teaching there was not a refuge for those who couldn't make it in business or the professions, but rather a commendable calling for college-educated African Americans. The faculty ran a tight ship where students were required to speak well, dress appropriately, and keep up with their lessons. Growing up in those days, a black kid could not realistically aspire to a big career in professional sports or entertainment like today, but he or she could aspire to a high school diploma because of I.M. Terrell. Its successes were celebrated by the entire black community. Over the years Terrell produced notable scholars, athletes, and musicians. Its graduates went on to serve on school boards and city councils, and the state legislature, and even have their names placed on buildings. They were the educated elite of the black community. Terrell's faculty was both beloved and honored by those graduates.[75]

Photo 20. Hazel Harvey Peace

Hazel Harvey Peace was an icon at I.M. Terrell High School for many years. Here in 1952 as counselor and dean of girls. From "I.M.T. Panther" Annual of 1952. Courtesy of Byron White of Fort Worth.

In the midst of economic depression, the 1930s saw some easing of Jim Crow. The reasons are complex and hard to assess, but it may be because working-class people were getting organized as never before and taking a determined stand against an unequal and unjust system, plus unlike in previous years the federal government was taking their side. Fort Worth's black community was also larger and more assertive than ever before, and the power of the Klan, which had been so dominant in the twenties, was fading.

Hazel Harvey Peace—Teaching generations of black schoolchildren[76]

Hazel Harvey Peace liked to say "I'm doing the best I can with what I got." That motto seemed to sum up her remarkable life. Fortunately for generations of black schoolchildren, this tiny woman was blessed with brains, a flair for teaching, and an unquenchable can-do spirit. She also demonstrated love and compassion in abundance for her students. The five-foot-tall woman with the steely gaze taught for forty-six years at I.M. Terrell High School and elsewhere, although Terrell students and teachers were always her first family. Principals described her as "a ball of fire," but her students called her "Mama Hazel." She did not set out to be a teacher; things just worked out that way. As she admitted, "I can't say teaching was my first love. I would say it turned into my first love."

She was born in Fort Worth to Allen and Georgia Harvey on August 4, 1907. For her entire life there would be questions about the date and place of her birth, but she herself never had any doubts. Hazel was a child prodigy, learning to read by the age of four. Growing up in Fort Worth's Seventh Ward, she spent as much time as possible in the Carnegie Public Library. Because of Jim Crow she could not read there but had to check out her books and leave. Still, she never lost her love of books and libraries. She attended James E. Guinn Elementary School, then went to Fort Worth Colored High School, graduating in 1919 at the age of thirteen. From there she went to Howard University, graduating in 1923. She returned to I.M. Terrell to teach, although still just a teenager herself. She was determined to prepare her students for college despite conventional wisdom that they should be content learning a vocation. Her debate students, for instance, learned how to do research in a college library and how to write college-level essays. Her "field" was whatever was required: English, drama, debate, history, she taught them all. Yet academic content was only part of her mission. What she was really teaching was "life," raising up the poorest of the poor by giving them knowledge. Before she was through with them, they were reciting Shakespeare and discussing the

French Revolution. She could not confine herself to one classroom any more than she could confine herself to one subject. She enlisted Terrell's shop teacher to help build sets for her drama productions. Eventually she became Dean of Girls at Terrell, a position that perfectly suited her talents. She helped Terrell girls with all sorts of problems, whether social, religious, or educational, that they could not take home. When she left Terrell in 1972 she was vice principal.

Meanwhile she continued her own education, enrolling in a theater course at Columbia University in New York City during the summers. In four years she earned a master's degree in English. But she did not stop there; she had an unquenchable thirst for knowledge. She did postgraduate work by correspondence at the University of Wisconsin and spent her summers studying at Vassar, Atlanta University, and Hampton College.

She was also a wife, married to Joe Peace, but in her professional life she never dropped her maiden name; she was always "Hazel Harvey Peace." They never had any children of their own, but she never lacked for family. The thousands of students who came through her classes over the years were her children. Joe Peace died in 1959. She was also a pillar of Baker Chapel African Methodist Episcopal Church.

She spent eighty-four years teaching, forty-six of them in the classroom After Terrell closed in 1972, a victim of desegregation, she went to work at Bishop College, which had moved to Dallas in 1961, as Student Affairs Director and Financial Aid Coordinator. She retired for good in 1981, and in the years that followed the awards started rolling in. Bishop College recognized her in 1985 as a "Texas Black Woman of Courage." In 1988 she received the Fort Worth Volunteer Award and the United Way Hercules Award in 1988. In 1992 Texas Wesleyan University awarded her a Doctor of Humane Letters, and in 1999 the Fort Worth Library renamed the children's section at the Central Branch the Hazel Harvey Peace Youth Center. Her portrait hangs there today. In 2001 she was an Olympic "Torchbearer" when it came through Texas on the way to the 2002 Winter Games in Salt Lake City. In 2007 the University of North Texas endowed a chair in her name in the School of Library and Information Sciences, making her the first African-American woman to be so honored in public education in Texas. Through all the awards and honors, she protested, "I don't like fanfare," which was another reason people loved her.

In her last years she remained a one-woman force of nature who had lived enough history for several books. She had been a witness to two world wars, Jim Crow segregation, the civil rights movement, and the election of the first blacks in Fort Worth. She wanted to pass that knowledge on to others to carry on the good fight. She also spoke to the black community from a unique position of authority:

> Many of our black parents have not had [educational] opportunities; therefore, it isn't possible for them to give all the motivation [their children need]. They can encourage them, make it possible for them to go to school every day, feed them well, clothe them, and even have the funds to send them to school. But there's something else that's got to be there. That's where the teacher comes in. She's got to be an extension of the home.

She was just as blunt the old days. Five years after I.M. Terrell closed, a reporter asked her if she missed it. "No," she said, "I don't miss it. I gave it the best I had."

Hazel Harvey Peace died on June 8, 2008, at the age of 100. Her death was not just the black community's loss; it was the entire city's loss. The word spread across the state and then went national. Her funeral was a public event, the first such funeral ever for an African American in Fort Worth. Not even William McDonald had been honored so. The memorial service at Baker Chapel six days later was standing-room-only. Fort Worth Mayor Mike Moncrief eulogized her place in Fort Worth history with these words: "She was, without a doubt, one of the most influential women in our city's history." Her former students in attendance represented a "Who's Who" of Fort Worth's black community, including Tarrant County Commissioner Roy Brooks, journalist Bob Ray Sanders, and educator-author Reby Cary. Professor James Cash, I.M

Terrell graduate and former TCU basketball star, flew in from Harvard. They all agreed that Hazel Harvey Peace had taught them the formula for success: “excellence, hard work, and fair play.”

NOTES

1. Perhaps second only to heavyweight champion Joe Louis, Paul Robeson was the best known black person in America in the 1930s and '40s. For a concise biography, see Arnold H. Lubasch, *Robeson: An American Ballad* (New York: Scarecrow Press, 2013). For an excellent discussion of the song and its place in the American consciousness, see Will Friedwald, *Stardust Melodies* (New York: Pantheon Books, 2002), 105–136.
2. The other was Farmers' Bank of Waco. Barr, *Black Texans*, 153–55.
3. Barr, *Black Texans*, 153–55.
4. Dallas's total population at the same time was 209,247, and Houston's was 203,394. San Antonio came in fourth at 122,698. *Dallas Morning News*, September 21, 1931. By comparison, in 2010, Fort Worth's black population numbered 140,133, or 19% of a total population of 736,200. *Fort Worth Star-Telegram*, February 18, 2011.
5. *Dallas Morning News*, July 22, 1931.
6. The Will Rogers Memorial Complex was the brainchild of Amon G.Carter, named for his friend and beloved humorist, Will Rogers who died in a plane crash in 1935. The money came from the Works Progress Administration (WPA), a New Deal agency created by Congress in 1935 to put unemployed citizens back to work on projects that would utilize their particular skills and create something that would serve the public for years to come. Ruby Schmidt, *Historical Guide*, 38 (Will Rogers Auditorium). Ibid. Roark, *Historical Guide*, 41–42 (T & P Station). Debbie M. Liles, *Will Rogers Coliseum* (Charleston, SC: Arcadia Publishers, 2012), 7, 41, 43, 53. WPA projects paid less than union wage scale to both blacks and whites.
7. The Terminal also included a separate waiting room for white women. Roark, *Historical Guide*, 41–42. Ironically, when the restored terminal was dedicated in 1999, a black former employee who had been there in 1931 was an honored guest for the occasion. *Fort Worth Star-Telegram*, October 31, 1999. For Growald, see Cary, *How We Got Over!* 2nd ed., p. 2. The NACW was founded in 1896 with that same motto. For Will Rogers Auditorium and the NACW, see Liles, 92-93.
8. For Randolph, see Robert W. Rydell, *World of Fairs* (Chicago: University of Chicago Press, 1993), 160–64. For Ames, see *Dallas Morning News*, November 8, 1931. For Elliott, see ibid., December 3, 1938. For the TCIC,

see Julia Anne McDonough, "Men and Women of Good Will: A History of the Commission on Interracial Cooperation and the Southern Regional Council, 1919-1954," Ph.D. Dissertation, University of Virginia, Charlottesville, 1993.

9. Astor, *The Right to Fight*, 140. *Dallas Morning News*, June 25, 1942.
10. For a history of the NACWC, see Deborah Gray White, *Too Heavy a Load: Black Women in Defense of Themselves, 1894–1994* (New York: W.W. Norton & Co., 1998). *Dallas Morning News*, August 7, 1921; October 13, 1931; and April 26, 1936.
11. *San Antonio Express*, May 13, 1901. *Dallas Morning News*, July 18, 1937.
12. *Dallas Morning News*, December 17 and 19, 1900; November 26, 1904; and February 7, 1937.
13. For Colored Progressive Club efforts, see *Fort Worth Register*, January 22, 1897. For black convict labor, see "State prison system competing with farmers" in "Letters from Readers," *Dallas Morning News*, October 26, 1932.
14. This incredible story may have been made up by the men to win points with their bosses. It is hard to imagine a white communist agitator singling out two black cotton-pickers. *Fort Worth Press*, August 29, 1933.
15. The survey was conducted informally among black recruits at Camp Bowie, so the sample was hardly scientific, merely empirical. *Fort Worth Star-Telegram*, March 13, 1919. For salary, see interview with Walter Caldwell, a retired porter, *Fort Worth Star-Telegram*, October 31, 1999.
16. *Dallas Morning News*, December 2 and 16, 1932; and November 7, 1940.
17. *Fort Worth Star-Telegram*, August 1 and 29, 1920. *Dallas Morning News*, September 4, 1922; September 4, 1923; August 27, 1929; August 29, 1935; September 3, 1940. For numbers, see *Dallas Morning News*, August 23, 1936.
18. *Dallas Morning News*, April 17, 1934.
19. In the 1920s and '30s, the TCIC is mentioned occasionally in the major Fort Worth and Dallas newspapers, the NAACP, never. For a history of the NAACP in Fort Worth, see Steven A. Reich, "Soldiers of Democracy," *Journal of American History* 82, no. 4 (March 1996): 1503. *Cf.*, Reby Cary, *The First! And the Foremost* (Fort Worth: Privately Printed, 2011), 263–64, hereafter Cary, *The First!*. Cary says the NAACP arrived in Fort Worth in 1938. For a history of the CIC, see John Egerton, *Speak Now against the Day* (New York: Alfred A. Knopf, 1994), 47–50, 605, hereafter Egerton, *Speak Now*. For the TCIC, see Shabazz, *Advancing Democracy*, 27, 30.

20. Cary, *The First!*, 263–64. *Fort Worth Star-Telegram*, August 9, 1956. *Dallas Morning News*, August 24, 1956.
21. The keynote speaker was Mrs. Jessie Daniel Ames, director of women's programs for the CIC. *Dallas Morning News*, November 8, 1931.
22. *Dallas Morning News*, December 8 and 9, 1934. If the estimate of the *Dallas Morning News* was anywhere close to accurate, this would have been one of the largest conventions ever held in Fort Worth up to this date.
23. *Dallas Morning News*, December 1, 1938. For a good general history, see Michael L. Gillette, "The Rise of the NAACP in Texas," *The Southwestern Historical Quarterly* 81, no. 4 (April 1978): 393–416.
24. Smith, *Negro Directory*, 45.
25. *Fort Worth Press*, September 28, 29, and 30, 1932.
26. *Fort Worth Press*, September 28, 1932.
27. *Dallas Morning News*, November 8, 1931; December 8, 1934. Proclamation of Mayor M.J. Hammond, Mayor & Council Proceedings, March 1938, Box 1, Folder 1, 1938 Proceedings.
28. For statistics on schools and students, see *Dallas Morning News*, December 3, 1938. For doctors and lawyers, see *ibid.*, February 7, 1937. For the best discussion of the issue of out-of-state scholarships, see Shabazz, *Advancing Democracy*.
29. *Dallas Morning News*, July 22, 1932. Lonnie Harris was a black Harris County voter who sued county election official S.S. Allwright for the right to vote in the Democratic primary. For a general history of the issue, see Darlene Clark Hine, *Black Victory: The Rise and Fall of the White Primary in Texas* (Columbia: University of Missouri Press, 2003), hereafter Hine, *Black Victory*.
30. *Dallas Morning News*, March 17, 1939. For constitutionality of Texas' white primaries, see *Grovey vs. Townsend*, 295 U.S. 45 (1935); and Carl Brent Swisher, "The Supreme Court and the South," *Journal of Politics* 10 (1948): 291–99, hereafter Swisher, "The Supreme Court and the South."
31. *Beaumont Enterprise*, November 3, 1944. Hine, *Black Victory*.
32. For Swor's visit, see *Dallas Morning News*, April 17, 1934. For others, see ibid., February 7, 1937.
33. William M. "Goose Neck Bill" McDonald, "Location and Erection of Negro High School," *The White Man and The Negro* 2, no. 10 (December 1933): 257.
34. *Dallas Morning News*, December 1, 1938.
35. Some of those houses were upgraded by later owners with electricity and indoor plumbing. Gooch, *Life of Lenora Rolla*, 23–24. Virginia McAlester

and Lee McAlester, *A Field Guide to American Houses* (New York: Alfred A. Knopf, 1984), 90. A few examples of those old shotgun houses still exist in Fort Worth today off East Rosedale. Some interest has been expressed in recent years to preserve them for historic purposes.

36. The same thing happened in Dallas, only with more serious consequences for racial peace and harmony. Lynn Landrum, "Hair-trigger Edge," *Dallas Morning News*, October 6, 1940.
37. Photos of the area, both before and after construction of the Ripley Arnold Project, are in the Fort Worth Housing Authority files, Series V, Photographs, Sub-series B, Misc. photographs, 1939-1962, Box 1, Fort Worth Library, Central Branch, Local History, Genealogy & Archives Unit.
38. Where the Ripley Arnold Project was built, the Tarrant County College Trinity River campus stands today. *Dallas Morning News*, April 5 and May 4, 1939.
39. *Dallas Morning News*, June 14, 1942; *Fort Worth Star-Telegram*, June 7, 2015; Richard Selcer, *Fort Worth: A Texas Original!* (Austin: Texas State Historical Association, 2004), 77–78.
40. Lynn Landrum, "Thinking Out Loud" (column), *Dallas Morning News*, October 6, 1940. The emphasis is included in the original.
41. *Dallas Morning News*, June 14, 1942.
42. *Fort Worth Press*, June 19 and June 20, 1939; *Fort Worth Star-Telegram*, June 19 and 20, 1939; *Dallas Morning News*, June 20, 1939. For Rosedale's numbers, see Scott Cummings, *Left Behind in Rosedale* (Bolder, CO: Westview Press, 1998), 19, hereafter Cummings, *Left Behind.*
43. *Fort Worth Press*, June 20, 1939; *Fort Worth Star-Telegram*, June 20, 1939; *Dallas Morning News*, June 20, 1939.
44. Cummings, *Left Behind*, 20–27 *ff. Fort Worth Press*, June 19 and 22, 1939.
45. The Slave Narratives exist in several forms today: *"Federal Writers' Project,", Slave Narratives: A Folk History of Slavery in the United States from Interviews with Former Slaves,* 17 vols. (Washington, D.C.: Library of Congress, 1941); *Born in Slavery: Slave Narratives from the "Federal Writers' Project," 1936–1938*, online at www.loc.gov/ammem/snhtml; and George P. Rawick, ed., *The American Slave: A Composite Autobiography* (Westport, CT: Greenwood Press, 1972–79).
46. Other former slaves in attendance that year (with ages in parentheses) included Sam Kilgore (94) and A.J. Anderson (90). *Fort Worth Star-Telegram*, June 19, 1939; *Dallas Morning News*, June 17, 1939.

47. *Fort Worth Star-Telegram*, May 7, 1922. Lucy had subsequently moved into another house with her daughters on East Pulaski. *Dallas Morning News*, June 17, 1939.
48. John Hickman is buried in the Trinity section of Oakwood Cemetery. His remarkable story is told in Bud Kennedy, "In My Opinion," *Fort Worth Star-Telegram*, November 12, 2005.
49. *Fort Worth Press*, June 11 and 29, 1938. Louise Beavers (1902–1962) appeared in *Imitation of Life* (1934), which made her a star for playing something besides the stereotypical "mammy." Her career tailed off into television work in the 1950s, and there is no indication that she ever came back to Fort Worth.
50. *The White Man and The Negro* 2, no. 4 (June 1933): 98.
51. See, for instance, Cab Calloway's appearance at the Texas Centennial in 1936 and the Macedonia Baptist Church choir's performance of "The Holy City" for the National Baptist Convention in Dallas in 1936. *Dallas Morning News*, June 16, 1936, and July 30, 1936.
52. The Greenleaf Café, owned by Oscar Cooper, was not just any café; it was a favorite meeting place in the black community. *Fort Worth Star-Telegram*, June 11 and 26, 1944 (for pre-show advertising and review); February 27, 2013 ("Overlooked Contributors").
53. The cause was to raise money for the Home Makers' Industrial School for Negro Girls. *Dallas Morning News*, October 13, 1918.
54. For Anderson's appearance at Mount Gilead, see Jones, *Renegades*, 285.
55. Even in cosmopolitan New York City, Anderson could not be put up in a first-class (white) hotel. Jim Haskins, *The Cotton Club* (New York: Hippocrene Books, 1994), 75; *Dallas Morning News*, November 19, 1931; and March 7, 1939.
56. Anderson went on to make her debut at the Metropolitan Opera House, New York City, on January 7, 1955, the first black singer to be admitted to "the Met." *Dallas Morning News*, January 29, 1941. *Cf.* Anderson's career with another legendary black opera star, Leontyne Price in Haskins, *Black Music*, 133–39. For race music, see ibid., 120. For interviews, see undated, unidentified clipping, "Marian Anderson Keeps Reporters Waiting at Press Session," in Lenora Rolla Papers.
57. For Anderson, see undated clipping in Lenora Rolla Papers. For Louis, see Sanders, *Calvin Littlejohn*, 167 and 172. For Rolla's interviews, see Gooch, *Life of Rolla*, 17, 20.
58. Like so many other black businesses, the Jim Hotel/"New Jim Hotel" was done in by desegregation in the 1960s. The place was finally razed in

1964 to make room for the Poly Freeway. It is celebrated today in art as part of Paula Blincoe Collins' mural at the Intermodal Transportation Center, Jones St. See Christopher Evans, Fort Worth Star-Telegram, June 30, 1991; and Cheryl L. Simon, "Jim Hotel," *Handbook of Texas Online* (www.tshaonline.org/handbook/online/articles).

59. This section is indebted to the pioneering work of Jan L. Jones, historian of Fort Worth entertainment and biographer of William Madison McDonald. *Chicago Defender*, October 12, 1929; January 12 and July 17, 1937; and May 28, 1938. The Egypt Club disappears from the public record after 1938. The circumstances and causes of its closing are unknown.
60. Little is known about Pat's Araby Club today except passing mention in the *Fort Worth Press*, the few odd photos in the collections of the Tarrant County Black Historical & Genealogical Society, and what exists in the collective historical memory of the black community. See *Fort Worth Press*, November 30, December 2 and 7, 1960; January 11, February 13, April 26, and June 20, 1961. There was also a white Club Araby in Dallas. *Dallas Morning News*, February 21 and December 11, 1961.
61. Chief of Police A.E. Dowell to City Manager Dudley L. Lewis, March 30, 1938, Mayor & Council Proceedings 1938, Box 1, File 4, 1938 Proceedings.
62. No author, "Texas Centennial," *New Handbook of Texas. Dallas Morning News*, June 19 and August 18, 1936, October 19, 1937. For vendors, see Jan Jones, *Billy Rose Presents. . . Casa Mañana* (Fort Worth: Texas Christian University Press, 1990), 99, hereafter Jones, *Casa Mañana.*
63. *Dallas Morning News*, August 18, 1936.
64. The *Dallas Morning News* also characterized the exhibition as a "History of Negro Life from Jungles to Now." *Dallas Morning News*, February 25, June 16, 18, and 20, 1936. Robert W. Rydell, *World of Fairs* (Chicago: University of Chicago Press, 1993), 176–182, hereafter Rydell, *World of Fairs.* Paul M. Lucko, "Hall of Negro Life," *New Handbook of Texas*, hereafter Lucko, *Handbook.*
65. Joe Louis, aka, the "Brown Bomber" was proclaimed the Heavyweight Champion of the World in 1937. Black poet and intellectual Langston Hughes said, "Each time Louis won a fight during the Depression years, thousands of black Americans. . . would throng out into the streets all across the land to march and cheer and yell and cry because of Joe's one-man triumphs." Langston Hughes, *Autobiography: The Collected Works of Langston Hughes*, vo. 14, ed. Joseph McLaren (Columbia: University

of Missouri Press, 2002), 307. Gaylon Polatti, "The Magic City and the Frontier," *Legacies Journal* 11, no. 1 (Spring 1999): 37–39.

66. Jones, *Casa Mañana*, 99.
67. *Dallas Morning News*, October 19, 1937.
68. World War II began in Europe in September 1939 when Germany invaded Poland. *Dallas Morning News*, January 20, 1939.
69. Unfortunately, Fort Worth readers had to read about the event in the Dallas newspaper. *Dallas Morning News*, October 15, 1939. The all-white Southwest Conference consisted of TCU, SMU, University of Texas, Texas A&M, Baylor, University of Arkansas, and Texas Tech University. It folded in 1996. The black Southwestern Athletic Conference, organized in 1920, still exists today.
70. Doggett, "Survey," 5.
71. The same was true in Dallas; the black community depended on the street car lines much more than the white community did. *Dallas Morning News*, October 6, 1940. For Riverside line, see ibid., August 23, 1932.
72. *Dallas Morning News*, April 11, 1930.
73. *Fort Worth Press*, September 27, 1932.
74. Smith, *Negro Directory*, 41. *Pittsburgh Courier*, Jan. 29, 1938. Crooms (1889–1958) is a forgotten figure today in both the black community and the religious community.
75. For the best overview of the I.M. Terrell phenomenon, see Samuel Wilson, "Vanished Legacies and the Lost Culture of I.M. Terrell High School in Segregated Fort Worth," Master's Thesis in History, University of Texas at Arlington, 2012.
76. Sources: Allen (Sherrod), 202–03. "Hazel Peace" in Thirteenth Federal Census (1910) Fourteenth Census (1920), and Fifteenth Census (1930), Fort Worth, Tarrant County, Texas, Microfilm Rolls No. T624_1591 (1910), T625_1848 (1920); and2392 (1930). *Fort Worth Star-Telegram*, May 23, 1977; February 20, 2002; March 13, 2005; August 4, 2007; June 9 and 14, 2008. *Dallas Morning News*, June 15, 2008. Her favorite saying, her mantra really, was recalled by former students at her funeral. *Fort Worth Star-Telegram*, June 14, 2008. "Teaching" quote comes from interview with Jackie Grey, *ibid.*, May 23, 1977. Note: The 1910 Census says she was born in Texas in 1893. The 1920 Census says she was born in Alabama in 1904. The 1930 Census says she was born in Texas in 1906. Obituary quote comes from Roy Brooks, *Fort Worth Star-Telegram*, June 9, 2008.

Chapter 8

World War II

Fighting a Different "Two-front War" for Blacks

World War II was the paramount event of the 1940s for all Americans regardless of race, but for African Americans, the struggle against the Axis was part of a more personal war for freedom and democracy. It became a "two-front war," not just in Europe and the Pacific, but on the home front.

The decade started literally with a bang in Dallas with a series of bombings in black neighborhoods, commencing in the spring and continuing into the fall in what one newspaper called "a year of racial troubles." The bombings were about the same old issue: blacks moving into all-white neighborhoods.[1]

Meanwhile, on the west side of the Trinity all was quiet. Fort Worth blacks faced the same oppression and felt the same resentments as their Dallas brethren, but were not trying to force their way into historically white neighborhoods at this point, thereby not provoking a violent white reaction. Still, the racial violence in Dallas was so close that Fort Worthers of both races could not help but feel a little anxious. The city had not experienced racial upheaval since 1913, and anyone alive who had been around then was willing to do almost anything to avoid another race riot. Most of Fort Worth's African Americans probably agreed with the black Dallas resident who advised, "Out of respect to peace and harmony, Negro and white ought not to live as next-door neighbors."[2]

By 1940, Jones St. was slipping as a business corridor for the black community after losing its residential population in earlier decades. It was now paved and lighted all the way from Weatherford down to Lancaster, home to hotels, restaurants, doctors' offices, barber shops, and beauty parlors. By the middle of the decade it had the Colored YMCA, the swanky Jim Hotel, the Colored Country Club, and the Red Cab Company. The glow had long since gone off Ninth St., formerly the principal black business corridor. Now it was bisected by multiple railroad tracks, increasingly given over to warehouse and industrial properties, and hemmed in on the south by not just the railroad reservation, but south of that, by a "wholesale, garage, and lumber-yard district owned by white capital."[3]

One big difference between Dallas and Fort Worth at this time was that Dallas' leading newspaper, the *Dallas Morning News*, had on its staff a strong advocate for the black community. Lynn W. Landrum was a white man who wrote columns with titles like, "They Want Protection," "Negro Opportunity," and "Patience Unparalleled" that called upon his fellow whites to extend justice and equality to their black neighbors. The *Fort Worth Star-Telegram* during these same years had no staff writer who advocated for the black community.[4]

Photo 21. "Colored YMCA"

Before the new suburban McDonald Branch YMCA was built in 1968, and when the Downtown YMCA at Fifth and Lamar was still segregated, black YMCA patrons had to go to the "Colored YMCA" at Fifteenth and Jones St. It closed when the McDonald branch opened. Public domain (Jack White website, "The Way We Were")

After December 7, 1941, no one gave much thought to advocating for the black community. The United States was at war, and African Americans heard their country's call just as surely as whites. They were not lacking in patriotism. The Prince Hall Masons, for instance, had for years opened their annual state conventions by standing and singing, "My Country, 'Tis of Thee," and the city's black schoolchildren opened every day with the Pledge of Allegiance just like white children. Still, African Americans had ambivalent feelings about the war. On the one hand, they felt no sympathy for the Axis powers; on the other hand, they could not help but feel that the struggle for freedom should begin at home. Black leaders responded to the call for national mobilization with the "Double V" (for Victory) campaign, which aimed not just for victory against the Axis powers, but also against Jim Crow. "If not now, when?" was their rallying cry[5]

One black Dallas resident in 1940 wrote this letter-to-the-editor, expressing the ambivalence felt by many African Americans:

> We are loyal, we are patriotic, yet in our enthusiasm we, white and black, fail to comprehend true Americanism. . . . When our homes are bombed, the same as those in . . . Poland, when our rights as citizens aren't respected, when we are segregated, ostracized, and contrived against, we oft times find it hard to differentiate between the situation here and abroad.[6]

During four years of war, 125,000 African Americans would fight for their country while another three million would take war-production jobs back home. The only black men in uniform Fort Worthers saw were those passing through town on the way to or from their posts. The city's experience with Camp Bowie's 3,000 blacks was only some twenty years in the past. Memories were still vivid enough that this time around, city fathers did not rush headlong into procuring another training camp for the city. Unlike Houston with Camp Logan, Fort Worth had not experienced any racial incidents, but city fathers were not about to tempt fate. The city was still socially conservative and overwhelmingly white, and in 1940 there was no Ben E. Keith to knock on War Department doors for another training camp. (Texas would indeed have another Camp Bowie in World War II, but it would be at Brownwood, not Fort Worth.)

Fort Worth enthusiastically jumped on both the patriotic bandwagon and the economic gravy-train by securing the Consolidated Vultee bomber plant. It and the adjacent Army Air Forces base were a win-win proposition for the city: millions of defense dollars that would pour into the local economy *and* there was absolutely no possibility that thousands of African Americans would descend on the city. Local workplace rules saw to that. Consolidated Vultee was a private concern that would operate under traditional Jim Crow practices. The War Department wanted airplanes, not a civil rights campaign.[7]

The $30 million construction project was built by the Corps of Engineers with local labor. Out of necessity, some of those workers were blacks. They did the dirty, heavy labor, but they still earned a regular government paycheck. The plant was up and running by March 1942, one hundred days ahead of schedule and by November 1943, it had 30,574 employees working in three eight-hour shifts, six days a week, assembling B-24 Liberators and other aircraft. To find that many workers, Consolidated Vultee had to depend on women and draft-exempt men, 11,577 of the former by the end of the war. While none of the jobs on the two assembly lines went to non-whites, somebody had to sweep the floors and clean the bathrooms, and that opened up opportunities for blacks that had not existed before.[8]

Housing was a touchier issue. All those thousands of workers had to have someplace to live, and there was nowhere near enough existing housing to meet the need. Unlike Dallas, Fort Worth had not been designated a "No. 1 critical labor market," so the federal government did not require color-blind labor and housing practices. Thus, not only could the city's white employers avoid hiring blacks, but the Fort Worth housing market for "war workers" was not held to federal standards. The burden did not fall too hard on people already living here. Most of the female workers hired were the wives, daughters, or sisters of local families, meaning they already had homes. Many newcomers to town also managed to find accommodations as some larger homes were turned into boarding houses. Any home-owner with an extra room or two could rent them out, making a little money and helping the war effort at the same time.

But none of these arrangements met the demand, so the National Housing Agency (NHA) threw up "ricky-ticky," barracks-style housing just across the road from the plant, later building two more sections of housing about a mile away. Named "Liberator Village" for the name of the airplane being built by the thousands at the plant, the living conditions were Spartan but provided affordable housing for 6,000 Consolidated

Vultee employees—none of whom were black. Administered by the Federal Public Housing Authority, Liberator Village operated under established Jim Crow practices, which meant segregated housing. Blacks who held menial jobs at the plant had to find housing elsewhere.[9]

Like many well-entrenched Jim Crow practices , housing restrictions for Liberator Village could be enforced in subtle ways. All applicants went through Consolidated Vultee's Personnel Department where they had to meet three qualifications: 1) employment at the plant; 2) job level (higher classification meant quicker approval); and 3) marital status (marrieds before unmarrieds). By #2 alone it was possible to keep out unwanted tenants. It was not necessary to put up signs saying "No Negroes Allowed."[10]

In other, subtle ways, it was clear from the outset that this was a white man's war. Every public high school in Fort Worth except I.M. Terrell had a Reserve Officer Training Cadet program (ROTC). I.M. Terrell boys were eligible for the draft and so had to register when they turned eighteen, but since they had no hope of becoming commissioned officers, the army regarded an ROTC program at Terrell as a waste of time and precious resources. Local black leaders did not rock the boat until the summer of 1944 when the Fort Worth chapter of the Texas Commission on Interracial Cooperation began pressuring the school board to set up a Terrell ROTC program starting with the new school year in September. The school superintendent said vaguely that he saw no reason "why they can't have a program," but that was as far as it went.[11]

The clear snub of the I.M. Terrell student body and lack of any pathway to commissioned status did not prevent Terrell boys from enlisting anyway. Lonnell Cooper, an I.M. Terrell graduate (1939), became the first African American from Tarrant County to enlist in the U.S. Marines when he signed up in 1942. He did his wartime service in rear areas, but he wore the uniform with pride, and being a veteran opened doors for him after the war.[12]

The war needed African Americans, and not just fighting men and defense plant workers. The entire population was expected to get behind the war effort although blacks who enlisted could look forward to most likely being assigned to either kitchen duty or a labor battalion. Young black men still faced conscription under the Selective Service Training Act of 1940, which was modeled on the World War I plan. It left the details of who was called up and who got a pass to local draft boards so long as they met their monthly quotas. Any young man, eighteen to thirty years of age, at least 5-feet tall, weighing a minimum of 105 pounds, having correctable vision and at least half his teeth, was eligible.

Like their white countrymen, not all African Americans were motivated to register for the draft, never mind enlisting. They knew that the second-class treatment they lived with in civilian life would not end when they put on a uniform. The U.S. Army was interested in "the most effective military use of colored troops," not social reform. Black recruits from Fort Worth did their basic training at camps in Louisiana or other sites in the Deep South. They had to ride segregated trains to get there, and when they arrived they faced more hardened racial attitudes than even back home. It is no surprise that few Fort Worth black men felt a patriotic tug at their hearts after December 7, 1941. As it turned out, there were more Reby Carys than Audie Murphys among young, draft-age blacks.[13]

Nevertheless, no matter how or why they entered service, African Americans from Fort Worth forged an exemplary record as soldiers. Two local men overcame enormous odds to become members of the legendary Tuskegee Airmen, that band of African-American pilots nicknamed for their Alabama training base. The two local fellows were John Briggs of Hurst and Claude R. Platte of Fort Worth. Twenty-year-old Johnny Briggs entered the service in 1942 and after graduating from Tuskegee flew 125 combat missions by the time the war ended, most of them in an outdated P-39 Bell Aircobra. Platte, who grew up on Fort Worth's south side, was seven years old when he saw his first airplane fly overhead on the way to Meacham Field in far north Fort Worth. He later packed a lunch and walked the seventeen miles to the field just to watch the planes come and go. When the war came, the twenty-one-year-old Platte, who had learned to fly in the meantime, went off to Tuskegee as a civilian flight instructor. He stayed in the service after the war and when blacks could fly again in 1948 he became one of the first African-American commissioned officers in the new U.S. Air Force. The Tuskegee Airmen achieved such a distinguished combat record flying air cover for American bombers over North Africa, Sicily, and southern Europe, despite flying mostly second-rate equipment, that they were collectively awarded a Congressional gold medal by a grateful nation. Their legend grew over the years until it came to be accepted that they had never lost a bomber to enemy fighters in hundreds of combat missions (not true). Still, at the end of the war they were disbanded and either sent home or reassigned. Would-be black pilots had to wait until U.S. armed forces were desegregated in 1948 before they got another chance to fly for their country.[14]

Back home, blacks learned to deal with wartime shortages and rationing just like whites. After the Office of Price Administration (OPA) in Washington imposed rationing, Tarrant County commissioners set up a War Price and Rationing Board in the courthouse. Members of the Board, all volunteers, took their job seriously, which was to distribute ration books for such commodities as sugar, meat, gasoline, and tires. A different "panel" handled each commodity.

"Black markets" sprang up dealing in rationed commodities like sugar and gasoline that could only be bought legally with ration coupons. Rumors arose among white citizens of Fort Worth that blacks were reporting their coupon books stolen and getting replacements, only to have the "stolen" books turn up on the black market. It made a perfect symmetry between skin color and illegal activity! The virulent rumors showed the fissures in the myth of wartime unity. Meanwhile, blacks were encouraged to buy war bonds (the cheapest cost $18.75), and black veterans were sent out by the government to push the bonds among their people. .[15]

With so many men away fighting, professional sports nearly dried up during the war. The 1941 professional baseball season was the last normal season for the next four years. To feed their sports addiction Americans had to turn to women's leagues and Negro Leagues. Charlie Mentesana organized a black football team in Dallas in September 1943 and challenged a Fort Worth outfit sponsored by white baseball legend Rogers Hornsby. They rented LaGrave Field and mounted a last-minute advertising blitz that brought out a mixed-race crowd that without even being told settled into their designated sections. The men on the field were either too old to be drafted or had day jobs in defense industries. Nobody pretended that the caliber of football being played could replace college ball or the real pros, but it was good enough for a nice fall night at the stadium.[16]

But LaGrave Field was always first and foremost a baseball stadium. Many summer nights, black baseball games brought out fans of both colors to watch teams of the Negro American League play. The star of that league was the legendary Satchel Paige who played for the Kansas City Monarchs. During the 1944 season, Paige and the Monarchs visited Fort Worth twice, once in April and again in September, to play the Cincinnati Clowns (baseball's version of the Harlem Globetrotters). At this date Paige was already thirty-eight-years old after toiling in the Negro Leagues for nineteen years, but he was still a successful pitcher who could sit down an opposing team in order, which is why the fans came out to see him. During his two Fort Worth appearances, an entire section of the LaGrave bleachers was reserved for "white fans."[17]

Even when Paige was not playing, black teams could fill the LaGrave stands during the war. The local nine, known as the "Black Panthers" at a time when that name had a whole different connotation than thirty years later, were one of the best in the Texas Negro League. When they played Hubbard City, another one of the better teams, admission was 50¢ for adults, 25¢ for children regardless of color. The only difference was blacks and whites sat in their own designated sections regardless of who was playing.[18]

When the war ended and white baseball returned for the 1946 season, the black teams either folded or returned to playing in dilapidated stadiums in little towns like Hubbard City while white teams reclaimed both the major leagues and the minor leagues. The wartime truce in race relations ended.

The readjustment was not just in baseball either. With the war winding down in 1945, blacks faced the same kind of issues as whites returning to civilian life. Black leaders were determined to call in the IOUs they had gotten from the government during four years of war. In 1946 Adam Clayton Powell, a black Democratic Congressman from New York, spoke to a large, overwhelmingly black audience at Will Rogers Memorial Auditorium. Although it was a weeknight and reason for the event was a lecture not entertainment, it was one of the largest gatherings of Fort Worth blacks ever seen in the city. "Gooseneck Bill" McDonald spoke first, then introduced Powell. The Congressman urged "Negroes" to fight for their rights "with the same kind of unity that won the war" while still disavowing any resort to violence. Speaking the next night to a Dallas audience, he went further, saying "We have fought for democracy. Now we want some of it. We are not going to let ourselves be thrown back to the rank of second-class citizens!" He also urged his audience to "be proud of your race—wear your color as a badge," a theme that was not heard publicly until the "Black Power" movement came along nearly two decades later. Powell spoke in six cities on his Texas tour before returning to the friendlier climes of New York City. His appearance in Fort Worth was so significant that the conservative *Star-Telegram* covered it both before and after the event. He left thousands of black Texans in his wake who had heard his message and were inspired, thereby putting white Texans on notice that challenges were coming to Jim Crow.[19]

Photo 22. William "Gooseneck Bill" McDonald

In 1946, New York Congressman Adam Clayton Powell visited Fort Worth. He was introduced to an appreciative audience in the I.M. Terrell High School auditorium by an animated Gooseneck Bill McDonald. Author's collections.

To begin with, there was the problem of what to do with thousands of black soldiers coming home after the war. If World War I were any guide, they would be quickly demobilized and sent back to their shotgun shacks and menial jobs. Not this time. Congress had decided to intervene to help the twelve million men who had served (8.3 million in the army) re-enter civilian life and prosper. The Servicemen's Readjustment Act of 1944, better known as the "G.I Bill of Rights," provided a broad range of benefits to veterans, without reference to race, that included weekly unemployment checks for up to a year while they looked for a regular job, up to three years of higher education (either academic or vocational), and low-interest loans to help them buy houses and set up small businesses. This smorgasbord of benefits replaced the simple cash bonuses handed out after earlier wars. A greatly expanded Veterans Administration (VA) was charged with distributing the money and enforcing compliance with all of the associated rules and regulations.

The postwar housing shortage was one area where the G.I. Bill made an enormous difference. While the shortage hit whites and blacks alike, the biggest difference was that historically blacks could not walk into any bank or savings and loan and take out a mortgage. The G.I. Bill promised to change the rules of the loan game. And it did, at least until it ran into long-held prejudices. Edward Williams was a black veteran of the war and a career soldier who used a G.I. loan to purchase a house in a white neighborhood on the Near South Side. Two weeks later on the night of February 28, 1946, while he, his wife, and daughter and son-in-law were sleeping, someone set off a bomb on his front porch. Fortunately, no one was hurt, but it was a sign that neither the war nor the G.I. Bill could change generations of bigoted thinking.[20]

Not even the G.I. Bill could help if there were no houses to be had in nicer neighborhoods either. It was clear that what was needed were new housing developments that welcomed blacks as well as whites. Oscar Chapman, a black Dallas entrepreneur, got a bank loan to erect multiple housing units in the Hutchins suburb specifically for black veterans who could now become home-owners under the G.I. Bill. Chapman built modest four- and five-room "cottages" that were inexpensive and could be thrown up quickly. The first batch of eight was ready for their new owners in the fall of 1946, and a second batch of nine was ready the next spring. These were no Levitt-style suburban tract houses, and seventeen scarcely put a dent in the demand. But Chapman's development was the start of a new era in north Texas. Unfortunately, Fort Worth did not have a local builder willing to take on the challenge of creating affordable housing for black veterans.[21]

Schooling was the other big area where the G.I. Bill rewrote the book. Four out of five World War II veterans chose to go back to school, creating enormous stresses on the nation's education system but also opening up higher education to the average male for the first time in American history. Over one million vets enrolled in colleges and universities under the G.I. Bill in 1946 alone. They could draw $90 a month in "subsistence" plus another $40 a month for books and tuition. The schools could not cope with the flood of new students. Old schools put up temporary buildings and created extension campuses; new schools sprang up like mushrooms to satisfy the demand—and to cash in on the $14.5 billion that Uncle Sam would eventually pump into the economy through the G.I. Bill.

Opening Up the Education System to Veterans and Others

In Fort Worth the first wave of veterans enrolling in classes included 800–900 African Americans who had served their country and saw a college diploma as their ticket to a better life—white-collar jobs, management positions, meaningful employment. While many white veterans took vocational courses in temporary classrooms set up at the Will Rogers Complex, those classes were closed to blacks. No one screamed discrimination, but five white veterans did secure a government loan to open the Southwestern College of Industrial Arts. They hired white teachers and a couple of black administrators to be dean and registrar then threw open the doors. Besides providing training in such things as auto mechanics, tailoring, and woodwork, the school applied directly to the VA for the $40 monthly tuition payments each student had coming to him. With money and students both pouring in, the school quickly grew "beyond all expectations."[22]

Most African Americans were not familiar with the workings of the education system; they did not know how to enroll in college, set up class schedules, and apply for their government benefits. When Dr. Felton G. Clark, the president of Southern University (a historically black college in New Orleans), came through the area he urged the black community to help their men-folk apply for their federal benefits and not let local bigotry discourage them. Only if they did, he told a Dallas audience, could they ever hope to "become self-supporting and handlers of their own business." The Negro Chamber of Commerce in Dallas began counseling veterans and helping them fill out the necessary paperwork. Fort Worth did not have a Negro Chamber of Commerce, but the word was spread from pulpits and through social clubs, and a grassroots movement sprang up.[23]

But the Southwestern College of Industrial Arts quickly ran into trouble with the government over its business practices. In August 1947 the VA withdrew its certification, and the FBI opened an investigation. It seemed at least 177 students were not attending classes, but the school was still collecting their tuition payments. Southwestern was forced to suspend classes, throwing its 900 students out on the street. Eventually, a federal grand jury indicted the five owners for fraud for filing false claims with the VA, the first such suit brought under the G.I. Bill in Texas. The trial opened in December 1947 and dragged on through February 1948. The defendants' lawyers attempted to point the finger at the two black administrators they had hired, but the prosecution shot holes in that argument. And black students testified that defendants had promised them gold watches "if we could get five new students for the school who would attend every day for a month." (A month was long enough to establish a paper trail for the VA.) It also came out that the school's operators were drawing salaries of $1,000 a month, also paid out of G.I. Bill money. (The black dean was only receiving $500 a month.). On Friday, February 13, the all-white jury found the defendants not guilty, pointing to poor oversight by the VA.[24]

In the meantime, the school had been reorganized as a non-profit organization. Two of the three new operators were the former dean and registrar, Elmer Williams and Reby Cary, respectively. (The third partner was the Rev. J.W. Washington.) There was still a big demand for vocational training for black veterans that the white community was not filling. With Uncle Sam writing the checks, they secured a charter of incorporation as a non-profit and changed the name to the W.M. McDonald School of Industrial Arts. They found space for classes in the Prince Hall Masonic Mosque on First Street. Still, they had a hard time getting VA certification until the legal case against the old school had been cleared up.[25]

Things were tougher for black veterans who wanted to pursue academic degrees rather than vocational training. To begin with, the investment of four years of a man's life while trying to live on a government check, with no job prospects after graduation except maybe teaching did not hold much appeal. At the time there were three institutions of higher education in Fort Worth—Texas Christian University, Texas Wesleyan College, and the Southwestern Baptist Seminary—but none of them admitted blacks. The nearest historically black colleges were halfway across the state, Bishop College in Marshall and Jarvis Christian College in Hawkins. (Jarvis was the black "branch" of TCU.) Academics in the black community were prized for their own sake, not because they held out the promise of lifetime employment.

While black entrepreneurs were busy opening store-front vocational schools hoping to cash in on Uncle Sam's largesse, African-American leaders with a different agenda gathered in Austin in the summer of 1946. They were there to petition the legislature to create a black branch of the state's flagship university. In August some 300 protesters representing 200 black organizations stood outside the Capitol to demand their share of the university's $60 million endowment. At the time, the state's only publicly funded black college was Prairie View A&M which was cut out of the "permanent fund" (endowment) that supported the University of

Texas and Texas A&M. It was not supposed to be that way. Back in 1882 the legislature had provisionally approved a black branch of the state university authorized by the constitution of 1876, but neither the 1882 legislature nor any subsequent legislature had ever passed the enabling legislation. Now, fifty-four years later, black leaders from all over Texas, including G.W. Williams and Mrs. A.S. Robinson of Fort Worth, were at the Capitol to collect on what they considered an unfulfilled promise made to them in 1882. Opinion among the protestors was divided over just where was the best place to locate a "Negro branch" of the state university. The Dallas-Fort Worth area was in the running along with Austin, Houston, and Waco. Each area or city had its advocates. An advocate of a different sort was University of Texas President T.S. Painter who supported the idea of a "statutory Negro university" in the system but only if it did not pull from the permanent fund, *i.e.,* compete with U.T. and Texas A&M. What he had in mind, he said, was "A real, bang-up, first-class school equal to any in the country, whose credits will be acceptable anywhere"—just so long as it was not in Austin and was not supported out of the permanent fund. There he drew the line.[26]

Various black spokespersons were heard, each making one pitch for creating a brand-new black, state-supported university and a second pitch for locating it in their hometown. The Dallas and Fort Worth representatives managed to bury their historic rivalry and speak with one voice, an approach that would have appalled Dallas-hating Amon Carter. Worse, the Fort Worth folks let their Dallas brethren take the lead. Scott Bower of the (white) Dallas Chamber of Commerce finessed the rivalry by arguing non-specifically for a "north Texas location" for the "Negro University." In the end all the speeches and advocacy added up to nothing, however. The legislature was not persuaded to create another state-supported university (for blacks) at this time, whether because they were being budget-conscious or out of racial prejudice or both is unclear. Most legislators probably believed that the existing, historically black colleges were adequate for the limited number of black students desiring higher education, that what was really needed was more vocational schools such as the Southwestern College of Industrial Arts. Many of the state's white citizens probably agreed with the *Dallas Morning News* that said in an editorial, "The State of Texas should just pay [any black] the difference in money between what it would cost him to go to school at Prairie View and what it would cost him to go to school outside Texas, including railroad fare to and from his Texas home."[27]

As a matter of fact, Texas was already paying what it called "scholarship differentials" for black residents forced to leave the state to complete their studies in medicine, dentistry, or law. The state paid the difference, including transportation costs, between what it would cost a black student to attend Prairie View and what it cost to get advanced training out of state. This was how the state avoided admitting qualified black students to the law, medicine, and dentistry programs at U.T. This is how Alexander B. Terrell, Riley Ranson, Robert Gilton, Mays C. Maxwell, and other black physicians over the years had been able to study at prestigious universities in other states; they were on the Texas plan. In 1934, Dr. Channing H. Tobias, a leader of the Colored Y.M.C.A. movement, told a convention of black Texas school teachers, "Texas has produced great Negroes." The problem, he went on to explain, was "They have to leave Texas to gain full expression of their genius," meaning to complete their education. Now in 1946, the Austin protesters returned home without any commitment from the legislature to keep black students studying for the professions at home. Still, they were not a total failure either; they had taken a stand and planted the seeds of change.[28]

Those seeds began to sprout the next year. In 1947 the legislature created Texas State University for Negroes in Houston, the first new school and the first black school in the U.T. system since Prairie View A&M joined. By 1950 U.T. Austin was a "going concern" that enrolled more than 2,000 students. That same year it capitulated again when the Supreme Court forced the school to end racist admission policies in its law and medical schools. Though the victory in Sweatt vs. Painter was definitely worth celebrating, it was not followed by a rush of black applicants. Before that could happen, the state's black secondary schools would have to produce more would-be doctors and lawyers.[29]

By 1952, eleven institutions of higher learning in Texas—three of them in the Dallas-Fort Worth area—admitted blacks. The local trio included Southwestern Baptist Theological Seminary, Brite College of the Bible (TCU), and Perkins Theological School (SMU). Brite was part of the TCU campus (just like Perkins was part of SMU's), but its admission policies were separate from TCU's. While Brite reflected the religious beliefs of the Disciples of Christ, TCU reflected the beliefs of its board of trustees and alumni. There was a similar difference of opinion between the Baptist Theological Seminary in Fort Worth, which had an open admissions policy, and Arlington Baptist College which did not. None of the three open-admissions schools, admirable as they were, posed any threat to Jim Crow. For the school year 1952–53, the Seminary only had four black students, Brite had three, and Perkins, five. They were hardly noticeable on their respective campuses, which was the whole point. The colleges with a miniscule black presence and those with none at all sang the same song publicly: they would do more if only they could get more "qualified Negro applicants."[30]

The NAACP's Three-Pronged Assault on Jim Crow

The NAACP experienced explosive growth in the 1940s, from 50,000 members at the beginning of the decade to almost 450,000 by 1946. Those numbers and the gains of World War II encouraged the leadership to adopt a more aggressive stance than in earlier times. Educational equality was the second prong of a three-pronged assault on racial segregation by the Texas branch of the organization in the 1940s. (The other two were political and social equality.) While the nation's attention had been on defeating the Axis powers in the first half of the decade, black Texans were waging a simultaneous war against the Jim Crow electoral system, specifically white primaries. It was a war not of bullets and bombs but of lawsuits and political maneuvering. The Texas NAACP had been fighting a losing battle for years after first taking the state to (federal) court in 1927. They were back in 1932 and 1935 with a series of lawsuits dubbed the "Texas primary cases." Every time they won in court (*Nixon vs. Herndon*, 1927, and *Nixon vs. Condon*, 1932), the legislature re-wrote the primary law to keep Texas primaries all-white. In 1937 the court ruled that political primaries, as "private matters," did not fall under the protections of the Fourteenth and Fifteenth Amendments.[31]

In 1944, NAACP lawyers tried again, reaching the Supreme Court, which ruled in *Smith vs. Allwright* that the state's all-white primaries were unconstitutional. The immediate impact of the decision was to open the door to more black participation in Texas elections, but the Democratic Party's old guard did not go quietly. The first chance black Texas Democrats had to participate fully in the electoral process came two years later. Upwards of 150,000 paid their poll tax in 1946 to be allowed to vote, but countless others did not exercise their constitutional right. Even if every possible black voter had cast a ballot, the best they could have hoped for was to elect a sympathetic white candidate such as Fort Worth's Frederick "Fitz" Lanham. When the state Democratic Party convened in Fort Worth in September 1948, it was Texas' first mixed-race convention in forty-four years. In protest, conservative attendees led by the Dallas delegation walked out, only to have their places taken by "dozens of negroes filing in to take the seats they had just vacated." It was a historic moment.[32]

The NAACP's motto in these years might well have been "heaven is not reached in a single bound." The victory over white primaries and the creation of Texas State University had taken most of the decade, and the biggest fight in its three-pronged strategy was still ahead—social equality. The organization decided to focus first on "recreation" facilities as opposed to public transportation or lodging. In the next few years blacks would challenge Jim Crow rules at state and city parks, municipal golf links, and stadiums, and Fort Worth blacks would be at the forefront of that fight.[33]

The "two-front war" was still being fought out four years after the Germans and Japanese surrendered, on the screens and in the movie theaters. In 1949 United Artists Pictures released *Home of the Brave*, a movie about a black G.I. on a wartime mission suffering more abuse from his fellow (white) soldiers than from the enemy. Very daring for its time, the movie played in Fort Worth at the Palace Theater in July 1949. During its one-week run the theater set aside its long-standing policy of not admitting blacks. Management "reserved" the balcony for blacks while whites had the main floor as always. Unfortunately, *Home of the Brave* was a one-week experiment that did not presage any long-term change in theater policy.[34]

Reby Cary—He *lived* Fort Worth history[35]

Reby Cary has both made and written history during a life that is now in its tenth decade. His distinguished record of public service is not just to the black community but to his city, state, and nation. He was born September 9, 1920 into a middle-class, deeply religious family. His father was Reverend Smith Cary, minister of Fort Worth's Rising Star Baptist Church. From Cary Sr. he learned to stand up for what's right. He never lacked in self-confidence and never meekly accepted Jim Crow segregation. He attended I.M. Terrell, High School, graduating in 1937. He enrolled in Prairie View A&M University and graduated in 1941with a Bachelor of Arts degree. He began working on a Master's degree but had to put that on hold after Pearl Harbor when Uncle Sam came calling. When a white man informed him about Pearl Harbor with these words, "We are in a war," he shot back it was not *his* war.

Conscription got Cary. Some young black men like future Hollywood stars Sammy Davis, Jr. and Sidney Poitier may have enlisted after Pearl Harbor, but not Cary. He did not feel the pull of patriotism, especially if he had to serve in a segregated army. He enlisted in the U.S. Coast

Guard, which at the time was the only branch of the service that did not relegate blacks to menial duty. What Cary did not know was the Coast Guard had been placed under the Navy for the duration, so he would still be on the front lines of the war. His train trip to the Coast Guard Academy at Manhattan Beach, Brooklyn, New York, was his first time out of Texas. (This was where black coast guard cadets trained.) After completing his training to be an apprentice seaman he was sent to Florida, where his first assignment was "kitchen patrol." He protested, citing his college degree, so he was sent to Atlantic City, New Jersey, to train as a radio man, becoming just the third black man in the Coast Guard to achieve that rating when he completed the course in 1943. He drew duty in the Pacific theater, where his ship was under fire in the Navy's assaults on Saipan (June 15–July 13, 1944) and Okinawa (April 1–June 22, 1945). During the war he also married a girl he had met at Prairie View A&M. Their marriage endured until she died in 2004.

At the war's end Cary was discharged in Louisiana. He was a radioman first-class, but he never considered making the Navy a career. After fighting for his country for three years, he came back to Fort Worth in a segregated rail car, the same way he had gone off to war in 1942. Nothing had changed for African Americans. He resumed work on his Master's degree at Prairie View, but now the G.I. Bill was paying for it. (He completed the degree in 1948 with a double major in history and political science.) When he went looking for work, he found it hard to get a job doing anything but menial work, even with two college degrees. As a veteran he could draw $20 a week in unemployment, but that was not his style. With a wife and the clock ticking on his G.I. benefits, he took a job as registrar at one of the new vocational schools for black veterans. When the school went under in 1947 he and two other black entrepreneurs reopened it in the Prince Hall Masonic Temple on First St. After the pool of black veterans dried up, the school closed again. Undaunted, he got his real estate license and opened up his own business, but never considered it a career. With his life drifting, he let a friend at Dunbar High School talk him into teaching there. Initially, he had little sympathy for the immature students who cared nothing for learning, but he wound up staying at Dunbar for nine years, even taking on counseling duties.

In 1967 when Tarrant County Junior College opened on south Loop 820, he moved over from Dunbar to TCJC's faculty. He was the first black instructor at TCJC and taught the first Black History course there. In 1969 he jumped to the University of Texas at Arlington (UTA), and again he was a pioneer as the first black full-time faculty member. Offended by the school's Johnny Reb mascot and Confederate flag emblem, he organized a successful campaign to do away with both. He stayed at UTA until 1978, rising to assistant professor and ultimately Associate Dean of Student Affairs, all the while working on a doctorate degree.

Politics drew him. He first entered politics in 1974, making a successful run for the Fort Worth School Board. He became the first African American ever to sit on that board. Making his victory all the more remarkable, was that he was elected at large, which meant he had to win a majority of votes in the city, white as well as black. He served on the School Board for four years. In 1979, he ran for the state legislature as a Democrat, representing District 95 on the south and east sides of Fort Worth. Again he won. He dropped off the school board and took a leave of absence from UTA.

Reby Cary's first love has always been writing and research. To date he has authored eighteen books on African-American history and Fort Worth, all of them self-published. Cary is present in all of his books, not just as the author, but also as a participant and observer. In 2008 he donated his personal papers to the Fort Worth Library. They are a principal source on the city's black history. For years, the School Board has considered naming a school for Cary. That honor will no doubt happen at some point in the future in recognition of his long service to his hometown.

Cary has fought a life-long battle against racial discrimination and ignorance. He has never backed down from a fight; on the contrary, he has picked more than a few. His values reflect those of his hero, Bill McDonald. He is a big believer in free enterprise, dismissive of both welfare and government regulations in general. He believes in old-fashioned values and individual initiative, making him at one time a rising star in the Republican party. He has been at the center of so much Fort Worth history, arguably the most articulate voice in the black community for more than half a century. As Benjamin Franklin said, "If you would be remembered, you must either write things worth reading or do things worth writing." Reby Cary has done both.

NOTES

1. *Dallas Morning News*, September 17, October 2, and December 4, 1940.
2. Wardell Wilson (Letters to the Editor) in *Dallas Morning News*, October 6, 1940.
3. For a list of businesses on different streets, see *Fort Worth City Directories*, 1926–1946, specifically the section at the back of each directory that matches street addresses and residents block by block. (Hard copies and microfiche). Fort Worth Library, Central Branch, Local History, Genealogy & Archives Unit. For "white capital," see Doggett, "Survey," 5.
4. For representative Landrum columns, see *Dallas Morning News*, October 6, 1940; February 25, 1941; June 24, 1946; June 20, and November 11, 1947.
5. Ira Katznelson, *Fear Itself: The New Deal and the Origins of Our Time* (New York: Liveright Publishing Corp., 2013), 340–41, hereafter, Katznelson, *Fear Itself*. For Prince Hall Masons, see *Proceedings of the (Annual) Most Worshipful Grand Lodge of Texas*, 1887-1929, Box 1, Archives, (Prince Hall) Grand Lodge of Texas, Fort Worth. The best account of the "Double V" campaign is James, *Double V*.
6. Wardell Wilson, *Dallas Morning News*, October 6, 1940.
7. Consolidated Vultee's main plant was in Los Angeles. The company was owned by a syndicate. For Consolidated Vultee's story, see Klein, *Call to Arms*, 455, 456–457.
8. Pate, *Arsenal*, 73–80; Janet L. Schmelzer, *Where the West Begins: Fort Worth and Tarrant County* (Northridge, CA: Windsor Publications, 1985), 77.
9. For "ricky-ticky," see Jerry Flemmons, *Amon: The Texan Who Played Cowboy for America* (Lubbock: Texas Tech University Press, 1998), 263.
10. For housing matters, including "Liberator Village," see Pate, *Arsenal*, 80, 118–120. Among the requirements of the new federal housing were that every house had to have "an inside toilet, a sewage connection for the kitchen sink, and running water from the city mains." The NHA, which was the top federal housing agency during the war, was headed by John B. Blanford. For requirements and other issues of being a "No. 1 critical labor market," see *Dallas Morning News*, September 25, 1943. See also "Time Frames" in *Fort Worth Star-Telegram*, September 30, 2013.
11. *Fort Worth Star-Telegram*, May 3, 1944.

12. Obituary, *Fort Worth Star-Telegram*, January 28, 2011. For Lonnell Cooper's full story, see sidebar.
13. It should be possible to take the census records from 1940 and match it up to the U.S. Army service records and determine exactly how many black men from Fort Worth served during the war. It would be a big job but a worthwhile one that would give us a better picture of local support for the war. White recruits from Texas did their basic infantry training at Camp Howze, Camp Maxey, Camp Swift, or Camp Wolters, Texas. Murphy was the eighteen-year-old, Kingston, Texas (white) youth who enlisted in the Army in 1942 and went on to become the most decorated soldier of World War II. U.S. Army policy was laid out in *Leadership and the Negro Soldier*, Army Service Forces Manual M5 (1940), discussed in "Debt of Honor," *U.S. News & World Report*, May 6, 1996, pp. 30-31.
14. For Briggs, see *Fort Worth Star-Telegram*, February 27, 2004. For Platte, see ibid., August 9, 2013. For an overview of the Tuskegee Airman, see J. Todd Moye, *Freedom Flyers: The Tuskegee Airmen of World War II* (New York: Oxford University Press, 2010. For debunking the Tuskegee legend, see interview with Warren Ludlum in Bob Johnson, "Pilot: Fighters Weren't Perfect," *Fort Worth Star-Telegram*, December 16, 2006.
15. Lee Kennett, *For the Duration* (New York: Charles Scribner's Sons, 1985), 133–38; *Dallas Morning News*, August 5, 1942; *Dallas Morning News*, July 6, 1944.
16. *Dallas Morning News*, September 26, 1943. For a general overview of wartime football, see Richard R. Lingeman, *Don't You Know There's A War On?* (New York: Paperback Library, 1970), 387–390.
17. *Fort Worth Star-Telegram*, April 21 and September 15, 1944.
18. *Fort Worth Star-Telegram*, April 26, 1944.
19. *Fort Worth Star-Telegram*, March 6 and 7, 1946; *Dallas Morning News*, March 8, 1946.
20. *Fort Worth Star-Telegram*, March 1, 1946; *Fort Worth Press*, March 1, 1946.
21. Neither Chapman nor any other black builder could hope to compete with the likes of William Levitt who parlayed a 1,500-acre potato field in Nassau County, New York, into hundreds of cheap houses for white families in the first post-war suburban development. For $6,900 a white veteran could buy a basic Cape-Cod box with a postage-stamp-sixed yard. Thus was born the first of several "Levittowns." *Dallas Morning News*, April 6, 1947.
22. The Southwestern College of Industrial Arts was one of fifteen vocational schools that sprang up in Texas after the war to take advantage of

the G.I. Bill, only to have their certifications yanked within two years. Others were in Dallas, Tyler, and Irving. *Dallas Morning News*, August 28, 1947. Reby Cary says the school was named McDonald College of Industrial Arts after local black icon Bill McDonald, but the newspapers refer to it as Southwestern. See Cary, *How We Got Over!*, 2nd ed., p. 2; and *Dallas Morning News*, November 14, 1947; and February 3, 7, and 12, 1948.

23. Reby Cary, *How We Got Over! Second Update on a Backward Look: A History of Blacks in Fort Worth*, 2nd ed. (Fort Worth: privately printed, 2006), 2, hereafter Cary, *How We Got Over!*, 2nd ed. *Dallas Morning News*, February 17, 1945.
24. *Dallas Morning News*, November 14 and December 2, 1947; February 5, 7, 12, 13, and 14, 1948.
25. During the legal difficulties of the school's operators, the newspapers took the usual Jim-Crow-era delight in the testimony of black witnesses. According to the *Dallas Morning News*, the black veterans unintentionally kept a federal grand jury "in stitches." *Dallas Morning News*, September 6 and November 18, 1947; February 2, 1948.
26. *Dallas Morning News*, August 9, 1946.
27. Earl Wadsworth Rand, president of Jarvis Christian College in Hawkins, TX, was one of the black leaders in Austin. Thirty years later he was still at Jarvis when this author taught there in the 1976–77 school year. At that time, Jarvis was still supported by the Disciples of Christ Church and still affiliated with TCU, and in such bad financial shape that it was barely hanging on. In other words, things had not changed since 1946! *Dallas Morning News*, August 9, 1946.
28. Terrell attended Harvard Medical School; Ransom attended Louisville (Kentucky) National Medical College; Gilton received his dentistry degree from Meharry College (Nashville, TN). Meharry was the first medical school in all of the South to admit blacks. A.B. Terrell was the first Fort Worth doctor to get his degree from some other school. Mays C. Maxwell, Jr. was the namesake son of the black theater impresario who operated the Ritz Theater on Calhoun St. in the 1940s. For schooling issues in general, see "Negro Education" in "Letters From Readers," *Dallas Morning News*, April 7, 1946. For Tobias quote, see ibid., December 9, 1934.
29. Sweatt vs. Painter, the fight to open the University of Texas law school, was decided by the U.S. Supreme Court in 1950. It was brought by Heman Marion Sweatt who applied and was denied admission in February 1946. The victory applied only to those degree programs (e.g., law)

that weren't available from Prairie View or Texas Southern University. W. Paige Keeton, "Sweatt vs. Painter," *New Handbook of Texas. Dallas Morning News*, February 2, 1950.

30. The Dallas/Fort Worth area's seven (white) institutions of higher learning were Texas Christian University (TCU), Southern Methodist University (SMU), Texas Wesleyan College, Arlington State College, Arlington Baptist College, Southwestern Theological Seminary, and North Texas State College. The eleven Texas schools were U.T., Austin; St. Edward's University, Austin; St. Mary's University, San Antonio; Southwestern Baptist Theological Seminary, Fort Worth; Amarillo College, Amarillo; Brite College of the Bible, Fort Worth; Howard County Junior College, Big Spring; Musical Arts Academy, Amarillo; Wayland College, Plainview; Del Mar College, Corpus Christi; and Southern Methodist University, Dallas. *Dallas Morning News*, December 7, 1952. The only history to date of breaking the color barrier at the big seven is William R. Simon, "Breaking the Color Bar at SMU," *Legacies Journal*, 24, no. 1 (Spring 2012): 32-42. *Cf.* "SMU Enrolls First Negro Freshman," *Dallas Express*, September 22, 1962.
31. Katznelson, *Fear Itself*, 341. The NAACP's three-pronged strategy was described by *Dallas Morning News* political editor Allen Duckworth in 1949 and revisited in ibid., February 2, 1950. The 1927 case was Nixon vs. Herndon, 273 U.S. 536; the 1932 case was Nixon vs. Condon, 286 U.S. 73; the 1935 case was Grovey vs. Townsend, 295 U.S. 45. For a discussion of all three cases and the long battle against Texas' white primaries, see Hine, *Black Victory*, and Conrey Bryson, *Dr. Lawrence A. Nixon and the White Primary* (El Paso, TX: Texas Western Press, 1993).
32. Fritz Lanham (1880-1965) was first elected to Congress from the Twelfth Congressional District, which included Fort Worth. He continued to represent the District and make his home in Fort Worth until 1947. See obituary, *Fort Worth Star-Telegram*, August 2, 1965. For Smith vs. Allwright, 321 U.S. 649 (1944), see Texas primary cases, see see Swisher, "The Supreme Court and the South," 298–99; Key, *Southern Politics*, 621–22; and Katznelson, *Fear Itself*, 185, 219. Poll tax numbers from *Fort Worth Star-Telegram*, March 7, 1946.
33. *Dallas Morning News*, February 2, 1950.
34. This story plus other evidence suggests that none of the Big 3 downtown movie houses—the Palace, Hollywood, and Worth—admitted blacks under any circumstances during the height of the Jim Crow era; it was not a matter of buying a ticket and sitting in the balcony. The director

of *Home of the Brave*, Stanley Kramer, went on to do two more "message movies" about race, *The Defiant Ones* (1958) and *Guess Who's Coming to Dinner* (1967), both of which played in Fort Worth. By the time of *Guess Who's Coming to Dinner*, the Big 3 movie houses were integrated. Jack Gordon's column, *Fort Worth Press*, July 14, 1949.

35. Sources: "An interview with Reby Cary by James Yeh," February 27, 2007, part of "Experiencing War: Stories from the Veterans History Project, The Library of Congress, available online at www.lcweb2.loc.gov/diglib/vhp-stories/loc.natlib.afc2001001.58790/transcript. Reby Cary Papers, An Inventory to the Collection, Biography, Fort Worth Library, Central Branch, Local History, Genealogy, & Archives Unit. "Reby Cary, Author, Historian: Paving the Way for Future Generations, www.rebycary.com/About. "Fort Worth Flashback: Reby Cary's Life, One of Patriotism, Service, Achievement," posted Nov. 11, 2012, www.fortworthtexas.gov/flashback/?id. For Davis' and Poitier's stories, see Roy Hoopes, *When the Stars Went to War* (New York: Random House, 1994), 336–37. During World War II, the Marine Corps as well as the armor, engineer, signal, and air branches of the Army did not accept blacks at all. The Navy only accepted blacks as cooks or stewards. The Coast Guard alone gave blacks a chance to train for all duties, including technical. Klein, *Call to Arms*, 119. For the debate on renaming an existing school for Cary, see *Fort Worth Star-Telegram*, August 12 and 14, 2013.

CHAPTER 9

THE EARLY CIVIL RIGHTS YEARS OR JIM CROW IN RETREAT

Following World War II, Jim Crow was in full retreat. The government's wartime appeal to black patriotism and the sacrifices made by black servicemen like the Tuskegee Airmen made the old ways increasingly harder to justify. New Deal liberals, still riding high in Washington, helped drive some of the first nails into the coffin—not in bold actions like the Voting Rights and Civil Rights acts of the 1960s, but in small ways.

The President's Committee on Fair Employment (PCFE), one of the most minor of federal agencies, took on racist "help-wanted" ads. Every newspaper had "classifieds"—they were an important revenue source —and those ads had always been blatantly racist, stating whether a potential employer wanted white or black workers. One 1944 ad in *the Fort Worth Press* said,

> Colored Men!
> Do you want a steady job with overtime?
> Apply 901 N. Throckmorton.

Another said,

> Male and Female, White and Colored
> Laborers and Butchers Needed
> Good pay—Plenty of Hours
> Apply Armour and Company
> North Fort Worth

The PCFE could not make law, but they asked the nation's employers to stop specifying race in their want ads. This, the third year of the war, was a good time to raise the issue since labor was still at a premium with so many men away fighting. But the PCFE's appeal, although well-intentioned, had little or no impact on hiring practices, at least in Fort Worth. Help-wanted ads continued to appear in the two leading newspapers specifying "white" or "colored." Not until the Civil Rights Act of 1964 creating the Equal Employment Opportunity Commission (EEOC) were race-specific want ads in newspapers and magazines prohibited.[1]

The war had interrupted many traditions, one of them being the celebration of Juneteenth, which was either halted for the duration or celebrated so quietly it did not make the news. The last celebration before the war had been marked by violence when a crowd of whites attacked the first black residence in their neighborhood. That is the only time in Fort Worth history when the "Colored holiday" provoked such an angry response. Eight years later, in 1947 with the war over less than two years, Juneteenth was back bigger than ever. It was the eighty-second anniversary of emancipation in Texas and the first public celebration of that date since the end of the war. Coming so soon after victory over the evil ideology of the Nazis gave added meaning to the date. Organizers got a parade permit, and the resulting parade brought out virtually every major church and civic organization in the black community. Six floats, several marching bands, and a troop of twenty-two horsemen made this a parade to remember. More significantly, it was the first *black* parade through downtown Fort Worth, on the same streets where the Klan had held its parades in the 1920s. Now, however, there were as many white faces as black in the crowd lining the parade route. Afterwards, black celebrants gathered for fun and games in Greenway Park, which was the city's designated "negro park." Swift and Armour, angling for a public relations coup, donated the meat for hotdogs and hamburgers.[2]

But if Fort Worth blacks expected a return to the more enlightened policies and practices of the New Deal, they were disappointed. With hardly a pause the nation went straight from World War II into the Cold War. The global fight against communism pushed civil rights issues to the back burner. All the money and effort invested in national security was money and effort that could not be invested in solving problems like poverty and race. Ironically, if America was truly the "Land of the Free," it was hard to wage war against the communist evil while America consigned millions of its own people to permanent second-class status. This contradiction was acknowledged in some measure. In the spirit of the Cold War, Texas Christian University offered black airmen at Carswell Air Force Base the chance to enroll in classes paid for by Uncle Sam, albeit only as extension students, meaning they could not attend classes on campus. This example of what we now call "distance learning" did not constitute a dramatic break with Jim Crow conventions; the black airmen did not attend classes on campus. TCU was not about to break with its sister schools in Texas when it came to holding the color line. The big battle over equal access to higher education still lay in the future.[3]

Enrolling African Americans in any capacity was a historic step for any local institution of higher learning, but just a foretaste of the changes that would rock Fort Worth in the 1950s. The decade began with some of the men who had shaped public opinion for decades passing from the scene: Bill McDonald died in 1950; Reverend J. Frank Norris, in 1952; and Amon G. Carter, "Mr. Fort Worth," in 1955. The city's new leadership included younger, more liberal men such as future mayors Edgar Deen and Bayard Friedman, attorney Jenkins Garrett, *Star-Telegram* editor Jack Butler, and U.S. Congressman Jim Wright. They did not identify so much with the Old South; they were not die-hard defenders of Jim Crow.[4]

The black community was also changing. A rising black middle class had finally found its voice. In addition to reading neighborhood newspapers and the occasional dry scholarly work like W.E.B. DuBois' *Black Reconstruction*, they were now snapping up slick magazines that targeted them specifically, such as *Ebony* and *Sepia* (formerly *Negro Achievements*). *Sepia* was a Fort-Worth-based, *Life*-magazine look-alike that was distributed nationally. It was published originally by the publisher-editor team of Horace J. Blackwell, Adelle Martin, and Beatrice Pringle under the banner of the Good Publishing Company. Later George Levitan bought out the original publishers. Besides being white, Levitan was a "practical businessman" who claimed to know what black readers wanted. He also published out of his Fort Worth offices three *True Confession*-type pulp magazines: *Bronze Thrills*, *Jive*, and *Hep*. Unfortunately, as the '50s turned into the '60s the black readership fell off, from a peak of 85,000 copies of each magazine sold monthly to only 65,000. Perhaps it was the hypocrisy of the publisher. Levitan shied away from civil rights issues and expressed a glaring insensitivity to the concerns of many of his readers: "I personally think Adam Clayton Powell is a reprobate and Mohammed Ali is a nut," he told an interviewer.[5]

Sepia focused on black entertainment and feel-good stories while the other three Levitan magazines were strictly "male" magazines. Levitan's stable of publications might have been aimed at the black market, but they completely missed the civil rights movement going on outside his offices. In Fort Worth the good fight was still being led by the NAACP. That worthy organization was not fighting alone, however. A grassroots organization, the Negro Citizens' Committee (NCC), led by Dr. Riley A. Ransom, joined the fight in 1953. The NCC worked closely with the NAACP without ever getting much recognition even locally. The NAACP was still pursuing the three-pronged strategy that had already targeted education and politics. Now the organization was ready to launch the third phase of its assault on Jim Crow.

THE PARKS AND RECREATION WARS

The NAACP now drew the battle lines over seemingly the mildest of social issues—access to white golf courses. Despite the apparent insignificance of golf as a civil rights issue, the target was not chosen lightly. Golf was a refined game played by upper-class whites; it was the sport of duffers, clubbers, and professionals. It was a game not traditionally given to high passions or physical confrontation like football and baseball. Anytime thousands of folks turned out at a football or baseball stadium anything could happen; there was no record of a riot ever during a round of golf.[6]

When Fort Worth Country Club opened in 1903 (in Arlington Heights), it boasted the city's first golf course. While Fort Worth's elite joined the national fad for the Scottish game, the only black face on the links belonged to the groundskeeper who "mowed the weeds and shooed the cows away." The fad grew so in the years that followed that in 1923 the city built a nine-hole municipal golf course half a mile southwest of TCU, naming it Worth Hills. Again, no black faces apart from groundskeepers were to be seen on the course. Still, some local blacks did take up the game and even manage to find a place to polish their skills. By 1941 some of the best black golfers in the state were calling Fort Worth home, and they hosted the first annual Southwestern Golf Open Tournament for Negroes.[7]

But they were still denied access to the city's three municipal courses (Worth Hills, Meadowbrook, Rockwood), so in June 1950, the Negro Golf Association petitioned the city council to open all three white courses to blacks plus build a golf course specifically for African Americans.[8] Simple economics combined with Jim Crow racism to torpedo the latter demand. Golf courses had never made economic sense when public usage was compared to cost the way stadiums and parks did. The small number of black golfers made building a black golf course even less cost-effective for the city than the white courses. Still, to keep black golfers off the white links, the Fort Worth Park Board announced disingenuously that it already had a black course in its plans. The site selected for this "Negro course" was on Trinity bottom land east of town, below I.M. Terrell High School. Park Superintendent Harry Adams promised a "negro playground" that would include a seventy-five-acre golf course and park on the river near the Greenway neighborhood "just as soon as we can get the land purchased." Greenway by this time had become not only the city's only black public park, but also the neighborhood that had grown up around the park. Carved out of river bottom land, Greenway Park already boasted picnic tables, playing fields, and a pond stocked with fish. It was the perfect location, or so it seemed, for a "Negro golf course" complete with a clubhouse, assuming the money could be found.[9]

But Adams made that promise without consulting the city council first. Those gentlemen dragged their feet, begging for more time while they built a "north-south expressway" (the future I-35) and completed various flood control measures in the works. The black community should have seen a red flag when Park Superintendent Adams mentioned that the flood control measures happened to be in the same area as the "negro playground." When built, not only would it be in the flood plain, but it would be right in the path of future flood-control projects, which did not bode well for its long-term viability.[10]

Two years passed, and the city continued to dither on a black golf course, while the white municipal courses were no closer to being thrown open than they had ever been. The city council tried to have it both ways, keeping white and black golfers happy while placating the NAACP by pouring $180,000 into the "negro playground," which became the Harmon Field Recreational Center and Golf Course for Negroes. The facility opened in 1954 on reclaimed river-bottom land little more than a long drive shot from the front door of I.M. Terrell. At the grand opening on June 13, Ross Trimble, chairman of the Fort Worth Recreation Board, applauded the fine facility, adding that he believed "Negroes will prefer to play golf on their own course rather than on any of the city's other [white] municipal layouts." The first week it was open, 350 black golfers played the Harmon course, paying green fees of 35¢ each on weekdays and 65¢ on weekends. But it was wishful thinking on Trimble's part if he thought Fort Worth blacks were going to be satisfied with access to a single (segregated) golf course, no matter how nice it might be. Never mind the fact that the first time the river rose, their course was going to be under water.[11]

City fathers congratulated themselves for having averted an expensive court battle or worse, public demonstrations. But they were premature. The local NAACP leadership was not willing to accept half a loaf; it was already preparing a legal challenge. On the very next Sunday (June 21) three black golfers led by Dr. C.W. Flint tried to gain admission to the Z. Boaz course. They were politely turned away and expressed genuine surprise to newspaper reporters. They were confused, they claimed, because Dallas had opened all its municipal courses to blacks two days earlier. Whatever misunderstanding there was, it had been compounded by black professional golfer Jesse Mitchell telling a gathering of black golfers in Fort Worth on Friday night, June 11, that the Dallas action opened the door for them; Jim Crow was dead on Fort Worth's municipal courses! Dr. Flint and friends found out otherwise on the twenty-first. The next Tuesday, representatives of the NCC showed up at the regular city council meeting to "humbly ask" that Fort Worth "follow the example" of other "large Texas cities" and change its policy on golf courses.[12]

The council ducked and dodged then handed the ball off to the Recreation Board, which was one of three city boards that operated "largely independent of the council." The Recreation Board scheduled time at their next meeting (June 25) to hear oral arguments why the city should/should not open white municipal courses to African American players. The NCC was there as were white groups expressing their opposition to the idea. One of their arguments was that if blacks were allowed to play the municipal courses, whites would stay away in droves, costing the city lost revenue. They also pointed out the blacks already had "their own" golf course, which got to the heart of the Jim Crow system—the idea that black and white citizens were not part of the same nation; blacks had their sandbox and whites had theirs and never the twain should meet. George Seaman, the spokesman of the opposition, could only offer one solution if the court ordered desegregation: privatize all the courses.[13]

The NAACP and the NCC could push and protest, but they could not sue in court unless they were personally affected by the golf ban; that was a principle in American jurisprudence. So in August, eight black golfers filed a discrimination suit in U.S. District Court charging the city with denying them their "full rights and privileges under the U.S. Constitution and laws." Named as defendants in the suit were the City of Fort Worth, the mayor, City Manager, City Secretary, Recreation Board chairman, and Recreation Board superintendent. Plaintiffs asked that all of the city's white municipal courses be opened immediately under temporary court order while the case worked its way through the legal system. Their legal strategy was to keep the case narrowly focused on breaking the golf color barrier. Their petition said they asked "only for golf-playing privileges; no other breakdown of segregation in city facilities—such as swimming—is asked." Plaintiffs' counsel anticipated a long fight that would probably end up in the U.S. Supreme Court.[14]

In the event, it took more than a year, but in November 1955 city officials had to admit to themselves they were going to lose the case. The word around the courthouse was that U.S. District Judge Joe E. Estes was about to announce his decision for the plaintiffs. A writer for the *Fort Worth Press* described the mood of city officials in just two sentences: "City officials today are resigned to having Negroes play on public golf courses built for whites. . . . They're hoping a decision on swimming pools can be delayed at least a year."[15]

The next day Judge Estes issued his decision which, as expected, was in favor of the plaintiffs. Within the next twenty-four hours, two things happened: A city Recreation Department spokesman announced that they would be continuing the segregation policy in all activities *except* golf. The second development came the next day (Thursday, November

10); four black golfers hit the links at Rockwood led by golf pro Jesse Mitchell who had been closely following the fight since the beginning. The *Fort Worth Press* reported, "Nothing out of the ordinary happened." That next weekend, black golfers showed up at all of the city's formerly white municipal courses with seventeen at Z. Boaz alone and only one at Worth Hills.[16]

Photo 23. Golfers with trophies

Black golfers went from playing on inferior public courses in the 1940s and early '50s to competing for trophies on first-class courses, public and private. Unidentified golfers, undated photo. Courtesy of Tarrant County Black Historical & Genealogical Society.

The golf-course war was a symbolic victory, nothing more—the first crack in the Jim Crow policies of the Fort Worth Recreation Department. Fighting a rear-guard action, a group of white golfers launched a drive to try to purchase the Meadowbrook golf course and return it to the Jim Crow fold. They contacted like-minded friends trying to raise enough money to buy it from the city and turn it into a private country club. They never could raise the money, so they either had to join one of the existing country clubs or learn to play with mixed groups on the municipal courses. Contrary to their fears, Judge Estes' ruling did not bring a mob of black golfers on the formerly white courses. On the contrary, the ruling produced few visible changes. A year later, the *Fort Worth Press* could report, "Only a few Negroes have taken advantage of the federal court order desegregating city golf courses." Most of the small company of black golfers in Fort Worth seemed to prefer to play the Harmon course, confirming the racist-sounding pronouncement of Ross Trimble two years earlier. Perhaps more significant than the number of black golfers out on the links was the subtle change that had occurred while no one was looking in newspaper coverage: The *Press* was now spelling "Negroes" with a capital "N," not a small "n" as in former days. This may have been the most significant signal that a sea change was occurring in local white thinking.[17]

In the end, it did not really matter how much black golfers preferred the Harmon putting greens and fairways; a year later the city council announced the course was being closed to make way for the north-south expressway (I-35) that was about to start construction. The expensive bone represented by the Harmon Center, thrown to the city's black residents, had all been for naught. Black golfers would no longer have to choose between "playing with their own" or playing white courses. The Interstate Highway Act of 1956 changed all that. Just like Texas Electric Service Company taking over Douglass Park for its power station on North Main in 1925, the black golf course had to give way to "progress." It was déjà vu. In neither instance were the city's black residents consulted, nor was any effort made to find alternative locations that would spare the black properties.[18]

The real prize in the golf-course war still lay ahead—the private country clubs where the city's V.I.P.s played golf. If the NAACP and its allies could gain admission to those exclusive havens of the rich and powerful, that would be a mortal blow to Jim Crow. The country clubs managed to hold the racial line for another three decades. Blacks were not admitted to any of the city's six clubs until Woodhaven broke ranks in 1985. Prior to that, the nearest country club that Fort Worth's black golfers could play on was Woodcrest in Grand Prairie, which was owned by the same people who owned Woodhaven. The fact that the same company operated two of its clubs on different racial policies in neighboring communities (Fort Worth and Grand Prairie) tells how slowly Fort Worth changed its racial attitudes over the years. Colonial Country Club did not throw open its doors—and its links—to blacks until 1991, and then only after the Professional Golfers' Association (PGA) took Alabama's Shoal Creek Country Club to court. In order to continue hosting the annual Colonial National Invitational Golf Tournament (NIT) the club had to integrate and integrate quickly. The board met with leaders of the Black Chamber of Commerce (BCC) and quickly rubber-stamped the applications of half a dozen African-American memberships including, for good measure, one for the BCC itself. Afterwards, everyone said all the right things. Someone even explained that this was not "tokenism" because the Club had accepted six black members while all they had to do to satisfy the PGA was accept one. As a result, Jim Crow was banished from Colonial Country Club, and the club has continued to host the prestigious NIT ever since.[19]

Somehow, the desegregation wars always seemed to start with golf courses and swimming pools, even before schools and public transportation. Civil rights activists followed that same game plan in Beaumont, Texas, during these same years. In Fort Worth, the 1950–55 legal assault on municipal golf courses proved to be just the opening salvo in the drive to desegregate all public recreation facilities. The next targets were the swimming pools and city parks. In November 1955, with the golf courses conquered, *Fort Worth Press* staff reporter John Ohendalski asked the rhetorical question, "City's Parks [and] Swimming Pools Next?" The answer was yes, but the battle would be more bitter, perhaps because blacks and whites swimming in the same water as opposed to playing on the same grass could be perceived as pushing racial equality too far.[20]

A pattern also emerged in the city's response to demands to integrate public facilities: delay as long as possible and promise 'em anything. When the swimming-pool wars opened in 1956, the city adopted the same strategy. Initially, the NAACP had only "requested" that city pools be desegregated in time for summer swimming season. At the time, there were five pools for whites and one for blacks. The latter was part of Dixie Park, an urban green space bounded by Rosedale, White, and Yuma streets. Originally a "private negro recreation park" like Douglass Park, it was acquired by the Recreation Department to relieve the pressure to open the white parks. The park with the white-sounding name included the usual playgrounds and picnic areas, but also a swimming pool and outdoor movie screen. If Dixie Park was intended to satisfy the demand for black recreation facilities, it was a failure. The city's black leaders were no longer satisfied with a single pool for the city's entire black population; they wanted access to all city pools, which otherwise were only open to blacks on a limited basis once a year (Juneteenth).[21]

As months passed and polite requests got no results, the NAACP threatened to take the city to court. In early June, with swimming season upon them, T. Gordon Ryan, head of the Recreation Department, tried the old golf-course dodge, issuing a public statement that "chances are bright" that a new "Negro" pool would be built "this summer or early fall." The projected location was the Como neighborhood, which already had Lake Como. Nonetheless, Como residents there were "joyful over the news" that they were getting a pool. A second black pool for the city may have already been in serious discussion even before the NAACP threatened legal action, but the timing of the announcement is still suspicious, as is the lack of hard numbers or a firm promise. Gordon Ryan did toss around some numbers: the Park Board would pay a third of the cost, and the city council would pay another third, while "I think we [the Recreation Board] can find the rest of the money." Significantly, no one on the city's side offered to put any of this in writing, and the city council only "hinted" that it would pony up one-third of the cost.

Still, the announcement put the NAACP in a bind. They did not want to turn their noses up at a new pool for the Como neighborhood. The reaction of the Como community did not help. A spokesperson for the community said she expected "people from all sections of the city will come and use the [new] pool." But the NAACP stood by its guns, issuing a statement that the pool would no doubt be "good for the [Como] community," but that it was still prepared to provide legal aid for "any Negro who is denied admission to white pools." And there things stood for at least one more summer.[22]

The old parks were still going in 2014, only not on front pages. It was not until 2014 that the city finally gave Mosier Valley, the city's oldest black community, its own public park. The council set aside four acres in February 2014, an action celebrated by the long-suffering residents of Mosier Valley as a major victory.[23]

Suitable venues for large black events such as concerts and conventions have always been hard to find. The black Masonic Temple (1907–1924) and its successor the Masonic Mosque along with I.M. Terrell High School filled some of the need. The city helped some by allowing blacks to schedule events in venues such as Will Rogers Auditorium, the North Side Coliseum, and Farrington Field so long as whites did not want to use those venues." In 1954 the city council opened another public venue, the decaying Pioneer Palace on South University. Left over from the 1936 Frontier Centennial, Pioneer Palace began alternating black and white high school "programs and dances" on weekends, not just out of fairness but to book the space as much as possible. The council decreed, "White youths will have use of the building on Friday nights, and Negro teenagers will hold their dances on Saturday nights." Accepting that the council's motives were not purely altruistic, it was still another small step in dismantling the old Jim Crow system.[24]

Integrating the Fort Worth Police Department (FWPD)

The bitterest segregation fights occurred over public services like the police department and school system. Both the FWPD and the Fort Worth Independent School District (FWISD) had to be dragged kicking and screaming into the civil rights era.

The FWPD caved first. Public pressure had been mounting for years to integrate the lily-white police force. Fort Worth was the last major city in the state to hire African-American officers—after Houston, Galveston, Austin, and San Antonio. Galveston had been hiring black officers since 1914. Dallas, the last of the lot, had changed its policy in 1937. Fort Worth city fathers fought change as long as possible, making a series of meaningless concessions. In the 1930s the FWPD employed a "Negro undercover agent" (a variation on the old special officer), but he never wore a uniform, appeared at roll call, or was issued a weapon. In 1946 commissioners passed an ordinance that actually forbade the department from hiring black officers. The explanation was the same old tired arguments that integration would destroy morale among white officers, that blacks lacked the moral fiber and good judgment to be policemen, and that white citizens would never accept armed black men lording it over them.[25]

Hiring black officers was just the first step. The bigger question was what duties they would perform. Even the most enlightened whites could not imagine black officers patrolling white neighborhoods, much less arresting white citizens. In 1946, Lynn Landrum, Dallas' outspoken advocate for an integrated police force, argued that black officers should be assigned only to their own neighborhoods, which was what Dallas had done.

> Police departments in other cities have found that a Negro detail can handle a Negro section of town better than a white detail can. . . . It makes a lot of difference whether a man fits in the area in which he is supposed to work. . . . the right sort of Negro policeman

> at work in Negro areas can be of great help to law enforcement, to the protection of property, and the safeguarding of lives."[26]

The FWPD was hardly convinced even by this approach. In 1948 five black applicants signed up to take the civil service exam for the department. Fort Worth had adopted municipal civil service in the 1920s, which presumably was color-blind, but it took another state law to require cities to certify all applicants according to test scores not other factors (*e.g.*, race). Fort Worth still found reasons not to hire African Americans for another four years. In 1949, Chief R.E. Dysart explained to the *Star-Telegram* why his department would not be hiring African Americans: "If these people were employed as policemen, they would have to work only as an isolated group and would be restricted to work among the Negro race." A police officer, he insisted, "should be able to work among all groups of people."[27]

Finally, in October 1952, the council took the plunge, hiring four "negro policemen." In an open letter to commissioners, Chief Roland Howerton did an about-face from the attitude of his predecessor: "I am thoroughly convinced that we have a need for this service (*i.e.*, black officers)." He went on to reassure doubters that black officers would only work "in the Negro sections of the city." At the city council meeting where the policy change was discussed, black spokesman Isaiah P. Anderson upbraided commissioners on their piecemeal approach to integrating city government: "This belated action of Fort Worth in hiring Negro policemen is very similar to not giving some form of employment to Negroes in its various departments." In the end, the vote was unanimous in favor of hiring black officers. Now, qualified candidates had to be found, which meant men who could pass both the oral and written civil service exams *and* were willing to accept the department's conditions on their employment.[28]

Before the end of the year the first black applicants had passed the exams, and on January 1, 1953, they started their probationary period. They were the first black men hired by the FWPD since Hagar Tucker eighty years before. Unlike Tucker, they also wore the uniform and drew the same pay as white officers. As part of their probation, Charles Wright, Jack Gray, Benny Griffin, and Travis Bell had to attend "police school" that represented the only training Fort Worth police receive before hitting the streets.

The black community celebrated the hirings as a historic victory, but their celebration turned out to be premature. Within six months two of the new men were let go for reasons never explained, leaving only Travis Bell and Charles Wright. Five more black candidates applied and took their civil service exams along with eighteen white applicants on June 5, 1953. Only two made the force because only two slots were open to blacks. An integrated force did not mean open competition; there were still only four positions open to African Americans.

With the two new hires, the department once more had filled its quota. The fight to open all divisions and positions in the FWPD was just beginning. The last bastion of Jim Crow on the force was the elite detective squad. In 1957 Chief Cato Hightower named two African Americans to the squad. One was Travis Bell and the other was Charles Wright. They did not last long, however. By 1963 there were no African Americans in the detective division. This was not just a holdover of Jim Crow practices. The plainclothes squad was composed of older men who had been seasoned by years in the uniformed ranks. That alone excluded younger men. The fact that the squad was all-white and saw blacks not as comrades but as perps merely justified the continuation of racist practice.[29]

The good intentions of Chief Howerton and the council did not last long. Six years after the first group of black officers hit the street, there remained only one black uniformed officer on the force; all the others had either quit or been driven off. Policemen are a close-knit club—the "thin blue line." Newcomers have to prove themselves to be accepted. Black officers never felt accepted, something that is crucial when a man is entrusting his life to his fellows every day. Anecdotal evidence also suggests that white veterans made life hell for the black officers. To begin with, department policy did just what they said it would do, assigning black officers only to black neighborhoods. On top of that, they could not ride in squad cars with white officers, drive squad cars regardless of whether they had a driver's license or not, or ride in the paddy wagon when transporting arrestees to jail. The ultimate insult may have been not being allowed to arrest white people or even stop them for questioning. In this regard, things had not changed since Hagar Tucker's time. In 1961 Lonnell Cooper learned the hard way that black officers were treated differently when they were injured in the line of duty, too. After being shot and seriously wounded, he had to wait for a black ambulance to be summoned, which took him to the segregated ward in St. Joseph's Hospital. All things considered, it is no wonder that the department had a hard time keeping its quota of black officers filled.[30]

The only officer from that first group of four black officers still in uniform in 1961 was Lonnell Cooper who went on to become a legend in the department. He survived being shunned, shamed, and shot. By 1967, the department had six black officers in uniform and additional men in training. The old quota system had even been discarded. As a department spokesman explained to a reporter, "We would like to have at least 50 [more], but we are having trouble getting men who qualify to apply."[31]

Photo 24. Lonnell Cooper (1923–2011)

Cooper was in the second class of black officers hired by the FWPD (1953) and the longest serving of any of them, retiring in 1980. Here, in his department annual photo as a rookie. Photo courtesy of Kevin Foster, Sgt. FWPD ret.

Photo 25. Lonnell Cooper, 2007

In 2007, Lonnell Cooper, retired for 27 years, attended the dedication ceremony for the Hagar Tucker historical marker at Oakwood Cemetery. Photo courtesy of Kevin Foster, Sgt. FWPD ret.

The Tarrant County District Attorney's office also changed with the times, hiring its first black assistant D.A. in 1959. Ollice Malloy, Jr. was a graduate of the University of Texas law school—a product of the victory nine years earlier to open UT's law school. Malloy went to work for District Attorney Doug Crouch, a liberal Democrat who became the first Tarrant County D.A. to hire African Americans. During nine controversial years in office (1959-66 and 1971-72), Crouch established a reputation as "a friend of the Negroes." In his first four years, besides Malloy, he hired three more African Americans. In the beginning, Assistant D.A. Malloy handled only "complaints from Negroes." (White members of the office handled prosecutions of black defendants.) Unfortunately, his first murder case did not go well; he lost. Whether the fact that there were only two black faces in the courtroom, Malloy's and the defendant's, had anything to do with the verdict is impossible to say. Despite losing, Malloy still made history since this was the first murder case in the history of Texas criminal justice argued by a black prosecutor. Within four years, he was helping prosecute cases regardless of the color of the defendant. Malloy's appointment was a reminder of a time only forty-four years earlier when black men like Jeff Daggett could not even enter the front door of the courthouse, much less get a respectful hearing of their complaints.[32]

Integrating Fort Worth Schools

As hidebound as the FWPD was, when it came to desegregating "with all deliberate speed," it moved faster than the FWISD. Segregated schools had always been part and parcel of their all-white neighborhoods. The school district made a practice of "dividing according to white elementary schools with Negro children directed to the nearest Negro elementary," however far away that was. It was a system that the white majority saw no reason to change. Neither did the elected school board, which could still insist in 1956 that Fort Worth had "the state's [most] outstanding system of Negro schools," but even if that were true, it was beside the point. The Supreme Court had struck down racially segregated schools in 1954 (*Brown vs. the Board of Education of Topeka, Kansas*), but the FWISD stubbornly resisted, and the Court's qualification that desegregation could proceed "with all deliberate speed" gave them plenty of wiggle room.[33]

While other school districts in Tarrant County, specifically Eagle Mountain and Grapevine, proceeded however reluctantly with integration (the term of preference at that time), the FWISD fought it every step of the way. The reaction of the school board to the decision was a mixture of self-delusion and rationalization. The day after the decision was announced in Washington, several board members were interviewed by *The Press*, and none of them was shy about offering his opinion. Said one, "There is no question but that in Fort Worth we have [always] given Negroes equal facilities." Another pointed out that the school board was "governed by state laws" and that "state legislators will have to act" before the board could do anything. Still another discounted the decision's impact on Fort Worth because "there are Negro high schools in every section of town" (a blatant untruth), and besides, "pupils will continue to want to go to the nearest school," meaning their neighborhood school, meaning white students in white schools. He seemed puzzled why blacks would even want to go to white schools. Several members prophetically anticipated "a number of private schools starting up" as a result of the decision. Perhaps the most incredulous comment came from the board member who believed "segregation may be abolished in the city" by the 1955–56 school year. Perhaps the smartest of the group was board president O.C. Armstrong who was conveniently out of town when the newspapers called for a comment.[34]

Some Fort Worth lawyers, none identified by name, predicted much more serious consequences if the color line were breached at the schoolhouse door. One warned that the day was coming when "Negroes will use city pools now reserved for whites, play on the same golf courses with whites, use the same restrooms in public buildings, and sit beside whites in buses!" As if that were not frightening enough, another opined that the last racial taboo was ultimately at risk in the aftermath of *Brown*: "I feel sure that whenever the Supreme Court gets ready. . . it will go so far as to say whites and Negroes may intermarry," he warned. Those same lawyers did hold out some hope that privately owned cafes, theaters, and hotels could continue to "bar or segregate Negroes" as they always had.[35]

The *Brown* decision may have stunned whites, but it was hardly a bolt out of the blue to the black community; they had been trying to dismantle the Jim Crow school system for years. Black leaders had openly challenged the status quo for the first time in 1951 when some black parents of Euless sued the Euless school district for not providing "equal facilities" for their children. A federal district judge found for the parents, but the Fifth Circuit Court in New Orleans reversed the lower court's ruling. Black Euless students continued to be bused to black Fort Worth schools.[36]

Long before the term "busing" entered the American vocabulary as shorthand for transporting children to schools outside their neighborhood it was normal practice in the black community when kids were bused to a segregated school far from their neighborhood. This was the case in particular for black kids when they moved up to high school because there was only one black high school for all of Tarrant County. Kids were bused in from outlying school districts and communities as far away as Weatherford in Parker County. Terrell served sixteen junior high "feeder" schools, which was more than any other high school in Texas. Some of the communities it served, like Euless, had just a handful of black families. Because its constituency was scattered all over the map, Terrell High School was an odd duck because school spirit was based on race, not ties to a particular neighborhood. And for decades the school board saw no reason to change things. In 1956 Board President Armstrong issued this statement: "The interests of all concerned would be best served, and the orderly and lawful operation of schools of the district would be best accomplished, by continuing the present [segregation] policy."[37]

During the Jim Crow years transporting black kids by bus to the nearest segregated school, often past several white schools along the way, was officially known as "transferring." Busing only became a heated issue to the majority of Americans after the courts ordered white kids transported out of their neighborhoods to black schools starting in 1969.

In 1954 some white leaders were predicting smugly that the *Brown* decision would fall hardest on black teachers. As school board member Leon Stewart explained, "Our Negro teachers are well-qualified," but hardly qualified to teach white children. In the future, he warned, if the school district followed a policy of hiring the best teachers regardless of race, that would mean fewer black teachers. He had put his finger on one of the hidden costs of Jim Crow: when large urban school systems were forced to cut back classroom staffing because of budget shortfalls, school closings, or other reasons, the axe always fell disproportionately on black teachers. They were laid off, and white teachers were moved into black classrooms.[38]

After the initial shock wore off, the Fort Worth School Board dug in its heels. Two years after the *Brown* decision, the board was still fighting a rearguard action. In the summer of 1956 with another school year looming they hit upon a neat solution to take the heat off while still meeting the legal requirements of *Brown.* At the end of the 1955–56 school year, they had announced the closing of the E. Van Zandt elementary school on Missouri Ave. because of low enrollment; it was down to just fifty-seven white students, ten fewer than the previous year. The problem was the surrounding neighborhood had been "turning black" for years, making the school a white island in an increasingly dark-hued sea. Meanwhile, black children from the neighborhood were being bused over to James E. Guinn School on the corner of East Rosedale and the South Freeway. Van Zandt held the key. As announced by School Superintendent Joe P. Moore, it would become the "first mixed Negro-white school in the city" if it re-opened *and* if "some of the white children remained." The scheme had the appeal of solving two problems in one stroke; most of the school's non-black students were Latinos who likewise did not fit comfortably with children in the "white" (Anglo) schools. Grouping black and Latino elementary students together in the same building would satisfy the law and solve the social problem in one fell swoop. It would also relieve over-crowding at James E. Guinn. Moore may have miscalculated, however, when he announced that the re-opened Van Zandt Elementary would have a black principal and black faculty because the parents of the few remaining white students there did not want to have their children relegated to what would obviously now be a second-class school. Superintendent Moore's scheme collapsed.[39]

The school board came up with another halfway measure for satisfying the letter if not the spirit of *Brown*. Since the most glaring discrepancy between black and white students was secondary schooling, the board proposed to create three new, all-black high schools by the clever stratagem of adding one grade a year to the three existing black junior highs—Kirkpatrick, Como, and Dunbar—starting with the 1954–55 school year. By this plan, they would graduate their first senior classes in the spring of 1957. The plan to "grow" black high schools rather than create them was approved and by the early 1960s Fort Worth had four black high schools counting I.M. Terrell. The problem was, this still did not put an end to racially segregated schooling. FWISD schools did not begin seriously desegregating until 1963.[40]

The first test case of the *Brown* decision locally came in Mansfield, nineteen miles southeast of Fort Worth, where a federal court had ordered "immediate integration" of the high school for the 1956–57 school year. The white community there reacted with fury, taking to the streets and hanging three black effigies from lamp poles. On Sunday, September 3, like-minded Fort Worth whites hanged a black effigy in the Riverside neighborhood. Their anger was about schools and housing and all the changes that had turned their world upside down.[41]

Meanwhile, the battle to desegregate Fort Worth schools went on behind closed doors led by L. Clifford Davis, a graduate of Howard University law school who was lead counsel for the NAACP in federal lawsuits to end segregation in Fort Worth and Mansfield schools. Fort

Worth officials were courteous and sympathetic; they were also adamant about preserving traditional neighborhood schools. For its part, the city's black community had a righteous cause they could rally around, and they refused to sit meekly by while the school board dragged its feet. In the summer of 1956, the local NAACP chapter made its biggest push yet by urging black parents to ignore the existing neighborhood enrollment system by putting their kids in any school they pleased for the coming school year. In response, School Board President Armstrong announced that Fort Worth schools would continue to operate under existing rules "unless the courts direct us to do otherwise." This was just before classes opened at the beginning of September, and he knew that no court was going to order anything so disruptive. At the same time, he was giving the board an out just in case they were forced to begin immediate desegregation: they were just following the federal mandate. He pleaded through the press that more time was needed to "make proper provisions for the integration of white and Negro students" while issuing a copy of the board's decision to all school principals with instructions to read it to any black parents who tried to enroll their kids outside of their neighborhood.[42]

When Mr. and Mrs. Herbert Teel and Mrs. Lois Kneeland showed up at Peter Smith Elementary and Carroll Peak Elementary, respectively, on the first day to enroll their kids, they were turned away, courteously but firmly. NAACP attorney L. Clifford Davis told a newspaper reporter the School Board's stand "might be the basis for a federal court suit," but he also equivocated, saying he "didn't know for sure." Although they did not know they were making history, the five Teel and Kneeland children were the vanguard in the full frontal assault on segregation in the FWISD. They left Peter Smith and Carroll Peak that day disappointed that they were not starting school like all the other children of Fort Worth, and their rebuff was soon forgotten as the nation turned its attention toward Central High School in Little Rock, Arkansas.[43]

Another way to change Jim Crow was by getting an African American on the school board. That was what Oran McGregor and his supporters were hoping to do when he became the first member of his race to run for the board in 1959. The black insurance agent challenged incumbent Atwood McDonald, one of the board's hard-liners who had held the line against change before the 1956–57 school year. McGregor lost for the at-large seat—7,995 votes to 1,475 votes—but like the Teel and Kneeland families, his challenge was another salvo in the long-running battle, and far from the last.[44]

That fall the NAACP filed yet another suit in federal court to "force the mixing of Negroes [and] whites in Fort Worth schools," as one newspaper described it. Named as defendants in the suit were the entire school board, School Superintendent Joe P. Moore, and the principals of Burton Hill and Peter Smith elementaries. The city's legal team managed to find an error in the lawsuit that allowed them to postpone the day of reckoning for a few more years at least.[45]

After being rebuffed in its first legal action, the NAACP went back to court in 1963. This time a different federal court ordered the school district to quit dragging its feet. The city's response was to produce a face-saving "Plan for Desegregation" that proposed integrating no more than one or two grades per year starting with the first grade in the 1963–64 school year. The school board touted it as a bold "stair-step plan," conveniently ignoring the fact that it had only been adopted as a result of a federal court order.[46]

They gave school desegregation a test run that summer at Trimble Technical High School. Summer school classes were opened up there to black students for the first time. On the first day (June 3), twenty black students showed up to take the "adult classes," and scarcely anyone noticed. White Fort Worth parents were not worried about adult classes; they were worried about their little Susies and Billies being forced to sit in the same classroom with "Negroes." In historical terms, however, those twenty students were the "Little Rock Nine" of Fort Worth, the vanguard of a sea change about to sweep over Fort Worth that had been held back for nine years, ever since the *Brown* decision.[47]

In the fall of 1963, the FWISD officially began integrating, beginning with the first grade. On Wednesday, September 4, twenty-nine black schoolchildren were enrolled at formerly all-white elementary schools. One Dallas newspaper described the day inaccurately as "[breaking] the classroom racial barrier for the first time." Nervous black parents with their first-graders in tow, bravely entered the doors of Lily B. Clayton, Theodore Willis, Charles E. Nash, Oakhurst, and Washington Heights school buildings. White parents escorted their own kids into the same buildings as countless parents had done before them to kick off the new school year, but it was obvious that things were different. Some white kids stopped and stared openly at the aliens in their midst. Uniformed policemen were present on all five campuses. Everything went peacefully. There were no demonstrations and no incidents, Chief Roland B. Howerton told the newspapers., which is not particularly surprising considering that no more than five or six black kids enrolled at any single school. It is easy to overlook five or six among scores. School officials starting with Superintendent Elden B. Busby were both proud and relieved. No one commented on the fact that the twenty-nine black kids who showed up were fewer than one-fourth of the eighty-five or so who had been cleared to be part of the first wave of desegregation of Fort Worth public schools in the 1963–64 school year. Superintendent Busby only said he expected more to show up in the days to come. Still, history was made that day; Fort Worth was the "last major city in Texas" to desegregate its public schools. It had been a long, difficult journey going back eighty-one years to the creation of the city's public school system in 1882.[48]

Photo 26. Desegregating Lily B. Clayton Elementary.

September 4, 1963, was D-Day at Lily B. Clayton Elementary, a Wednesday. This was the day Lily B. Clayton was de-segregated. This photograph shows the arrival of Kenneth Ray Blakey with his mother to begin his first day of classes. Courtesy of *Fort Worth Star-Telegram* Photograph Collection, Special Collections, University of Texas at Arlington Library, Arlington, TX.

Full integration was not achieved in the FWISD until the fall of 1967 when formerly all-white senior high schools enrolled their first black students, among them those historic bastions of white supremacy, Paschal and Arlington Heights high schools. By that date, however, many white parents had already bailed out, enrolling their children in exclusive white private schools like Fort Worth Country Day and Trinity Valley. The relative tranquility and high educational standards of private schools had a powerful attraction for middle-class parents.

The FWISD's foot-dragging, stair-step plan provoked an exasperated U.S. Fifth Circuit Court in 1971 to order the closing of some historically black schools and the forced busing of their students to white schools.

Thus busing came to Fort Worth. To ease the transition, the city appointed a Bi-racial Advisory Committee headed up by black activist and long-time city staffer Bertha Collins, to oversee things. In Collins, the city met its match. She butted heads with administrators, publicly accused the city council of "dragging its feet," and fought for free lunch programs and other benefits for Fort Worth's black schoolchildren.[49]

It may be no coincidence that Bertha Collins died in 1981, and the city found itself back in federal court in 1983, this time to "amend" its desegregation plan nearly twenty years after its schools had been declared unconstitutional. The battle over schools epitomized the halting, painful pace of civil rights in Fort Worth, but one can also see the glass as half-full because the city was able to avoid the violence and bitter divisions that marked desegregation in so many other cities, including our sister city to the east.[50]

All of Fort Worth's black children were not reduced to attending inferior public facilities or waiting to be admitted to segregated white public schools. A group of determined, middle-class black citizens got together in 1959 and created the Little Tommy Tucker Pla-Skool. They purchased a suitable building at 801 Verbena and hired staff and faculty to operate first grade ("primary"), nursery, and kindergarten classes. Three board members handled day-to-day operations: Tom E. Andrews (president) and his daughters, Willa Green and Myrtle Lewis. As impressive as the school's ambition was, its tuition-based program was not an option for most of Fort Worth's black community.[51]

Photo 27. Little Tommy Tucker Pla-Skool advertisement.

Not all black children were relegated to segregated public schools in the early 1960s. Some fortunate children were enrolled in private schools like the Little Tommy Tucker Pla-Skool, which struggled to provide quality education in a congenial environment on a shoe-string budget. From 1960 I.M. Terrell "Panther" Annual, courtesy of Byron White of Fort Worth.

Good Times Amidst the Bad

The 1940s were not all war all the time. Even in the midst of war, people still craved fun, and there were plenty of nightclubs and dance halls to satisfy that craving. The center of black night-life in Fort Worth was the Rosedale-Evans Ave. axis. Two of the more popular clubs there were the Zanzibar Club and the Aquarium Club. Over the years, some top acts such as Charlie Pride and Jackie Wilson played the Zanzibar. The Aquarium Club was a classy, two-story place that offered jazz concerts on Sundays, R&B and big-band sounds during the weeknights.

Jacksboro Highway going west out of Fort Worth was home to more daring *and* more dangerous clubs. Some offered "black and tan" shows that put black and white performers on the same stage although not at the same time. One of those was Abe & Pappy's Club (at Twelfth and Jacksboro Highway), which pushed the Jim Crow envelope to draw larger crowds who wanted something different. Some clubs pushed the envelope too far. The Skyliner Ballroom had white men performing with black women, which came under what city ordinance defined as "moral perversion." The Fort Worth police raided the place in 1953.[52]

Music critics steered clear of most black venues and not just out of fear for their personal safety. They considered African-American performers with the exception of the occasional opera singer like Marian Anderson "novelty acts," that is, having no intrinsic musical value. That meant when major black performers like Jackie Wilson or Joe Liggins came to town, they were virtually ignored by white newspapers and radio stations.

Music had its own set of rules under Jim Crow. What was called "race music" had been around for years in the form of jump and blues, but it did not break through into the mainstream until Joe Liggins' huge postwar hit, "The Honeydripper," which was propelled by a driving beat and honking saxophone to the top of the race charts for twenty-three weeks (September 1945 to January 1946) then crossed over to the pop charts where it reached No. 12, the highest position for any race record to that date. (In black parlance, a "honeydripper" was a smooth-talking lady's man.) Based on that success, Liggins formed his own band, gave them the name of his big hit, and went out on tour, reaching north Texas in 1951, but not Fort Worth. Kids living on the west side of the Trinity had to go to the Cavalcade of Blues in Dallas to hear the Honeydrippers' raucous good-time sound.

For whites curious about all aspects of black culture, there were always opportunities to see how the other half lived if one had an adventurous spirit. For night owls who appreciated jazz and rhythm and blues (R&B), the Bluebird Night Club in Como was the place to go. By the mid-50s, white sports fans could watch talented black baseball players play against white talent at LaGrave Field, something that had been denied them in previous decades. In 1955 the home-town Cats had future hall-of-famer Maury Wills on the team. Wills was the first black player on the Cats, which at the time was a farm team of the Brooklyn Dodgers. The stands at LaGrave Field were still segregated, but even the most die-hard segregationist could admire the smooth-fielding Wills playing shortstop for the Cats. Black baseball fans had to follow their hero on the radio or by standing outside the fence listening to the game. Years later after he hung up his glove, Wills held fond memories of Fort Worth, saying the hometown fans never "taunted or abused" him during the single season he played here before being called up to the majors.[53]

Fort Worth's black teenagers did not have a lot of choices when it came to hearing their kind of music. Most black entertainers who toured were adult oriented; if they were not big enough to be booked into the Masonic Mosque, they played the tough clubs out on Jacksboro Highway or East Lancaster. Local teenagers had to be mostly content with hearing their favorites on the radio or buying the latest hit, like Liggins' second hit, "Pink Champagne," in "colored" record shops. Some white shops like Record Town near TCU also carried race music, but it was not a big seller by that name. Liggins was something special. Before Chuck Berry did it, Liggins was writing most of his own stuff in both pop and spiritual genres, but he did not have Berry's timing, coming along during the transition years between the big band sound of the 1940s and rock and roll in the mid-fifties. Local teenagers did not know it, but what they heard at his 1951 Dallas appearance was the same driving back-beat, electric guitar, and energetic vocals soon to be known as rock and roll. *Billboard Magazine*, the Bible of the popular music industry, helped the cause of popularizing black music by replacing the objectionable term "race music" with the more commercial "rhythm and blues" (R&B).[54]

As the popularity of R&B spread, it broke down color barriers and caught the attention of the white masters of the music industry. The

Dallas Morning News managed to find a young black group willing to buck the musical trend. Their name was the Hi-Lo's and their spokesman, Chuck Burroughs, told the newspaper that he and his band mates had "no truck with that type of music," adding, "We wouldn't record one of those [rock and roll] songs if we were starving. . . . It [*sic*] lacks quality, and surely it isn't beautiful." The highly stylized language as quoted by the reporter makes it sound like young Chuck was being paraphrased, but this was the kind of quotation that reassured white readers who heard in R&B and R&R the beginning of the decline of Western civilization. For lining up on the white side of the musical divide, the Hi-Lo's got to play nice (white) venues like the Greater Dallas Club, and they were even rumored to be negotiating a television deal. Their writer, Bobby Batson, had a "bundle of manuscripts just waiting to be discovered." The fact that the Hi-Lo's never broke out, never even put a single record on the charts, says all that needs to be said about the viability of black groups who turned up their noses at the new music. This was same year the movie *Blackboard Jungle* came out, introducing the movie-going public to rock and roll music (The movie's theme song was "Rock Around the Clock"). The wave of the future was Little Richard and Chuck Berry, not the Hi-Lo's, and most black Fort Worth teenagers recognized that fact.[55]

The Fort Worth music scene did not have a (black) promoter like Howard Lewis or big-name venues like Lewis' Rose Room or the Cavalcade of Blues, both in Dallas. Lewis was one of the most powerful promoters of "Negro talent" in the Southwest. He was plugged into what was known as the "Chitlin' Circuit," which allowed him to book the hottest black acts like Ruth Brown, Louis Jordan, Dinah Washington, the Clovers into Dallas. And if they played Dallas, most acts made the thirty-mile trip west to play Fort Worth.[56]

On its own, Fort Worth would have found it almost impossible to attract the big-name acts, but Fort Worth could piggyback on Dallas bookings as long as they played by the rules of the game. Both cities were part of Howard Lewis' territory, and black promoters on the chitlin' circuit respected each other's territory, so all local bookings had to go through Lewis. No sensible Fort Worth promoter would dare try to end-run Lewis. Fortunately, the Dallas promoter had nothing against Fort Worth. On the contrary, he could improve his bottom line by booking his acts into both cities even though Fort Worth crowds were always smaller. The problem with Fort Worth was not just the smaller size of the black population; it was the dearth of first-rate venues. For years, Will Rogers' management would not stoop to booking black R&B acts so Fort Worth fans had to settle for small-time black performers like Ray Sharpe (at least before he broke out nationally) or the Red Hearts, a popular Dallas R&B group.

One of the most popular club venues was the Skyliner Ballroom on Jacksboro Highway, which catered to both black and white audiences although never on the same night. But the biggest regular venue for black acts was the Masonic Mosque on First St. near the river. Ruth Brown, the Atlantic Records recording star known in the 1950s as the "Queen of R&B," played "the Mosque" on November 14, 1959. Turning their auditorium into a major venue for black musical acts was the best thing the black Masons had going for them in the '50s because the Masonic Order was a dying force in American life. After the Masonic Mosque, the next biggest venue which could be rented by blacks was the North Side Coliseum. It seated four or five thousand people, but acoustics were problematic, and it was only available if no white booking agent wanted the same date. Unlike at the Masonic Mosque, white acts always got first dibs on the Coliseum, even bumping black acts that were already booked.[57]

To attempt to fill the gap between the high-brow tastes of the black middle class and the jive joints that catered to the young and the "hep," black elites in Dallas and Fort Worth formed the Dallas-Fort Worth Concert Bureau (DFWCB) in 1949. While claiming to represent both cities, it was dominated by its Dallas members including its president, Viol V. Dixon. They brought in church choirs, concert pianists, and opera singers—no vulgar R&B here! —booking the best venues in both towns, *i.e.*, the State Fair auditorium in Dallas and Will Rogers Auditorium in Fort Worth. Single-performance tickets for these shows started at 30¢ for the back of the balcony and went up to $2.40 for the best seats on the main floor. Season tickets for a package of four shows started at 60¢ and went up to $4.80. Considering the classy venues and the times, not surprisingly there was still separate seating for blacks and whites. The 1950 season included a "new Negro music series" that started off with "noted Negro basso" Kenneth Spencer. There is no record of how big the audience was, that night or any other night. The aim was more to uplift and show off rather than entertain, which did not bode well. The DFWCB could not match the cachet of the symphony orchestra, and the performers it featured, like the Mount Zion Baptist Church choir and Dallas Negro Piano Quartet, did not have the pull of major national acts. It didn't help that the major newspapers referred to it condescendingly as the "Negro Bureau." Nevertheless, the board had high ambitions. In the first year, they announced plans to establish a "teaching center of [black] music" and offer scholarships to worthy students from the area. Like the rest of the dream, those plans never got off the ground. The black middle class and a handful of white liberals could simply not support such dreams.[58]

For black teenagers or anyone with the same musical tastes, Fort Worth had its own black radio station dating back to World War II. Station KCNC went on the air (AM) in 1943 and gave Jimmy Clemons, later a black radio celebrity, his start as a young disc jockey. KCNC's successors at 970 on the AM dial were KWBC (1946–53), then KNOK (1953–1979). KWBC was launched on a wing and a $70,000 prayer by the Worth Broadcasting Company (part of the Associated Broadcasters family). It was a small-market, 1,000-watt station that targeted both the Hispanic and black audiences. It was the local station that introduced Fort Worth listeners to R&B music thanks to the Dean McClain show in 1950: one hour of R&B programming to test the waters. In 1953 management changed the call letters to KNOK and mixed country, Spanish-language, and R&B programming. Four years later, they refocused the programming exclusively at the black audience, featuring besides R&B music, the

"Negro Spiritual Hour," the "Gospel Music Train," and "Blues at Sunset." Starting in 1957, KNOK AM signed off at sunset, switching to KNOK FM until dawn (simulcasting). The black community's shifting demographics were reflected in the station's address changes. KWBC's studio was at Ninth and Main; KNOK's was at 3601 Kimbo on the north side of town.[59]

In 1960 KNOK jumped on the rock-and-roll bandwagon with local boy Delbert McClinton's cross-over country/R&R hit, "Wake Up Baby." By that date, KNOK had already established itself as Fort Worth's R&B station of choice. In the next few years Jimmy Clemons became KNOK's star personality in addition to being the city's best-known black DJ. One of his fellow DJs was Jerry Thomas, a 1948 graduate of I.M. Terrell who went to work at KNOK in 1955. As the city's only R&B station, KNOK attracted both black and white listeners at a time when WFAA, KFJZ, and KXOL had almost exclusively white audiences. In 1968 KNOK jumped on the new FM bandwagon when it began broadcasting at 107.5 on the FM dial.[60]

KNOK was the voice of black Fort Worth for twenty years. That gave the KNOK crew the right to host the major black acts that came through town, such as the Supremes and James Brown. By the time Jerry Thomas retired he had risen from DJ to news reporter and ultimately program director. In 2008 he was inducted into the Texas Radio Hall of Fame.[61]

Radio broadcasting helped break down the barriers between races because Jim Crow could not dictate what kind of music a person listened to on the radio. Many white listeners got their first introduction to R&B on KNOK or a station just like it, and it is significant that big-name white artists like Boz Scaggs and Jimmie Vaughan listed Fort Worth's KNOK early in their careers.[62]

Television was harder for blacks to break into. It took a bigger investment to get into, there was only a handful of TV stations in the early years as opposed to hundreds of radio stations, and it was harder for white audiences to accept black faces in their homes as opposed to "race music" on the radio. Jerry Thomas was the first black broadcaster to break into TV in the Fort Worth market. He successfully made the jump from radio to the small independent station KTVT as host of a show that took the then-radical step of covering events and personalities in the black community called "What About People?" KTVT's management was not so much trail-blazing as desperate. They needed to fill so many hours with local programming, and the selection was slim. (Another KTVT local program was "Slam-Bang Theater" with Icky Twerp.) Still, Thomas' "neutral features," closely trimmed hair, and mellifluous voice ("like chocolate flowing over ice cream") was not off-putting to whites who happened to tune in to his show.[63]

Entertainment, like athletics, was a path out of the Jim Crow ghetto. Black music had cross-over appeal, and black DJs became that friendly voice between songs to their regular listeners, the first black "friend" many whites had. Radio and television gave the "Kings of the Airwaves," whether on radio or TV, an invaluable platform for promoting black culture and black issues as well as opening doors for all the people behind the celebrities such as sound men and camera men. Jerry Thomas was a rare talent who was ahead of his time. He was not just a radio and TV personality; he was also an accomplished stage actor and newspaper publisher. He used his KNOK fame to start the Lake Como Theater Guild in 1960 and the Sojourner Truth theater company in 1972, and was co-founder of *La Vida News*, a black newspaper that is still published today. He also became the first black president of the Fort Worth Catholic Schools Diocese.[64]

Joe Liggins was a popular performer when he came through town, but he could not hold a candle to another "Joe" who blurred the distinction between entertainment and sports. As a musical talent Joe Louis did not have a pinch of the musical talent of Joe Liggins, but the former heavyweight boxing champion had infinitely more name recognition. He had been the darling of black Americans in the 1930s and '40s and even white fans grudgingly accepted him as the best there was in the ring. After he retired from boxing Louis tried to parlay his boxing fame into a musical and comedy act, which he called "The Big Rhythm and Blues Show." He took it on the road and came through north Texas. In 1953 Dallas promoter Howard Lewis brought him to Dallas where he played Burnett baseball field in front of a mixed-race audience. Fort Worth blacks who had a car or could catch the inter-city bus made the thirty-mile trip to see their hero, not necessarily catch his singing and dancing. Three years later, having given up his stage career, Louis came to Fort Worth as a retired heavyweight boxing champ but still a hero to the students of I.M. Terrell, where he spoke.[65]

Another black athlete-hero also in the entertainment business was tennis great Arthur Ashe. He was one of the rising stars of the game, and the only black player on the professional circuit, when he came to Fort Worth in 1965 to play in the Colonial National Invitational Tennis tournament. He won the men's singles title on April 18 against Fred Stolle, winner of the recent French Open. Three years later Ashe was ranked number one in the world. He is still the only African American to win the Colonial Invitational tennis title. It was a long way from the first black tennis tournament in Fort Worth in 1931, played on the asphalt courts of Greenway Park.[66]

PUBLIC HOUSING AND THE NEIGHBORHOOD WARS

Things came to a head in residential living post-World War II. The local housing shortage caused by the war did not disappear after VJ-Day. Many members of both races who had been drawn to Fort Worth by the booming wartime economy stayed on. In particular, the black population was larger than ever before, and they needed housing. They had outgrown the old neighborhoods, not just in terms of sheer numbers but in their expectations and economic status. They desired first-class housing or what one newspaper columnist summed up as "a good roof, a nice yard, and a pleasant neighborhood. . . close to churches, schools, and parks."[67]

Areas like Rock Island Bottom and Chambers Hill that had once contained both well-to-do and poor blacks were no longer satisfactory to the rising middle class. "Black flight" left those neighborhoods in precipitous decline. The situation was complicated because as white businesses and suburbs expanded westward, blacks living on the west side of town were forced to vacate the area except for the Lake Como enclave. On the east side, the historic lines between white and black neighborhoods blurred as middle-class blacks went looking for better housing and refused to be limited by outmoded Jim Crow thinking. They soon learned that relocating in white neighborhoods could provoke a nasty fight even quicker than integrating schools.[68]

The breaching of the color line that had begun on the Near South Side in the 1920s resumed with a vengeance in the 1950s. (see chap. 4) The 1944 G.I. Bill opened the door, but there were many Americans looking for better living conditions who did not qualify for veterans' benefits. Federal housing policy after World War II was a continuation of New Deal policies that took direct aim at poverty-stricken inner cities. Congress got the ball rolling with the 1949 Housing Act that spoke of eliminating "sub-standard and other inadequate housing through the clearance of slums and blighted areas, and the realization . . . of a decent home and a suitable living environment for every American family." In the years that followed, Congress expanded on the original landmark legislation with supplemental housing acts in 1954, 1956, 1957, and 1961.[69]

Fort Worth's original public housing projects, built in 1940, were inadequate to meet the rising demand. Things moved slowly. Housing decisions still had to respect traditional Jim Crow attitudes, justified by the argument that "the Negro does not want to live among white people." By 1951 federal bureaucrats were talking about "slum clearance" and the critical need for additional "public housing." The hectoring from Washington would only get worse over the next decade. The basic question was not whether long-standing black sub-standard housing needed to be replaced, but what kind of housing it was going to be replaced with and who was going to pay for it. As one advocate argued in classic bureaucratic jargon, "We have a mass of low-earnings families now living in distressingly inadequate quarters. Their needs justify housing by either public or private benefaction and subsidy." Fort Worth's resident housing scholar, TCU Sociology Professor Robert Talbert, stated that "urban blight" was holding the "metropolis" back, dragging it down. Sub-standard housing could be eliminated, he proposed, with sweeping slum-clearance projects.[70]

The cruel logic of urban slum clearance did not bode well for historic black neighborhoods on the Near East Side and Near South Side, two of the three concentrations of black residents. (The third was Como.) Replacing existing black housing with new housing in this quadrant would not upset the city's neighborhood racial balance. White neighborhood growth could still move into undeveloped lands on the west side of the city (the Wedgwood, Westcliff, Tanglewood, and Ridglea areas).

By the 1950s the Near South Side along the East Rosedale axis was home to schools, churches, and black-owned businesses. The last-named included Dixie Park, Drake's Cafeteria, and the Grand and Rosedale theaters. A black family could enjoy an all-day Saturday or Sunday outing and not stray more than a couple of blocks off Rosedale. Nice, black-owned homes up and down Humboldt and Terrell were occupied by doctors, pastors, educators, and bankers. It was the most exclusive black residential section of Fort Worth. And the population of the Near South Side was on the march, moving north into Riverside, which had been overwhelmingly white since its beginnings in 1899. Riverside was roughly bounded by Beach Street on the east and Riverside Dr. on the west and by Northeast Twenty-eighth on the north and present-day State Highway 121 on the south.[71]

Another black neighborhood which might also be considered part of the Near East Side, was anything but middle-class. It was bounded by Bewley Mills on the north, present-day I-30 on the south, the Santa Fe-Rock Island tracks on the west, and Live Oak on the east. There were

383 sub-standard houses there, making it "the most dilapidated area of the city." The Chamber of Commerce and city council regularly received complaints about the unsanitary conditions and criminal activity there. It was an eyesore clearly visible from the Dallas-Fort Worth turnpike that was constructed in 1957 and I-35 (the North-South Freeway), completed three years later. City councilman Tommy Thompson said it "created a most unfavorable impression" on visitors coming into town on either of those two arteries. The city did not know what to do with it other than tear it down, but that would require "finding housing for the persons displaced."[72]

In the 1950s both the Near South Side and Near East Side areas were devastated by construction of the north-south and east-west freeways, which wiped out many homes, throwing their owners onto an already tight housing market. The completed freeways also isolated those areas (neighborhoods) from the rest of the city and caused property values to plummet. To replace demolished housing and relieve the housing shortage in the black community, in 1954 the city built Cavile Place, off East Rosedale, the last of the old-fashioned public housing projects built in Fort Worth. It was named for pioneering black teacher James A. Cavile. (see chap. 2) The Federal Housing Administration had approved Fort Worth for additional units of public housing in 1948, but it took the city another six years to select a site and come up with plans. The 300 units that became Cavile Place were constructed on Etta St. They were of modest size and maintained by federal subsidies. They were intended to take the pressure off housing in the Riverside and Poly neighborhoods. Unfortunately for their builders, they were not the kind of housing middle-class blacks wanted to move into.[73]

Meanwhile, Como, still the only black neighborhood on the west side, was in the best shape of any of the city's historic black neighborhoods. It consisted of numerous small, tidy bungalows laid out on neat residential streets. There were thriving businesses nearby and proud schools, and crime was low. Rather than being surrounded by railroad tracks and freeways, Como was a quiet suburban neighborhood adjoining the nice white neighborhoods of Ridglea and River Crest. As recently as the 1920s the neighborhood had been predominantly white; it would be 99 percent black in a few more years.[74]

These were Fort Worth's historic black neighborhoods as defined by law and custom in the 1950s. The problem was not just the lack of housing stock but that the existing stock was in "poor or dilapidated condition," what the city manager called "slum buildings." Something had to be done. Soon-to-be-famous white-neighborhood-buster Lloyd G. Austin later explained the frustration he and others felt: "[Black] People were *tired* of living like they were living."[75]

The alternatives to just packing up and leaving town amounted to three options: 1) hope private developers constructed new black residential additions; 2) petition the federal government for more public housing; or 3) for those who could afford it, move into historically white neighborhoods. Each of these options posed its own set of problems. In 1955 the council rejected the city manager's recommendation to apply for federal subsidies to build more public housing. Four years later he was back seeking an additional 274 units of public housing. One council member offered a resolution to place additional units on Chambers Hill, near I.M. Terrell High School, replacing the "slums" that were there. The council agreed that the existing slums needed clearing, but could not reach agreement on constructing more public housing on the land. After the Fort Worth Real Estate Board came out strongly against "the city getting in the housing business," the era of public housing projects like Cavile Place and Butler came to an end. City Manager L.P. Cookingham thereafter shifted his efforts to "private real estate interests," calling on them to "shoulder the responsibility for rebuilding substandard areas of the city."[76]

Only one white developer had already stepped up to the plate but not to rebuild sub-standard housing. What Howard G. Patterson, President of the Western Management Corporation, had in mind was creating a brand-new neighborhood of single-family homes, schools, and churches for upscale blacks. There would be no public housing units, no shotgun houses, just quality homes all with lawns and garages, neatly spaced on quiet residential streets, indistinguishable from nicer white neighborhoods. He launched his project in 1952, getting the city council to annex 135 acres of undeveloped land adjacent to the Stop Six neighborhood. The boundaries were Rosedale on the north, Ramey Ave. on the south, Stalcup on the west, and Cravens Rd. (now SE Loop 820) on the east. Naming it "Carver Heights" after the legendary black agronomist, George Washington Carver, he laid it out as a model community, what the promotional literature called "an exclusive neighborhood of restricted home-sites." Carver Heights had "protective deed restrictions" like the nicest white neighborhoods had always had, but his deed restrictions were not aimed at maintaining racial segregation but at keeping out commercial development, specifically the saloons and night clubs that had been the bane of black neighborhoods since the beginning. The city granted his deed restrictions.[77]

When it came to marketing the lots in Carver Heights, Patterson worked with L.V. Johnson, an African-American realtor. The city's black leadership got behind Patterson, even putting out flyers urging blacks to "Own a New Modern Home of your choice in LOVELY CARVER HEIGHTS." The Carver Heights Addition was an unqualified success as the first post-World-War-II suburb in Fort Worth built specifically for African Americans. While national attention focused on the "Levittowns" being built by William Levitt on the east coast, all with race restrictions, Howard Patterson was a pioneer in creating the suburban dream for African Americans. Nearly 900 houses were constructed, virtually all in the same ranch style that was so popular in white suburban developments of the day. Residents included a state representative, three city council members, and a criminal court judge in addition to numerous teachers, lawyers, and businessmen. Eventually, Carver Heights residents secured a state "historic" designation meaning the houses could not be torn down or substantially altered from their original form without state permission. Reby Cary would say many years later that they had sought the historic designation to "keep the prefab homes out," which was what the Levittown model was all about. There was one big problem with Carver Heights: it was a one-off success. Other developers did not follow Patterson's lead and build more middle-class housing for the black community.[78]

Without more middle-class black housing on the drawing boards, there was only one thing to be done: move into white neighborhoods, which would inevitably be interpreted as hostile take-overs. The experiences on the Near South Side and in Poly had shown what happened when white neighborhoods were integrated: confrontation, white flight, or both. Later research would show that there is a tipping point, *i.e.*, the percentage of minorities that whites will accept moving into the neighborhood; it is 8 percent, after which white residents pack up and move. In the 1950s, white residents in the Van Zandt and Riverside neighborhoods were not willing to wait until the percentage reached 8 percent before taking action.[79]

Both Van Zandt and Riverside bordered on historic black neighborhoods, which meant that when African-Americans went house-hunting, they did not have to look far to find something better than what they had. And closing a deal on a new home was remarkably easy because not every white home-owner felt a sense of racial solidarity. Some were willing to sell to anyone who came up with the money, and real estate agents were focused on the bottom line.

The trouble started on the Near South Side again, in an area known as the Van Zandt neighborhood, which was roughly east of Missouri Ave., south of E. Hattie, and north of E. Allen Ave. This was the same area that had been rocked by a series of bombings in 1925 and '26. Since then blacks had continued to move into the area quietly with the transformation accelerating after World War II. In February 1946 a black family bought the house at 824 E. Maddox, which happened to be the same street that had been a flashpoint of the events of 1925. Several black families now lived on the street. The house at 824 had a "history." It had been bombed "several years before" after a black family bought it and moved in. The family hurriedly moved out. Now it had a new black owner, Edward Williams. His white neighbors seemed friendly at first, but that changed two weeks later. On the night of February 28, a dynamite bomb placed on the front porch rocked the house. No one was hurt. Police conducted an investigation but the perpetrator was never caught.[80] (See story of Edward Williams, Chap. 7)

The Maddox St. bombing was just the opener. A week later a few blocks away on Missouri Ave. a bomb went off at three in the morning. This time the target was a black-owned beauty shop. The place was wrecked but no one was injured. The owner had been warned not to open, but she did so anyway after informing police of the threat. The police investigated but no arrests resulted.[81]

The transformation of the Van Zandt and Terrell Heights neighborhoods proceeded rapidly after World War II. What had once been all-white neighborhoods became mixed and then predominantly black within a few years. Mostly the transformation proceeded quietly, but still the Near South Side was hardly a model of what the city's white power structure liked to call "the Fort Worth Way" of peaceful resolution..[82]

But it was in Riverside that the racial tinderbox exploded into mass demonstration and headline news. It is one of the most wrenching and dramatic stories in Fort Worth history. The difference between Riverside and Poly (1939) or the Near South Side (1925–26, 1946) was that events in Riverside played out before a much larger audience.

The battle lines were drawn in the early 1950s when Riverside was still a quiet, leafy neighborhood just east of the Trinity, connected to downtown by the Belknap St. bridge. It was a mixture of middle-class and working-class families who sent their children to Oakhurst and Bonnie Brae elementaries and Riverside High School and did their shopping at Leonard's. They lived in neat, little framed houses with tree-shaded yards but no porches; some houses also had attached garages. It was a proud, close-knit neighborhood unmarred by vacant houses and overgrown lots.

The axes of the neighborhood were Riverside Dr. running north and south, and Belknap running east and west. The heart of the area was the intersection called "Six Points" where Belknap, Riverside Dr., and Race came together. In 1905, when only about 1,500 people called Riverside home, it was described as part of the "suburban chain encircling the city." A street car line built in 1909 provided a faster connection to the city, but Riverside's development did not really take off until Fort Worth annexed it in 1922. As late as 1950, there was still truck farming in the nearby Trinity River bottoms.[83]

By that date numerous small businesses had sprung up on Race, Sylvania, and Belknap while on the western edge of Riverside was the newer Oakhurst Addition. Also on the west was the area known as "the Rock Island Bottom," a no-man's land separating Riverside from downtown, created by the river bottom and the Rock Island railroad tracks. That area had long been home to African Americans, and as the Rock Island residents climbed up the ladder they dreamed of moving into nicer neighborhoods. They did not have to look far; Riverside was right next door geographically but another world socially.

A contributing factor to the social upheaval was Riverside's flood history. The area was hit hard by floods in 1922 and 1949. The 1949 deluge left the Rock Island and Greenway neighborhoods under water, driving their residents to look for homes elsewhere. Some white residents in Riverside also decided to leave, putting their houses up for sale before another flood came along. This threw the neighborhood open, and blacks with good jobs at the nearby steel and flour mills were interested, especially because the houses were now below-market-value, and real estate brokers like L.V. Johnson were eager to handle the sales. Later, after all the racial trouble erupted in Riverside, Johnson would defend his role, saying, "The white people came to me [to sell]. I never went to them." Regardless of who made the first move, the results were like poking a hornets' nest. Until 1953, the north end of the Riverside neighborhood, between Belknap and NE 28th, was solidly white. That was the year

Lawrence Peters, an African-American employee at Ralston Purina Mills, closed on a house at 109 North Judkins. L.V. Johnson brokered the sale.[84]

Photo 28. Silver Dollar Café

In the 1940s, the Rock Island Bottom neighborhood was a thriving community of residences and businesses, such as the Silver Dollar service station and café, owned by Albert Huey-You, managed by Mary Allen (on left). Courtesy of Mary Allen, LeCarolyn Moreland, and the Brooks family.

For the conspiracy-minded, Lawrence Peters was just the opening wedge in what the *Dallas Morning News* called a "disturbing Southern trend" —namely, the breaching of the long-standing color barrier between adjacent black and white neighborhoods by "a single Negro family" acting as the advance agent for the onslaught of "Negroes" to follow. The first sale panicked other white families to sell out and pretty soon "all or almost all white residents sell to Negroes." Another block conquered! Or at least that's the way the conspirators saw it, an insidious plot with the same tactic is repeated over and over until an entire neighborhood was taken over. According to the local Cassandras, this was exactly what had happened in the Van Zandt neighborhood; they did not want to see it happen to their neighborhood. It was no coincidence that the headquarters of the Ku Klux Klan in Fort Worth was on Riverside Dr. (intersection of Riverside Dr. and E. Lancaster). Riverside was prime recruiting ground for the KKK. Their fury was directed as much at the NAACP as at the black families moving into the neighborhood because they blamed the NAACP for orchestrating the assault. Whether the whole thing was orchestrated or spontaneous, it was entirely legal.[85]

Lawrence Peters' ordeal began as soon as he moved into his new house in August 1953 with what a Dallas newspaper euphemistically described as "vigorous protests." It would escalate as more houses on the block went up for sale and were bought by blacks. Peters' response to the hate campaign was to hunker down and ride out the storm. He installed floodlights to light up his yard at night and slept with a rifle by his side. About three months after moving in, on a Sunday night, another house on the block recently purchased by a black family was torched. Fortunately, the new owners had not moved in yet, and the fire was extinguished by the quick action of the Fire Department before it could do much damage. But that was not the end of it. Later that same night, someone attached a dynamite bomb to Peters' car, parked in front of his house. The explosion destroyed the car, "rocking the neighborhood," but did not injure anyone. If not related to it, the bombing had certainly been encouraged by a wave of home bombings in black Dallas neighborhoods in 1950 and '51. There, no group claimed credit for similar bombings, but Texas Rangers made some arrests and authorities filed charges.[86]

The Fort Worth bombing followed a similar script. No group claimed credit for blowing up Lawrence Peters' car either, and perfunctory investigations by the Fort Worth police and fire departments produced no suspects. But if the Riverside Merchants and Homeowners Association were not guilty of the bombing, they were more than willing to explain it away. Their leader dismissed it as nothing but a set-up by friends of the so-called victim to "gain sympathy for Negroes and stir up hatred." The victim himself refused to sit idly by and be accused of lying or worse; he decided to be proactive. Peters called FBI headquarters in

Washington, D.C. and somehow got put through to Director J. Edgar Hoover who "promised a [federal] investigation." No FBI agents ever showed up in Riverside, however. Meanwhile, the real estate agent who had sold Peters the house was outed and began receiving threatening letters and phone calls.[87]

When white Riverside residents couldn't run off Lawrence Peters or keep out other black families, they themselves began to bail out. Some simply moved across Sylvania into the Oakhurst Addition where whites still ruled. Those who stayed in Riverside, however, did not give up the fight. They could draw some comfort from the fact that whites still held the balance of power, controlling the neighborhood schools and the business strips on Sylvania and Race. North of the 100 block of North Judkins, Riverside was still as solidly white as ever. But Lawrence Peters was only round one. Three years later Riverside would erupt again.

Round two in the Battle for Riverside occurred on the 200 block of North Judkins, one block north of Lawrence Peters' house. In September 1956, Lloyd G. Austin moved his family (wife Macie and daughter Georgina) into a house on the all-white 200 block of North Judkins. The Austins should have been welcomed as good neighbors. They were part of the rising black middle class, a two-income family trying to escape a slum, not create one. He drove a truck for a local grain company, and she was a long-time employee of Stripling's Department Store downtown. Lloyd had grown up in the nearby Rock Island Bottom, one of a family of thirteen living in a little three-room house. "We slept on the floor on pallets we made from quilts," is the way he described his upbringing. As a boy his first job had been keeping an eye on farmers' trucks at the Jones St. public market for which the owners paid him a dime a truck. When he got the chance to move out of Rock Island Bottom, he jumped at it.[88]

The sale of his new house was brokered by Curtis Helmer, a white real estate agent with more interest in the color green than in black and white. The white residents of the block saw things differently and reacted with outrage when they saw their new neighbors moving in on Saturday morning, September 1. Things moved fast from that point. E.G. Brown, the white leader and self-appointed spokesman of the Riverside Merchants and Homeowners' Association, paid Austin a neighborly visit that same day, advising him that he and his family would never be welcome in the neighborhood and trouble would surely follow if they tried to stay. He even offered to return Austin's equity—in cash—but Austin turned him down. Before departing, Brown offered a final warning: Personally he would never be party to violence, he said, but he "could not guarantee the actions of other neighbors." The next day, Brown called a whites-only meeting at Riverside Elementary where he called the presence of the Austins the first step in "an insidious plot by the NAACP" to integrate their schools. (It was indeed a good question where the Austins intended to send their daughter to school.) He closed the meeting with a call for "peaceful protest to show the sentiment of the people." His audience was having none of it. They roared, "Let's go up and give those niggers hell and talk about it later!" Then a mob of 150 angry whites, many of them young males who were not even residents of Riverside, set off for 209 North Judkins. They gathered in the yard and spilled over into the street. Someone hung an African-American effigy from the maple tree in the front yard. (The effigy was intended as both a warning to Austin and a statement of solidarity with Mansfield whites who were at that moment fighting to keep their high school segregated.) Before long, the mob began chanting, "Nigger get out!" like fans cheering at a football game.[89]

Austin barricaded his doors and placed himself at his front window with a couple of .22-caliber rifles. He had no intention of making a last stand, so he called the police, imploring them to come protect him and his family. The dispatcher asked if anyone was hurt. "Not yet," he replied. Two white officers finally arrived, but they stood to one side refusing to intervene as the number of protestors kept growing. Their attitude also grew more belligerent as their numbers increased. Fearing that a full-blown riot was about to erupt, the officers on the scene called dispatch to ask for backup. In the meantime, reporters from all local newspapers and television stations had showed up.[90]

North Judkins presented a dramatic contrast in urban life in just a two-block stretch that included the 100 and 200 blocks. While the 200 block was filled with angry whites and nervous police officers, one block to the south across an intersection that served as a racial dividing line the street was lined with black-owned homes except for one white family. Now a group of thirty or forty black residents stood quietly at the intersection watching the situation, but making no attempt to come to Austin's aid. They no doubt realized that to do so would provoke a full-fledged street brawl. The white mob ignored the blacks gathered at the intersection and continued to focus its fury on the Austins. They did not even back down when Captain J.D. Dunwoody arrived and told them, "We can't run that Negro out of the house; it's his home!"[91]

As the situation tottered between a demonstration and a full-scale riot, a gunshot rang out. It came from the window where Lloyd Austin stood with his .22s. Depending on who is telling the story, the bullet either buried itself in the ground at the mob's feet or struck the radiator of one of their cars. Reporters on the scene believed Austin had "aimed low" although they also reported that one young man claimed the bullet had gone through the hood of his automobile. Whatever the case, the story grew in the retelling in subsequent years, taking on Wild West overtones with Austin in the role of the courageous homesteader defending his farm from a lynch mob by firing a warning shot over their heads. Whatever the truth of the matter, the shot accomplished Austin's objective of driving the crowd back, but they reacted by hurling bottles at the house. It was about this time that Police Chief Cato Hightower arrived on the scene with a dozen men. Using a bullhorn he ordered everyone to go home which finally produced the desired effect. But it was not over.[92]

For the next week, Hightower posted officers on the block. A total of ten men armed with tear-gas guns "and other weapons" patrolled the block and manned barricades at either end. They let through only persons who lived on the block and those who had legitimate business there. Demonstrators and gawkers were turned away. It had been decades since a Fort Worth cop had walked a neighborhood beat, but that was exactly what they were doing now. They would remain for a week to insure that peace had once more descended on North Judkins. The media lost interest a lot sooner.[93]

The Battle for Riverside did not end that Sunday night in September, and its effects were felt far beyond that leafy stretch of North Judkins. On Monday, E.G. Brown "and his followers" announced that they would try to get Lloyd and Macie Austin fired from their jobs. When one newspaper contacted the personnel manager at Stripling's for a statement, he called Mrs. Austin "an old and trusted employee" and said he knew nothing about her being fired. A few days later, both employers apparently caved in to public pressure because the Austins were dismissed without cause. (Lloyd subsequently got his job back after his union intervened.)[94]

Meanwhile, at the regular Tuesday night meeting of the city council, the Riverside Merchants and Homeowners' Association filled the chamber to ask that the police posted on Judkins be withdrawn because their very presence only encouraged further "Negro encroachment." The police stayed. Brown informed the council that Austin had offered to sell out for $1,350 on Monday, but was talked out of it by the NAACP trying to keep things stirred up. The situation remained tense for the remainder of the week, and the Austins were not the only target of angry whites. A bomb went off in front of real-estate agent Curtis Helmer's house. Fortunately, no one was injured.[95]

Downtown, the city council was getting desperate. They did the only thing they knew how: appoint a bi-racial, mediation committee (five whites and five blacks). The committee met with Lloyd Austin in the offices of a bank, urging him to give in "for the good of the community." Even the African-American committee members urged him to find someplace else to live. When he refused to budge, the meeting concluded on a frosty note. In the end, Lloyd and Macie Austin stayed put and did not have any more trouble. Their white neighbors either adjusted or moved out, and the black residential advance continued northward through Riverside.[96]

Lloyd Austin never saw himself as a civil rights crusader. As he later explained it, he did not set out to make history. "All we wanted to do was have a nice place to live," he told a *Star-Telegram* reporter in 2013. After his brush with history, Austin heard a higher calling. He quit his job with the grain company to get ordained as a Baptist minister. When he eventually retired in 2005 as a spry eighty-nine-year-old, he was pastor of the St. John Missionary Baptist Church in Mosier Valley, a venerable congregation with a hundred-year-old tradition. Maybe he wasn't a crusader, but Austin continued his battle for fairness and equality from the pulpit of St. John's, never forgetting his humble beginnings or his welcome to North Judkins St. in 1956.[97]

Tellingly, the racial upheaval in Riverside was scarcely covered in the Fort Worth newspapers although reporters from both the *Star-Telegram* and *Press* were on the scene during the worst of it. To find out what was happening in their own town, Fort Worth residents had to read the Dallas newspapers. It is not hard to understand why the conspiracy of silence. The two major Fort Worth papers were loathe to show the ugly underbelly of their city. Dallas editors were not so squeamish. The enforced silence served to perpetuate the myth that Fort Worth did not have race problems, only Dallas had race problems. The reality was that Fort Worth was sweeping its racial problems under the rug.

Photo 29. North Judkins St.

North Judkins St. looking south toward the 200 block. Author's photo.

Photo 30. North Judkins St.

In the early 1950s North Judkins St. was the scene of angry confrontations between white and black home-owners. The dividing line was between the 100 and 200 blocks. Fifty-plus years later the street is peaceful, but State Highway 183 (the Airport Freeway) bisects it where the black-white line used to be. This view is looking north toward the 200 block. Author's photographs.

The Battle for Riverside pitted longtime residents of one of the city's humbler neighborhoods against newcomers who were a different color and even lower on the socio-economic scale. The same clash of cultures struck another working-class neighborhood, Morningside, only without all the *sturm und drang*. Until the mid-1950s Morningside was just another lily-white Near Southside neighborhood. In the next decade it would be transformed into virtually an African-American neighborhood. The same occurred in the Polytechnic area during the same years: First one black family would move in, then another and another, until the trickle turned into a flood. Whites saw it as an invasion; blacks saw it as "opening up" the neighborhood. Either way, it always seemed to follow the same script of one house in one neighborhood at a time. Most white home-owners did not get too worked up until blacks became the majority, then they sold out and moved to a new neighborhood. It was what Jack Moseley in 1967 called "a quiet revolution in Negro housing."[98]

It was a different story in ritzier neighborhoods like Tanglewood, Ridglea, and River Crest. Those neighborhoods could keep out black interlopers simply by being too pricey; they did not have to mount an organized, openly racist resistance. The houses were expensive, property taxes and insurance rates were high, and neighborhood associations had tough rules. Blacks simply could not afford to buy a house in those areas even if they had wanted to. In Riverside, by contrast, the houses were more modestly priced, so Riverside became the first racial battleground in Fort Worth and the first all-white neighborhood to be "broken" by the rising black middle class.

That battle produced another unexpected result. To counter the efforts of the Riverside Merchants and Homeowners Association, black activists formed the Negro Citizens' Committee in 1953. Organized with no grand goals in mind or long-term strategy, the committee soon discovered it had lots more work to do than merely standing up to the Riverside Merchants and Homeowners Association; they also took on the city Recreation Department to break the all-white golf courses. In that battle they flexed their muscle by filing the 1955 lawsuit that broke the color-barrier at the city's municipal golf courses. In the early years of the modern civil rights struggle in Fort Worth, the Negro Citizens' Committee proved a valuable, local ally to the NAACP and other national civil rights organizations.[99]

And events in Riverside only turned up the heat on white home-owners in other neighborhoods not to sell to blacks. In May 1959 when Betty Crill listed her ten-room house on the South Side, where she and her mother (both white) had lived for years, her white neighbors reacted with fury. It was not that she was selling, it was that she had listed the house with a black real estate dealer, which practically guaranteed that a black family would be buying it. After the Southeast Civic League, a white home-owners' association, organized resistance to the sale, she started receiving threatening phone calls. On Friday night, May 15, a crowd of thirty people gathered menacingly in her front yard, and although they finally left without doing any damage, they had made their point. Crill was not unsympathetic, but as she explained her predicament to a Dallas reporter, "We can't rent the place, and we held out as long as we could because we didn't want to hurt the neighbors." She and her mother left, and the house remained on the market.[100]

The 1949 flood shook up the housing market in the city and not just in Riverside; the Rock Island Bottom, just downriver from Riverside, was also affected. The flood waters virtually wiped out the neighborhood whose residents were slammed twice because they did not have insurance to rebuild. They fled to Riverside and other areas not as hard hit, either displacing white residents or competing with them for affordable housing.[101]

By the late 1960s the city had six historic black neighborhoods: Lake Como, Stop Six, Riverside, the North Side, and Morningside-South Side. Already, North Side was becoming home to a large influx of Latinos, diluting the black population there until it was once again in the position of a permanent minority. The Near South Side, south of Lancaster and east of Main, would lose much of its single-family housing to freeway construction (I-30 and I-35) and expansion of the hospital district followed by "re-development" for white "yuppies." By contrast, the demographics of Como, Stop Six, and Riverside would not change much over the years. The biggest difference is that nowadays historic black neighborhoods are euphemistically referred to as "blighted" or "under-served areas of the city." They are still at the end of the line when it comes to financial investment and municipal services.

Although the historic lines between black and white neighborhoods have been all but obliterated, property taxes and zoning laws still keep most blacks out of high-end neighborhoods like Tanglewood and Overton Park. Other neighborhoods such as Wedgwood, South Hills, and Eastern Hills today have large black populations, which if they are not the majority now, will be some day based on current demographic trends. The suburban white flight of the 1950s and '60s has turned into flight behind high walls. Well-to-do whites have moved into "gated communities" concentrated in the far north and far west parts of town. The walls of those exclusive developments not only keep out criminals but also poor people and anyone else who does not fit the owners' profile.[102]

There have always been different standards for white and black neighborhoods. Not even all the civil rights progress of the 1960s changed that. In 1970, when the sort of "modular housing" that had first been introduced with Levittown in 1947, began to arrive in north Texas, Fort Worth's city manager expressed reservations about pre-fabricated construction. Was it up to the standards of traditional, custom-built housing? He warned that "the [building] technique could require changes in city codes." Significantly, however, he had no problem with modular housing going into Carver Heights, a black neighborhood, with or without code changes, only into more strictly zoned areas of the city (read that "white neighborhoods").[103]

Photo 31. Jax Beer coming to a neighborhood near you

Jax Beer, out of Jacksonville, Florida, was not considered a premier brand among whites, but had a huge presence in the black community, both as a product and as an employer. Courtesy of Tarrant County Black Historical & Genealogical Society.

Breaking the Color Barrier in Retail

The racial lines in retail were never as hard and fast as in schools, housing, and transportation. In particular, the beer and soft drink distributors aggressively courted the black community. Coca Cola, Pepsi Cola, Nehi soft drinks, Jax, Lone Star, and Schlitz beer companies, and Wonder Bread were just a few of the brands beloved by black consumers. The soft drink companies sponsored school events; the beer distributors paid regular visits to black-owned bars and night clubs, and their logos were all over the walls. The relationship was a two-way street because some of the best jobs a black man could get were driving a delivery truck or being a sales representative for one of the major distributors. They were paid well, got to wear a uniform, and could earn generous sales rewards.

Even the white downtown merchants always kept one eye on the color line and the other on the bottom line. When the color line was finally breached it was not so much due to a courageous stand by the NAACP or the Negro Citizens' Committee but to bottom-line business decisions made by the leading merchants. Marvin and O.B. (Obie) Leonard of Leonard's Department Store were the first of the big downtown store owners to repudiate segregation. Ever since opening their general merchandising store in 1918, they had made it policy to welcome all customers regardless of social or economic status. That was why they priced their goods as low as possible: to serve the broadest possible spectrum of the shopping public. They adopted the Walmart model before there was a Walmart. As a result, for forty-six years working-class folks took their business to Leonard's because they could buy practically anything and at a good price, too.[104]

Blacks also liked shopping at Leonard's. The store toed the line when it came to restrooms, drinking fountains, buying on credit, and the other essentials of Jim Crow, but blacks also knew they got good value for their dollar there, and the owners went beyond the call of duty to make African Americans feel welcome. The phenomenally popular "Toyland" that they created in the basement every Christmas dispensed with segregation, and whenever black churches had out-of-town VIPs come in, the pastors always knew they could bring their guests to Leonard's cafeteria "where Marvin let them eat for free." By contrast, Stripling Department Store's "Pink Rooster" restaurant did not even have segregated seating; they did not serve blacks at all.[105]

More importantly, Leonard's treated their black employees remarkably well. For their biography of Marvin Leonard, historians Walter and Victoria Buenger interviewed former black store employees among whom they discovered a legacy of good feelings from their days at Leonard's.

They "felt welcome there" which made them willing to overlook the routine segregation rules. Leonard's was not as upscale as Stripling's ("Fort Worth's Quality Department Store") or Monnig's, much less Meacham's or The Fair, but it did a booming business that was the envy of its competitors. Even in the 1920s when Marvin Leonard was a card-carrying member of the Ku Klux Klan, the store was never as hard-nosed about racial segregation as the other downtown stores. That line was drawn more clearly in 1956 after racial conflict erupted on North Judkins Street. Stripling's management dismissed Macie Austin who had worked at the store as an elevator operator and maid for thirteen years. When word of her firing got around, black middle-class shoppers who by this date had charge accounts with the store, cancelled those accounts in protest. This was the first civil rights boycott on record in Fort Worth history. But their numbers were too few to force Stripling's to change its attitude.[106]

A couple of blocks away, change came down from the top at Leonard's although Marvin and Obie were careful not to stick their necks out too far. They were businessmen, not crusading reformers. By the mid-1950s, Leonard's was thriving like no other downtown store, and Marvin Leonard could see the writing on the wall. Recent Supreme Court decisions and local demographic trends both suggested that Jim Crow was falling into disfavor. In a series of low-key changes he ordered the "Colored" and "Whites Only" signs taken down all over the store, and seating in both employees' and customers' cafeterias thrown open. Leonard's biographers do not pinpoint an exact date for the policy change but put the changes in the 1956–57 years. Jenkins Garrett, Marvin Leonard's long-time lawyer and advisor, provides both a month and a year: February 1960. Regardless of the exact date, Leonard's Department Store was ahead of the competition.

Garrett admitted the decision was not driven by simple altruism. At the time, black customers made up only "15 to 30% of our trade." Marvin Leonard made the call but only after thinking on it a long time. On the one hand, he didn't want to concede a significant pool of customers; on the other hand, there was always the risk that he might lose a substantial number of white customers if black customers were treated the same. In the end, the gamble paid off, and the Jim Crow walls began tumbling down, not just at Leonard's but all over downtown. Historian Tim Madigan salutes Leonard's as "the first major Fort Worth institution to abandon segregation." That is only true if by "institution" we mean retail merchants. Municipal golf courses and the FWPD had already desegregated. Still, there is no denying that Marvin and Obie Leonard led the way among downtown merchants. Jenkins Garrett recalled in an interview with Madigan that the other big merchants were "relieved" that the Leonards took the first step, thus not putting the target on their backs if it turned out to be a bad idea. Within three years, however, every downtown department store, theater, and restaurant had thrown open its doors. As civil rights leader Marion J. Brooks explained, "The business establishment decided to put profits ahead of prejudice."[107]

In the meantime, the winds of change had been sweeping through municipal government and in the words of the *Fort Worth Press*, "shattering tradition." African Americans were appointed to two of the "top three citizens' boards" for the first time ever: the Park Board and the Library Board. (The Recreation Board was the third citizens' board.) Dr. Marion J. Brooks joined the Park Board; the Rev. C.A. Holliday joined the Library Board. These were not elected positions, but Fort Worth had a strong tradition of citizen involvement in running the city so they were important positions. The Park and Library departments of the city had been quietly integrating for several years, but this was the first time blacks had been put in policy-making positions. As *The Press* said, these appointments "launched a [new] Fort Worth era."[108]

During the Jim Crow era a small group of black professionals provided all the basic needs of the black community, such as this pharmacy, *ca.* 1930s. The clothing and the neat appearance of the place show the pride that the owner took in his businesses. Courtesy of Fort Worth collector Gregory Dow.

Lonnell Cooper—Serving and Protecting[109]

By the time Lonnell Erskine Cooper died in 2011 at the age of 87, few Fort Worthers were aware of what a pioneer he had been. But the Fort Worth Police Department (FWPD) knew, especially the Black Officers' Association, because Lonnell was the last surviving member of six determined black men who broke the department's color barrier in 1953.

He was born in Fort Worth on May 24, 1923, to Oscar and Maude Cooper. The family lived in a segregated city, but Lonnell had the advantage of growing up in a home with both a mother and father. Almost as important, Oscar Cooper had a steady job that allowed him to keep food on the table and a roof over their heads. Lonnell attended I.M. Terrell High School and graduated in 1939. He began college at Prairie View A&M before World War II came along and changed everything. His nation called and he chose to join the all-white Marine Corps, the most segregated branch of the armed forces. But this was wartime, and the Marines needed a few good men. It was 1942, and Lonnell was in the first group of African Americans accepted by the Marines. It was the first of several color barriers he broke down in his lifetime. In 1945 he came home and went to work for the U.S. Public Health Service where he might have been content to retire in a nice civil service job, but he learned that the FWPD was finally hiring African Americans. When two of the initial class of four recruits quit during their probationary period, Cooper stepped up as a replacement. His obvious intelligence and military record, plus scoring a 95 on the civil service exam, got him hired. It was hardly a dream job. He successfully completed probation but still had to endure the snubs of veteran white officers, exclusion from social activities, and either no backup or a slow response in dangerous situations on the street. One by one the first class of black officers quit until by 1959 he was the only remaining black man on the force.

In November 1961 he was gunned down outside a nightclub, almost dying from two gunshot wounds before he received medical treatment. He was back at work ten months later. His "red badge of courage" even won him a measure of acceptance from his fellow officers. Still, unwelcome as a partner by white officers, he worked mostly in the youth and communications divisions during the rest of his twenty-seven-year career. In 1968 he helped set up the department's community relations division, created to avert the racial violence going on in other American cities at the time. He made sergeant in 1972, the department's first black sergeant. More than once he was recognized as "Officer of the Year" by a department that had once shunned him. He also won the Liberty

Bell Award for "encouraging freedom under the law." In 1980 he retired with honors.

But he was not done with law enforcement. He still wanted to "serve and protect." The following year he became Tarrant County's first black constable when he was elected to the new Precinct No. 8. He ran unopposed two more times before taking his badge off for good in 1987. He spent his final years an emeritus officer of the FWPD. On January 24, 2011, Lonnell Cooper died and was buried in the Dallas-Fort Worth National Cemetery alongside other military service veterans.

There was never any quit in Lonnell Cooper. Jim Ewing, in 2011 director of the community relations division that Cooper had helped create, said this about Cooper's fortitude: "The average person, being abused and shot and all of that would have just given up." Instead, his quiet strength and conscientious service coupled with a sterling character made him a role model for future generations of black young people. As Tarrant County Commissioner Roy Brooks explained, "He was one of the first that any of us black kids saw wearing a police uniform. . . . He was a mentor, an advocate, an example." One of those Cooper inspired was Douglas Wright who became Tarrant County's first black police chief with the Forest Hill Police Department. Cooper also lived long enough to see a historic marker placed in Oakwood Cemetery in 2006 honoring his trailblazing predecessor, Hagar Tucker.

NOTES

1. *Fort Worth Star-Telegram*, May 18, June 9, September 16, 1944. The EEOC was created by Title VII of the 1964 Civil Rights Act. The Commission began its work in July 1965, and one of its first acts was prohibiting such ads. James T. Patterson, *The Eve of Destruction* (New York: Basic Books, 2012), 207, 211.
2. For 1939 Juneteenth, see *Fort Worth Press*, June 20, 1939; *Fort Worth Star-Telegram*, June 19, 1939; and *Dallas Morning News*, June 20, 1939. For 1947 celebration, see *Fort Worth Press* and *Fort Worth Star-Telegram*, June 20, 1947. For Juneteenth recollections of those days, see interview with Cecil Williams, *Fort Worth Star-Telegram*, June 13, 2003.
3. For Carswell airmen, see black newspaper *Fort Worth Mind*, October 26, 1951 (reprinted in "Black History Month" chronology, *Fort Worth Star-Telegram*, February 27, 1991).
4. Edgar Deen was mayor of Fort Worth twice, 1947–1951 and 1953–55. Bayard Friedman was mayor of Fort Worth 1963–65. Jenkins Garrett was Marvin Leonard's lawyer who engineered the end of Jim Crow segregation in Leonard's Department Store. Fort Worth-born Jim Wright began his four-decade career in Congress in 1954 from Texas' 12th Congressional district despite the fervent opposition of publisher Amon Carter. In 1956, Wright refused to sign the segregationist "Southern Manifesto" with most of his Southern colleagues in Congress, marking him as a liberal and a maverick. *Fort Worth Star-Telegram*, July 24, 2004.
5. Allen (Sherrod), *Grace and Gumption*, 196–97. For Levitan, see *Dallas Morning News*, April 2, 1967.
6. Robert J. Robertson, *Fair Ways* (College Station: Texas A&M University Press, 2005), 75–76, hereafter Robertson, *Fair Ways*.
7. For golf background, see *Fort Worth Telegram*, November 16, 1902; and Mack Williams, "In Old Fort Worth: How 'Pasture Pool' Became Golf," *Fort Worth News-Tribune*, Bicentennial Ed. (Fort Worth: privately printed by Mack H. and Madeline C. Williams, 1975), 34. Robert J. Robertson, *Fair Ways*, 75–76.
8. There were actually four white municipal courses in the city: Worth Hills in the TCU area, Rockwood on Jacksboro Highway, Z. Boaz in the far west side, and Meadow on the far east side. But the petition did not

include Meadowbrook, perhaps because the neighborhood and the regular players on the course were adamantly anti-black.

9. *Fort Worth Press*, June 7, 1950. For Greenway's facilities, see Sohmer, "Rock Island Bottom," 60–61.
10. *Fort Worth Press*, June 7, 1950.
11. Harry Taylor, the City's Recreation Director, agreed with Trimble. *Fort Worth Star-Telegram* June 4, 1954. For green fees, see ibid., June 21, 1954. See also Houston *Informer*, June 26 and July 7, 1954.
12. The exact date when Fort Worth municipal courses were thrown open is not clear. Bob Ray Sanders in his book on Fort Worth photographer Calvin Littlejohn, includes a photograph purporting to show a black woman teeing it up at Worth Hills on June 19, 1951. Sanders, *Calvin Littlejohn*, 85. *Cf. Dallas Morning News*, June 13, 1954.
13. The other two boards were the Parks Board and the Library Board. *Fort Worth Press*, May 15, 1961; *Fort Worth Star-Telegram*, June 21, 1954; Robertson, *Fair Ways*, 76.
14. *Fort Worth Star-Telegram*, August 1, 1954.
15. *Fort Worth Press*, November 9, 1955.
16. The other three were James Clemons, Vernon Jenkins, and J.W. Parker. *Fort Worth Press*, November 11 and 14, 1955.
17. Meadowbrook had been a private country club until the 1930s when it went bankrupt and was taken over by the city. *Fort Worth Press*, November 10, 1955; and May 13, 1956.
18. Signed into law by President Eisenhower in June 1956, this law subsidized a 42,500-mile system of limited-access highways linking all major cities in the country, including I-30 and I-35 through Fort Worth. For impact on Harmon golf course, see *Fort Worth Star-Telegram* February 5, 1957. For Douglass Park, see Richard Selcer, "Historic Marker Application for Douglass and McGar Parks," Vertical files, Fort Worth Public Library, Central Branch, Local History, Genealogy, & Archives Unit.
19. *Fort Worth Star-Telegram*, April 27, 1991, pp. 1, 27 A, and 10B. *Dallas Morning News*, May 2 and 9, 1991.
20. *Fort Worth Press*, November 10, 1955. For Beaumont, see Shabazz, *Advancing Democracy*, 170–71.
21. Dixie Park had been a playground for the local black community since at least 1932. Ironically, the name "Dixie" with all its Deep South, racist connotation, was quite popular for black recreation venues—*e.g.*, Dixie Theater, Dixie Tavern, Dixie Park. "Federal Writers' Project," pp. 21,389–90 (microfiche).

22. The five neighborhood white pools were at Kellis Park, Sycamore Park, Forest Park, Marine Creek Park, and Sylvania. In 1956 the newest of these was twenty years old, and their operation constituted a huge drain on the Recreation Department's annual budget. The Dixie Park address was 1125 Fabons St. *Fort Worth Press*, June 7, 1956.
23. For Negro Athletic Park and Greenway, see *Fort Worth City Directory*, 1926–27 and 1928. For Mosier Valley, see "Mosier Valley. . . Finally Gets a Park," *Fort Worth Star-Telegram*, February 12, 2014.
24. Jones, *Renegades*, 285; *Fort Worth Press*, June 10, 1954.
25. W. Marvin Dulaney, *Black Police in America* (Bloomington: Indiana University Press, 1996), 35–36; *Dallas Morning News*, October 19, 1937; Bob Ray Sanders, "Commentary," *Fort Worth Star-Telegram*, March 2, 2003. Galveston even had "negro detectives" in addition to blacks on the uniformed force. *Fort Worth Star-Telegram*, July 24, 1914. For "undercover," see *Fort Worth Press*, October 1, 1952.
26. Lynn W. Landrum, "Police Protection," *Dallas Morning News*, October 21, 1946.
27. Those first, ultimately rejected applicants were Clarence Arthur Pollard, Ollice Maloy Thomas, Lawrence Leroy Thomas, Edward Leroy Willis, and Robert B. Howard. *Fort Worth Press*, February 24, 1948. For Dysart, see *Fort Worth Star-Telegram*, December 12, 1949.
28. *Fort Worth Press*, October 1, 1952. Bob Ray Sanders, "Commentary," *Fort Worth Star-Telegram*, March 2, 2003. For Anderson, see *Fort Worth Defender and Baptist Herald*, October 2, 1952.
29. Detective candidates had to pass another exam besides the civil service exams to make the squad. It has been suggested by FWPD veterans that the first black detectives were personally promoted by Chief Hightower outside the regular chain of command as a concession to racial sensitivities. FWPD records are silent on the subject. For Hightower's action, see *Fort Worth Press*, October 1, 1952; and March 26, 1957. The names come from email correspondence with retired Fort Worth officer J.D. Roberts, June 28, 2013.
30. Bob Ray Sanders, "Commentary," ibid., March 2, 2003; Sanders, *Calvin Littlejohn*, 75.
31. In 2013 a former officer in the department had the same complaint: not enough qualified black candidates. There must be a reason things have not changed in 46 years. Jack Moseley, "The Negro in Fort Worth. . . Getting a Job . . . and Keeping It," No. 2 in a 4-part series, *Fort Worth Press*,

August 28, 1967, hereafter Moseley with the title, number, and date of the article.

32. The other three were receptionist, switchboard operator, and clerk, low-level positions granted, but still ground-breaking. *Dallas Morning News*, January 2, 1959; and November 10, 1963. For Malloy's history-making turn, see *Fort Worth Press*, October 4, 1959. Following the *Sweatt vs. Painter* Supreme Court decision (1950), Mallory was one of several black law students who enrolled for the 1950–51 school year. For an overview of the decision, see W. Paige Keeton, "Sweatt vs. Painter," *New Handbook of Texas*.
33. On May 17, 1954, the Court handed down the first part of the famous decision that barred racial segregation in the nation's public schools, the result of a suit brought by the NAACP on behalf of eleven-year-old Linda Brown. The second part of the decision, the implementation order, came on May 31, 1955. These are known collectively as "Brown I" and "Brown II." The Court's ruling did not set a deadline and left implementation up to local school boards and state judges, saying only that "a prompt and reasonable start" should be made "with all deliberate speed." This wording became the loophole that many school districts used to escape or at least delay indefinitely the Court order. For a good overview of a very complicated matter, see John A. Kirk, "Crisis at Central High School," *History Today* 57, no. 9 (September 2007); 23–29. *Fort Worth Press*, May 18, 1954. For "outstanding system," see *Fort Worth Press*, May 11, 1956.
34. In 1958, Eagle Mountain school district merged with Saginaw to form a single district. For Eagle Mountain and Grapevine, see Bill Fairley, "Tarrant Chronicles," *Fort Worth Star-Telegram*, February 10, 1999. *Fort Worth Press*, May 18, 1954.
35. *Fort Worth Press*, May 18, 1954.
36. *Dallas Morning News*, July 3, 1951.
37. In 1957 Kirkpatrick and Como (black) high schools opened to relieve some of the pressure on I.M. Terrell. "De-segregation of Fort Worth Schools," vertical files in Billy W. Sills Archives. For school board quote, see *Fort Worth Star-Telegram*, August 9, 1956.
38. *Fort Worth Press*, May 18, 1954. For axing black teachers, see Goldstein, *Teacher Wars*, 118.
39. *Fort Worth Press*, July 6, 1956.
40. For a discussion of the high school plan, see Bob Ray Sanders, "FW Schools Have Come a Long Way in 60 Years," *Fort Worth Star-telegram*, May 18, 2014.

41. *Dallas Morning News*, September 4, 1956.
42. In 1955 the Little Rock School Board opened Horace Mann High School to blacks while allowing white students to transfer out to another, all-white school. In February 1956 the NAACP sued the school board. Then on the morning of September 4, 1957, a group of nine black students attempted to integrate all-white Central High School. When they were turned away by a white mob of 400 protesters backed by Arkansas National Guardsmen, the first school crisis of the modern civil rights era was launched. Twenty-one days later the students returned, this time backed by troops of the 101st Airborne. For full story of Little Rock, see Elizabeth Jacoway, *Turn Away Thy Son* (New York: The Free Press, 2006). L. Clifford Davis' story is related in *Fort Worth Star-Telegram*, May 9, 2014. Davis began his civil rights crusade in Arkansas in 1947 before moving to Fort Worth. In 2014 the Tarrant County Bar Association honored Davis's 65-year-career with its Blackstone Award for a professional lifetime of "integrity and courage."
43. For all the maneuvering by the FWISD and NAACP in Fort Worth, one must read the *Dallas Morning News*, August 24 and September 5, 1956.
44. *Dallas Morning News*, April 5, 1959.
45. *Fort Worth Press*, October 1 and 2, 1959.
46. *Dallas Morning News*, September 5, 1963.
47. *Dallas Morning News*, September 5, 1963.
48. *Dallas Morning News*, September 5, 1963.
49. Bill Fairley, "Tarrant Chronicles," *Fort Worth Star-Telegram*, May 17, 2000.
50. "De-segregation of Fort Worth Schools," vertical files, Billy W. Sills Archives.
51. Information derived from Little Tommy Tucker Pre-School promotional literature for the 1962-63 school year. Their slogan was, "Your child's home away from home." Personal Collections of Fort Worth's Dalton Hoffman.
52. This material is based on extensive research done by Fort Worth researcher and archivist Max Hill who is writing a book on the subject of Fort Worth entertainment.
53. For Lonnell Cooper et al., see Bob Ray Sanders, "One of Fort Worth's First Is Also One of Its Finest," *Fort Worth Star-Telegram*, March 2, 2003. For school desegregation, see ibid., August 9, 1956. For Wills, see Madigan, "Out at Home," Part 3 in a 7-part series, "The Color of Hate," ibid., October 8, 2002; and Guinn, *Panthers*, 107-08.

54. Richard Lingeman, *The Noir Forties* (New York: Nation Books, 2012), 69-73, hereafter Lingeman, *Noir Forties. Dallas Morning News*, December 13, 1951.
55. *Dallas Morning News*, December 18, 1955.
56. The "Chitlin' Circuit" was a chain of black-operated venues across the country where rising black acts played segregated nightspots before raucous crowds for small paychecks. It emerged informally in the 1930s and included stops from Indianapolis to Houston. Preston Lauterbach, *The Chitlin' Circuit, And the Road to Rock 'n' Roll* (New York: W.W. Norton, 2011), 10, 89, 159. Lingeman, *Noir Forties*, 75.
57. Ray Sharpe had a national hit in 1962 with "Linda Lu." Regarding the acoustics at the North Side Coliseum, *The Critic* (black newspaper) praised the coliseum as "the ideal place for concerts," but recollections of others are that the acoustics were not that good and standards in 1915 may have been different than decades later. See *The Critic*, December 18, 1915. Sanders, *Calvin Littlejohn*, 159, 160, 165. Mark A. Nobles, *Fort Worth's Rock and Roll Roots* (Charleston, SC: Arcadia Publishing, 2011), 26, 27, 30, hereafter Nobles, *Rock and Roll.*
58. Program for 1950 season comes from newspaper advertising. See reporting and advertising in *Dallas Morning News*, February 23, September 7, October 4, 1949; and March 26, 1950.
59. Key dates and programming in Fort Worth's black radio history come from www.dfwRetroplex.com and www.DFWRadioHistory.com.
60. For Clemons, see *Fort Worth Press*, October 6, 1963. For Thomas, see obituary, *Fort Worth Star-Telegram*, January 1, 2013.
61. Thomas obituary, *Fort Worth Star-Telegram*, January 1, 2013. www.DFWRadioHistory.com.
62. Obituary, *Fort Worth Star-Telegram*, January 1, 2014.
63. Obituary, *Fort Worth Star-Telegram*, January 1, 2014.
64. Obituary, *Fort Worth Star-Telegram*, January 1 and 2 (electronic), 2014. For Sojourner Truth Theater Guild, see Jones, *Renegades*, 289.
65. In his 1956 visit, Louis had lunch at I.M. Terrell High School, another historic moment in a long series of historic moments at the school. Sanders, *Calvin Littlejohn*, 167, 172. *Dallas Morning News*, July 11 and August 3, 1953.
66. Ashe (1943–1993) won 35 professional titles before retiring in 1980. He is also the only African American male to date to win a U.S. Open singles title. *Fort Worth Star-Telegram*, "Time Frames," February 17, 2014.

67. The quote comes from newspaper columnist Lynn W. Landrum, "Negro Housing," *Dallas Morning News*, January 17, 1947. Unfortunately, Landrum's voice was not echoed in the Fort Worth newspapers.
68. For Westside flight, see Doggett, ""Survey," 6. Most black residential pockets, such as Chambers Hill, had no distinct identity, so their history cannot be easily traced. Not so the Rock Island bottom. See Sohmer, "Rock Island Bottom."
69. Sohmer, "Rock Island Bottom," 83. For a general discussion of postwar federal housing policy, see Scott Greer, *Urban Renewal and American Cities* (Indianapolis, IN: Bobbs-Merrill, 1965).
70. Landrum, "Thinking Out Loud," *Dallas Morning News*, January 6, 1951. Robert Talbert, *Cowtown Metropolis: Case Study of a City's Growth and Structure* (Fort Worth: Texas Christian University Press, 1956), 188.
71. For a typical black family outing on the Near South Side in 1961, see Phyllis Allen, "Turn Back Time," *Fort Worth Star-Telegram*, September 8, 2007.
72. *Fort Worth Press*, October 15, 1959.
73. *Fort Worth Press*, October 15 and 23, 1959. *Fort Worth Star-Telegram*, June 7, 2015.
74. 98 percent of the 1,655 families (6,910 individuals) living in Como in 1967 were black. Moseley, "City's Negro Population Quiet, Busy" (No. 1), August 24, 1967. Victoria and Walter L. Buenger, *Texas Merchant: Marvin Leonard and Fort Worth* (College Station: Texas A&M University Press, 1998), 141–42, hereafter Buenger, *Texas Merchant.*
75. *Fort Worth Press*, October 15, 1959. Austin quote comes from Jim Jones, "Beloved Pastor Returning to Church for Celebration," *Fort Worth Star-Telegram*, June 29, 2013, hereafter Jones, "Beloved Pastor."
76. *Fort Worth Press*, October 15, 23, and 30, 1959.
77. Reby Cary, *Carver Heights* (Fort Worth: privately published, 2010), 1–2, hereafter Cary, *Carver Heights*. For advertising copy, see *The Fort Worth Mind*, August 17, 1956, in "Carver Heights" vertical file, Local History, Archives, and Genealogy Unit, Central Branch, Fort Worth Library. Bob Ray Sanders, "Fort Worth's Historic Carver Heights," *Fort Worth Star-Telegram*, November 27, 2010, hereafter Sanders, "Carver Heights."
78. Cary, *Carver Heights*, 1–2. Note: Contrary to the author's sweeping claim, Carver Heights was not "the first black community in Fort Worth where whites never lived." (p. 1) Even discounting historic slum districts like "Little Africa," that honor still belongs to the Booker T. Washing-

ton Addition (1907). See Chap. 4. Sanders, "Carver Heights." For Cary on "prefab," see *Fort Worth Star-Telegram*, September 25, 2014.

79. For an explanation of the 8 percent figure, see "The Happy Façade of Race," *U.S. News & World Report*, April 8, 2002, p. 8.
80. As in the 1925-26 series of bombings, this one was reported in *The Press* but not the *Star-Telegram*. *Fort Worth Press*, March 1, 1946.
81. The second bombing was reported in both major Fort Worth dailies. *Fort Worth Press*, March 4, 1946 and *Fort Worth Star-Telegram*, March 4, 1946.
82. *Fort Worth Press*, July 6, 1956.
83. *Fort Worth Telegram*, June 25, 1905. *Dallas Morning News*, June 15, 1909
84. Sanders, *Calvin Littlejohn*, 82–84 (with photographs). For Johnson, see *Dallas Morning News*, November 18, 1953; and July 15, 1969.
85. *Dallas Morning News*, September 3 and 4, 1956. For motivation, see Jones, "Beloved Pastor."
86. The wave of Dallas bombings started in February 1950 and lasted into 1951. Shabazz, *Advancing Democracy*, 105–06.
87. While Peters' phone call is reported in the newspaper, it seems unlikely that he was put through to the Great Man himself, but even if it was, it is doubtful he got any sympathy. The legendary FBI Director was himself a racist. For Peters' story, see *Dallas Morning News*, November 3, 5, 6, and 18, 1953; and September 3, 1956. See also Tim Madigan, "Showdown on Judkins Street," *Fort Worth Star-Telegram*, October 6, 2002, Part 1 in 7-part series on "How the Jim Crow Era Shamed and Shaped Our City," pp. 1 and 16-22A, hereafter Madigan, "Showdown."
88. *Dallas Morning News*, September 3, 4, and 5, 1956. Jones, "Beloved Pastor."
89. Jones, "Beloved Pastor." *Dallas Morning News*, September 3 and 4, 1956.
90. *Dallas Morning News*, September 3 and 4, 1956.
91. *Dallas Morning News*, September 3 and 4, 1956.
92. An unidentified Dallas reporter believed the shot had been fired into the ground while acknowledging that a white youth claimed the shot hit his car. *Dallas Morning News*, September 4, 1956. That youth was later identified and interviewed by the *Fort Worth Star-Telegram*'s Tim Madigan. His name was Stephen Shoemaker, and he still insisted forty years later that the bullet struck the radiator of his "prized, two-door Chevy." See Madigan, "Showdown," 19A.
93. *Dallas Morning News*, September 4, 1956.
94. Ironically, Stripling's prided itself on being enlightened. They had liberal hiring policies when it came to blacks and advertised in the black

community, including the I.M. Terrell High School Annual and the *Lake Como Weekly*. Madigan, "Showdown," 19 and 21A.

95. *Dallas Morning News*, September 5, 1956. Madigan, "Showdown," 19 and 21A.
96. Jones, "Beloved Pastor." Madigan, "Showdown," 19 and 21A. *Dallas Morning News*, September 5, 1956.
97. Austin was pastor of St. John Missionary Baptist Church from 1964 to 2005. Thereafter he was pastor emeritus and a popular guest preacher at other black churches in the area. *Fort Worth Star-Telegram*, February 12, 2014. Jones, "Beloved Pastor;" and December 22, 2014, "After 111 Years, Fort Worth Church Knows It Belongs."
98. The existence of a master plan or strategy has never been proven, but some white observers thought they detected a "pattern," and Paul Sims, the black leader of the Community Action Program, seemed to admit as much to a reporter in 1967. Moseley, "Negro Has Come a Long Way in Housing" (No. 3), August 27, 1967.
99. *Fort Worth Star-Telegram*, June 21, 1954.
100. *Dallas Morning News*, May 17, 1959.
101. Sohmer, "Rock Island Bottom," 75–76. For lack of insurance, see *Fort Worth Star-Telegram*, May 18, 1949.
102. Moseley, "City's Negro Population Quiet, Busy" (No. 1), August 24, 1967. For re-development of Southside, see *Fort Worth Star-Telegram*, July 25, 2003 and June 19, 2006; and Dan McGraw, "The South (side) Rises Again," *Fort Worth Weekly*, June 10-16, 2009. For "underserved," see *Fort Worth Star-Telegram*, December 1, 2004; and February 12, 2014. For "blighted," see ibid., June 4, 2005.
103. The appeal of modular housing was that it could lower the cost of house construction by thousands of dollars. The reservations concerned how sturdy and durable the units were. *Dallas Morning News*, March 19, 1970.
104. The full albeit admiring story of the Leonard brothers is told in Buenger, *Texas Merchant*.
105. Buenger, *Texas Merchant*, 118, 144–45, and 153. For many years Leonard's, like other downtown retailers, did not give credit to black shoppers. At different dates, each store changed its policy so that African Americans could get a credit card. Historically, not granting credit cards to blacks was standard retail practice in the South. For "Toyland," see ibid., 144.

106. For Marvin Leonard, the KKK and black preachers, see Buenger, *Texas Merchant,* 64–66. For Macie Austin and Stripling's, see Madigan, "Showdown," p. 19A. For Buenger's views, see Madigan, "Signs of Change," 6th of a 7-part series, "The Color of Hate," ibid., October 12, 2002, p. 8F.
107. For the story of Leonard's history-making change, see Buenger, *Texas Merchant,* 118, 144–45; and Tim Madigan, "Signs of Change," Part 6 in the series, ibid., October 12, 2002, pp. 1, 6-8F. For Brooks, see Buenger, *Texas Merchant,* 143.
108. *Fort Worth Press,* May 21, 1961.
109. Sources: Christopher Evans, "A Drive through History—Two African-American Brothers," *Fort Worth Star-Telegram,* March 14, 1993; and Obituary, ibid., January 26, 20011; Bob Ray Sanders, "Commentary" (editorial), ibid., March 2, 2003. Vertical file, Fort Worth Public Library, Central Branch, Local History, Genealogy, & Archives Unit; and www.findagrave.com ("Find a Grave Memorial" #64743808).

Chapter 10

Jim Crow R.I.P.

The Later Civil Rights Years

The King Comes To Fort Worth

1963 was the year of the historic 250,000-person March on Washington that climaxed with Martin Luther King, Jr.'s "I Have a Dream" speech at the Lincoln Memorial. Years later, Fort Worth blacks would look back on 1963 as "the year the [civil rights] movement began" although few were aware of the planned march and Fort Worth did not send a delegation. Fort Worth was largely insulated from the national civil rights movement at this point. Among those who did attend was Lenora Rolla who was in Chicago at the time and traveled to Washington from there. It changed her life.[1]

According to Rolla, the civil rights movement almost passed Fort Worth by. When she returned home from Washington, D.C. (riding on a segregated train), she was "energized" to bring the fight to Fort Worth. Her dedication to change elevated her in the eyes of the local black community, but the march changed nothing in the near run; it was just an item in the newspapers. No civil rights marches or sit-ins occurred in Fort Worth. The Southern Christian Leadership Conference and Urban League were not even represented in Fort Worth while the NAACP and NCC kept low profiles and played by the rules. To their credit, city fathers were not totally insensitive to the racial issues of the day. They made sincere attempts to build bridges to the black community. In 1956, 1960, and 1963, three different mayors appointed bi-racial "commissions" to help ease the transition from Jim Crow in the wake of the Supreme Court's *Brown* decision (1954). They tapped "responsible" community leaders of both races to serve on these commissions, with "responsible" meaning they were not only respected but unlikely to rock the boat by demanding immediate change. Each of these commissions opted for the carrot over the stick. While white members urged white businesses to open their doors to blacks, black members urged their people to be calm and patient—the same message blacks had heard since emancipation.[2]

Fort Worth remained peaceful but hardly progressive. Later, some white residents would applaud how the city's power elite handled desegregation. Ruth Castillon, the first woman reporter at the *Star-Telegram,* told an interviewer years later, "I think it's great that Fort Worth and the *Star-Telegram* could do so many things without making big headlines." Castillon and most of her white peers saw nothing wrong with taking it slow and easy. But for those on the other side of the racial divide, change could not come fast enough. One black community leader later said of those years, "One reason Fort Worth has been free of racial violence is that we have not had radical Negro ministers," by which she meant the kind of church leaders who led marches and organized boycotts.[3]

One of the most "radical" black church leaders of the 1950s, Martin Luther King, Jr., was actually in Fort Worth three years after the success of the Montgomery Bus Boycott that made him a national figure. He was in Fort Worth in October 1959 at the invitation of a group of Brite Divinity School professors who shared his faith in the social gospel. King was not on a speaking tour; he was here by invitation. He spoke to a predominantly black audience at the normally segregated Majestic Theater (1101 Commerce) on October 29, which by that date was no longer a first-run movie house. On this night the Majestic relaxed its long-standing, whites-only policy, making general seating available to African Americans for the first time. The place was only about one-third filled with about 400 turning out to hear him speak on the topic, "A Great Time to Be Alive." Local lore says that the crowd was so small not because the speaker was relatively unknown but because blacks were "afraid they'd get fired if somebody found out they went." The evening also featured noted African-American gospel singer and hometown celebrity Francine Morrison performing.[4]

Before his appearance, King visited with a small group of civil rights activists and church members in the home of Harold and Alberta Lunger. Dr. Harold Lunger was a Brite Divinity School professor at TCU who lived in the Worth Hills neighborhood near TCU. King's visit inspired an entire body of popular lore in the later telling and retelling, after he had become a martyr to the Great Cause. Part of black lore involves what this group said or what that group thought, and is unverifiable today. Another part of the lore surrounding that visit is admiration for the courage it took for the Lungers to host King in an "all-white neighborhood." At the time of his visit, King's agenda included recruiting young black ministers to join a new civil rights organization he was spearheading: the Southern Christian Leadership Conference. Sitting in the Lungers' living room, he appealed to the Lungers and their friends and colleagues to put their religious faith to work in the cause of a great social movement: racial equality. Despite the warm welcome he received from Fort Worth's black community on that occasion, King's visit scarcely stirred a ripple in history. This was the only time he ever visited Fort Worth. Only years later would people talk about that visit in awed terms.[5]

Taking Down Jim Crow Brick by Brick

The Jim Crow barriers would eventually come down, although whether it was the work of bi-racial commissions or powerful men working behind the scenes is hard to say. In the latter category were the movers and shakers who directed city affairs from their perch in the Fort Worth Club eleven floors above Seventh St. (306 West Seventh). It has almost been forgotten with the passage of time that the tone of race relations in those days was set not at city hall but in the Fort Worth Club where some of the city's most powerful men gathered, known to critics and admirers alike as "the Seventh Street Gang." Its membership included bankers, retail merchants, oil men, and newspaper publishers. Their names constituted a Who's Who of Fort Worth: H.B. "Babe" Fuqua; J. Lee Johnson, Jr.; W.K. Stripling (son of W.C. Stripling); Marvin Leonard; Sid Richardson; and Amon Carter to name a few. One pair of authors say they played "the decisive role" in desegregating downtown. In September 1956 they attempted to mediate the North Judkins St. conflict. Five members of the Seventh St. Gang and five black leaders convened with the Austins at the First National Bank to try to resolve things amicably. The black leaders were carefully chosen to include only moderate men from the black upper class who had long intermingled with the white establishment and were as interested in avoiding confrontation as the Seventh Street Gang. Discussion and mediation of racial issues basically meant the blacks "seeing reason" and giving in on issues like housing, transportation, and access to downtown stores and restaurants. The leader of the negotiation with the Austins in 1956 was First National Bank President J. Lee Johnson, Jr. It was his bank, not the Club, where the negotiation was held, perhaps because blacks were not allowed in the Club except as hired staff.[6]

In the end it took more than the titans of the Fort Worth Club to end Jim Crow; it took the collective efforts of ordinary folks of both races —courageous African Americans willing to take a stand and "righteous whites" willing to dismantle Jim Crow because it was the right thing to do, not because they were pressured by the Seventh Street Gang or ordered to do so by Washington, D.C. One of the first whites to speak out was Madeleine Williams, a newspaper reporter working for the *Star-Telegram* in 1950 who was ordered by her editor, Cullum Greene, to write a piece on the annual Juneteenth celebration. Instead of turning in a generic story on how much fun blacks had on "their" day, she began asking questions at city hall. "What law says Negroes can't use the city parks except on Juneteenth? What city ordinance?" The answer from the city attorney was "no law" and "no ordinance." It was just the way things had always been done. That's how she wrote her story, and that's the way the newspaper published it. Looking back years later, she called it, "the most far-reaching, unmentioned story of my newspaper career."[7]

Then there were a few downtown store managers. One managed one of the Big Three movie houses located on the namesake street (aka, "theater row") where the Seventh Street Gang held sway. In the mid-1960s this theater manager broke the color barrier by quietly hiring the first black employee on theater row. He might have assigned her to janitorial duties behind the scenes, but he put her out front, in the ticket window and behind the concessions counter. Just as important, he backed her 100 percent when some white patrons resisted buying their popcorn from her. The manager of Fort Worth's Piccadilly Cafeteria on Houston was no crusader either, but he quietly served black customers even though his long-time white customers were shocked at seeing a black face that did not belong to a bus boy or a server behind the steam tables. Local managers like these two could make all the difference in the world. By comparison, the hard-nosed racist attitude of the manager of the Dallas Piccadilly Cafeteria in 1964 provoked that city's largest civil rights demonstration of the decade. [8]

Another of those righteous whites was Don Taylor, the golf pro at the city's Worth Hills Golf Course (where TCU's fraternity and sorority houses, baseball and soccer fields, and running track are now located). In 1959, four years after the city's public courses were thrown open to blacks, most of those courses still made black golfers feel unwelcome. Not Worth Hills thanks to Taylor. One evening on the way into the clubhouse he noticed two black golfers on the practice greens. He walked over and asked them, "You want to play out here [meaning the links]?"

Responded one, "I didn't know if we could."

Said Taylor, "You fellows can play out here anytime you want to." From then on there were never any questions at Worth Hills about the course being booked up or popular tee times being unavailable. As Orville Person, one of the golfers who encountered Taylor that day, told an interviewer many years later, "I felt welcomed."[9]

TCU chipped away at segregation in its own quiet way. Back in 1935 when "Jim Crow" was practically a member of the board at most schools, TCU became the first white college or university in the South to invite a black debate team to campus. TCU's debate team challenged the legendary Wiley College Forensic Society, who would lose just one intercollegiate contest between 1930 and 1940. The Horned Frogs in those same years were better known for their football teams than their debate teams. As hosts, TCU's students and faculty were gracious and welcoming. (Wiley won the debate.) Sixteen years later, TCU was again in the vanguard when it offered extension courses to black airmen at Carswell Air Force base. Brite Divinity School, part of TCU's campus, began admitting African Americans even before its parent university did. In athletics TCU also stepped out. In 1965 the university gave a basketball scholarship to James Cash, making him the first black basketball player in the Southwest Conference. (He graduated with a degree four years later.) In their commitment to racial equality the TCU family showed themselves to be quite progressive over the years.[10]

Which is not to say TCU was a paragon of progressivism when it came to race. The board of trustees did not change its policy on admitting black students until January 1964, and two of the thirty-two trustees adamantly opposed the change. Chancellor James Moudy, recalling the historic decision years later, gave them the benefit of the doubt, saying only that "They either didn't think it was the right time to admit blacks, or they didn't think blacks belonged at TCU at all." At the time, only TCU and Rice of all the schools in the Southwest Conference were still 100 percent segregated.[11]

In the meantime, blacks were not waiting for the white establishment to throw open the doors; they were busy fighting battles on several fronts, including segregated city buses. In 1944, an unnamed, twenty-six-year-old black woman objected to being asked to move to the back of the bus to make room for white riders. When the white driver attempted to move her forcibly, she scratched his face. Police arrested her at the next stop, and she was charged with disturbing the peace, which was a lighter charge than she might have faced. A few years later, Fort Worth even had its own Rosa Parks, the famous instigator of the Montgomery bus boycott (1955–56). Four years before the world heard of Rosa Parks, Fort Worth's Essie B. Sturges refused to move to the back of a Fort Worth bus. The date was December 7, 1951, a Friday, and she had just boarded the packed bus at the Lake Como stop. When a vacant seat opened up near the front at the next stop, she grabbed it. A white girl got on at the same time, and the driver told her to move to the back. When she refused, he got off and called the police. They came and arrested Essie for violating Sections 4-6, Chapter 10 of the City Code titled "Separation of the Races." She was released after posting a $10 bond, and trial was set for December 28 in corporation court. Like Parks, Sturges was a seamstress and some would say even resembled Parks. Also like Parks, she was more than a simple domestic looking for a seat on a bus. Sturges was a musician and a writer strongly committed to civil rights. Something odd happened when she got to court. Nearly a hundred supporters greeted her, filling Judge Gilmartin's courtroom. City prosecutor Tom Chapman did not want to prosecute the case, stating that "the evidence was insufficient to establish a case." The Judge dismissed the charges on the spot, and city fathers chalked up another victory for "the Fort Worth way," also known as "quiet diplomacy." Maybe, maybe not. Essie Sturges still filed a civil rights suit in federal court against the Fort Worth Transit Company. Ultimately, however, the case must have been dismissed because no record of it can be found.[12]

There would be no boycott of the Fort Worth bus system. Like Parks, Sturges challenged Jim Crow on the most basic level, public transportation, but unlike Parks she did not change history. So Rosa Parks is honored today as the only woman ever to "lie in honor" in the U.S. Capitol rotunda while Essie Sturges has been largely forgotten. Fort Worth buses went right on segregating blacks and white, just like the department stores and public schools.

The city revisited its segregationist policies on public transportation nearly sixty years after the issue first arose with regards to street cars. By 1962 nothing much had changed since the 1905 city council ordered seating on street cars to be segregated. When buses replaced street cars, it seemed reasonable to those in authority to continue the same policy. Now, nearly sixty years after the law had been laid down, it took simple economics to bring about change. Segregated seating ended more because the ridership on city buses had changed than because official attitudes about racial mixing had changed. By the 1960s the city bus system was mainly being used by black residents who could not afford an automobile. A white bus driver, Frank Foster, years later recalled those days this way: "Integration on the buses was so gradual you hardly noticed it." In 1962 it seemed only natural when the city hired its first black bus driver, Willis Pace. He had already put in eighteen years with the city as a janitor with the transportation department when he got his break. In his new job he blossomed, and his regulars loved him. Black riders would wait patiently at the stops as other buses came and went just so they could ride on his bus. They knew they would be treated with respect, and they considered it "an honor" to ride with him.[13]

The Fort Worth City Council was slow to get on board with the civil rights movement although not as slow as the FWPD and FWISD. In fact the gentlemen who ran those agencies were missing in action for most of the 1950s. When racial problems came up, they deferred to the Seventh Street Gang. The solution was not simply getting a black member on the city council. Operating under the council's purview were a score of "citizens' boards" overseeing the day-to-day operations of the various departments. The big three citizens' boards, so-called because they operated largely independent of the council, were the Parks, Recreation, and Library boards. Blacks had been appointed to other boards over the years, but not the big three. Not until the spring of 1961 did the council even take up the question of appointing "a Negro" to one of those boards. At the time, one unnamed councilman said he knew of "several Negro citizens who would make good board members" without naming any names. Attention focused on either the Park or Recreation departments as areas that blacks would know more about, but nothing came of it for several more years. Slow and steady was the Fort Worth mantra.[14]

The low-key nature of the civil rights movement in Fort Worth did not mean that nothing changed, only that much of the change was effected by ordinary citizens stepping up and doing the right thing even if sometimes reluctantly. While other cities were going up in flames or experiencing clashes between the authorities and angry demonstrators in the '60s, no one in Fort Worth was standing in the schoolhouse doorway or torching neighborhoods. Good people quietly accepted the need for change and took action, people like Marvin Leonard and Garrett Jenkins, the pair who first broke the color barrier among downtown Fort Worth merchants by taking down the "Colored" and "Whites Only" signs in Leonard's Department Store. [15]

Seeking to avoid confrontation and violence, however, Fort Worth's black leadership may have been too accommodating. They were always willing to meet at the Fort Worth National Bank or some other bastion of white power to compromise, to delay, to "reason together" in the words of Martin Luther King, Jr. What they were not ready to do was march in the streets, sit in at lunch counters, picket country clubs, or get themselves arrested for civil disobedience. They were not spineless men, just cautious and law-abiding. One contemporary, Paul Sims, said, "Many Negroes do not want to be considered pushy by the whites." In speaking of the older generation, he explained that they had grown up in a maids-and-chauffeur culture which taught them to bow and scrape and bite their tongues. Dr. Marion Jack Brooks, for instance, was no angry young man but a middle-aged physician who was all about "supporting the community" and "organizing" people. When Martin Luther King, Jr. was delivering his "I Have a Dream" speech in Washington, D.C. in August 1963, Brooks and his five children were protesting not in Fort Worth but outside the governor's mansion in Austin. Dr. Brooks could never be a fire-breathing militant although he belonged to two of the most militant groups of the era, the Black Panthers and the Student Non-violent Coordinating Committee. It was probably because of those associations that local FBI agents kept an eye on him.[16]

Dr. J.M. Burnett was another mild-mannered pillar of the black community. In 1956 he was invited to join the mediation group attempting to defuse the Judkins St. situation. He sided with the whites, urging Lloyd Austin to give in. George Flemmings, leader of the Fort Worth chapter of the NAACP, spoke at school board and city council meetings and filed lawsuits trying to get the city to do the right thing. Lenora Rolla was another activist out of the "Why-can't-we-all-get-along?" mould who was never less than unfailingly polite and respectful of authority. Together they raised up—and in Rolla's case taught—a generation of black Fort Worth kids to obey the rules. The "Black Power" movement may have flourished in cities like Detroit and Oakland, but it never made any headway in Fort Worth. When the Nation of Islam began making a lot of noise in the late 1950s, Black Muslims were dismissed in Fort Worth newspapers as "Negro cultists" and "lawless thugs" preaching "the supremacy of the colored races." And that opinion came from no less than civil rights activist and future Supreme Court Justice Thurgood Marshall! It was the considered opinion of conservative stalwarts that integration in the United States was moving "steadily forward," and "massive resistance" to it was over. How wrong they proved to be.[17]

Fort Worth went about its tried-and-true way of dealing with racial issues as if this were still the nineteenth century instead of the middle of the twentieth century. In 1963 city fathers appointed yet another bi-racial group to smooth Fort Worth's transition to a truly integrated community;

this one was dubbed the "Civil Rights Commission." It harked back to a time in the early part of the century when Progressives routinely created commissions of experts to solve every sticky problem, be it social or economic. The latest civil rights commission benefitted from the work of those that preceded it. Their biggest victory was getting all downtown department stores, restaurants, theaters, and hotels to follow Leonard Brothers' lead by taking down the "Colored" and "Whites Only" signs. The commission even had one African-American member, Harold Odom, a Federal Housing Administration employee and store owner. Odom took his position as liaison between the two races very seriously. He discouraged the more impatient members of the black community from staging sit-ins and other extreme forms of public protest, and when City Hall announced on the ninety-eighth anniversary of Juneteenth that public facilities were still not open to all, he took a philosophical, long-term view: "There is no need to try to prove anything or test anything now," he said. "It is over." That same month (June) the Fort Worth School Board finally began registering African-American students in formerly all-white schools.[18]

John F. Kennedy's Visit

1963 also marked a return to the past for the city's black schoolchildren in another sense. When Theodore Roosevelt visited Fort Worth in 1905 in a combination campaign swing and vacation, a choir of 600 black children turned out to serenade him with the "Star-Spangled Banner." Fifty-eight years later another president visited Fort Worth and was also musically entertained by the city's black youth. This time it was John F. Kennedy, making his second visit to Fort Worth. The visit got off to a rocky start even before the president and First Lady arrived. The White House advance staff in charge of making arrangements noted with concern that Fort Worth planners had completely excluded the city's black population from activities. The main event was to be a breakfast hosted by the Chamber of Commerce at the Hotel Texas on the morning of November 22. Not a single African American was on the original invitation list until the advance team advised the Chamber that President and Mrs. Kennedy would not attend unless blacks were represented. The Chamber scrambled to come up with an additional forty tickets, which it gave to Dr. Marion Brooks to distribute among the city's African-American Democratic supporters.[19]

With a little prodding, the Chamber also included other representatives of the black community in the festivities. They tapped the Dunbar High School band to be one of four high school bands that would serenade the president and First Lady along their way back to Carswell Air Force Base. Dunbar's band was placed about halfway through the route on the southeast corner of Jacksboro Highway and Highway 183. The ninety proud students dressed in their uniforms were bused to the site early that morning and waited several hours for the motorcade to come by. (There would be no stopping.) School officials and parents felt some concern that the students would be at risk standing on the side of the road in an all-white community (River Oaks), but the kids themselves were glad to be out of school and getting to play an original composition for the president of the United States. When the motorcade approached they started playing like mad and continued as it turned left onto Highway 183 and rolled out of sight. Later, after they got back to school, they learned the president had been shot and killed in Dallas. But no one could ever take away from them that they were the last bit of Fort Worth hospitality enjoyed by the Kennedys on their way out of town that historic day.[20]

The clash over black participation in the day's events was not the only disagreement the presidential party had with local officials. Entrenched Jim Crow practices and the historic racism of the Texas Democratic Party threatened to derail the visit before it ever left Washington. Among the advance team was an African American who was denied admission through the front entrance of the Hotel Texas. The president's men threatened to pull the entire presidential party from the hotel and stay elsewhere unless the entire team was treated with the same respect, whereupon hotel management backed down.

None of these issues became public knowledge at the time, and after the tragedy of November 22, they were largely forgotten until the 50th Anniversary. The positives that came out of it were the changes made in staging the event, albeit under pressure, so that afterwards it became harder to ignore African Americans in planning major events, and the pride felt forever thereafter by the ninety students and their school in being part of the president's visit. Kennedy's brief visit both directly and indirectly helped break down racial barriers that had long gone unchallenged.[21]

November 22, 1963, is also notable in the history of Fort Worth's black community for another reason related to President Kennedy's visit. Two photographers that day captured an image of the President reaching out in the crowd in front of the Hotel Texas to take the hand of a tall, well-dressed black man in a sea of white faces. Both Cecil Stoughton, traveling White House photographer, and William Allen, a photographer for the *Dallas Times-Herald*, saw something special in the moment that made them both snap the shutter. It is a striking image, iconic even, because it evokes Michelangelo's painting of God reaching out to Man on the ceiling of the Sistine Chapel. Sadly, the mystery black man has never been identified.[22]

Photo 33. President John F. Kennedy in Fort Worth

President Kennedy gave his next-to-the-last public speech in Fort Worth on the morning of November 22, 1963, about 9:00, on a parking lot across Eighth St. from the Hotel Texas. Afterwards he greeted an enthusiastic crowd, including this unidentified tall black man who reaches through the throng of people. Photo by *Dallas Times-Herald* photographer William Allen, Courtesy of Scott Barker.

Not until 1967 did Fort Worth officially go on record opposing racial discrimination. At least that was the way the *Fort Worth Press* put it. That was the year the council created a fifteen-member Community Relations Commission to cope with the "urgent and explosive problem" of race relations. The final vote was seven to two after language in the original ordinance giving the commission the power to "investigate and educate" had been stripped out. Opponents argued that the commission was a "left-wing" subterfuge to create a "police review board." One of the dissenting votes was cast by Mayor DeWitt McKinley who favored continuing his own appointed "human relations board" over creating a new agency by ordinance. The Community Relations Commission did not solve all of Fort Worth's race and ethnic problems, but it did smooth relations during the final years of the decade, marked elsewhere in the country by riots and assassinations.[23]

Progress on the Football Field and the Basketball Court

Athletics did as much as anything to break down racial barriers. That had always been true whether it was Jesse Owens and Joe Louis in the 1930s or Jackie Robinson in the 1940s. Whites could sit in the bleachers and cheer talent regardless of the color, and if that talent was on the home team, so much the better. Fort Worth's legendary high school basketball coach, Robert Hughes, won 1,333 games during his forty-seven-year career (1958–2005), making him the winningest high school boys' basketball coach of all time. He won thirty-five district championships and five state titles, first at I.M. Terrell then at Dunbar High School after 1968. Along the way he put Fort Worth basketball on the map. Hughes' Terrell teams played in the Prairie View Interscholastic League (PVIL), which governed black high school athletics in Texas during its Jim Crow era (1920–1967). Those teams never got a chance to go up against the best white teams because white schools played in the University Interscholastic League (UIL), but after he moved to Dunbar, his teams continued to win against all competition. With his motto, "Never, ever let anyone outwork you," he produced more than athletes; he produced men of character.[24]

One of Hughes' Terrell players was James Cash, who broke the color barrier in Southwest Conference basketball when he played for TCU from 1965 to 1968. Cash helped take TCU to a "final four" berth in the NCAA tournament in 1968, but basketball was just his ticket out of the ghetto. After graduating from TCU he went on to become the first black professor at Harvard Business School and later an associate dean. The forgotten part of his story is that Cash was a product of the public school system. Ironically, he was one of the best arguments that black schools could produce not just athletes, but students every bit the equal of their white counterparts from Paschal, Arlington Heights, and other distinguished white high schools.[25]

The accomplishments of Robert Hughes and the I.M. Terrell basketball program largely overshadowed the accomplishments of Kirkpatrick High School on the North Side. Kirkpatrick began as a junior high in 1950 then after the *Brown* decision (1954) grew into a full-fledged high school. The Kirkpatrick Wildcats never had more than about 125 boys to draw on in grades 10 through 12. Like I.M Terrell, the school was a member of the Prairie View Interscholastic League. It began a remarkable championship run in 1961 when it won the Class 3A championship in basketball under Coach Lester Beene. The Wildcats won three more basketball state titles in the next decade (1964, 1967, and 1971). Going I.M. Terrell one better, the Kirkpatrick football team also made history. Under Coach Gerald Beal they won back-to-back state titles in 1962 and 1963. During that magical two-year run, legendary TCU football coach Abe Martin called them "the best high school [football] team he had ever seen," regardless of race or school classification. In December 1962 the Wildcats won their first football championship at Farrington Field finishing the season 9–1. They were crowned state champions in December 1963, just two weeks after President Kennedy's visit to Fort Worth. But instead of being a time of celebration, it was a time of national mourning following the president's assassination that pushed the Wildcats' accomplishments off the front pages of the newspaper. And none of Kirkpatrick's titles ever got into the record books because the UIL kept all the records for Texas high school athletics in those years. In 1971 the FWISD closed Kirkpatrick High School under its federally mandated desegregation plan, thereby ending any chance Kirkpatrick had of adding to its laurels. To this day, Kirkpatrick holds the record among Fort Worth high schools for winning more championships than any other school, and it is the only Fort Worth high school to win a state football championship in any league. But as Coach Beal told an interviewer many years later, what was most important was that "his kids had the opportunity to experience some things that they never would have without Kirkpatrick," a sense of pride in community and self. The same applies to Dunbar's accomplishments in basketball. Those two high schools were the "shining light" of their neighborhoods, and more than that, they were shining lights for the entire black community. Their accomplishments were the whole community's accomplishments.[26]

Off the football field and basketball court, the victories were measured in smaller increments. In 1970 the *Fort Worth Star-Telegram* became the second big-city newspaper in the state to hire a black reporter (Cecil Johnson). The hiring was first vetted with business and community leaders. The fact that Fort Worth's first family of publishing, the Carters, owned the newspaper had a lot to do with how smoothly it went down. Once the Carter family got behind something, it was a done deal.[27]

The "Fort Worth Way"?

It has always been a matter of pride among Fort Worth leaders that the black and white communities could "come together" to solve any problem. What this really meant was keeping a lid on troubling issues so as not to embarrass the city. There is more than a little self-serving mythology in the official version of things although the record does show that Fort Worth has had less racial turmoil than many cities including Dallas. On the surface at least race relations appeared to be a model of civility and tolerance, dubbed the "Fort Worth Way," which name was neither original nor completely candid. Dallas officials called their approach the "Dallas Way," and other Southern cities also liked to think that they had discovered the secret of peaceful race relations. The secret, if there was one, is not hard to discover: the dominant group dictated the rules of the game to the minority group.[28]

In 1963, Raymond Buck, president of the Fort Worth Chamber of Commerce, told the *Star-Telegram*, "The climate of thought between all parties concerned and their representatives has been constructive and indicative of sensible solutions." Voices on both sides of the racial divide agreed. It is not only white leaders who have sung the praises of the Fort Worth Way. "We just get things done peacefully," Mt. Zion pastor L.B. George told a reporter in 1996. And in 2014 Judge Clifford Davis said, "We did not have the resistance in Fort Worth that many other Southern communities experienced. There were people of good will in Fort Worth that would respond to our efforts to bring about fair play and opportunity." Fort Worth's Way was all about the two races working out problems together, behind the scenes, by sitting down and talking things out. "Mutual respect" was the term often used on both sides. Bert Williams, the black golfer who helped break the color barrier at Colonial Country Club, generously put it this way in 2005: "There is no problem that can't be resolved by the two races working together." A local (white) historian concurs, claiming that by 1963, "All of Fort Worth's restaurants, hotels, department stores (including their lunch counters, rest rooms, and other facilities), theaters, athletic contests, and churches were open to all persons without regard to race." While that characterization is a bit over-drawn, it is not completely wrong either.[29]

The full story is more complicated. By 1963 the "Whites Only" signs had been removed in downtown businesses, but African Americans still felt unwelcome in many retail establishments and were still refused service in some, such as the Pink Rooster restaurant in Monnig's Department Store. What the Fort Worth Way really meant was that the black community played the game by the rules as they were set down by the whites who ran the city and settled for whatever concessions were offered. One long-time observer of the local scene put it this way many years later:

> If a black elected or appointed official pushes for substantive change that will improve quality of life for black people, that person will be "cut off"—denied the financial backing needed to win and hold office. . . . The minorities who have been embraced most by [white power-brokers] generally are the people who

> have been the least challenging and who are seen as having some usefulness to the people on the top.[30]

Thanks partly to the behind-the-scenes work of the Seventh Street Gang and the "Good Government League," in 1964 Tarrant County elected its first black public official, Leonard L. Haynes who was voted onto the original board of Tarrant County Junior College when TCJC was a single, wind-swept campus on SW Loop 820. Haynes's "day job" was pastoring a black church (St. Andrews United Methodist). The Reverend Haynes was followed in 1967 by Dr. Edward Guinn, the first black member of the city council.[31] Unlike most early black leaders, Edward Guinn did not come out of the black church. He owed his political success to being a team player. Dr. Guinn was a well-respected physician when he ran for his first political office. He had grown up in Fort Worth on the genteel Near South Side (on Terrell Ave.) and attended I.M. Terrell High School before getting his college degree from Prairie View Normal and Industrial College (now Prairie View A&M University). He served four years on the city council before passing the torch. Today, Dr. Guinn is honored as "one of the most active and innovative council members in city history," irrespective of race.[32]

Waiting for Jim Crow to die a natural death took decades. Change came in increments achieved by a few visionary black leaders willing to sit down at the table and discuss problems, as opposed to those whom Clifford Davis has called "hell-raisers." They were willing to push the boundaries, but always stopped short of open confrontation. It is arguable whether the incendiary methods of angry black Dallas leaders like John Wiley Price and Al Lipscomb would have accomplished any more than these men did or any faster.[33]

One explanation for the relatively peaceful race relations in Fort Worth over the years is that the black population of Fort Worth has always lacked the numbers to make a difference at the polls. In the nineteenth century, the numbers hovered around 6 percent of the total population compared to 20 percent in Dallas. The relatively peaceful relations of which Fort Worth is so proud has led activists like John Wiley Price to label Fort Worth accommodationists, "handkerchief head Negroes," and Fort Worth itself, "the Aunt Jemima capital of the world."[34]

When cities began erupting in race riots in the mid-sixties starting with the Watts neighborhood of Los Angeles, Fort Worth officials began to worry whether the Fort Worth Way could really guarantee racial harmony. Riots erupted all over the country every summer from 1965 through 1968. In May 1970, Dallas Cowboys football player Pettis Norman participated in a civil rights march through downtown Dallas that brought out hundreds of people in peaceful protest. Yet, a few years later upon returning to Dallas he found the city in "racial turmoil," what he called "the most dangerous time Dallas has ever had."[35]

Fort Worth's racial vibe at the end of the 1960s was entirely different. Police Chief Cato Hightower, who had witnessed the Riverside upheaval first-hand in 1956, took pains to stay ahead of the problem. He put his officers through riot training, and in 1968 the department opened its first "storefront" substation, putting it in the predominantly black Near South Side. The idea was to put officers in the neighborhood so they could head off residents' complaints before those complaints escalated into confrontations. Another Hightower initiative to "improve the image of the Department among Negroes and reduce the chance of race riots" was to enroll his officers in psychology classes at TCU. For all his admirable initiatives, two things Hightower was not willing to do was abolish the *de facto* quota system for blacks in the FWPD or actively recruit officers in the black community. The bones that the FWPD threw to the black community became part of Chief Hightower's legacy, helping to perpetuate the myth that Fort Worth had some magic formula for avoiding racial strife.[36]

A remarkable event occurred in Fort Worth in April 1968 following the assassination of Martin Luther King, Jr. in Memphis, Tennessee, on April 4. The whole nation was in mourning, white as well as black. In several cities, angry blacks also rioted in the streets. In Fort Worth an alliance of churches across all faiths, headed by Dr. Marion Brooks, needed just three days to put together a memorial service at TCU's Daniel Meyers Coliseum. Fort Worthers of all colors packed the place to hear prayers, readings, tributes, and testimonials to the man who more than any other spoke for his people. This was also the man Fort Worth had barely noticed when he came to town nine years earlier. Truly, "the times they were a-changin'".[37]

Looking back over the early civil rights years, it seems like the black vanguard in the war against Jim Crow were all quiet, unassuming men and women like Essie Sturges, Lloyd Austin, and Willis Pace, not angry and itching for a fight, but not accommodationists either. They were just people of conscience who had decided not to take it any longer. Despite being on the bottom of the social scale and having no obvious advantages in the fight for equality, they were not lacking in confidence. Willis Pace, as his son recalled, "didn't set out to be the first black bus driver; he just believed he could do anything." Pace had no schooling growing up. He was more the norm than the exception. These people were not college educated or even well-connected. They were not even the pride of I.M. Terrell. Willis Pace did not know how to read until he taught himself at the same time as his son when the latter was in kindergarten. What they lacked in education these civil rights pioneers made up for in hard work over the years, whether it be as maids or janitors or whatever the low-paying job, and when the time came to challenge the status quo, they did so. While some of their better educated, more articulate brethren got the headlines and the memorials, they changed things. Only a few of them are recognized today. The Fort Worth Transportation Authority honored Pace by declaring February 16, 2001, "Willis S. Pace Day." Lloyd Austin will forever be "the beloved pastor" of the St. John Missionary Baptist Church in Mosier Valley.[38]

Jim Crow was difficult to dismantle not just because whites held all the power, but because the two races had so many historic bonds holding them together. The system was mutually beneficial to a lot of people on both sides of the racial divide. For instance, some white-owned businesses made a good living catering to the black community, specifically beer distributors like Jax and Schlitz. Because so much of their regular business was in the black community, they employed black drivers and sales reps and even supervisors. Nobody seemed to complain as long as the suds flowed and the cash registers *ka-chinged.*

A more intimate relationship existed between the black wage-earners and the white employers they served for so many years. This was particularly true of domestics who worked in the homes of affluent white families. Those black maids and butlers, waiters and yard men were practically members of the family. They kept house, looked after their employers' children, were often picked up at their doorsteps by their employers and even transported to the doctor when they were sick. The same sort of personal relationships across racial lines could be found in the city's private clubs. The familial bond was not quite a strong, but white club members took a personal interest in the black staff who served meals, opened doors, and caddied golf games for them. They stopped to chat and inquired about their families. There are numerous pictures in the archives of such bastions of white power as River Crest and Colonial country clubs of white members posing with uniformed black staff. Club lore is also full of stories about people like Oscar Kirby who worked as the chef at River Crest Country Club for many years. He was beloved by club members for running an excellent kitchen and "watching with a sharp eye that every detail was met" to their satisfaction.[39]

Faithful black domestics like Oscar Kirby labored behind the scenes serving Fort Worth high society, and at the end of the day they returned to their humble digs in Como or on the Near South Side. Their perks included nice uniforms and getting to eat the same food as their employers and even take the leftovers home with them for their own families. They received Christmas gifts at Christmastime and usually bonuses at the end of the year. At Colonial Country Club, black caddies got to use the links on Mondays when the club was officially closed. In effect, they were "shadow golfers" playing "shadow games" unseen by the white membership. No municipal course was as nice as the club courses, even if blacks could only play after hours. Still, those caddies were so beloved by the white members that one unnamed black caddy became the subject of an oil portrait by River Crest club member Vivian Sloan Yarbrough. Without their black staff, places like River Crest and Colonial would not have been able to keep the doors open. But it was not the perks, the uniforms, or the leftovers that made the jobs special; it was the status that came with the job; it was being treated with respect and even affection by their employers.[40]

Of course, there was a down side to these heart-warming relationships: the black servant had to swallow whatever humiliations came with the job, and they were only "part of the family" so long as it suited their white employers. One long-time maid told how a white lady was always waiting for her when she got off the bus that brought her to work, demanding help in zipping up her dress. Another long-time black female employee of a country club filled in wherever needed all over the club and was adored by the members, but that did not prevent the club from summarily letting her and all the rest of the black staff go when it embarked on a major renovation. In her case, when the club reopened months later, her job was no longer there. She did not even receive severance pay.[41]

Such serving relationships knitted the black and white communities together and made it hard for members of the black community to support protests and demonstrations for larger political purposes. Issues like voting rights and segregated schools did not tend to come up when dishes were being washed and yards mowed, nor did they come up when Christmas bonuses were being handed out. It took angry people who were fed up to bring about change.

The Jim Crow system in Fort Worth would eventually collapse under its own weight, helped along by a combination of changing attitudes, crusading reformers (both black and white), and federal mandates. The city was spared the worst of the civil rights violence of the 1960s. There were no last rites for Jim Crow; it was quietly buried. But the harm it did could never be erased.

Photo 34. Amon Carter and driver

"Driving Mr. Amon"? Newspaper publisher and Fort Worth icon Amon Carter with unidentified chauffeur in front of River Crest Country Club, no date. Courtesy of Special Collections, Mary Couts Burnett Library, Texas Christian University.

Notes

1. "The year the movement began. . ." comes from Lenora Rolla, founder of the Tarrant County Black Historical & Genealogical Society, in an interview in *Fort Worth Star-Telegram*, September 27, 1999.
2. Many years later, the mythology of the March on Washington and "I Have a Dream" speech is that they actually changed anything in Fort Worth; they didn't. For Rolla, see *Fort Worth Star-Telegram*, September 27, 1999. The mayors were Jack Garrison (1955–57), Tom McCann (1957–61), and Bayard Friedman (1963–65). For the work of the 1956 and '60 commissions, see Buenger, *Texas Merchant*, 143.
3. Tim Madigan, "Jim Crow Lives," last of a 7-part series, "The Color of Hate," *Fort Worth Star-Telegram*, October 13, 2002. Quote is by the Rev. C.A. Holliday of Greater St. James Baptist Church. Moseley, "Ministers Help Keep Peace" (No. 2), August 25, 1967.
4. King's one-time appearance at the Majestic Theater was captured on film by peripatetic black photographer Calvin Littlejohn. That image is part of the Calvin Littlejohn Photography Archive, Dolph Briscoc Center for American History, University of Texas at Austin. Quote comes from Maryellen Hicks at an MLK Day observance, *Fort Worth Star-Telegram*, January 18, 2015.
5. Bud Kennedy, "The True Meaning of the MLK Holiday," *Fort Worth Star-Telegram*, January 18, 2013; and "MLK's Fort Worth Visit Fades from Memory," ibid., January 18, 2015. Harold Lunger was a Disciples of Christ minister and legendary professor who taught at Brite Divinity School for two decades, retiring in 1977. He died in 2002. *Fort Worth Star-Telegram*, May 27, 2002.
6. For list of "Seventh Street Gang" members and "decisive role," see Buenger, "Texas Merchant," 143. For Judkins St., see Madigan, "Showdown," p. 19A.
7. What Williams did not mention is that the city's parks had also been off-limits to the Mexican population. See *Fort Worth Star-Telegram*, September 9, 1921. For "Juneteenth," see Williams' story, see "How Reporter's Question Opened Parks to Negroes," *Fort Worth News-Tribune*, July 2-4, 1976, p. 14; and Bill Fairley, "Tales from Where the West Begins," *Fort Worth Star-Telegram*, June 18, 1997.

8. The Big Three downtown movie houses for many years were the Worth, the Hollywood, and the Palace. The names of the persons involved here are withheld upon their request although the stories have been vouchsafed by one of the principals. For Dallas Piccadilly, see "They Stood Their Ground," *Dallas Morning News*, July 23, 2006. The protest on the sidewalk in front of the cafeteria lasted 28 days.
9. Harriet, *Missing Link*, 60.
10. For the story of Wiley's visit, see E.R. Bills, "Great Debate," *Fort Worth Magazine* 17, no. 2 (February 2014): 60-61. Despite its admirable record, TCU lagged behind North Texas State College (1956), SMU (1962), and Arlington State College (1962) in integrating its student body.
11. *Fort Worth Star-Telegram*, December 20, 1999.
12. Rosa Parks was the Birmingham seamstress-activist who launched the 381-day boycott when she refused to give up her seat on a city bus to a white man, earning her the title, "Mother of the Civil Rights Movement." For an unvarnished view of Rosa Parks, see Douglas Brinkley, *Rosa Parks*, Penguin Lives Series (New York: Viking Press, 2000). For Fort Worth's 1944 bus case, see *Fort Worth Press*, July 5, 1944. For her stand, Essie Sturges lost her job at a local laundry. She died in 1985 at the age of 75. See Allen (Sherrod), *Grace and Gumption*, 201-02; and Bob Ray Sanders, "A Local Woman, a Different Bus, Same Bias," and "Bus Case Settled the Fort Worth Way," *Fort Worth Star-Telegram*, February 19 and 21, 2003. For "quiet diplomacy," see *Dallas Morning News*, December 20, 1990.
13. For Foster, see Bill Fairley, "Tarrant Chronicles," *Fort Worth Star-Telegram*, March 10, 1999. For Pace, see recollections of his son in his obituary. Ibid., June 27, 2002.
14. *Fort Worth Press*, May 15, 1961.
15. Tim Madigan, "Signs of Change," Part 6 in "The Color of Hate" series, *Fort Worth Star-Telegram*, October 12, 2002.
16. Brooks' characterization comes from recollections of Roy Brooks (son) and others in *Fort Worth Star-Telegram*, February 10, 2013. It was Roy Brooks who said his father was being watched by the FBI. Paul Sims was Community Action Program supervisor in the late 1960s. For Sims' quote, see Moseley, "Ministers Help Keep Peace" (No. 2), August 25, 1967.
17. *Fort Worth Press*, October 22, 1959.
18. For Odom and city commission, see Bud Kennedy, "Today Is a Historic Date for Fort Worth," *Fort Worth Star-telegram*, June 21, 2013. Fort Worth Technical High School is now Green B. Trimble Technical High School at 1003 W. Cannon St. (same address). The name was changed in 1967

in honor of Green B. Trimble, the principal who started the vocational programs at the school. In the old FWISD, black students were frequently shunted off into vocational programs considered more suitable for them than a college-directed academic course of study. *Cf.* Brian D. Behnken, "The 'Dallas Way': Protest, Response, and the Civil Rights Experience in Big D and Beyond," *The Southwestern Historical Quarterly* 111, no. 1 (July 1987): ix-29, hereafter Behnken, "The Dallas Way."

19. These nearly forgotten details did not come to light until fifty years later, on the occasion of the 50th anniversary of JFK's 1963 visit to Fort Worth. Exhibition materials at the Fort Worth Public Library (Central Branch), the Amon Carter Museum of American Art, and The University of Texas at Arlington Library. *Fort Worth Star-Telegram*, October 27, 2013.
20. At the time, I.M. Terrell's band was the oldest and largest black high school band in the city, but Dunbar got the honor, reportedly due to a coin flip between the two principals. See recollections of columnist Bob Ray Sanders, *Fort Worth Star-Telegram*, November 27, 2013, p. 13B. The other three high school bands selected were Poly's, Arlington Heights', and Castleberry's. The four bands were stationed at intervals along the Presidential route, starting with the Poly's "Marching 100" band on the courthouse steps. In 1963 Dunbar was still a combined junior-senior high school; the senior high did not get their own building until 1967. The story of the band performing for President Kennedy comes from the *Fort Worth Press*, November 21, 1963. For some reason, it is not told in the *Star-Telegram.* The story is retold in *Fort Worth: Outpost on the Trinity*, rev. ed., 254, and recalled by some who were there in "Students Played Hearts out for President," *Fort Worth Star-Telegram*, November 22, 2013, on the occasion of the 50th anniversary of the event. Ironically, that day the Poly marching band played their signature song for the Kennedys, "Dixie," which was not in the repertoire of the Dunbar band. For Poly, see "Fifty Years Later, Band to Reunite," *Fort Worth Star-Telegram*, September 23, 2013. JFK's first visit to Fort Worth was in 1960 when he was campaigning for president.
21. *Fort Worth Star-Telegram*, October 27 and November 22, 2013.
22. The photograph, blown up to larger-than-life proportions, was the centerpiece of a JFK exhibition at the UTA Library for the 50th Anniversary of the president's death. Stoughton's photo is among the collections of the Kennedy Presidential Library. Allen's photograph is owned by the Sixth Floor Museum (Dallas) today. The Allen photo, taken at street level,

gives a much clearer view of the mystery man. The photos were taken about 9:00 AM that morning.

23. *Fort Worth Press*, July 3, 1967.
24. For Hughes' legendary career, see *Fort Worth Star-Telegram*, February 12, 2004; and April 26, 2005. For motto, see interview on the occasion of being nominated for the Naismith Memorial Basketball Hall of Fame in 2015. He fell short of the required number of votes this first time, but still owns a High School Coach of the Year award (2003) and Wooten Lifetime Achievement award (2010). *Ibid.*, February 15 and April 7, 2015.
25. Cash graduated from I.M. Terrell in 1965. His athletic legacy has been recognized many times, including a place on the list of history-making Texans in the 75-year-history of the NCAA basketball tournament. *Fort Worth Star-Telegram*, March 17, 2013; and February 14, 2014.
26. The Kirkpatrick name lives on today at the same location as a middle school. The state trophies of the high school teams are on view in a trophy case in the front hall. Years after Kirkpatrick's and I.M. Terrell's great runs, the UIL finally got around to "grand-fathering" those PVIL teams into its record books. *Fort Worth Star-Telegram*, December 18, 2001 (Bud Kennedy's column); November 12, 2010; March 8, 2015.
27. For Cecil Johnson, see Madigan, "Our Own Sins," Part 5 in the series, ibid., October 10, 2002. The *Star-Telegram* was three years behind its Dallas rival, the *Dallas Morning News*, which hired Julia Scott Reed as a columnist in 1967. *Dallas Morning* News, September 9, 1967; *Dallas Express*, September 9, 1967.
28. For "Fort Worth Way," see Christine Stanley and Jeff Prince, "Hushed Up and Unhappy," *Fort Worth Weekly*, August 3–9, 2005, p.11, hereafter Stanley and Prince, "Hushed Up." For Dallas, see Behnken, "The Dallas Way," ix-29; and Jim Schutze, *The Accommodation: The Politics of Race in an American City* (New York: Citadel Press, 1987). Likewise, Robert A. Goldberg, "Racial Change on the Southern Periphery: The Case of San Antonio, Texas, 1960–1965," *The Journal of Southern History* 49, no. 3 (August 1983): 349–374.
29. For Buck, see Bill Fairley, "Tarrant Chronicles," *Fort Worth Star-Telegram*, February 24, 1999. For George, see Stanley and Prince, "Hushed Up." For Davis, see *Fort Worth Star-Telegram*, May 9, 2014. For historian, see Buenger, *Texas Merchant*, 142.
30. Katie Sherrod, "Power: Who Runs Fort Worth?" *D Magazine* 22, no. 11 (November 1995): 113.

31. For "working together," see this author's interview with black city councilman Frank Moss, June 6, 1999. Recounting the story of Dallas' civil rights travails was the 2006 Dallas exhibit, "Call to Action." Fort Worth has never acknowledged it had any travails. "They Stood Their Ground," *Dallas Morning News*, July 23, 2006. For Haynes, see Bob Ray Sanders, "Role of Black Preachers in Fort Worth on Exhibit," *Fort Worth Star-Telegram*, May 21, 2014. For other pioneering African-American leaders, see "Black Citizens Concerned with the Bicentennial in "Fort Worth: The Black Prospective [*sic*]," Fort Worth Library, Central Branch, Local History, Archives and Genealogy Unit, 1976.
32. Cecil Johnson, "Making Progress—Blacks and the City Council," *Fort Worth Star-Telegram*, April 16, 2000. Tim Madigan, "Out at Home," 3rd in a 7-part series, "The Color of Hate," ibid., October 8, 2002, p. 3E.
33. Price and Lipscomb were for many years colleagues in the Dallas civil rights movement, Price on the Dallas County Commission and Lipscomb on the city council. Both have well-earned reputations as provocateurs in race relations. See for instance, "Price Challenges Blacks in Fort Worth to Step up Fight against Racism," *Dallas Morning News*, December 20, 1990. Davis quote comes from conversation with author, July 26, 2014.
34. For statistics, see *Fort Worth Daily Gazette*, September 28, 1890. They come from U.S. Census data but are impossible to check against the original source today because the 1890 federal census results burned up in a fire in Washington, D.C. For John Wiley Price, see Stanley and Prince, "Hushed Up," 11; and Bob Ray Sanders, "In My Opinion," *Fort Worth Star-Telegram*, December 13, 2006.
35. Brian Jensen, *Where Have all Our Cowboys Gone?* (Lanham, MD: Taylor Trade Publishing, 2001), 43–45.
36. *Dallas Morning News*, April 4, 1968.
37. A copy of the program from that remarkable event is preserved in the TCBH&GS Collections, Series II (Individual Collections), Box 1, File 8. The quote is from a Bob Dylan protest song, "The Times, They Are A-changin'" (1963).
38. Information on Willis Pace comes from obituary, *Fort Worth Star-Telegram*, June 27, 2002. For Austin, see ibid., June 29, 2013.
39. See interview with Kirby when he was 92. *Fort Worth Press*, June 11, 1954.
40. For Colonial, see Robert J. Robertson, *Fair Ways* (College Station: Texas A&M University Press, 2005), 73–74. For River Crest, see photos and text in Hollace Ava Weiner, *River Crest Country Club: The First 100 Years, 1911–2011* (Fort Worth: River Crest Country Club, 2011), 27, 155, 416,

418, 443, hereafter Weiner, *River Crest.* "The Caddy" by Vivian Sloan Yarbrough, oil on canvas (1933), the collection of Edmund P. Cranz. Used with permission for the cover of this book.

41. The names of the employees and their employers are omitted here out of respect for all of the parties involved. For some, feelings are still sensitive even after many years.

Chapter 11

The Race Is Not Always to the Swift

There is an old saying that "victory is not always to the strong nor the race to the swift." The struggle for black equality, often summed-up as "the civil rights movement," was a marathon not a sprint, and marathons are not won in the first hundred yards or even the first ten miles. They are won by perseverance and determination over the long run. Fort Worth's black community has been in a marathon since the tiny outpost was planted on the bluffs over the Trinity in 1849. Some would say the struggle (race) is still going on. The black community has triumphed over slavery, Jim Crow, and the glass ceiling, but the race is not over. There are more miles to be run, more battles to be fought.

As the 1960s wound down, "Jim Crow is dead! Long live Jim Crow!" might have served as a battle cry, paraphrasing the traditional proclamation of the English when one king dies and the crown passes immediately to his successor. Thanks to civil rights legislation and court decisions, racial segregation was legally dead, only to be replaced by school busing, quotas, and the glass ceiling in the 1970s. Bill McDonald had likewise died, only to be replaced by J.W. Webber as the paragon of black success and the city's richest African American. He operated a string of nursing homes and was the president of an insurance company and a funeral home. He owned a big house in a nice, integrated neighborhood and did not have to look up to any man. He was the new Bill McDonald.[1]

Some things, however, had not changed. J.W. Webber and Bill McDonald were exceptional. Both had achieved the American Dream, yet as a black minister pointed out in 1967,

> Ninety-nine percent of all Negroes are [still] employed by whites. Ninety-eight percent of all the home mortgages are [still] held by whites. Whites hold ninety-nine percent of all the car notes. [2]

In other words, whites still held the keys to the kingdom. Booker T. Washington might have seen an object lesson in those numbers; he always said only when the black man achieved economic equality could he hope to achieve full equality with the white man, but for most African Americans it was the same old same old.

MUSIC HATH POWER

The racial walls did not come down all at once; progress was halting, marked by countless small victories along the way. Music played a critical role in bringing those walls down. Fort Worth produced several notable black musical talents in the twentieth century that crossed all racial lines. As in so many other areas, I. M. Terrell was the launching pad for success. Indeed, the school was a music factory that turned out such acclaimed twentieth-century musicians as Ornette Coleman, Curtis Ousley, Dewey Redman, Cornell Dupree, Charles Moffett, and Ray Sharpe. Their success was in addition to the collective accomplishments of the I.M. Terrell band, which was recognized as one of the finest high school bands in the state.[3]

Among the school's musical alumni, the most famous were jazz innovator Ornette Coleman and "rockabilly" performer Ray Sharpe. Coleman was born in Fort Worth in 1930 and played in the I. M. Terrell band until being kicked out for excessive improvising. He hit the road, first to New Orleans then eventually to Los Angeles where by the 1960s he was one of the leaders of the "free jazz" movement. In 2007 he received a Pulitzer Prize for his music. Ray Sharpe was likewise born in Fort Worth (1938) and attended I.M. Terrell. He found his inspiration in country music, traditionally a white genre, and honed his craft by performing in local, chitlin' circuit clubs. He hit nationally in 1959 with the top 10 hit "Linda Lu." American Bandstand and European tours followed. One of his Los Angeles session musicians in the early 1960s was Jimi Hendrix before Hendrix became a superstar in his own right.[4]

Photo 35. Ornette Coleman

The musical pioneer Ornette Coleman (1930–2015), best known as a saxophonist, made his last appearance in Fort Worth when he opened the Caravan of Dreams with his band on October 1, 1983. Courtesy of *Fort Worth Star-Telegram* Photograph Collection, Special Collections, University of Texas at Arlington Library, Arlington, TX.

It took rock and roll to introduce a mass white audience to black music and black musicians. Baby-boomers (those born between 1946 and 1964) regardless of color embraced the music of Motown, Chuck Berry, and James Brown among others. By the end of the 1960s white teenagers and their parents alike could openly enjoy what was once called "race music." One of the most sensational performers of the late '60s was Jimi Hendrix, the only black rock-and-roller playing psychedelic, electric-driven rock and roll. Fans did not care what color Hendrix was because he played with a blistering intensity like no one else, making musical history by obliterating the old racial lines in rock and roll. Fort Worth kids got to see Hendrix on February 18, 1968. How times had changed since Marian Anderson appeared at Will Rogers Auditorium before a mostly white audience in dark suits and long dresses! Now white teenagers sat beside black teenagers in reserved seating, many in jeans and T-shirts, listening to the psychedelic sounds of the Jimi Hendrix Experience.[5]

When the Caravan of Dreams, the personal dream of billionaire Ed Bass, opened in downtown Fort Worth on October 1, 1983, the first act booked into the upscale club was Ornette Coleman and his Prime Time ensemble. Even more surreal, two days earlier, Mayor Bob Bolen had proclaimed September 29 "Ornette Coleman Day" and presented him the key to the city. Coleman was thus the first black man ever presented the key to the city in Fort Worth, an ancient and curiously quaint method of honoring someone. Not William McDonald, not I.M. Terrell, not James E. Guinn, for all their contributions, had ever been so honored by their hometown.[6]

Today, black music and black theater thrive in Fort Worth, attracting a mixed racial audience as a matter of course. For cultural purists this had created a new set of problems. A century ago ragtime music did not reach the vast white audience until it was co-opted by white publishers, the same fate that befell rhythm and blues, funk, and rap music. Black theater has had a tough time of it because of the limited audience for live theater regardless of color. In 1972 the Sojourner Truth Players (STP) of

Fort Worth were founded by Rudy Eastman, Erma Lewis, Paul Sims, and others to expand the audience for high-quality African-American drama beyond the college crowd. The results were lauded by all, but that did not keep the STP from folding after a decade. Meanwhile, in 1981, Eastman founded the Jubilee Players and secured the financial backing to open a home theater for them, first in Poly then downtown at 506 Main where it still operates today. The Jubilee Theater has never had the audience or the financial backing of the older Stage West and Casa Mañana venues. Selling black culture to white audiences in a more elevated form than humorous stereotypes, "race music," and saintly "biopics" has always been a hard sell.[7]

Neighborhood Lines Blurred

The progress of Fort Worth's black community over the decades can be traced through the city's black neighborhoods. Historically, as populations shift, neighborhoods rise and fall; it is a fact of urban life. In the 1950s, Fort Worth's black population shifted southward from the Rock Island bottom, Stop Six, and Chambers Hill to Morningside, Carver Heights, and Forest Hills. The *Fort Worth Press* in 1967 called it "a quiet revolution in Negro housing." By that year blacks could live in any neighborhood in the city where they could afford to buy a house. There were still pockets of poverty, what *The Press* called "Negro slums," and there were 643 poor black families living in public housing.[8]

"Black flight" to the suburbs, paralleling white flight, meant the steady downward slide of some black areas. East Lancaster turned into what the *Star-Telegram* called "the homeless district," marked by the Union Gospel Mission, the Salvation Army Center, and the Presbyterian Night Shelter. In between are a lot of boarded-up buildings and overgrown lots. Farther south, E. Rosedale was taken over by prostitutes and drug dealers. The future of these once-vibrant thoroughfares is still in doubt.[9]

Meanwhile, other historically black neighborhoods have been completely wiped off the map, not by demographic shifts but by public policy. This was the fate of Battercake Flats, Chambers Hill, Rock Island Bottom, and the Ripley Arnold Project. Each of those neighborhoods has its own story to tell.

Battercake Flats is gone and good riddance, wiped out in the 1920s by levee construction on the Trinity and slum clearance. No one misses Battercake Flats, and its residents were people with homes and families and they had to live somewhere. They were a community that was uprooted and scattered, and they were not the last to suffer that fate.

The old Chambers Hill neighborhood exists today only in the form of the Butler Housing Project. Freeway construction and slum clearance wiped out most of the housing that used to stand there. The Butler Project and nearby I.M. Terrell are the only reminders that this area was once a vibrant if poor community.

The residents of the Ripley Arnold Project were uprooted en masse in 2001 when the Fort Worth Housing Authority sold the 48-acre site to Radio Shack for $20 million. At the time there were 520 people living there, all of whom had to be relocated somewhere else to make way for progress. Ripley Arnold had long been considered an eyesore and an embarrassment, and the Radio Shack deal was the justification to finally demolish it. The residents did not get a vote on whether they wanted to move or not; they were all gone in the next two years. Before construction began there was more concern with saving the trees on the site than finding new homes for the former residents.[10]

Rock Island Bottom is the saddest case of all. For fifty years it was a vibrant, close-knit neighborhood until the 1949 flood devastated the area. That was followed by the one-two punch of desegregation and construction of the North-South Freeway (I-35), which went right through the middle of the neighborhood. Today the old Rock Island Bottom neighborhood is nothing but a fond memory in the minds of its elderly former residents who may be forgiven a little nostalgia for a time when they represented the best of black Fort Worth.[11]

All of these former neighborhoods rested on shaky foundations. The residents were never able to put down deep roots because they never knew if they would be living there tomorrow. With no political clout at city hall and no solid economic base, they were subject to forces beyond their control. Each of those historic black neighborhoods began life on marginal land, and when that land became desirable for some grander purpose, their days were numbered.

"Re-development" and "eminent domain" are terms that no black neighborhood ever wants to hear. Late in the nineteenth century, the poor residents of Calhoun and Jones streets were displaced by the tracks of the Missouri, Kansas & Texas (1881), the Gulf, Colorado & Santa Fe (1881), the Fort Worth & Denver City (1882), and the Chicago, Rock Island & Texas (1893), which collectively created a second "reservation" on the east side of the city. In another deal with the city in 1907 the Chicago, Rock Island & Texas laid spur tracks on East Seventh between Grove and Calhoun. That deal led to the proliferation of warehouses on the east side of the city that pushed out the last of the area's long-time residents.

It did not stop with the railroads. In 1924 Douglass Park was sold to Texas Electric Service Company to build its power plant, thus removing the city's only black public park from the board. In the 1950s the construction of the North-South Freeway wiped out entire streets besides dividing neighborhoods. And in 2003 Radio Shack purchased the prime real estate out from under the residents of Butler Project. It has been a familiar story for more than a hundred years.[12]

Neighborhoods are comprised of homes, and residential housing has always been one of the defining elements of Jim Crow, starting with shotgun houses and later on, "the projects." Shotgun houses, also known as "row houses," were the early twentieth century's version of "affordable housing." These relics of Jim Crow are not hard to find, however, if one goes looking. Dozens of them could be seen in the 1950s and '60s just off

I-35 below the Purina and Bewley Mills grain elevators. Those have since been torn down, and most would say "good riddance." In the twenty-first century examples of shotgun houses still exist on the North Side and Near South Side, some barely recognizable thanks to improvements over the years, others looking pretty much the same as they did when they were built. They are reminders of a bygone ago although it seems likely they will continue to be occupied for many years to come. The issue nowadays is whether to bulldoze them in the name of urban renewal or save them in the name of historic preservation.[13]

Housing continues to be a sensitive area today. In 2013 a study commissioned by the city's Community Development Council showed that "some groups, primarily African Americans and Hispanics, face barriers to fair housing." This was not front-page headlines, but the specifics of the problem in the twenty-first century support the old adage, "the more things change, the more they remain the same." Blacks, it seems, are charged higher interest rates on loans and have twice the rejection rate as whites in the application process. The result, as one advocate pointed out, is that blacks [and other minorities] have "a very difficult time finding housing outside of the poverty areas," meaning traditional black neighborhoods like Stop Six, Como and the Near South Side.[14]

In 2014 the Texas Department of Housing and Community Affairs recognized "Fort Worth's tremendous need for affordable rental housing," and announced the first massive public-housing project in the city since 1940 for 302 units. It's the same old problem; only the name has changed. Instead of being called a "housing project" it is now called "affordable housing" or "housing options for low-income tenants."[15]

By 1990, 20 percent of Fort Worth's population was black, but more importantly African Americans were no longer an unrepresented population living in the shadows. They occupied positions of importance in public life sitting on the city council, county commissioners' court, and the school board.[16]

Storming the Corridors of Power

The presence of blacks in the corridors of power did not happen by accident. In the 1970s citizens approved single-member voting districts, which meant that henceforward blacks could run for elected office from districts where they had a large population with an expectation of winning, as opposed to the older method of running at large thereby diluting the black vote. The results were dramatic in the years that followed. In 1977, Walter Beatrice Barbour became the first African American elected to the city council, representing District 5 (the Stop Six community). This was the same year Maryellen Hicks became Fort Worth's first black municipal court judge. In 1983, Governor Mark White appointed her to an open seat on the district court, and she was elected in her own right the following year. In 1983 Governor Bill Clements appointed L. Clifford Davis to fill an unfinished term as judge of Criminal District Court No. 2. Davis won the seat in his own right the following year, and served as a visiting judge around the state after leaving office in 1988. In 1987 Virginia Nell Webber, following in the footsteps of Walter Barbour, became just the second black woman elected to the city council, serving until 1997. In 1989 Dionne Bagsby became the first woman *and* the first black elected to Tarrant County Commissioners' Court. After leaving stepping down in 2004 she served on the boards of the Fort Worth Symphony, Jubilee Theater, and Presbyterian Night Shelter. Only one of those three organizations was a black organization, demonstrating that black leaders had even achieved cross-over appeal in the white bastions of power in the private sector.[17]

Among all the newcomers who took their place at the table in recent decades, none was more satisfying than Walter Dansby, appointed FWISD School Superintendent in 2012. Dansby was a forty-year veteran of the school system who had paid his dues climbing the career ladder. Beyond that, however, was the symbolism of his appointment as the first Africa-American school superintendent in the city's history. It was, it should be remembered, the Fort Worth school board that had stubbornly resisted desegregation for nine years after the *Brown* decision. They had fought change more even than the police department, more than the city or county, more than the big downtown retail merchants. It took until 2012 for Fort Worth blacks to get one of their own as superintendent of schools. Long before that date a majority of Fort Worth's 83,000 public-school children were non-white.[18]

All of these people earned their positions through hard work and political smarts; they did not ride the coat-tails of political correctness into office. And they all continued to serve the larger Fort Worth community after leaving office by such things as fighting the AIDS epidemic, supporting public education, working with the American Association of Retired Persons, and mentoring the next generation of leadership. Today, every aspect of Fort Worth culture and politics is racially integrated. Those battles have been won. The problem, however, is not diversifying the top rungs of society; it is moving blacks off the bottom rung of the socio-economic ladder. That is the last fight in the historic civil rights movement.

One of the most important although often overlooked steps on the long road to equality is laying claim to one's history. Progress means not just fixing the present but also fixing history insofar as possible. Take Oliver Knight's classic history of the city, *Fort Worth: Outpost on the Trinity*, which has been in print continuously since 1953. An epilogue added to the 1990 edition attempted to update Fort Worth's black history in three pages. The authors concluded that "ending segregation was probably easier for Fort Worth than it was for most cities in the South." They cite an amusing incident when a "busload" of black "Freedom Riders" came to Fort Worth determined to integrate the segregated lunch counter at the Worth Hotel Coffee Shop. They entered the restaurant apparently determined to provoke a confrontation that would make a statement. If so, their plans were derailed by two veteran white waitresses, Minnie and Alma who seated them at the counter, took their orders, and served them, all without missing a beat. The would-be protesters in the end paid their bills and retreated to their bus, defeated by Fort Worth's old-fashioned, Southern hospitality. The authors end with this observation: "Things went that way all over Fort Worth. Fort Worth simply ceased to be a segregated city." Wishful thinking. Cities do not suddenly cease to be segregated. Someone or a lot of people have to push for change. It may be behind the scenes or in the streets, but someone has to rock the boat before change will occur.[19]

The story of the Freedom Riders is a wonderful story, but it lacks such vital details as the participants' full names and the date when it occurred to verify it. There is also the problem that the famous "Freedom Riders" of the early 1960s who traveled via interstate buses through the Deep South never got as far west as Fort Worth. The story therefore must remain apocryphal until further evidence is forthcoming. But what is absolutely true is that segregation in Fort Worth did not simply "cease to be." That's part of the mythology perpetuated by a white historical community still a little fuzzy on black history.

And that is nothing new. As far back as 1909, Fort Worth old-timer J.B. Roberts related his reminiscences in the *Star-Telegram*. Part of his recollections was how even in its formative years, Fort Worth had been a city "populated by men, women, and children, old and young, *black and white* [emphasis added], who even that far back had an abiding faith in the future greatness of the place." This sounds more like a press release out of the Amon Carter school of civic boosterism than a historical description, and for that reason it must be discounted. But it also shows that white Fort Worthers have been painting a rosy picture of the city's race relations for more than a hundred years.[20]

A community must own its past before it can lay claim to its future. Perhaps the first step in that commitment in Fort Worth came in April 1977 when the Tarrant County Black Historical and Genealogical Society was launched—thanks largely to the vision of one woman, Lenora Rolla. Her personal papers, collected during seven decades of civil rights activism in Fort Worth, formed the basis of the Society's collections then and still do. The city of Fort Worth had to fight the University of Texas at Austin for her papers. Fortunately, there were those in Fort Worth who recognized the importance of keeping such a rich collection here. After Rolla's death in 2002 the papers were placed with the Fort Worth Library where they could be readily accessed by researchers now and in the future. The Society maintains a museum at a separate location that serves as a clearinghouse for the precious artifacts and documents of the city's black history.

The re-discovery of the city's black history has proceeded quietly with only the occasional historic marker dedication or a "Black History Month" column in the newspaper to mark it. In 2006 a headstone and marker were placed on the grave of Hagar Tucker (Fort Worth's first black policeman) in Old Trinity Cemetery (today part of Oakwood Cemetery). The dedication ceremony brought out not just the usual historical types, but the Fort Worth Black Officers' Association. In 2011 another historic marker was placed on the site of the former Douglass Park. In 2009 the photographs of Calvin Littlejohn were published thanks to the combined efforts of Bob Ray Sanders and Ron Abram. It was a major publishing event. And every year that same Bob Ray Sanders writes a series of articles and editorials in the *Star-Telegram*, typified by a 2014 column, "Black History Month: Embrace It, Don't Resent It."[21]

Littlejohn had long been recognized as an important figure in the city's black history. Other African Americans, not nearly so well known, have emerged from the shadows in recent years. Enoch Jackson was the classic "fish out of water" because for nearly forty years he was the caretaker at Temple Beth-El. He might have been completely forgotten in Fort Worth history if not for events on the night of May 28–29, 1946, and the efforts of Fort Worth historian Hollace Weiner. There are undoubtedly other African Americans out there relegated to the shadows of Fort Worth history until someone shines a spotlight on them.

Photo 36. Lenora Rolla

In February 1988, two Fort Worth legends came together: Lenora Rolla—educator, archivist—and I.M. Terrell High School. She was returning to dedicate a historical marker for the school. Rolla graduated from Fort Worth Colored High School in 1921, then taught there for years. Courtesy of *Fort Worth Star-Telegram* Photograph Collection, Special Collections, University of Texas at Arlington Library, Arlington, TX.

In recent years change has come in small but significant ways. In 1988 Fort Worth hosted the largest convention ever held in the city up to that date: the African Methodist Episcopal Church. Not only were the thousands of delegates a financial shot in the arm to the economy, but it was appropriate that the descendants of the same group that had formed the city's first organized black church in 1870 were back and filling the convention center 118 years later. In the wake of that event the city's Convention & Visitors' Bureau put out a major effort to attract more black conventions to Fort Worth.[22]

In 2001, Jim and Gloria Austin created the National Cowboys of Color Museum & Hall of Fame to honor the African American contribution to our Western heritage. It was the first institution dedicated to that purpose in the country. Fort Worth's African American history has several entries on the national BlackPast.Org website. These are clear signs that Fort Worth is a different world today, hardly perfect, but much better than it was a century and more ago.[23]

In 2003 the FWPD celebrated "50 Years of Blacks in Blue," harking back to when the first class of black officers was hired in 1953. The harsh words of Police Chief Dysart in 1949 are long forgotten. Nearly one-third of the FWPD today is black, and they work in every division of the department and neighborhood of the city. Today, the only color that matters is the blue of the uniform.

On June 25, 2011, the Most Worshipful Prince Hall Grand Lodge of Texas held a ribbon-cutting to open the Wilbert M. Curtis Library-Museum. A long time coming, the museum is a repository for all things related to black Masonry in Fort Worth and Tarrant County, some of it dating back to the 1800s. As Grand Master Curtis said in his dedication, "We will now be able to tell our own story." Appropriately, the museum is on Martin Luther King Freeway. It is not just the treasures stored at the site; it is the all-too-rare accomplishment of creating a repository for African-American history and culture. It is a museum, library, and archive all rolled into one. The Wilbert M. Curtis Library-Museum is just the second such depository in Fort Worth after the Tarrant County Black Historical and Genealogical Society. They are fighting a rear-guard action to preserve black history.[24]

The Fort Worth Library today plays a key role in spotlighting the city's black history through a series of programs, especially but not exclusively during Black History Month every year. In 2012, a program on Dr. Marion Brooks brought out family descendants and others, both black and white, interested in the pioneering local physician who just happened to be black. A lot more programs and historic markers will be necessary to rescue Fort Worth's black history from obscurity.

The city now has statues to six notable men in Fort Worth history: Ripley Arnold, Will Rogers, Quanah Parker, Charles Tandy, John F. Kennedy, and Bill Pickett. One of those statues, located in the stockyards, is of a black man. Bill Pickett's claim to fame is that he was a champion bull-dogger whose distinctive style of bringing down a bull made him a legend in rodeo history. Having broken the "statuary" color barrier, there is no reason there cannot be more statues in the future to notable black Fort Worthers, say Bill McDonald or Francine Morrison.[25]

Fort Worth has always bragged that our race relations are more peaceable, more collegial than those of our sister city to the east. Dallas endured a series of residential bombings in 1940 and public demonstrations in the 1970s. Fort Worth has had only a few "isolated incidents," as the newspapers call them. Dallas had John Wiley Price; Fort Worth had Lenora Rolla and Hazel Harvey Peace. These things are on the surface. Looking beneath the surface, we are forced to face certain uncomfortable facts. For instance, Fort Worth's black community did experience bombings and riots, which we have conveniently forgotten, and Dallas had a black chamber of commerce fifty-three years before Fort Worth (1926 vs. 1979). According to its website, the Fort Worth Metropolitan Black Chamber of Commerce "champions the cause of African American businesses and entrepreneurs working to get their piece of the economic pie," which still paints the struggle for equality in terms of "us" vs. "them." On the touchy subject of reparations for slavery, the Fort Worth city council in 2004 approved a resolution calling on Congress to "study the effects of slavery and discrimination and whether governmental reparations are needed." In 2014 the Dallas County Board of Commissioners passed a resolution offered by John Wiley Price supporting reparations payments.[26]

Mechanisms are in place today such as the Fort Worth Minority Leaders and Citizens' Council to keep us from slipping back into the bad old days of overt racial prejudice. The Fort Worth Police Department compiles statistics annually that distinguish between black-on-black and black-on-white crime, presumably showing it is sensitive to the problem of racial profiling.

Yet the ghosts of the past still haunt us. In 1988 the A.M.E. Church conventioneers on the way out of town groused about the "shabby treatment" they had received, including a shortage of hotel rooms and "inadequate restaurant service downtown." Some could not help but wonder if that was because of their color. When asked if they would ever return to Fort Worth, one A.M.E. church official replied, "Maybe in the next millennium." They have not been back since.[27]

In 2002 when the *Fort Worth Star-Telegram* ran a seven-part series on "The Color of Hate: How the Jim Crow Era Shamed and Shaped Our City," the editors felt obliged to explain why they were re-opening old wounds. The series was generally well-received, but one letter to the editor probably spoke for many readers: "I was a child in the '60s, and I didn't know any of this stuff then, and I don't care to know about it now, and I don't want my children to know."[28] As long as we refuse to face our past we can never move on. We don't want to live in the past, but we want to know our past because from knowing comes understanding. It starts with acknowledging that Fort Worth's black community has never been all this or all that, and at the end of the day both black and white communities want the same things: respect, a good life, and a better future for their children.

Here in the twenty-first century, Fort Worth's black community is still plagued by the same old problems: lack of housing, lack of opportunity, blighted neighborhoods; in other words, being marginalized. Only the terms of the argument have changed: instead of lamenting the evils of institutionalized segregation, the discussion now is about assessing blame and calculating the costs of fixing the problems. Having achieved equal status before the law, blacks have come up against the "glass ceiling" of reality. For instance, although the "Rosedale corridor" through the heart of the Near South Side neighborhood has been targeted for redevelopment for years, the going is slow. For instance, in the spring of 2013 the street was widened and new lighting and traffic islands added. However, it took the city more than a year to put up the signage on the cross streets. And Mosier Valley was approved for a city park in February 2014, but that is not the same thing as having a city park like most white neighborhoods. At the time of the announcement, a spokesman for the city's Parks and Community Services Department explained that Mosier Valley Park has to get in the "queue," which includes creating a "master plan" that acknowledges both the historical and environmental factors. The only thing the city could promise as of 2014 was a "ceremony" to announce the acquisition of the land and "just to recognize the history of Mosier Valley." Who knows when an actual park will be built?[29]

Wrestling with the Past

The dismantling of Jim Crow in the 1960s came at a steep price. Historically, persecution and bigotry had pushed African Americans to close ranks and to honor their own, embracing the occasional victory in the courts or on the playing field as a milestone on the journey to equality. But the civil rights movement for all its accomplishments proved a mixed blessing; black schools closed down, black businesses could not compete, and black churches struggled to attract young members. Juneteenth was one of the most notable casualties of civil rights success. For many years it had been *the* African-American holiday, more meaningful to

African-American residents of Texas even than the Fourth of July. Its importance on the black calendar may have peaked in 1947 with the big parade through downtown Fort Worth. In the years that followed, the day retained its meaning as a social event in the black community. In 1974 more than 10,000 people crowded into Sycamore Park, and the following year 18,000-plus gathered there, making Sycamore the new Greenway as a gathering spot for the black community.[30]

As Jim Crow barriers fell, however, Juneteenth lost much of its historic significance. It became almost an embarrassing reminder of the bad old days, and how it took white soldiers to free black slaves. Cecil Williams, a long-time black resident of Fort Worth, lamented a few days before the celebration in 2003, "Juneteenth isn't what it used to be." He explained why: "It used to be a big holiday. . . . The spirit and knowledge of the day isn't as strong as it used to be. Over the years each generation has strayed further and further away from celebrating the day." The days when the city's black residents gather by the thousands in Greenway Park or Sycamore Park to celebrate something that happened in 1865 will never return. Today, blacks can picnic in any city park they wish, go to a movie, hang out at the mall, or take in a baseball game if the Texas Rangers are at home. Every year the *Star-Telegram* reminds its readers of the importance of Juneteenth. In the early years the newspaper did not even mention it unless trouble occurred.[31]

Photo 37. Juneteenth celebration

By 1958, the annual Juneteenth holiday was so ingrained in the fabric of the community that Convair, the city's biggest employer, sponsored a major celebration for its employees and their families at Convair Recreation Area, and even produced a souvenir book of the event. Courtesy of Fort Worth collector Dalton Hoffman.

Ironically, even as its meaning was fading, Juneteenth was being elevated as an important date on the calendar. In 1980 the legislature made it an official state holiday, and in the years since it has been appropriated as a national event inspiring laudatory editorials and countless newspaper columns. Today forty-one states and the District of Columbia observe Juneteenth, and Congress has taken up the proposal to make it a National Day of Observance similar to Flag Day. Locally, however, it is hardly a red-letter date on the calendar.[32]

What happened to Juneteenth is Martin Luther King Day (the third Monday in January), which was declared a national holiday in 1983. For black Americans it is important because it honors one of their own instead of recalling an 1865 proclamation by a white Army officer. King's martyrdom to the cause of freedom and equality simply adds to the popular appeal. Truth be told, Juneteenth celebrations are as much reminders of Jim Crow as of emancipation. That fact was underscored by the long-standing tradition of only opening two city parks to blacks on that date: Forest Park and the Botanical Gardens. Also galling was the fact that white businesses largely funded the day's activities, and special sections for whites were set aside at all the events. It is no wonder the younger generation of African Americans prefers to recognize a different date on the calendar. Tarrant County blacks have commemorated MLK Day in a big way ever since 1984. The day includes the sort of festivities that used to mark Juneteenth, starting with a parade through downtown. Besides speeches and performances by high school bands, a scholarship awards ceremony is also part of the activities now.[33]

There are other casualties of desegregation. The whole black business corridor that grew up on Jones and East Ninth and East Fourth is gone, a victim of changing times and changing attitudes. Black customers, like white, will do their shopping at the stores that give them the best selection at the best price, and black retailers could not compete. In 1992 the president of the Black Chamber of Commerce said, "African-American business is in worse financial shape now than it was before the civil rights movement broke the back of racial segregation in the 1960s."[34]

In some ways, education was in the same sinking boat as retail. Beloved I.M. Terrell High School was boarded up in 1973, bringing down the curtain on an educational and cultural icon after half a century. Similarly, James E. Guinn Elementary closed in 1980 after sixty-three years, its teachers and students parceled out among other, predominantly white schools. These all-black schools—and we can add to them Riverside Colored School (1911-1936)—instilled strong values as well as the 3Rs in their students. Ironically, although they were inferior to white schools in terms of facilities and resources, they were still remembered by their alumni years later with "fondness and pride." Everyone agreed, the faculty and students had been more like "a great family than a school." In 1985, I.M. Terrell alumni gathered for an "All Student" Reunion that was so big they had to hold it in the Convention Center. A "Who's Who" of black Fort Worth showed up that included gospel songbird Francine Morrison, Dr. Marion Brooks, Rev. R.V. Jones, and too many others to mention. In the end, however, the ideal of racial equality trumped the pride, family atmosphere, and high standards of these monuments to black education.[35]

Another casualty of the victory over Jim Crow was an independent black press. At the height of its influence in the late 1940s, when there were at least 155 black-owned newspapers in the country and most white papers did not have a single black person on staff, the black pres spoke for the community. It was downhill after that. Once the *Fort Worth Press* and *Star-Telegram* began covering news out of the black community that could not be categorized as either crime or high-jinks, the writing was on the wall. Perhaps nothing symbolized the changing times more than when the major newspapers started capitalizing the word "Negro" and referring to black men by their last name preceded by "Mr." The black-owned press tried to hang on by filling a niche, like the *Lake Como Monitor*, or appealing to black pride like the *Texas Times* or *La Vida News*, but in terms of staff, advertising revenue, and national coverage, they simply could not compete. The only stories the black press could bring a fresh perspective to were civil rights stories and when black celebrities like Joe Louis or Adam Clayton Powell came to town.[36]

Today we have one daily newspaper in Fort Worth to cover all the news in town, regardless of race or ethnicity. The *Star-Telegram* is no longer locally owned; its policies and practices are set by corporate headquarters in a distant city, and it has a diverse staff. Southern or even white prejudices no longer shape the news. But local news has also suffered, as neighborhood events, marriages, deaths, and the life are no longer covered in detail. Like in so many other areas, something has been gained but something had been lost.

Lenora Rolla—Woman on a mission[37]

Lenora Rolla wore many hats during her ninety-seven years, but no matter the hat she happened to be wearing at any given time, she was always a tireless advocate for the rights of women and African Americans. Her humble origins make her story all the more amazing as she literally came up from poverty, a broken home, and discrimination to become a role model for all who knew her.

She was born Lenora Butler on March 4, 1904, in Palestine, Texas. Her parents were Richard and Amanda Butler, a farmer and a maid. She grew up in Anderson County hearing her grandmother's stories about the bad old days of slavery. But life was still tough for African Americans even forty years after emancipation. Many years later, someone would ask her if she remembered when bacon was 10¢ a pound. She responded that her family wasn't worried about 10¢-a-pound bacon; they ate liver because it was only 5¢ a pound.

Before she was five, her mother moved to Fort Worth in search of work, finding it as a domestic in the home of a white family, leaving Lenora back in east Texas. The girl got to spend her summers with her mother until she was fourteen, then she joined her mother in Fort Worth to attend high school because Anderson County had no high school for blacks. Fort Worth Colored High School was a Mecca for black students from all over Tarrant County who wanted to learn more than simple reading, writing and 'rithmitic. Lenora took Latin and literature and other academic courses, graduating in 1921. But she wanted more. She began taking correspondence courses from Prairie View A&M and Bishop College while supporting herself as a substitute teacher at her alma mater. Looking for a new challenge and more income, she went to work for her uncle in the insurance business, one of the few lines of work where blacks could run their own show. She sold "street policies" for the next twenty years.

Church was always central to her life. As a twelve-year-old in 1916 she went down front to be baptized at Southside Christian Church, and her commitment never wavered for the rest of her life. Still in her twenties, she took a job with the Southern Christian Institute in Edwards, Mississippi, moving in to the girls' dormitory. But she was drawn back to Fort Worth where she went to work as a proof-reader for a black newspaper while selling insurance on the side. She really found her niche in life as a community activist in a community short of black female role models. In 1936 she went to Washington, D.C. to work for Mary McLeod Bethune, a living legend who had been appointed by President Franklin Roosevelt to lead the "Negro Affairs" division of the National Youth Administration. There she got to know not just Bethune but also First Lady Eleanor Roosevelt. She was inspired to become a "Bethunite," as Mary McLeod Bethune's followers called themselves. Their leader was a 5'4" ball of fire with a silver tongue who defied black leadership stereotypes with her gender and "ebony" skin tone.

Lenora was still in Washington when the war came in 1941. She went to work for the U.S. Maritime Commission in the clerical and typing pool. At the end of the war she received a War Service Certificate in recognition of her hard work. During the war she also continued her college education at Howard University in the city. On a trip back to Fort Worth she met and fell in love with Jacob Rolla, a member of the Southside Christian Church. He followed her back to Washington where they married on June 22, 1944. Later that year they returned to Fort Worth for good. He worked for the railroad, and she went back to teaching at her old high school (now I.M. Terrell). Their marriage endured until Jacob died in 1984.

While teaching, she took the federal civil service exam, scoring 85.6 out of 100. When she encountered the same old Jim Crow barriers in federal employment, she left in 1949 to become a licensed funeral director, which was another way to serve the black community. In 1951 she gave civil service another try, again passing the test with ease to become the first black female postal clerk in Fort Worth.

As she got older, she devoted more and more time to public service and church work. She joined the Tarrant County Precinct Workers' Council, an advocacy group in majority-black precincts. She was now a member of the East Annie St. Christian Church and attended every annual convention of the National Christian Missionary Convention. She addressed the World Convention of the United Christian Missionary Society in 1953, served as president of the Christian Women's Fellowship, 1954–55, and was selected for the board of the Fort Worth Area Council of Churches. She was never just a token member of any group or organization.

She could never be content doing just one thing. In 1952 she returned to newspapering as managing editor of the *Dallas Express*, the oldest black newspaper in Texas. In that capacity, she covered the beginning of the modern civil rights movement in Montgomery, Alabama. In 1955 she was tapped by Jarvis Christian College, a historically black institution, to be Dean of Women. She continued to divide her time between gainful employment and community service. In the 1960s while sitting on the executive committee of the Tarrant County Community Action Agency, she attended the Urban Training Center in Chicago. They put Rolla and her fellow students on the mean streets of Chicago with nothing but a toothbrush, a comb, and $4.50 in their pockets. Their assignment: To find a way to survive for three days without begging or committing a crime. Also while in Chicago, she learned about Martin Luther King, Jr.'s "March on Washington." She took the train to be a part of the historic moment and came home to Fort Worth reinvigorated to fight for black civil rights.

Rolla did not slow down in her later years. She worked to revitalize the predominantly black Near South Side and secure historical markers for black landmarks in the city. Perhaps her most notable work was preserving the city's black history. She spearheaded the effort to establish the Tarrant

County Black Historical & Genealogical Society. In the beginning it was a lonely, one-woman fight, but over the years she recruited allies and supporters. In 1977 the Tarrant County Black Historical and Genealogical Society was formally launched in her home with twenty-one charter members. In 1980 the Society moved into its permanent home in the historic A.L. Boone house at 1120 East Humboldt. In May 2011 the Lenora Rolla Heritage Center Museum opened there. In 1986 she was inducted into the Black Woman's Hall of Fame. Two years later she received the Carter G. Woodson Memorial Award for "making significant positive change in a local [black] community." On the occasion of her ninety-fifth birthday in 1999, Mayor Kenneth Barr declared March 4 "Lenora Butler Rolla Day" in Fort Worth.

On June 29, 2001, Lenora Rolla died at her home, surrounded by friends and admirers. The *Star-Telegram*, a newspaper that would have ignored her passing in earlier years, eulogized her as a "tireless activist to preserve local history," calling her "feisty" and "no-nonsense." People came from all over the country to attend her funeral. One speaker simply said of her passing, she had been "promoted to glory."

Lenora Rolla's life and accomplishments are impossible to sum up in a few sentences. Her causes were legion: education, church, the poor, civil rights, black history, women's issues, and historic preservation, to name just the best-known. She mixed with "kings and commoners," talking to troubled youths then attending a formal affair to chat with luminaries President Lyndon Johnson, Congressman Jim Wright, or Black Panther founder Stokely Carmichael. She never had any children of her own, but she mentored generations of Fort Worth's black children with wise words and an exemplary life. She devoted her life to learning and teaching, two sides of the same coin. She was a believer in the hard-work-and-self-help philosophy of Frederick Douglass, Booker T. Washington and Mary McLeod Bethune. She once said, "I have no advice for people who are down and out. Faith is what they need, and I can't give that to anybody." She never had the time to write her own life story. She was too busy changing the world and preserving her community's history. That is too bad because it is easy to forget that her life was not one success after another. She struggled her entire life, but through it all she persevered, proving that the good people do also lives after them.

Enoch Jackson—Black *Shammas*, Jewish Hero[38]

Many white churches over the years employed black "porters" (janitors), among them First Baptist Church. Their beloved, long-time janitor was Balaam Shaw. In 1927, First Baptist preacher J. Frank Norris announced that he would baptize Shaw in the church baptistery, which so outraged some church members that Norris called it off.

Enoch Jackson and Temple Beth-El had a much happier ending because he was more than just a janitor. He was also a beloved member of the Temple Beth-El family for four decades even though he was not born Jewish nor did he convert to Judaism. In 1927 Beth-El was looking for a new janitor when Rabbi Harry Merfeld met Jackson while traveling in the northeast. Jackson was a skilled handyman, having learned those skills with Ringling Brothers Circus. Prior to that he had performed on the vaudeville stage, singing, tap-dancing, and telling jokes as the opening act for such big-name stars as Mae West. When Jackson left Ringling Brothers he was looking for new adventures. That is when he met Rabbi Merfeld who persuaded him to come to Fort Worth and work for Temple Beth-El. What helped make up his mind was that his grandmothers had been Jewish, and he had always been curious about that part of his heritage.

He may have started as a janitor, but he became much more than that over the years that followed. In Yiddish, he was what is known as a *shammas*—someone who "not only cleans the synagogue and polishes the silver but also manages the premises and cares for its people." In Jewish lore, the *shammas* is the "guardian" of the synagogue in an almost mystical sense. Jackson was adopted by the Temple Beth-El family, learning Hebrew, and helping members of "the Sisterhood" translate the words inscribed on the Passover seder plate. He gladly performed any duty asked of him, including directing traffic in the parking lot for worship services.

But Jackson won immortality in the history of Temple Beth-El in the early-morning hours of August 29, 1946, when the building caught fire. Only a few months earlier the congregation had paid off the last installment of its thirty-year mortgage; the building was now theirs, free and clear. Then disaster struck. The cause of the fire has never been established although it seems to have started in the basement social hall. It grew into a three-alarm blaze before the fire department finally put it out. Jackson was the only one present at the time. He could have fled the burning building, and no one would have thought the less of him, but instead of saving himself, he dashed into the sanctuary to save priceless Torah scrolls. Jackson's place in Temple history was forever set. He remained *shammas* at Temple Beth-el for another twenty-two years before retiring in 1968, by which date the black janitor with the Old-Testament name had more tenure at Beth-El than any rabbi in the congregation's history. Interviewed by the *Star-Telegram*, he said his favorite Jewish holiday was Yom Kippur (the Day of Atonement) because the focus on meditation made it a time of peace and quiet around the Temple.

In "blaxploitation" movies of the 1970s, a "shamus" was a black, kick-butt private detective, the most famous example being Richard Roundtree's "Shaft" in the movie of the same name. Thanks to Enoch Jackson, "shammas" (same pronunciation, different spelling) conjures up a far nobler image.

NOTES

1. The assertion that Webber was the richest African American in Fort Worth comes from Moseley, "Negro Has Come a Long Way in Housing," (No. 3), August 27, 1967.
2. Quote is by the Reverend C.A. Holliday, Moseley, "City's Negro Population Quiet, Busy" (No. 1), August 24, 1967.
3. Ousley (1934–1971), who performed under the stage name "King Curtis," was a soul, jazz, and R&B artist. Redman (1931–2006) was a jazz artist. Moffett (1929–1997) was also a jazz artist. The I.M. Terrell band made its mark with hand-me-down instruments and little recognition in the white press.
4. Randolph Denard Ornette Coleman, born in Fort Worth in 1930, started playing the saxophone at age fourteen. He went on to become a founder of the free jazz movement. He was still performing almost up to his death on June 11, 2015. John Litweiler, *Ornette Coleman: A Harmolodic Life* (London: Quartet Books, 1992). For Ray Sharpe, see Gerard Herzhaft, ed., *Encyclopedia of the Blues*, 2nd ed. (Fayetteville: University of Arkansas Press, 1997). Coleman was not the only "world-class" jazz artist to come out of I.M. Terrell. Other notable names include James Hamilton, Willie Crenshaw, Prince Lawsha, Nathaniel Scott, Charles Moffatt, William Lawsha, Charles Scott, Dewey Redman, and Thomas Reese.
5. The Jimi Hendrix Experience consisted of the band's namesake plus Noel Redding on bass and Mitch Mitchell on drums. Jimi did not incinerate his guitar on stage that night as he did four months later at the Monterey Pop Festival, Monterey, CA., but he still electrified the audience with his blues-informed psychedelic rock. Nobles, *Rock and Roll*, 27, 79. Additional details of Hendrix's 1967 Fort Worth appearance come from author's own recollections.
6. The Caravan of Dreams, at 312 Houston, was best described as a "performing arts center," a combination theater, nightclub, and rooftop garden that helped spark the Bass-led revival of downtown Fort Worth. It was distinguished from street level by its unique geodesic dome visible above the roof line. It enjoyed a good run before closing in 2001. *Fort Worth Star-Telegram*, September 29 and October 2, 1983; May 12, 2014.
7. Eastman was a product of Paul Quinn College before settling in Fort Worth. Jones, *Renegades*, 291–94.

8. "Negro Has Come a Long Way in Housing," *Fort Worth Press*, August 27, 1967.
9. "Homelessness in Fort Worth," a state-of-the city report in *Fort Worth Star-Telegram*, October 19, 2014.
10. Ironically, in less than six years, with its finances in free fall, Radio Shack was ready to abandon its "world-class" river-front headquarters and find cheaper digs. *Fort Worth Star-Telegram*, January 9, 2003; November 12 and 15 (Mitch Schnurman editorial), 2009.
11. Sohmer, "Rock Island Bottom," 44–112.
12. The North-South Freeway practically obliterated Crump and Harding streets, taking out, for instance, the Negro YWCA at 1916 Crump. Sharpe, *One Hundred Years*, n.p.
13. Fort Worth historian Charles Liddell has photographed surviving examples of shotgun houses in Fort Worth. Those photos can be seen on the website www.fortwortharchitecture.com in the "Jack White Photos" section. Three or four examples are just off East Rosedale. Ironically, Rosedale itself has been redeveloped for the twenty-first century while the shotgun houses are relics of the 1920s or earlier.
14. *Fort Worth Star-Telegram*, September 26, 2013.
15. *Fort Worth Star-Telegram*, January 29, 2014.
16. For statistic, see *Fort Worth Star-Telegram*, May 6, 1991.
17. By contrast, Dallas still had not adopted single-member voting districts two decades later. *Dallas Morning News*, December 20, 1990. For Bagsby, see "The Legacy of Dionne Bagsby," *Fort Worth Star-Telegram*, April 2, 2005. "Political Pioneers Reflect on Progress," ibid., February 28, 2008. For Barbour, see obituary, ibid., February 4, 2015.
18. Dansby was pushed out of office by the school board two years later for unspecified reasons. Though his tenure was cut short and did not end well, that does not make him any less a pioneer in Fort Worth race relations. *Fort Worth Star-Telegram*, June 3 and 4, 2014.
19. Knight, *Fort Worth*, 247.
20. See J.B. Roberts, "When Fort Worth Was a Frontier Town Twenty-five Years Ago," *Fort Worth Star-Telegram*, December 12, 1909. Amon Carter owned the *Star-Telegram*.
21. For Tucker, see Bob Ray Sanders, "Tombstone Is Tribute to Historic First in City," *Fort Worth Star-Telegram*, July 23, 2006. See also Sanders, "Black History Month. . . ," ibid., February 12, 2014.
22. *Dallas Morning News*, June 18, 1992.

23. Today, the Austins' creation has grown into the National Multicultural Western Heritage Museum.
24. "Telling Our Own Story," the dedication of the Wilbert M. Curtis Texas Prince Hall Library Museum, http://phoenixmasonry.org/telling_our_own_story.htm.
25. Francine Reese Morrison, known as the "Songbird of the South" and "God's Ambassador of Song," is an internationally known gospel singer and recording artist, born in Fort Worth in 1938.
26. Dallas' resolution was "non-binding," and after it passed some commissioners claimed to have been misled about what it said. *Fort Worth Star-Telegram*, May 19, 2004; and June 19, 2014. For Fort Worth Chamber, see www.fwmbcc.org.
27. *Dallas Morning News*, June 18, 1992.
28. "Letters, faxes and e-mails to the Editor" in response to the "Color of Hate" series, printed in *Fort Worth Star-Telegram*, November 3, 2002.
29. For park, see "Mosier Valley. . . Finally Gets Park," *Fort Worth Star-Telegram*, February 12, 2014.
30. For numbers, see Reby Cary, "Bicentennial and Juneteenth, 1976; Black Leadership in Fort Worth," *Fort Worth, The Black Prospective* [*sic*], p. 3.
31. *Fort Worth Star-Telegram*, June 13, 2003; and June 19, 2014 (editorial).
32. For the nationalization of Juneteenth, *Fort Worth Star-Telegram*, June 19, 1013.
33. MLK, Jr. Day has been officially observed as a "floating holiday" since January 20, 1986. For its history in Fort Worth, see *Fort Worth Star-Telegram*, January 15, 2014. White businesses donated food and drink and sometimes even underwrote the entertainment. For white involvement in earlier Juneteenth celebrations, see *Fort Worth Star-Telegram*, Junc 19, 1939; and *Fort Worth Press*, June20, 1939.
34. *Dallas Morning News*, June 19, 1992.
35. "Family" quote comes from James A. Hamilton referring to the black schools of his own day. Hamilton, *History and Directory*, 42. On February 14, 1988, a Texas state historical marker was dedicated at I.M. Terrell High School, with Lenora Rolla doing the unveiling honors. The following decade, after major remodeling and renovation, I.M. Terrell was reborn as an elementary school and FWISD computer operations center. In 2014 it was suggested as the "perfect site" for the District's Visual and Performing Arts Academy. *Fort Worth Star-Telegram*, December 3, 2014. For Riverside Colored School and quotation, see Susan Kline, application for historic marker for Riverside [Colored] School, 1999, Sec. 8, p. 11,

Billy W. Sills Archives. For 1985 reunion, see program, etc. in TCBH&GS Collections, Series II (Individual Collections), Box 1, File 1. Samuel Wilson, "Vanished Legacies and the Lost Culture of I.M. Terrell High School in Segregated Fort Worth," Master of Arts thesis in History, University of Texas at Arlington, 2012.

36. Katznelson, *Fear Itself,* 341. *La Vida,* which started publishing in 1957, is Tarrant County's only black newspaper. (It is published out of Arlington.) It covers black news and cultural events that the *Star-Telegram* overlooks. The *Lake Como Monitor* was started by W.H. Wilburn in the 1940s and published until the 1980s. Random copies have survived but not the complete run. It is another lost artifact of the times. Ironically, Powell had caused a black newspaper, the *Pittsburgh Courier,* to be censored by the U.S. Government during the war for subversive statements comparing the treatment of blacks in America to Jews in Germany. Katznelson, *Fear Itself,* 342.

37. Sources: "Lenora Rolla," unpublished autobiographical MS. in Lenora Rolla Papers. Allen (Sherrod), *Grace and Gumption,* pp. 194-99. Gooch, *Life of Rolla.* "Black History Month Timeline: Lenora Rolla," *Fort Worth Star-Telegram,* February 26, 2004. SCI was operated by the Disciples of Christ Church from 1882 until 1953 when it merged with Tougaloo College, and the campus was closed. It offered courses from elementary grades through college and was not accredited until 1931. Rolla went there to teach, not attend school. For "glory," see Gooch, "Life Events of Lenora Rolla," n. p., *Life of Rolla.*

38. Sources: Hollace Ava Weiner, ed., *Beth-El Congregation Centennial: Fort Worth, Texas, 1902-2002* (Fort Worth: Beth-El Temple, 2002), 43–44, 97. *Fort Worth Star-Telegram,* August 29, 1946. "Enoch Jackson" in Dept. of Health Services, Center for Health Statistics, State of California, *California Death Index, 1940–1997* (also available online, Ancestry.com, *California, Death Index, 1940–1997*). David R. Stokes, *The Shooting Salvationist* (Hanover, NH: Steerforth Press, 2011), 130.

Chapter 12

A Few Conclusions

Immersing oneself in a subject allows a writer to take certain liberties, one of which is drawing certain conclusions. I would be presumptuous to claim to completely understand the black experience, but I can make some observations about what I have learned.

One of the big differences between the black community in the past versus now is the message they hear from their own. Back in the early twentieth century, local black leaders preached the gospel of "self-sufficiency" and "self-dependency" as the path to success; today it is about empowerment, affirmative action, and political activism. The message delivered then, in particular from the pulpit, was, "Don't be angry, don't be hatin'; pull yourself up by your bootstraps and make a success of yourself!" And with that message came a big dollop of a thank-you to all the white people who had "helped and encouraged the negro to rise." Those messages would never fly today, but in 1905 and 1921 they were applauded by black audiences.[1]

The black ideal back then was not the multi-millionaire professional athlete or entertainer but the educated professional, the minister, the Pullman porter. When they think of success, African Americans can aim higher today, but the values represented by those doctors, ministers, porters seem to have gotten lost somewhere along the way when it seems every teenager wants to be a rapper or basketball player.

We still struggle with the legacy of slavery and Jim Crow. That legacy is not a simple matter of "whites bad, blacks good"; it is more nuanced than that. For instance, grateful whites frequently extended their favor to black servants who had served them long and faithfully. There is nothing wrong with such kindness except that it was always a one-way street; all the power was on one side. In the nineteenth century, John Pratt, Hagar Tucker, and Dan Daggett were all taken under the wing of benevolent whites. (See Chap. 2) Pratt, Tucker, and Daggett were proud men, but they were never allowed to forget the source of their good fortune. Their like could still be found during the modern civil rights era. For twenty-two years Walter Williams managed the Men's Tavern at River Crest Country Club. Dressed in a tuxedo and displaying impeccable manners, he served the club's wealthy clientele with aplomb. As he himself observed, a good sense of humor was invaluable. In 1976 Williams died of a heart attack, still on the job, at the age of forty-six. His funeral was packed with white country-club members come to pay their final respects. But though he was beloved by them, he would never have been considered their equal, no matter how long he worked there or how well he ran the Men's Tavern. Williams was part of the legacy of centuries of race relations that an Emancipation Proclamation or even a constitutional amendment could not change. What African Americans like John Pratt, Hagar Tucker, Jeff Daggett, and Walter Williams did was to help build bridges between the two races.[2]

Some things have not changed. The black church remains the heart and soul of the black community. The first regular gatherings of the freedmen during Reconstruction were for the purpose of worshiping, even before they had buildings to worship in. Years later, the black church provided valuable business and social contacts in the community and took the lead in the civil rights movement. Today the oldest organized black groups in

Fort Worth call places like Allen Chapel and Morning Chapel home. Their legacy can be seen in the celebration of anniversaries, such as the 111th anniversary of Paradise Missionary Baptist Church in 2014. The guest preacher for that occasion was ninety-one-year-old Lloyd Austin, who played a leading role at the dawn of the modern civil rights struggle in Riverside in the 1950s. Those black churches with 100-year-old histories will probably still be around in another 100 years.

Memory is a funny thing, especially collective historical memory. We learn one kind of history in school; we learn a different kind from those around us. That is because history is not just what happened; it is what people *believe* happened or want to believe happened. For the black community whose history is mostly oral, the problems of memory and perception are magnified. This is not to suggest that African Americans have a monopoly on selective historical memory, just that it plays such a large part in how they remember their history. In the absence of hard research and use of all the historian's tools, Fort Worth's black history contains many myths, some harmless, some misleading. Most white Fort Worth residents, including this author, grew up with little or no knowledge of the black community living in our midst. Some examples that came to light in the course of researching this book: J.L. Terry was an elderly white Fort Worth resident when he was interviewed for the "Federal Writers' Project" in the 1930s. Recalling the old days, he remembered when African-American Sol Bragg was executed for assaulting a white woman. The problem is, that's not what happened. Bragg was hanged for murder, and the victim was male. Then there was Lee M. Hammond, a (white) FWISD employee for thirty years who was interviewed for a Mack Williams "In Old Fort Worth" column. As Hammond remembered things, "all pupils north of the river" attended Marine Common School, at least until after annexation. He did not remember, if he ever knew, that there was once a Yellow Row Colored School north of the river (see Chap. 4). More recently, Madeleine Williams, Mack Williams' wife and a respected journalist in her own right, remembered conducting a one-woman crusade in 1950 to get "Fort Worth parks and golf courses opened to Negroes immediately." Also not true.[3]

Collective historical memory works in several ways. Take Evans Plaza, for instance, on the Near South Side. In 2011 the city declared the area a "community space" to help revive the blighted, black neighborhood around it. The central element of the Plaza was a timeline in stone inscribed with the names of distinguished African Americans who had contributed to Fort Worth history and culture, one of whom was Miss Sue Huffman, who was certainly distinguished but *not* African American. She was a highly educated woman and dedicated teacher but 100 percent white! In sifting through Fort Worth history searching for worthy subjects, the historical team behind the timeline latched onto Miss Huffman as a role model and declared her "the first African American to bear the title of superintendent of schools of the city of Fort Worth." The truth is, in 1881 city fathers were not appointing African Americans to run anything. After an uproar in the newspapers, the mistake was corrected, but no one ever explained how she got on the timeline in the first place. All we know is that the research was done by "a voluntary advisory committee" who turned their work over to "city staffers" who created the timeline. An egregious mistake was literally carved in stone, which makes it harder to correct. A spokesman for the African American community only made things worse by trying to explain that an African American woman *could* have been appointed school superintendent because "many blacks in Fort Worth at that time owned land and businesses." (Also not true.) Careless research compounded by faulty knowledge of history and an excess of political correctness produces bad history.[4]

The aim of the present work is to make a start at setting the record straight. The authors of *Fort Worth, The Black Prospective* [*sic*] in 1976 expressed the same hope that their work would "serve as a stimulus to inspire some of our local historians to dig into the very roots of Fort Worth and present a portrait of blacks as they really were." The current author was in the middle of graduate school at TCU in 1976. Now, nearly four decades later, that challenge is being answered with this and other works that are coming out soon.[5]

This work does not claim to be the last word on the history of Fort Worth's black community. More than 165 years of black history cannot be fully told even in 500 pages, and that leaves unanswered the question of who will read it. If this work blazes a trail, it will have accomplished its purpose. Hopefully, it will smoke out some more of those all-important primary source documents that the best history is written from. There are members of Fort Worth's black community who have letters, photos, and clippings that will help fill in the yawning gaps in the public record. There are also oral history interviews to do, recording the recollections of people who have lived in Fort Worth all their lives as did their parents and grandparents before them. The rich subject of black Fort Worth history could easily become a lifetime project for someone. But not the present author. I did not set out to produce a *magnum opus.* It is my hope that this modest work can serve as the starting point for a more in-depth study, that it might inspire others to take up the work. If it serves that function, then we have accomplished what we set out to accomplish.

The pity is that to date there is not a single published academic history that puts the history of Fort Worth blacks in context, not a single article in a scholarly journal, not a single balanced biography of a black leader to date. What often passes for a primary source, historic markers, are barely a blip on the radar. Of the 331 Texas State Markers in Tarrant County in 2009, only seven were about African-American history. Since that date a dozen or more markers have been added to the count, but only one of them dealing with African-American history (the Douglass-McGar Park marker). We have to ask why no one has taken up the challenge to write a scholarly history or even more makers. With two exceptions—octogenarian Reby Cary and *Star-Telegram* columnist Bob Ray Sanders—all the heavy lifting has been done by white historians. It does not have to be that way. Henry Louis Gates, Jr., the Harvard professor and historian of African-American history, has written about "Growing up

Colored" in Piedmont, West Virginia, in the 1950s. Piedmont is not much different from Fort Worth fifty or a hundred years ago, so his story in many ways parallels the story of any young African American growing up in Fort Worth at that time, but we are still waiting for that person to write about "Growing up Colored" in Fort Worth.[6]

History is a subject that does not appeal to most African Americans for complex reasons, one of which is that when African Americans look at our nation's history they do not see themselves in any of the leading roles. The familiar story of American history has always been about whites and for whites. This is not to say that black history can only be written by black historians, but it is telling that not a single history of Fort Worth's black community has been produced by a black academic.

A related question is how do we get the black community to "own" their own history? There is some truth to the idea that black history can best be told from the black perspective, but the telling has to be balanced with rigorous scholarship. It is not enough to have lived the story. Nor is it enough to trot out a few old-timers during Black History Month every year to reminisce about the bad old days.

The pre-civil-rights era left us with an awkward legacy that we still wrestle with today. Part of that legacy is a list of proscribed terms we can no longer use, and not just "negro" and "colored," which no one with any sense still uses. Even "mulatto," which has the sanction of being in the dictionary, has been banished from both scholarly dialogue and polite conversation. Other, more obscure terms that were perfectly acceptable a hundred years ago, specifically "yellow negro" and "maroon," are not just quaint but virtually unknown today. Yet they are part of the historical record. If we lose all knowledge of what those terms mean, how are we to understand statements like the one in the *Fort Worth Democrat* in 1879—"Some of our maroon colored citizens are getting altogether too fresh"—or the one in the *Fort Worth Telegram* in 1903 saying Milton Taylor, a "yellow negro," got off the train from Indian Territory and was arrested? When we scrub certain terms out of the dialogue for scholars and laymen alike, we lose a part of our history, and we need all of that history to understand how we got to where we are today. At one time, "yellow negro," "blue-gum negro," and "maroon" were part of the vernacular used by whites and blacks alike. "Yellow Negroes" were light-skinned African Americans whose fair complexions may have come from mixed parents, making it another term for mulatto. "Blue-gum negro" was a term rooted in superstition used to describe someone possessing "the most depraved qualities of his race." Blue-gums went with "short teeth" as a descriptive; superstition said the bite from such a person was as poisonous as the bite of a rattlesnake. Whites pooh-poohed the superstition, but appropriated the term to describe the most despicable blacks. Jefferson Davis, slave-owner and the only president of the Confederacy (1861–65), reportedly once said there was only one thing worse than a "blue-gum Negro," and that was hell.[7]

These terms need to be kept alive as part of our collective history, which is not to say in daily conversation, but in historical memory so that we can fully understand those distant days. They give us insight into the thinking of our predecessors, and remind us that the past is indeed a "foreign country" as the saying goes.

When it comes to writing the black history of our city, we have more raw materials than one might imagine. The *Chicago Defender*, the nation's leading black newspaper for decades, is now online and contains more than 3,000 references to contemporary persons and events in Fort Worth. Both of Fort Worth's leading white dailies in the modern era took up the challenge of trying to tell the story fairly. In 1967 at the height of the civil rights movement, Jack Moseley wrote a four-part series in the *Fort Worth Press*, "The Negro in Fort Worth," whose very title reflected the times. Moseley focused on population (Part 1), the church (Part 2), housing (Part 3), and jobs (Part 4). The series was full of positive accomplishments and hope for the future. Thirty-five years later, another newspaper reporter, Tim Madigan, revisited the subject, but Madigan's focus was not all the positive accomplishments and hope but all the ugliness spawned by the city's long history of racism. Apparently racism was a bigger subject in 2002 or else the *Star-Telegram* was willing to make a bigger commitment to telling the story. Madigan's excellent seven-part series, titled "The Color of Hate," reminded readers how bad things used to be, including the years covered by Moseley. Moseley's approach was more statistical, Madigan's was more evocative.[8]

This volume was partly inspired by their work. But whereas Moseley's work reflected the can-do spirit of the Sixties and Madigan saw nothing but hate, in the twenty-first century we need to move beyond those two polarizing views and see the bigger picture. The truth is, Fort Worth blacks in the early days created a vibrant community within the boundaries set by Jim Crow. They were a long way from Martin Luther King, Jr.'s "mountain top," but they were not living in abject fear for their lives either. Even if they were not terrorized, they were still treated as second-class citizens by the larger white community.

One of Tim Madigan's most telling episodes was about the lynching of Fred Rouse in 1921 (see Chap. 4). Rouse was hanged by a mob of white vigilantes in the dark of night, but he was not lynched just because he was black; he was lynched because he was a black strikebreaker who shot two striking Swift workers. He would probably have suffered the same fate had he been white; being black just compounded his crime in the mob's eyes. The point here is not to argue that Fred Rouse was not lynched, but to point out that his lynching was more complicated than a simple night-rider episode. The history of Fort Worth's black community is also more complicated than a simple litany of outrages perpetrated by whites and relieved occasionally by the appearance of a black hero.[9]

The legends warm our hearts, but they also obscure the truth. The Fort Worth black community has its share of cherished legends about the "old days" and about beloved figures. One such legend about Hazel Harvey Peace came up on the occasion of her 100th birthday in 2007. The Dean of UNT's School of Library and Information Sciences, which had endowed a chair in her honor, told the audience how she used to go to the Fort Worth Public Library to check out books, but because of her race she was not permitted to browse the stacks. She could only request the books she wanted at the check-out counter and wait while the librarian retrieved them then she had to leave. Yet, according to Ms. Peace herself in newspaper interviews, she went to the library as a girl, checked out her own books, and took them home to read. The two stories are close enough to be accepted as more or less the same, but they are not the same. One paints a far grimmer picture of Jim Crow as a cruel, mindless system. The other sounds more historical. The library ladies in the old days were not crusading civil rights activists, but they were not heartless bigots either. Ms. Peace did state that later, while teaching at I.M. Terrell, she took her students to the TCU Library to do research because they were not allowed to use the reference materials in (as opposed to checking them out of) the Fort Worth Library. Presumably, the librarians at TCU Library welcomed them.[10]

All the memorial plaques and "Black History Months" cannot cover up the fact that there is still a strong undercurrent of anger in the black community. The cover story of the *Fort Worth Weekly* for August 3–9, 2005, was provocatively titled, "Hushed Up and Unhappy," which the subtitle explained referred to "Fort Worth's black leaders [who] won't stay quiet much longer." The article is built around interviews with several prominent black leaders old enough to recall the bad, old days and who don't see much improvement going on forty years. Said Reverend Roosevelt Sutton, "They should call the city council 'Mary Kay' because it's all cosmetic." Most of the black leaders interviewed for the story were either current or retired ministers of historically black congregations, which gave them a sympathetic audience to their strongly worded opinions.[11]

When read in the current climate of peaceful co-existence, their words sound like the manifesto of some sixties black-power radical. But the black community still feels it has much to be angry about, especially with law enforcement and the judicial system. Going back a century and more, race relations always seem to start with the police. Nothing, it sometimes seems, has changed. In September 2011, black leaders stated they were tired of the pervasive "bullying, intimidating and threatening" by Fort Worth police officers. They called on Police Chief Jeff Halstead to resign. All this came shortly before the announcement that a Tarrant County grand jury had no-billed a white officer in the fatal shooting of a black motorist.[12]

Often overlooked is that fact that indifference can be just as destructive as overt racism, and the leadership of Fort Worth has been just as guilty of this over the years. One example is the re-developed East Rosedale. The street is the central axis of the black community on the east side, and city leaders proudly point to it as Exhibit A in the city's commitment to uplift the Near South Side. But it took more than two years for the city to get around to something as simple as putting up signage to mark the cross streets on East Rosedale. This is Exhibit A that proves the more things change, the more they stay the same.

Coming to grips with the past can take many forms. Evans Plaza is one. Another is public art. In a burst of good intentions, the city has belatedly sought to recognize the contributions of African Americans to our city's history by commissioning commemorative artworks. On February 24, 2002, an alliance of interests came together at the Intermodal Transportation Center (ITC) on Jones to dedicate "The Historic Wall" by Denton artist Paula Blincoe Collins. The five panels that compose the sculpture in clay recognize the black contribution to Fort Worth's economic and cultural life from 1865 to 1940. Four years in the making, "The Wall" has already been seen by the thousands of travelers who passed through the ITC daily, far more than would ever read an old-fashioned history book. A few blocks south of the ITC in the main hall of the Texas & Pacific Terminal on Lancaster is a "mural sculpture" by Cleburne sculptor Jeff Gottfried titled "Freedom Train." In simple profile it traces the role played by African Americans in the history of railroad transportation in this country. Both "The Historic Wall" and the

"Freedom Train" are modern works with an old-fashioned sensibility. If they don't add anything to our historical knowledge they at least raise public consciousness.[13]

One last conclusion I came to in the course of this study is that after all the mythology is scraped away, Fort Worth's black community has much to be proud of. Despite a century's worth of repression and degradation, it produced vibrant neighborhoods and men and women of accomplishment. Just to name two, I.M. Terrell and Como were beacons of light. The irony is that both were products of segregation. Terrell-graduate James Cash said many years after leaving his hometown, "Growing up in totally segregated Fort Worth helped prepare me for many of the things I faced [and overcame]."[14]

Fort Worth today is 22 percent black and that percentage will continue growing in the years to come. Sometime in the next two-to-three decades according to demographers, Fort Worth's minorities will become the majority, and the present white majority will find itself in the unfamiliar position of being the minority. Already in the first decade of the twenty-first century, the combined African-American-Hispanic population of the Fort Worth-Dallas metroplex grew by more than 600,000 while the Anglo population fell by 156,732. During that same period, the black population of Texas grew by 11 percent. At some point in the not-too-distant future these two demographic trends will cross, and it will be a brand-new world. Today's minorities will be tomorrow's majority. They will own not only the present, but also the past because every generation rewrites the past to reflect its own experiences and values. How will the historians of the future write Fort Worth's history? Not the same way as the current generation and certainly not the same way as our predecessors. All that the current generation of historians can do is try to leave an accurate record of the past, not colored by our own cultural biases and racial perspectives. Unfortunately, every year that passes sees the sources for our community's black history recede that much further from living memory. The burden is on current historians to leave as accurate a record as possible so that those who follow can build on it. We want our children and our children's children to be able to read the history of the *entire* Fort Worth community, not just one segment of it.[15]

Understanding where we came from helps us know where we are going. "Us" today means all of Fort Worth, not just black or white or brown Fort Worth. We can no longer leave half our history to mythology and vague memories. In 2014 a Fort Worth author wrote, "Little has been published on Fort Worth's African-American community, and the potential does not seem hopeful." It is hoped that this work can be the first step toward remedying that failure.[16]

Notes

1. See addresses delivered by various black speakers to black audiences, *Fort Worth Telegram*, August 28, 1905; and *Fort Worth Star-Telegram*, October 12, 1921.
2. Information on Walter Williams comes from Weiner, *River Crest*, 418, and personal interviews.
3. For J.L. Terry's story, see fnt. 28 in the present volume. For Hammond, see "In Old Fort Worth: 'The First Time I Saw Fort Worth," in Mack Williams, ed., *In Old Fort Worth: The Story of a City and Its People as Published in The News-Tribune in 1976 and 1977* (Fort Worth: privately printed, 1986), 117. For Madeleine Williams, see Williams, "How Reporter's Question Opened Parks to Negroes," *Fort Worth News-Tribune*, July 2–4, 1976, p. 14. Williams' columns on Fort Worth history ran in the *Fort Worth News-Tribune* for years.
4. For Sue Huffman, see Linda P. Campbell, "A Mistaken Milestone Makes It into a Fort Worth Landmark," *Fort Worth Star-Telegram*, August 11, 2011; and Knight, *Fort Worth*, 49, 150. Mrs. Huffman lost her job as superintendent after a few months when the public-school proposal collapsed. It was reborn the next year with Alexander Hogg as superintendent.
5. *Fort Worth, The Black Prospective* [*sic*].
6. Henry Louis Gates, Jr., "Growing up Colored," *American Heritage Magazine* 62, no. 2 (Summer 2012): 56–63.
7. *Fort Worth Daily Democrat*, September 4, 1879. *Fort Worth Telegram*, October 29, 1903. For "yellow negroes," see *Fort Worth Morning Register*, September 17, 1901. For Jefferson Davis and "blue-gum negroes," see *Fort Worth Register*, July 21, 1897.
8. Moseley, "The Negro in Fort Worth," *Fort Worth Press*, August 24, 25, 27, and 28, 1967. Tim Madigan, "The Color of Hate," *Fort Worth Star-Telegram*, seven-part series, October 6, 7, 8, 9, 10, 12, and 13, 2002.
9. Madigan compares Lloyd and Macie Austin, the black couple who broke the color barrier in the Riverside neighborhood, with Rosa Parks, "the Alabama seamstress whose desire to rest her weary feet" and sparked the historic Montgomery bus boycott in 1955. The problem is, Parks was no foot-weary domestic but a dedicated civil rights activist, and the Austins were just a hard-working couple trying to move up the ladder. Tim Madi-

gan, "Showdown on Judkins St.," *Fort Worth Star-Telegram*, October 6, 2002.

10. This author remembers growing up in Fort Worth in the 1950s and going to the public library to check out books and seeing black kids browsing in the stacks. That does not mean they were welcome to stay and read their choices, but at least they were allowed in the stacks in those years. *Fort Worth Star-Telegram*, May 23, 1977.
11. Christine Stanley and Jeff Prince, "Hushed Up and Unhappy," *Fort Worth Weekly*, August 3–9, 2005, p. 11.
12. Reviewed along with other notable events in the tenure of outgoing Chief Halstead in 2014. *Fort Worth Star-Telegram*, November 11, 2014.
13. For the dedication of the Collins mural, see Bob Ray Sanders, "Station Mural," *Fort Worth Star-Telegram*, February 24, 2002.
14. *Fort Worth Star-Telegram*, February 14, 2014.
15. The statistics come from *Fort Worth Star-Telegram*, August 9, 2013.
16. Rich, *Fort Worth*, 166.

Bibliography

PRIMARY SOURCES

Bundy, William Oliver. *Life of William Madison McDonald.* Fort Worth: Bunker Printing & Book Co., 1925. Bundy was an African-American contemporary and huge admirer of McDonald; he was not a trained historian or biographer.

Cary, Reby. *We've Come This Far: A 2007 Retrospective on African Americans in Fort Worth and Tarrant County.* Fort Worth, TX: Privately Printed, 2007. For a list of Cary's books covering the entire history of the black community in Fort Worth from his own unique perspective, see "Secondary Sources" below.

"Federal Writers' Project." Research Data: Fort Worth and Tarrant County, Texas. Series I. 77 vols. with Index and on microfiche. Fort Worth Public Library Unit, 1941. Fort Worth Library. Central Branch. Local History, Genealogy, & Archives Unit.

Fort Worth, City of. Records of the City of Fort Worth. Planning Dept. Series III. 2 boxes. Fort Worth Library. Central Branch. Local History, Genealogy, & Archives Unit.

Fort Worth City Directory, 1877–1928. Microfiche. Fort Worth Library, Central Branch, Local History, Genealogy, & Archives Unit.

Fox, George. "End of an Era." In *Lives and Voices: A Collection of American Jewish Memoirs,* edited by Stanley F. Chyet, 279–281. Philadelphia, PA: Jewish Publication Society, 1972.

Gammel, H.N.P., compiler. *The Laws of Texas, 1822–1897.* 10 vols. Austin: The Gammel Book Co., 1898.

Gibson, W.H., Sr. *History of the United Brothers of Friendship and Sisters of the Mysterious Ten: A Negro Order.* Louisville, KY, 1897,. repr. Forgotten Books, 2012.

Graves, Edward. *The Invisible Chains.* Fort Worth: self-published, 1991. One man's take on African-American culture against a predominantly white, racist American society. Anything but cool and balanced!

Hall, Ron, and Denver Moore. *Same Kind of Different as Me: A Modern-Day Slave, an International Art Dealer, and the Unlikely Woman Who Bound Them Together.* Nashville, TN: Thomas Nelson, 2008. Moore is a TCU graduate who met Hall, a homeless man, while volunteering at the Union Gospel Mission.

Hamilton, William (former slave). See Handler, Zeke.

Handler, Zeke. "Interviews with former slaves." Fort Worth Public Library. Central Branch. Local History, Genealogy, & Archives Unit. Also cited in Mack Williams, ed. *The News-Tribune in Old Fort Worth* 13, no.1 (July 2, 3, 4, 1976): 15.

Hoffman, Dalton, Collections of. Hoffman is a lifelong collector of Fort Worth memorabilia, comprising his private holdings, which he has generously made available to researchers over the years.

Horace, Lillian, Collection. Tarrant County Black Historical & Genealogical Society Collections. Series II, 4 Boxes. Fort Worth Library, Central Branch, Local History & Genealogy Dept.

Hughes, Lyn. *An Anthology of Respect: The Pullman Porters National Historic Registry of African Americans Railroad Employees.* Chicago: Hughes Peterson Publishers, 2009.

Kilgore, Sam (former slave). See Handler, Zeke. "Interviews with Former Slaves."

Kinch, Samuel E., Jr. "Amon Carter: Publisher-Salesman." Master's thesis, University of Texas, , January, 1965.

Kirvin, Johnnie F. *Hey Boy! Hey George. The Pullman Porter: A Memoir.* Los Angeles: Privately printed by Carla S. Kirvin, 2009. This book is not specifically about a Fort Worth resident but is a very helpful volume understanding the life of the Pullman Porter during the golden age of train travel.

Landrum, Lynn W. *Dallas and the Trinity.* Dallas: A.H. Belo Corp. 1933.

Lubbock, Francis. *Six Decades in Texas, Or, Memoirs of Francis Richard Lubbock*. Edited by C.W. Raines. Austin: Pemberton Press, 1968. First published, Austin, TX: Ben C. Jones & Co., 1900.

Minton, J. "The Houston Riot and Courts-Martial of 1917." Carver Community Cultural Center, n.d. Military Reference Branch. National Archives & Records Administration. Washington, D.C.

Olmsted, Frederick Law. *A Journey Through Texas*. 1857. New York: Time-Life Educational, 1982.

_______. *Journeys and Explorations in the Cotton Kingdom*. 1861. Charleston, SC: Nabu Press, 2010.

Paddock, Capt. B.B., ed. *A Twentieth Century History and Biographical Record of North and West Texas*. Chicago: The Lewis Publishing Co., 1906.

Prince Hall Masons. *Proceedings of the Most Worshipful "Communication"* [convention] *of the Grand Lodge of Texas*. Annual, 1887–1929. Prince Hall Grand Lodge of Texas. Fort Worth, TX. The 1887 *Proceeding* was the 12th convention of the Texas lodges, but the first one in the Grand Lodge collections.

__________. *Souvenir Book, Masonic Golden Jubilee, 1875–1925*. Fort Worth: privately printed, 1925. Collections of the Prince Hall Grand Lodge of Texas, Fort Worth, TX.

Rawick, George P., ed. *The American Slave: A Composite Autobiography*. Series I and II, 10 Vols. Westport, CT.: Greenwood Press, 1972, 1979. Another form of the *Slave Narratives* that were collected, 1937–39.

Roberts, J.B. "Memories of an Early Police Reporter," *Fort Worth News-Tribune*, July 2–4, 1976, pp. 28–29.

Rolla, Lenora. Unpublished autobiographical MS. Vertical files. Fort Worth Library. Central Branch. Local History, Genealogy, & Archives Unit.

Ruffin, Edmund. *The Diary of Edmund Ruffin*. Edited by William Kaufman Scarborough. Baton Rouge: Louisiana State University Press, 1972–1989.

Slave Narratives. Federal Writers' Project. 17 volumes. Washington, D.C.: Library of Congress, Manuscript Division, 1940. These are actually field notes made by interviewers of 2,300 elderly African Americans who were once slaves and answered a standard set of questions posed by the interviewers. Various forms of the *Narratives* exist.

Smith, J. H. *Negro Directory of Fort Worth, Texas, 1937–1938.* "A listing of churches, schools, businesses and fraternal, civic, social organizations, and other activities," not residents. Collections of Fort Worth collector Dalton Hoffman.

Tarrant County Black Historical & Genealogical Society Archives. Fort Worth Public Library. Central Branch. Local History, Genealogy, & Archives Unit.

Terrell, I. M. High School. Yearbook (*The Tidings*). 1922 and 1923. Fort Worth, TX: published by the senior classes, 1922, 1923.

Terrell, J.C. *Reminiscences of the Early Days of Fort Worth.* Fort Worth, TX: TCU Press, 1999. First published Fort Worth: Texas Printing Company, 1906.

Turner, Ida. "Memoir." One box, 10 folders. Fort Worth Library. Central Branch. Local History, Genealogy, & Archives Unit.

Tyler, Ronnie C., and Lawrence R. Murphy, eds. *Slave Narratives of Texas.* 1974. Austin, TX: State House Press, 1997.

United States Federal Census, Tarrant County and Fort Worth, Ninth (1870)–Fifteenth (1930) On microfilm.

Williams, Mack H., ed. "In Old Fort Worth." *The News-Tribune.* 1975–1986. Collected columns based on interviews with old-timers.

Williams, Mack H., ed. *In Old Fort Worth: The Story of a City and Its People as Published in* The News Tribune *in 1976 and 1977.* Fort Worth: privately printed by Mack H. and Madeleine C. Williams, 1986.

Williams, Madeleine, "How Reporter's Question Opened Parks to Negroes," *Fort Worth News-Tribune*, July 2-4, 1976, p. 14.

Wilson, Jamie (former slave). See Handler, Zeke. "Interviews with Former Slaves."

PRIMARY SOURCES —ARCHIVES AND COLLECTIONS

Allen Frances, Collection. Tarrant County Archives. Dr. Daisy Emery Allen, 1876–1958, was a longtime resident and physician of Fort Worth.

Beth-El (Jewish) Congregation Archives. Fort Worth, Texas.

Billy W. Sills Center for Archives. Fort Worth Independent School District. 2720 Cullen St., Fort Worth, TX, 76107.

Calvin Little john Photography Archive. Dolph Briscoe Center for American History. University of Texas at Austin.

Cary, Reby. Collected Papers. 23 boxes in 8 series with an inventory. Fort Worth Library. Central Branch. Local History, Genealogy, & Archives Unit.

Cervantez, Brian. "Lone Star Booster: The Life of Amon G. Carter." Doctoral dissertation for the University of North Texas, History Dept., 2011.

Collins, Bertha Papers. Fort Worth Library. Central Branch. Local History, Genealogy, and Archives Unit. Collins (1915–1891) was a civil rights activist and long-time member of city government who witnessed a lot of history first-hand.

Davis, L. Clifford (Judge). Conversation with on occasion of Western Heritage Symposium, July 26, 2014.

Duckworth Papers, Allen, 1944-1962. Dolph Briscoe Center for American History, University of Texas at Austin. Duckworth was the long-time political editor for the *Dallas Morning News.*

Fort Worth, City of, Records of the City of Fort Worth. Series I. Mayor & Council Proceedings. 2 boxes. Fort Worth Library Central Branch. Local History, Genealogy & Archives Unit.

Fort Worth Housing Authority, Series V, Photographs, Sub-series B. Miscellaneous Photographs, 1939-1962. Fort Worth Library. Central Branch. Local History, Genealogy & Archives Unit.

Fort Worth Independent School District Archives. See Billy W. Sills Center for Archives.

Fort Worth Library. Miscellaneous Manuscripts. Inventory to the Collection. Central Branch. Local History, Genealogy and Archives Unit.

"From the Pasture to the Hill: A Community Heritage Celebration." Exhibition sponsored by Arlington Historical Society. Fielder House Museum. Arlington, TX. June 27–Sept. 15, 1999.

Hill, Byron. Interview with. March 12, 2015. Hill is a resident of Fort Worth and fourth generation descendant of John Chisum and Jensie.

"Historic Marker Application for Douglass and McGar Parks." 2009. Richard Selcer. Vertical Files. Fort Worth Library. Central Branch. Local History, Genealogy, & Archives Unit.

"Historic Marker Application for Grave of Hagar Tucker." 2005. Richard Selcer. Vertical Files. Fort Worth Library. Central Branch. Local History, Genealogy, & Archives Unit.

Lake, Mary Daggett. Papers. Series I-XII. 52 boxes with finding aid. Fort Worth Library. Central Branch. Local History, Genealogy, & Archives Unit. Lake (1881–1955) was the daughter of a distinguished pioneering Fort Worth family and the wife of a distinguished cattleman who wrote for many years for the local newspapers.

Lenora Rolla Heritage Center, 1020 E. Humbolt St. Extensive collections maintained by the Tarrant County Black Historical & Genealogical Society.

Littlejohn, Calvin. Collected papers. See Calvin Littlejohn Photographic Archive.

Martin, John Edward, Papers. Tarrant County Archives. Martin, 1846-1914, was a long-time resident of Fort Worth, an attorney and judge.

Mayor & Council Proceedings. See Fort Worth, City of.

McCutcheon, D.N. Letter to wife ("Mrs. G.A. McCutcheon"). September 8, 1926. Author's collections.

McDonough, Julia Anne. "Men and Women of Good Will: A History of the Commission on Interracial Cooperation and the Southern Regional Council, 1919–1954. Ph.D. Dissertation. University of Virginia. Charlottesville, VA. 1993.

Peak Family Papers. Tarrant County Archives. Fort Worth, TX. Includes correspondence, writings, and various documents of the various family members, Jefferson, Junius, Juliette, Carroll, Howard, *et al.*

Prince Hall Masons Grand Lodge of Texas, Archives. 3433 Martin Luther King Freeway, Fort Worth, TX. 76119. Collections consist of documents and photos, all in the process of being organized.

Reby Cary Papers. See Cary, Reby Collected Papers.

Roach, Diana. Scrapbooks (4). Donated to Tarrant County Black Historical & Genealogical Society, Oct. 22, 2012.

Roberts, J.D. (retired Fort Worth police officer). Email correspondence, June 28, 2013.

Rolla, Lenora, Papers. Vertical files, Fort Worth Library, Central Branch, Local History, Genealogy, and Archives Unit. See also Lenora Rolla Heritage Center.

Sills, Billy W. Center. See Billy W. Sills Center for Archives of the Fort Worth ISD.

Tarrant County Tax Records. Microfilm. Fort Worth Library, Central Branch. Local History, Genealogy, & Archives Unit.

Ward, Russell B. "Panther City Progressives." Master's Thesis (1995). Texas A&M University. College Station, TX, 1995.

Williams, Joyce M. "Women in Fort Worth History," unpublished MS of a talk presented as part of Centennial Celebration, 1999.Vertical files. Fort Worth Library. Central Branch. Local History, Genealogy, & Archives Unit.

SECONDARY SOURCES

Abbott, Lynn, and Doug Seroff. *Out of Sight: The Rise of African-American Popular Music, 1889–1895.* Jackson: University Press of Mississippi, 2009.

"African-American Historic Places, Fort Worth, Texas." Planning Department, City of Fort Worth. n.d. Tarrant County Black Historical & Genealogical Society Collections.

Alexander, Michelle. *The New Jim Crow: Mass Incarceration in the Age of Colorblindness.* New York: The New Press, 2010.

Alter, Judy. *Extraordinary Texas Women.* Fort Worth, TX: TCU Press, 2007.

Arnold, Ann. *A History of the Fort Worth Medical Community.* Arlington, TX: Landa Press, 2002.

_________. *Camp Meeting to Cathedral: Fort Worth's Historic Congregations.* Arlington, TX: Landa Press, 2004.

Astor, Gerald. *The Right to Fight: A History of African Americans in the Military.* Cambridge, MA: Da Capo Press, 1998.

Atkinson, Jim, and Judy Wood. *Fort Worth's Huge Deal.* Fort Worth: Self-published, 2010.

Aulbach, Louis, Linda C. Gorski, and Robbie Morin. *Camp Logan, Houston, Texas, 1917–1919: A World War I Emergency Training Center.* Houston: Louis F. Aulbach Pub., 2014.

Barbeau, Arthur E., and Florette Henri. *The Unknown Soldiers: African American Troops in World War I.* New York: Da Capo Press, 1996.

Barr, Alwyn, *The African Texans, Texans All.* College Station: Texas A&M University Press, 2004.

______. *Black Texans: A History of African American Texas, 1528–1995.* 2nd ed. Norman: University of Oklahoma Press, 1996.

______, and Robert A. Calvert, eds. *Black Leaders: Texans for Their Times.* Austin: Texas State Historical Association, 1981.

Bartley, Numan V. *The New South, 1945–1980.* Baton Rouge: Louisiana State University Press, 1995.

Beckner, Chrisanne. *100 African-Americans Who Shaped American History.* San Mateo, CA: Bluewood Books, 1995.

Beth-El Congregation Centennial. Fort Worth: Beth-El Congregation, 2002. See also on-line.

Blackmon, Douglas A. *Slavery by Another Name: The Re-enslavement of Black Americans from the Civil War to World War II.* New York: Random House, Anchor Books, 2009.

Blackwelder, Julia Kirk. *Styling Jim Crow: African American Beauty Training during Segregation.* College Station: Texas A&M University Press, 2003.

Brinkley, Douglas. *Rosa Parks.* Penguin Lives Series. New York: Viking Press, 2000.

Brooks, Tilford. *America's Black Musical Heritage.* New York: Prentice-Hall, 1984.

Bryson, Conrey. *Dr. Lawrence A. Nixon and the White Primary.* Rev. ed. Southwestern Studies Series. El Paso, TX: Texas Western Press, 1993.

Burrell, Tom. *Brainwashed: Challenging the Myth of Black Inferiority.* New York: SmileyBooks, 2010.

Bute, E.L., and H.J.P. Harmer. *The Black Handbook: The People, History and Politics of Africa and the African Diaspora.* London, U.K.: Cassell, 1997. The book has some factual errors, *e.g.*, the "Brownsville Incident," but is a good quick read on African-American history.

Buenger, Victoria, and Walter L. Buenger. *Texas Merchant: Marvin Leonard and Fort Worth.* College Station: Texas A&M University Press, 1998.

Campbell, Randolph B. *An Empire for Slavery: The Peculiar Institution in Texas 1821–1865.* Baton Rouge: Louisiana State University Press, 1989.

Cary, Reby. *Born to Win.* Fort Worth, TX: Privately Printed, 2009.

_______. *Bringing the Past into Focus: Blacks' Sheaves in Fort Worth and the Inner City Ring.* Fort Worth, TX: Privately Printed, 2006.

_______. *Carver Heights: Where the "Best" Begins: A Roll Call of Pioneers, et al.* Fort Worth, TX: Privately Printed, 2010.

_______. *Cinderella Kid "Remastered": Historical Imprints of Blacks in Fort Worth—Tarrant County, From Slavery to 2009.* Fort Worth: Privately Printed, 2009.

_______. *First, The! And the Foremost: A Flash-back Portfolio of Blacks in Fort Worth and Tarrant County.* Fort Worth: Privately Printed, 2011.

________. *How We Got Over! Update on a Backward Look: A History of Blacks in Fort Worth.* Fort Worth, TX: Privately Printed, 2005.

________. *How We Got Over! Second Update on a Backward Look: A History of Blacks in Fort Worth.* 2nd ed. Fort Worth, TX: Privately Printed, 2006.

________. *I Tried to Tell You!: "A Wake-up Call to Blacks and Hispanics": They Wouldn't Publish It.* Fort Worth, TX: Zebra Printing Co., 2004.

________. *Princes Shall Come out of Egypt, Texas, and Fort Worth.* Pittsburgh, PA: Dorrance Publishing Co., 2002.

_______. *Step up, A: The Way Makers: Who Did What? A Chronicle of Black Progress in Fort Worth and Tarrant County.* Fort Worth, TX: Privately Printed, 2010.

________. *We've Come This Far: A 2007 Retrospective on African Americans in Fort Worth and Tarrant County.* Fort Worth, TX: Privately Printed, 2007.

Caver, Joseph, Jerome Ennels, and Daniel Haulman. *The Tuskegee Airmen: An Illustrated History, 1939–1949.* Montgomery, AL: NewSouth Books, 2011.

Chalk. Ocania. *Pioneers of Black Sport.* New York: Dodd, Mead, 1975.

Chyet, Stanley F., ed. *Lives and Voices: A Collection of American Jewish Memoirs.* Philadelphia, PA: Jewish Publication Society, 1972.

Cummings, Scott. *Left Behind in Rosedale: Race Relations and the Collapse of Community Institutions.* 2nd ed. Boulder, CO: Westview Press, 1998.

Dalessandro, Robert J., and Gerald Torrence. *Willing Patriots: Men of Color in the First World War.* Atglen, PA: Schiffer, 2009.

Davis, Allen F. *Spearheads for Reform: The Social Settlements and the Progressive Movement, 1890-1914.* Rev. Ed. New Brunswick, NJ: Rutgers University Press, 1966.

Diedrich, Maria. *Love Across Color Lines: Ottilie Assing and Frederick Douglass.* New York: Hill and Wang, 1999.

Directory of Negro Business Enterprises and Professions of Fort Worth, Texas. Fort Worth: Hornet Publishing Company, 1921. The *Directory* is in the Lenora Rolla Papers, Box C, Tarrant County Black Historical and Genealogical Society, Local History, Genealogy & Archives Dept., Central Branch, Fort Worth Library.

Donald, Graeme. *They Got It Wrong: SCIENCE. All the Facts That Turned Out to Be Science Fiction.* New York: Reader's Digest, 2013.

Dulaney, W. Marvin. *Black Police in America.* Bloomington: Indiana University Press, 1996.

Egerton, John. *Speak Now against the Day: The Generation before the Civil Rights Movement in the South.* New York: Alfred A. Knopf, 1994.

Fink Rob. *Playing in Shadows: Texas and Negro League Baseball.* Lubbock: Texas Tech University Press, 2010.

Flemmons, Jerry. *Amon: The Texas Who Played Cowboy for America.* Lubbock: Texas Tech University Press, 1998.

Fort Worth, The Black Prospective [*sic.*]. no author. Fort Worth: Black Citizens Concerned with the Bicentennial, 1976. A bound copy of this slim volume is in the collections of the Fort Worth Library.

Fort Worth Colored History and Directory (1909). Compiled and published by J.A. Hamilton. Tarrant County Black Historical and Genealogical Society Archives. Fort Worth Library. Central Branch. Local History, Genealogy, & Archives Unit. See also *History and Directory of Fort Worth. . .*

Friedwald, Will. *Stardust Melodies: The Biography of Twelve of America's Most Popular Songs.* New York: Pantheon Books, 2002.

Gable, John Allen. *The Bull Moose Years: Theodore Roosevelt and the Progressive Party.* Port Washington, NY: Kennikat Press, 1978.

Garrett, Julia Kathryn. *Fort Worth: A Frontier Triumph.* Austin, TX: Encino Press, 1972. Reprinted, Fort Worth, TX: Texas Christian University Press, 1995.

Geisel, Paul N. *Historical Vignette of the Black Population of Fort Worth, Texas.* Part of the Statistical and Geographical Abstract of the Black Population in the United States. College Park, MD: Dr. Charles M. Christian and the Dept. of Geography, University of MD, 1991. Located in the collections of the Fort Worth Library, Central Branch, Local History, Genealogy, and Archives Unit.

Glasrud, Bruce, ed. *Anti-Black Violence in Twentieth-Century Texas.* College Station: Texas A&M University Press, 2015.

Glass, Charles. *The Deserters: A Hidden History of World War II.* New York: Penguin Books, 2013.

Goldstein, Dana. *The Teacher Wars: A History of America's Most Embattled Profession.* New York: Doubleday, 2014.

Gooch, Augusta. *Life of Lenora Rolla: A Citizen Shapes Her World.* Seattle, WA: CreateSpace Independent Publishing Platform, 2013.

Gordon, Sarah. *Passage to Union: How the Railroads Transformed American Life, 1829–1929.* Chicago: Ivan R. Dee, 1997.

Graham, Lawrence Otis. *Our Kind of People: Inside America's Black Upper Class.* New York: HarperCollins, 1998.

Greer, Scott. *Urban Renewal and American Cities.* Indianapolis: Bobbs-Merrill, 1965.

Grob, Gerald N. *Workers and Utopia: A Study of Ideological Conflict in the American Labor Movement, 1865–1900.* Evanston, IL: Northwestern University Press, 1961.

Guinn, Jeff. *When Panthers Roared: The Fort Worth Cats and Minor League Baseball.* Fort Worth: Texas Christian University Press, 1999.

Hall, Colby D. *History of Texas Christian University: A College of the Cattle Frontier.* 1947. Fort Worth, TX: TCU Press, 2014.

Harries, Meirion, and Susie Harries. *The Last Days of Innocence: America at War, 1917–1918.* New York: Random House, 1997.

Harriet, Ramona M. *A Missing Link: The Journey of African Americans in Golf.* 2nd ed. Florida: privately printed by Ramona Merriwether Harriet, 2013.

Haskins, James. *Black Music in America: A History through Its People.* New York: HarperCollins Publishers, 1987.

_______. *The Cotton Club.* New York: Hippocrene Books, 1994.

Heintze, Michael R. *Private Black Colleges in Texas, 1865–1954.* College Station: Texas A&M University Press, 1985.

Herzhaft, Gerard, ed. *Encyclopedia of the Blues.* Fayetteville: University of Arkansas Press, 1997.

Hine, Darlene Clark. *Black Victory: The Rise and Fall of the White Primary in Texas.* Columbia: University of Missouri Press, 2003.

Hine, Thomas. *The Rise and Fall of the American Teenager.* New York: Avon Books, 1999.

History and Directory of Fort Worth, Giving an Account of Its Early Settlers, Founders, and Growth. J.A. Hamilton. Fort Worth: privately printed, 1907. The Library of Congress has 2 copies, or a poorly transcribed copy is available online.

Homan, Lynn, and Thomas Reilly. *Black Knights: The Story of the Tuskegee Airmen.* Gretna, LA: Pelican Publishing Company, 2001.

Hoopes, Roy. *When the Stars Went to War: Hollywood and World War II.* New York: Random House, 1994.

Jackson, Kenneth T. *The Ku Klux Klan in the City, 1915–1930.* 2nd ed. Chicago: Ivan R. Dee, 1992.

Jacoway, Elizabeth. *Turn Away Thy Son: Little Rock, the Crisis That Shocked the Nation.* New York: The Free Press, 2006.

James, Rawn, Jr. *The Double V: How Wars, Protest, and Harry Truman Desegregated America's Military.* New York: Bloomsbury Press, 2013.

Jensen, Brian. *Where Have All Our Cowboys Gone?* Lanham, MD: Taylor Trade Publishing, 2001.

Jones, Jan L. *Billy Rose Presents... Casa Mañana.* Fort Worth: Texas Christian University Press, 1990.

_________. *Renegades, Showmen, and Angels: A Theatrical History of Fort Worth from 1873–2001.* Fort Worth: Texas Christian University Press, 2006.

Katznelson, Ira. *Fear Itself: The New Deal and the Origins of Our Time.* New York: W.W. Norton, 2013.

Keith, Jeanette. *Fever Season: The Story of a Terrifying Epidemic and the People Who Saved a City.* New York: Bloomsbury Press, 2012.

________. *Rich Man's War, Poor Man's Fight: Race, Class and Power in the Rural South During the First World War.* Chapel Hill: University of North Carolina Press, 2004.

Kelbaugh, Ross. *Introduction to African-American Photographs, 1840–1950.* Gettysburg, PA: Thomas Publications, 2007.

Kennett, Lee. *For the Duration: The United States Goes to War: Pearl Harbor–1942.* New York: Charles Scribner's Sons, 1985.

Key, V.O., Jr. *Southern Politics in State and Nation.* New York: Alfred A. Knopf, 1950.

Klein, Maury. *A Call to Arms: Mobilizing America for World War II.* New York: Bloomsbury Press, 2013.

Kline, Susan Allen. *Fort Worth Parks.* Images of America series. Charleston, SC: Arcadia Publishing, 2010.

Knight, Oliver. *Fort Worth: Outpost on the Trinity.* Norman: University of Oklahoma Press, 1953. Reprinted by TCU Press with a new introduction, 1990.

Kossie-Chernyshev, Karen. *Recovering Five Generations of Hence: The Life and Writings of Lillian Jones Horace.* College Station: Texas A&M University Press, 2013.

Ladino, Robyn Duff. *Desegregating Texas Schools: Eisenhower, Shivers, and the Crisis at Mansfield High.* Austin: University of Texas Press, 1996.

Lane, Ann J. *The Brownsville Affair: National Crisis and Black Reaction.* Port Washington, NY: Kennikat Press, 1971.

Lanning, Michael Lee. *The African-American Soldier: From Crispus Attucks to Colin Powell.* Secaucus, NJ: Birch Lane Press, 1997.

Lauterbach, Preston. *The Chitlin' Circuit, And the Road to Rock 'n' Roll.* New York: W.W. Norton, 2011.

Levine, Bruce. *The Fall of the House of Dixie: The Civil War and the Social Revolution that Transformed the South.* New York: Random House, 2013.

Lewis, David Levering. *When Harlem Was in Vogue.* New York: Alfred A. Knopf, 1981.

Liles, Debbie M. *Will Rogers Coliseum.* Images of America Series. Charleston, SC: Arcadia Publishers, 2012.

Lingeman, Richard. *Don't You Know There's A War On? The American Home Front, 1941–1945.* New York: Paperback Library, G.P. Putnam's Sons, 1970.

_________. *The Noir Forties: The American People from Victory to Cold War.* New York: Nation Books, 2012.

Licht, Walter. *Industrializing America: The Nineteenth Century.* The American Movement Series. Baltimore: The Johns Hopkins University Press, 1995.

Litweiler, John. *Ornette Coleman: A Harmolodic Life.* London: Quartet Books, 1992.

Lowry, Beverly. *Her Dreams of Dreams: The Rise and Triumph of Madam C.J. Walker.* New York: Alfred A. Knopf, 2003.

Lubasch, Arnold H. *Robeson: An American Ballad.* Lanham, MD: Scarecrow Press, 2013.

Massey, Sara R., ed. *Black Cowboys of Texas.* College Station: Texas A&M University Press, 2000.

McAlester, Virginia, and Lee McAlester. *A Field Guide to American Houses.* New York: Alfred A. Knopf, 1984.

McCaslin, Richard B. *Tainted Breeze: The Great Hanging at Gainesville, Texas, 1862.* Baton Rouge: Louisiana State University Press, 1994.

McDaniel, Pete. *Uneven Lies: The Heroic Story of African-Americans in Golf.* Greenwich, CT: American Golfer, 2000.

McFeely, William S. *Frederick Douglass.* New York: W.W. Norton, 1991.

Mjagkij, Nina. *Loyalty in Time of Trial: The African American Experience during World War I.* African American History Series. Lanham, MD: Rowman & Littlefield Publishers, 2011.

Morgan, Philip. *Slave Counterpoint: Black Culture in the Eighteenth-Century Chesapeake and Lowcountry.* Williamsburg, VA: Omohundro Institute of Early American History and Culture, 1998.

Morning Chapel Christian Methodist Episcopal Church History, 1873–1977. Fort Worth, TX: The Church (1977?). In the collections of Fort Worth Library.

Moye, J. Todd. *Freedom Flyers: The Tuskegee Airmen of World War II.* Oxford Oral History Series. New York: Oxford University Press, 2010.

Mullins, Marion Day, compiler. *A History of the Woman's Club of Fort Worth, 1923–1973.* Fort Worth, TX: The Woman's Club, 1973.

Musto, David F. *The American Disease: Origins of Narcotic Control.* 3rd ed. New York: Oxford University Press, 1999.

Nalty, Bernard C. *Strength for the Fight: A History of Black Americans in the Military.* New York: The Free Press, 1986.

Newberry, Kevin. *Texas Golf: The Best of the Lone Star State.* Houston: Gulf Publishing, 1998.

Nichols, Mike. *Lost Fort Worth.* Charleston, SC: The History Press, 2014.

Nobles, Mark A. *Fort Worth's Rock and Roll Roots.* Images of America Series. Charleston, SC: Arcadia Publishing, 2011.

Oates, Paula, ed. *Celebrating 150 Years: The Pictorial History of Fort Worth, Texas, 1849–1999.* Fort Worth, TX: Landmark Publishing, 1999.

Paddock, B.B., ed. *Fort Worth and the Texas Northwest.* 4 vols. Chicago: Lewis Publishing Co., 1922.

Pate, J'Nell. *Arsenal of Defense: Fort Worth's Military Legacy.* Denton: Texas State Historical Association, 2011.

Patterson, James T. *The Eve of Destruction: How 1965 Transformed America.* New York: Basic Books, 2012.

Perkins, Clay. *The Fort in Fort Worth.* Keller, TX: Cross-Timbers Heritage Publishing Co., 2001.

Pickering, David, and Judy Falls. *Brush Men and Vigilantes: Civil War Dissent in Texas.* College Station: Texas A&M University Press, 2000.

Presswood, Mark, and Chris Holaday. *Baseball in Fort Worth.* Charleston, SC: Arcadia Publishers, 2004.

Putnam, Robert D. *Bowling Alone: The Collapse and Revival of American Community.* New York: Simon & Schuster, 2001.

Reynolds, Donald E. *Editors Make War: Southern Newspapers in the Secession Crisis.* 2nd ed. Carbondale: Southern Illinois University Press, 2006.

__________. *Texas Terror: The Slave Insurrection Panic of 1860 and the Secession of the Lower South.* Baton Rouge: Louisiana State University Press, 2007.

Rich, Harold. *Fort Worth: Outpost, Cowtown, Boomtown.* Norman: University of Oklahoma Press, 2014.

Richardson, Rupert N., Ernest Wallace, and Adrian N. Anderson. *Texas: The Lone Star State.* 4th ed. Englewood Cliffs, NJ: Prentice-Hall, 1981.

Ritterhouse, Jennifer. *Growing Up Jim Crow: The Racial Socialization of Black and White Southern Children, 1890–1940.* Chapel Hill: University of North Carolina Press, 2006.

Roark, Carol, ed. *Fort Worth and Tarrant County: An Historical Guide.* Fort Worth: Tarrant County Historical Society and TCU Press, 2003. This is a revised and expanded version of the 1884 *Historical Guide* by Ruby Schmidt. See below.

Robertson, Robert J. *Fair Ways: How Six Black Golfers Won Civil Rights in Beaumont, Texas.* College Station: Texas A&M University Press, 2005.

Rucker, Walter C., Jr., and James N. Upton, eds. *Encyclopedia of American Race Riots.* 2 vols. Westport, CT: Greenwood Press, 2006.

Runstedtler, Theresa. *Jack Johnson, Rebel Sojourner: Boxing in the Shadow of the Global Color Line.* Berkeley: University of California Press, 2012.

Rydell, Robert W. *World of Fairs: The Century-of-Progress Expositions.* Chicago: University of Chicago Press, 1993.

Sanders, Bob Ray. *Calvin Littlejohn: Portrait of a Community in Black and White.* Fort Worth, TX: TCU Press, 2009.

Sanders, Drew. *The Garden of Eden: The Story of a Freedmen's Community in Texas.* Fort Worth, TX: TCU Press, 2015.

Schmelzer, Janet L. *Where the West Begins: Fort Worth and Tarrant County.* Northridge, CA: Windsor Publications, 1985.

Schmidt, Ruby, ed. *Fort Worth and Tarrant County: An Historical Guide.* A project of the Tarrant County Historical Society. Fort Worth: Texas Christian University Press, 1984.

Schutze, Jim. *The Accommodation: The Politics of Race in an American City.* New York: Citadel Press, 1987.

Selcer, Richard. *Fort Worth: A Texas Original!* Austin: Texas State Historical Association, 2004.

__________. *Fort Worth Characters.* Denton: University of North Texas Press, 2009.

__________, et al. *Legendary Watering Holes: The Saloons That Made Texas Famous.* College Station: Texas A&M University Press, 2004.

__________, and Kevin S. Foster. *Written in Blood: The History of Fort Worth's Fallen Lawmen, Vol. 2: 1910–1928.* Denton: University of North Texas Press, 2011.

Shabazz, Amilcar. *Advancing Democracy: African Americans and the Struggle for Access and Equality in Higher Education in Texas.* Chapel Hill: University of North Carolina Press, 2004.

Sharpe, Laurene, comp. and ed. *One Hundred Years of the Black Man in Fort Worth.* Vol. 1: *Early Life, Church Life, Black Pioneers, Together with Dates and Events to Remember.* Fort Worth: Privately Printed (L. Sharpe & Co.), 1973. This rare booklet is in the collections of the Fort Worth Library, Central Branch, Local History, Genealogy, & Archives Unit.

Sherrod, Katie, ed. *Grace and Gumption: Stories of Fort Worth Women.* Fort Worth, TX: TCU Press, 2007.

Smallwood, James. *Time of Hope, Time of Despair: Black Texans during Reconstruction.* London: Kennikat, 1981.

Stephens, A. Ray. *Texas: A Historical Atlas.* Norman: University of Oklahoma Press, 2010.

Stokes, David R. *The Shooting Salvationist: J. Frank Norris and the Murder Trail That Captivated America.* Hanover, NH: Steerforth Press, 2011.

Streitmatter, Roger. *Voices of Revolution: The Dissident Press in America.* New York: Columbia University Press, 2001.

Talbert, Robert. *Cowtown Metropolis: Case Study of a City's Growth and Structure.* Fort Worth: Texas Christian University Press, 1956.

Taylor, Quintard. *In Search of the Racial Frontier: African Americans in the American West, 1528–1990.* New York: W.W. Norton & Company, 1998.

Turner, Stephanie Hayes, Stephanie Cole, and Rebecca Sharpless, eds. *Texas Women: Their Histories, Their Lives.* Athens: University of Georgia Press, 2015.

Tye, Larry. *Rising from the Rails: Pullman Porters and the Making of the Black Middle Class.* New York: Henry Holt and Company, 2004.

Tyler, Ron, et al., eds. *New Handbook of Texas, The.* 6 vols. Austin: Texas State Historical Association, 1996.

Van Zandt, Khleber. *Force without Fanfare: The Autobiography of K.M. Van Zandt.* Edited by Sandra L. Myres. Fort Worth: Texas Christian University Press, 1968.

Warner, Jay. *On This Day in Black Music History.* Milwaukee, WI.: Hal Leonard, 2006.

Waskow, Arthur I. *From Race Riot to Sit-in: 1919 and the 1960s.* Garden City, NY: Anchor Books, 1966.

Weaver, John D. *The Brownsville Raid.* New York: W.W. Norton, 1970.

Weiner, Hollace Ava. *Jewish Stars in Texas: Rabbis and Their Work.* College Station: Texas A&M University Press, 1999.

___________ , ed. *Beth-El Congregation Centennial: Fort Worth, Texas, 1902–2002.* Fort Worth: Beth-El Temple, 2002.

White, Deborah Gray. *Too Heavy a Load: Black Women in Defense of Themselves, 1894–1994.* New York: W.W. Norton & Co., 1998.

White, Lonnie J. *Panthers to Arrowheads: the 36th (Texas-Oklahoma Division in World War I).* Austin: Presidial Press, 1984.

White, Walter. *Rope and Faggot: A Biography of Judge Lynch.* New York: Alfred A. Knopf, 1929; repr. as volume in Intellectual Heritage Series, Notre Dame, IN: University of Notre Dame Press, 2002.

Williams, Chad L. *Torchbearers of Democracy: African American Soldiers in the World War I Era.* John Hope Franklin Series in African American History and Culture. Chapel Hill: University of North Carolina Press, 2010.

Williams, Joyce E. *Black Community Control: A Study of Transition in a Texas Ghetto.* New York: Praeger Publishers, 1973.

Williams, Mack, ed. *In Old Fort Worth* Fort Worth: Privately Published, 1986.

Wood, Amy Louise. *Lynching and Spectacle: Witnessing Racial Violence in America, 1890–1940.* New Directions in Southern Studies. Chapel Hill: University of North Carolina Press, 2009.

Willis, Libby. *Fort Worth's Oakhurst Neighborhood.* Images of America Series. Charleston, SC: Arcadia Publishing, 2014.

Winegarten, Ruthe, and Janet G. Humphrey. *Black Texas Women: 150 Years of Trial and Triumph.* Austin: University of Texas Press, 1995.

Wynn, Neil A. *The African American Experience during World War II.* African American History Series. Lanham, MD: Rowman & Littlefield Publishers, 2010.

PERIODICAL ARTICLES, ENCYCLOPEDIA ENTRIES, CHRONOLOGIES, THESES, AND DISSERTATIONS

Batts, Jan. "On the Shores of Lake Como." *Fort Worth Magazine* 9, no. 8 (August 2006): 108–113.

Bills, E.R. "Great Debate. *Fort Worth Magazine* 17, no. 2 (February 2014): 60–61.

Behnken, Brian D. "The 'Dallas Way': Protest, Response, and the Civil Rights Experience in Big D and Beyond." *The Southwestern Historical Quarterly* 111, no. 1 (July 1987): ix–29.

Cartwright, Gary. "Community, Edward W. Guinn, When Duty Calls in Fort Worth's Worst Neighborhood, the Doctor Is In." *Texas Monthly*. September 1999.

Casseday-Blair, Jennifer, and Paul K. Harral. "Members Only." *Fort Worth Magazine* 16, no. 5 (May 2013): 88–94. A history of Fort Worth' private clubs from 1906 to the present.

Chamber Letter. Newsletter of the Fort Worth Chamber of Commerce, 1984–1994. Vertical files. Fort Worth Library, Central Branch, Local History, Genealogy & Archives Unit.

"Chronology of the Fort Worth Independent School District." Roy Housewright, compiler. Billy W. Sills Center for Archives. Fort Worth ISD.

Crisis, The. Nov. 1910 *ff*. Official magazine of the National Association for the Advancement of Colored People, published monthly out of New York. Edited by W.E.B. DuBois 1910–1934.

Critic, The. Newspaper devoted to culture and the arts; began publication in December 1915.

Dallas Express, The. Weekly African-American newspaper published 1892-1970. Founded by W.E. King. Published in its middle years by a white owner. Available on-line through "The Portal to Texas History." www.texashistory.unt.edu.]

Dallas Morning News. Various issues.

"Debt of Honor: Seven Black Heroes. . . nominated for the Medal of Honor." *U.S. News & World Report*. May 6, 1996. Pp. 28-42.

Defender, The (Chicago). Various issues.

Doggett, Dorothy Lasseter. "Survey of Fort Worth's Negro Schools." M.A. Thesis. Dept. of Education. Texas Christian University. Fort Worth, TX. 1927. Copy found in Mary Couts Burnett Library, Special Collections, TCU.

Fairley, Bill. "Tales from Where the West Begins" and "Tarrant Chronicles." *Fort Worth Star-Telegram*. 1997-2002. A series by an amateur Fort Worth historian examining various times, topics, and figures in local history. Most of his columns on black history coincide with annual Black History Month or Juneteenth. See in particular, June 18, 1997; February 3 10, 17, and 24, and March 10, 1999; February 23 and May 17, 2000; February 19 and June 19, 2002.

Fairley, Bill. "Memoirs Offer Rich Look at Past." 4-part series based on *The Slave Narratives* in "Tales from Where the West Begins." *Fort Worth Star-Telegram.* February 5, 12, 19, and 26, 1997.

Foroohar, Rana. "Reinventing High School." *Time Magazine.* February 24, 2014. Pp. 22–29.

Fort Worth Gazette. Various issues, in daily and weekly editions, all on the same microfilm rolls.

Fort Worth Mail-Telegram. This was one of the forerunners of the *Star-Telegram,* absorbed by the latter in 1907. A few assorted issues are preserved with the early *Star-Telegram* on microfilm.

Fort Worth Mind, The. R.L. "Pie" Melton was the founder and chief reporter of the newspaper.

Fort Worth News-Tribune. Published by Mack and Madeleine Williams, 1970–1986.

Fort Worth Press.

Fort Worth Record.

Fort Worth Register (aka, *Fort Worth Morning Register*). A scattering of issues from 1897 through 1901 are preserved on microfilm.

Fort Worth Telegram/Star-Telegram. The *Fort Worth Star* and *Fort Worth Telegram* were two separate newspapers until 1909. Surviving pre-1909 issues of both papers are preserved on microfilm with the *Star-Telegram.*

Fort Worth Magazine.

Freeman Newspaper. Published in Indianapolis, Indiana, April 9, 1913.

Gates, Henry Louis, Jr., "Growing up Colored." *American Heritage Magazine* 62, no. 2 (Summer 2012): 56–63.

Gillette, Michael L. "The Rise of the NAACP in Texas." *The Southwestern Historical Quarterly* 81, no. 4 (April 1978): 393–416.

Goldberg, Robert A. "Racial Change on the Southern Periphery: The Case of San Antonio, Texas, 1960-1965." *The Journal of Southern History* 49. no. 3 (August 1983): 349–374.

Graham, Lawrence Otis. "Living in a Class Apart: The Separate World of America's Black Elite." *U.S. News & World Report*, February 15, 1999, pp. 48–52.

Hales, Douglas. "Paul Quinn College." *The New Handbook of Texas*, Ron Tyler, et al., eds. Austin: Texas State Historical Assoc., 1996. Vol. 5. Pp. 97-98.

Hill, Max. "William Trezevant, Jr." *Footprints, the* Magazine of *Fort Worth Genealogical Society* 47, no. 3 (August 2004): 107.

Hodges, Eudora. "Lawrence Steel [*sic.*]—Early Settler." *Footprints, the Magazine of the Fort Worth Genealogical Society* 34, no. 4 (November, 1991): 197-200.

Holzer, Harold, "Secession Fever Revisited." *Civil War Times* 24, no. 2 (May 2011): 21–22.

Hopkins, Ken. "Searching for Stick Town." Research notes in "Stick Town" vertical file of Local History, Archives, and Genealogy Unit, Central Branch, Fort Worth Library.

Houston Post. Various dates.

Karaim, Reed. "Vigilante Justice." *American History Magazine* 46, no. 6 (Feb. 2012): 50–55.

Keehn, David. "Strong Arm of Secession," *North & South Magazine* 10, no. 6 (June 2008): 42–55.

Keeton, W. Page. "Sweatt vs. Painter." *The New Handbook of* Texas. Ron Tyler, et al., eds. Austin: Texas State Historical Association, 1996. Vol. 6. Pp. 168-69.

Kirk, John A. "Crisis at Central High," *History Today* 57, no. 9 (September, 2007): 23–29.

Lake Como Monitor. Founded by W.H. Wilburn in 1941.

Ling, Peter. "The Media Made Malcolm." *History Today* 62, no. 1 (January 2012): 49–55.

Madigan, Tim. "The Color of Hate: How the Jim Crow Era Shamed and Shaped Our City." Photographs by Rodger Mallison and Jeffrey Washington. Seven-part series. *Fort Worth Star-Telegram,* October 6-13, 2002.

Moneyhon, Carl H. "Black Codes." *The New Handbook of Texas.* Ron Tyler, *et al,* eds. Austin: Texas State Historical Association, 1996. Vol. 1, p. 562.

Moseley, Jack. "The Negro in Fort Worth." Four-part series. *Fort Worth Press.* August 24–28, 1967.

Munches-Forde, Lady George. "History of the Negro in Fort Worth—Syllabus for a High School Course." M.A. Thesis. Education Dept. Fisk University. Nashville, TN, 1941.

News-Tribune, The. "In Old Fort Worth." See Williams, Mack, ed.

Palmer, Robert. "Ornette Coleman and the Circle with a Hole in the Middle." *The Atlantic Monthly* 230, no. 6 (December 1972): 91–93.

Phillips, Edward Hake. "Teddy Roosevelt in Texas, 1905." *West Texas Historical Association Year Book* 51 (1980): 58–67.

Polatti, Gaylon. "The Magic City and the Frontier: How Dallas and Fort Worth Celebrated the Texas Centennial." *Legacies: A History Journal for Dallas and North Central Texas* 13, no. 1 (Spring 1999): 37–39.

"Progress of Abolition, The." *Civil War Times* 48, no. 6 (December 2009).

Reich, Steven A. "Soldiers of Democracy: Black Texans and the Fight for Citizenship, 1917-1921." *Journal of American History* 82, no. 4 (March 1996): 1478–1504.

Selcer, Richard. "When Streetcars Roamed Fort Worth." *Fort Worth Magazine* 15, no. 12 (December 2012): 58–63.

Sherrod, Katie. "Power: Who Runs Fort Worth?" *D Magazine* 22, no. 11 (November 1995): 86–91*ff.*

Simon, Cheryl L. "Jim Hotel." *Handbook of Texas Online* (www.tshaonline.org/handbook/articles) .

Simon, William R. "Breaking the Color Bar at SMU." *Legacies: A History Journal for Dallas and North Central Texas* 24, no. 1 (Spring 2012): 32–42.

Smith, Thomas H. "A Poor Pilgrim of Sorrow: 'Sin Killer' Griffin and Dallas Revivals." *Legacies: A History Journal for Dallas and North Central Texas* 17, no. 2 (Fall 2005): 4–11.

Sohmer, Rebecca R. "Fort Worth's Rock Island Bottom: A Social Geography of an African-American Neighborhood." M.A. Thesis. Syracuse University. Syracuse, New York. 1997. Copy held by Fort Worth Library.

Standifer, Ben H., Jr. "The Black Business District, 1900–1940." Term Paper for TCU History Course No. 3970. History of Fort Worth from Its Beginnings. Fall term 1998. Collections of Fort Worth Library.

Stanley, Christine, and Jeff Prince. "Hushed Up and Unhappy: Fort Worth's Black Leaders Won't Stay Quiet Much Longer." *Fort Worth Weekly*. August 3–9, 2005. Pp. 8-14.

Swisher, Carl Brent. "The Supreme Court and the South." *Journal of Southern Politics* 10 (1948): 291–99.

Texas Almanac for 1871, and Emigrant's Guide to Texas. See "Tarrant County." Austin, 1871 (also available in digital form through The Portal to Texas History).

Texas State Gazette (Austin). Various dates.

White Man and the Negro, The. Vol. 1, No. 7 (Sept. 1933); Vol. 2, No. 4 (June 1933); and Vol. 2, No. 10 (Dec. 1933).

Williams, Mack H. and Madeline C., eds. "In Old Fort Worth." Collected columns from the *Fort Worth News-Tribune*, Bicentennial ed. (1975).

Willis, Libby. "History of the Oakhurst Neighborhood, Fort Worth, Texas." Unpublished address, 2006. In author's possession.

Wilson, Samuel. "Vanished Legacies and the Lost Culture of I.M. Terrell High School in Segregated Fort Worth." Master's Thesis in History, University of Texas at Arlington, 2012.

WEBSITES

www.100thww2.org. [The website of the 100th Infantry Division Association]

www.aphiliprandolphmuseum.com. (The website of the A. Philip Randolph Museum. Randolph was the organizer and head of the Brotherhood of Pullman Porters.]

www.bethelfw.org. (online source for the 100-year history of the Beth-El (Jewish) Congregation, *Beth-El Centennial*)

www.blackpast.org. (An online reference guide to African American History)

www.cah.utexas.edu. (on-line archive of Calvin Littlejohn's work in 2 sections, "Online Exhibits" and "Digital Media Repository")

www.dfwRetroplex.com. (website maintained by Mike Shannon, tracing the history of Dallas-fort Worth radio and television from 1920-2005.)

www.findagrave.com. (Find a Grave Memorial website)

www.fwmbcc.org (Fort Worth Metropolitan Black Chamber of Commerce)

www.tshaonline.org/handbook/africanamericans. [This is the *Handbook of African American Texas*, part of the online *New Handbook of Texas* created by the Texas State Historical Association. It is in digital form only, more than 850 entries in more than 30 categories.]

www.hometownbyhandlebar.com (website of former *Fort Worth Star-Telegram* columnist and current local historian Mike Nichols)

www.lcweb2.loc.gov/diglib/vhp-stories/loc.natlib.afc2001001.58790/transcript?ID. (The transcript of an interview with Reby Cary by James Yeh for the Veterans History Project, Library of Congress, February 27, 2007).

www.library.unt.edu/news/digital-projects-unit/portal-texas-history. (The Portal to Texas History, University of North Texas.

www.loc.gov/ammem/snhtml. [The 17 volumes of "Slave Narratives" assembled by the Federal Writers' Project between 1936 and 1938. The "Texas Narratives" are in Vol. XVI.]

www.lonesentry.com. ["The Story of the Century: The Story of the 100th Infantry Division"]

www.mwphglotx.org. (Prince Hall Masonic Grand Lodge of Texas)

www.nauticalcharts.noaa.gov/history/CivilWar (Unique, color-coded, 1861 map based on eighth U.S. census, showing distribution of the nation's slave population; in the collections of the National Oceanic and Atmospheric Administration, Central Library, catalogued by the NOAA as "Charting a More Perfect Union." Puts Tarrant County's slave population in historical perspective.)

http://phoenixmasonry.org/telling_our_own_story.htm. ("Telling Our Own Story: Wilbert M. Curtis, Texas Prince Hall Library Museum Unveiled," June 25, 2011)

www.polkmiller.com (The music and story of musician Polk Miller, 1844-1913)

www.tshaonline.org (The Handbook of Texas Online, the classic source for all things Texan, now more than half a century old.)

www.TSHAonline.org (same site but specifically for *The Handbook of African-American Texas*, new in 2013 from the Texas State Historical Association)

www.vahistorical.org ("Unknown No Longer."A database of 1,500+ slave names created by Virginia Historical Society)

www.vulture.com. (A movie review website of Will Leitch and Tim Grierson that reviews all of Spike Lee's 22 films, *ca.* 2012.)

www.ymcafw.org/About-YMCA/YMCA-History. (A brief institutional history of the YMCA of Metropolitan Fort Worth, including the McDonald branch)

Index